FOCUS ON LITERATURE

ACTION

PEOPLE

VIEWPOINTS

FORMS

AMERICA

IDEAS

HOUGHTON MIFFLIN COMPANY   BOSTON

Atlanta   Dallas   Geneva, Illinois   Lawrenceville, New Jersey   Palo Alto   Toronto

PHILIP McFARLAND

FRANCES FEAGIN

SAMUEL HAY

STELLA S.F. LIU

FRANK McLAUGHLIN

NORMA WILLSON

FOCUS ON LITERATURE

AMERICA

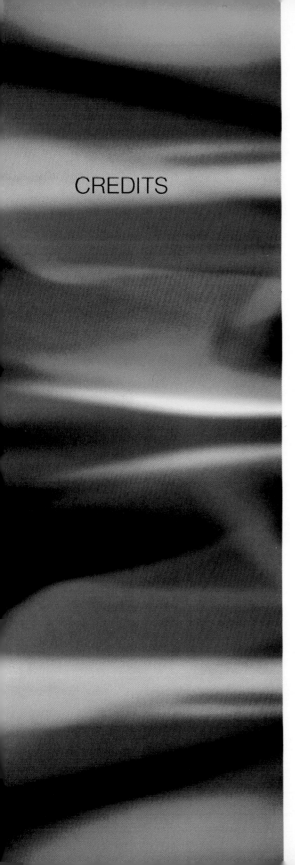

CREDITS

Acosta, Teresa. "My Mother Pieced Quilts," from *Festival de Flor y Canto: An Anthology of Chicano Literature,* © 1976 by El Centro Chicano, published by University of Southern California Press.

Adams, Abigail. Letter, reprinted by permission of the publishers from *Adams Family Correspondence,* Vol. I, L.H. Butterfield, ed., Cambridge, Massachusetts: The Belknap Press of Harvard University Press, © 1963 by the Massachusetts Historical Society.

Agee, James. *The Bride Comes to Yellow Sky,* copyright © 1958 by Theasquare Productions, Inc. From *Agee on Film,* Vol. 2, by James Agee. Copyright © 1960 by The James Agee Trust. Used by permission of Grosset & Dunlap, Inc.

Agüeros, Jack. "A Puerto Rican Pilgrimage," excerpted from *The Immigrant Experience,* edited by Thomas C. Wheeler. Copyright © 1971 by The Dial Press. Reprinted by permission of The Dial Press.

Alurista. "it is said," from *Nationchild Plumaroja,* Tolteca Publications, 1972; P.O. Box 8251, San Diego 92102.

Bahe, Liz Sohappy. "Farewell," from *Carriers of the Dream Wheel,* published by Harper & Row. All efforts to locate the copyright holder of this selection have proved unsuccessful. An appropriate fee for this use will be reserved by the publisher.

Baldwin, James. "Tell Me How Long the Train's Been Gone." Excerpts from *Tell Me How Long the Train's Been Gone* by James Baldwin. Copyright © 1968 by James Baldwin. Reprinted by permission of The Dial Press. Slightly adapted.

Bambara, Toni Cade. "Blues Ain't No Mockin Bird," copyright © 1971 by Toni Cade Bambara. Reprinted from *Gorilla, My Love,* by Toni Cade Bambara, by permission of Random House, Inc.

Baraka, Imamu Amiri. "Preface to a Twenty Volume Suicide Note," copyright © 1961 by LeRoi Jones. Reprinted by permission of Corinth Books.

Benét, Stephen Vincent. "The Devil and Daniel Webster," from *The Selected Works of Stephen Vincent Benét.* Copyright, 1936, by The Curtis Publishing Company. Copyright renewed © 1964 by Thomas C. Benét, Stephanie B. Mahin, and Rachel B. Lewis. Reprinted by permission of Brandt & Brandt.

Berriault, Gina. "The Stone Boy," first published by *Mademoiselle.* Copyright © 1957 by Gina Berriault. By permission of Toni Strassman, Agent. Slightly adapted.

Bontemps, Arna. "To a Young Girl Leaving the Hill Country," reprinted by permission of Harold Ober Associates Incorporated. Copyright © 1963 by Arna Bontemps.

1986 Impression

Library of Congress Catalog Card Number: 76-53136

ISBN: 0-395-29362-6

Giovanni. "Poetry," from *The Women and the Men,* copyright © 1976, Nikki Giovanni.

Hayden, Robert. "Runagate Runagate" and "Those Winter Sundays" by Robert Hayden, from *Selected Poems.* Copyright © 1966 by Robert Hayden. Reprinted by permission of October House.

Hemingway, Ernest. "Old Man at the Bridge" (copyright 1938 Ernest Hemingway) is reprinted by permission of Charles Scribner's Sons from *The Short Stories of Ernest Hemingway* by E. Hemingway.

Houston, Jeanne Wakatsuki and James D. Houston. "What Is Pearl Harbor?" From the book *Farewell to Manzanar,* by Jeanne Wakatsuki Houston and James D. Houston. Reprinted by permission of Houghton Mifflin Company. Copyright © 1973 by James D. Houston.

Hughes, Langston. "Let America Be America Again," reprinted by permission of Harold Ober Associates Incorporated. Copyright 1938 by Langston Hughes. Renewed.

Hurston, Zora Neale. "The Inside Search," abridged from *Dust Tracks on a Road* by Zora Neale Hurston. Copyright 1942 by Zora Neale Hurston. Copyright © renewed 1970 by John C. Hurston. Reprinted by permission of J. B. Lippincott Company.

Jackson, Shirley. "The Lottery," from *The Lottery* by Shirley Jackson. Copyright 1948, 1949 by Shirley Jackson. Reprinted with the permission of Farrar, Straus & Giroux, Inc.

Jeffers, Robinson. "Hurt Hawks," copyright 1928 and renewed 1956 by Robinson Jeffers. Reprinted from *The Selected Poetry of Robinson Jeffers,* by permission of Random House, Inc.

Johnson, James Weldon. "The Creation," from *God's Trombones* by James Weldon Johnson. Copyright 1927 by The Viking Press, Inc., copyright © renewed 1955 by Grace Nail Johnson. Reprinted by permission of The Viking Press.

Joseph, Chief. "I Have Heard Talk and Talk," from *Nimrod,* vol. 16, no. 2, Spring/Summer 1972 as adapted by Francine Ringold, Editor, *Nimrod.*

King, Martin Luther, Jr. Abridgment of "The Day of Days, December 5" from *Stride Toward Freedom* by Martin Luther King, Jr. Copyright © 1958 by Martin Luther King, Jr. Reprinted by permission of Harper & Row, Publishers, Inc.

Lardner, Ring. "Haircut" (copyright 1925 Ellis A. Lardner) is reprinted by permission of Charles Scribner's Sons from *The Love Nest and Other Stories* by Ring Lardner.

Levertov, Denise. "Laying the Dust," from *Here and Now.* Copyright © 1957 by Denise Levertov. Reprinted by permission of New Directions Publishing Corporation.

Lowell, Amy. "Patterns," from the book *The Complete Poetical Works of Amy Lowell,* by Amy Lowell. Reprinted by permission of Houghton Mifflin Company. Copyright 1955 by Houghton Mifflin Company.

Lowell, Robert. "Water," from *For the Union Dead,* by Robert Lowell. Copyright © 1962, 1964 by Robert Lowell. Reprinted with the permission of Farrar, Straus and Giroux, Inc.

McCullers, Carson. "A Tree A Rock A Cloud," from the book *Collected Short Stories* and the novel *The Ballad of the Sad Cafe,* by Carson McCullers. Reprinted by permission of Houghton Mifflin Company. Copyright 1955 by Carson McCullers.

McKay, Claude. "The Tropics in New York," from *The Selected Poems of Claude McKay,* copyright 1953 by Twayne Publishers, Inc. Reprinted with the permission of Twayne Publishers, a division of G. K. Hall & Co., Boston.

MacLeish, Archibald. "Ars Poetica," from the book *Collected Poems 1917–1952,* by Archibald MacLeish. Reprinted by permission of Houghton Mifflin Company. Copyright 1952 by Archibald MacLeish.

Mailer, Norman. "First Hour on the Moon," excerpted from *Of a Fire on the Moon,* copyright © 1969, 1970 by Norman Mailer. Includes material from *First on the Moon,* by Armstrong, Collins, and Aldrin. Copyright © 1970, Little, Brown & Co. Inc.

Masters, Edgar Lee. "Lucinda Matlock" and "George Gray," from *Spoon River Anthology* by Edgar Lee Masters. Copyright by the Macmillan Company 1914, 1915, 1942. "Silence,"

credits continued on page 671

ABOUT THE editors

Philip McFarland teaches at Concord Academy in Massachusetts, where he has served for a number of years as Chairman of the English Department. He earned his B.A. at Oberlin College in Ohio, and he received a Master's Degree and First Class Honors in English Literature at Cambridge University in England. Mr. Mc-Farland has published a novel and a biography of Washington Irving. He is also the co-author of several high school texts in literature and composition.

Frances Feagin is a former teacher of English at Albany High School in Albany, Georgia. She received her B.A. and M.Ed. from Mercer University in Macon, Georgia. She has had extensive teaching experience at the secondary level, including five years as Supervisor of English, and has been involved in the continuing study and revision of local curricula.

Samuel Hay is Chairman of the Department of Communications and Theater Arts at Morgan State University. A graduate of Bethune-Cookman College, he received an M.A. from Johns Hopkins University and a Ph.D. from Cornell University. He has taught high school English, speech, and drama. Dr. Hay is a playwright and the author of numerous articles on black literature.

Stella S.F. Liu is an Associate Professor of Education at Wayne State University in Detroit, Michigan. Dr. Liu received her B.A. from Yenching University in China and her Ph.D. from the University of California at Berkeley; she is a recipient of an outstanding dissertation award from the International Reading Association. Dr. Liu has had extensive experience as a teacher, reading specialist, and reading coordinator at both the elementary and secondary levels.

Frank McLaughlin, co-founder and editor of *Media and Methods* magazine, is an Associate Professor at Fairleigh Dickinson University in New Jersey. A graduate of St. Joseph's College in Philadelphia, Mr. McLaughlin received his M.A. from Villanova University. Formerly an English teacher and department chairman, he continues to work in high schools as coordinator of teaching interns. He has written numerous articles for *Media and Methods* and other publications.

Norma Willson is Chairwoman of the English Department at West High School in Torrance, California. A graduate of Kansas State College, she received an M.A. from the University of Southern California. She is a frequent speaker at national and state conferences on topics relating to the image of women in society and education, particularly in textbooks.

Marcella Johnson is Instructional Supervisor and Specialist in Communication Skills for the Instructional Planning Division of the Los Angeles Unified School District. As consultant for the Focus on Literature Series, she reviewed the selections written by and about members of minority groups.

ConTenTs

AMERICAN VOICES

FICTION

NONFICTION

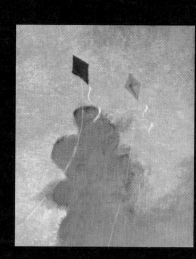

POETRY

DRAMA

THEMES

VALUES

VISIONS

REALITIES

FICTION

Rip Van Winkle

WASHINGTON IRVING

[The following tale was found among the papers of the late Diedrich
Knickerbocker, an old gentleman of New York, who was very curious in
the Dutch history of the province, and the manners of the descendants
from its primitive settlers. His historical researches, however, did not lie
so much among books as among men; for the former are lamentably
scanty on his favourite topics; whereas he found the old burghers, and
still more their wives, rich in that legendary lore so invaluable to true
history. Whenever, therefore, he happened upon a genuine Dutch family,
snugly shut up in its low-roofed farmhouse, under a spreading sycamore,
he looked upon it as a little clasped volume of black-letter, and studied it
with the zeal of a bookworm.

The result of these researches was a history of the province during
the reign of the Dutch governors, which he published some years since.
There have been various opinions as to the literary character of his work,
and, to tell the truth, it is not a whit better than it should be. Its chief
merit is its scrupulous accuracy, which indeed was a little questioned on
its first appearance, but has since been completely established; and it is
now admitted into all historical collections as a book of unquestionable
authority. . . .]

Whoever has made a voyage up the Hudson must remember the
Kaatskill Mountains. They are a dismembered branch of the great Appalachian family, and are seen away to the west of the river, swelling up to
a noble height, and lording it over the surrounding country. Every change
of season, every change of weather, indeed, every hour of the day, produces some change in the magical hues and shapes of these mountains,
and they are regarded by all the good wives, far and near, as perfect ba-
rometers. When the weather is fair and settled, they are clothed in blue
and purple, and print their bold outlines on the clear evening sky; but
sometimes, when the rest of the landscape is cloudless, they will gather a
hood of gray vapours about their summits, which, in the last rays of the
setting sun, will glow and light up like a crown of glory.

At the foot of these fairy mountains, the voyager may have descried
the light smoke curling up from a village, whose shingle-roofs gleam
among the trees, just where the blue tints of the upland melt away into

the fresh green of the nearer landscape. It is a little village, of great antiquity, having been founded by some of the Dutch colonists in the early time of the province, just about the beginning of the government of the good Peter Stuyvesant (may he rest in peace!) and there were some of the houses of the original settlers standing within a few years, built of small yellow bricks brought from Holland, having latticed windows and gable fronts, surmounted with weathercocks.

In that same village, and in one of these very houses (which, to tell the precise truth, was sadly time-worn and weather-beaten), there lived, many years since, while the country was yet a province of Great Britain, a simple, good-natured fellow, of the name of Rip Van Winkle. He was a descendant of the Van Winkles who figured so gallantly in the chivalrous days of Peter Stuyvesant, and accompanied him to the siege of Fort Christina. He inherited, however, but little of the martial character of his ancestors. I have observed that he was a simple, good-natured man; he was, moreover, a kind neighbour, and an obedient, henpecked husband. Indeed, to the latter circumstance might be owing that meekness of spirit which gained him such universal popularity; for those men are most apt to be obsequious and conciliating abroad who are under the discipline of shrews at home. Their tempers, doubtless, are rendered pliant and malleable in the fiery furnace of domestic tribulation; and a curtain-lecture is worth all the sermons in the world for teaching the virtues of patience and long-suffering. A termagant[1] wife may, therefore, in some respects, be considered a tolerable blessing; and, if so, Rip Van Winkle was thrice blessed.

Certain it is, that he was a great favourite among all the good wives of the village, who, as usual with the amiable sex, took his part in all family squabbles; and never failed, whenever they talked those matters over in their evening gossipings, to lay all the blame on Dame Van Winkle. The children of the village, too, would shout with joy whenever he approached. He assisted at their sports, made their playthings, taught them to fly kites and shoot marbles, and told them long stories of ghosts, witches, and Indians. Whenever he went dodging about the village he was surrounded by a troop of them, hanging on his skirts,[2] clambering on his back, and playing a thousand tricks on him with impunity; and not a dog would bark at him throughout the neighbourhood.

The great error in Rip's composition was an insuperable aversion to all kinds of profitable labour. It could not be from the want of assiduity or perseverance, for he would sit on a wet rock, with a rod as long and

---

[1] *termagant* (tûr′mə-gənt): a quarrelsome scold; a shrew.
[2] *skirts:* coat-tails.

heavy as a Tartar's lance, and fish all day long without a murmur, even though he should not be encouraged by a single nibble. He would carry a fowling-piece on his shoulder for hours together, trudging through woods and swamps, and up hill and down dale, to shoot a few squirrels or wild pigeons. He would never refuse to assist a neighbour even in the roughest toil, and was a foremost man at all country frolics for husking Indian corn or building stone fences; the women of the village, too, used to employ him to run their errands, and to do such little odd jobs as their less obliging husbands would not do for them. In a word, Rip was ready to attend to anybody's business but his own; but as to doing family duty, and keeping his farm in order, he found it impossible.

In fact, he declared it was of no use to work on his farm; it was the most pestilent little piece of ground in the whole country; everything about it went wrong, and would go wrong, in spite of him. His fences were continually falling to pieces; his cow would either go astray, or get among the cabbages; weeds were sure to grow quicker in his fields than anywhere else; the rain always made a point of setting in just as he had some out-of-door work to do; so that though his patrimonial estate had dwindled away under his management, acre by acre, until there was little more left than a mere patch of Indian corn and potatoes, yet it was the worst conditioned farm in the neighbourhood.

His children, too, were as ragged and wild as if they belonged to no-body. His son Rip, an urchin begotten in his own likeness, promised to inherit the habits, with the old clothes, of his father. He was generally seen trooping like a colt at his mother's heels, equipped in a pair of his father's cast-off galligaskins,[3] which he had much ado to hold up with one hand, as a fine lady does her train in bad weather.

Rip Van Winkle, however, was one of those happy mortals, of foolish, well-oiled dispositions, who take the world easy, eat white bread or brown, whichever can be got with least thought of trouble, and would rather starve on a penny than work for a pound. If left to himself, he would have whistled life away in perfect contentment; but his wife kept continually dinning in his ears about his idleness, his carelessness and the ruin he was bringing on his family. Morning, noon, and night, her tongue was incessantly going, and everything he said or did was sure to produce a torrent of household eloquence. Rip had but one way of replying to all lectures of the kind, and that, by frequent use, had grown into a habit. He shrugged his shoulders, shook his head, cast up his eyes, but said nothing. This, however, always provoked a fresh volley from his wife; so that he was fain to draw off his forces, and take to the outside of

---

[3] *galligaskins:* loose breeches.

the house—the only side which, in truth, belongs to a henpecked husband.

Rip's sole domestic adherent was his dog Wolf, who was as much
henpecked as his master; for Dame Van Winkle regarded them as companions in idleness, and even looked upon Wolf with an evil eye, as the
cause of his master's going so often astray. True it is, in all points of
spirit befitting an honourable dog, he was as courageous an animal as
ever scoured the woods; but what courage can withstand the ever-during
and all-besetting terrors of a woman's tongue? The moment Wolf entered
the house his crest fell, his tail drooped to the ground, or curled between
his legs, he sneaked about with a gallows air, casting many a sidelong
glance at Dame Van Winkle, and at the least flourish of a broomstick or
ladle he would fly to the door with yelping precipitation.

Times grew worse and worse with Rip Van Winkle as years of matrimony rolled on; a tart temper never mellows with age, and a sharp tongue is the only edged tool that grows keener with constant use. For a long while he used to console himself, when driven from home, by frequenting a kind of perpetual club of the sages, philosophers, and other idle personages of the village, which held its sessions on a bench before a small inn, designated by a rubicund[4] portrait of His Majesty, George the Third. Here they used to sit in the shade through a long, lazy summer's day, talking listlessly over village gossip, or telling endless sleepy stories about nothing. But it would have been worth any statesman's money to have heard the profound discussions that sometimes took place, when by chance an old newspaper fell into their hands from some passing traveller. How solemnly they would listen to the contents, as drawled out by Derrick Van Bummel, the schoolmaster, a dapper, learned little man, who was not to be daunted by the most gigantic word in the dictionary; and how sagely they would deliberate upon public events some months after they had taken place.

The opinions of this junta[5] were completely controlled by Nicholas Vedder, a patriarch of the village, and landlord of the inn, at the door of which he took his seat from morning till night, just moving sufficiently to avoid the sun and keep in the shade of a large tree; so that the neighbours could tell the hour by his movements as accurately as by a sundial. It is true he was rarely heard to speak, but smoked his pipe incessantly. His adherents, however (for every great man has his adherents), perfectly understood him, and knew how to gather his opinions. When anything that was read or related displeased him, he was observed to smoke his pipe vehemently, and to send forth short, frequent, and angry puffs; but when pleased, he would inhale the smoke slowly and tranquilly, and emit it in light and placid clouds; and sometimes, taking the pipe from his mouth, and letting the fragrant vapour curl about his nose, would gravely nod his head in token of perfect approbation.

From even this stronghold the unlucky Rip was at length routed by his termagant wife, who would suddenly break in upon the tranquillity of the assemblage and call the members all to naught; nor was that august personage, Nicholas Vedder himself, sacred from the daring tongue of this terrible virago,[6] who charged him outright with encouraging her husband in habits of idleness.

---

[4] *rubicund:* rosy or ruddy complexioned.
[5] junta (hŏŏn'tə): a group (usually military) who have seized power.
[6] *virago* (vĭ-rä'gō): a noisy, domineering woman.

Poor Rip was at last reduced almost to despair; and his only alternative, to escape from the labour of the farm and clamour of his wife, was to take gun in hand and stroll away into the woods. Here he would sometimes seat himself at the foot of a tree, and share the contents of his wallet with Wolf, with whom he sympathised as a fellow sufferer in persecution. "Poor Wolf," he would say, "thy mistress leads thee a dog's life of it; but never mind, my lad, while I live thou shalt never want a friend to stand by thee!" Wolf would wag his tail, look wistfully in his master's face; and if dogs can feel pity, I verily believe he reciprocated the sentiment with all his heart.

In a long ramble of the kind on a fine autumnal day, Rip had unconsciously scrambled to one of the highest parts of the Kaatskill Mountains. He was after his favourite sport of squirrel-shooting, and the still solitude had echoed and reëchoed with the reports of his gun. Panting and fatigued, he threw himself, late in the afternoon, on a green knoll, covered with mountain herbage, that crowned the brow of a precipice. From an opening between the trees he could overlook all the lower country for many a mile of rich woodland. He saw at a distance the lordly Hudson, far, far below him, moving on his silent but majestic course, with the reflection of a purple cloud, or the sail of a lagging bark, here and there sleeping on its glassy bottom, and at last losing itself in the blue highlands.

On the other side he looked down into a deep mountain glen, wild, lonely, and shagged, the bottom filled with fragments from the impending cliffs, and scarcely lighted by the reflected rays of the setting sun. For some time Rip lay musing on this scene; evening was gradually advancing; the mountains began to throw their long, blue shadows over the valleys; he saw that it would be dark long before he could reach the village, and he heaved a heavy sigh when he thought of encountering the terrors of Dame Van Winkle.

As he was about to descend, he heard a voice from the distance, hallooing: "Rip Van Winkle! Rip Van Winkle!" He looked round, but could see nothing but a crow winging its solitary flight across the mountain. He thought his fancy must have deceived him, and turned again to descend, when he heard the same cry ring through the still evening air: "Rip Van Winkle! Rip Van Winkle!"—at the same time Wolf bristled up his back, and giving a low growl, skulked to his master's side, looking fearfully down into the glen. Rip now felt a vague apprehension stealing over him; he looked anxiously in the same direction, and perceived a strange figure slowly toiling up the rocks, and bending under the weight of something he carried on his back. He was surprised to see any human being in this lonely and unfrequented place; but supposing it to be some one of the neighbourhood in need of his assistance, he hastened down to yield it.

On nearer approach he was still more surprised at the singularity of the stranger's appearance. He was a short, square-built old fellow, with thick bushy hair, and a grizzled beard. His dress was of the antique Dutch fashion—a cloth jerkin strapped round the waist—several pair of breeches, the outer one of ample volume, decorated with rows of buttons down the sides, and bunches at the knees. He bore on his shoulder a stout keg that seemed full of liquor, and made signs for Rip to approach and assist him with the load. Though rather shy and distrustful of this new acquaintance, Rip complied with his usual alacrity; and mutually relieving one another, they clambered up a narrow gully, apparently the dry bed of a mountain torrent. As they ascended, Rip every now and then heard long, rolling peals, like distant thunder, that seemed to issue out of a deep ravine, or rather cleft, between lofty rocks, towards which their rugged path conducted. He paused for an instant, but supposing it to be the muttering of one of those transient thunder-showers which often take place in mountain heights, he proceeded. Passing through the ravine, they came to a hollow, like a small amphitheatre,[7] surrounded by perpendicular precipices, over the brinks of which impending trees shot their branches, so that you only caught glimpses of the azure sky and the bright evening cloud. During the whole time Rip and his companion had laboured on in silence; for though the former marvelled greatly what could be the object of carrying a keg of liquor up this wild mountain, yet there was something strange and incomprehensible about the unknown, that inspired awe and checked familiarity.

On entering the amphitheatre, new objects of wonder presented themselves. On a level spot in the centre was a company of odd-looking personages playing at ninepins. They were dressed in a quaint, outlandish fashion; some wore short doublets, others jerkins,[8] with long knives in their belts, and most of them had enormous breeches of similar style with that of the guide's. Their visages, too, were peculiar: one had a large beard, broad face, and small, piggish eyes; the face of another seemed to consist entirely of nose, and was surmounted by a white sugar-loaf hat, set off with a little red cock's tail. They all had beards of various shapes and colours. There was one who seemed to be the commander. He was a stout old gentleman, with a weather-beaten countenance; he wore a laced doublet, broad belt and hanger, high-crowned hat and feather, red stockings, and high-heeled shoes, with roses in them. The whole group re-

---

[7] *amphitheatre:* an oval or round structure with seats rising from a central arena.
[8] *doublets . . . jerkins:* close-fitting jackets . . . vests.

minded Rip of the figures in an old Flemish painting, in the parlour of Dominie Van Shaick, the village parson, and which had been brought over from Holland at the time of the settlement.

What seemed particularly odd to Rip was, that, though these folks were evidently amusing themselves, yet they maintained the gravest faces, the most mysterious silence, and were, withal, the most melancholy party of pleasure he had ever witnessed. Nothing interrupted the stillness of the scene but the noise of the balls, which, whenever they were rolled, echoed along the mountains like rumbling peals of thunder.

As Rip and his companion approached them, they suddenly desisted from their play, and stared at him with such fixed, statuelike gaze, and such strange, uncouth, lack-lustre countenances, that his heart turned within him, and his knees smote together. His companion now emptied the contents of the keg into large flagons, and made signs to him to wait upon the company. He obeyed with fear and trembling; they quaffed the liquor in profound silence, and then returned to their game.

By degrees Rip's awe and apprehension subsided. He even ventured, when no eye was fixed upon him, to taste the beverage, which he found had much of the flavour of excellent hollands.[9] He was naturally a thirsty soul, and was soon tempted to repeat the draught.[10] One taste provoked another; and he reiterated his visits to the flagon so often that at length his senses were overpowered, his eyes swam in his head, his head gradually declined, and he fell into a deep sleep.

On waking, he found himself on the green knoll whence he had first seen the old man of the glen. He rubbed his eyes—it was a bright, sunny morning. The birds were hopping and twittering among the bushes, and the eagle was wheeling aloft, and breasting the pure mountain breeze. "Surely," thought Rip, "I have not slept here all night." He recalled the occurrences before he fell asleep. The strange man with a keg of liquor—the mountain ravine—the wild retreat among the rocks—the woebegone party at ninepins—the flagon—"Oh! that flagon! that wicked flagon!" thought Rip—"what excuse shall I make to Dame Van Winkle?"

He looked round for his gun, but in place of the clean, well-oiled fowling-piece, he found an old firelock lying by him, the barrel encrusted with rust, the lock falling off, and the stock worm-eaten. He now suspected that the grave roisterers of the mountain had put a trick upon him, and, having dosed him with liquor, had robbed him of his gun. Wolf, too, had disappeared, but he might have strayed away after a squirrel or partridge. He whistled after him, and shouted his name, but

[9] *hollands:* Dutch ale.
[10] *draught* (drăft): amount taken in at a single swallow.

all in vain; the echoes repeated his whistle and shout, but no dog was to be seen.

He determined to revisit the scene of the last evening's gambol, and if he met with any of the party to demand his dog and gun. As he rose to walk he found himself stiff in the joints, and wanting in his usual activity. "These mountain beds do not agree with me," thought Rip, "and if this frolic should lay me up with a fit of the rheumatism, I shall have a blessed time with Dame Van Winkle!" With some difficulty he got down into the glen; he found the gully up which he and his companion had ascended the preceding evening; but to his astonishment a mountain stream was now foaming down it, leaping from rock to rock, and filling the glen with babbling murmurs. He, however, made shift to scramble up its sides, working his toilsome way through thickets of birch, sassafras, and witch-hazel, and sometimes tripped up or entangled by the wild grape-vines that twisted their coils or tendrils from tree to tree, and spread a kind of network in his path.

At length he reached to where the ravine had opened through the cliffs to the amphitheatre; but no traces of such opening remained. The rocks presented a high, impenetrable wall, over which the torrent came tumbling in a sheet of feathery foam, and fell into a broad deep basin, black from the shadows of the surrounding forest. Here, then, poor Rip was brought to a stand. He again called and whistled after his dog; he was only answered by the cawing of a flock of idle crows, sporting high in air about a dry tree that overhung a sunny precipice; and who, secure in their elevation, seemed to look down and scoff at the poor man's perplexities. What was to be done? The morning was passing away, and Rip felt famished for want of his breakfast. He grieved to give up his dog and gun; he dreaded to meet his wife; but it would not do to starve among the mountains. He shook his head, shouldered the rusty firelock, and, with a heart full of trouble and anxiety, turned his steps homewards.

As he approached the village he met a number of people, but none whom he knew, which somewhat surprised him, for he had thought himself acquainted with every one in the country round. Their dress, too, was of a different fashion from that to which he was accustomed. They all stared at him with equal marks of surprise, and whenever they cast their eyes upon him, invariably stroked their chins. The constant recurrence of this gesture induced Rip, involuntarily, to do the same, when, to his astonishment, he found his beard had grown a foot long!

He had now entered the skirts of the village. A troop of strange children ran at his heels, hooting after him, and pointing at his gray beard. The dogs, too, not one of which he recognised for an old acquaintance, barked at him as he passed. The very village was altered; it was larger and more populous. There were rows of houses which he had never seen before, and those which had been his familiar haunts had disappeared. Strange names were over the doors—strange faces at the windows— everything was strange. His mind now misgave him; he began to doubt whether both he and the world around him were not bewitched. Surely this was his native village, which he had left but the day before. There stood the Kaatskill Mountains—there ran the silver Hudson at a dis- tance—there was every hill and dale precisely as it had always been. Rip was sorely perplexed. "That flagon last night," thought he, "has addled my poor head sadly!"

It was with some difficulty that he found the way to his own house, which he approached with silent awe, expecting every moment to hear the shrill voice of Dame Van Winkle. He found the house gone to de- cay—the roof fallen in, the windows shattered, and the doors off the hinges. A half-starved dog that looked like Wolf was skulking about it. Rip called him by name, but the cur snarled, showed his teeth, and passed on. This was an unkind cut indeed. "My very dog," sighed poor Rip, "has forgotten me!"

He entered the house, which, to tell the truth, Dame Van Winkle had always kept in neat order. It was empty, forlorn, and appparently abandoned. This desolateness overcame all his cunnubial[11] fears—he called loudly for his wife and children—the lonely chambers rang for a moment with his voice, and then all again was silence.

He now hurried forth, and hastened to his old resort, the village inn—but it, too, was gone. A large, rickety wooden building stood in its place, with great gaping windows, some of them broken and mended with old hats and petticoats, and over the door was painted: The Union Hotel, by Jonathan Doolittle. Instead of the great tree that used to shelter the quiet little Dutch inn of yore, there now was reared a tall naked pole, with something on the top that looked like a red nightcap, and from it was fluttering a flag, on which was a singular assemblage of stars and stripes;—all this was strange and incomprehensible. He recognised on the sign, however, the ruby face of King George, under which he had smoked so many a peaceful pipe; but even this was singularly metamor- phosed.[12] The red coat was changed for one of blue and buff, a sword was held in the hand instead of a sceptre, the head was decorated with a cocked hat, and underneath was painted in large characters: GENERAL WASHINGTON.

---

[11] *connubial:* having to do with marriage.
[12] *metamorphosed:* transformed.

There was, as usual, a crowd of folk about the door, but none that Rip recollected. The very character of the people seemed changed. There was a busy, bustling, disputatious tone about it, instead of the accustomed phlegm [13] and drowsy tranquillity. He looked in vain for the sage Nicholas Vedder, with his broad face, double chin, and fair long pipe, uttering clouds of tobacco smoke instead of idle speeches; or Van Bummel, the schoolmaster, doling forth the contents of an ancient newspaper. In place of these, a lean, bilious-looking fellow, with his pockets full of handbills, was haranguing vehemently about rights of citizens—elections—members of Congress—liberty—Bunker Hill—heroes of '76—and other words, which were a perfect Babylonish jargon to the bewildered Van Winkle.

The appearance of Rip, with his long grizzled beard, his rusty fowling-piece, his uncouth dress, and an army of women and children at his heels, soon attracted the attention of the tavern politicians. They crowded round him, eyeing him from head to foot with great curiosity. The orator bustled up to him, and, drawing him partly aside, inquired "on which side he voted." Rip stared in vacant stupidity. Another short but busy little fellow pulled him by the arm, and, rising on tiptoe, inquired in his ear "whether he was Federal or Democrat." Rip was equally at a loss to comprehend the question; when a knowing, self-important old gentleman, in a sharp cocked hat, made his way through the crowd, putting them to the right and left with his elbows as he passed, and planting himself before Van Winkle, with one arm akimbo, the other resting on his cane, his keen eyes and sharp hat penetrating, as it were, into his very soul, demanded in an austere tone "what brought him to the election with a gun on his shoulder and a mob at his heels; and whether he meant to breed a riot in the village."—"Alas! gentlemen," cried Rip, somewhat dismayed, "I am a poor, quiet man, a native of the place, and a loyal subject of the King, God bless him!"

Here a general shout burst from the bystanders—"A Tory! a Tory! a spy! a refugee! hustle him! away with him!" It was with great difficulty that the self-important man in the cocked hat restored order; and, having assumed a tenfold austerity of brow, demanded again of the unknown culprit what he came there for and whom he was seeking. The poor man humbly assured him that he meant no harm, but merely came there in search of some of his neighbours, who used to keep about the tavern.

"Well—who are they?—name them."

Rip bethought himself a moment, and inquired: "Where's Nicholas Vedder?"

---

[13] *phlegm* (flĕm): sluggishness.

There was a silence for a little while, when an old man replied, in a thin, piping voice: "Nicholas Vedder! Why, he is dead and gone these eighteen years! There was a wooden tombstone in the churchyard that used to tell all about him, but that's rotten and gone too."

"Where's Brom Dutcher?"

"Oh, he went off to the army in the beginning of the war; some say he was killed at the storming of Stony Point—others say he was drowned in a squall at the foot of Anthony's Nose. I don't know—he never came back again."

"Where's Van Bummel, the schoolmaster?"

"He went off to the wars, too, was a great militia general, and is now in Congress."

Rip's heart died away at hearing of these sad changes in his home and friends, and finding himself thus alone in the world. Every answer puzzled him, too, by treating of such enormous lapses of time, and of matters which he could not understand: war—Congress—Stony Point— he had no courage to ask after any more friends, but cried out in despair: "Does nobody here know Rip Van Winkle?"

"Oh, Rip Van Winkle!" exclaimed two or three, "oh, to be sure! that's Rip Van Winkle yonder, leaning against the tree."

Rip looked, and beheld a precise counterpart of himself, as he went up the mountain; apparently as lazy, and certainly as ragged. The poor fellow was now completely confounded. He doubted his own identity, and whether he was himself or another man. In the midst of his bewilderment, the man in the cocked hat demanded who he was, and what was his name.

"God knows," exclaimed he, at his wit's end; "I'm not myself—I'm somebody else—that's me yonder—no—that's somebody else got into my shoes—I was myself last night, but I fell asleep on the mountain, and they've changed my gun, and everything's changed, and I'm changed, and I can't tell what's my name, or who I am!"

The bystanders began now to look at each other, nod, wink significantly, and tap their fingers against their foreheads. There was a whisper, also, about securing the gun, and keeping the old fellow from doing mischief, at the very suggestion of which the self-important man in the cocked hat retired with some precipitation. At this critical moment a fresh, comely woman pressed through the throng to get a peep at the gray-bearded man. She had a chubby child in her arms, which, frightened at his looks, began to cry. "Hush, Rip," cried she, "hush, you little fool; the old man won't hurt you." The name of the child, the air of the mother, the tone of her voice, all awakened a train of recollections in his mind. "What is your name, my good woman?" asked he.

"Judith Gardenier."

"And your father's name?"

"Ah, poor man, Rip Van Winkle was his name, but it's twenty years since he went away from home with his gun, and never has been heard of since—his dog came home without him; but whether he shot himself, or was carried away by the Indians, nobody can tell. I was then but a little girl."

Rip had but one question more to ask; but he put it with a faltering voice:

"Where's your mother?"

"Oh, she, too, had died but a short time since; she broke a blood-vessel in a fit of passion [14] at a New England peddler."

---

[14] *fit of passion:* fit of rage.

There was a drop of comfort, at least, in this intelligence. The honest man could contain himself no longer. He caught his daughter and her child in his arms. "I am your father!" cried he—"young Rip Van Winkle once—old Rip Van Winkle now!—Does nobody know poor Rip Van Winkle?"

All stood amazed, until an old woman, tottering out from among the crowd, put her hand to her brow, and peering under it in his face for a moment, exclaimed: "Sure enough! It is Rip Van Winkle—it is himself! Welcome home again, old neighbour. Why, where have you been these twenty long years?"

Rip's story was soon told, for the whole twenty years had been to him as but one night. The neighbours stared when they heard it; some were seen to wink at each other, and put their tongues in their cheeks; and the self-important man in the cocked hat, who, when the alarm was over, had returned to the field, screwed down the corners of his mouth, and shook his head—upon which there was a general shaking of the head throughout the assemblage.

It was determined, however, to take the opinion of old Peter Vanderdonk, who was seen slowly advancing up the road. He was a descendant of the historian of that name, who wrote one of the earliest accounts of the province. Peter was the most ancient inhabitant of the village, and well versed in all the wonderful events and traditions of the neighbourhood. He recollected Rip at once, and corroborated[15] his story in the most satisfactory manner. He assured the company that it was a fact, handed down from his ancestor the historian, that the Kaatskill Mountains had always been haunted by strange beings. That it was affirmed that the great Hendrick Hudson, the first discoverer of the river and country, kept a kind of vigil there every twenty years, with his crew of the Half Moon; being permitted in this way to revisit the scenes of his enterprise, and keep a guardian eye upon the river and the great city called by his name. That his father had once seen them in their old Dutch dresses playing at ninepins in a hollow of the mountain; and that he himself had heard, one summer afternoon, the sound of their balls, like distant peals of thunder.

To make a long story short, the company broke up and returned to the more important concerns of the election. Rip's daughter took him home to live with her; she had a snug, well-furnished house, and a stout, cheery farmer for a husband, whom Rip recollected for one of the urchins that used to climb upon his back. As to Rip's son and heir, who was the ditto of himself, seen leaning against the tree, he was employed

---

[15] *corroborated* (kə-rŏb'ə-rā-tĕd): confirmed; supported.

to work on the farm; but evinced an hereditary disposition to attend to anything else but his business.

Rip now resumed his old walks and habits; he soon found many of his former cronies, though all rather the worse for the wear and tear of time; and preferred making friends among the rising generation, with whom he soon grew into great favour.

Having nothing to do at home, and being arrived at that happy age when a man can be idle with impunity, he took his place once more on the bench at the inn door, and was reverenced as one of the patriarchs of the village, and a chronicle of the old times "before the war." It was some time before he could get into the regular track of gossip, or could be made to comprehend the strange events that had taken place during his torpor: [16] how that there had been a Revolutionary war—that the country had thrown off the yoke of old England—and that, instead of being a subject of His Majesty, George III, he was now a free citizen of the United States. Rip, in fact, was no politician; the changes of states and empires made but little impression on him; but there was one species of despotism under which he had long groaned, and that was—petticoat government. Happily that was at an end; he had got his neck out of the yoke of matrimony, and could go in and out whenever he pleased, without dreading the tyranny of Dame Van Winkle. Whenever her name was mentioned, however, he shook his head, shrugged his shoulders, and cast up his eyes; which might pass either for an expression of resignation to his fate or joy at his deliverance.

He used to tell his story to every stranger that arrived at Mr. Doolittle's hotel. He was observed, at first, to vary on some points every time he told it, which was, doubtless, owing to his having so recently awakened. It at last settled down precisely to the tale I have related, and not a man, woman, or child in the neighbourhood but knew it by heart. Some always pretended to doubt the reality of it, and insisted that Rip had been out of his head, and that this was one point on which he always remained flighty. The old Dutch inhabitants, however, almost universally gave it full credit. Even to this day they never hear a thunderstorm of a summer afternoon about the Kaatskill, but they say Hendrick Hudson and his crew are at their game of ninepins; and it is a common wish of all henpecked husbands in the neighbourhood, when life hangs heavy on their hands, that they might have a quieting draught out of Rip Van Winkle's flagon.

---

[16] *torpor:* stupor.

NOTE

The foregoing tale, one would suspect, had been suggested to Mr. Knickerbocker by a little German superstition about the Emperor Frederick der Rothbart, and the Kypphäuser mountain: the subjoined note, however, which he had appended to the tale, shows that it is an absolute fact, narrated with his usual fidelity.

"The story of Rip Van Winkle may seem incredible to many, but nevertheless I give it my full belief, for I know the vicinity of our old Dutch settlements to have been very subject to marvellous events and appearances. Indeed, I have heard many stranger stories than this, in the villages along the Hudson; all of which were too well authenticated to admit of a doubt. I have even talked with Rip Van Winkle myself, who, when last I saw him, was a very venerable old man, and so perfectly rational and consistent on every other point, that I think no conscientious person could refuse to take this into the bargain; nay, I have seen a certificate on the subject taken before a country justice and signed with a cross, in the justice's own handwriting. The story, therefore, is beyond the possibility of a doubt.

"D.K."

DISCUSSION

1. As Rip becomes accustomed to the changed times, why do you suppose he prefers "making friends among the rising generation" to renewing friendships with his old cronies?

2. Rip would console himself in the old days before his adventure by sitting with "the perpetual club of the philosophers, sages, and other idle personages of the village." Look back at the description of these "personages." What is the author's attitude toward them? How can you tell?

3. "The late Diedrich Knickerbocker," supposed author of this story, is purely fictitious. What tongue-in-cheek statement in the "Note" helps give this away?

4. The author surrounds the story of Rip with false claims for its truthfulness and pokes fun at Rip, his wife, the inhabitants of the village, and even the American Revolution. Is the author serious about anything? What do you think he wanted to show the readers of this tale? (Look back at the introduction to the story before you answer.)

5. Decide whether you agree or disagree with this statement and explain your reasons: the plot of this story is far more important than either the characters or the setting.

For further activities, see page 56.

This story is taken from Melville's novel *Redburn*. Wellingborough Redburn, here referred to by his nickname "Buttons," is a fictional version of Melville himself on his own first voyage.

New York to Liverpool

HERMAN MELVILLE

The anchor being secured, a steam tug-boat with a strong name, the Hercules, took hold of us; and away we went past the long line of shipping, and wharves, and warehouses; and rounded the green south point of the island where the Battery[1] is, and passed Governor's Island, and pointed right out for the Narrows, which is the entrance to New York Harbor from sea. When you go out of these Narrows on a long voyage, it seems like going out into the broad highway, where not a soul is to be seen. For far away and away, stretches the great Atlantic Ocean; and all you can see beyond is where the sky comes down to the water. It looks lonely and desolate enough, and I could hardly believe, as I gazed around me, that there could be any land beyond, or any place like Europe or England in the great wide world. It seemed too strange, and wonderful, and altogether incredible, that there could really be cities and towns and villages and green fields and hedges and farm-yards and orchards, away over that wide blank of sea, and away beyond the place where the sky came down to the water. And to think of steering right out among those waves, and leaving the bright land behind, and the dark night coming on, too, seemed wild and fool-hardy.

About sunset we got fairly "outside," and well may it so be called; for I felt thrust out of the world. Then the breeze began to blow, and the sails were loosed, and hoisted; and after a while, the steam-boat left us, and for the first time I felt the ship roll, a strange feeling enough, as if it were a great barrel in the water. Shortly after, I observed a swift little schooner running across our bows, and re-crossing again and again; and while I was wondering what she could be, she suddenly lowered her sails, and two men took hold of a little boat on her deck, and launched it overboard as if it had been a chip. Then I noticed that our pilot, a red-faced man in a rough blue coat, who to my astonishment had all this time been giving orders instead of the captain; I noticed that he began to button up his coat to the throat, like a prudent person about leaving a house at night in a lonely square, to go home; and he left the giving orders to the chief mate, and stood apart talking with the captain, and put his hand into his pocket, and gave him some newspapers.

And in a few minutes, when he had stopped our headway, and allowed the little boat to come alongside, he shook

[1] *Battery:* old fort overlooking New York harbor.

hands with the captain and officers and bade them good-bye, without saying a syllable of farewell to me and the sailors; and so he went laughing over the side, and got into the boat, and they pulled him off to the schooner, and then the schooner made sail and glided under our stern, her men standing up and waving their hats, and cheering; and that was the last we saw of America.

The second day out of port, the decks being washed down and breakfast over, the watch was called, and the mate set us to work.

It was a very bright day. The sky and water were both of the same deep hue; and the air felt warm and sunny; so that we threw off our jackets. I could hardly imagine that this was the same ocean, now so beautiful and blue, that during part of the night-watch had rolled along so black and forbidding.

There were little traces of sunny clouds all over the heavens; and little fleeces of foam all over the sea; and the ship made a strange, musical noise under her bows, as she glided along, with her sails all still. It seemed a pity to go to work at such a time; and if we could only have sat in the windlass[2] again; or if they would have let me go out on the bowsprit[3] and lay down between the *man-ropes*[4] there, and look over at the fish in the water, and think of home, I should have been almost happy for a time.

I had now completely got over my seasickness, and felt very well; so that I could now look around me, and make observations.

And truly, though we were at sea, there was much to behold and wonder at to me, who was on my first voyage. What most amazed me was the sight of the great ocean itself, for we were out of sight of land. All round us, on both sides of the ship, ahead and astern, nothing was to be seen but water—water—water; not a single glimpse of green shore, not the smallest island, or speck of moss any-where. Never did I realise till now what the ocean was: how grand and majestic, how solitary, and boundless, and beauti-ful and blue; for that day it gave no to-kens of squalls or hurricanes, such as I had heard my father tell of; nor could I imagine how anything that seemed so playful and placid, could be lashed into rage, and troubled into rolling avalanches of foam, and great cascades of waves, such as I saw in the end.

But what seemed perhaps the most strange to me of all, was a certain won-derful rising and falling of the sea; I do not mean the waves themselves, but a sort of wide heaving and swelling and sinking all over the ocean. It was some-thing I can not very well describe; but I know very well what it was, and how it affected me. It made me almost dizzy to look at it; and yet I could not keep my eyes off it, it seemed so passing[5] strange and wonderful.

I felt as if in a dream all the time; and when I could shut the ship out, al-most thought I was in some new, fairy

---

[2] *windlass:* device for raising or lowering objects by winding or unwinding rope around a cylinder.
[3] *bowsprit:* pole projecting from the bow.
[4] *man-ropes:* ropes used as guardrails or supports.

[5] *passing:* very.

world, and expected to hear myself called to, out of the clear blue air, or from the depths of the deep blue sea. But I did not have much leisure to indulge in such thoughts; for the men were now getting some *stun'-sails*[6] ready to hoist aloft, as the wind was getting fairer[7] and fairer for us; and these stun'-sails are light canvas which are spread at such times, away out beyond the ends of the yards,[8] where they overhang the wide water, like the wings of a great bird.

For my own part, I could do but little to help the rest, not knowing the name of anything, or the proper way to go about aught. Besides, I felt very dreamy, as I said before; and did not exactly know where, or what I was; everything was so strange and new.

At last we hoisted the stun'-sails up to the top-sail yards; and as soon as the vessel felt them, she gave a sort of bound like a horse, and the breeze blowing more and more, she went plunging along, shaking off the foam from her bows, like foam from a bridle-bit.[9] Every mast and timber seemed to have a pulse in it that was beating with life and joy; and I felt a wild exulting in my own heart, and felt as if I would be glad to bound along so round the world.

Then was I first conscious of a wonderful thing in me, that responded to all the wild commotion of the outer world; and went reeling on and on with the planets in their orbits, and was lost in one delirious throb at the center of the All. A wild bubbling and bursting was at my heart, as if a hidden spring had just gushed out there; and my blood ran tingling along my frame, like mountain brooks in spring freshets.

Yes! yes! give me this glorious ocean life, this salt-sea life, this briny, foamy life, when the sea neighs and snorts, and you breathe the very breath that the great whales respire! Let me roll around the globe, let me rock upon the sea; let me race and pant out my life, with an eternal breeze astern, and an endless sea before!

But how soon these raptures abated, when after a brief idle interval, we were again set to work, and I had a vile commission to clean out the chicken coops, and make up the beds of the pigs in the long-boat.[10]

Miserable dog's life is this of the sea! commanded like a slave, and set to work like a donkey! vulgar and brutal men lording it over me. Yes, yes blow on, ye breezes, and make a speedy end to this abominable voyage!

I must now tell of my first going aloft at sea.

It happened on the second night out of port, during the middle watch, when the sea was quite calm, and the breeze was mild.

The order was given to loose the *main-skysail,* which is the fifth and highest sail from deck. It was a very small sail, and from the forecastle[11] looked no bigger than a cambric pocket-handkerchief.

---

[6] *stun'-sails:* studding sails; small sails added in a fair wind.
[7] *fairer:* coming more nearly from behind the ship.
[8] *yards:* horizontal poles supporting tops of square sails.
[9] *bridle-bit:* bar put in horse's mouth to control or restrain.

[10] *long-boat:* largest of the ship's utility boats.
[11] *forecastle* (fōk'səl): deck area at the bow.

But I have heard that some ships carry still smaller sails, above the skysail; called *moon-sails,* and *sky-scrapers,* and *cloud-rakers.* But I shall not believe in them till I see them; a *skysail* seems high enough in all conscience; and the idea of anything higher than that seems preposterous. Besides, it looks almost like tempting heaven, to brush the very firmament so, and almost put the eyes of the stars out; when a flaw [12] of wind, too, might very soon take the conceit out of these cloud-defying *cloud-rakers.*

Now, when the order was passed to loose the skysail, an old Dutch sailor came up to me, and said,"Buttons, my boy, it's high time you be doing something; and it's boy's business, Buttons, to loose de royals, [13] and not old men's business, like me. Now, d'ye see dat leetle fellow way up dare? *dare,* just behind dem stars dare: well, tumble up, now, Buttons, I zay, and looze him; way you go, Buttons."

All the rest joining in, and seeming unanimous in the opinion, that it was high time for me to be stirring myself, and doing *boy's business,* as they called it, I made no more ado, but jumped into the rigging. Up I went, not daring to look down, but keeping my eyes glued, as it were, to the shrouds, [14] as I ascended.

It was a long road up those stairs, and I began to pant and breathe hard, before I was half way. But I kept at it till I got to the *Jacob's Ladder;* [15] and they may well call it so, for it took me almost into

the clouds; and at last, to my own amazement, I found myself hanging on the sky-sail-yard, holding on might and main to the mast; and curling my feet round the rigging, as if they were another pair of hands.

For a few moments I stood awe-stricken and mute. I could not see far out upon the ocean, owing to the darkness of the night; and from my lofty perch, the sea looked like a great, black gulf, hemmed in, all round, by beetling [16] black cliffs. I seemed all alone, treading the midnight clouds, and every second, expected to find myself falling—falling—falling, as I have felt when the nightmare has been on me.

I could but just perceive the ship below me, like a long narrow plank in the water; and it did not seem to belong at all to the yard, over which I was hanging. A gull, or some sort of sea-fowl, was flying round the truck [17] over my head, within a few yards of my face; and it almost frightened me to hear it, it seemed so much like a spirit, at such lofty and solitary height.

Though there was a pretty smooth sea, and little wind; yet, at this extreme elevation, the ship's motion was very great; so that when the ship rolled one way, I felt something as a fly must feel, walking the ceiling; and when it rolled the other way, I felt as if I was hanging along a slanting pine tree.

But presently I heard a distant, hoarse noise from below; and though I could not make out anything intelligible, I knew it was the mate hurrying me. So in a nervous, trembling desperation, I

---

[12] *flaw:* sudden gust.
[13] *royals:* sails next below the skysails.
[14] *shrouds:* ropes steadying the tops of masts.
[15] *Jacob's Ladder:* named for ladder to heaven (Genesis 28:12) that Jacob saw in a dream.

[16] *beetling:* overhanging.
[17] *truck:* round tip of mast.

went to casting off the *gaskets,* or lines tying up the sail; and when all was ready, sung out as I had been told, to *"hoist away!"* And hoist they did, and me too along with the yard and sail; for I had no time to get off, they were so unexpectedly quick about it. It seemed like magic; there I was going up higher and higher; the yard rising under me, as if it were alive, and no soul in sight. Without knowing it at the time, I was in a good deal of danger, but it was so dark that I could not see well enough to feel afraid—at least on that account; though I felt frightened enough in a promiscuous[18] way. I only held on hard, and made good the saying of old sailors, that the last person to fall overboard from the rigging is a landsman, because he grips the ropes so fiercely; whereas old tars are less careful, and sometimes pay the penalty.

It was on a Sunday we made the Banks of Newfoundland; a drizzling, foggy, clammy Sunday. You could hardly see the water, owing to the mist and vapor upon it; and everything was so flat and calm, I almost thought we must have somehow got back to New York, and were lying at the foot of Wall-street again in a rainy twilight. The decks were dripping with wet, so that in the dense fog, it seemed as if we were standing on the roof of a house in a shower.

I tried to recall all my pleasant, sunny Sundays ashore; and tried to imagine what they were doing at home; and whether our old family friend, Mr. Bridenstoke, would drop in, with his silver-mounted tasseled cane, between

churches, as he used to; and whether he would inquire about myself.

But it would not do. I could hardly realize that it was Sunday at all. Everything went on pretty much the same as before. There was no church to go to; no place to take a walk in; no friend to call upon. I began to think it must be a sort of second Saturday; a foggy Saturday, when schoolboys stay at home reading Robinson Crusoe.

What is this that we sail through? What palpable obscure?[19] What smoke and reek, as if the whole steaming world were revolving on its axis, as a spit?

It is a Newfoundland Fog; and we are yet crossing the Great Banks, wrapt in a mist, that no London in the Novemberest November ever equaled. The chronometer[20] pronounced it noon; but do you call this midnight or mid-day? So dense is the fog, that though we have a fair wind, we shorten sail for fear of accidents; and not only that, but here am I, mounted aloft on a sort of belfry, the top of the *"Sampson-Post,"* a lofty tower of timber, so called; and tolling the ship's bell, as if for a funeral.

This is intended to proclaim our approach, and warn all strangers from our track.

Dreary sound! toll, toll, toll, through the dismal mist and fog.

The bell is green with verdigris,[21] and damp with dew; and the little cord attached to the clapper, by which I toll it,

---

[18] *promiscuous:* confused.

[19] *palpable obscure:* darkness thick enough to touch; quotation from Milton's *Paradise Lost*, Book II.
[20] *chronometer:* very accurate ship's timepiece.
[21] *verdigris:* crust of copper sulfate or chloride formed on metal exposed to air and seawater for a long period of time.

now and then slides through my fingers, slippery with wet.

The most strange and unheard-of noises came out of the fog at times: a vast sound of sighing and sobbing. What could it be? This would be followed by a spout, and a gush, and a cascading commotion, as if some fountain had suddenly jetted out of the ocean.

Seated on my Sampson-Post, I stared more and more, and suspended my duty as a sexton. But presently some one cried out—*"There she blow! whales! whales close alongside!"*

A whale! Think of it! whales close to *me,*—would my own brother believe it? I dropt the clapper as if it were red-hot, and rushed to the side; and there, dimly floating, lay four or five long, black snaky-looking shapes, only a few inches out of the water.

Can these be whales? Monstrous whales, such as I had heard of? I thought they would look like mountains on the sea; hills and valleys of flesh! regular krakens,[22] that made it high tide, and inundated continents, when they descended to feed!

It was a bitter disappointment, from which I was long in recovering. I lost all respect for whales; and began to be a little dubious about the story of Jonah,[23] for how could Jonah reside in such an insignificant tenement; how could he have had elbowroom there? But perhaps, thought I, the whale, which according to Rabbinical traditions[24] was a female one, might have expanded to receive him like an anaconda, when it swallows an elk and leaves the antlers sticking out of its mouth.

Nevertheless, from that day, whales greatly fell in my estimation.

On the next day, the fog lifted; and by noon, we found ourselves sailing through fleets of fishermen at anchor. They were very small craft; and when I beheld them, I perceived the force of that sailor saying, intended to illustrate restricted quarters, or being *on the limits. It is like a fisherman's walk,* say they, *three steps and overboard.*

Lying right on the track of the multitudinous ships crossing the ocean between England and America, these little vessels are sometimes run down, and obliterated from the face of the waters; the cry of the sailors ceasing with the last whirl of the whirlpool that closes over their craft. Their sad fate is frequently the result of their own remissness in keeping a good look-out by day, and not having their lamps trimmed, like the wise virgins,[25] by night.

We were still on the Banks, when a terrific storm came down upon us, the like of which I had never before beheld, or imagined. The rain poured down in sheets and cascades; the scupper holes could hardly carry it off the decks; and in bracing the yards we waded about almost up to our knees; everything floating about, like chips in a dock.

This violent rain was the precursor of a hard squall, for which we duly pre-

---

[22] *krakens:* sea monsters.
[23] *Jonah:* Biblical prophet who lived three days inside a whale.
[24] *Rabbinical traditions:* Hebrew commentaries on the Bible.

[25] *lamps trimmed . . . wise virgins:* from Matthew 25, New Testament.

pared, taking in our canvas to double-reefed topsails. [26]

The tornado came rushing along at last, like a troop of wild horses before the flaming rush of a burning prairie. But after bowing and cringing to it awhile, the good Highlander was put off before it; and with her nose in the water, went wallowing on, ploughing milk-white waves, and leaving a streak of illuminated foam in her wake.

It was an awful scene. It made me catch my breath as I gazed. I could hardly stand on my feet, so violent was the motion of the ship. But while I reeled to and fro, the sailors only laughed at me; and bade me look out that the ship did not fall overboard; and advised me to get a hand-spike, and hold it down hard in the weather-scuppers, to steady her wild motions. But I was now getting a little too wise for this foolish kind of talk; though all through the voyage, they never gave it over.

This storm past, we had fair weather until we got into the Irish Sea.

The morning following the storm, when the sea and sky had become blue again, the man aloft sung out that there was a wreck on the lee-beam. [27] We bore away for it, all hands looking eagerly toward it, and the captain in the mizzen-top [28] with his spy-glass. Presently, we slowly passed alongside of it.

It was a dismantled, water-logged schooner, a most dismal sight, that must have been drifting about for several long weeks. The bulwarks were pretty much gone; and here and there the bare *stanchions,* or posts, were left standing, splitting in two the waves which broke clear over the deck, lying almost even with the sea. The foremast was snapt off less than four feet from its base; and the shattered and splintered remnant looked like the stump of a pine tree thrown over in the woods. Every time she rolled in the trough of the sea, her open main-hatchway yawned into view; but was as quickly filled, and submerged again, with a rushing, gurgling sound, as the water ran into it with the lee-roll.

At the head of the stump of the mainmast, about ten feet above the deck, something like a sleeve seemed nailed; it was supposed to be the relic of a jacket, which must have been fastened there by the crew for a signal, and been frayed out and blown away by the wind.

Lashed, and leaning over sideways against the taffrail, [29] were three dark, green grassy objects, that slowly swayed with every roll, but otherwise were motionless. I saw the captain's glass directed toward them, and heard him say at last, "They must have been dead a long time." These were sailors, who long ago had lashed themselves to the taffrail for safety; but must have famished.

Full of the awful interest of the scene, I surely thought the captain would lower a boat to bury the bodies, and find out something about the schooner. But we did not stop at all, passing on our course, without so much as learning the

[26] *double-reefed topsails:* sails made smaller by *reefing,* or tying down sections with short pieces of line.
[27] *lee-beam:* area on side away from wind at widest point of ship.
[28] *mizzen-top:* platform around rear mast (mizzenmast) below its topsail.

[29] *taffrail:* railing around the stern.

schooner's name, though every one supposed her to be a New Brunswick lumberman. [30]

On the part of the sailors, no surprise was shown that our captain did not send off a boat to the wreck; but the steerage passengers [31] were indignant at what they called his barbarity. For me, I could not but feel amazed and shocked at his indifference; but my subsequent sea experiences have shown me, that such conduct as this is very common, though not, of course, when human life can be saved.

So away we sailed, and left her; drifting, drifting on, a garden spot for barnacles, and a playhouse for the sharks.

At sea, the sailors are continually engaged in *"parceling," "serving,"* [32] and in a thousand ways ornamenting and repairing the numberless shrouds and stays; mending sails, or turning one side of the deck into a rope-walk, where they manufacture a clumsy sort of twine, called *spun-yarn.* This is spun with a winch. [33] For material, they use odds and ends of old rigging called *"junk,"* the yarns of which are picked to pieces, and then twisted into new combinations, something as most books are manufactured.

This "junk" is bought at the junk shops along the wharves; outlandish looking dens, generally subterranean, full of old iron, old shrouds, spars, rusty blocks, and superannuated tackles; and kept by villainous looking old men, in tarred trowsers, and with yellow beards like oakum. [34] They look like wreckers; [35] and the scattered goods they expose for sale involuntarily remind one of the sea-beach, covered with keels and cordage, swept ashore in a gale.

I was now as nimble as a monkey in the rigging, and at the cry of *"tumble up there, my hearties, and take in sail,"* I was among the first ground-and-lofty tumblers, that sprang aloft at the word.

But the first time we reefed top-sails of a dark night, and I found myself hanging over the yard with eleven others, the ship plunging and rearing like a mad horse, till I felt like being jerked off the spar; then, indeed, I thought of a feather-bed at home, and hung on with tooth and nail; with no chance for snoring. But a few repetitions, soon made me used to it; and before long, I tied my reef-point as quickly and expertly as the best of them; never making what they called a *"granny-knot,"* [36] and slipt down on deck by the bare stays, instead of the shrouds. It is surprising, how soon a boy overcomes his timidity about going aloft. For my own part, my nerves became as steady as the earth's diameter, and I felt as fearless on the royal yard, as Sam Patch on the cliff of Niagara. [37] To my amazement, also, I found, that running up the rigging at sea, especially during a squall, was much easier than while lying in port.

---

[30] *lumberman:* ship carrying cargo of lumber.
[31] *steerage passengers:* those paying lowest fare, with quarters below decks.
[32] *"parceling," "serving":* parceling involves binding canvas strips around rope to keep it dry; serving is winding wire around stays to prevent fraying.
[33] *winch:* winding device turned by a crank.

[34] *oakum:* fiber salvaged from old rope.
[35] *wreckers:* salvagers of wrecked vessels.
[36] *"granny-knot":* incorrectly made square knot; it will slip rather than hold.
[37] *Sam Patch . . . Niagara:* Patch dived into the river from a cliff at Niagara Falls.

For as you always go up on the windward side, and the ship leans over, it makes more of a *stairs* of the rigging; whereas, in harbor, it is almost straight up and down.

Besides, the pitching and rolling only imparts a pleasant sort of vitality to the vessel; so that the difference in being aloft in a ship at sea, and a ship in harbor, is pretty much the same, as riding a real live horse and a wooden one. And even if the live charger should pitch you over his head, *that* would be much more satisfactory, than an inglorious fall from the other.

I took great delight in furling the top-gallant sails and royals in a hard blow; which duty required two hands on the yard.

There was a wild delirium about it; a fine rushing of the blood about the heart; and a glad, thrilling, and throbbing of the whole system, to find yourself tossed up at every pitch into the clouds of a stormy sky, and hovering like a judgment angel between heaven and earth, both hands free, with one foot in the rigging, and one somewhere behind you in the air. The sail would fill out like a balloon, with a report like a small cannon, and then collapse and sink away into a handful. And the feeling of mastering the rebellious canvas, and tying it down like a slave to the spar, and binding it over and over with the *gasket,* had a touch of pride and power in it, such as young King Richard must have felt, when he trampled down the insurgents of Wat Tyler. [38]

As for steering, they never would let me go to the helm, except during a calm, when I and the figurehead on the bow were about equally employed.

The reason why they gave me such a slender chance of learning to steer was this. I was quite young and raw, and steering a ship is a great art, upon which much depends; especially the making a short passage; for if the helmsman be a clumsy, careless fellow, or ignorant of his duty, he keeps the ship going about in a melancholy state of indecision as to its precise destination; so that on a voyage to Liverpool, it may be pointing one while to Gibraltar, then for Rotterdam, and now for John o' Groats; [39] all of which is worse than wasted time. Whereas, a true steersman keeps her to her work night and day and tries to make a bee-line from port to port.

Then, in a sudden squall, inattention or want of quickness at the helm might make the ship *"lurch to"*—or *"bring her by the lee."* And what those things are, the cabin passengers would never find out, when they found themselves going down, down, down, and bidding good-bye forever to the moon and the stars.

And they little think, many of them, fine gentlemen and ladies that they are, what an important personage, and how much to be had in reverence, is the rough fellow in the pea-jacket, whom they see standing at the wheel, now cocking his eye aloft, and then peeping at the compass, or looking out to windward.

---

[38] *Wat Tyler:* led unsuccessful peasant revolt against King Richard II, in 1381.

[39] *John o' Groats:* the northernmost point of Great Britain.

Why, that fellow has all your lives and eternities in his hand; and with one small and almost imperceptible motion of a spoke, in a gale of wind, might give a vast deal of work to surrogates and lawyers, in proving last wills and testaments.

The Highlander was not a greyhound, not a very fast sailer; and so, the passage, which some of the packet ships[40] make in fifteen or sixteen days, employed us about thirty.

At last, one morning, I came on deck, and they told me that Ireland was in sight.

Ireland in sight! A foreign country actually visible! I peered hard, but could see nothing but a bluish, cloud-like spot to the northeast. Was that Ireland? Why, there was nothing remarkable about that; nothing startling. If *that's* the way a foreign country looks, I might as well have stayed at home.

Now what, exactly, I had fancied the shore would look like, I can not say; but I had a vague idea that it would be something strange and wonderful. However, there it was; and as the light increased and the ship sailed nearer and nearer, the land began to magnify, and I gazed at it with increasing interest.

Presently a fishing-boat drew near, and I rushed to get a view of it; but it was a very ordinary looking boat, bobbing up and down, as any other boat would have done; yet, when I considered that the solitary man in it was actually a born native of the land in sight; that in

all probability he had never been in America, and knew nothing about my friends at home, I began to think that he looked somewhat strange.

He was a very fluent fellow, and as soon as we were within hailing distance, cried out—"Ah, my fine sailors, from Ameriky, ain't ye, my beautiful sailors?" And concluded by calling upon us to stop and heave a rope. Thinking he might have something important to communicate, the mate accordingly backed the main yard, and a rope being thrown, the stranger kept hauling in upon it, and coiling it down, crying, "pay out! pay out, my honeys; ah! but you're noble fellows!" Till at last the mate asked him why he did not come alongside, adding, "Haven't you enough rope yet?"

"Sure and I have," replied the fisherman, "and it's time for Pat to cut and run!" and so saying, his knife severed the rope, and with a Kilkenny[41] grin, he sprang to his tiller, put his little craft before the wind, and bowled away from us, with some fifteen fathoms of our towline.

"And may the Old Boy[42] hurry after you, and hang you in your stolen hemp, you Irish blackguard!" cried the mate, shaking his fist at the receding boat, after recovering from his first fit of amazement.

Here, then, was a beautiful introduction to the eastern hemisphere: fairly robbed before striking soundings.[43] This

---

[41] *Kilkenny:* county in southeastern Ireland.
[42] *Old Boy:* the Devil.
[43] *soundings:* water shallow enough for sounding (measuring) line to reach bottom.

[40] *packet ships:* ships with set schedules.

trick upon experienced travelers certainly beat all I had ever heard about the wooden nutmegs and bass-wood pumpkin seeds of Connecticut. And I thought if there were any more Hibernians[44] like our friend Pat, the Yankee peddlers might as well give it up.

The next land we saw was Wales. It was high noon, and a long line of purple mountains lay like banks of clouds against the east.

With a light breeze, we sailed on till next day, when we made Holyhead and Anglesea.[45] Then it fell almost calm, and what little wind we had, was ahead; so we kept tacking to and fro, just gliding through the water, and always hovering in sight of a snow-white tower in the distance, which might have been a fort, or a light-house. I lost myself in conjectures as to what sort of people might be tenanting that lonely edifice, and whether they knew anything about us.

The third day, with a good wind over the taffrail, we arrived so near our destination, that we took a pilot at dusk.

He, and everything connected with him were very different from our New York pilot. In the first place, the pilot boat that brought him was a plethoric[46] looking sloop-rigged boat, with flat bows, that went wheezing through the water; quite in contrast to the little gull of a schooner, that bade us adieu off Sandy Hook.

Aboard of her were ten or twelve other pilots, fellows with shaggy brows, and muffled in shaggy coats, who sat grouped together on deck like a fire-side of bears, wintering in Aroostook.[47] They must have had fine sociable times, though, together; cruising about the Irish Sea in quest of Liverpool-bound vessels; smoking cigars, drinking brandy-and-water, and spinning yarns; till at last, one by one, they are all scattered on board of different ships, and meet again by the side of a blazing sea-coal fire in some Liverpool taproom, and prepare for another yachting.

Now, when the English pilot boarded us, I stared at him as if he had been some wild animal just escaped from the Zoological Gardens; for here was a real live Englishman, just from England. Nevertheless, as he soon fell to ordering us here and there, and swearing vociferously in a language quite familiar to me, I began to think him very common-place, and considerable of a bore after all.

After running till about midnight, we *"hove-to"* near the mouth of the Mersey;[48] and next morning, before daybreak, took the first of the flood;[49] and with a fair wind, stood into the river; which, at its mouth, is quite an arm of the sea. Presently, in the misty twilight, we passed immense buoys, and caught sight of distant objects on shore, vague and shadowy shapes, like Ossian's ghosts.[50]

---

[44] *Hibernians:* Hibernia is the Latin name for Ireland.
[45] *Holyhead and Anglesea:* islands of northern Wales.
[46] *plethoric:* overloaded.

[47] *Aroostook:* area of northern Maine.
[48] *Mersey:* river which flows past Liverpool.
[49] *flood:* rising tide.
[50] *Ossian's ghosts:* from ancient Irish legends, retold by "Ossian" (J. Mcpherson).

As I stood leaning over the side, and trying to summon up some image of Liverpool, to see how the reality would answer to my conceit; and while the fog, and mist, and gray dawn were investing every thing with a mysterious interest, I was startled by the doleful, dismal sound of a great bell, whose slow intermitting tolling seemed in unison with the solemn roll of the billows. I thought I had never heard so boding a sound; a sound that seemed to speak of judgment and the resurrection, like belfry-mouthed Paul of Tarsus.[51] This was the famous *Bell-Buoy;* no one can give ear to it, without thinking of the sailors who sleep far beneath it at the bottom of the deep.

As we sailed ahead the river contracted. The day came, and soon, passing two lofty land-marks on the Lancashire shore, we rapidly drew near the town, and at last, came to anchor in the stream.

[51] *belfry-mouthed Paul of Tarsus:* apostle Paul, author of much of the New Testament.

DISCUSSION

1. The emotions that "Buttons" feels on his first ocean journey range from awe to misery. What experiences convince him that seafaring life is the best he can choose? What experiences lead him to think it a "miserable dog's life"? Which feeling do you think wins out?

2. From the way he tells about his experiences and the kinds of things he says, how would you describe Buttons?

3. *Redburn,* the work from which this selection comes, could be called an apprenticeship novel, the story of a young person learning about the world. Look up the word *apprenticeship.* In what ways is Buttons an apprentice?

4. Setting is an important element in Melville's writing. Having spent much time at sea, he writes of it with clarity and realism. Which passages did you find most effective in conveying the experience of sailing?

For further activities, see page 56.

THE BLACK CAT

EDGAR ALLAN POE

For the most wild, yet most homely narrative which I am about to pen, I neither expect nor solicit belief. Mad indeed would I be to expect it, in a case where my very senses reject their own evidence. Yet, mad am I not—and very surely do I not dream. But tomorrow I die, and today I would unburden my soul. My immediate purpose is to place before the world, plainly, succinctly, and without comment, a series of mere household events. In their consequences, these events have terrified—have tortured—have destroyed me. Yet I will not attempt to expound them. To me, they have presented little but horror—to many they will seem less terrible than *baroques*.[1] Hereafter, perhaps, some intellect may be found which will reduce my phantasm to the commonplace—some intellect more calm, more logical, and far less excitable than my own, which will perceive, in the circumstances I detail with awe, nothing more than an ordinary succession of very natural causes and effects.

From my infancy I was noted for the docility and humanity of my disposition. My tenderness of heart was even so conspicuous as to make me the jest of my companions. I was especially fond of animals, and was indulged by my parents with a great variety of pets. With these I spent most of my time, and never was so happy as when feeding and caressing them. This peculiarity of character grew with my growth, and, in my manhood, I derived from it one of my principal sources of pleasure. To those who have cherished an affection for a faithful and sagacious dog, I need hardly be at the trouble of explaining the nature or the intensity of the gratification thus derivable. There is something in the unselfish and self-sacrificing love of a brute, which goes directly to the heart of him who has had frequent occasion to test the paltry friendship and gossamer fidelity of mere *Man*.

I married early, and was happy to find in my wife a disposition not uncongenial with my own. Observing my partiality for domestic

---

[1] *baroques:* flamboyant and exaggerated.

pets, she lost no opportunity of procuring those of the most agreeable kind. We had birds, goldfish, a fine dog, rabbits, a small monkey, and *a cat.*

This latter was a remarkably large and beautiful animal, entirely black, and sagacious to an astonishing degree. In speaking of his intelligence, my wife, who at heart was not a little tinctured with superstition, made frequent allusion to the ancient popular notion, which regarded all black cats as witches in disguise. Not that she was ever *serious* upon this point—and I mention the matter at all for no better reason than that it happens, just now, to be remembered.

Pluto—this was the cat's name—was my favorite pet and playmate. I alone fed him, and he attended me wherever I went about the house. It was even with difficulty that I could prevent him from following me through the streets.

Our friendship lasted, in this manner, for several years, during which my general temperament and character—through the instrumentality of the Fiend Intemperance—had (I blush to confess it) experienced a radical alteration for the worse. I grew, day by day, more moody, more irritable, more regardless of the feelings of others. I suffered myself to use intemperate language to my wife. At length, I even offered her personal violence. My pets, of course, were made to feel the change in my disposition. I not only neglected, but ill-used them. For Pluto, however, I still retained sufficient regard to restrain me from maltreating him, as I made no scruple of maltreating the rabbits, the monkey, or even the dog, when by accident, or through affection, they came in my way. But my disease grew upon me—for what disease is like Alcohol!—and at length even Pluto, who was now becoming old, and consequently somewhat peevish—even Pluto began to experience the effects of my ill temper.

One night, returning home, much intoxicated, from one of my haunts about town, I fancied that the cat avoided my presence. I seized him; when, in his fright at my violence, he inflicted a slight wound upon my hand with his teeth. The fury of a demon instantly possessed me. I knew myself no longer. My original soul seemed, at once, to take its flight from my body; and a more than fiendish malevolence, gin-nurtured, thrilled every fibre of my frame. I took from my waistcoat-pocket a pen-knife, opened it, grasped the poor beast by the throat, and deliberately cut one of its eyes from the socket! I blush, I burn, I shudder, while I pen the damnable atrocity.

When reason returned with the morning—when I had slept off the fumes of the night's debauch—I experienced a sentiment half of horror, half of remorse, for the crime of which I had been guilty; but it was, at best, a feeble and equivocal feeling, and the soul remained untouched. I again plunged into excess, and soon drowned in wine all memory of the deed.

In the meantime the cat slowly recovered. The socket of the lost eye presented, it is true, a frightful appearance, but he no longer appeared to suffer any pain. He went about the house as usual, but, as might be expected, fled in extreme terror at my approach. I had so much of my old heart left, as to be at first grieved by this evident dislike on the part of a creature which had once so loved me. But this feeling soon gave place to irritation. And then came, as if to my final and irrevocable overthrow, the spirit of PERVERSENESS. Of this spirit philosophy takes no account. Yet I am not more sure that my soul lives, than I am that perverseness is one of the primitive impulses of the human heart—one of the indivisible primary faculties, or sentiments, which give direction to the character of Man. Who has not, a hundred times, found himself committing a vile or a silly action, for no other reason than because he knows he should *not?* Have we not a perpetual inclination, in the teeth of our best judgment, to violate that which is *Law,* merely because we understand it to be such? This spirit of perverseness, I say, came to my final overthrow. It was this unfathomable longing of the soul *to vex itself*—to offer violence to its own nature—to do wrong for the wrong's sake only—that urged me to continue and finally to consummate the injury I had inflicted upon the unoffending brute. One morning, in cool blood, I slipped a noose about its neck and hung it to the limb of a tree;—hung it with the tears streaming from my eyes, and with the bitterest remorse at my heart;—hung it *because* I knew that it had loved me, and *because* I felt it had given me no reason of offence;—hung it *because* I knew that in so doing I was committing a sin—a deadly sin that would so jeopardize my immortal soul as to place it—if such a thing were possible—even beyond the reach of the infinite mercy of the Most Merciful and Most Terrible God.

On the night of the day on which this cruel deed was done, I was aroused from sleep by the cry of fire. The curtains of my bed were in flames. The whole house was blazing. It was with great difficulty that my wife, a servant, and myself, made our escape from the conflagration. The destruction was complete. My entire worldly wealth was swallowed up, and I resigned myself thenceforward to despair.

I am above the weakness of seeking to establish a sequence of cause and effect, between the disaster and the atrocity. But I am detailing a chain of facts—and wish not to leave even a possible link imperfect. On the day succeeding the fire, I visited the ruins. The walls, with one exception, had fallen in. This exception was found in a compartment wall, not very thick, which stood about the middle of the house, and against which had rested the head of my bed. The plastering had here, in great measure, resisted the action of the fire—a fact which I attributed to its having been recently spread. About this wall a dense crowd were collected, and many persons seemed to be examining a particular portion of it with very minute and eager attention. The words "strange!" "singular!" and other similar expressions, excited my curiosity. I approached and saw, as if graven in *bas relief* upon the white surface, the figure of a gigantic *cat.* The impression was given with an accuracy truly marvellous. There was a rope about the animal's neck.

When I first beheld this apparition—for I could scarcely regard it as less—my wonder and my terror were extreme. But at length reflection came to my aid. The cat, I remembered, had been hung in a garden adjacent to the house. Upon the alarm of fire, this garden had been immediately filled by the crowd—by some one of whom the animal must have been cut from the tree and thrown, through an open window, into my chamber. This had probably been done with the view of arousing me from sleep. The falling of other walls had compressed the victim of my cruelty into the substance of the freshly spread plaster; the lime of which, with the flames, and the *ammonia* from the carcass, had then accomplished the portraiture as I saw it.

Although I thus readily accounted to my reason, if not altogether to my conscience, for the startling fact just detailed, it did not the less fail to make a deep impression upon my fancy. For months I could not rid myself of the phantasm of the cat; and, during this period, there came back into my spirit a half-sentiment that seemed, but was not, remorse. I went so far as to regret the loss of the animal, and to look about me, among the vile haunts which I now habitually frequented, for another pet of the same species, and of somewhat similar appearance, with which to supply its place.

One night as I sat, half stupified, in a den of more than infamy, my attention was suddenly drawn to some black object, reposing upon the head of one of the immense hogsheads of Gin, or of Rum, which constituted the chief furniture of the apartment. I had been looking steadily at the top of this hogshead for some minutes, and what now caused me surprise was the fact that I had not sooner perceived the object thereupon. I approached it, and touched it with my hand. It was a black cat—a very large one—fully as large as Pluto, and closely resembling him in every respect but one. Pluto had not a white hair upon any portion of his body; but this cat had a large, although indefinite splotch of white, covering nearly the whole region of the breast.

Upon my touching him he immediately arose, purred loudly, rubbed against my hand, and appeared delighted with my notice. This, then, was the very creature of which I was in search. I at once offered to purchase it of the landlord; but this person made no claim to it—knew nothing of it—had never seen it before.

I continued my caresses, and, when I prepared to go home, the animal evinced a disposition to accompany me. I permitted it to do so; occasionally stooping and patting it as I proceeded. When it reached the house it domesticated itself at once, and became immediately a great favorite with my wife.

For my own part, I soon found a dislike to it arising within me. This was just the reverse of what I had anticipated; but I know not how or why it was—its evident fondness for myself rather disgusted and annoyed. By slow degrees, these feelings of disgust and annoyance rose into the bitterness of hatred. I avoided the creature; a certain sense of shame, and the remembrance of my former deed of cruelty, preventing me from physically abusing it. I did not, for some weeks, strike, or otherwise violently ill use it; but gradually—very gradually—I came to look upon it with unutterable loathing, and to flee silently from its odious presence, as from the breath of a pestilence.

What added, no doubt, to my hatred of the beast, was the discovery, on the morning after I brought it home, that, like Pluto, it also had been deprived of one of its eyes. This circumstance, however, only endeared it to my wife, who, as I have already said, possessed, in a high degree, that humanity of feeling which had once been my distinguishing trait, and the source of many of my simplest and purest pleasures.

With my aversion to this cat, however, its partiality for myself seemed to increase. It followed my footsteps with a pertinacity which it would be difficult to make the reader comprehend. Whenever I sat, it would crouch beneath my chair, or spring upon my knees, covering me with its loathsome caresses. If I arose to walk it would get between my feet and thus nearly throw me down, or, fastening its long and sharp claws in my dress, clamber, in this manner, to my breast. At such times, although I longed to destroy it with a blow, I was yet withheld from so doing, partly by a memory of my former crime, but chiefly—let me confess it at once—by absolute *dread* of the beast.

This dread was not exactly a dread of physical evil—and yet I should be at a loss how otherwise to define it. I am almost ashamed to own—yes, even in this felon's cell, I am almost ashamed to own—that the terror and horror with which the animal inspired me, had been

heightened by one of the merest chimeras it would be possible to conceive. My wife had called my attention, more than once, to the character of the mark of white hair, of which I have spoken, and which constituted the sole visible difference between the strange beast and the one I had destroyed. The reader will remember that this mark, although large, had been originally very indefinite; but, by slow degrees—degrees nearly imperceptible, and which for a long time my Reason struggled to reject as fanciful—it had, at length, assumed a rigorous distinctness of outline. It was now the representation of an object that I shudder to name—and for this, above all, I loathed, and dreaded, and would have rid myself of the monster *had I dared*—it was now, I say, the image of a hideous—of a ghastly thing—of the GALLOWS!—oh, mournful and terrible engine of Horror and of Crime—of Agony and of Death!

And now was I indeed wretched beyond the wretchedness of mere Humanity. And *a brute beast*—whose fellow I had contemptuously destroyed—*a brute beast* to work out for *me*—for me a man, fashioned in the image of the High God—so much of insufferable woe! Alas! neither by day nor by night knew I the blessing of Rest any more! During the former the creature left me no moment alone; and, in the latter, I started, hourly, from dreams of unutterable fear, to find the hot breath of *the thing* upon my face, and its vast weight—an incarnate Nightmare that I had no power to shake off—incumbent eternally upon my *heart!*

Beneath the pressure of torments such as these, the feeble remnant of the good within me succumbed. Evil thoughts became my sole intimates—the darkest and most evil of thoughts. The moodiness of my usual temper increased to hatred of all things and of all mankind; while, from the sudden, frequent, and ungovernable outbursts of a fury to which I now blindly abandoned myself, my uncomplaining wife, alas! was the most usual and the most patient of sufferers.

One day she accompanied me, upon some household errand, into the cellar of the old building which our poverty compelled us to inhabit. The cat followed me down the steep stairs, and, nearly throwing me headlong, exasperated me to madness. Uplifting an axe, and forgetting, in my wrath, the childish dread which had hitherto stayed my hand, I aimed a blow at the animal which, of course, would have proved instantly fatal had it descended as I wished. But this blow was arrested by the hand of my wife. Goaded, by the interference, into a rage more than demoniacal, I withdrew my arm from her grasp and buried the axe in her brain. She fell dead upon the spot, without a groan.

This hideous murder accomplished, I set myself forthwith, and with entire deliberation, to the task of concealing the body. I knew that I could not remove it from the house, either by day or by night, without the risk of being observed by the neighbors. Many projects entered my mind. At one period I thought of cutting the corpse into minute fragments, and destroying them by fire. At another, I resolved to dig a grave for it in the floor of the cellar. Again, I deliberated about casting it in the well in the yard—about packing it in a box, as if merchandize, with the usual arrangements, and so getting a porter to take it from the house. Finally I hit upon what I considered a far better expedient than either of these. I determined to wall it up in the cellar—as the monks of the middle ages are recorded to have walled up their victims.

For a purpose such as this the cellar was well adapted. Its walls were loosely constructed, and had lately been plastered throughout with a rough plaster, which the dampness of the atmosphere had prevented from hardening. Moreover, in one of the walls was a projection, caused by a false chimney, or fireplace, that had been filled up, and made to resemble the rest of the cellar. I made no doubt that I could readily displace the bricks at this point, insert the corpse, and wall the whole up as before, so that no eye could detect anything suspicious.

And in this calculation I was not deceived. By means of a crowbar I easily dislodged the bricks, and, having carefully deposited the body against the inner wall, I propped it in that position, while, with little trouble, I re-laid the whole structure as it originally stood. Having procured mortar, sand, and hair, with every possible precaution, I prepared a plaster which could not be distinguished from the old, and with this I very carefully went over the new brick-work. When I had finished, I felt satisfied that all was right. The wall did not present the slightest appearance of having been disturbed. The rubbish on the floor was picked up with the minutest care. I looked around triumphantly, and said to myself—"Here at least, then, my labor has not been in vain."

My next step was to look for the beast which had been the cause of so much wretchedness; for I had, at length, firmly resolved to put it to death. Had I been able to meet with it, at the moment, there could have been no doubt of its fate; but it appeared that the crafty animal had been alarmed at the violence of my previous anger, and forebore to present itself in my present mood. It is impossible to describe, or to imagine, the deep, the blissful sense of relief which the absence of the detested creature occasioned in my bosom. It did not make its appearance during the night—and thus for one night at least, since its introduction into the house, I soundly and tranquilly slept; aye, *slept,* even with the burden of murder upon my soul!

The second and the third day passed, and still my tormentor came not. Once again I breathed as a free man. The monster, in terror, had fled the premises forever! I should behold it no more! My happiness was supreme! The guilt of my dark deed disturbed me but little. Some few inquiries had been made, but these had been readily answered. Even a search had been instituted—but of course nothing was to be discovered. I looked upon my future felicity as secured.

Upon the fourth day of the assassination, a party of the police came, very unexpectedly, into the house, and proceeded again to make rigorous investigation of the premises. Secure, however, in the inscrutability of my place of concealment, I felt no embarrassment whatever. The officers bade me accompany them in their search. They left no nook or corner unexplored. At length, for the third or fourth time, they descended into the cellar. I quivered not in a muscle. My heart beat calmly as that of one who slumbers in innocence. I walked the cellar from end to end. I folded my arms upon my bosom, and roamed easily to and fro. The police were thoroughly satisfied and prepared to depart. The glee at my heart was too strong to be restrained. I burned to say if but one word, by way of triumph, and to render doubly sure their assurance of my guiltlessness.

"Gentlemen," I said at last, as the party ascended the steps, "I delight to have allayed your suspicions. I wish you all health, and a little more courtesy. By the bye, gentlemen, this—this is a very well constructed house." (In the rabid desire to say something easily, I scarcely knew what I uttered at all)—"I may say an *excellently* well constructed house. These walls—are you going, gentlemen?—these walls are solidly put together;" and here, through the mere phrenzy of bravado, I rapped heavily, with a cane which I held in my hand, upon that very portion of the brick-work behind which stood the corpse of the wife of my bosom.

But may God shield and deliver me from the fangs of the Arch-Fiend! No sooner had the reverberation of my blows sunk into silence, than I was answered by a voice from within the tomb!—by a cry, at first muffled and broken, like the sobbing of a child, and then quickly swelling into one long, loud, and continuous scream, utterly anomalous and inhuman—a howl—a wailing shriek, half of horror and half of triumph, such as might have arisen only out of hell, conjointly from the throats of the damned in their agony and of the demons that exult in the damnation.

Of my own thoughts it is folly to speak. Swooning, I staggered to the opposite wall. For one instant the party upon the stairs remained motionless, through extremity of terror and of awe. In the next, a dozen stout arms were toiling at the wall. It fell bodily. The corpse, already greatly decayed and clotted with gore, stood erect before the eyes of the spectators. Upon its head, with red extended mouth and solitary eye of fire, sat the hideous beast whose craft had seduced me into murder, and whose informing voice had consigned me to the hangman. I had walled the monster up within the tomb!

DISCUSSION

1. Why do you think the story is called "The Black Cat" when *two* black cats play important roles?

2. How do you explain the narrator's aversion to the second cat, when he had taken it home expecting to grow fond of it?

3. Which of the following statements seems to you to best describe "The Black Cat": (a) this is the story of a man's gradual self-destruction; or (b) this is the story of a man who was the victim of a revengeful and supernatural cat? Explain.

For further activities, see page 56.

The Revolt of 'Mother'

MARY E. WILKINS FREEMAN

Father!"

"What is it?"

"What are them men diggin' over there in the field for?"

There was a sudden dropping and enlarging of the lower part of the old man's face, as if some heavy weight had settled therein; he shut his mouth tight, and went on harnessing the great bay mare. He hustled the collar on to her neck with a jerk.

"Father!"

The old man slapped the saddle upon the mare's back.

"Look here, father, I want to know what them men are diggin' over in the field for, an' I'm goin' to know."

"I wish you'd go into the house, mother, an' 'tend to your own affairs," the old man said then. He ran his words together, and his speech was almost as inarticulate as a growl.

But the woman understood; it was her most native tongue. "I ain't goin' into the house till you tell me what them men are doin' over there in the field," said she.

Then she stood waiting. She was a small woman, short and straight-waisted like a child in her brown cotton gown. Her forehead was mild and benevolent between the smooth curves of gray hair; there were meek downward lines about her nose and mouth; but her eyes, fixed upon the old man, looked as if the meekness had been the result of her own will, never of the will of another.

They were in the barn, standing before the wide open doors. The spring air, full of the smell of growing grass and unseen blossoms, came in their faces. The deep yard in front was littered with farm wagons and piles of wood; on the edges, close to the fence and the house, the grass was a vivid green, and there were some dandelions.

The old man glanced doggedly at his wife as he tightened the last buckles on the harness. She looked as immovable to him as one of the rocks in his pastureland, bound to the earth with generations of blackberry vines. He slapped the reins over the horse, and started forth from the barn.

"*Father!*" said she.

The old man pulled up. "What is it?"

"I want to know what them men are diggin' over there in that field for."

"They're diggin' a cellar, I s'pose, if you've got to know."

"A cellar for what?"

"A barn."

"A barn? You ain't goin' to build a barn over there where we was goin' to have a house, father?"

The old man said not another word. He hurried the horse into the farm wagon, and clattered out of the yard, jouncing as sturdily on his seat as a boy.

The woman stood a moment looking after him, then she went out of the barn across a corner of the yard to the house. The house, standing at right angles with the great barn and a long reach of sheds and out-buildings, was infinitesimal compared with them. It was scarcely as commodious for people as the little boxes under the barn eaves were for doves.

A pretty girl's face, pink and delicate as a flower, was looking out of one of the house windows. She was watching three men who were digging over in the field which bounded the yard near the road line. She turned quietly when the woman entered.

"What are they digging for, mother?" said she. "Did he tell you?"

"They're diggin' for—a cellar for a new barn."

"Oh, mother, he ain't going to build another barn?"

"That's what he says."

A boy stood before the kitchen glass combing his hair. He combed slowly and painstakingly, arranging his brown hair in a smooth hillock over his forehead. He did not seem to pay any attention to the conversation.

"Sammy, did you know father was going to build a new barn?" asked the girl.

The boy combed assiduously.

"Sammy!"

He turned, and showed a face like his father's under his smooth crest of hair. "Yes, I s'pose I did," he said, reluctantly.

"How long have you known it?" asked his mother.

" 'Bout three months, I guess."

"Why didn't you tell of it?"

"Didn't think 'twould do no good."

"I don't see what father wants another barn for," said the girl, in her sweet, slow voice. She turned again to the window, and stared out at the digging men in the field. Her tender, sweet face was full of a gentle distress. Her forehead was as bald and innocent as a baby's with the light hair strained back from it in a row of curl-papers. She was quite large, but her soft curves did not look as if they covered muscles.

Her mother looked sternly at the boy. "Is he goin' to buy more cows?"

The boy did not reply; he was tying his shoes.

"Sammy, I want you to tell me if he's goin' to buy more cows."

"I s'pose he is."

"How many?"

"Four, I guess."

His mother said nothing more. She went into the pantry, and there was a clatter of dishes. The boy got his cap from a nail behind the door, took an old arithmetic from the shelf, and started for school. He was lightly built, but clumsy. He went out of the yard with a curious spring in the hips, that made his loose home-made jacket tilt up in the rear.

The girl went to the sink, and began to wash the dishes that were piled up there. Her mother came promptly out of the pantry, and shoved her aside. "You wipe 'em," said she, "I'll wash. There's a good many this mornin'."

The mother plunged her hands vigorously into the water, the girl wiped the plates slowly and dreamily. "Mother," said she, "don't you think it's too bad father's going to build that new barn, much as we need a decent house to live in?"

Her mother scrubbed a dish fiercely. "You ain't found out yet we're women-folks, Nanny Penn," said she. "You ain't seen enough of men-folks yet to. One of these days you'll find it out, an' then you'll know that we know only what men-folks think we do, so far as any use of it goes, an' how we'd ought to reckon men-folks in with Providence, an' not complain of what they do any more than we do of the weather."

"I don't care; I don't believe George is anything like that, anyhow," said Nanny. Her delicate face flushed pink, her lips pouted softly, as if she were going to cry.

"You wait an' see. I guess George Eastman ain't no better than other men. You hadn't ought to judge father, though. He can't help it, 'cause he don't look at things jest the way we do. An' we've been pretty comfortable here, after all. The roof don't leak—ain't never but once—that's one thing. Father's kept it shingled right up."

"I do wish we had a parlor."

"I guess it won't hurt George Eastman any to come to see you in a nice clean kitchen. I guess a good many girls don't have as good a place as this. Nobody's ever heard me complain."

"I ain't complained either, mother."

"Well, I don't think you'd better, a good father an' a good home as you've got. S'pose your father made you go out an' work for your livin'? Lots of girls have to

that ain't no stronger an' better able to than you be."

Sarah Penn washed the frying-pan with a conclusive air. She scrubbed the outside of it as faithfully as the inside. She was a masterly keeper of her box of a house. Her one living-room never seemed to have in it any of the dust which the friction of life with inanimate matter produces. She swept, and there seemed to be no dirt to go before the broom; she cleaned, and one could see no difference. She was like an artist so perfect that he has apparently no art. Today she got out a mixing bowl and a board, and rolled some pies, and there was no more flour upon her than upon her daughter who was doing finer work. Nanny was to be married in the fall, and she was sewing on some white cambric and embroidery. She sewed industriously while her mother cooked; her soft milk-white hands and wrists showed whiter than her delicate work.

"We must have the stove moved out in the shed before long," said Mrs. Penn. "Talk about not havin' things, it's been a real blessin' to be able to put a stove up in that shed in hot weather. Father did one good thing when he fixed that stove-pipe out there."

Sarah Penn's face as she rolled her pies had the expression of meek vigor which might have characterized one of the New Testament saints. She was making mince-pies. Her husband, Adoniram Penn, liked them better than any other kind. She baked twice a week. Adoniram often liked a piece of pie between meals. She hurried this morning. It had been later than usual when she began, and she wanted to have a pie baked for dinner. However deep a resentment she might be forced to hold against her husband, she would never fail in sedulous attention to his wants.

Nobility of character manifests itself at loop-holes when it is not provided with large doors. Sarah Penn's showed itself to-day in flaky dishes of pastry. So she made the pies faithfully, while across the table she could see, when she glanced up from her work, the sight that rankled in her patient and steadfast soul—the digging of the cellar of the new barn in the place where Adoniram forty years ago had promised her their new house should stand.

The pies were done for dinner. Adoniram and Sammy were home a few minutes after twelve o'clock. The dinner was eaten with serious haste. There was never much conversation at the table in the Penn family. Adoniram asked a blessing, and they ate promptly, then rose up and went about their work.

Sammy went back to school, taking soft sly lopes out of the yard like a rabbit. He wanted a game of marbles before school, and feared his father would give him some chores to do. Adoniram hastened to the door and called after him, but he was out of sight.

"I don't see what you let him go for, mother," said he. "I wanted him to help me unload that wood."

Adoniram went to work out in the yard unloading wood from the wagon. Sarah put away the dinner dishes, while Nanny took down her curl-papers and changed her dress. She was going down to the store to buy some more embroidery and thread.

When Nanny was gone, Mrs. Penn went to the door. "Father!" she called.

"Well, what is it!"

"I want to see you jest a minute, father."

"I can't leave this wood nohow. I've got to git it unloaded an' go for a load of gravel afore two o'clock. Sammy had ought to helped me. You hadn't ought to let him go to school so early."

"I want to see you jest a minute."

"I tell ye I can't, nohow, mother."

"Father, you come here." Sarah Penn stood in the door like a queen; she held her head as if it bore a crown; there was that patience which makes authority royal in her voice. Adoniram went.

Mrs. Penn led the way into the kitchen, and pointed to a chair. "Sit down, father," said she; "I've got somethin' I want to say to you."

He sat down heavily; his face was quite stolid, but he looked at her with restive eyes. "Well, what is it, mother?"

"I want to know what you're buildin' that new barn for, father?"

"I ain't got nothin' to say about it."

"It can't be you think you need another barn?"

"I tell ye I ain't got nothin' to say about it, mother; an' I ain't goin' to say nothin'."

"Be you goin' to buy more cows?"

Adoniram did not reply; he shut his mouth tight.

"I know you be, as well as I want to. Now, father, look here"—Sarah Penn had not sat down; she stood before her husband in the humble fashion of a Scripture woman—"I'm goin' to talk real plain to you; I never have sence I married you, but I'm goin' to now. I ain't never complained, an' I ain't goin' to complain now, but I'm goin' to talk plain. You see this room here, father; you look at it well. You see there ain't no carpet on the floor, an' you see the paper is all dirty, an' droppin' off the wall. We ain't had no new paper on it for ten year, an' then I put it on myself, an' it didn't cost but ninepence a roll. You see this room, father; it's all the one I've had to work in an' eat in an' sit in sence we was married. There ain't another woman in the whole town whose husband ain't got half the means you have but what's got better. It's all the room Nanny's got to have her company in; an' there ain't one of her mates but what's got better, an' their fathers not so able as hers is. It's all the room she'll have to be married in. What would you have thought, father, if we had had our weddin' in a room no better than this? I was married in my mother's parlor, with a carpet on the floor, an' stuffed furniture, an' a mahogany card-table. An' this is all the room my daughter will have to be married in. Look here, father!"

Sarah Penn went across the room as though it were a tragic stage. She flung open a door and disclosed a tiny bedroom, only large enough for a bed and bureau, with a path between. "There, father," said she—"there's all the room I've had to sleep in forty year. All my children were born there—the two that died, an' the two that's livin'. I was sick with a fever there."

She stepped to another door and opened it. It led into the small, ill-lighted pantry. "Here," said she, "is all the buttery I've got—every place I've got for my dishes, to set away my victuals in, an' to keep my milkpans in. Father, I've been takin' care of the milk of six cows in this place, an' now you're goin' to build a new barn, an' keep more cows, an' give me more to do in it."

She threw open another door. A narrow crooked flight of stairs wound upward from it. "There, father," said she, "I want you to look at the stairs that go up to them two unfinished chambers that are all the places our son an' daughter have had to sleep in all their lives. There ain't a prettier girl in town nor a more ladylike one than Nanny, an' that's the place she has to sleep in. It ain't so good as your horse's stall; it ain't so warm an' tight."

Sarah Penn went back and stood before her husband. "Now, father," said she, "I want to know if you think you're doin' right an' accordin' to what you profess. Here, when we was married, forty year ago, you promised me faithful that we should have a new house built in that lot over in the field before the year was out. You said you had enough money, an' you wouldn't ask me to live in no such place as this. It is forty year now, an' you've been makin' more money, an' I've been savin' of it for you ever since, an' you ain't built no house yet. You've built sheds an' cowhouses an' one new barn, an' now you're goin' to build another. Father, I want to know if you think it's right. You're lodgin' your dumb beasts better than you are your own flesh an' blood. I want to know if you think it's right."

"I ain't got nothin' to say."

"You can't say nothin' without ownin' it ain't right, father. An' there's another thing—I ain't complained; I've got along forty year, an' I s'pose I should forty more, if it wasn't for that—if we don't have another house. Nanny she can't live with us after she's married. She'll have to go somewhere else to live away from us, an' it don't seem as if I could have it so, noways, father. She wasn't ever strong. She's got considerable color, but there wasn't never any backbone to her. I've always took the heft of everything off her, an' she ain't fit to keep house an' do everything herself. She'll be all worn out inside of a year. Think of her doin' all the washin' an' ironin' an' bakin' with them soft white hands an' arms, an' sweepin'! I can't have it so, noways, father."

Mrs. Penn's face was burning; her mild eyes gleamed. She had pleaded her little cause like a Webster; she had ranged from severity to pathos; but her opponent employed that obstinate silence which makes eloquence futile with mocking echoes. Adoniram arose clumsily.

"Father, ain't you got nothin' to say?" said Mrs. Penn.

"I've got to go off after that load of gravel. I can't stan' here talkin' all day."

"Father, won't you think it over, an' have a house built there instead of a barn?"

"I ain't got nothin' to say."

Adoniram shuffled out. Mrs. Penn went into her bedroom. When she came out, her eyes were red. She had a roll of unbleached cotton cloth. She spread it out on the kitchen table, and began cutting out some shirts for her husband. The men over in the field had a team to help them this afternoon; she could hear their halloos. She had a scanty pattern for the shirts; she had to plan and piece the sleeves.

Nanny came home with her embroidery, and sat down with her needlework. She had taken down her curl-papers, and there was a soft roll of fair hair like an aureole over her forehead; her face was as delicately fine and clear as porcelain. Suddenly she looked up, and the tender red flamed all over her face and neck. "Mother," said she.

"What say?"

"I've been thinking—I don't see how we're goin' to have any—wedding in this room. I'd be ashamed to have his folks come if we didn't have anybody else."

"Mebbe we can have some new paper before then; I can put it on. I guess you won't have no call to be ashamed of your belongin's."

"We might have the wedding in the new barn," said Nanny, with gentle pettishness. "Why, mother, what makes you look so?"

Mrs. Penn had started, and was staring at her with a curious expression. She turned again to her work, and spread out a pattern carefully on the cloth. "Nothin'," said she.

Presently Adoniram clattered out of the yard in his two-wheeled dump cart, standing as proudly upright as a Roman charioteer. Mrs. Penn opened the door and stood there a minute looking out; the halloos of the men sounded louder.

It seemed to her all through the spring months that she heard nothing but the halloos and the noises of saws and hammers. The new barn grew fast. It was a fine edifice for this little village. Men came on pleasant Sundays, in their meeting suits and clean shirt bosoms; and stood around it admiringly. Mrs. Penn did not speak of it, and Adoniram did not mention it to her, although sometimes, upon a return from inspecting it, he bore himself with injured dignity.

"It's a strange thing how your mother feels about the new barn," he said, confidentially, to Sammy one day.

Sammy only grunted after an odd fashion for a boy; he had learned it from his father.

The barn was all completed ready for use by the third week in July. Adoniram had planned to move his stock in on Wednesday; on Tuesday he received a letter which changed his plans. He came in with it early in the morning. "Sammy's been to the post-office," said he, "an' I've got a letter from Hiram." Hiram was Mrs. Penn's brother, who lived in Vermont.

"Well," said Mrs. Penn, "what does he say about the folks?"

"I guess they're all right. He says he thinks if I come up country right off there's a chance to buy jest the kind of a horse I want." He stared reflectively out of the window at the new barn.

Mrs. Penn was making pies. She went on clapping the rolling-pin into the crust, although she was very pale, and her heart beat loudly.

"I dun' know but what I'd better go," said Adoniram. "I hate to go off jest now, right in the midst of hayin', but the ten-acre lot's cut, an' I guess Rufus an' the others can git along without me three or four days. I can't get a horse round here to suit me, nohow, an' I've got to have another for all that wood-haulin' in the fall. I told Hiram to watch out, an' if he got wind of a good horse to let me know. I guess I'd better go."

"I'll get out your clean shirt an' collar," said Mrs. Penn calmly.

She laid out Adoniram's Sunday suit and his clean clothes on the bed in the little bedroom. She got his shaving-water and razor ready. At last she buttoned on his collar and fastened his black cravat.

Adoniram never wore his collar and cravat except on extra occasions. He held his head high, with a rasped dignity. When he was all ready, with his coat and hat brushed, and a lunch of pie and cheese in a paper bag, he hesitated on the threshold of the door. He looked at his wife, and his manner was definitely apologetic. "*If* them cows come today, Sammy can drive 'em into the new barn," said he; "an' when they bring the hay up, they can pitch it in there."

"Well," replied Mrs. Penn.

Adoniram set his shaven face ahead and started. When he had cleared the door-step, he turned and looked back with a kind of nervous solemnity. "I shall be back by Saturday if nothin' happens," said he.

"Do be careful, father," returned his wife.

She stood in the door with Nanny at her elbow and watched him out of sight. Her eyes had a strange, doubtful expression in them; her peaceful forehead was contracted. She went in, and about her baking again. Nanny sat sewing. Her wedding-day was drawing nearer, and she was getting pale and thin with her steady sewing. Her mother kept glancing at her.

"Have you got that pain in your side this mornin'?" she asked.

"A little."

Mrs. Penn's face, as she worked, changed, her perplexed forehead smoothed, her eyes were steady, her lips firmly set. She formed a maxim for herself, although incoherently with her unlettered thoughts. "Unsolicited opportunities are the guide-posts of the Lord to the new roads of life," she repeated in effect, and she made up her mind to her course of action.

"S'posin' I *had* wrote to Hiram," she muttered once, when she was in the pantry—"s'posin' I had wrote, an' asked him if he knew of any horse? But I didn't, an' father's goin' wa'n't none of my doin'. It looks like a providence." Her voice rang out quite loud at the last.

"What you talkin' about, mother?" called Nanny.

"Nothin'."

Mrs. Penn hurried her baking; at eleven o'clock it was all done. The load of hay from the west field came slowly down the cart track, and drew up at the new barn. Mrs. Penn ran out. "Stop!" she screamed, "stop!"

The men stopped and looked; Sammy upreared from the top of the load, and stared at his mother.

"Stop!" she cried out again. "Don't you put the hay in that barn; put it in the old one."

"Why, he said to put it in here," returned one of the haymakers, wonderingly. He was a young man, a neighbor's son, whom Adoniram hired by the year to help on the farm.

"Don't you put the hay in the new barn; there's room enough in the old one, ain't there?" said Mrs. Penn.

"Room enough," returned the hired man, in his thick, rustic tones. "Didn't need the new barn, nohow, far as room's concerned. Well, I s'pose he changed his mind." He took hold of the horses' bridles.

Mrs. Penn went back to the house. Soon the kitchen windows were darkened, and a fragrance like warm honey came into the room.

Nanny laid down her work. "I thought father wanted them to put the hay into the new barn?" she said, wonderingly.

"It's all right," replied her mother.

Sammy slid down from the load of hay, and came in to see if dinner was ready.

"I ain't goin' to get a regular dinner to-day, as long as father's gone," said his mother. "I've let the fire go out. You can have some bread an' milk an' pie. I thought we could get along." She set out some bowls of milk, some bread, and a pie on the kitchen table. "You'd better eat your dinner now," said she. "You might jest as well get through with it. I want you to help me afterwards."

Nanny and Sammy stared at each other. There was something strange in their mother's manner. Mrs. Penn did not eat anything herself. She went into the pantry, and they heard her moving dishes while they ate. Presently she came out with a pile of plates. She got the clothes-basket out of the shed, and packed them in it. Nanny and Sammy watched. She brought out cups and saucers, and put them in with the plates.

"What you goin' to do, mother?" inquired Nanny, in a timid voice. A sense of something unusual made her tremble, as if it were a ghost. Sammy rolled his eyes over his pie.

"You'll see what I'm goin' to do," replied Mrs. Penn. "If you're through, Nanny, I want you to go up-stairs an' pack up your things; an' I want you, Sammy, to help me take down the bed in the bedroom."

"Oh, mother, what for?" gasped Nanny.

"You'll see."

During the next few hours a feat was performed by this simple, pious New England mother which was equal in its way to Wolfe's storming of the Heights of Abraham. It took no more genius and audacity of bravery for Wolfe to cheer his wondering soldiers up those steep precipices, under the sleeping eyes of the enemy, than for Sarah Penn, at the head of her children, to move all their little household goods into the new barn while her husband was away.

Nanny and Sammy followed their mother's instructions without a murmur; indeed, they were overawed. There is a certain uncanny and superhuman quality about all such purely original undertakings as their mother's was to them. Nanny went back and forth with her light load, and Sammy tugged with sober energy.

At five o'clock in the afternoon the little house in which the Penns had lived for forty years had emptied itself into the new barn.

Every builder builds somewhat for unknown purposes, and is in a measure a prophet. The architect of Adoniram Penn's barn, while he designed it for the comfort of four-footed animals, had planned better than he knew for the comfort of humans. Sarah Penn saw at a glance its possibilities. Those great box-stalls, with quilts hung before them, would make better bedrooms than the one she had occupied for forty years, and there was a tight carriage-room. The harness-room, with its chimney and shelves would make a kitchen of her dreams. The great middle space would make a parlor, by-and-by, fit for a palace. Up-stairs there was as much room as down. With partitions and windows, what a house would there be! Sarah looked at the row of stanchions before the allotted space for cows, and reflected that she would have her front entry there.

At six o'clock the stove was up in the harness room, the kettle was boiling, and the table set for tea. It looked as home-like as the abandoned house across the yard had ever done. The young hired man milked, and Sarah directed him calmly to bring the milk to the new barn. He came gaping, dropping little blots of foam from the brimming pails on the grass. Before the next morning he had spread the story of Adoniram Penn's wife moving into the new barn all over the little village. Men assembled in the store and talked it over, women with shawls over their heads scuttled into each other's houses before their work was done. Any deviation from the ordinary course of life in this quiet town was enough to stop all progress in it. Everybody paused to look at the staid, independent figure on the side track. There was a difference of opinion with regard to her. Some held her to be insane; some, of a lawless and rebellious spirit.

Friday the minister went to see her. It was in the forenoon, and she was at the barn door shelling peas for dinner. She looked up and returned his salutation with dignity, then she went on with her work.

She did not invite him in. The saintly expression of her face remained fixed, but there was an angry flush over it.

The minister stood awkwardly before her, and talked. She handled the peas as if they were bullets. At last she looked up, and her eyes showed the spirit that her meek front had covered for a lifetime.

"There ain't no use talkin', Mr. Hersey," said she. "I've thought it all over an' over, an' I believe I'm doin' what's right. I've made it the subject of prayer, an' it's betwixt me an' the Lord an' Adoniram. There ain't no call for nobody else to worry about it."

"Well, of course, if you have brought it to the Lord in prayer, and feel satisfied that you are doing right, Mrs. Penn," said the minister, helplessly. His thin gray-bearded face was pathetic. He was a sickly man; his youthful confidence had cooled; he had to scourge himself up to some of his pastoral duties as relentlessly as a Catholic ascetic, and then he was prostrated by the smart.

"I think it's right jest as much as I think it was right for our forefathers to come over here from the old country 'cause they didn't have what belonged to 'em," said Mrs. Penn. She arose. The barn threshold might have been Plymouth Rock from her bearing. "I don't doubt you mean well, Mr. Hersey," said she, "but there are things people hadn't ought to interfere with. I've been a member of the church for over forty years. I've got my own mind an' my own feet, an' I'm goin' to think my own thoughts an' go my own way, an' nobody but the Lord is goin' to dictate to me unless I've a mind to have him. Won't you come in an' set down? How is Mis' Hersey?"

"She is well, I thank you," replied the minister. He added some more perplexed apologetic remarks; then he retreated.

He could expound the intricacies of every character study in the Scriptures, he was competent to grasp the Pilgrim Fathers and all historical innovators, but Sarah Penn was beyond him. He could deal with primal cases, but parallel ones worsted him. But, after all, although it was aside from his province, he wondered more how Adoniram Penn would deal with his wife than how the Lord would. Everybody shared the wonder. When Adoniram's four new cows arrived, Sarah ordered three to be put in the old barn, the other in the house shed where the cooking-stove had stood. That added to the excitement. It was whispered that all four cows were domiciled in the house.

Towards sunset on Saturday, when Adoniram was expected home, there was a knot of men in the road near the new barn. The hired man had milked, but he still hung around the premises. Sarah Penn had supper all ready. There were brown-bread and baked beans and a custard pie; it was the supper that Adoniram loved on a Saturday night. She had on a clean calico, and she bore herself imperturbably. Nanny and Sammy kept close at her heels. Their eyes were large, and Nanny was full of nervous tremors. Still there was to them more pleasant excitement than anything else. An inborn confidence in their mother over their father asserted itself.

Sammy looked out of the harness-room window. "There he is," he announced, in an awed whisper. He and Nanny peeped around the casing. Mrs.

Penn kept on about her work. The children watched Adoniram leave the new horse standing in the drive while he went to the house door. It was fastened. Then he went around to the shed. That door was seldom locked, even when the family was away. The thought how her father would be confronted by the cow flashed upon Nanny. There was a hysterical sob in her throat. Adoniram emerged from the shed and stood looking about in a dazed fashion. His lips moved; he was saying something, but they could not hear what it was. The hired man was peeping around a corner of the old barn, but nobody saw him.

Adoniram took the new horse by the bridle and led him across the yard to the new barn. Nanny and Sammy slunk close to their mother. The barn doors rolled back, and there stood Adoniram, with the long mild face of the great Canadian farm horse looking over his shoulder.

Nanny kept behind her mother, but Sammy stepped suddenly forward, and stood in front of her.

Adoniram stared at the group. "What on airth you all down here for?" said he. "What's the matter over to the house?"

"We've come here to live, father," said Sammy. His shrill voice quavered out bravely.

"What"—Adoniram sniffed—"what is it smells like cookin'?" said he. He stepped forward and looked in the open door of the harness-room. Then he turned to his wife. His old bristling face was pale and frightened. "What on airth does this mean, mother?" he gasped.

"You come in here, father," said Sarah. She led the way into the harness-room and shut the door. "Now, father," said she, "you needn't be scared. I ain't crazy. There ain't nothin' to be upset over. But we've come here to live, an' we're goin' to live here. We've got jest as good a right here as new horses an' cows. The house wasn't fit for us to live in any longer, an' I made up my mind I wa'n't goin' to stay there. I've done my duty by you forty year, an' I'm goin' to do it now; but I'm goin' to live here. You've got to put in some windows and partitions; an' you'll have to buy some furniture."

"Why, mother!" the old man gasped.

"You'd better take your coat off an' get washed—there's the wash basin—an' then we'll have supper."

"Why, mother!"

Sammy went past the window, leading the new horse to the old barn. The old man saw him, and shook his head speechlessly. He tried to take off his coat, but his arms seemed to lack the power. His wife helped him. She poured some water into the tin basin, and put in a piece of soap. She got the comb and brush, and smoothed his thin gray hair after he had washed. Then she put the beans, hot bread, and tea on the table. Sammy came in, the family drew up. Adoniram sat looking dazedly at his plate, and they waited.

"Ain't you goin' to ask a blessin', father?" said Sarah.

And the old man bent his head and mumbled.

All through the meal he stopped eating at intervals, and stared furtively at his wife; but he ate well. The home food tasted good to him, and his old frame was too sturdily healthy to be affected by his mind.

But after supper he went out, and sat down on the step of the smaller door at the right of the barn, through which he had meant his Jerseys to pass in stately file, but which Sarah designed for her front house door, and he leaned his head on his hands.

After the supper dishes were cleared away and the milk-pans washed, Sarah went out to him. The twilight was deepening. There was a clear green glow in the sky. Before them stretched the smooth level of field; in the distance was a cluster of hay-stacks like the huts of a village; the air was very cool and calm and sweet. The landscape might have been an ideal one of peace.

Sarah bent over and touched her husband on one of his thin, sinewy shoulders. "Father!"

The old man's shoulders heaved: he was weeping.

"Why, don't do so, father," said Sarah.

"I'll—put up the—partitions, an'—everything you—want, mother."

Sarah put her apron up to her face; she was overcome by her own triumph.

Adoniram was like a fortress whose walls had no active resistance, and went down the instant the right besieging tools were used. "Why, mother," he said, hoarsely, "I hadn't no idee you was so set on't as all this comes to."

DISCUSSION

1. "We'd ought to reckon men-folks in with Providence, an' not complain of what they do any more than we do of the weather," Sarah tells her daughter Nanny. Yet she "revolts" so openly against her husband that the whole community is shocked. What do you learn in the course of the story about Sarah's character that makes her "revolt" believable?

2. What is Sarah's attitude toward Adoniram? Is she loyal or disloyal? Does she respect him or resent him? Does she feel love or dislike for him? Use quotations from the story to back up your answers.

3. In the three previous stories, the reader is *told* everything that happens: in "Rip Van Winkle" by an *omniscient* (all-knowing) *narrator* who looks with amusement on his subject, in "New York to Liverpool" and "The Black Cat" by the voice of the person to whom the events supposedly happened. In this story, however, we see something new—both the characters and the plot are presented through *dialogue*, what the characters say to each other. We get to know three of the four main characters almost completely through dialogue. Which character are we told about through paragraphs of direct description as well as dialogue? Is this direct description necessary? Could the story stand without it? Explain.

For further activities, see page 56.

VOCABULARY

Rip Van Winkle (page 2)

The following words may or may not be familiar to you, but their meanings can be guessed from their context. Look back at the passages in which these words are found, and then choose a synonym as close to the meaning of the word in its context as possible.

chivalrous (p. 3)	pestilent (p. 4)	quaffed (p. 9)
obsequious (p. 3)	dapper (p. 6)	reiterated (p. 9)
impunity (p. 3)	adherents (p. 6)	firelock (p. 9)
assiduity (p. 3)	approbation (p. 6)	roisterers (p. 9)

The Black Cat (page 33)

Substitute words from the following list for the words in bold type in the story below. Then pick three of the words and explain why they are more vivid or have a richer meaning in this context than the word they replace.

apparition	malevolence	atrocity
conflagration	perverseness	debauch
bravado		

I was at one time a quiet man who loved all animals. But I drank to excess and spent my evenings in *a state of intemperance.* It was then that I became possessed with *hatred,* especially toward my cat. In a drunken state, I was guilty of an *act of violence*—I cut out one of its eyes. Even then my *willfulness* was not entirely gone; I hanged the cat. That same evening my house was destroyed by a *fire*. This disaster, and seeing the *picture* of the hanged cat in the wall, changed my life for the worse. Nothing would satisfy me until a second cat came into my life. Eventually, however, my anger at the second cat led me to try to kill it. I killed my wife instead. I walled up her body in the cellar. When the police came to investigate, I rapped on the cellar wall with my cane in a great show of *bravery.* I came to regret that act—I had walled the living cat up within the tomb.

The Revolt of Mother (page 43)

Choose the word in parentheses that best completes each of the following phrases.

1. As inarticulate as (a city, an orator, a growl)
2. As benevolent as a (cow, missionary, thief)
3. As infinitesimal as (a building, an insect, a grain)
4. As assiduously as a (bee, lake, wind)
5. As commodious as (a box, an auditorium, an ashtray)
6. As sedulous as a (talker, hard worker, listener)
7. As stolid as a (stone, town crier, funeral director)
8. As restive as a (bloodhound, cow, swan)
9. As obstinate as a (mule, fairy, plant)
10. As rustic as a (cosmopolite, farmer, fireman)

COMPOSITION

Rip Van Winkle (page 2)

1. Suppose you had fallen asleep on this day ten years ago, and had not waked again until this very morning. Picture yourself lying in bed, with your eyes just opened, expecting to see around you what you would have seen at that time. Write a description of that self and that world; then wake yourself up and describe the bewildering changes that greet you and your reactions.

2. Rip Van Winkle and his wife, with such very different approaches to life, had made certain adjustments in order to live with each other. What characteristic of each gave the other the most difficulty? Write a paragraph from the viewpoint of Rip; what does his wife do that bothers him most? Write a second paragraph from the viewpoint of his wife; what does he do that maddens her? How do they (consciously or unconsciously) punish each other by their actions?

The Black Cat (page 33)

"Perverseness is one of the primitive impulses of the human heart. . . . Who has not, a hundred times, found himself committing a vile or a silly action, for no other reason than because he knows he should *not*?" Using this quotation from the story as your topic, write a few paragraphs agreeing or disagreeing with what it says.

HAIRCUT

RING LARDNER

I got another barber that comes over from Carterville and helps me out Saturdays, but the rest of the time I can get along all right alone. You can see for yourself that this ain't no New York City and besides that, the most of the boys works all day and don't have no leisure to drop in here and get themselves prettied up.

You're a newcomer, ain't you? I thought I hadn't seen you round before. I hope you like it good enough to stay. As I say, we ain't no New York City or Chicago, but we have pretty good times. Not as good, though, since Jim Kendall got killed. When he was alive, him and Hod Meyers used to keep this town in an uproar. I bet they was more laughin' done here than any town its size in America.

Jim was comical, and Hod was pretty near a match for him. Since Jim's gone, Hod tries to hold his end up just the same as ever, but it's tough goin' when you ain't got nobody to kind of work with.

They used to be plenty fun in here Saturdays. This place is jam-packed Saturdays, from four o'clock on. Jim and Hod would show up right after their supper, round six o'clock. Jim would set himself down in that big chair, nearest the blue spittoon. Whoever had been settin' in that chair, why they'd get up when Jim come in and give it to him.

You'd of thought it was a reserved seat like they have sometimes in a theayter. Hod would generally always stand or walk up and down, or some Saturdays, of course, he'd be settin' in this chair part of the time, gettin' a haircut.

Well, Jim would set there a w'ile without openin' his mouth only to spit, and then finally he'd say to me, "Whitey,"—my right name, that is, my right first name, is Dick, but everybody round here calls me Whitey—Jim would say, "Whitey, your nose looks like a rosebud to-night. You must of been drinkin' some of your aw de cologne."

So I'd say, "No, Jim, but you look like you'd been drinkin' some-thin' of that kind or somethin' worse."

Jim would have to laugh at that, but then he'd speak up and say, "No, I ain't had nothin' to drink, but that ain't sayin' I wouldn't like somethin'. I wouldn't even mind if it was wood alcohol."

Then Hod Meyers would say, "Neither would your wife." That would set everybody to laughin' because Jim and his wife wasn't on very good terms. She'd of divorced him only they wasn't no chance to get alimony and she didn't have no way to take care of herself and the kids. She couldn't never understand Jim. He *was* kind of rough, but a good fella at heart.

Jim and Hod had all kinds of sport with Milt Sheppard. I don't suppose you've seen Milt. Well, he's got an Adam's apple that looks more like a mushmelon. So I'd be shavin' Milt and when I'd start to shave down here on his neck, Hod would holler, "Hey, Whitey, wait a minute! Before you cut into it, let's make up a pool and see who can guess closest to the number of seeds."

And Jim would say, "If Milt hadn't of been so hoggish, he'd of ordered a half a cantaloupe instead of a whole one and it might not of stuck in his throat."

All the boys would roar at this and Milt himself would force a smile, though the joke was on him. Jim certainly was a card!

There's his shavin' mug, settin' on the shelf, right next to Charley Vail's. "Charles M. Vail." That's the druggist. He comes in regular for his shave, three times a week. And Jim's is the cup next to Charley's. "James H. Kendall." Jim won't need no shavin' mug no more, but I'll leave it there just the same for old times' sake. Jim certainly was a character!

Years ago, Jim used to travel for a canned goods concern over in Carterville. They sold canned goods. Jim had the whole northern half of the State and was on the road five days out of every week. He'd drop in here Saturdays and tell his experiences for that week. It was rich.

I guess he paid more attention to playin' jokes than makin' sales. Finally the concern let him out and he come right home here and told everybody he'd been fired instead of sayin' he'd resigned like most fellas would of.

It was a Saturday and the shop was full and Jim got up out of that chair and says, "Gentlemen, I got an important announcement to make. I been fired from my job."

Well, they asked him if he was in earnest and he said he was and nobody could think of nothin' to say till Jim finally broke the ice himself. He says, "I been sellin' canned goods and now I'm canned goods myself."

You see, the concern he'd been workin' for was a factory that made canned goods. Over in Carterville. And now Jim said he was canned himself. He was certainly a card!

Jim had a great trick that he used to play w'ile he was travelin'. For instance, he'd be ridin' on a train and they'd come to some little town like, well, like, we'll say, like Benton. Jim would look out the train window and read the signs on the stores.

For instance, they'd be a sign, "Henry Smith, Dry Goods." Well, Jim would write down the name and the name of the town and when he got to wherever he was goin' he'd mail back a postal card to Henry Smith at Benton and not sign no name to it, but he'd write on the card, well, somethin' like "Ask your wife about that book agent that spent the afternoon last week," or "Ask your Missus who kept her from gettin' lonesome the last time you was in Carterville." And he'd sign the card, "A Friend."

Of course, he never knew what really come of none of these jokes, but he could picture what *probably* happened and that was enough.

Jim didn't work very steady after he lost his position with the Carterville people. What he did earn, doin' odd jobs round town, why he spent pretty near all of it on gin and his family might of starved if the stores hadn't of carried them along. Jim's wife tried her hand at dressmakin', but they ain't nobody goin' to get rich makin' dresses in this town.

As I say, she'd of divorced Jim, only she seen that she couldn't support herself and the kids and she was always hopin' that some day Jim would cut out his habits and give her more than two or three dollars a week.

They was a time when she would go to whoever he was workin' for and ask them to give her his wages, but after she done this once or twice, he beat her to it by borrowin' most of his pay in advance. He told it all round town, how he had outfoxed his Missus. He certainly was a caution!

But he wasn't satisfied with just outwittin' her. He was sore the way she had acted, tryin' to grab off his pay. And he made up his mind he'd get even. Well, he waited till Evans's Circus was advertised to come to town. Then he told his wife and two kiddies that he was goin' to take them to the circus. The day of the circus, he told them he would get the tickets and meet them outside the entrance to the tent.

Well, he didn't have no intentions of bein' there or buyin' tickets or nothin'. He got full of gin and laid round Wright's poolroom all day. His wife and the kids waited and waited and of course he didn't show up. His wife didn't have a dime with her, or nowhere else, I guess. So she finally had to tell the kids it was all off and they cried like they wasn't never goin' to stop.

Well, it seems, w'ile they was cryin', Doc Stair came along and he asked what was the matter, but Mrs. Kendall was stubborn and wouldn't tell him, but the kids told him and he insisted on takin' them and their mother in the show. Jim found this out afterwards and it was one reason why he had it in for Doc Stair.

Doc Stair come here about a year and a half ago. He's a mighty handsome young fella and his clothes always look like he has them made to order. He goes to Detroit two or three times a year and w'ile he's there he must have a tailor take his measure and then make him a suit to order. They cost pretty near twice as much, but they fit a whole lot better than if you just bought them in a store.

For a w'ile everybody was wonderin' why a young doctor like Doc Stair should come to a town like this where we already got old Doc Gamble and Doc Foote that's both been here for years and all the practice in town was always divided between the two of them.

Then they was a story got round that Doc Stair's gal had throwed him over, a gal up in the Northern Peninsula somewheres, and the reason he come here was to hide himself away and forget it. He said himself that he thought they wasn't nothin' like general practice in a place like ours to fit a man to be a good all round doctor. And that's why he'd came.

Anyways, it wasn't long before he was makin' enough to live on, though they tell me that he never dunned nobody for what they owed him, and the folks here certainly has got the owin' habit, even in my business. If I had all that was comin' to me for just shaves alone, I could go to Carterville and put up at the Mercer for a week and see a different picture every night. For instance, they's old George Purdy— but I guess I shouldn't ought to be gossippin'.

Well, last year, our coroner died, died of the flu. Ken Beatty, that was his name. He was the coroner. So they had to choose another man to be coroner in his place and they picked Doc Stair. He laughed at first and said he didn't want it, but they made him take it. It ain't no job that anybody would fight for and what a man takes out of it in a year would just about buy seeds for their garden. Doc's the kind, though, that can't say no to nothin' if you keep at him long enough.

But I was goin' to tell you about a poor boy we got here in town—Paul Dickson. He fell out of a tree when he was about ten years old. Lit on his head and it done somethin' to him and he ain't never been right. No harm in him, but just silly. Jim Kendall used to call him cuckoo; that's a name Jim had for anybody that was off their head, only he called people's head their bean. That was another of his gags, callin' head bean and callin' crazy people cuckoo. Only poor Paul ain't crazy, but just silly.

You can imagine that Jim used to have all kinds of fun with Paul. He'd send him to the White Front Garage for a left-handed monkey wrench. Of course they ain't no such a thing as a left-handed monkey wrench.

And once we had a kind of a fair here and they was a baseball game between the fats and the leans and before the game started Jim

called Paul over and sent him way down to Schrader's hardware store
to get a key for the pitcher's box.

They wasn't nothin' in the way of gags that Jim couldn't think up,
when he put his mind to it.

Poor Paul was always kind of suspicious of people, maybe on account of how Jim had kept foolin' him. Paul wouldn't have much to
do with anybody only his own mother and Doc Stair and a girl here
in town named Julie Gregg. That is, she ain't a girl no more, but pretty
near thirty or over.

When Doc first came to town, Paul seemed to feel like here was a
real friend and he hung around Doc's office most of the w'ile; the
only time he wasn't there was when he'd go home to eat or sleep or
when he seen Julie Gregg doin' her shoppin'.

When he looked out Doc's window and seen her, he'd run downstairs and join her and tag along with her to the different stores. The
poor boy was crazy about Julie and she always treated him mighty
nice and made him feel like he was welcome, though of course it
wasn't nothin' but pity on her side.

Doc done all he could to improve Paul's mind and he told me
once that he really thought the boy was gettin' better, that they was
times when he was as bright and sensible as anybody else.

But I was goin' to tell you about Julie Gregg. Old Man Gregg was
in the lumber business, but got to drinkin' and lost the most of his
money and when he died, he didn't leave nothin' but the house and
just enough insurance for the girl to skimp along on.

Her mother was a kind of a half invalid and didn't hardly ever
leave the house. Julie wanted to sell the place and move somewheres
else after the old man died, but the mother said she was born here
and would die here. It was tough on Julie, as the young people round
this town—well, she's too good for them.

She's been away to school and Chicago and New York and different places and they ain't no subject she can't talk on, where you take
the rest of the young folks here and you mention anything to them
outside of Gloria Swanson or Tommy Meighan and they think you're
delirious. Did you see Gloria in Wages of Virtue? You missed somethin'!

Well, Doc Stair hadn't been here more than a week when he
come in one day to get shaved and I recognized who he was as he
had been pointed out to me, so I told him about my old lady. She's
been ailin' for a couple of years and either Doc Gamble or Doc Foote,
neither one, seemed to be helpin' her. So he said he would come out

and see her, but if she was able to get out herself, it would be better to bring her to his office where he could make a completer examination.

So I took her to his office and w'ile I was waitin' for her in the reception room, in come Julie Gregg. When somebody comes in Doc Stair's office, they's a bell that rings in his inside office so as he can tell they's somebody to see him.

So he left my old lady inside and come out to the front office and that's the first time him and Julie met and I guess it was what they call love at first sight. But it wasn't fifty-fifty. This young fella was the slickest lookin' fella she'd ever seen in this town and she went wild over him. To him she was just a young lady that wanted to see the doctor.

She'd came on about the same business I had. Her mother had been doctorin' for years with Doc Gamble and Doc Foote and without no results. So she'd heard they was a new doc in town and decided to give him a try. He promised to call and see her mother that same day.

I said a minute ago that it was love at first sight on her part. I'm not only judgin' by how she acted afterwards but how she looked at him that first day in his office. I ain't no mind reader, but it was wrote all over her face that she was gone.

Now Jim Kendall, besides bein' a jokesmith and a pretty good drinker, well, Jim was quite a lady-killer. I guess he run pretty wild durin' the time he was on the road for them Carterville people, and besides that, he'd had a couple little affairs of the heart right here in town. As I say, his wife could of divorced him, only she couldn't.

But Jim was like the majority of men, and women, too, I guess. He wanted what he couldn't get. He wanted Julie Gregg and worked his head off tryin' to land her. Only he'd of said bean instead of head.

Well, Jim's habits and his jokes didn't appeal to Julie and of course he was a married man, so he didn't have no more chance than, well, than a rabbit. That's an expression of Jim's himself. When somebody didn't have no chance to get elected or somethin', Jim would always say they didn't have no more chance than a rabbit.

He didn't make no bones about how he felt. Right in here, more than once, in front of the whole crowd, he said he was stuck on Julie and anybody that could get her for him was welcome to his house and his wife and kids included. But she wouldn't have nothin' to do with him; wouldn't even speak to him on the street. He finally seen he wasn't gettin' nowheres with his usual line so he decided to try the rough stuff. He went right up to her house one evenin' and when she opened the door he forced his way in and grabbed her. But she broke loose and before he could stop her, she run in the next room and locked the door and phoned to Joe Barnes. Joe's the marshal. Jim could hear who she was phonin' to and he beat it before Joe got there.

Joe was an old friend of Julie's pa. Joe went to Jim the next day and told him what would happen if he ever done it again.

I don't know how the news of this little affair leaked out. Chances is that Joe Barnes told his wife and she told somebody else's wife and they told their husband. Anyways, it did leak out and Hod Meyers had the nerve to kid Jim about it, right here in this shop. Jim didn't deny nothin' and kind of laughed it off and said for us all to wait; that lots of people had tried to make a monkey out of him, but he always got even.

Meanw'ile everybody in town was wise to Julie's bein' wild mad over the Doc. I don't suppose she had any idea how her face changed when him and her was together; of course she couldn't of, or she'd of kept away from him. And she didn't know that we was all noticin' how many times she made excuses to go up to his office or pass it on the other side of the street and look up in his window to see if he was there. I felt sorry for her and so did most other people.

Hod Meyers kept rubbin' it into Jim about how the Doc had cut him out. Jim didn't pay no attention to the kiddin' and you could see he was plannin' one of his jokes.

One trick Jim had was the knack of changin' his voice. He could make you think he was a girl talkin' and he could mimic any man's voice. To show you how good he was along this line, I'll tell you the joke he played on me once.

You know, in most towns of any size, when a man is dead and needs a shave, why the barber that shaves him soaks him five dollars for the job; that is, he don't soak *him,* but whoever ordered the shave. I just charge three dollars because personally I don't mind much shavin' a dead person. They lay a whole lot stiller than live customers. The only thing is that you don't feel like talkin' to them and you get kind of lonesome.

Well, about the coldest day we ever had here, two years ago last winter, the phone rung at the house w'ile I was home to dinner and I answered the phone and it was a woman's voice and she said she was Mrs. John Scott and her husband was dead and would I come out and shave him.

Old John had always been a good customer of mine. But they live seven miles out in the country, on the Streeter road. Still I didn't see how I could say no.

So I said I would be there, but would have to come in a jitney and it might cost three or four dollars besides the price of the shave. So she, or the voice, it said that was all right, so I got Frank Abbott to drive me out to the place and when I got there, who should open the door but old John himself! He wasn't no more dead than, well, than a rabbit.

It didn't take no private detective to figure out who had played me this little joke. Nobody could of thought it up but Jim Kendall. He certainly was a card!

I tell you this incident just to show you how he could disguise his voice and make you believe it was somebody else talkin'. I'd of swore it was Mrs. Scott had called me. Anyways, some woman.

Well, Jim waited till he had Doc Stair's voice down pat; then he went after revenge.

He called Julie up on a night when he knew Doc was over in Carterville. She never questioned but what it was Doc's voice. Jim said he must see her that night; he couldn't wait no longer to tell her somethin'. She was all excited and told him to come to the house. But he said he was expectin' an important long distance call and wouldn't she please forget her manners for once and come to his office. He said they couldn't nothin' hurt her and nobody would see her and he just *must* talk to her a little w'ile. Well, poor Julie fell for it.

Doc always keeps a night light in his office, so it looked to Julie like they was somebody there.

Meanw'ile Jim Kendall had went to Wright's poolroom, where they was a whole gang amusin' themselves. The most of them had drank plenty of gin, and they was a rough bunch even when sober. They was always strong for Jim's jokes and when he told them to come with him and see some fun they give up their card games and pool games and followed along.

Doc's office is on the second floor. Right outside his door they's a flight of stairs leadin' to the floor above. Jim and his gang hid in the dark behind these stairs.

Well, Julie come up to Doc's door and rung the bell and they was nothin' doin'. She rung it again and rung it seven or eight times. Then she tried the door and found it locked. Then Jim made some kind of a noise and she heard it and waited a minute, and then she says, "Is that you, Ralph?" Ralph is Doc's first name.

They was no answer and it must of came to her all of a sudden that she'd been bunked. She pretty near fell downstairs and the whole gang after her. They chased her all the way home, hollerin', "Is that you, Ralph?" and "Oh, Ralphie, dear, is that you?" Jim says he couldn't holler it himself, as he was laughin' too hard.

Poor Julie! She didn't show up here on Main Street for a long, long time afterward.

And of course Jim and his gang told everybody in town, everybody but Doc Stair. They was scared to tell him, and he might of never knowed only for Paul Dickson. The poor cuckoo, as Jim called him, he was here in the shop one night when Jim was still gloatin' yet over what he'd done to Julie. And Paul took in as much of it as he could understand and he run to Doc with the story.

It's a cinch Doc went up in the air and swore he'd make Jim suffer. But it was a kind of a delicate thing, because if it got out that he had beat Jim up, Julie was bound to hear of it and then she'd know that Doc knew and of course knowin' that he knew would make it worse for her than ever. He was goin' to do somethin', but it took a lot of figurin'.

Well, it was a couple days later when Jim was here in the shop again, and so was the cuckoo. Jim was goin' duck-shootin' the next day and had came in lookin' for Hod Meyers to go with him. I happened to know that Hod had went over to Carterville and wouldn't be home till the end of the week. So Jim said he hated to go alone and he guessed he would call it off. Then poor Paul spoke up and said if Jim would take him he would go along. Jim thought a w'ile and then he said, well, he guessed a half-wit was better than nothin'.

I suppose he was plottin' to get Paul out in the boat and play some joke on him, like pushin' him in the water. Anyways, he said Paul could go. He asked him had he ever shot a duck and Paul said no, he'd never even had a gun in his hands. So Jim said he could set in the boat and watch him and if he behaved himself, he might lend him his gun for a couple of shots. They made a date to meet in the mornin' and that's the last I seen of Jim alive.

Next mornin', I hadn't been open more than ten minutes when Doc Stair come in. He looked kind of nervous. He asked me had I seen Paul Dickson. I said no, but I knew where he was, out duck-shootin' with Jim Kendall. So Doc says that's what he had heard, and he couldn't understand it because Paul had told him he wouldn't never have no more to do with Jim as long as he lived.

He said Paul had told him about the joke Jim had played on Julie. He said Paul had asked him what he thought of the joke and the Doc had told him that anybody that would do a thing like that ought not to be let live.

I said it had been a kind of a raw thing, but Jim just couldn't resist no kind of a joke, no matter how raw. I said I thought he was all right at heart, but just bubblin' over with mischief. Doc turned and walked out.

At noon he got a phone call from old John Scott. The lake where Jim and Paul had went shootin' is on John's place. Paul had come runnin' up to the house a few minutes before and said they'd been an accident. Jim had shot a few ducks and then give the gun to Paul and told him to try his luck. Paul hadn't never handled a gun and he was nervous. He was shakin' so hard that he couldn't control the gun. He let fire and Jim sunk back in the boat, dead.

Doc Stair, bein' the coroner, jumped in Frank Abbott's flivver and rushed out to Scott's farm. Paul and old John was down on the shore of the lake. Paul had rowed the boat to shore, but they'd left the body in it, waitin' for Doc to come.

Doc examined the body and said they might as well fetch it back to town. They was no use leavin' it there or callin' a jury, as it was a plain case of accidental shootin'.

Personally I wouldn't never leave a person shoot a gun in the same boat I was in unless I was sure they knew somethin' about guns. Jim was a sucker to leave a new beginner have his gun, let alone a half-wit. It probably served Jim right, what he got. But still we miss him round here. He certainly was a card!

Comb it wet or dry?

DISCUSSION

1. How much can we find out about the barber from the last full paragraph of the story alone? Is there a difference between the barber's view of Jim and the author's view of him? Explain. What is the effect of the barber's repeating, "He certainly was a card!"?

2. The author of "The Black Cat," Edgar Allan Poe, thought that the single most important thing in a story was a strong total effect. He said that if the writer's "very initial sentence tend not to the outbringing of this effect, then he has failed in his first step." Would Poe have approved of the first paragraph of "Haircut"? Why or why not?

3. Like "The Black Cat," this story is told in the *first person;* that is, the narrator calls himself "I." Why do you think the author chose a barber to tell the story? Why do you think the author chose a narrator who would think Jim was "a card" or "a caution," rather than someone who saw Jim as cruel and destructive?

A Visit of Charity

EUDORA WELTY

It was mid-morning—a very cold, bright day. Holding a potted plant before her, a girl of fourteen jumped off the bus in front of the Old Ladies' Home, on the outskirts of town. She wore a red coat, and her straight yellow hair was hanging down loose from the pointed white cap all the little girls were wearing that year. She stopped for a moment beside one of the prickly dark shrubs with which the city had beautified the Home, and then proceeded slowly toward the building, which was of whitewashed brick and reflected the winter sunlight like a block of ice. As she walked vaguely up the steps she shifted the small pot from hand to hand; then she had to set it down and remove her mittens before she could open the heavy door.

"I'm a Campfire Girl. . . . I have to pay a visit to some old lady," she told the nurse at the desk. This was a woman in a white uniform who looked as if she were cold; she had close-cut hair which stood up on the very top of her head exactly like a sea wave. Marian, the little girl, did not tell her that this visit would give her a minimum of only three points in her score.

"Acquainted with any of our residents?" asked the nurse. She lifted one eyebrow and spoke like a man.

"With any old ladies? No—but—that is, any of them will do," Marian stammered. With her free hand she pushed her hair behind her ears, as she did when it was time to study Science.

The nurse shrugged and rose. "You have a nice *multiflora cineraria* there," she remarked as she walked ahead down the hall of closed doors to pick out an old lady.

There was loose, bulging linoleum on the floor. Marian felt as if she were walking on the waves, but the nurse paid no attention to it. There was a smell in the hall like the interior of a clock. Everything was silent until, behind one of the doors, an old lady of some kind cleared her throat like a sheep bleating. This decided the nurse. Stopping in her tracks, she first extended her arm, bent her elbow, and leaned forward from the hips—all to examine the watch strapped to her wrist; then she gave a loud double-rap on the door.

"There are two in each room," the nurse remarked over her shoulder.

"Two what?" asked Marian without thinking. The sound like a sheep's bleating almost made her turn around and run back.

One old woman was pulling the door open in short, gradual jerks, and when she saw the nurse a strange smile forced her old face dangerously awry. Marian, suddenly propelled by the strong, impatient arm of the nurse, saw next the side-face of another old woman, even older, who was lying flat in bed with a cap on and a counterpane drawn up to her chin.

"Visitor," said the nurse, and after one more shove she was off up the hall.

Marian stood tongue-tied; both hands held the potted plant. The old woman, still with that terrible, square smile (which was a smile of welcome) stamped on her bony face, was waiting. . . . Perhaps she said something. The old woman in bed said nothing at all, and she did not look around.

Suddenly Marian saw a hand, quick as a bird claw, reach up in the air and pluck the white cap off her head. At the same time, another claw to match drew her all the way into the room, and the next moment the door closed behind her.

"My, my, my," said the old lady at her side.

Marian stood enclosed by a bed, a washstand and a chair; the tiny room had altogether too much furniture. Everything smelled wet—even the bare floor. She held onto the back of the chair, which was wicker and felt soft and damp. Her heart beat more and more slowly, her hands got colder and colder, and she could not hear whether the old women were saying anything or not. She could not see them very clearly. How dark it was! The window shade was down, and the only door was shut. Marian looked at the ceiling. . . . It was like being caught in a robbers' cave, just before one was murdered.

"Did you come to be our little girl for a while?" the first robber asked.

Then something was snatched from Marian's hand—the little potted plant.

"Flowers!" screamed the old woman. She stood holding the pot in an undecided way. "Pretty flowers," she added.

Then the old woman in bed cleared her throat and spoke. "They are not pretty," she said, still without looking around, but very distinctly.

Marian suddenly pitched against the chair and sat down in it.

"Pretty flowers," the first old woman insisted. "Pretty—pretty. . . ."

Marian wished she had the little pot back for just a moment—she had forgotten to look at the plant herself before giving it away. What did it look like?

"Stinkweeds," said the other old woman sharply. She had a bunchy white forehead and red eyes like a sheep. Now she turned them toward Marian. The fogginess seemed to rise in her throat again, and she bleated, "Who—are—you?"

To her surprise, Marian could not remember her name. "I'm a Campfire Girl," she said finally.

"Watch out for the germs," said the old woman like a sheep, not addressing anyone.

"One came out last month to see us," said the first old woman.

A sheep or a germ? wondered Marian dreamily, holding onto the chair.

"Did not!" cried the other old woman.

"Did so! Read to us out of the Bible, and we enjoyed it!" screamed the first.

"Who enjoyed it!" said the woman in bed. Her mouth was unexpectedly small and sorrowful, like a pet's.

"We enjoyed it," insisted the other. "You enjoyed it—I enjoyed it."

"We all enjoyed it," said Marian, without realizing that she had said a word.

The first old woman had just finished putting the potted plant high, high on the top of the wardrobe, where it could hardly be seen from below. Marian wondered how she had ever succeeded in placing it there, how she could ever have reached so high.

"You mustn't pay any attention to old Addie," she now said to the little girl. "She's ailing today."

"Will you shut your mouth?" said the woman in bed. "I am not."

"You're a story."

"I can't stay but a minute—really, I can't," said Marian suddenly. She looked down at the wet floor and thought that if she were sick in here they would have to let her go.

With much to-do the first old woman sat down in a rocking chair—still another piece of furniture!—and began to rock. With the fingers of one hand she touched a very dirty cameo pin on her chest. "What do you do at school?" she asked.

"I don't know . . ." said Marian. She tried to think but she could not.

"Oh, but the flowers are beautiful," the old woman whispered. She seemed to rock faster and faster; Marian did not see how anyone could rock so fast.

"Ugly," said the woman in bed.

"If we bring flowers——" Marian began, and then fell silent. She had almost said that if Campfire Girls brought flowers to the Old Ladies' Home, the visit would count one extra point, and if they took a Bible with them on the bus and read it to the old ladies, it counted double. But the old woman had not listened, anyway; she was rocking and watching the other one, who watched back from the bed.

"Poor Addie is ailing. She has to take medicine—see?" she said, pointing a horny finger at a row of bottles on the table, and rocking so high that her black comfort shoes lifted off the floor like a little child's.

"I am no more sick than you are," said the woman in bed.

"Oh, yes you are!"

"I just got more sense than you have, that's all," said the other old woman, nodding her head.

"That's only the contrary way she talks when *you all* come," said the first lady with sudden intimacy. She stopped the rocker with a neat pat of her feet and leaned toward Marian. Her hand reached over—it felt like a petunia leaf, clinging and just a little sticky.

"Will you hush! Will you hush!" cried the other one.

Marian leaned back rigidly in her chair.

"When I was a little girl like you, I went to school and all," said the old woman in the same intimate, menacing voice. "Not here—another town. . . ."

"Hush!" said the sick woman. "You never went to school. You never came and you never went. You never were anything—only here. You never were born! You don't know anything. Your head is empty, your heart and hands and your old black purse are all empty, even that little old box that you brought with you you brought empty—you showed it to me. And yet you talk, talk, talk, talk, talk all the time until I think I'm losing my mind! Who are you? You're a stranger—a perfect stranger! Don't you know you're a stranger? Is it possible that they have actually done a thing like this to anyone—sent them in a stranger to talk, and rock, and tell away her whole long rigmarole? Do they seriously suppose that I'll be able to keep it up, day in, day out, night in, night out, living in the same room with a terrible old woman—forever?"

Marian saw the old woman's eyes grow bright and turn toward her. This old woman was looking at her with despair and calculation in her face. Her small lips suddenly dropped apart, and exposed a half circle of false teeth with tan gums.

"Come here, I want to tell you something," she whispered. "Come here!"

Marian was trembling, and her heart nearly stopped beating altogether for a moment.

"Now, now, Addie," said the first old woman. "That's not polite. Do you know what's really the matter with old Addie today?" She, too, looked at Marian; one of her eyelids drooped low.

"The matter?" the child repeated stupidly. "What's the matter with her?"

"Why, she's mad because it's her birthday!" said the first old woman, beginning to rock again and giving a little crow as though she had answered her own riddle.

"It is not, it is not!" screamed the old woman in bed. "It is not my birthday, no one knows when that is but myself, and will you please be quiet and say nothing more, or I'll go straight out of my mind!" She turned her eyes toward Marian again, and presently she said in the soft, foggy voice, "When the worst comes to the worst, I ring this bell, and the nurse comes." One of her hands was drawn out from under the patched counterpane—a thin little hand with enormous black freckles. With a finger which would not hold still she pointed to a little bell on the table among the bottles.

"How old are you?" Marian breathed. Now she could see the old woman in bed very closely and plainly, and very abruptly, from all sides, as in dreams. She wondered about her—she wondered for a moment as though there was nothing else in the world to wonder about. It was the first time such a thing had happened to Marian.

"I won't tell!"

The old face on the pillow, where Marian was bending over it, slowly gathered and collapsed. Soft whimpers came out of the small open mouth. It was a sheep that she sounded like—a little lamb. Marian's face drew very close, the yellow hair hung forward.

"She's crying!" She turned a bright, burning face up to the first old woman.

"That's Addie for you," the old woman said spitefully.

Marian jumped up and moved toward the door. For the second time, the claw almost touched her hair, but it was not quick enough. The little girl put her cap on.

"Well, it was a real visit," said the old woman, following Marian through the doorway and all the way out into the hall. Then from behind she suddenly clutched the child with her sharp little fingers. In an affected, high-pitched whine she cried, "Oh, little girl, have you a penny to spare for a poor old woman that's not got anything of her own? We don't have a thing in the world—not a penny for candy—not a thing! Little girl, just a nickel—a penny——"

Marian pulled violently against the old hands for a moment before she was free. Then she ran down the hall, without looking behind her and without looking at the nurse, who was reading *Field & Stream* at her desk. The nurse, after another triple motion to consult her wrist watch, asked automatically the question put to visitors in all institutions: "Won't you stay and have dinner with *us?*"

Marian never replied. She pushed the heavy door open into the cold air and ran down the steps.

Under the prickly shrub she stooped and quickly, without being seen, retrieved a red apple she had hidden there.

Her yellow hair under the white cap, her scarlet coat, her bare knees all flashed in the sunlight as she ran to meet the big bus rocketing through the street.

"Wait for me!" she shouted. As though at an imperial command, the bus ground to a stop.

She jumped on and took a big bite out of the apple.

DISCUSSION

1. At the end of the story Marian retrieves a *red* apple she has hidden under a bush. Then she *runs*, with her *yellow* hair and her *scarlet* coat and her bare knees all *flashing* in the *sunlight* and *jumps* onto the bus. To round out this picture of brightness and energy, Marian takes a *big bite* out of her red apple, so that we can almost feel its juiciness. All of this is an extreme contrast to the Old Ladies' Home Marian has just left. Beginning with the first paragraph of the story, find five or six of the words or *images* (word pictures) the author uses to describe the Home or the people in it. Taken together, what is their effect?

2. "She's mad because it's her birthday!" the first old woman says about Addie. Do you think it really was Addie's birthday? If it was not, why would the first old woman say that it was? If it was, why would Addie deny it? As a result of this incident, Marian experiences something completely new. What is it, and why is it so new to Marian?

3. To whom is the author more sympathetic—Marian or the old women? Is she sympathetic to either? Explain.

THE LOTTERY

SHIRLEY JACKSON

The morning of June 27th was clear and sunny, with the fresh warmth of a full-summer day; the flowers were blossoming profusely and the grass was richly green. The people of the village began to gather in the square, between the post office and the bank, around ten o'clock; in some towns there were so many people that the lottery took two days and had to be started on June 26th, but in this village, where there were only about three hundred people, the whole lottery took less than two hours, so it could begin at ten o'clock in the morning and still be through in time to allow the villagers to get home for noon dinner.

The children assembled first, of course. School was recently over for the summer, and the feeling of liberty sat uneasily on most of them; they tended to gather together quietly for a while before they broke into boisterous play, and their talk was still of the classroom and the teacher, of books and reprimands. Bobby Martin had already stuffed his pockets full of stones, and the other boys soon followed his example, selecting the smoothest and roundest stones; Bobby and Harry Jones and Dickie Delacroix—the villagers pronounced this name "Delacroy"—eventually made a great pile of stones in one corner of the square and guarded it against the raids of the other boys. The girls stood aside, talking among themselves, looking over their shoulders at the boys, and the very small children rolled in the dust or clung to the hands of their older brothers or sisters.

Soon the men began to gather, surveying their own children, speaking of planting and rain, tractors and taxes. They stood together, away from the piles of stones in the corner, and their jokes were quiet and they smiled rather than laughed. The women, wearing faded house dresses and sweaters, came shortly after their menfolk. They greeted one another and exchanged bits of gossip as they went to join their husbands. Soon the women, standing by their husbands, began to call to their children, and the children came reluctantly, having to be called four or five times. Bobby Martin ducked under his mother's grasping hand and ran, laughing, back to the pile of stones. His father spoke up sharply, and Bobby came quickly and took his place between his father and his oldest brother.

The lottery was conducted—as were the square dances, the teen-age club, the Halloween program—by Mr. Summers, who had time and energy to devote to civic activities. He was a round-faced, jovial man and he ran the coal business, and people were sorry for him, because he had no children and his wife was a scold. When he arrived in the square, carrying the black wooden box, there was a murmur of conversation among the villagers, and he waved and called, "Little late today, folks." The postmaster, Mr. Graves, followed him, carrying a three-legged stool, and the stool was put in the center of the square and Mr. Summers set the black box down on it. The villagers kept their distance, leaving a space between themselves and the stool, and when Mr. Summers said, "Some of you fellows want to give me a hand?" there was a hesitation before two men, Mr. Martin and his oldest son, Baxter, came forward to hold the box steady on the stool while Mr. Summers stirred up the papers inside it.

The original paraphernalia for the lottery had been lost long ago, and the black box now resting on the stool had been put into use even before Old Man Warner, the oldest man in town, was born. Mr. Summers spoke frequently to the villagers about making a new box, but no one liked to upset even as much tradition as was represented by the black box. There was a story that the present box had been made with some pieces of the box that had preceded it, the one that had been constructed when the first people settled down to make a village here. Every year, after the lottery, Mr. Summers began talking again about a new box, but every year the subject was allowed to fade off without anything's being done. The black box grew shabbier each year; by now it was no longer completely black but splintered badly along one side to show the original wood color, and in some places faded or stained.

Mr. Martin and his oldest son, Baxter, held the black box securely on the stool until Mr. Summers had stirred the papers thoroughly with his hand. Because so much of the ritual had been forgotten or discarded, Mr. Summers had been successful in having slips of paper substituted for the chips of wood that had been used for generations.

Chips of wood, Mr. Summers had argued, had been all very well when the village was tiny, but now that the population was more than three hundred and likely to keep on growing, it was necessary to use something that would fit more easily into the black box. The night before the lottery, Mr. Summers and Mr. Graves made up the slips of paper and put them in the box, and it was then taken to the safe of Mr. Summer's coal company and locked up until Mr. Summers was ready to take it to the square next morning. The rest of the year, the box was put away, sometimes one place, sometimes another; it had spent one year in Mr. Graves' barn and another year underfoot in the post office, and sometimes it was set on a shelf in the Martin grocery and left there.

There was a great deal of fussing to be done before Mr. Summers declared the lottery open. There were the lists to make up—of heads of families, heads of households in each family, members of each household in each family. There was the proper swearing-in of Mr. Summers by the postmaster, as the official of the lottery; at one time, some people remembered, there had been a recital of some sort, performed by the official of the lottery, a perfunctory, tuneless chant that had been rattled off duly each year; some people believed that the official of the lottery used to stand just so when he said or sang it, others believed that he was supposed to walk among the people, but years and years ago this part of the ritual had been allowed to lapse. There had been, also, a ritual salute, which the official of the lottery had had to use in addressing each person who came up to draw from the box, but this also had changed with time, until now it was felt necessary only for the official to speak to each person approaching. Mr. Summers was very good at all this; in his clean white shirt and blue jeans, with one hand resting carelessly on the black box, he seemed very proper and important as he talked interminably to Mr. Graves and the Martins.

Just as Mr. Summers finally left off talking and turned to the assembled villagers, Mrs. Hutchinson came hurriedly along the path to the square, her sweater thrown over her shoulders, and slid into place in the back of the crowd. "Clean forgot what day it was," she said to Mrs. Delacroix, who stood next to her, and they both laughed softly. "Thought my old man was out back stacking wood," Mrs. Hutchinson went on, "and then I looked out the window and the kids was gone, and then I remembered it was the twenty-seventh and came a-running." She dried her hands on her apron, and Mrs. Delacroix said, "You're in time, though. They're still talking away up there."

Mrs. Hutchinson craned her neck to see through the crowd and found her husband and children standing near the front. She tapped Mrs. Delacroix on the arm as a farewell and began to make her way through the crowd. The people separated good-humoredly to let her through; two or three people said, in voices just loud enough to be heard across the crowd, "Here comes your Missus, Hutchinson," and "Bill, she made it after all." Mrs. Hutchinson reached her husband, and Mr. Summers, who had been waiting, said cheerfully, "Thought we were going to have to get on without you, Tessie." Mrs. Hutchinson said, grinning, "Wouldn't have me leave m'dishes in the sink, now, would you, Joe?" and soft laughter ran through the crowd as the people stirred back into position after Mrs. Hutchinson's arrival.

"Well, now," Mr. Summers said soberly, "guess we better get started, get this over with, so's we can go back to work. Anybody ain't here?"

"Dunbar," several people said. "Dunbar, Dunbar."

Mr. Summers consulted his list. "Clyde Dunbar," he said. "That's right. He's broke his leg, hasn't he? Who's drawing for him?"

"Me, I guess," a woman said, and Mr. Summers turned to look at her. "Wife draws for her husband," Mr. Summers said. "Don't you have a grown boy to do it for you, Janey?" Although Mr. Summers and everyone else in the village knew the answer perfectly well, it was the business of the official of the lottery to ask such questions formally. Mr. Summers waited with an expression of polite interest while Mrs. Dunbar answered.

"Horace's not but sixteen yet," Mrs. Dunbar said regretfully. "Guess I gotta fill in for the old man this year."

"Right," Mr. Summers said. He made a note on the list he was holding. Then he asked, "Watson boy drawing this year?"

A tall boy in the crowd raised his hand. "Here," he said. "I'm drawing for m'mother and me." He blinked his eyes nervously and ducked his head as several voices in the crowd said things like "Good fellow, Jack," and "Glad to see your mother's got a man to do it."

"Well," Mr. Summers said, "guess that's everyone. Old Man Warner make it?"

"Here," a voice said, and Mr. Summers nodded.

A sudden hush fell on the crowd as Mr. Summers cleared his throat and looked at the list. "All ready?" he called. "Now, I'll read the names—heads of families first—and the men come up and take a paper out of the box. Keep the paper folded in your hand without looking at it until everyone has had a turn. Everything clear?"

The people had done it so many times that they only half listened to the directions; most of them were quiet, wetting their lips, not looking around. Then Mr. Summers raised one hand high and said, "Adams." A man disengaged himself from the crowd and came forward. "Hi, Steve," Mr. Summers said, and Mr. Adams said, "Hi, Joe." They grinned at one another humorlessly and nervously. Then Mr. Adams reached into the black box and took out a folded paper. He held it firmly by one corner as he turned and went hastily back to his place in the crowd, where he stood a little apart from his family, not looking down at his hand.

"Allen," Mr. Summers said. "Anderson. . . . Bentham."

"Seems like there's no time at all between lotteries any more," Mrs. Delacroix said to Mrs. Graves in the back row. "Seems like we got through with the last one only last week."

"Time sure goes fast," Mrs. Graves said.

"Clark. . . . Delacroix."

"There goes my old man," Mrs. Delacroix said. She held her breath while her husband went forward.

"Dunbar," Mr. Summers said, and Mrs. Dunbar went steadily to the box while one of the women said, "Go on, Janey," and another said, "There she goes."

"We're next," Mrs. Graves said. She watched while Mr. Graves came around from the side of the box, greeted Mr. Summers gravely, and selected a slip of paper from the box. By now, all through the crowd there were men holding the small folded papers in their large hands, turning them over and over nervously. Mrs. Dunbar and her two sons stood together, Mrs. Dunbar holding the slip of paper.

"Harburt. . . . Hutchinson."

"Get up there, Bill," Mrs. Hutchinson said, and the people near her laughed.

"Jones."

"They do say," Mr. Adams said to Old Man Warner, who stood next to him, "that over in the north village they're talking of giving up the lottery."

Old Man Warner snorted. "Pack of crazy fools," he said. "Listening to the young folks, nothing's good enough for *them*. Next thing you know, they'll be wanting to go back to living in caves, nobody work any more, live *that* way for a while. Used to be a saying about 'Lottery in June, corn be heavy soon.' First thing you know, we'd all be eating stewed chickweed and acorns. There's *always* been a lottery," he added petulantly. "Bad enough to see young Joe Summers up there joking with everybody."

"Some places have already quit lotteries," Mrs. Adams said.

"Nothing but trouble in *that*," Old Man Warner said stoutly. "Pack of young fools."

"Martin." And Bobby Martin watched his father go forward. "Overdyke. . . . Percy."

"I wish they'd hurry," Mrs. Dunbar said to her older son. "I wish they'd hurry."

"They're almost through," her son said.

"You get ready to run tell Dad," Mrs. Dunbar said.

Mr. Summers called his own name and then stepped forward precisely and selected a slip from the box. Then he called, "Warner."

"Seventy-seventh year I been in the lottery," Old Man Warner said as he went through the crowd. "Seventy-seventh time."

"Watson." The tall boy came awkwardly through the crowd. Someone said, "Don't be nervous, Jack," and Mr. Summers said, "Take your time, son."

"Zanini."

After that, there was a long pause, a breathless pause, until Mr. Summers, holding his slip of paper in the air, said, "All right, fellows." For a minute, no one moved, and then all the slips of paper were opened. Suddenly, all the women began to speak at once, saying, "Who is it?," "Who's got it?," "Is it the Dunbars?," "Is it the Watsons?" Then the voices began to say, "It's Hutchinson. It's Bill," "Bill Hutchinson's got it."

"Go tell your father," Mrs. Dunbar said to her older son.

People began to look around to see the Hutchinsons. Bill Hutchinson was standing quiet, staring down at the paper in his hand. Suddenly, Tessie Hutchinson shouted to Mr. Summers, "You didn't give him time enough to take any paper he wanted. I saw you. It wasn't fair!"

"Be a good sport, Tessie," Mrs. Delacroix called, and Mrs. Graves said, "All of us took the same chance."

"Shut up, Tessie," Bill Hutchinson said.

"Well, everyone," Mr. Summers said, "that was done pretty fast, and now we've got to be hurrying a little more to get done in time." He consulted his next list. "Bill," he said, "you draw for the Hutchinson family. You got any other households in the Hutchinsons?"

"There's Don and Eva," Mrs. Hutchinson yelled. "Make *them* take their chance!"

"Daughters draw with their husbands' families, Tessie," Mr. Summers said gently. "You know that as well as anyone else."

"It wasn't *fair*," Tessie said.

"I guess not, Joe," Bill Hutchinson said regretfully. "My daughter draws with her husband's family, that's only fair. And I've got no other family except the kids."

"Then, as far as drawing for familes is concerned, it's you," Mr. Summers said in explanation, "and as far as drawing for households is concerned, that's you, too. Right?"

"Right," Bill Hutchinson said.

"How many kids, Bill?" Mr. Summers asked formally.

"Three," Bill Hutchinson said. "There's Bill, Jr., and Nancy, and little Dave. And Tessie and me."

"All right, then," Mr. Summers said. "Harry, you got their tickets back?"

Mr. Graves nodded and held up the slips of paper. "Put them in the box, then," Mr. Summers directed. "Take Bill's and put it in."

"I think we ought to start over," Mrs. Hutchinson said, as quietly as she could. "I tell you it wasn't *fair*. You didn't give him time enough to choose. *Every*body saw that."

Mr. Graves had selected the five slips and put them in the box, and he dropped all the papers but those onto the ground, where the breeze caught them and lifted them off.

"Listen, everybody," Mrs. Hutchinson was saying to the people around her.

"Ready, Bill?" Mr. Summers asked, and Bill Hutchinson, with one quick glance around at his wife and children, nodded.

"Remember," Mr. Summers said, "take the slips and keep them folded until each person has taken one. Harry, you help little Dave." Mr. Graves took the hand of the little boy, who came willingly with him up to the box. "Take a paper out of the box, Davy," Mr. Summers said. Davy put his hand into the box and laughed. "Take just *one* paper," Mr. Summers said. "Harry, you hold it for him." Mr. Graves took the child's hand and removed the folded paper from the tight fist and held it while little Dave stood next to him and looked up at him wonderingly.

"Nancy next," Mr. Summers said. Nancy was twelve, and her school friends breathed heavily as she went forward, switching her skirt, and took a slip daintily from the box. "Bill, Jr.," Mr. Summers said, and Billy, his face red and his feet over-large, nearly knocked the box over as he got a paper out. "Tessie," Mr. Summers said. She hesitated for a minute, looking around defiantly, and then set her lips and went up to the box. She snatched a paper out and held it behind her.

"Bill," Mr. Summers said, and Bill Hutchinson reached into the

box and felt around, bringing his hand out at last with the slip of paper in it.

The crowd was quiet. A girl whispered, "I hope it's not Nancy," and the sound of the whisper reached the edges of the crowd.

"It's not the way it used to be," Old Man Warner said clearly. "People ain't the way they used to be."

"All right," Mr. Summers said. "Open the papers. Harry, you open little Dave's."

Mr. Graves opened the slip of paper and there was a general sigh through the crowd as he held it up and everyone could see that it was blank. Nancy and Bill, Jr., opened theirs at the same time, and both beamed and laughed, turning around to the crowd and holding their slips of paper above their heads.

"Tessie," Mr. Summers said. There was a pause, and then Mr. Summers looked at Bill Hutchinson, and Bill unfolded his paper and showed it. It was blank.

"It's Tessie," Mr. Summers said, and his voice was hushed. "Show us her paper, Bill."

Bill Hutchinson went over to his wife and forced the slip of paper out of her hand. It had a black spot on it, the black spot Mr. Summers had made the night before with the heavy pencil in the coal company office. Bill Hutchinson held it up, and there was a stir in the crowd.

"All right, folks," Mr. Summers said. "Let's finish quickly."

Although the villagers had forgotten the ritual and lost the original black box, they still remembered to use stones. The pile of stones the boys had made earlier was ready; there were stones on the ground with the blowing scraps of paper that had come out of the box. Mrs. Delacroix selected a stone so large she had to pick it up with both hands and turned to Mrs. Dunbar. "Come on," she said. "Hurry up."

Mrs. Dunbar had small stones in both hands, and she said, gasping for breath, "I can't run at all. You'll have to go ahead and I'll catch up with you."

The children had stones already, and someone gave little Davy Hutchinson a few pebbles.

Tessie Hutchinson was in the center of a cleared space by now, and she held her hands out desperately as the villagers moved in on her. "It isn't fair," she said. A stone hit her on the side of the head.

Old Man Warner was saying, "Come on, come on, everyone." Steve Adams was in the front of the crowd of villagers, with Mrs. Graves beside him.

"It isn't fair, it isn't right," Mrs. Hutchinson screamed, and then they were upon her.

DISCUSSION

1.   When did you first notice that something ominous was taking place? Now look back even further and see if you can find any earlier *foreshadowing,* or clues as to what is to come.

2.   "There's *always* been a lottery," Old Man Warner says. What details in the story tell you that the villagers are acting out a long-standing tradition? Why do you think the author made the traditional aspect of the lottery so important?

3.   The theme of the scapegoat is a very old one. Look up the word *scapegoat* in the dictionary, or read about the original scapegoat in the book of Leviticus, chapter 16, in the Bible. Do you think the scapegoat tradition may have had something to do with the origins of the lottery? Do you think the lottery may have begun for some other reasons? Explain.

4.   The *theme* of a literary work is its underlying idea. Often themes are difficult to sum up; a story can have more than one theme; and in some stories, theme is much less important than character or mood. However, we can safely say that the theme of "From New York to Liverpool" is the awesomeness of the sea; that the theme of "Haircut" is how cruelty and evil can go unrecognized. Try your hand at stating the theme or themes of "The Lottery."

5.   In the last story, "A Visit of Charity," the brightness of the sunlight and the little girl's clothes made the Old Ladies' Home even more depressing and dismal in contrast. Much of the force and horror of this story comes from a contrast, too. What contrast makes "The Lottery" so memorable?

6.   Old Man Warner makes a highly *ironic* statement when he hears that a neighboring village is considering giving up the lottery: "First thing you know, we'd all be eating stewed chickweed and acorns." Irony always arises from contrast. A statement or a situation is ironic when the underlying meaning is different from the surface meaning. The situation in "Haircut" is ironic because the barber who tells the story does not see the truth about it. Old Man Warner's statement is ironic because he implies that without the lottery the village would return to an uncivilized state, while, we, the readers, see the lottery as barbaric and uncivilized. What other statement does Old Man Warner make that is also ironic?

For further activities, see page 114.

Tell Me How Long the Train's Been Gone

JAMES BALDWIN

My brother, Caleb, was seventeen when I was ten. We were very good friends. In fact, he was my best friend and, for a very long time, my only friend.

I do not mean to say that he was always nice to me. I got on his nerves a lot, and he resented having to take me around with him and be responsible for me when there were so many other things he wanted to be doing. Therefore, his hand was often up against the side of my head, and my tears caused him to be punished many times. But I knew, somehow, anyway, that when he was being punished for my tears, he was not being punished for anything he had done to me; he was being punished because that was the way we lived; and his punishment, oddly, helped unite us. More oddly still, even as his great hand caused my head to stammer and dropped a flame-colored curtain before my eyes, I understood that he was not striking *me*. His hand leaped out because he could not help it, and I received the blow because I was there. And it happened, sometimes, before I could even catch my breath to howl, that the hand that had struck me grabbed me and held me, and it was difficult indeed to know which of us was weeping. He was striking, striking out, striking out, striking out; the hand asked me to forgive him. I felt his bewilderment through the membrane of my own. I also felt that he was trying to teach me something. And I had no other teachers.

For our father—how shall I describe our father?—was a ruined Barbados peasant, exiled in a Harlem which he loathed, where he never saw the sun or sky he remembered, where life took place neither indoors nor without, and where there was no joy. By which I mean no joy that he remembered. Had he been able to bring with him any of the joy he had felt on that far-off island, then the air of the sea and the impulse to dancing would sometimes have transfigured our dreadful rooms. Our lives might have been very different.

But no, he brought with him from Barbados only black rum and blacker pride and magic incantations, which neither healed nor saved.

He did not understand the people among whom he found himself; they had no coherence, no stature and no pride. He came from a race which had been flourishing at the very dawn of the world—a race greater and nobler than Rome or Judea, mightier than Egypt—he came from a race of kings, kings who had never been taken in battle, kings who had never been slaves. He spoke to us of tribes and empires, battles, victories and monarchs of whom we had never heard—they were not mentioned in our textbooks—and invested us with glories in which we felt more awkward than in the secondhand shoes we wore. In the stifling room of his pretensions and expectations, we stumbled wretchedly about, stubbing our toes, as it were, on rubies, scraping our shins on golden caskets, bringing down, with a childish cry, the splendid purple tapestry on which, in pounding gold and scarlet, our destinies and our inheritance were figured. It could scarcely have been otherwise, since a child's major attention has to be concentrated on how to fit into a world which, with every passing hour, reveals itself as merciless.

If our father was of royal blood and we were royal children, our father was certainly the only person in the world who knew it. The landlord did not know it; our father never mentioned royal blood to *him*. When we were late with our rent, which was often, the landlord threatened, in terms no commoner had ever used before a king, to put us in the streets. He complained that our shiftlessness, which he did not hesitate to consider an attribute of the race, had forced him, an old man with a weak heart, to climb all these stairs to plead with us to give him the money we owed him. And this was the last time; he wanted to make sure we understood that this was the last time.

Our father was younger than the landlord, leaner, stronger, and bigger. With one blow, he could have brought the landlord to his knees. And we knew how much he hated the man. For days on end, in the wintertime, we huddled around the gas stove in the kitchen, because the landlord gave us no heat. When windows were broken, the landlord took his time about fixing them; the wind made the cardboard we stuffed in the windows rattle all night long; and when snow came, the weight of the snow forced the cardboard inward and onto the floor. Whenever the apartment received a fresh coat of paint, we bought the paint and did the painting ourselves; we killed the rats. A great chunk of the kitchen ceiling fell one winter, narrowly missing our mother.

We all hated the landlord with a perfectly exquisite hatred, and we would have been happy to see our proud father kill him. We would have been glad to help. But our father did nothing of the sort. He stood before the landlord, looking unutterably weary. He made excuses. He apologized. He swore that it would never happen again. (We knew that it *would* happen again.) He begged for time. The landlord would finally go down the stairs, letting us and all the neighbors know how goodhearted he was, and our father would walk into the kitchen and pour himself a glass of rum.

But we knew that our father would never have allowed any black man to speak to him as the landlord did, as policemen did, as storekeepers and welfare workers and pawnbrokers did. No, not for a moment. He would have thrown him out of the house. He would certainly have made a black man know that he was not the descendant of slaves! He had made them know it so often that he had almost no friends among them, and if we had followed his impossible lead, we would have had no friends, either. It was scarcely worthwhile being the descendant of kings if the kings were black and no one had ever heard of them.

And it was because of our father, per-

haps, that Caleb and I clung to each other, in spite of the great difference in our ages; or, in another way, it may have been precisely the difference in our ages that made the clinging possible. I don't know. It is really not the kind of thing anyone can ever know. I think it may be easier to love the really helpless younger brother, because he cannot enter into competition with one on one's own ground, or on any ground at all, and can never question one's role or jeopardize one's authority. In my own case, certainly, it did not occur to me to compete with Caleb, and I could not have questioned his role or his authority, because I needed both. He was my touchstone, my model and my only guide.

Anyway, our father, dreaming bitterly of Barbados, despised and mocked by his neighbors and all but ignored by his sons, held down his unspeakable factory job, spread his black gospel in bars on the weekends, and drank his rum. I do not know if he loved our mother. I think he did.

They had had five children—only Caleb and I, the first and the last, were left, We were both dark, like our father; but two of the three dead girls had been fair, like our mother.

She came from New Orleans. Her hair was not like ours. It was black, but softer and finer. The color of her skin reminded me of the color of bananas. Her skin was as bright as that, and contained that kind of promise, and she had tiny freckles around her nose and a small black mole just above her upper lip. It was the mole, I don't know why, which made her beautiful. Without it, her face might have been merely sweet, merely pretty. But the mole was funny. It had the effect of making one realize that our mother liked funny things, liked to laugh. The mole made one look at her eyes—large, extraordinary dark eyes, eyes which seemed always to be amused by something, eyes which looked straight out, seeming to see everything, seeming to be afraid of nothing. She was a soft, round, plump woman. She liked nice clothes and dangling jewelry, which she mostly didn't have, and she liked to cook for large numbers of people, and she loved our father.

She knew him—knew him through and through. I am not being coy or colloquial but bluntly and sadly matter-of-fact when I say that I will now never know what she saw in him. What she saw was certainly not for many eyes; what she saw got him through his working week and his Sunday rest; what she saw saved him. She saw that he was a man. For her, perhaps, he was a great man. I think, though, that, for our mother, any man was great who aspired to become a man: this meant that our father was very rare and precious. I used to wonder how she took it, how she bore it—his rages, his tears, his cowardice.

On Saturday nights, he was almost always evil, drunk and maudlin. He came home from work in the early afternoon and gave our mother some money. It was never enough, of course, but he always kept enough to go out and get drunk. She never protested, at least not as far as I know. Then she would go out shopping. I would usually go with her, for Caleb would almost always be out somewhere, and our mother didn't like the idea of leaving me alone in the house. And this was probably, after all, the best possible arrangement. People who disliked our father were sure (for that very reason) to like our mother;

and people who felt that Caleb was growing to be too much like his father could feel that I, after all, might turn out like my mother. Besides, it is not, as a general rule, easy to hate a small child. One runs the risk of looking ridiculous, especially if the child is with his mother.

And especially if that mother is Mrs. Proudhammer. Mrs. Proudhammer knew very well what people thought of Mr. Proudhammer. She knew, too, exactly how much she owed in each store she entered, how much she was going to be able to pay, and what she had to buy. She entered with a smile, ready.

"Evening. Let me have some of them red beans there."

"Evening. You know, you folks been running up quite a little bill here."

"I'm going to give you something on it right now. I need some cornmeal and flour and some rice."

"You know, I got my bills to meet, too, Mrs. Proudhammer."

"Didn't I just tell you I was going to pay? I want some cornflakes too, and some milk." Such merchandise as she could reach, she had already placed on the counter.

"When do you think you're going to be able to pay this bill? All of it, I mean."

"You know I'm going to pay it just as soon as I can. How much does it all come to? Give me that end you got there of that chocolate cake." The chocolate cake was for Caleb and me. "Well, now you put this against the bill." Imperiously, as though it were the most natural thing in the world, she put two or three dollars on the counter.

"You lucky I'm softhearted, Mrs. Proudhammer."

"Things sure don't cost this much

downtown—you think I don't know it? Here." And she paid him for what she had bought. "Thank you. You been mighty kind."

And we left the store. I often felt that in order to help her, I should have filled my pockets with merchandise while she was talking. But I never did, not only because the store was often crowded or because I was afraid of being caught by the storekeeper, but because I was afraid of humiliating her. When I began to steal, not very much later, I stole in stores that were not in our neighborhood, where we were not known.

When we had to do "heavy" shopping, we went marketing under the bridge at Park Avenue—Caleb, our mother and I; and sometimes, but rarely, our father came with us. The most usual reason for heavy shopping was that some relatives of our mother's, or old friends of both our mother's and our father's, were coming to visit. We were certainly not going to let them go away hungry—not even if it meant, as it often did mean, spending more than we had. In spite of what I have been suggesting about our father's temperament, and no matter how difficult he may sometimes have been with us, he was much too proud to offend any guest of his; on the contrary, his impulse was to make them feel that his home was theirs; and besides, he was lonely, lonely for his past, lonely for those faces which had borne witness to that past. Therefore, he would sometimes pretend that our mother did not know how to shop, and our father would come with us, under the bridge, in order to teach her.

There he would be, then, uncharacteristically, in shirtsleeves, which made him look rather boyish; and as our mother

showed no desire to take shopping lessons from him, he turned his attention to Caleb and me. He would pick up a fish, opening the gills and holding it close to his nose. "You see that? That fish looks fresh, don't it? Well, that fish ain't as fresh as I am, and I *been* out of the water. They done doctored that fish. Come on." And we would walk away, a little embarrassed but, on the whole, rather pleased that our father was so smart.

Meantime, our mother was getting the marketing done. She was very happy on days like this, because our father was happy. He was happy, odd as his expression of it may sound, to be out with his wife and his two sons. If we had been on the island that had been witness to his birth, instead of the unspeakable island of Manhattan, he felt that it would not have been so hard for us all to trust and love each other. He sensed, and I think he was right, that on that other, never to be recovered island, his sons would have looked on him very differently, and he would have looked very differently on his sons. Life would have been hard there, too; we would have fought there, too, and more or less blindly suffered and more or less blindly died. But we would not have been (or so it was to seem to all of us forever) so wickedly menaced by the mere fact of our relationship, would not have been so frightened of entering into the central, most beautiful and valuable facts of our lives. We would have been laughing and cursing and tussling in the water, instead of stammering under the bridge; we would have known less about vanished African kingdoms and more about each other. Or, not at all impossibly, more about both.

If it was summer, we bought a watermelon, which either Caleb or our father carried home, fighting with each other for this privilege. They looked very like each other on those days—both big, both black, both laughing.

Caleb always looked absolutely helpless when he laughed. He laughed with all his body, perhaps touching his shoulder against yours, or putting his head on your chest for a moment, and then careening off you, halfway across the room or down the block. I will always hear his laughter. He was always happy on such days, too. If our father needed his son, Caleb certainly needed his father. Such days, however, were rare—one of the reasons, probably, that I remember them now.

Eventually, we all climbed the stairs into that hovel which, at such moments, was our castle. One very nearly felt the drawbridge rising behind us as our father locked the door.

The bathtub could not yet be filled with cold water and the melon placed in the tub, because this was Saturday, and, come evening, we all had to bathe. The melon was covered with a blanket and placed on the fire escape. Then we unloaded what we had bought, rather impressed by our opulence, though our father was always, by this time, appalled by the money we had spent. I was always sadly aware that there would be nothing left of all this once tomorrow had come and gone and that most of it, after all, was not for us, but for others.

Our mother was calculating the pennies she would need all week—carfare for our father and for Caleb, who went to a high school out of our neighborhood; money for the life insurance; money for

milk for me at school; money for light and gas; money put away, if possible, toward the rent. She knew just about what our father had left in *his* pockets and was counting on him to give me the money I would shortly be demanding to go to the movies. Caleb had a part-time job after school and already had his movie money. Anyway, unless he was in a very good mood or needed me for something, he would not be anxious to go to the movies with me.

Our mother never insisted that Caleb tell her where he was going, nor did she question him as to how he spent the money he made. She was afraid of hearing him lie, and she did not want to risk forcing him to lie. She was operating on the assumption that he was sensible and had been raised to be honorable and that he, now more than ever, needed his privacy.

But she was very firm with him, nevertheless. "I do not want to see you rolling in here at three in the morning, Caleb. I want you here in time to eat, and you know you got to take your bath."

"Yes, indeed, ma'am. Why can't I take my bath in the morning?"

"Don't you start being funny. You know you ain't going to get up in time to take no bath in the morning."

"Don't nobody want you messing around in that bathroom all morning long, man," said our father. "You just git back in the house like your ma's telling you."

"Besides," I said, "you never wash out the tub."

Caleb looked at me in mock surprise and from a great height, allowing his chin and his lids simultaneously to drop and swiveling his head away from me.

"I see," he said, "that everyone in this

family is ganging up on me. All right, Leo. I was planning to take you to the show with me, but now I've changed my mind."

"I'm sorry," I said quickly. "I take it back."

"You take *what* back?"

"What I said—about you not washing out the tub."

"Ain't no need to take it back," our father said stubbornly. "It's true. A man don't take back nothing that's true."

"So *you* say," Caleb said, with a hint of a sneer. But before anyone could possibly react to this, he picked me up, scowling into my face, which he held just above his own. "You take it back?"

"Leo ain't going to take it back," our father said.

Now I was in trouble. Caleb watched me, a small grin on his face. "You take it back?"

"Stop teasing that child, and put him down," our mother said. "The trouble ain't that Caleb don't wash out the tub—he just don't wash it out very clean."

"I never knew him to wash it out," our father said, "unless I was standing behind him."

"Well, ain't neither one of you much good around the house," our mother said.

Caleb laughed and set me down. "You didn't take it back," he said.

I said nothing.

"I guess I'm just going to have to go on without you."

Still, I said nothing.

"You going to have that child to crying in a minute," our mother said. "If you going to take him go on and take him. Don't do him like that."

Caleb laughed again. "I'm going to

take him. The way he got them eyes all ready to water, I'd better take him somewhere." We walked toward the door. "But you got to make up *your* mind," he said to me, "to say what *you* think is right."

I grabbed Caleb's hand, the signal for the descent of the drawbridge. Our mother watched us cheerfully as we walked out; our father watched us balefully. Yet there was a certain humor in his face, too, and a kind of pride.

"Dig you later," Caleb said, and the door closed behind us.

The hall was dark, smelling of cooking, of stale wine, of rotting garbage. We dropped down the stairs, Caleb going two at a time, pausing at each landing, briefly, to glance back up at me. I dropped down behind him as fast as I could. When I reached the street level, Caleb was already on the stoop, joking with some of his friends, who were standing in the doorway—who seemed always to be in the doorway.

I didn't like Caleb's friends, because I was afraid of them. I knew the only reason they didn't try to make life hell for me, the way they made life hell for a lot of the other kids, was because they were afraid of Caleb. I went through the door, passing between my brother and his friends, down to the sidewalk, feeling, as they looked briefly at me and then continued joking with Caleb, what they felt—that here was Caleb's round-eyed, frail and useless sissy of a little brother. They pitied Caleb for having to take me out. On the other hand, they also wanted to go to the show, but didn't have the money. Therefore, in silence, I could crow over them even as they despised me. But this was always a terribly

risky, touch-and-go business, for Caleb might, at any moment, change his mind and drive me away.

I always stood, those Saturday afternoons, in fear and trembling, holding on to the small shield of my bravado, while waiting for Caleb to come down the steps of the stoop, away from his friends, to me. I braced myself, always, for the moment when he would turn to me, saying, "Okay, kid. You run along. I'll see you later."

This meant that I would have to go the movies by myself and hang around in front of the box office, waiting for some grown-up to take me in. I could not go back upstairs, for this would be informing my mother and father that Caleb had gone off somewhere after promising to take me to the movies.

Neither could I simply hang around, playing with the kids on the block. For one thing, my demeanor, as I came out of the house, very clearly indicated that I had better things to do than play with *them;* for another, they were not terribly anxious to play with *me;* and, finally, my remaining on the block would have had exactly the same effect as my going upstairs. To remain on the block after Caleb's dismissal was to put myself at the mercy of the block and to put Caleb at the mercy of our parents.

So I prepared myself, those Saturdays, to respond with a cool "Okay. See you later," and then to turn indifferently away, and walk. This was surely the most terrible moment. The moment I turned away, I was committed, I was trapped, and I then had miles to walk, so it seemed to me, before I would be out of sight, before the block ended and I could turn onto the avenue. I wanted to run out of that block, but I never did. I never looked back. I forced

myself to walk very slowly, looking neither right nor left, striving to seem at once distracted and offhand; concentrating on the cracks in the sidewalk and stumbling over them; trying to whistle, feeling every muscle in my body, feeling that all the block was watching me, and feeling, which was odd, that I deserved it.

And then I reached the avenue, and turned, still not looking back, and was released from those eyes at least; but now I faced other eyes, eyes coming toward me. These eyes were the eyes of children stronger than me, who would steal my movie money; these eyes were the eyes of white cops, whom I feared, whom I hated with a literally murderous hatred; these eyes were the eyes of old folks, who might wonder what I was doing on this avenue by myself.

And then I got to the show. Sometimes someone would take me in right away, and sometimes I would have to stand there and wait, watching the faces coming to the box office. And this was not easy, since I didn't, after all, want everyone in the neighborhood to know I was loitering outside the movie house waiting for someone to take me in. If it came to our father's attention, he would kill both Caleb and me.

Eventually, I would see a face which looked susceptible. I would rush up to him—it was usually a man, for men were less likely to be disapproving—and whisper, "Take me in," and give him my dime. Sometimes the man simply took the dime and disappeared inside; sometimes he gave my dime back to me and took me in anyway. Sometimes I ended up wandering around the streets—but I couldn't wander into a strange neighborhood, because I would be beaten up if I did—until I figured the show was out. It was dangerous to get home too early, and, of course, it was practically lethal to arrive too late. If all went well, I could cover for Caleb, saying that I had left him with some boys on the stoop. Then, if *he* came in too late, it could not be considered my fault.

But if wandering around this way was not without its dangers, neither was it without its discoveries and delights. I discovered subways. I discovered, that is, that I could ride on subways by myself and, furthermore, that I could usually ride for nothing. Sometimes, when I ducked under the turnstile, I was caught, and sometimes great black ladies seized on me as a pretext for long, very loud, ineffably moral lectures about wayward children breaking their parents' hearts. Sometimes, doing everything in my power not to attract their attention, I endeavored to look as though I were in the charge of a respectable-looking man or woman, entering the subway in their shadow and sitting very still beside them. It was best to try to sit *between* two such people, for each would automatically assume that I was with the other. There I would sit, then, in a precarious anonymity, watching the people, listening to the roar, watching the lights of stations flash by. It seemed to me that nothing was faster than a subway train, and I loved the speed, because the speed was dangerous.

For a time, during these expeditions, I simply sat and watched the people. Lots of people would be dressed up, for this was Saturday night. The women's hair would be all curled and straightened, and the lipstick on their full lips looked purple and make-believe against the dark skins of their faces. They wore very fancy capes or coats, in wonderful colors, and long dresses, and sometimes they had jewels in their hair, and sometimes they wore flowers on their dresses. They were almost as beautiful as movie stars. And so the men with them seemed to think.

The hair of the men was slick and wavy, brushed up into pompadours; or they wore very sharp hats, brim flicked down dangerously over one eye, with perhaps one flower in the lapel of their many-colored suits. They laughed and talked with their girls, but quietly, for there were white people in the car. The white people would scarcely ever be dressed up and did not speak to each other at all—only read their papers and stared at the advertisements. But they fascinated me more than the colored people did, because I knew nothing at all about them and could not imagine what they were like.

Underground, I received my first apprehension of New York neighborhoods and, underground, first felt what may be called a civic terror. I very soon realized that after the train had passed a certain point, going uptown or downtown, all the colored people disappeared. The first time I realized this, I panicked and got lost. I rushed off the train, terrified of what these white people might do to me, with no colored person around to protect me—even to scold me, even to beat me; at least, their touch was familiar, and I knew that they did not, after all, intend to kill me—and got on another train only because I saw a black man on it. But almost everyone else was white.

The train did not stop at any of the stops I remembered. I became more and more frightened, frightened of getting off the train and frightened of staying on it, frightened of saying anything to the man and frightened that he would get off the train before I could say anything to him. He was my salvation, and he stood there in the unapproachable and frightening form that salvation so often takes. At each stop, I watched him with despair. . . .

Finally, I tugged at the man's sleeve. He looked down at me with a gruff, amused concern; then, reacting, no doubt to the desperation in my face, he bent closer.

I asked him if there was a bathroom on the train.

He laughed, "No," he said, "but there's a bathroom in the station." He looked at me again. "Where're you going?"

I told him that I was going home.

"And where's home?"

I told him.

This time he did not laugh. "Do you know where you are?" he said.

I shook my head. At that moment, the train came into a station, and after several hours, it rolled to a stop. The doors opened, and the man led me to the bathroom. I ran in, and I hurried, because I was afraid he would disappear. But I was glad he had not come in with me.

When I came out, he stood waiting for me. "Now," he said, "you in Brooklyn. You ever hear of Brooklyn? What you doing out here by yourself?"

"I got lost," I said.

"I *know* you got lost. What I want to know is how *come* you got lost? Where's your mama? Where's your daddy?"

I almost said that I didn't have any, because I liked his face and his voice and was half hoping to hear him say that *he* didn't have any little boy and would just as soon take a chance on me. But I told him

that my mama and daddy were at home.

"And do they know where *you* are?"

I said, "No." There was a pause.

"Well, I know they going to make your tail hot when they see you." He took my hand. "Come on."

And he led me along the platform and then down some steps and along a narrow passage and then up some steps onto the opposite platform. I was very impressed by this maneuver; in order to accomplish the same purpose, I had always left the subway station and gone up into the street. Now that the emergency was over, I was in no great hurry to leave my savior. I asked him if he had a little boy.

"Yes," he said, "and if *you* was my little boy, I'd paddle your behind so you couldn't sit down for a week."

I asked him how old was his little boy, what was his name and if his little boy was at home.

"He *better* be at home!" He looked at me and laughed. "His name is Jonathan. He ain't but five years old." His gaze refocused, sharpened. "How old are you?"

I told him that I was ten, going on eleven.

"You a pretty bad little fellow," he said then.

I tried to look repentant, but I would not have dreamed of denying it.

"Now, look here," he said, "this here's the uptown side. Can you read, or don't you never go to school?" I assured him that I could read. "Now, to get where you going, you got to change trains." He told me where. "Here, I'll write it down for you." He found some paper in his pockets but no pencil. We heard the train coming. He looked about him in helpless annoyance, looked at his watch, looked at me.

"It's all right. I'll tell the conductor."

But the conductor, standing between two cars, had rather a mean pink face.

My savior looked at him dubiously. "He *might* be all right. But we better not take no chances." He pushed me ahead of him into the train. "You know you right lucky that I got a little boy? If I didn't, I swear I'd just let you go on and *be* lost. You don't know the kind of trouble you going to get me in at home. My wife ain't *never* going to believe *this* story."

I told him to give me his name and address and I would write a letter to his wife and to his little boy, too.

This caused him to laugh harder than ever. "You only say that because you know I ain't got no pencil. You are one . . . shrewd little boy."

I told him that then maybe we should get off the train and that I would go back home with him.

This made him grave. "What does your father do?"

This question made me uneasy. I stared at him for a long time before I answered. "He works in a—" I could not pronounce the word—"he has a job."

He nodded. "I see. Is he home now?"

I really did not know, and I said I did not know.

"And what does your mother do?"

"She stays home."

Again he nodded. "You got any brothers or sisters?"

I told him no.

"I see. What's your name?"

"Leo."

"Leo what?"

"Leo Proudhammer."

He saw something in my face. "What do you want to be when you grow up, Leo?"

"I want to be—" and I had never said this before—"I want to be a—a movie actor. I want to be a—actor."

"You pretty skinny for that," he said.

"That's all right," I told him. "Caleb's going to teach me to swim. That's how you get big."

"Who's Caleb?"

I opened my mouth, I started to speak. I checked myself as the train roared into a station. He glanced out the window, but did not move. "He swims," I said.

"Oh," he said after a very long pause, during which the doors slammed and the train began to move. "Is he a good swimmer?"

I said that Caleb was the best swimmer in the world.

"Okay," my savior said, "okay," and put his hand on my head again and smiled at me.

I asked him what his name was.

"Charles," he said, "Charles Williams. But you better call me *Uncle* Charles, you little devil, because you have certainly ruined my Saturday night." The train came into a station. "Here's where we change," he said.

We got out of the train and crossed the platform and waited.

"Now," he said, "this train stops exactly where you going. Tell me where you going."

I stared at him.

"I want you," he said, "to tell me exactly where you *going*. I can't be fooling with you all night."

I told him.

"You sure that's right?"

I told him I was sure.

"I got a very good memory," he said. "Give me your address. Just say it, I'll remember it."

So I said it, staring into his face as the train came roaring in.

"If you don't go straight home," he said, "I'm going to come see your daddy, and when we find you, you'll be mighty sorry." He pushed me into the train and put one shoulder against the door. "Go on, now," he said, loud enough for all the car to hear. "Your mama'll meet you at the station where I told you to get off." He repeated my subway stop, pushed the angry door with his shoulder, and then said gently, "Sit down, Leo." He remained in the door until I sat down. "So long, Leo," he said then, and stepped backward out. The doors closed. He grinned at me and waved, and the train began to move.

I waved back. Then he was gone, the station was gone, and I was on my way back home.

I never saw that man again, but I made up stories about him, I dreamed about him, I even wrote a letter to him and his wife and his little boy, but I never mailed it.

I never told Caleb anything about my solitary expeditions. I don't know why. I think he might have liked to know about them. I suppose, finally, at bottom, I said nothing because my expeditions belonged to me.

Another time, it was raining, and it was still too early for me to go home. I felt very, very low that day. It was one of the times that my tongue and my body refused to obey me, and I had not been able to work up the courage to ask anyone to take

me in to the show. The ticket taker was watching me, or so I thought, with a hostile suspicion. Actually, it's very unlikely he was thinking at all, and certainly not of me. But I walked away from the show, because I could no longer bear his eyes, or anybody's eyes.

I walked the long block east from the movie house. The street was empty, black and glittering. The water soaked through my coat at the shoulders, and water dripped down my neck from my cap. I began to be afraid. I could not stay out in the rain, because then my father and mother would know I had been wandering the streets. I would get a beating, and, though Caleb was too old to get a beating, he and my father would have a terrible fight, and Caleb would blame it all on me and would not speak to me for days.

I began to hate Caleb. I wondered where he was. I started in the direction of our house, only because I did not know what else to do. Perhaps Caleb would be waiting for me on the stoop.

The avenue, too, was very long and silent. Somehow, it seemed old, like a picture in a book. It stretched straight before me, endless, and the streetlights did not so much illuminate it as prove how dark it was. The rain was falling harder. Cars sloshed by, sending up sheets of water. From the bars, I heard music, faintly, and many voices. Straight ahead of me a woman walked, very fast, head down, carrying a shopping bag. I reached my corner and crossed the wide avenue. There was no one on my stoop.

Now I was not even certain what time it was; but I knew it wasn't time yet for the show to be over. I walked into my hallway and wrung out my cap. I was sorry that I had not made someone take me in to the show, because now I did not know what to do. I *could* go upstairs and say that we had not liked the movie and had left early and that Caleb was with some boys on the stoop. But this would sound strange, and Caleb, who would not know what story I had told, would, therefore, be greatly handicapped when he came home.

I could not stay in my hallway, because my father might not be at home and might come in. I could not go into the hallway of another building, because if any of the kids who lived in the building found me, they would have the right to beat me up. I could not go back out into the rain. I stood next to the big, cold radiator, and I began to cry. But crying wasn't going to do me any good, either, especially as there was no one to hear me.

So I stepped out on my stoop again and stood there for a long time, wondering what to do. Then I thought of a condemned house, around the corner from us. We played there sometimes, though it was very dangerous and we were not supposed to. What possessed me to go there now, I don't know, except that I could not think of another dry place in the whole world. I started running east, down our block. I turned two corners and came to the house, with its black window sockets. The house was completely dark. I had forgotten how afraid I was of the dark, but the rain was drenching me. I ran down the cellar steps and clambered into the house through one of the broken windows. I squatted there in a still, dry dread, not daring to look into the house but staring outward. I was holding my breath. I heard an endless scurrying

in the darkness, a perpetual busyness, and I thought of rats, of their teeth and ferocity and fearful size, and I began to cry again.

I don't know how long I squatted there this way or what was in my mind. I listened to the rain and the rats. Then I was aware of another sound—I had been hearing it for a while without realizing it. This was a moaning sound, a sighing sound, a sound of strangling, which mingled with the sound of the rain and with a muttering, cursing human voice. The sounds came from the door that led to the backyard.

I wanted to stand, but I crouched lower; wanted to run, but could not move. Sometimes the sounds seemed to come closer, and I knew that this meant my death; sometimes they diminished or ceased altogether, and then I knew that my assailant was looking for me. I looked toward the backyard door, and I seemed to see, silhouetted against the driving rain, a figure, half bent, moaning, leaning against the wall, in indescribable torment; then there seemed to be two figures, sighing and grappling, moving so quickly that it was impossible to tell which was which, two creatures, each in a dreadful, absolute, silent single-mindedness attempting to strangle the other! . . .

Then everything was still, all movement ceased. Then I heard only the rain and the scurrying of the rats. It was over; one of them, or both of them, lay stretched out, dead or dying in this filthy place. It happened in Harlem every Saturday night. I could not catch my breath to scream. Then I heard a laugh, a low, happy, wicked laugh, and the figure turned in my direction and seemed to start toward me.

Then I screamed and stood straight up,

bumping my head on the window frame and losing my cap, and scrambled up the cellar steps. I ran head down, like a bull, away from that house and out of that block. I ran up the steps of my stoop and bumped into Caleb.

"Where . . . have you been? Hey! What's the matter with you?"

I had jumped up on him, almost knocking him down, trembling and sobbing.

"You're *soaked.* Leo, what's the matter? Where's your cap?"

But I could not say anything. I held him around the neck with all my might, and I could not stop shaking.

"Come on, Leo," Caleb said, in a different tone, "tell me what's the matter." He pried my arms loose and held me away from him, so that he could look into my face. "Oh, little Leo. Little Leo. What's the matter, baby?" He looked as though he were about to cry himself, and this made me cry harder than ever. He took out his handkerchief and wiped my face and made me blow my nose. My sobs began to lessen, but I could not stop trembling. He thought that I was trembling from cold, and he rubbed his hands roughly up and down my back and rubbed my hands between his. "What's the matter?"

I did not know how to tell him.

"Somebody try to beat you up?"

I shook my head. "No."

"What movie did you see?"

"I didn't go. I couldn't find nobody to take me in."

"And you just been wandering around in the rain all night?"

"Yes."

He sat down on the hallway steps. "Oh, Leo." Then, "You mad at me?"

I said, "No. I was scared."

He nodded. "I reckon you were, man." He wiped my face again. "You ready to go upstairs? It's getting late."

"Okay."

"How'd you lose your cap?"

"I went in a hallway to wring it out—and—I put it on the radiator, and I heard some people coming—and—I ran away, and I forgot it."

"We'll say you forgot it in the movies."

"Okay."

We started up the stairs.

"Leo," he said, "I'm sorry about tonight. I'm really sorry. I won't let it happen again. You believe me?"

"Sure. I believe you." I smiled up at him.

He squatted down. "Give us a kiss."

I kissed him.

"Okay. Climb up. I'll give you a ride. Hold on, now."

He carried me piggyback up the stairs.

DISCUSSION

1.   At the end of the story, Caleb says, "Leo, I'm sorry about tonight. . . . I won't let it happen again. You believe me?" Leo replies, "Sure, I believe you." Is Leo telling the truth do you think? If not, why would he say, "I believe you"? Is whether or not "it" happens again really important? Explain.

2.   "The hand that struck me grabbed me and held me," the narrator says about Caleb; and, "I felt his bewilderment through . . . my own. I also felt that he was trying to teach me something." In a way these statements sum up the story. How do they fit the boys' situation at home—how are Caleb and Leo pulled in two directions? What things might confuse them about who they are and what their place in the world is? If Caleb is trying to teach Leo something, what might it be?

3.   The boys' mother is described in the paragraph on pages 87 and 88 beginning, "She came from New Orleans." How much do you find out about the mother from the first half of the paragraph alone? The technique of presenting a character in a story is called *characterization.* How else is the mother characterized in this story?

4.   In the first part of the story the narrator speaks as an adult, looking back at his childhood and commenting on his parents in a way a child could not. How does this change in the last part of the story? What is the effect of this change—does it make the story more or less dramatic? More or less emotionally affecting? Explain.

For further activities, see page 114.

THE STONE BOY GINA BERRIAULT

Arnold drew his overalls and raveling gray sweater over his naked body. In the other narrow bed his brother Eugene went on sleeping, undisturbed by the alarm clock's rusty ring. Arnold, watching his brother sleeping, felt a peculiar dismay; he was nine, six years younger than Eugie, and in their waking hours it was he who was subordinate. To dispel emphatically his uneasy advantage over his sleeping brother, he threw himself on the hump of Eugie's body.

"Get up! Get up!" he cried.

Arnold felt his brother twist away and saw the blankets lifted in a great wing, and, all in an instant, he was lying on his back under the covers with only his face showing, like a baby, and Eugie was sprawled on top of him.

"Whassa matter with you?" asked Eugie in sleepy anger, his face hanging close.

"Get up," Arnold repeated. "You said you'd pick peas with me."

Stupidly, Eugie gazed around the room as if to see if morning had come into it yet. Arnold began to laugh derisively, making soft, snorting noises, and was thrown off the bed. He got up from the floor and went down the stairs, the laughter continuing, like hiccups, against his will. But when he opened the staircase door and entered the parlor, he hunched up his shoulders and was quiet because his parents slept in the bedroom downstairs.

Arnold lifted his .22-caliber rifle from the rack on the kitchen wall. It was an old lever-action Winchester that his father had given him because nobody else used it any more. On their way down to the garden he and Eugie would go by the lake, and if there were any ducks on it he'd take a shot at them. Standing on the stool before the cupboard, he searched on the top shelf in the confusion of medicines and ointments for man and beast and found a small yellow box of .22 cartridges. Then he sat down on the stool and began to load his gun.

It was cold in the kitchen so early, but later in the day, when his mother canned the peas, the heat from the wood stove would be almost unbearable. Yesterday she had finished preserving the huckleberries that the family had picked along the mountain, and before that she had canned all the cherries his father had brought from the warehouse in Corinth. Sometimes, on these summer days, Arnold would deliberately come out from the shade where he was playing and make himself as uncomfortable as his mother was in the kitchen by standing in the sun until the sweat ran down his body.

Eugie came clomping down the stairs and into the kitchen, his head drooping with sleepiness. From his perch on the stool Arnold watched Eugie slip on his green knit cap. Eugie didn't really need a cap; he hadn't had a haircut in a long time and his brown curls grew thick and matted, close around his ears and down his neck, tapering there to a small whorl. Eugie passed his left hand through his hair before he set his cap down with his right. The very way he slipped his cap on was an announcement of his status; almost everything he did was a reminder that he was eldest—first he, then Nora, then Arnold— and called attention to how tall he was (almost as tall as his father), how long his legs were, how small he was in the hips, and what a neat dip above his buttocks his thick-soled logger's boots gave him. Arnold never tired of watching Eugie offer silent praise unto himself. He wondered, as he sat enthralled, if when he got to be Eugie's age he would still be undersized and his hair still straight.

Eugie eyed the gun. "Don't you know this ain't duck season?" he asked gruffly, as if he were the sheriff.

"No, I don't know," Arnold said with a snigger.

Eugie picked up the tin washtub for the peas, unbolted the door with his free hand and kicked it open. Then, lifting the tub to his head, he went clomping down the back steps. Arnold followed, closing the door behind him.

The sky was faintly gray, almost white. The mountains behind the farm made the sun climb a long way to show itself. Several miles to the south, where the range opened up, hung an orange mist, but the valley in which the farm lay was still cold and colorless.

Eugie opened the gate to the yard and the boys passed between the barn and the row of chicken houses, their feet stirring up the carpet of brown feathers dropped by the molting chickens. They paused before going down the slope to the lake. A fluky morning wind ran among the shocks of wheat that covered the slope. It sent a shimmer northward across the lake, gently moving the rushes that formed an island in the center. Killdeer, their white markings flashing, skimmed the water, crying their shrill, sweet cry. And there at the south end of the lake were four wild ducks, swimming out from the willows into open water.

Arnold followed Eugie down the slope, stealing, as his brother did, from one shock of wheat to another. Eugie paused before climbing through the wire fence that divided the wheat field from the marshy

pasture around the lake. They were screened from the ducks by the willows along the lake's edge.

"If you hit your duck, you want me to go in after it?" Eugie asked.

"If you want," Arnold said.

Eugie lowered his eyelids, leaving slits of mocking blue. "You'd drown 'fore you got to it, them legs of yours are so puny," he said.

He shoved the tub under the fence and, pressing down the center wire, climbed through into the pasture.

Arnold pressed down the bottom wire, thrust a leg through, and leaned forward to bring the other leg after. His rifle caught on the wire and he jerked at it. The air was rocked by the sound of the shot. Feeling foolish, he lifted his face, baring it to an expected shower of derision from his brother. But Eugie did not turn around. Instead, from his crouching position, he fell to his knees and then pitched forward onto his face. The ducks rose up crying from the lake, cleared the mountain background and beat away northward across the pale sky.

Arnold squatted beside his brother. Eugie seemed to be climbing the earth, as if the earth ran up and down, and when he found he couldn't scale it he lay still.

"Eugie?"

Then Arnold saw it, under the tendril of hair at the nape of the neck—a slow rising of bright blood. It had an obnoxious movement, like that of a parasite.

"Hey, Eugie," he said again. He was feeling the same discomfort he had felt when he had watched Eugie sleeping; his brother didn't know that he was lying face down in the pasture.

Again he said, "Hey, Eugie," an anxious nudge in his voice. But Eugie was as still as the morning about them.

Arnold set his rifle on the ground and stood up. He picked up the tub and, dragging it behind him, walked along by the willows to the garden fence and climbed through. He went down on his knees among the tangled vines. The pods were cold with the night, but his hands were strange to him, and not until some time had passed did he realize that the pods were numbing his fingers. He picked from the top of the vine first, then lifted the vine to look underneath for pods and then moved on to the next.

It was a warmth on his back, like a large hand laid firmly there, that made him raise his head. Way up on the slope the gray farmhouse was struck by the sun. While his head had been bent the land had grown bright around him.

When he got up his legs were so stiff that he had to go down on
his knees again to ease the pain. Then, walking sideways, he dragged
the tub, half full of peas, up the slope.

The kitchen was warm now; a fire was roaring in the stove with a
closed-up, rushing sound. His mother was spooning eggs from a pot of
boiling water and putting them into a bowl: Her short brown hair was
uncombed and fell forward across her eyes as she bent her head. Nora
was lifting a frying pan full of trout from the stove, holding the handle
with a dish towel. His father had just come in from bringing the cows
from the north pasture to the barn, and was sitting on the stool, un-
buttoning his red plaid Mackinaw.

"Did you boys fill the tub?" his mother asked.

"They ought of by now," his father said. "They went out of the
house an hour ago. Eugie woke me up comin' downstairs. I heard you
shootin'—did you get a duck?"

"No," Arnold said. They would want to know why Eugie wasn't
coming in for breakfast, he thought. "Eugie's dead," he told them.

They stared at him. The pitch crackled in the stove.

"You kids playin' a joke?" his father asked.

"Where's Eugene?" his mother asked scoldingly. She wanted,
Arnold knew, to see his eyes, and when he had glanced at her she put
the bowl spoon down on the stove and walked past him. His father
stood up and went out the door after her. Nora followed them with
little skipping steps, as if afraid to be left alone.

Arnold went into the barn, down along the foddering passage past
the cows waiting to be milked, and climbed into the loft. After a few
minutes he heard a strange, terrifying sound coming toward the house.
His parents and Nora were returning from the willows, and sounds
sharp and terrible as knives were rising from his mother's breast and
carrying over the sloping fields. But as he listened, the reason for the
cries ran more swiftly away from him as the cries drew closer. In a
short while he heard his father go down the back steps, slam the car
door and drive away.

Arnold lay still as a fugitive, listening to the cows eating close by.
If his parents never called him, he thought, he would stay up in the
loft forever, out of the way. In the night he would sneak down for a
drink of water from the faucet over the trough and for whatever food
they left for him by the barn.

The rattle of his father's car as it turned down the lane recalled
him to the present. He heard the voices of his Uncle Andy and Aunt
Alice as they and his father went past the barn to the lake. He could
feel the morning growing heavier with sun. Someone, probably Nora,

had let the chickens out of their coops and they were cackling in the yard.

After a while another car turned down the road off the highway. The car drew to a stop and he heard the voices of strange men. The men also went past the barn and down to the lake. The undertakers, whom his father must have phoned from Uncle Andy's house, had arrived from Corinth. Then he heard everybody come back and heard the car turn around and leave.

"Arnold!" It was his father calling from the yard.

He climbed down the ladder and went out into the sun, picking wisps of hay from his overalls.

Corinth, nine miles away, was the county seat. Arnold sat in the front seat of the old Ford between his father, who was driving, and Uncle Andy; no one spoke. Uncle Andy was his mother's brother, and he had been fond of Eugie because Eugie had resembled him. Andy had taken Eugie hunting and had given him a knife and a lot of things, and now Andy, his eyes narrowed, sat tall and stiff beside Arnold.

Arnold's father parked the car before the courthouse. It was a two-story brick building with a lamp on each side of the bottom step. They went up the wide stone steps, Arnold and his father going first, and entered the darkly paneled hallway. The shirt-sleeved man in the sheriff's office said that the sheriff was at Carlson's Parlor examining the Curwing boy.

Andy went off to get the sheriff while Arnold and his father waited on a bench in the corridor. Arnold felt his father watching him, and he lifted his eyes with painful casualness to the announcement, on the opposite wall, of the Corinth County Annual Rodeo, and then to the clock with its loudly clucking pendulum. After he had come down from the loft his father and Uncle Andy had stood in the yard with him and asked him to tell them everything, and he had explained to them how the gun had caught on the wire. But when they had asked him why he hadn't run back to the house to tell his parents, he had had no answer—all he could say was that he had gone down into the garden to pick the peas. His father had stared at him in a pale, puzzled way, and it was then that he had felt his father and the others set their cold, turbulent silence against him. Arnold shifted on the bench, his only feeling a small one of compunction imposed by his father's eyes.

At a quarter past nine Andy and the sheriff came in. They all went into the sheriff's private office, and Arnold was sent forward to sit in the chair by the sheriff's desk; his father and Andy sat down on the bench against the wall.

The sheriff lumped down into his swivel chair and swung toward Arnold. He was an old man with white hair like wheat stubble. His restless green eyes made him seem not to be in his office but to be hurrying and bobbing around somewhere else.

"What did you say your name was?" the sheriff asked.

"Arnold," he replied, but he could not remember telling the sheriff his name before.

"Curwing?"

"Yes."

"What were you doing with a .22, Arnold?"

"It's mine," he said.

"Okay. What were you going to shoot?"

"Some ducks," he replied.

"Out of season?"

He nodded.

"That's bad," said the sheriff. "Were you and your brother good friends?"

What did he mean—good friends? Eugie was his brother. That was different from a friend, Arnold thought. A best friend was your own age, but Eugie was almost a man. Eugie had had a way of looking at him, slyly and mockingly and yet confidentially, that had summed up how they both felt about being brothers. Arnold had wanted to be with Eugie more than with anybody else but he couldn't say they had been good friends.

"Did they ever quarrel?" the sheriff asked his father.

"Not that I know," his father replied. "It seemed to me that Arnold cared a lot for Eugie."

"Did you?" the sheriff asked Arnold.

If it seemed so to his father, then it was so. Arnold nodded.

"Were you mad at him this morning?"

"No."

"How did you happen to shoot him?"

"We was crawlin' through the fence."

"Yes?"

"An' the gun got caught on the wire."

"Seems the hammer must of caught," his father put in.

"All right, that's what happened," said the sheriff. "But what I want you to tell me is this. Why didn't you go back to the house and tell your father right away? Why did you go and pick peas for an hour?"

Arnold gazed over his shoulder at his father, expecting his father to have an answer for this also. But his father's eyes, larger and even lighter blue than usual, were fixed upon him curiously. Arnold picked at a callus in his right palm. It seemed odd now that he had not run back to the house and wakened his father, but he could not remember why he had not. They were all waiting for him to answer.

"I come down to pick peas," he said.

"Didn't you think," asked the sheriff, stepping carefully from word to word, "that it was more important for you to go tell your parents what had happened?"

"The sun was gonna come up," Arnold said.

"What's that got to do with it?"

"It's better to pick peas while they're cool."

The sheriff swung away from him, laid both hands flat on his desk. "Well, all I can say is," he said across to Arnold's father and Uncle Andy, "he's either a moron or he's so reasonable that he's way ahead of us." He gave a challenging snort. "It's come to my notice that the most reasonable guys are mean ones. They don't feel nothing."

For a moment the three men sat still. Then the sheriff lifted his hand like a man taking an oath. "Take him home," he said.

Andy uncrossed his legs. "You don't want him?"

"Not now," replied the sheriff. "Maybe in a few years."

Arnold's father stood up. He held his hat against his chest. "The gun ain't his no more," he said wanly.

Arnold went first through the hallway, hearing behind him the heels of his father and Uncle Andy striking the floor boards. He went down the steps ahead of them and climbed into the back seat of the car. Andy paused as he was getting into the front seat and gazed back at Arnold, and Arnold saw that his uncle's eyes had absorbed the knowingness from the sheriff's eyes. Andy and his father and the sheriff had discovered what made him go down into the garden. It was because he was cruel, the sheriff had said, and didn't care about his brother. Was that the reason? Arnold lowered his eyelids meekly against his uncle's stare.

The rest of the day he did his tasks around the farm, keeping apart from the family. At evening, when he saw his father stomp tiredly into the house, Arnold did not put down his hammer and leave the chicken coop he was repairing. He was afraid that they did not want him to eat supper with them. But in a few minutes another fear that they would go to the trouble of calling him and that he would be made conspicuous by his tardiness made him follow his father into the house. As he went through the kitchen he saw the jars of peas standing in rows on the workbench, a reproach to him.

No one spoke at supper, and his mother, who sat next to him, leaned her head in her hand all through the meal, curving her fingers over her eyes so as not to see him. They were finishing their small, silent supper when the visitors began to arrive, knocking hard on the back door. The men were coming from their farms now that it was growing dark and they could not work any more.

Old Man Matthews, gray and stocky, came first, with his two sons, Orion, the elder, and Clint, who was Eugie's age. As the callers entered the parlor, where the family ate, Arnold sat down in a rocking chair, the narrow one with the tall back. Even as he had been undecided before supper whether to remain outside or take his place at the table, he now thought that he should go upstairs, and yet he stayed to avoid being conspicuous by his absence. If he stayed, he thought, as he always stayed and listened when visitors came, they would see that he was only Arnold and not the person the sheriff thought he was. He sat with his arms crossed and his hands tucked into his armpits and did not lift his eyes.

The Matthews men had hardly settled down around the table, after Arnold's mother and Nora had cleared away the dishes, when another car rattled down the road and someone else rapped on the back door. This time it was Sullivan, a spare and sandy man, so nimble of gesture and expression that Arnold had never been able to catch more than a few of his meanings. Sullivan, in dusty jeans, sat down in the other rocker, shot out his skinny legs and began to talk in his fast way, recalling everything that Eugene had ever said to him. The other men interrupted to tell of occasions they remembered, and after a time Clint's young voice, hoarse like Eugene's had been, broke in to tell about the time Eugene had beat him in a wrestling match.

Out in the kitchen the voices of Orion's wife and of Mrs. Sullivan mingled with Nora's voice but not, Arnold noticed, his mother's. Then dry little Mr. Cram came, leaving large Mrs. Cram to sit in. No one asked Arnold to get up and he was unable to rise. He knew that the story had got around to them during the day about how he had gone and picked peas after he had shot his brother, and he knew that although they were talking only about Eugie they were thinking about him and if he got up, if he moved even his foot, they would all be alerted. Then Uncle Andy arrived and leaned his tall, lanky body against the doorjamb and there were two men standing.

Presently Arnold was aware that the talk had stopped. He knew without looking up that the men were watching him.

"Not a tear in his eye," said Andy, and Arnold knew that it was his uncle who had gestured the men to attention.

"He don't give a hoot, is that how it goes?" asked Sullivan, trippingly.

"He's a reasonable fellow," Andy explained. "That's what the sheriff said. It's us who ain't reasonable. If we'd of shot our brother, we'd of come runnin' back to the house, crying' like a baby. Well, we'd of been unreasonable. What would of been the use of actin' like that? If your brother is shot dead, he's shot dead. What's the use of gettin' emotional about it? The thing to do is go down to the garden and pick peas. Am I right?"

The men around the room shifted their heavy, satisfying weight of unreasonableness.

Matthews' son Orion said: "If I'd of done what he done, Pa would've hung my pelt by the side of that big coyote's in the barn."

Arnold sat in the rocker until the last man had filed out. While his family was out in the kitchen bidding the callers good night and the cars were driving away down the dirt lane to the highway, he picked up one of the kerosene lamps and slipped quickly up the stairs. In his room he undressed by lamplight, although he and Eugie had always undressed in the dark, and not until he was lying in his bed did he blow out the flame. He felt nothing, not any grief. There was only the same immense silence and crawling inside of him; it was the way the house and fields felt under a merciless sun.

He woke suddenly. The night was big and still. He knew that his father was out in the yard, closing the doors of the chicken houses so that the chickens could not roam out too early and fall prey to the coyotes that came down from the mountains at daybreak. The sound that had wakened him was the step of his father as he got up from the rocker and went quietly, creakingly down the back steps. And he knew that his mother was awake in her bed.

Throwing off the covers, he rose swiftly, went down the stairs and across the dark parlor to his parents' room. He rapped on the door.

"Mother?"

From the closed room her voice rose to him, a seeking and retreating voice. "Yes?"

"Mother?" he asked insistently. He had expected her to realize that he wanted to go down on his knees by her bed and tell her that Eugie was dead. She did not know it yet, nobody knew it, and yet she was sitting up in bed, waiting to be told, waiting for him to confirm her dread. He had expected her to tell him to come in, to allow him to dig his head into her blankets and tell her about the terror he had felt when he had knelt beside Eugie. He had come to clasp her in his arms and, in his terror, to pommel her with his head. He put his hand upon the knob.

"Go back to bed, Arnold," she called sharply.

But he waited.

"Go back! Is night when you get afraid?"

At first he did not understand. Then, silently, he left the door and for a stricken moment stood by the rocker. Outside everything was still. The fences, the shocks of wheat seen through the window before him were so still it was as if they moved and breathed in the daytime and had fallen silent with the lateness of the hour. It was a silence that seemed to observe his father, a figure moving alone around the yard, his lantern casting a circle of light by his feet. In a few minutes his father would enter the dark house, the lantern still lighting his way.

Arnold was suddenly aware that he was naked. He had thrown off his blankets and come down the stairs to tell his mother how he felt about Eugie, but she had refused to listen to him and his nakedness had become unpardonable. At once he went back up the stairs, fleeing from his father's lantern.

At breakfast he kept his eyelids lowered as if to deny the humiliating night. Nora, sitting at his left, did not pass the pitcher of milk to him and he did not ask for it. He would never again, he vowed, ask them for anything, and he ate his fried eggs and potatoes only because everybody ate meals—the cattle ate, and the cats; it was customary for everybody to eat.

"Nora, you gonna keep that pitcher for yourself?" his father asked.

Nora lowered her head unsurely.

"Pass it on to Arnold," his father said.

Nora put her hands in her lap.

His father picked up the metal pitcher and set it down at Arnold's plate.

Arnold, pretending to be deaf to the discord, did not glance up, but relief rained over his shoulders at the thought that his parents recognized him again. They must have lain awake after his father had come in from the yard: had they realized together why he had come down the stairs and knocked at their door?

"Bessie's missin' this morning," his father called out to his mother, who had gone into the kitchen. "She went up to the mountain last night and had her calf, most likely. Somebody's got to go up and find her 'fore the coyotes get the calf."

That had been Eugie's job, Arnold thought. Eugie would climb the cattle trails in search of a newborn calf and come down the mountain carrying the calf across his back, with the cow running along behind him, mooing in alarm.

Arnold ate the few more forkfuls of his breakfast, put his hands on the edge of the table and pushed back his chair. If he went for the calf he'd be away from the farm all morning. He could switch the cow down the mountain slowly, and the calf would run along at its mother's side.

When he passed through the kitchen his mother was setting a kettle of water on the stove. "Where you going?" she asked awkwardly.

"Up to get the calf," he replied, averting his face.

"Arnold?"

At the door he paused reluctantly, his back to her, knowing that she was seeking him out, as his father was doing, and he called upon his pride to protect him from them.

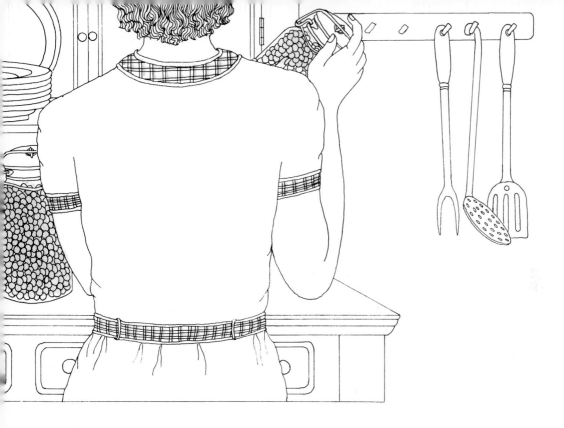

"Was you knocking at my door last night?"

He looked over his shoulder at her, his eyes narrow and dry.

"What'd you want?" she asked humbly.

"I didn't want nothing," he said flatly.

Then he went out the door and down the back steps, his legs trembling from the fright his answer gave him.

DISCUSSION

1. What was going through Arnold's mind that made him refuse to answer his mother's question?

2. The way the shooting incident is described gives us a clue about Arnold's reaction. The whole story is told in the *third person,* that is, the narrator is not an "I" character in the story. But the point of view is limited, or *personal*—the author has, figuratively, put herself inside the body and mind of Arnold. We see everything through his eyes. Keep this in mind as you reread the account of the shooting. How does this moment by moment description help to explain why Arnold went on to pick the peas? How does the description of his picking the peas make his reaction even clearer and more understandable? What other details in the story help you understand the things about Arnold's behavior that upset and puzzle his relatives and neighbors?

VOCABULARY

Tell Me How Long the Train's Been Gone (page 85)

A.   An image or an unexpected word can make a mental or a physical state suddenly clear to us:

> "I always stood, those Saturday afternoons, in fear and trembling, holding onto the small shield of my bravado."

> "We hated the landlord with a perfectly exquisite hatred."

> "In the stifling room of his [the father's] pretensions and expectations, we stumbled wretchedly about, stubbing our toes, as it were, on rubies, scraping our shins on golden caskets, bringing down, with a childish cry, the splendid purple tapestry on which, in pounding gold and scarlet, our destinies and our inheritance were figured."

> "I felt his bewilderment through the membrane of my own."

> "His great hand dropped a flame-colored curtain before my eyes."

Translate each of these statements into its literal meaning. Then experiment with finding a fresh and precise image, or just the right word, to convey a sensation or mental state. Use three or four of the starters listed below, or make up your own.

> fear (any kind)
> feeling that there's no way out of a situation
> feeling that you've just done something as well as it can be done
> sudden anger
> relief that something unpleasant is over

B.   Instead of telling what the words in bold type mean in the following sentences, tell what they *don't* mean. In other words, define them by stating their opposites.

1.   If there is anything she *loathes,* it is Boston cream pie.
2.   I see that your crab grass is *flourishing* this year.
3.   He would do anything except *jeopardize* his class standing.
4.   My dear, this is the wrong moment to be *coy.*
5.   The later it got, the more *maudlin* he became.
6.   She eyed the cameraman *dubiously.*
7.   Their chances for victory look more and more ***precarious.***

COMPOSITION

The Lottery (page 75)

Are there any traditions that we cling to "because that's the way it's always been done"? Should any of these be examined again and reconsidered? Choose a tradition and either defend it or argue that it should be changed.

Tell Me How Long the Train's Been Gone (page 85)

"A child's major attention has to be concentrated on how to fit into a world which, with every passing hour, reveals itself as merciless," the narrator says. State your agreement or disagreement with this idea in a few paragraphs; or propose your own idea of what "a child's major attention has to be concentrated on."

REVIEW

1. In which story or stories, of the nine in this unit, can the following be found?

   a fictional author
   a first-person narrator
   an omniscient point of view with a third-person narrator
   a personal point of view (limited to one character in the story)
       with a third-person narrator
   dialect (the speech of a region or group that differs from
       standard English)
   humor
   irony
   dialogue

2. Which stories had the strongest total effect?
3. In which stories, did the narrator seem most distant from the characters? most involved?

SENSORY
WORDS

COMPOSITION

Our lives are made up of a succession of experiences, some pleasant, some unpleasant, some memorable, some forgettable. All of these experiences we come to know through our five senses (of sight, smell, hearing, taste, and touch).

If we want to share our experiences with others, we can do it best by using words that appeal to the senses of our listeners and readers. *Scalding, screech, rotting, sour, radiance,* are all *sensory words.* Writers use such words often. Indeed, stories and novels are in large part simply a record of a succession of experiences and the emotions that those experiences awaken. Thus, the writer of fiction must constantly be remembering or imagining sense impressions: what the participants in an action would have seen, heard, smelled, tasted, and felt. If the writer then uses words that accurately describe those impressions, we as readers will be able to share the experiences of the characters in the story.

Look, for example, at Melville's description of a boy's nighttime climb to the precarious top of a ship's mast at sea (page 22). What emotions was Buttons feeling at the top? "For a few moments I stood awe-stricken and mute." What could he see from up there? "I could not see far out upon the ocean, owing to the darkness of the night. . . . I could but just perceive the ship below me, like a long narrow plank in the water." What did he hear? A gull was flapping overhead around the truck, "and it almost frightened me to hear it." That sound he heard, and "a distant, hoarse noise from below," which was the voice of the mate hurrying the boy about his task. And what motions did he experience? "Though there was a pretty smooth sea, and little wind; yet, at this extreme elevation, the ship's motion was very great; so that when the ship rolled one way, I felt something as a fly must feel, walking the ceiling; and when it rolled the other way, I felt as if I was hanging along a slanting pine-tree. . . ."

Sensory words and images help express his experiences vividly, as they will help communicate experiences you may want to share.

ABOUT THE SELECTIONS

1. These selections present a number of different worlds—among them a Catskill village in Colonial times, a sailing ship at sea, a New England farm, a district in New York City. Which world did you come to know best? Describe that world as clearly as you can. Try to evoke more than merely the appearance of the world. What sounds, what smells would a visitor to that world encounter?

2. Several characters in this section might benefit from sympathetic counsel. Arnold at the end of "The Stone Boy," the speakers who tell the stories of "The Black Cat" and "Haircut," Rip upon his return to his village, are all in need of help. What advice would you offer one such character? Address your remarks to that person directly.

3. To which senses does the following passage appeal? Identify the sensory words and comment on how they help communicate the experience that the passage describes.

> It was a warmth on his back, like a large hand laid firmly there, that made him raise his head. Way up on the slope the gray farmhouse was struck by the sun. While his head had been bent the land had grown bright around him.

ON YOUR OWN

1. Think of an unusual experience, one you have had or can vividly imagine. What does it feel like to run at top speed around a track, to ski down a mountain, do somersaults down a golf-course slope, or squeeze through a tight space under the front porch? Or what does stagefright or seasickness or hunger or total exhaustion feel like? In a page describe one such experience as fully and accurately as you can.

2. "Haircut" tells an entire story as a *monologue*—one person speaking throughout without interruption. Write a page of monologue yourself, perhaps by imagining someone on the telephone. See how much individuality, character, and interest you can develop within the limits of a single individual's speaking voice.

3. Look back at the description of the boys' mother in "Tell Me How Long the Train's Been Gone" (on pages 86 and 87). Write your own description of someone, making it about the same length as Baldwin's. Try his method of picking out physical details, letting one lead to another, and using them to show something about the person. Finish off with a few general statements about the person, as Baldwin does. Pick them carefully, to finish off the description and portray the character as fully and interestingly as you can.

4. Use sensory words and descriptive details to develop the following situation. How would it look, sound, smell, feel?

> At sunset, on the back porch of a farm house, a woman waits to welcome her father, an old man approaching over the nearby hill in a buggy. He arrives, and the two greet each other affectionately in the back yard.

NONFICTION

Speech to the Virginia Convention

PATRICK HENRY

. . . This is no time for ceremony. The question before the house is one of awful moment[1] to this country. For my own part, I consider it as nothing less than a question of freedom or slavery. And in proportion to the magnitude of the subject ought to be the freedom of the debate. . . . Should I keep back my opinions at such a time, through fear of giving offense, I should consider myself as guilty of treason toward my country, and of an act of disloyalty toward the Majesty of Heaven, which I revere above all earthly kings.

Mr. President, it is natural to man to indulge in the illusions of hope. We are apt to shut our eyes against a painful truth, and listen to the song of that siren[2] till she transforms us into beasts. Is this the part of wise men, engaged in a great and arduous struggle for liberty? . . . For my part, whatever anguish of spirit it may cost, I am willing to know the whole truth, to know the worst and provide for it.

I have but one lamp by which my feet are guided, and that is the lamp of experience. I know of no way of judging of the future but by the past. And judging by the past, I wish to know what there has been in the conduct of the British ministry for the last ten years to justify those hopes with which gentlemen have been pleased to solace themselves and the house? Is it that insidious smile with which our petition has been lately received? Trust it not, sir: it will prove a snare to your feet. Suffer not yourselves to be betrayed with a kiss.[3] Ask yourselves how gracious reception of our petition comports[4] with those warlike preparations[5] which cover our waters and darken our land. Are fleets and armies necessary to a work of love and reconciliation? . . . What means this martial array, if its purpose be not to force us to submission? Can gentlemen assign any other possible motive for it? Has Great Britain any enemy in this quarter of the world, to call for all this accumulation of navies and armies? No, sir, she has none. They are meant for us: they can be meant for no other. They are sent over to bind and rivet upon us those chains which the British ministry have been so long forging. And what have we to oppose to them? Shall we try argument? Sir, we have been trying that for the last ten years. Have we anything new to offer upon the subject? Nothing. We have held the subject up in every light of which it is capable; but it has been all in vain. Shall we resort to entreaty and humble supplication? What terms shall we find

---

[1] *awful moment:* profound importance.
[2] *siren:* one of a group of women in Greek mythology who lured sailors to destruction by their songs. Henry seems to have the Greek hero Odysseus in mind; his men were turned into beasts by the enchantress Circe.
[3] *betrayed with a kiss:* Jesus was betrayed by a kiss from Judas.
[4] *comports:* agrees.
[5] *warlike preparations:* Henry made his address on March 23. On April 19 British and American forces clashed at Lexington and Concord.

which have not been already exhausted? Let us not, I beseech you, sir, deceive ourselves longer.

Sir, we have done everything that could be done to avert the storm which is now coming on. We have petitioned; we have remonstrated; we have supplicated; we have prostrated ourselves before the throne, and have implored its interposition to arrest the tyrannical hands of the ministry and Parliament. Our petitions have been slighted; our remonstrances have produced additional violence and insult; our supplications have been disregarded; and we have been spurned with contempt from the foot of the throne! In vain, after these things, may we indulge the fond hope of peace and reconciliation. There is no longer any room for hope. If we wish to be free, if we mean to preserve inviolate those inestimable privileges for which we have been so long contending, if we mean not basely to abandon the noble struggle in which we have been so long engaged, and which we have pledged ourselves never to abandon until the glorious object of our contest shall be obtained—we must fight! I repeat it, sir, we must fight! An appeal to arms and to the God of Hosts is all that is left us!

They tell us, sir, that we are weak—unable to cope with so formidable an adversary. But when shall we be stronger? Will it be the next week, or the next year? Will it be when we are totally disarmed, and when a British guard shall be stationed in every house? Shall we gather strength by irresolution and inaction? . . .

It is in vain, sir, to extenuate[6] the matter. Gentlemen may cry, Peace, Peace—but there is no peace. The war is actually begun! The next gale that sweeps from the north will bring to our ears the clash of resounding arms! Our brethren are already in the field! Why stand we here idle? . . . Is life so dear, or peace so sweet, as to be purchased at the price of chains and slavery? Forbid it, Almighty God! I know not what course others may take; but as for me, give me liberty or give me death!

---

[6] *extenuate:* minimize the seriousness of.

DISCUSSION

1.   Some members of the Virginia Convention were in favor of arming themselves against England; others were not. What does Patrick Henry say that should change the minds of those not in favor? Pick out those statements of his that you feel are most effective.

2.   Do you think Henry is appealing to the hearts or to the minds of his listeners? Explain, using examples from the speech.

3.   In his speech, Henry makes two literary *allusions*, references to works he assumes his audience will recognize. One allusion is to Greek poetry, the other to the Bible. What does his use of these allusions tell you about him? What does their use suggest about Henry's audience?

For further activities, see page 150.

THE DECLARATION OF INDEPENDENCE

THOMAS JEFFERSON

When in the course of human events, it becomes necessary for one people to dissolve the political bands which have connected them with another and to assume among the powers of the earth the separate and equal station to which the laws of Nature and of Nature's God entitle them, a decent respect to the opinions of mankind requires that they should declare the causes which impel them to the separation.

We hold these truths to be self-evident: that all men are created equal; that they are endowed by their Creator with certain unalienable[1] rights; that among these are life, liberty, and the pursuit of happiness; that to secure these rights, governments are instituted among men, deriving their just powers from the consent of the governed; that whenever any form of government becomes destructive of these ends, it is the right of the people to alter or to abolish it and to institute new government, laying its foundation on such principles and organizing its powers in such form as to them shall seem most likely to effect their safety and happiness. Prudence, indeed, will dictate that governments long established should not be changed for light and transient causes; and accordingly all experience hath shown that mankind are more disposed to suffer, while evils are sufferable, than to right themselves by abolishing the forms to which they are ac-

[1] *unalienable:* incapable of being transferred or given up.

customed. But when a long train of abuses and usurpations pursuing invariably the same object evinces a design to reduce them under absolute despotism, it is their right, it is their duty, to throw off such government and to provide new guards for their future security. Such has been the patient sufferance of these colonies; and such is now the necessity which constrains them to alter their former systems of government. The history of the present king of Great Britain is a history of repeated injuries and usurpations, all having in direct object the establishment of an absolute tyranny over these states. To prove this, let facts be submitted to a candid world.

[Here follows a detailed list of the colonies' grievances against the British king and parliament.]

In every stage of these oppressions we have petitioned for redress in the most humble terms: our repeated petitions have been answered only by repeated injury. A prince whose character is thus marked by every act which may define a tyrant is unfit to be the ruler of a free people.

Nor have we been wanting in attention to our British brethren. We have warned them from time to time of attempts by their legislature to extend an unwarrantable jurisdiction over us. We have reminded them of the circumstances of our emigration and settlement here. We have appealed to their native justice and magnanimity, and we have conjured[2] them by the ties of our common kindred to disavow these usurpations, which would inevitably interrupt our connections and correspondence. They too have been deaf to the voice of justice and of consanguinity.[3] We must, therefore, acquiesce in the necessity which denounces[4] our separation and hold them, as we hold the rest of mankind, enemies in war, in peace, friends.

---

[2] *conjured:* called upon or implored solemnly.
[3] *consanguinity:* blood relationship.
[4] *denounces:* here, proclaims, announces.

We, therefore, the representatives of the united states of America, in general congress, assembled, appealing to the Supreme Judge of the world for the rectitude of our intentions, do, in the name and by authority of the good people of these colonies, solemnly publish and declare that these united colonies are and of right ought to be free and independent states; that they are absolved from all allegiance to the British crown; and that all political connection between them and the state of Great Britain is and ought to be totally dissolved; and that as free and independent states, they have full power to levy war, conclude peace, contract alliances, establish commerce, and to do all other acts and things which independent states may of right do. And for the support of this declaration, with a firm reliance on the protection of divine Providence, we mutually pledge to each other our lives, our fortunes and our sacred honor.

DISCUSSION

1.   What self-evident truths did Jefferson list in the Declaration? From whom, according to the Declaration, does a government derive its powers? What, according to Jefferson, prevents people from revolting "for light and transient causes"?

2.   At the Continental Congress in 1776, Thomas Jefferson was chosen to write the Declaration of Independence. John Adams suggested him because he thought Jefferson had a "happy talent for composition." In the Declaration, find examples of this talent that you think are particularly effective.

3.   One of the purposes of the Declaration was to persuade other nations that the Americans' cause was a just one. What idea or specific passages in the Declaration do you think a foreign government might find most persuasive? Why?

For further activities, see page 150.

ABIGAIL ADAMS

writes to her husband

Braintree March 31, 1776

. . . I long to hear that you have declared an inde-
pendancy—and by the way in the new Code of Laws which I suppose
it will be necessary for you to make I desire you would Remember the
Ladies, and be more generous and favourable to them than your ancestors. Do not put such unlimited power into the hands of the Husbands.
Remember all Men would be tyrants if they could. If perticuliar care
and attention is not paid to the Laidies we are determined to foment a
Rebelion, and will not hold ourselves bound by any Laws in which we
have no voice, or Representation.

That your Sex are Naturally Tyrannical is a Truth so thoroughly established as to admit of no dispute, but such of you as wish
to be happy willingly give up the harsh title of Master for the more
tender and endearing one of Friend. Why then, not put it out of the
power of the vicious and the Lawless to use us with cruelty and indig-
nity with impunity. Men of Sense in all Ages abhor those customs
which treat us only as the vassals of your Sex. Regard us then as
Beings placed by providence under your protection and in immitation of
the Supreem Being make use of that power only for our happiness.

FROM **Self-Reliance**

RALPH WALDO EMERSON

I read the other day some verses written by an eminent painter which were original and not conventional. The soul always hears an admonition in such lines, let the subject be what it may. The sentiment they instill is of more value than any thought they may contain. To believe your own thought, to believe that what is true for you in your private heart is true for all men—that is genius. Speak your latent conviction, and it shall be the universal sense. . . . A man should learn to detect and watch that gleam of light which flashes across his mind from within, more than the luster of the firmament of bards and sages.[1] Yet he dismisses without notice his thought, because it is his. In every work of genius, we recognize our own rejected thoughts; they come back to us with a certain alienated majesty. Great works of art have no more affecting lesson for us than this. They teach us to abide by our spontaneous impresson with good-humored inflexibility then most when the whole city of voices is on the other side. Else tomorrow a stranger will say with masterly good sense precisely what we have thought and felt all the time, and we shall be forced to take with shame our own opinion from another.

There is a time in every man's education when he arrives at the conviction that envy is ignorance; that imitation is suicide; that he must take himself for better for worse as his portion; that though the wide universe is full of good, no kernel of nourishing corn can come to him but through his toil bestowed on that plot of ground which is given to him to till. The power which resides in him is new in nature, and none but he knows what that is which he can do, nor does he know until he has tried. . . .

Trust thyself: every heart vibrates to that iron string. Accept the place the divine providence has found for you, the society of your contemporaries, the connection of events. Great men have always done so, and confided themselves childlike to the genius of their age, betraying their perception that the absolutely trustworthy was seated at their heart, working through their hands, predominating in all their being. . . .

What pretty oracles nature yields us on this text in the face and behavior of children, babes, and even brutes! That divided and rebel

[1] *bards and sages:* poets and philosophers.

mind, that distrust of sentiment because our arithmetic has computed the strength and means opposed to our purpose, these have not. Their mind being whole, their eye is as yet unconquered, and when we look in their faces we are disconcerted. Infancy conforms to nobody; all conform to it; so that one babe commonly makes four or five out of the adults who prattle and play to it. So God has armed youth and puberty and manhood no less with its own piquancy and charm, and made it enviable and gracious and its claims not to be put by, if it will stand by itself. Do not think the youth has no force, because he cannot speak to you and me. Hark! in the next room his voice is sufficiently clear and emphatic. It seems he knows how to speak to his contemporaries. Bashful or bold then, he will know how to make us seniors very unnecessary.

The nonchalance of boys who are sure of a dinner, and would disdain as much as a lord to do or say aught to conciliate one, is the healthy attitude of human nature. A boy is in the parlor what the pit[2] is in the playhouse; independent, irresponsible, looking out from his corner on such people and facts as pass by, he tries and sentences them on their merits, in the swift, summary way of boys, as good, bad, interesting, silly, eloquent, troublesome. He cumbers himself never about consequences, about interests; he gives an independent, genuine verdict. You must court him; he does not court you. But the man is as it were clapped into jail by his consciousness. As soon as he has once acted or spoken with *éclat*[3] he is a committed person, watched by the sympathy or the hatred of hundreds whose affections must now enter into his account.

What I must do is all that concerns me, not what the people think. This rule, equally arduous in actual and in intellectual life, may serve for the whole distinction between greatness and meanness. It is the harder because you will always find those who think they know what is your duty better than you know it. It is easy in the world to live after the world's opinion; it is easy in solitude to live after our own; but the great man is he who in the midst of the crowd keeps with perfect sweetness the independence of solitude.

The objection to conforming to usages that have become dead to you is that it scatters your force. It loses your time and blurs the impression of your character. If you maintain a dead church, contribute

[2] *pit:* the spectators in the cheapest seats.
[3] *éclat* (ā-klä′): brilliance.

to a dead Bible-society, vote with a great party either for the government or against it, spread your table like base housekeepers—under all these screens I have difficulty to detect the precise man you are: and of course so much force is withdrawn from your proper life. But do your work, and I shall know you. Do your work, and you shall reinforce yourself. . . .

For nonconformity the world whips you with its displeasure. And therefore a man must know how to estimate a sour face. The bystanders look askance on him in the public street or in the friend's parlor. If this aversion had its origin in contempt and resistance like his own he might well go home with a sad countenance; but the sour faces of the multitude, like their sweet faces, have no deep cause, but are put on and off as the wind blows and a newspaper directs. . . .

The other terror that scares us from self-trust is our consistency; a reverence for our past act or word because the eyes of others have no other data for computing our orbit than our past acts, and we are loath to disappoint them.

But why should you keep your head over your shoulder? Why drag about this corpse of your memory, lest you contradict somewhat[4] you have stated in this or that public place? Suppose you should contradict yourself; what then? It seems to be a rule of wisdom never to rely on your memory alone, scarcely even in acts of pure memory, but to bring the past for judgment into the thousand-eyed present and live ever in a new day. . . .

A foolish consistency is the hobgoblin of little minds, adored by little statesmen and philosophers and divines. With consistency a great soul has simply nothing to do. He may as well concern himself with his shadow on the wall. Speak what you think now in hard words and tomorrow speak what tomorrow thinks in hard words again, though it contradict every thing you said today.—"Ah, so you shall be sure to be misunderstood?" Is it then so bad to be misunderstood? Pythagoras was misunderstood, and Socrates, and Jesus, and Luther, and Copernicus, and Galileo, and Newton, and every pure and wise spirit that ever took flesh. To be great is to be misunderstood.

I suppose no man can violate his nature. . . . There will be an agreement in whatever variety of actions, so they be each honest and natural in their hour. For of one will, the actions will be harmonious, however unlike they seem. These varieties are lost sight of at a little distance, at a little height of thought. One tendency unites them all. The voyage of the best ship is a zigzag line of a hundred tacks. See

---

[4] *somewhat:* something.

the line from a sufficient distance, and it straightens itself to the average tendency. Your genuine action will explain itself and will explain your other genuine actions. Your conformity explains nothing. . . .

I hope in these days we have heard the last of conformity and consistency. Let the words be gazetted and ridiculous henceforward. Instead of the gong for dinner, let us hear a whistle from the Spartan[5] fife. Let us never bow and apologize more. A great man is coming to eat at my house. I do not wish to please him; I wish that he should wish to please me. I will stand here for humanity, and though I would make it kind, I would make it true. Let us affront and reprimand the smooth mediocrity and squalid contentment of the times and hurl in the face of custom and trade and office the fact which is the upshot of all history, that there is a great responsible Thinker and Actor working wherever a man works; that a true man belongs to no other time or place but is the center of things. . . . Every true man is a cause, a country, and an age; requires infinite spaces and numbers and time fully to accomplish his design; and posterity seem to follow his steps as a train of clients. A man Caesar is born, and for ages after we have a Roman Empire. Christ is born, and millions of minds so grow and cleave to his genius that he is confounded with virtue and the possible of man.[6] An institution is the lengthened shadow of one man. . . .

And truly it demands something godlike in him who has cast off the common motives of humanity and has ventured to trust himself for a taskmaster. High be his heart, faithful his will, clear his sight, that he may in good earnest be doctrine, society, law, to himself, that a simple purpose may be to him as strong as iron necessity is to others!

If our young men miscarry in their first enterprises, they lose all heart. If the young merchant fails, men say he is *ruined.* If the finest genius studies at one of our colleges and is not installed in an office within one year afterwards in the cities or suburbs of Boston or New York, it seems to his friends and to himself that he is right in being disheartened and in complaining the rest of his life. A sturdy farm lad from New Hampshire or Vermont, who in turn tries all the professions, who *teams it, farms it, peddles,* keeps a school, preaches, edits a newspaper, goes to Congress, buys a township, and so forth, in successive years, and always like a cat falls on his feet, is worth a hun-

---

[5] *Spartan:* The ancient Greek city of Sparta was famous for its strict discipline and complete absence of luxury in all aspects of life.

[6] *confounded . . . man:* confused with virtue and the limit of human achievement.

dred of these city dolls. He walks abreast with his days and feels no shame in not "studying a profession," for he does not postpone his life, but lives already. He has not one chance, but a hundred chances.

Insist on yourself; never imitate. Your own gift you can present every moment with the cumulative force of a whole life's cultivation; but of the adopted talent of another you have only an extemporaneous half possession. That which each can do best, none but his Maker can teach him. No man yet knows what it is, nor can, till that person has exhibited it. Where is the master who could have taught Shakespeare? Where is the master who could have instructed Franklin, or Washington, or Bacon, or Newton? Every great man is a unique.

The civilized man has built a coach, but has lost the use of his feet. He is supported on crutches, but lacks so much support of muscle. He has a fine Geneva watch, but he fails of the skill to tell the hour by the sun. A Greenwich nautical almanac[7] he has, and so being sure of the information when he wants it, the man in the street does not know a star in the sky. The solstice he does not observe; the equinox he knows as little; and the whole bright calendar of the year is without a dial in his mind. His notebooks impair his memory; his libraries overload his wit; the insurance office increases the number of accidents; and it may be a question whether machinery does not encumber; whether we have not lost by refinement some energy, by a Christianity, entrenched in establishments and forms, some vigor of wild virtue. For every Stoic[8] was a Stoic; but in Christendom where is the Christian?

. . . It is only as a man puts off all foreign support and stands alone that I see him to be strong and to prevail. He is weaker by every recruit to his banner. Is not a man better than a town? Ask nothing of men, and in the endless mutation, thou only firm column must presently appear the upholder of all that surrounds thee. He who knows that power is inborn, that he is weak because he has looked for good out of him and elsewhere, and, so preceiving, throws himself unhesitatingly on his thought, instantly rights himself, stands in the erect position, commands his limbs, works miracles; just as a man who stands on his feet is stronger than a man who stands on his head.

---

[7] *nautical almanac:* tables showing the exact position of the moon at noon and midnight of each day, from which seamen calculate their position.

[8] *Stoic:* member of an ancient philosophical sect believing that people should be free from passion and calmly accept all things as the result of divine will.

So use all that is called Fortune. Most men gamble with her, and gain all, and lose all, as her wheel rolls. But do thou leave as unlawful these winnings, and deal with Cause and Effect, the chancellors of God. In the Will work and acquire, and thou has chained the wheel of Chance and shall sit hereafter out of fear from her rotations. A political victory, a rise of rents, the recovery of your sick or the return of your absent friend, or some other favorable event raises your spirits, and you think good days are preparing for you. Do not believe it. Nothing can bring you peace but yourself. Nothing can bring you peace but the triumph of principles.

DISCUSSION

1. A healthy human nature should resemble, Emerson says, "the nonchalance of boys who are sure of a dinner." Why? What characterizes the attitude of such boys?

2. What two "terrors" prevent us from trusting ourselves?

3. What distinction does Emerson make between greatness and meanness?

4. *Style* is a combination of many things: what kind of words are used; whether the sentences are short or long, complex or simple; whether the writing sounds rhythmic or abrupt and jerky; whether the writer uses many adjectives or relies on strong nouns and verbs; whether the language is formal or informal, whether ideas are carefully organized or loosely strung together. Different styles are used for different purposes. A style can be called, among many other things, journalistic, poetic, scientific, sincere, artificial. Anything that you say to describe the *way* an author writes, the way he or she fits words and ideas together, is describing that author's style.

One word that has been used to describe Emerson's style is "aphoristic." An *aphorism* is a short, memorable statement of some principle or truth, for example, "To be great is to be misunderstood." What other aphorisms can you find?

What is another way you could describe Emerson's style in this essay? You might pick a sentence or paragraph and tell how it is different from most modern writing—what you see in magazines or newspapers.

For further activities, see page 150.

FROM Life on the Mississippi

SAMUEL CLEMENS

When I was a boy, there was but one permanent ambition among my comrades in our village [1] on the west bank of the Mississippi River. That was, to be a steamboatman. We had transient ambitions of other sorts, but they were only transient. When a circus came and went, it left us all burning to become clowns. . . . Now and then we had a hope that, if we lived and were good, God would permit us to be pirates. These ambitions faded out, each in its turn; but the ambition to be a steamboatman always remained.

Once a day a cheap, gaudy packet arrived upward from St. Louis, and another downward from Keokuk. Before these events, the day was glorious with expectancy; after them, the day was a dead and empty

[1] *village:* Hannibal, Missouri.

thing. Not only the boys, but the whole village, felt this. After all these years I can picture that old time to myself now, just as it was then: the white town drowsing in the sunshine of a summer's morning; the streets empty, or pretty nearly so; one or two clerks sitting in front of the Water Street stores, with their splint-bottomed chairs tilted back against the walls, chins on breasts, hats slouched over their faces, asleep—with shingle-shavings enough around to show what broke them down; a sow and a litter of pigs loafing along the sidewalk, doing a good business in watermelon rinds and seeds; two or three lonely little freight piles scattered about the "levee;" a pile of "skids"[2] on the slope of the stone-paved wharf, and the fragrant town drunkard asleep in the shadow of them; two or three wood flats at the head of the wharf, but nobody to listen to the peaceful lapping of the wavelets against them; the great Mississippi, the majestic, the magnificent Mississippi, rolling its mile-wide tide along, shining in the sun; the dense forest away on the other side; the "point" above the town, and the "point" below, bounding the river-glimpse and turning it into a sort of sea, and withal a very still and brilliant and lonely one. Presently a film of dark smoke appears above one of those remote "points;" instantly a Negro drayman, famous for his quick eye and prodigious voice, lifts up the cry, "S-t-e-a-m-boat a-comin'!" and the scene changes! The town drunkard stirs, the clerks wake up, a furious clatter of drays follows, every house and store pours out a human contribution, and all in a twinkling the dead town is alive and moving. Drays, carts, men, boys, all go hurrying from many quarters to a common center, the wharf. Assembled there, the people fasten their eyes upon the coming boat as upon a wonder they are seeing for the first time.

And the boat *is* rather a handsome sight, too. She is long and sharp and trim and pretty; she has two tall, fancy-topped chimneys, with a gilded device of some kind swung between them; a fanciful pilot-house, all glass and "gingerbread," perched on top of the "texas" deck behind them; the paddle-boxes are gorgeous with a picture or with gilded rays above the boat's name; the boiler-deck, the hurricane-deck, and the texas deck are fenced and ornamented with clean white railings; there is a flag gallantly flying from the jack-staff; the furnace doors are open and the fires glaring bravely; the upper decks are black with passengers; the captain stands by the big bell, calm, imposing, the envy of all; great volumes of the blackest smoke are rolling and tumbling out of the chimneys—a husbanded grandeur created with a

---

[2] *skids:* low platforms on which cargo is placed for handling.

bit of pitch-pine just before arriving at a town; the crew are grouped on the forecastle;[3] the broad stage is run far out over the port bow, and an envied deck-hand stands picturesquely on the end of it with a coil of rope in his hand; the pent steam is screaming through the gauge-cocks; the captain lifts his hand, a bell rings, the wheels stop; then they turn back, churning the water to foam, and the steamer is at rest. Then such a scramble as there is to get aboard, and to get ashore, and to take in freight and to discharge freight, all at one and the same time; and such a yelling and cursing as the mates facilitate it all with! Ten minutes later the steamer is under way again, with no flag on the jack-staff and no black smoke issuing from the chimneys. After ten more minutes the town is dead again, and the town drunkard asleep by the skids once more.

My father was a justice of the peace, and I supposed he possessed the power of life and death over all men, and could hang anybody that offended him. This was distinction enough for me as a general thing; but the desire to be a steamboatman kept intruding, nevertheless. I first wanted to be a cabin-boy, so that I could come out with a white apron on and shake a table-cloth over the side, where all my old comrades could see me; later I thought I would rather be the deck-hand who stood on the end of the stage-plank with the coil of rope in his hand, because he was particularly conspicuous. But these were only day-dreams—they were too heavenly to be contemplated as real possibilities. By and by one of our boys went away. He was not heard of for a long time. At last he turned up as apprentice engineer or "striker" on a steamboat. This thing shook the bottom out of all my Sunday-school teachings. That boy had been notoriously worldly, and I just the reverse; yet he was exalted to this eminence, and I left in obscurity and misery. There was nothing generous about this fellow in his greatness. He would always manage to have a rusty bolt to scrub while his boat tarried at our town, and he would sit on the inside guard and scrub it, where we all could see him and envy him and loathe him. And whenever his boat was laid up he would come home and swell around the town in his blackest and greasiest clothes, so that nobody could help remembering that he was a steamboatman; and he used all sorts of steamboat technicalities in his talk, as if he were so used to them that he forgot common people could not understand them. He would speak of the "labboard"[4] side of a horse in an

---

[3] *forecastle* (fōk′səl): section of the forward part of the boat.
[4] *labboard:* larboard or port (left).

easy, natural way that would make one wish he was dead. And he was always talking about "St. Looy" like an old citizen; he would refer casually to occasions when he was "coming down Fourth Street," or when he was "passing by the Planter's House," or when there was a fire and he took a turn on the brakes of "the old Big Missouri;" and then he would go on and lie about how many towns the size of ours were burned down there that day. Two or three of the boys had long been persons of consideration among us because they had been to St. Louis once and had a vague general knowledge of its wonders, but the day of their glory was over now. They lapsed into a humble silence, and learned to disappear when the ruthless "cub"-engineer approached. This fellow had money, too, and hair-oil. Also an ignorant silver watch and a showy brass watch-chain. He wore a leather belt and used no suspenders. If ever a youth was cordially admired and hated by his comrades, this one was. No girl could withstand his charms. He "cut out" every boy in the village. When his boat blew up at last, it diffused a tranquil contentment among us such as we had not known for months. But when he came home the next week, alive, renowned, and appeared in church all battered up and bandaged, a shining hero, stared at and wondered over by everybody, it seemed to us that the partiality of Providence for an undeserving reptile had reached a point where it was open to criticism.

This creature's career could produce but one result, and it speedily followed. Boy after boy managed to get on the river. The minister's son became an engineer. The doctor's and the postmaster's sons became "mud clerks"; the wholesale liquor dealer's son became a barkeeper on a boat; four sons of the chief merchant, and two sons of the county judge, became pilots. Pilot was the grandest position of all. The pilot, even in those days of trivial wages, had a princely salary—from a hundred and fifty to two hundred and fifty dollars a month, and no board to pay. Two months of his wages would pay a preacher's salary for a year. Now some of us were left disconsolate. We could not get on the river—at least our parents would not let us.

So, by and by, I ran away. I said I would never come home again till I was a pilot and could come in glory. But somehow I could not manage it. I went meekly aboard a few of the boats that lay packed together like sardines at the long St. Louis wharf, and humbly inquired for the pilots, but got only a cold shoulder and short words from mates and clerks. I had to make the best of this sort of treatment for the time being, but I had comforting day-dreams of a future when I should be a great and honored pilot, with plenty of money, and could kill some of these mates and clerks and pay for them.

Months afterward the hope within me struggled to a reluctant death, and I found myself without an ambition. But I was ashamed to go home. I was in Cincinnati, and I set to work to map out a new career. I had been reading about the recent exploration of the river Amazon by an expedition sent out by our government. It was said that the expedition, owing to difficulties, had not thoroughly explored a part of the country lying about the headwaters, some four thousand miles from the mouth of the river. It was only about fifteen hundred miles from Cincinnati to New Orleans, where I could doubtless get a ship. I had thirty dollars left; I would go and complete the exploration of the Amazon. This was all the thought I gave to the subject. I never was great in matters of detail. I packed my valise, and took passage on an ancient tub called the *Paul Jones,* for New Orleans. For the sum of sixteen dollars I had the scarred and tarnished splendors of "her" main saloon principally to myself, for she was not a creature to attract the eye of wiser travelers.

What with lying on the rocks four days at Louisville, and some other delays, the poor old *Paul Jones* fooled away about two weeks in making the voyage from Cincinnati to New Orleans. This gave me a chance to get acquainted with one of the pilots, and he taught me how to steer the boat, and thus made the fascination of river life more potent than ever for me.

I soon discovered two things. One was that a vessel would not be likely to sail for the mouth of the Amazon under ten or twelve years; and the other was that the nine or ten dollars still left in my pocket would not suffice for so impossible an exploration as I had planned, even if I could afford to wait for a ship. Therefore it followed that I must contrive a new career. The *Paul Jones* was now bound for St. Louis. I planned a siege against my pilot, and at the end of three hard days he surrendered. He agreed to teach me the Mississippi River from New Orleans to St. Louis for five hundred dollars, payable out of the first wages I should receive after graduating. I entered upon the small enterprise of "learning" twelve or thirteen hundred miles of the great Mississippi River with the easy confidence of my time of life. If I had really known what I was about to require of my faculties, I should not have had the courage to begin. I supposed that all a pilot had to do was to keep his boat in the river, and I did not consider that that could be much of a trick, since it was so wide.

The boat backed out from New Orleans at four in the afternoon, and it was "our watch" until eight. Mr. Bixby, my chief, "straightened her up," plowed her along past the sterns of the other boats that lay at the Levee, and then said, "Here, take her; shave those steamships as close as you'd peel an apple." I took the wheel, and my heartbeat fluttered up into the hundreds; for it seemed to me that we were about to scrape the side off every ship in the line, we were so close. I held my breath and began to claw the boat away from the danger; and I had my own opinion of the pilot who had known no better than to get us into such peril, but I was too wise to express it. In half a minute I had a wide margin of safety intervening between the *Paul Jones* and the ships; and within ten seconds more I was set aside in disgrace, and Mr. Bixby was going into danger again and flaying me alive with abuse of my cowardice. I was stung, but I was obliged to admire the easy confidence with which my chief loafed from side to side of his wheel, and trimmed the ships so closely that disaster seemed ceaselessly imminent. When he had cooled a little he told me that the easy water was close ashore and the current outside, and therefore we must hug the bank, up-stream, to get the benefit of the former, and stay well out, down-stream, to take advantage of the latter. In my own mind I resolved to be a down-stream pilot and leave the up-streaming to people dead to prudence.

Now and then Mr. Bixby called my attention to certain things. Said he, "This is Six-Mile Point." I assented. It was pleasant enough information, but I could not see the bearing of it. I was not conscious that it was a matter of any interest to me. Another time he said, "This is Nine-Mile Point." Later he said, "This is Twelve-Mile Point." They were all about level with the water's edge; they all looked about alike to me; they were monotonously unpicturesque. I hoped Mr. Bixby would change the subject. But no; he would crowd up around a point, hugging the shore with affection, and then say: "The slack water ends here, abreast this bunch of China trees; now we cross over." So he crossed over. He gave me the wheel once or twice, but I had no luck. I either came near chipping off the edge of a sugar plantation, or I yawed too far from shore, and so dropped back into disgrace again and got abused.

The watch was ended at last, and we took supper and went to bed. At midnight the glare of a lantern shone in my eyes, and the night watchman said:

"Come, turn out!"

And then he left. I could not understand this extraordinary procedure; so I presently gave up trying to, and dozed off to sleep. Pretty soon the watchman was back again, and this time he was gruff. I was annoyed. I said:

"What do you want to come bothering around here in the middle

of the night for? Now, as like as not, I'll not get to sleep again
tonight."

The watchman said:

"Well, if this ain't good, I'm blessed."

The "off-watch" was just turning in, and I heard some brutal
laughter from them, and such remarks as "Hello, watchman! ain't the
new cub turned out yet? He's delicate, likely. Give him some sugar in
a rag, and send for the chambermaid to sing 'Rock-a-by Baby,' to him."

About this time Mr. Bixby appeared on the scene. Something like
a minute later I was climbing the pilot-house steps with some of my
clothes on and the rest in my arms. Mr. Bixby was close behind, commenting. Here was something fresh—this thing of getting up in the
middle of the night to go to work. It was a detail in piloting that had
never occurred to me at all. I knew that boats ran all night, but somehow I had never happened to reflect that somebody had to get up out
of a warm bed to run them. I began to fear that piloting was not quite
so romantic as I had imagined it was; there was something very real
and worklike about this new phase of it.

It was a rather dingy night, although a fair number of stars were
out. The big mate was at the wheel, and he had the old tub pointed at
a star and was holding her straight up the middle of the river. The
shores on either hand were not much more than half a mile apart, but
they seemed wonderfully far away and ever so vague and indistinct.
The mate said:

"We've got to land at Jones's plantation, sir."

The vengeful spirit in me exulted. I said to myself, "I wish you
joy of your job, Mr. Bixby; you'll have a good time finding Mr. Jones's
plantation such a night as this; and I hope you never *will* find it as
long as you live."

Mr. Bixby said to the mate:

"Upper end of the plantation, or the lower?"

"Upper."

"I can't do it. The stumps there are out of water at this stage. It's
no great distance to the lower, and you'll have to get along with that."

"All right, sir. If Jones don't like it, he'll have to lump it, I
reckon."

And then the mate left. My exultation began to cool and my wonder to come up. Here was a man who not only proposed to find this
plantation on such a night, but to find either end of it you preferred. I
dreadfully wanted to ask a question, but I was carrying about as many
short answers as my cargo-room would admit of, so I held my peace.
All I desired to ask Mr. Bixby was the simple question whether . . . he

was going to find that plantation on a night when all plantations were exactly alike and all of the same color. But I held in. I used to have fine inspirations of prudence in those days.

Mr. Bixby made for the shore and soon was scraping it, just the same as if it had been daylight. And not only that, but singing:

> "Father in heaven,
> the day is declining," etc.

It seemed to me that I had put my life in the keeping of a peculiarly reckless outcast. Presently he turned on me and said:

"What's the name of the first point above New Orleans?"

I was gratified to be able to answer promptly, and I did. I said I didn't know.

"Don't *know?*"

This manner jolted me. I was down at the foot again, in a moment. But I had to say just what I had said before.

"Well, you're a smart one!" said Mr. Bixby. "What's the name of the *next* point?"

Once more I didn't know.

"Well, this beats anything. Tell me the name of *any* point or place I told you."

I studied awhile and decided that I couldn't.

"Look here! What do you start out from, above Twelve-Mile Point, to cross over?"

"I—I—don't know."

"You—you—don't know?" mimicking my drawling manner of speech. "What *do* you know?"

"I—I—nothing, for certain."

"By the great Cæsar's ghost, I believe you! You're the stupidest dunderhead I ever saw or ever heard of, so help me Moses! The idea of *you* being a pilot—*you!* Why, you don't know enough to pilot a cow down a lane."

Oh, but his wrath was up! He was a nervous man, and he shuffled from one side of his wheel to the other as if the floor was hot. He would boil awhile to himself, and then overflow and scald me again.

"Look here! What do you suppose I told you the names of those points for?"

I tremblingly considered a moment, and then the devil of temptation provoked me to say:

"Well, to—to—be entertaining, I thought."

This was a red rag to the bull. He raged and stormed so (he was crossing the river at the time) that I judged it made him blind, because he ran over the steering-oar of a trading-scow. Of course the traders sent up a volley of red-hot profanity. Never was a man so grateful as Mr. Bixby was; because he was brimful, and here were subjects who could *talk back*. He threw open a window, thrust his head out, and such an irruption followed as I never had heard before. The fainter and farther away the scowmen's curses drifted, the higher Mr. Bixby lifted his voice and the weightier his adjectives grew. You could have drawn a seine[5] through his system and not caught curses enough to disturb your mother with. Presently he said to me in the gentlest way:

"My boy, you must get a little memorandum-book; and every time I tell you a thing, put it down right away. There's only one way to be a pilot, and that is to get this entire river by heart. You have to know it just like A B C."

That was a dismal revelation to me; for my memory was never loaded with anything but blank cartridges. However, I did not feel discouraged long. I judged that it was best to make some allowances, for doubtless Mr. Bixby was "stretching." Presently he pulled a rope and struck a few strokes on the big bell. The stars were all gone now, and the night was as black as ink. I could hear the wheels churn along the bank, but I was not entirely certain that I could see the shore. The voice of the invisible watchman called up from the hurricane-deck:

"What's this, sir?"

"Jones's plantation."

I said to myself, "I wish I might venture to offer a small bet that it isn't." But I did not chirp. I only waited to see. Mr. Bixby handled the engine-bells, and in due time the boat's nose came to the land, a torch glowed from the forecastle, a man skipped ashore, . . . and the next moment we were standing up the river again, all serene. I reflected deeply awhile, and then said—but not aloud—"Well, the finding of that plantation was the luckiest accident that ever happened; but it couldn't happen again in a hundred years." And I fully believed it *was* an accident, too.

By the time we had gone seven or eight hundred miles up the river, I had learned to be a tolerably plucky up-stream steersman, in daylight; and before we reached St. Louis I had made a trifle of progress in night work, but only a trifle. I had a note-book that fairly bristled with the names of towns, "points," bars, islands, bends, reaches, etc.; but the information was to be found only in the note-book—none of it was in my head. It made my heart ache to think I had only got

---

[5] *seine* (sān): fishing net.

half of the river set down; for as our watch was four hours off and four hours on, day and night, there was a long four-hour gap in my book for every time I had slept since the voyage began.

My chief was presently hired to go on a big New Orleans boat, and I packed my satchel and went with him. She was a grand affair. When I stood in her pilot-house I was so far above the water that I seemed perched on a mountain; and her decks stretched so far away, fore and aft, below me, that I wondered how I could ever have considered the little *Paul Jones* a large craft.

When I returned to the pilot-house St. Louis was gone, and I was lost. Here was a piece of river which was all down in my book, but I could make neither head nor tail of it: you understand, it was turned around. I had seen it when coming up-stream, but I had never faced about to see how it looked when it was behind me. My heart broke again, for it was plain that I had got to learn this troublesome river *both ways.*

The pilot-house was full of pilots, going down to "look at the river." What is called the "upper river" (the two hundred miles between St. Louis and Cairo, where the Ohio comes in) was low; and the Mississippi changes its channel so constantly that the pilots used to always find it necessary to run down to Cairo to take a fresh look, when their boats were to lie in port a week; that is, when the water was at a low stage. . . .

All visiting pilots were useful, for they were always ready and willing, winter or summer, night or day, to go out in the yawl and help buoy the channel or assist the boat's pilots in any way they could. They were likewise welcomed because all pilots are tireless talkers, when gathered together, and as they talk only about the river they are always understood and are always interesting. Your true pilot cares nothing about anything on earth but the river, and his pride in his occupation surpasses the pride of kings.

We had a fine company of these river inspectors along this trip. There were eight or ten, and there was abundance of room for them in our great pilot-house. Two or three of them wore polished silk hats, elaborate shirt-fronts, diamond breastpins, kid gloves, and patent-leather boots. They were choice in their English, and bore themselves with a dignity proper to men of solid means and prodigious reputation as pilots. The others were more or less loosely clad, and wore upon their heads tall felt cones that were suggestive of the days of the Commonwealth.

I was a cipher[6] in this august company, and felt subdued, not to say torpid. I was not even of sufficient consequence to assist at the wheel when it was necessary to put the tiller hard down in a hurry; the guest that stood nearest did that when occasion required—and this was pretty much all the time, because of the crookedness of the channel and the scant water. I stood in a corner; and the talk I listened to took the hope all out of me. One visitor said to another:

"Jim, how did you run Plum Point, coming up?"

"It was in the night, there, and I ran it the way one of the boys on the *Diana* told me; started out about fifty yards above the wood-pile on the false point, and held on the cabin under Plum Point till I raised the reef—quarter less twain—then straightened up for the middle bar till I got well abreast the old one-limbed cottonwood in the bend, then got my stern on the cottonwood, and head on the low place above the point, and came through a-booming—nine and a half."

"Pretty square crossing, an't it?"

---

[6] *cipher:* person without influence or value.

"Yes, but the upper bar's working down fast."

Another pilot spoke up and said:

"I had better water than that, and ran it lower down; started out from the false point—mark twain—raised the second reef abreast the big snag in the bend, and had quarter less twain."

One of the gorgeous ones remarked:

"I don't want to find fault with your leadsmen, but that's a good deal of water for Plum Point, it seems to me."

There was an approving nod all around as this quiet snub dropped on the boaster and "settled" him. And so they went on talk-talk-talking. Meantime, the thing that was running in my mind was, "Now, if my ears hear aright, I have not only to get the names of all the towns and islands and bends, and so on, by heart, but I must even get up a warm personal acquaintanceship with every old snag and one-limbed cottonwood and obscure wood-pile that ornaments the banks of this river for twelve hundred miles; and more than that, I must actually know where these things are in the dark, unless these guests are gifted with eyes that can pierce through two miles of solid blackness. I wish the piloting business was in Jericho and I had never thought of it."

At dusk Mr. Bixby tapped the big bell three times (the signal to land), and the captain emerged from his drawing-room in the forward end of the "texas," and looked up inquiringly. Mr. Bixby said:

"We will lay up here all night, captain."

"Very well, sir."

That was all. The boat came to shore and was tied up for the night. It seemed to me a fine thing that the pilot could do as he pleased, without asking so grand a captain's permission. I took my supper and went immediately to bed, discouraged by my day's observations and experiences. My late voyage's note-booking was but a confusion of meaningless names. It had tangled me all up in a knot every time I had looked at it in the daytime. I now hoped for respite in sleep; but no, it reveled all through my head till sunrise again, a frantic and tireless nightmare.

Next morning I felt pretty rusty and low-spirited. We went booming along, taking a good many chances, for we were anxious to "get out of the river" (as getting out to Cairo was called) before night should overtake us. But Mr. Bixby's partner, the other pilot, presently grounded the boat, and we lost so much time getting her off that it was plain the darkness would overtake us a good long way above the mouth. This was a great misfortune, especially to certain of our visiting pilots whose boats would have to wait for their return, no matter how long that might be. It sobered the pilot-house talk a good deal.

Coming up-stream, pilots did not mind low water or any kind of darkness; nothing stopped them but fog. But down-stream work was different; a boat was too nearly helpless, with a stiff current pushing behind her; so it was not customary to run down-stream at night in low water.

There seemed to be one small hope, however; if we could get through the intricate and dangerous Hat Island crossing before night, we could venture the rest, for we would have plainer sailing and better water. But it would be insanity to attempt Hat Island at night. So there was a deal of looking at watches all the rest of the day, and a constant ciphering upon the speed we were making; Hat Island was the eternal subject; sometimes hope was high and sometimes we were delayed in a bad crossing, and down it went again. For hours all hands lay under the burden of this suppressed excitement; it was even communicated to me, and I got to feeling so solicitous about Hat Island, and under such an awful pressure of responsibility, that I wished I might have five minutes on shore to draw a good, full, relieving breath, and start over again. We were standing no regular watches. Each of our pilots ran such portions of the river as he had run when coming up-stream, because of his greater familiarity with it; but both remained in the pilot-house constantly.

An hour before sunset Mr. Bixby took the wheel, and Mr. W. stepped aside. For the next thirty minutes every man held his watch in his hand and was restless, silent, and uneasy. At last somebody said, with a doomful sigh:

"Well, yonder's Hat Island—and we can't make it."

All the watches closed with a snap, everybody sighed and muttered something about its being "too bad, too bad—ah, if we could *only* have got here half an hour sooner!" and the place was thick with the atmosphere of disappointment. Some started to go out, but loitered, hearing no bell-tap to land. The sun dipped behind the horizon, the boat went on. Inquiring looks passed from one guest to another; and one who had his hand on the door-knob and had turned it, waited, then presently took away his hand and let the knob turn back again. We bore steadily down the bend. More looks were exchanged, and nods of surprised admiration—but no words. Insensibly the men drew together behind Mr. Bixby, as the sky darkened and one or two dim stars came out. The dead silence and sense of waiting became oppressive. Mr. Bixby pulled the cord, and two deep, mellow notes from the big bell floated off on the night. Then a pause, and one more note was struck. The watchman's voice followed, from the hurricane-deck:

"Labboard lead, there! Stabboard lead!"

The cries of the leadsmen began to rise out of the distance, and were gruffly repeated by the wordpassers on the hurricane-deck.

"M-a-r-k three! M-a-r-k three! Quarter-less-three! Half twain! Quarter twain! M-a-r-k twain! Quarter-less—"

Mr. Bixby pulled two bell-ropes, and was answered by faint jinglings far below in the engine-room, and our speed slackened. The steam began to whistle through the gauge-cocks. The cries of the leadsmen went on—and it is a weird sound, always, in the night. Every pilot in the lot was watching now, with fixed eyes, and talking under his breath. Nobody was calm and easy but Mr. Bixby. He would put his wheel down and stand on a spoke, and as the steamer swung into her (to me) utterly invisible marks—for we seemed to be in the midst of a wide and gloomy sea—he would meet and fasten her there. Out of the murmur of half-audible talk, one caught a coherent sentence now and then—such as:

"There; she's over the first reef all right!"

After a pause, another subdued voice:

"Her stern's coming down just *exactly* right, by *George!*"

"Now she's in the marks; over she goes!"

Somebody else muttered:

"Oh, it was done beautiful—*beautiful!*"

Now the engines were stopped altogether, and we drifted with the current. Not that I could see the boat drift, for I could not, the stars being all gone by this time. This drifting was the dismalest work; it held one's heart still. Presently I discovered a blacker gloom than that which surrounded us. It was the head of the island. We were closing right down upon it. We entered its deeper shadow, and so imminent seemed the peril that I was likely to suffocate; and I had the strongest impulse to do *something,* anything, to save the vessel. But still Mr. Bixby stood by his wheel, silent, intent as a cat, and all the pilots stood shoulder to shoulder at his back.

"She'll not make it!" somebody whispered.

The water grew shoaler and shoaler, by the leadsman's cries, till it was down to:

"Eight-and-a-half! E-i-g-h-t feet! E-i-g-h-t- feet! Seven-and—"

Mr. Bixby said warningly through his speaking-tube to the engineer:

"Stand by, now!"

"Ay, ay, sir!"

"Seven-and-a-half! Seven feet! *Six*-and—"

We touched bottom! Instantly Mr. Bixby set a lot of bells ringing, shouted through the tube, *"Now,* let her have it—every ounce you've got!" then to his partner, "Put her hard down! snatch her! snatch her!" The boat rasped and ground her way through the sand, hung upon the apex of disaster a single tremendous instant, and then over she went! And such a shout as went up at Mr. Bixby's back never loosened the roof of a pilot-house before!

There was no more trouble after that. Mr. Bixby was a hero that night; and it was some little time, too, before his exploit ceased to be talked about by river-men.

Fully to realize the marvelous precision required in laying the great steamer in her marks in that murky waste of water, one should know that not only must she pick her intricate way through snags and blind reefs, and then shave the head of the island so closely as to brush the overhanging foliage with her stern, but at one place she must pass almost within arm's reach of a sunken and invisible wreck that would snatch the hull timbers from under her if she should strike it, and destroy a quarter of a million dollars' worth of steamboat and cargo in five minutes, and maybe a hundred and fifty human lives into the bargain.

The last remark I heard that night was a compliment to Mr. Bixby, uttered in soliloquy and with unction by one of our guests. He said:

"By the Shadow of Death, but he's a lightning pilot!"

DISCUSSION

1.   How does Samuel Clemens's life on the riverboat differ from the way he had imagined it?

2.   Clemens tells a lot about Mr. Bixby. Describe Mr. Bixby as clearly and as accurately as you can from Clemens's comments and from *dialogue* (see page 55).

3.   "About this time Mr. Bixby appeared on the scene. Something like a minute later I was climbing the pilot-house steps with some of my clothes on and the rest in my arms. Mr. Bixby was close behind, commenting." Here, Clemens smoothly passes over an incident that you should be able to picture rather vividly in your mind. What happened? What is the effect of underplaying it in this way?

4.   "Why, you don't know enough to pilot a cow down a lane," Mr. Bixby tells young Clemens. But he is exaggerating. Surely Clemens isn't that ignorant. Such exaggeration, usually for comic effect, is called *hyperbole*. What other examples can you find?

For further activities, see page 150.

Chief Joseph was the leader of the Nez Percé people. The U.S. Government broke treaty after treaty with them, and the Nez Percé decided to move to Canada. After a 1700-mile march, they were finally turned back by the U.S. Army.

I Have Heard Talk and Talk

Speech by **CHIEF JOSEPH**

I have heard talk and talk, but nothing is done.
Good words do not last long unless they amount to something.
Words do not pay for my dead people.
They do not pay for my country
Now overrun by white men. . . .
Good words will not give my people good health and stop them
    from dying.
Good words will not get my people a home where they can live in peace
    and take care of themselves.
I am tired of talk that comes to nothing.
It makes my heart sick when I remember all the good words
    and broken promises. . . .
You might as well expect the rivers to run backward
You who expect a man born free to be content penned up forbidden to
    go where he pleases. . . .
I have asked some of the great white chiefs
"Where do you get authority to say to the Indian that he shall stay in
    one place, while we see white men going where they please."
They cannot tell me.
Let me be a free man—
Free to travel,
Free to stop,
Free to work,
Free to trade where I choose,
Free to choose my own teachers,
Free to follow the religion of my fathers,
Free to think and talk and act for myself—and I will obey every law, or
    submit to the penalty.

VOCABULARY

Speech to the Virginia Convention (page 120)

patriotism	freedom
treason	liberty
tyranny	contempt
bravery	peace

The words listed above are abstract words. That is, they represent thoughts and ideas, not objects. They are also emotional words. When we see or hear them we have an almost immediate positive or negative reaction. But what do these words really mean? Without referring to a dictionary, define these words. Are they "positive" or "negative" words? When you have finished your definitions, see if you and your classmates have come to the same conclusions.

Life on the Mississippi (page 133)

Samuel Clemens chose his pen name, Mark Twain, from sea jargon. *Mark twain* really means "by the mark of two fathoms." Sea jargon is frequently used in conversation, although when most of us use these terms, we are not aware of their literal meanings. How many of the following expressions, which have their origin in sailing, do you recognize? What are their nonliteral meanings? What are their literal meanings? What others can you think of?

from stem to stern	dead reckoning
hit the deck	shipshape
keep an even keel	walk the plank
run a tight ship	batten down the hatches

COMPOSITION

Speech to the Virginia Convention (page 120)

Not all members of the Virginia Convention were prepared to take arms against England. Patrick Henry's speech was intended to change their minds. Presumably it did. But suppose you had been there. And suppose that after listening to Patrick Henry's rousing speech, you did not change your mind. How would you have answered Patrick Henry? Write a speech in which you present your side. Try to finish your speech with a memorable last line.

The Declaration of Independence (page 122)

When Jefferson submitted the Declaration of Independence to the delegates of the Continental Congress, many of the delegates began immediately to edit the document, suggesting changes here and there. Reluctantly Jefferson agreed to make the changes. The document was then accepted and has remained unchanged ever since. Read the Declaration again. Then, in a paragraph or so, explain the changes you feel might now be desirable—to make the document more modern or clearer in some way, for example. If you would make no changes, explain why.

Letter from Abigail Adams (page 125)

While John Adams was attending the Continental Congress in Philadelphia, he exchanged frequent letters with his wife Abigail. The letter on page 125 was written by Abigail to John before the Declaration was completed. Write a letter that you think Abigail might have written to John after she read the Declaration. If you wish, try to use her style, but use contemporary spelling.

Self-Reliance (page 126)

Nothing great was ever achieved without enthusiasm.
A friend is a person with whom I may be sincere. Before him, I may think aloud.
The reward of a thing well done is to have done it.
Popularity is for dolls; a hero cannot be popular.
Keep cool; it will all be one a hundred years hence.
What you are stands over you the while, and thunders so loud I cannot hear what you say to the contrary.

The statements above are all quotations taken from various essays by Ralph Waldo Emerson. Choose one that you agree with and explain why you do. Choose one you don't agree with and explain why you don't. Be sure you understand the quotations before you start to write.

Life on the Mississippi (page 133)

From this selection, it would seem that Samuel Clemens did not do very well as an apprentice riverboat pilot. He tells us the ways in which he fails. But these incidents are told from his point of view. How would Mr. Bixby tell them? Write a few anecdotes about Samuel Clemens's experiences as you think Mr. Bixby would tell them, using the dialogue you think he would use.

FROM

MY LIFE

ISADORA DUNCAN

As my mother had divorced my father when I was a baby in arms, I
had never seen him. Once, when I asked one of my aunts whether I
had ever had a father, she replied, "Your father was a demon who
ruined your mother's life." After that I always imagined him as a demon in a picture book, with horns and a tail, and when other children
at school spoke of their fathers, I kept silent.

When I was seven years old, we were living in two very bare
rooms on the third floor, and one day I heard the front door bell ring
and, on going out into the hall to answer it, I saw a very good-looking
gentleman in a top hat who said:

"Can you direct me to Mrs. Duncan's apartment?"

"I am Mrs. Duncan's little girl," I replied.

"Is this my Princess Pug?" said the strange gentleman. (That had
been his name for me when I was a baby.)

And suddenly he took me in his arms and covered me with tears
and kisses. I was very much astonished at this proceeding and asked
him who he was. To which he replied with tears, "I am your father."

I was delighted at this piece of news and rushed in to tell the
family.

"There is a man there who says he is my father."

My mother rose, very white and agitated, and, going into the next
room, locked the door behind her. One of my brothers hid under the
bed and the other retired to a cupboard, while my sister had a violent
fit of hysterics.

"Tell him to go away, tell him to go away," they cried.

I was much amazed, but being a very polite little girl, I went into
the hall and said:

"The family are rather indisposed, and cannot receive today," at
which the stranger took me by the hand and asked me to come for a
walk with him.

We descended the stairs into the street, I trotting by his side in a
state of bewildered enchantment to think that this handsome gentleman was my father, and that he had not got horns and a tail, as I had
always pictured him.

He took me to an ice cream parlour and stuffed me with ice
cream and cakes. I returned to the family in a state of the wildest excitement and found them in a terribly depressed condition.

"He is a perfectly charming man and he is coming tomorrow to
give me more ice cream," I told them.

But the family refused to see him, and after a time he returned to
his other family at Los Angeles.

After this I did not see my father for some years, when he suddenly appeared again. This time my mother relented sufficiently to see him, and he presented us with a beautiful house which had large dancing rooms, a tennis court, a barn, and a windmill. This was due to the fact that he had made a fourth fortune. In his life he had made three fortunes and lost them all. This fourth fortune also collapsed in course of time and with it the house, etc., disappeared. But for a few years we lived in it and it was a harbour of refuge between two stormy voyages.

It was owing to my mother that, as children, our entire lives were permeated with music and poetry. In the evenings she would sit at the piano and play for hours, and there were no set times for rising or going to bed, nor any discipline in our lives. On the contrary, I think my mother quite forgot about us, lost in her music or declaiming poetry, oblivious of all around her. One of her sisters, too, our aunt Augusta, was remarkably talented. She often visited us and would have performances of private theatricals. She was very beautiful, with black eyes and coal black hair, and I remember her dressed in black velvet "shorts" as Hamlet. She had a beautiful voice and might have had a great career as a singer, had it not been that everything relating to the theatre was looked upon by her father and mother as pertaining to the Devil. I realise now how her whole life was ruined by what would be difficult to explain nowadays—the Puritan spirit of America. The early settlers in America brought with them a psychic sense which has never been lost entirely. And their strength of character imposed itself upon the wild country. . . . They were always trying to tame themselves as well, with disastrous results artistically!

From her earliest childhood my aunt Augusta had been crushed by this Puritan spirit. Her beauty, her spontaneity, her glorious voice were all annihilated.[1] What was it that made men at that time exclaim, "I would rather see my daughter dead than on the stage"? It is almost impossible to understand this feeling nowadays, when great actors and actresses are admitted to the most exclusive circles.

I suppose it was due to our Irish blood that we children were always in revolt against this Puritanical tyranny.

One of the first effects of our removal to the large house my father gave us, was the opening of my brother Augustin's theatre in the barn. I remember he cut a piece out of the fur rug in the parlour to use as a beard for Rip Van Winkle, whom he impersonated in so real-

---

[1] *annihilated:* destroyed.

istic a manner that I burst into tears, as I watched him from a cracker box in the audience. We were all very emotional and refused to be repressed.

The little theatre grew and became quite celebrated in the neighbourhood. Later on this gave us the idea of making a tournée[2] on the coast. I danced, Augustin recited poems, and afterwards we acted a comedy in which Elizabeth and Raymond also took part. Although I was only twelve years old at the time and the others still in their teens, these tournées down the coast at Santa Clara, Santa Rosa, Santa Barbara, and so forth, were very successful.

The dominant note of my childhood was the constant spirit of revolt against the narrowness of the society in which we lived, against the limitations of life and a growing desire to fly eastward to something I imagined might be broader. How often I remember haranguing the family and my relations, and always ending with, "We *must* leave this place, we shall never be able to accomplish anything here."

Of all the family I was the most courageous, and when there was absolutely nothing to eat in the house, I was the volunteer who went to the butcher and through my wiles induced him to give me mutton chops without payment. I was the one sent to the baker, to entice him to continue credit. I took a real adventurous pleasure in these excursions, especially when I was successful, as I generally was. I used to dance all the way home with joy, bearing the spoils and feeling like a highwayman. This was a very good education, for from learning to wheedle ferocious butchers, I gained the technique which enabled me afterwards to face ferocious managers.

I remember once, when I was quite a baby, finding my mother weeping over some things which she had knitted for a shop and which had been refused. I took the basket from her, and putting one of the knitted caps on my head and a pair of knitted mittens on my hands, I went from door to door and peddled them. I sold everything and brought home twice the money mother would have received from the shop.

When I hear fathers of families saying they are working to leave a lot of money for their children, I wonder if they realise that by so doing they are taking all the spirit of adventure from the lives of those children. For every dollar they leave them makes them so much the weaker. The finest inheritance you can give to a child is to allow it to make its own way, completely on its own feet. Our teaching led my

---

[2] *tournée:* a round of visits.

sister and me into the richest houses in San Francisco. I did not envy these rich children; on the contrary, I pitied them. I was amazed at the smallness and stupidity of their lives, and, in comparison to these children of millionaires, I seemed to be a thousand times richer in everything that made life worthwhile.

Our fame as teachers increased. We called it a new system of dancing, but in reality there was no system. I followed my fantasy and improvised, teaching any pretty thing that came into my head. One of my first dances was Longfellow's poem, "I shot an arrow into the air." I used to recite the poem and teach the children to follow its meaning in gesture and movement. In the evenings my mother played to us while I composed dances. A dear old lady friend who came to spend the evening with us very often, and who had lived in Vienna, said I reminded her of Fanny Elssler, and she would recount to us the triumphs of Fanny Elssler. "Isadora will be a second Fanny Elssler," she would say, and this incited me to ambitious dreams. She told my mother to take me to a famous ballet teacher in San Francisco, but his lessons did not please me. When the teacher told me to stand on my toes I asked him why, and when he replied "Because it is beautiful," I said that it was ugly and against nature and after the third lesson I left his class, never to return. This stiff and commonplace gymnastics which he called dancing only disturbed my dream. I dreamed of a different dance. I did not know just what it would be, but I was feeling out towards an invisible world into which I divined I might enter if I found the key. My art was already in me when I was a little girl, and it was owing to the heroic and adventurous spirit of my mother that it was not stifled. I believe that whatever the child is going to do in life should be begun when it is very young. I wonder how many parents realise that by the so-called education they are giving their children, they are only driving them into the commonplace, and depriving them of any chance of doing anything beautiful or original. But I suppose this must be so, or who would supply us with the thousands of shop and bank clerks, etc., who seem to be necessary for organised civilised life.

My mother had four children. Perhaps by a system of coercion and education she might have turned us into practical citizens, and sometimes she lamented, "Why must all four be artists and not one practical?" But it was her own beautiful and restless spirit that made us artists. My mother cared nothing for material things and she taught us a fine scorn and contempt for all such possessions as houses, furniture, belongings of all kinds. It was owing to her example that I have never worn a jewel in my life. She taught us that such things were trammels. [3]

After I left school I became a great reader. There was a public library in Oakland, where we then lived, but no matter how many miles we were from it, I ran or danced or skipped there and back. The librarian was a very wonderful and beautiful woman, a poet of California, Ina Coolbrith. She encouraged my reading and I thought she always looked pleased when I asked for fine books. She had very beautiful eyes that glowed with burning fire and passion. Afterwards I learnt that at one time my father had been very much in love with her. She was evidently the great passion of his life and it was probably by the invisible thread of circumstance that I was drawn to her.

At that time I read all the works of Dickens, Thackeray, Shakespeare, and thousands of novels besides, good and bad, inspired books and trash—I devoured everything. I used to sit up at night, reading until dawn by the light of candles' ends which I had collected during the day. I also started to write a novel, and at this time I edited a newspaper, all of which I wrote myself, editorials, local news and short stories. In addition I kept a journal, for which I invented a secret language, for at this time I had a great secret. I was in love.

Besides the classes of children, my sister and I had taken some older pupils to whom she taught what was then called "Society dancing," the valse, mazurka, polka, and so forth, and among these pupils were two young men. One was a young doctor and the other a chemist. The chemist was amazingly beautiful and had a lovely name—Vernon. I was eleven years old at the time, but looked older as I had my hair up and my dresses long. Like the heroine of Rita, I wrote in my journal that I was madly, passionately in love, and I believe that I was. Whether Vernon was conscious of it or not, I do not know. At that age I was too shy to declare my passion. We went to balls and dances where he danced almost every dance with me and afterwards I sat up until the small hours recounting to my journal the terrifying thrills which I felt, "floating," as I put it, "in his arms." During the day he worked in a drug store in the main street and I walked miles just to pass the drug store once. Sometimes I mustered up enough courage to go in and say, "How do you do?" I also found out the house where he lodged, and I used to run away from home in the evening to watch the light in his window. This passion lasted two years and I believed that I suffered quite intensely. At the end of the two years he

---

[3] *trammels:* hindrances or confinements.

announced his approaching marriage to a young girl in Oakland society. I confined my agonised despair to my journal and I remember the day of the wedding and what I felt as I saw him walking down the aisle with a plain girl in a white veil. After that I never saw him.

The last time I danced in San Francisco, there came into my dressing-room a man with snow-white hair, but looking quite young and extremely beautiful. I recognised him at once. It was Vernon. I thought that after all these years I might tell him of the passion of my youth. I thought he would be amused, but he was extremely frightened and talked about his wife, the plain girl, who it seems is still alive, and from whom his affections have never deviated. How simple some people's lives can be!

That was my first love. I was madly in love, and I believe that since then I have never ceased to be madly in love.

DISCUSSION

1.   How does Isadora feel on seeing Vernon again after so many years?

2.   The author says "I seemed to be a thousand times richer in everything that made life worthwhile" (page 156). Richer than whom? Why does she think so? Do you agree?

3.   The style of dancing—her own style—that Isadora Duncan became famous for was considered quite revolutionary. In this selection she expresses ideas about parents' responsibilities toward their children that some people might call revolutionary. What are those ideas? How do you feel about them?

For further activities, see page 214.

THE OTHER LADY

VIRGINIA SORENSEN

Actually I saw her on only two occasions. Yet they were both so dramatic that she seems to figure larger in my childhood than some of the people I knew well for years. I have been told that she was rather ordinary, and that may be. I only know she was not ordinary when I saw her, either time. The first time, of course, she was in love, and therefore transfigured. The other time she was totally bereft. The dates, April and November of the same year, are entirely too symbolic, but this I cannot help. I invent the time still less than the emotion.

That a young woman should be in love with my tall handsome grandfather, then in his late fifties, seemed perfectly natural to me from the beginning. But that my grandmother should be upset I was fascinated to hear, because she was not the sort of person who ever got upset. She was so square and firm and impassive that one kissed her when she came for a visit as one might kiss a wall. One did not think of her as a wall that protected or obscured, or even as a barrier, for she refused her grandchildren nothing. One did not think particularly, either, of the words "strong" and "good," though both were true. She was simply *there,* like the house in which one has been born and in which one therefore habitually lives. . . . When I overheard my parents saying that she had gone to bed and lay biting her nails to the quick because of a certain letter she had found in Grandfather's traveling coat, I could scarcely imagine it. But I was so interested that the vision of it would not leave my mind.

Grandfather had traveled as far back as I could remember. Once he had managed a big store of his own, but in some great depression—"the Cleveland depression" I think it was—his store had been lost. So his undeniable salesmanship talents were sold to the Mormon Church, whose great Zion's Cooperative Mercantile Institution still bears the sign of the watchful Eye of God. Every few weeks his travels brought him to our valley, several hundred miles south of Salt Lake City, and the evenings he spent with us were like towering peaks over the gentle sunny plains of our village life. He was over six feet tall, an expansive Dane, and kissing him was an experience big and complete. He opened his arms and you entered an enchanted masculine warmth; he had the smooth clean feel of a fine gentleman. Best of all, his embrace was never overdone. Almost instantly he held you off and looked at you, and then the wonder was his voice and his laugh. "And since last time," he would say, "how has it been?"

It was usually on Friday that he came, completing his circuit for the weekend, and sometimes he met us when we came from the Friday afternoon matinee. I was so proud to walk on Main Street beside him that I still feel the stretch of my lifted chin when I think of it. His black suit, his gloves, his hat, his immaculate shirt front and tie, his glossy shoes—among the farmers of our community he was shining light, and it could be they resented him, I do not know. He even carried a fine stick, like a man on a stage, but this went under his arm when he held my hand and my sister's hand, one on either side. He had acted for a time in the Salt Lake Theater, and certainly his voice was theatrically rich. He had to know everything that had happened to us, about our marks at school, about the Primary Show we had appeared in, the new songs we had learned. Invariably something we had accomplished must have a reward, and the reward was always a new silver dollar. *New* is the important thing: Grandfather's Dollars were always fresh from the mint. No money ever made can have felt or looked so much like *money* as those great round Western dollars he gave to us. To this day I still feel, when I happen to see one, that it must be worth a dozen dollar bills. We saved our Grandfather Dollars, laying them carefully upon tinted cotton in pretty boxes as if they were jewels.

It was a week before Easter that I overheard the news about Grandmother. She had been expected to visit us during the spring holidays. It was after supper and Dad sat frowning over a letter from one of his sisters, "Why, it's ridiculous," he said. "Father never had anything to do with another woman. Somebody with a hat shop, over in Ephraim. Have you ever heard of her?"

"Only that she makes pretty hats," Mother said.

Something about the way she said it made Dad angry right away. "Well, I won't have you trotting over there to find out!" he said.

"Why not?" Mother asked, looking lively.

"Because I don't believe a word of it. Women——" He looked at the letter again. "They imagine things."

"If it's not true, why shouldn't I go?" Mother asked. "A good many women here get their Easter hats from her. They say she studied millinery in the East."

Dad said No, absolutely No, forever No. But the very next afternoon, which was a Saturday, we left as soon as he had gone back to work after noon. We were back in plenty of time for Mother to get supper.

It is odd to remember how far seven miles seemed in those days. When I go back to Utah now, those two little towns seem almost one to me, they are so close together. The houses, too, that I always thought spacious and elegant are really quite small and commonplace. How shall one be sure of anything at all then? But they say a vision is partly the eye that perceives it, as the ear must record the falling of a tree. That day I fell in love with the most beautiful pink bonnet ever

made, and it is no wonder that I have remembered its creator, there in her charming little shop, as a woman of surpassing
loveliness and generosity.

Before we arrived I was set for
drama.

Mother said to us, energetically steering as she spoke (for she always drove as
if the car must be made to go by her own
force), "We're going for *hats,* you understand? I don't want either of you letting
on we came to see *her.*"

Helen, almost two years my senior,
looked sidewise at me, and I thought she
meant to enforce Mother's words, so I
made a face at her. But presently she
said to Mother, "Well, anyway, we *do* get
hats, don't we?"

"Of course we get hats! That's what
I told you we were going for."

"But if we take hats home, Dad will
know where we went."

The car lurched. Mother deliberately
drove it off the road and stopped. Immediately, as always when Mother stopped
the car, the engine died. She turned to us,
but with her gloved hands still clutching
the wheel. "Naturally I meant to tell
your father the minute we got home."
Her voice was severe. *"I'll* tell him," she
said, looking at me, for I was always the
one to spill everything at the wrong time.

"I only thought——" Helen, began,
and stopped suddenly, staring ahead.

"What did you think?" Mother
asked. "Honestly, you'd think your father
and I could talk about something, just
ourselves, just once in a while!" She
looked at us with a kind of hopeless anger. "If I catch either of you repeating
one word of this outside of the family, I'll

spank you good. Do you hear? I shouldn't
have brought you."

My eyes were on my sister's face,
which was turning redder and redder. She
knew something I did not; I could tell it.
And I had believed she told me everything. She and I had agreed that we
could speak of anything together—even
of things Mother called "nasty" and
would not speak about any more than
she would breathe a word of scandal. It
was a good joke between us how Mother
would *not* notice a mess even when she
was physically involved in cleaning it up.
This, I think, was part of her English-
ness; with the English, I've noticed since,
nobody cares whether a thing is *done,*
just so it is not mentioned.

But Mother was noticing Helen's
face. "Did you read that letter?" she demanded. "If you did——"

"No. No, I didn't! I didn't even see
any letter," Helen said, but her eyes
looked set, suddenly, as if she fought to
hold her tears.

"Then what was it you thought?"

"Nothing. I didn't think anything."

"You did. I can tell you did." Mother's voice sharpened. "Has anybody been
saying anything?" she asked in despair.

"No. It was only that I——" Helen
paused one long second and then
plunged. "It was just that I saw Grandfather. Last week when I went over with
Mr. Reid, when he brought the books
over." Mr. Reid was the County Superin-
tendent of Schools, a kindly man who
sometimes let his daughters and their
friends go along, up and down the

county, on errands he had to make.

"You saw him! You couldn't—— He wasn't even down last week," Mother said.

I must confess that I enjoyed the look on her face. Overcome as I was that Helen had not told me, I was fascinated and full of admiration as well that she had not told Mother. Imagine keeping such a thing to yourself! I could no more have done that than I could have stopped breathing. Mother seemed to hang onto the wheel; Helen wept into her hands. At last Mother's voice came again, hollowly. "Was he with *her?*"

"He was there by her store. They were laughing and talking."

"On the street? Right there on Main Street?" Mother cried.

"She was on the step, holding the door open."

"Was he—could you tell? Was he going in?" She paused terribly. "Or coming out?"

"I don't know. We went on by, and nobody saw him but me. When we came back they weren't there."

Mother leaned forward on the wheel, rubbing her forehead back and forth. "Why didn't you tell us?" she asked. "You should have come right home and told us."

Helen turned her eyes to me then, and I'm sure mine were asking accusingly, Why didn't you tell *me?* She could have told me, whether or not she was able to tell Mother. "I thought he'd come for supper," she said miserably. "I thought maybe he wanted it to be a surprise."

"But when he didn't come? And when we got that letter——"

"I didn't think about it. I don't know——" She was really saying she didn't want it to be true.

We sat in silence. Then Mother lifted her head again, decisively. "Well!" she said. "Well, then! I think it's high time we came over!" The car roared and went lurching onto the road again; Mother did not glance behind her, for after all nothing much except hayracks ever came along that road. In two minutes we came to a stop every bit as decisive as the start, exactly in front of the little shop, by a rusted hitching post. A sign said "Hat Shoppe" in elegant black letters over a window filled with the very breath of a feminine spring.

Mother looked at the place and then at herself in the little mirror at the side of the car. Firmly she removed her old winter hat and laid it on the back seat. "Well, come on!" she said.

I expected from the look on her face that she meant to march right in and start shouting something important, maybe the Ten Commandments. But she paused at the window. She looked carefully at the hats, each on a little white pedestal wound with ribbons. I spun, agitated as a top, on the step, wanting whatever it was going to be to happen now, at once, but Mother leaned to the glass, intent as if searching for a clue.

"The straws are pretty," she said in her most ordinary shopping voice.

But then I saw the pink hat. And for a time I saw nothing else, nothing in the window or in the street or in the entire universe. That spring, for a change, it was fashionable again even for grown women to be fussy and feminine. For little girls a kind of poke-bonnet was the rage, and this was such a bonnet—but more, much much more. It had that certain indefinable quality that only a few hats have in this world, a peculiar saucy excitement in its very shape, not too decorative, but only *so*—— One fancied one's face deep within, rosy and mysterious with the freckles mercifully hidden. Frankly sentimental, the hat was made of rows of pink satin ribbon that were all one piece, even the two lengths to tie, turning upon themselves, with every stitch invisible. Mother too has always remembered it. Two very blue forget-me-nots with tiny yellow centers sat at the very edge of the crown, their stems tucked in. At the foot of the pedestal lay a small blue bouquet upon a frail flower of pink handkerchief.

"Oh, *Mother*. . . ." I could scarcely breathe. I was already seeing myself as I came into Sunday School, my eyes watchful from their deep pink place, the pink handkerchief in my hand, the flowers pinned to my collar, against my throat. "Mother, can I try it on? Can I? Can I?"

"There's no price on it. We'll see. It's probably too expensive," Mother said.

"I think it's babyish," said Helen.

"Babyish? Just because it's pink and blue?" I cried out as if she had taken the Lord's name in vain.

"Well, I like plain straw," she said. She was trying to please Mother; I did not even glance at the hat she pointed out.

Mother nodded. "I'd really thought of straw," she said. And I clutched at her then, saying, "Oh, Mother . . ." the way I'd learned to do long since. "I'll put all my allowance——"

"You've 'put' all your allowance on ten different things already and you know it," she said firmly. "Please don't be silly just now. Especially not just now." She turned toward the step and opened the door.

So it was I entered the Shoppe in a daze of selfish concern, a thousand times less interested in the other lady herself than in her proprietorship of the fabulous pink hat. She was sewing when we came in, sitting at a machine in one corner of the little room, surrounded with the makings of her bonnets. Spools of ribbons stood on a shelf behind her, the colors shaded light to dark, like a rainbow. There were cards of lace, piles of flowers and handkerchiefs, an array of colored feathers. There were shapes for hats of various kinds, some of straw and some of stiff white tape. I noted much of this right away, with the sort of ardent concern with which one views the house where his love was born.

I remember how tall and thin she looked when she rose, perhaps because I had been thinking of her in terms of Grandmother, who was short and very plump. Her cheeks went red and she lifted her hands at once to push her hair from her forehead, as a woman will do when a man enters a room unexpectedly. She knew us. She spoke to Mother at once by her name.

As I recall it, Mother was the more flustered of the two. She said at once that we had come to look at hats, to my horror adding, "I'd thought of simple straws for the girls—little sailors, I think. There's one in the window."

"Mother——" I sought her hand. "The pink one—ask if I can try on the pink one——"

The lady looked at me. She smiled. "It's very pretty, isn't it?" she said. "I just finished it this morning."

"I'm really not interested in anything that dressy," Mother said hastily. "Something simple—a little shade, their faces burn so all summer."

I knew she meant that my hat was too expensive, and suddenly, acknowledging the truth of what she had said of my allowance, and also, I imagine, inspired by the present drama, I cried out: "Mother, I'll pay all of my Grandfather Dollars, every single one!"

Mother gave me a terrible look. Helen gave me a terrible pinch. But I did not mind either one, for the lady proceeded at once to the window and lifted up not only the obnoxious straw but the pink hat as well, spinning a bit on its cunning pedestal. "There," she said, setting it down in front of the mirror by the wall. "A pretty girl like you should have a pretty hat."

I would have given my life for her on the spot. She could have done anything and I would have forgiven her. At that moment I truly believe she could have tied up my handsome and beloved grandfather in a gunny sack and carried him off to the North Pole and I would not have offended her by objecting. Even my bosom friend, in her wildest adoration, had never gone so far as to suggest that I was pretty. How I really looked in the hat I have no idea, but it was a creation that even enhanced its pedestal, so it

might have enhanced me. The lady drew it over my head and expertly tied the ribbons into an enchanting bow under my left ear. I stood gazing into the glass.

Mother stood still. Helen gave a nervous giggle. Then, with a determined look, Mother reached over and looked at the price tag which was apparently hanging at the back of my neck. I saw her do it, in the glass.

"I promise, I'll give *all*——" I began again.

It was the lady herself who interrupted. "You must let me give it to her," she said to Mother. Her face was scarlet but Mother looked quite pale. With those words our whole errand, the whole truth, was laid instantly bare.

"Why, I wouldn't think of such a thing!" Mother said.

"I'd be so glad if you would," the lady said, and leaned on her shaking fingers on a table laden with hats. "If we could be friends—all of us——" Then, shockingly, she used my grandfather's given name. "He'd be so pleased," she said.

Without another word, Mother turned and left the shop. Helen stumbled after. And there I stood, crowned in my rosy splendor, not knowing what to do.

"Please take it," the lady said.

But of course I could not. I could never wear such a creation home, or explain it. I lifted a heavy hand and slipped the bow undone. I'm sure no ballad bridegroom was ever torn from his bride with more anguish than I felt as I slipped that hat from my head and laid it reverently down. Mother was starting the car. When

I heard the engine roaring, I flew in a panic to the door. One second I paused there, saying, "It's the prettiest hat in the world!" and the door slammed after me.

"Get in!" Mother said.

All the way home she blamed herself and me, turn and turn about. Dad always knew best, she said, why hadn't she remembered that? And I—I had spoiled everything with that silly pink hat, talking about Grandfather. But before we came into our street we decided, like conspirators, that since we had no hats to explain we needn't confess our escapade, after all. We stopped at Brown's for ice-cream sundaes and then went to our own hat shop where we thought quite simply about hats and bought two for shade. I can't say I was entirely reconciled about the pink one, either that day or for many days thereafter. I only say it was one of many lessons in that same sort of resignation and that I would have done without them all if I could.

It must have been the following week that Grandfather was waiting for us after the Friday matinee. He was standing behind the little copper rail in front of the ticket window, watching the stream of children come out. We were always dazed, coming into the blast of level afternoon light from the flickering dark. Grandfather looked unreal for a while, as the whole world did. But his hand was reassuring, and his hug strong. I thought, "So he still loves us; he still comes to see us too," and felt wildly happy as we walked along Main Street. Yet when we turned at our corner and he asked, familiarly, "And how has it been since last time?" there was a long moment when we could not think what to say. He spoke again himself before either of us could answer, his voice as usual, teasing and gay. "I hear you offered all your silver dollars for a bonnet."

Suddenly, dreadfully, Helen broke from his hand and began to run. When we came to our gate, in the first deep silence I had ever known with my grandfather, she had disappeared. I looked up at his face as he carefully fastened the gate after us, and for the first time in my life felt the sorrow of being beside a person I loved and yet helplessly apart. For a moment his face sagged, deep lines gathered above his white collar. And then he pushed out his lower lip and his chin came up in a way that was particularly his; he took my hand again and we walked around the path which curved against the lawn. As we climbed the steps to the porch, the front door opened and Dad came out.

He spoke to me, holding the door wide. "Go in," he said. I went in and the door closed after me. Instantly I was at the window looking onto the porch, filled with terror. Wasn't Grandfather to come in to supper, to laugh, to talk, to tell all the wonderful comical things that had happened since the last time? I suppose I knew. It seems to me I knew what was said between them, every syllable, though it isn't possible that I really heard. I knew from their mouths, their gestures. Grandfather held out his hand and it simply stood there, on the air.

Then Grandfather's hand fell at his side and he turned and went down the steps and around the path and through the gate and down the street, out of sight. None of us ever saw him alive again.

The news of his death came from California the next November. The divorce had happened quickly, in Nevada, and he was married again at once. But one day, not long afterward, he was cranking a car and fell, so we were told, and died in the street. He was brought back to Utah to be buried in the family plot.

I remember the feeling of importance amidst my sorrow; I was to stay out of school and to travel on the train. The fact of death was impossible to believe, especially about Grandfather, and so I did not really believe it until I saw it. I looked into the coffin only once, and it was a long time before the vision of Grandfather in his black suit and fine tie and gloves and hat and stick overcame again the dreadful unnatural vision of him lying in pure white with his eyes closed and his shoes sticking oddly up into the air. There was a curious cap on his head and his hands were folded over an apron of bright green, embroidered with patterns of leaves, the Mormon burial clothes. All afternoon everybody kept kissing everybody, which was to me a difficult trial. I remember my turn coming with each aunt and uncle, each distant cousin, and with poor Grandmother it was worst of all for she tasted of salt and trembled, another creature than the hearty woman I had always known, almost as different as Grandfather himself.

It was from the midst of the family kissing that I first saw the other lady. She stood against the wall, beside the door, completely alone. If anybody spoke to her or looked at her, I did not see it. As for kissing, of course that was out of the question, one advantage at least of her position. After that, from deep among the scores of cousins and second cousins and third cousins, I kept seeking her out, and have no idea whether my fascination was only curiosity or whether I felt pity too. The pity may have come later; how can one be sure? I only know that I see her now as unmistakably as I see Grandfather, in slim black, unrelieved from top to toe by any ornament, or by even so much as the shine of a button. At the funeral she followed the family, far behind Grandmother and her long procession of tall sons and daughters, her grandchildren, her brothers and sisters, nephews and nieces. The lady came down the aisle, walking alone; I saw from my important place on the end of the front row that there was now one spot of pure white upon her, a handkerchief she held in her right hand.

Later I saw her at the graveside. It was then she caught my eye, once, but I quickly looked at the ground again. She was wearing a very tight and very ugly black hat, and none of her hair was showing. She who had so many pretty hats. It was certain, then, that she no longer cared for hats or for anything.

Dad had to return home that night, for there was nobody to relieve him at his work next morning. We left for the train soon after the fabulous dinner that followed the funeral. When we came to the depot, the other lady was there, sitting in

the waiting room, alone on a long straight-backed bench. I will never forget Mother in the next moment. She stood for a time like a person about to jump into the sea, her face streaked and her hat awry. And then she rushed suddenly over to the other lady and sat down and they cried together. Dad said nothing. He made no sign of recognition, then or later, on the train. I knew he was remembering, as I was, the last time Grandfather had come to our house, holding out his hand.

The lady sat alone on the train, far down the aisle on the other side. The train was overheated and soot drifted along the sills of the windows. The conductor turned the lights out, except for a small one at either end of the car, and everybody slept. Once in a while the train stopped, people moved a little, murmuring together, and slept again. I remember waking for the last time looking up half-stupefied at Mother standing over me.

Beside her was the other lady, with a little satchel and the ugly black hat in her hand. Her hair was tumbled and her face flushed. "I would so like to kiss her, if I may," she said.

Mother said, "Of course."

The lady leaned down over me and I felt the brief warm pressure of her lips. She smelled of something sweet, barely spiced, and a great flood of excited love came over me. I moved close. The train was stopping; she walked hurriedly down the aisle. I could hear Dad talking with the conductor in the vestibule, and turned to press my face against the window. I saw her walk alone across the lighted platform and then, presently, as the train started once again, she disappeared from sight.

DISCUSSION

1. The Other Lady, referring to the pink hat, says to the author, "You must let me give it to you." Why are these words so significant? How does everyone react to that statement?

2. What do you think of the Other Lady? Does your opinion of her ever change? If so, when and how?

3. Virginia Sorensen obviously loved her grandfather very much. She does not say so in those words. How does she tell us? Find lines in the selection that let you know how she felt about him.

4. "Actually I saw her only twice," the author says about the Other Lady. Why then do you think these incidents have remained so long in the author's memory?

For further activities, see page 214.

A Christmas Memory

TRUMAN CAPOTE

Imagine a morning in late November. A coming of winter morning more than twenty years ago. Consider the kitchen of a spreading old house in a country town. A great black stove is its main feature; but there is also a big round table and a fireplace with two rocking chairs placed in front of it. Just today the fireplace commenced its seasonal roar.

A woman with shorn white hair is standing at the kitchen window. She is wearing tennis shoes and a shapeless gray sweater over a summery calico dress. She is small and sprightly, like a bantam hen; but, due to a long youthful illness, her shoulders are pitifully hunched. Her face is re-markable—not unlike Lincoln's, craggy like that, and tinted by sun and wind; but it is delicate too, finely boned, and her eyes are sherry-colored and timid. "Oh my," she exclaims, her breath smoking the windowpane, "it's fruitcake weather!"

The person to whom she is speaking is myself. I am seven; she is sixty-something. We are cousins, very distant ones, and we have lived to-gether—well, as long as I can remember. Other people inhabit the house, relatives; and though they have power over us, and frequently make us cry, we are not, on the whole, too much aware of them. We are each other's best friend. She calls me Buddy, in memory of a boy who was formerly her best friend. The other Buddy died in the 1880s, when she was still a child. She is still a child.

"I knew it before I got out of bed," she says, turning away from the window with a purposeful excitement in her eyes. "The courthouse bell sounded so cold and clear. And there were no birds singing; they've gone to warmer country, yes indeed. Oh, Buddy, stop stuffing biscuit and fetch our buggy. Help me find my hat. We've thirty cakes to bake."

It's always the same: a morning arrives in November, and my friend, as though officially inaugurating the Christmas time of year that exhila-rates her imagination and fuels the blaze of her heart, announces: "It's fruitcake weather! Fetch our buggy. Help me find my hat."

The hat is found, a straw cartwheel corsaged with velvet roses out-of-doors has faded: it once belonged to a more fashionable relative. To-gether, we guide our buggy, a dilapidated baby carriage, out to the gar-den and into a grove of pecan trees. The buggy is mine; that is, it was bought for me when I was born. It is made of wicker, rather unraveled,

Capote: prounced kə-pō′tē.

and the wheels wobble like a drunkard's legs. But it is a faithful object; springtimes, we take it to the woods and fill it with flowers, herbs, wild fern for our porch pots; in the summer, we pile it with picnic paraphernalia and sugar-cane fishing poles and roll it down to the edge of a creek; it has its winter uses, too: as a truck for hauling firewood from the yard to the kitchen, as a warm bed for Queenie, our tough little orange and white rat terrier who has survived distemper and two rattlesnake bites. Queenie is trotting beside it now.

Three hours later we are back in the kitchen hulling a heaping buggyload of windfall pecans. Our backs hurt from gathering them: how hard they were to find (the main crop having been shaken off the trees and sold by the orchard's owners, who are not us) among the concealing leaves, the frosted, deceiving grass. Caarackle! A cheery crunch, scraps of miniature thunder sound as the shells collapse and the golden mound of sweet oily ivory meat mounts in the milk-glass bowl. Queenie begs to taste, and now and again my friend sneaks her a mite, though insisting we deprive ourselves. "We mustn't, Buddy. If we start, we won't stop. And there's scarcely enough as there is. For thirty cakes." The kitchen is growing dark. Dusk turns the window into a mirror: our reflections mingle with the rising moon as we work by the fireside in the firelight. At last, when the moon is quite high, we toss the final hull into the fire and, with joined sighs, watch it catch flame. The buggy is empty, the bowl is brimful.

We eat our supper (cold biscuits, bacon, blackberry jam) and discuss tomorrow. Tomorrow the kind of work I like best begins: buying. Cherries and citron, ginger and vanilla and canned Hawaiian pineapple, rinds and raisins and walnuts and whiskey and oh, so much flour, butter, so many eggs, spices, flavorings: why, we'll need a pony to pull the buggy home.

But before these purchases can be made, there is the question of money. Neither of us has any. Except for skinflint sums persons in the house occasionally provide (a dime is considered very big money); or what we earn ourselves from various activities: holding rummage sales, selling buckets of hand-picked blackberries, jars of homemade jam and apple jelly and peach preserves, rounding up flowers for funerals and weddings. Once we won seventy-ninth prize, five dollars, in a national football contest. Not that we know a fool thing about football. It's just that we enter any contest we hear about: at that moment our hopes are centered on the fifty-thousand-dollar Grand Prize being offered to name a new brand of coffee (we suggested "A.M."; and, after some hesitation, for my friend thought it perhaps sacrilegious, the slogan "A.M.! Amen!"). To tell the truth, our only *really* profitable enterprise was the Fun and

Freak Museum we conducted in a backyard woodshed two summers ago. The Fun was a stereopticon[1] with slide views of Washington and New York lent us by a relative who had been to those places (she was furious when she discovered why we'd borrowed it); the Freak was a three-legged biddy chicken hatched by one of our own hens. Everybody hereabouts wanted to see that biddy: we charged grownups a nickel, kids two cents. And took in a good twenty dollars before the museum shut down due to the decease of the main attraction.

But one way and another we do each year accumulate Christmas savings, a Fruitcake Fund. These moneys we keep hidden in an ancient bead purse under a loose board under the floor under a chamber pot under my friend's bed. The purse is seldom removed from this safe location except to make a deposit, or, as happens every Saturday, a withdrawal; for on Saturdays I am allowed ten cents to go to the picture show. My friend has never been to a picture show, nor does she intend to: "I'd rather hear you tell the story, Buddy. That way I can imagine it more. Besides, a person my age shouldn't squander their eyes. When the Lord comes, let me see Him clear." In addition to never having seen a movie, she has never: eaten in a restaurant, traveled more than five miles from home, received or sent a telegram, read anything except funny papers and the Bible, worn cosmetics, cursed, wished someone harm, told a lie on purpose, let a hungry dog go hungry. Here are a few things she has done, does do: killed with a hoe the biggest rattlesnake ever seen in this country (sixteen rattles), dip snuff[2] (secretly), tame hummingbirds (just try it) till they balance on her finger, tell ghost stories (we both believe in ghosts) so tingling they chill you in July, talk to herself, take walks in the rain, grow the prettiest japonicas in town, know the recipe for every sort of old-time Indian cure, including a magical wart-remover.

Now, with supper finished, we retire to the room in a faraway part of the house where my friend sleeps in a scrap-quilt-covered iron bed painted rose pink, her favorite color. Silently, wallowing in the pleasures of conspiracy, we take the bead purse from its secret place and spill its contents on the scrap quilt. Dollar bills, tightly rolled and green as May buds. Somber fifty-cent pieces, heavy enough to weight a dead man's eyes. Lovely dimes, the liveliest coin, the one that really jingles. Nickels and quarters, worn smooth as creek pebbles. But mostly a hateful heap of bitter-odored pennies. Last summer others in the house contracted to pay us a penny for every twenty-five flies we killed. Oh, the carnage[3] of

---

[1] *stereopticon:* optical device used to project the enlarged image of a picture.
[2] *snuff:* finely ground tobacco that can be inhaled into the nostrils.
[3] *carnage:* massive slaughter.

August: the flies that flew to heaven! Yet it was not work in which we took pride. And, as we sit counting pennies, it is as though we were back tabulating dead flies. Neither of us has a head for figures; we count slowly, lose track, start again. According to her calculations, we have $12.73. According to mine, exactly $13. "I do hope you're wrong, Buddy. We can't mess around with thirteen. The cakes will fall. Or put somebody in the cemetery. Why, I wouldn't dream of getting out of bed on the thirteenth." This is true: she always spends thirteenths in bed. So, to be on the safe side, we subtract a penny and toss it out the window.

Of the ingredients that go into our fruitcakes, whiskey is the most expensive, as well as the hardest to obtain: State laws forbid its sale. But everybody knows you can buy a bottle from Mr. Haha Jones. And the next day, having completed our more prosaic shopping, we set out for Mr. Haha's business address, a "sinful" (to quote public opinion) fish-fry and dancing café down by the river. We've been there before, and on the same errand; but in previous years our dealings have been with Haha's wife, an iodine-dark Indian woman with brassy peroxided hair and a dead-tired disposition. Actually, we've never laid eyes on her husband, though we've heard that he's an Indian too. A giant with razor scars across his cheeks. They call him Haha because he's so gloomy, a man who never laughs. As we approach his café (a large log cabin festooned inside and out with chains of garish-gay naked light bulbs and standing by the river's muddy edge under the shade of river trees where moss drifts through the branches like gray mist) our steps slow down. Even Queenie stops prancing and sticks close by. People have been murdered in Haha's café. Cut to pieces. Hit on the head. There's a case coming up in court next month. Naturally these goings on happen at night when the colored lights cast crazy patterns and the victrola wails. In the daytime Haha's is shabby and deserted. I knock at the door, Queenie barks, my friend calls: "Mrs. Haha, ma'am? Anyone to home?"

Footsteps. The door opens. Our hearts overturn. It's Mr. Haha Jones himself! And he *is* a giant; he *does* have scars; he *doesn't* smile. No, he glowers at us through Satan-tilted eyes and demands to know: "What you want with Haha?"

For a moment we are too paralyzed to tell. Presently my friend half-finds her voice, a whispery voice at best: "If you please, Mr. Haha, we'd like a quart of your finest whiskey."

His eyes tilt more. Would you believe it? Haha is smiling! Laughing, too. "Which one of you is a drinkin' man?"

"It's for making fruitcakes, Mr. Haha. Cooking."

This sobers him. He frowns. "That's no way to waste good whiskey." Nevertheless, he retreats into the shadowed café and seconds later

appears carrying a bottle of daisy-yellow unlabeled liquor. He demon-
strates its sparkle in the sunlight and says: "Two dollars."

We pay him with nickels and dimes and pennies. Suddenly, as he
jangles the coins in his hand like a fistful of dice, his face softens. "Tell
you what," he proposes, pouring the money back into our bead purse,
"just send me one of them fruitcakes instead."

"Well," my friend remarks on our way home, "there's a lovely man.
We'll put an extra cup of raisins in *his* cake."

The black stove, stoked with coal and firewood, glows like a lighted
pumpkin. Eggbeaters whirl, spoons spin round in bowls of butter and
sugar, vanilla sweetens the air, ginger spices it; melting, nose-tingling
odors saturate the kitchen, suffuse the house, drift out to the world on
puffs of chimney smoke. In four days our work is done. Thirty-one
cakes, dampened with whiskey, bask on window sills and shelves.

Who are they for?

Friends. Not necessarily neighbor friends: indeed, the larger share is
intended for persons we've met maybe once, perhaps not at all. People
who've struck our fancy. Like President Roosevelt. Like the Reverend and
Mrs. J. C. Lucey, Baptist missionaries to Borneo who lectured here last
winter. Or the little knife grinder who comes through town twice a year.
Or Abner Packer, the driver of the six o'clock bus from Mobile, who ex-
changes waves with us every day as he passes in a dust-cloud whoosh.

Or the young Wistons, a California couple whose car one afternoon broke down outside the house and who spent a pleasant hour chatting with us on the porch (young Mr. Wiston snapped our picture, the only one we've ever had taken). Is it because my friend is shy with everyone *except* strangers that these strangers, and merest acquaintances, seem to us our truest friends? I think yes. Also, the scrapbooks we keep of thank-you's on White House stationery, time-to-time communications from California and Borneo, the knife grinder's penny post cards, make us feel connected to eventful worlds beyond the kitchen with its view of a sky that stops.

Now a nude December fig branch grates against the window. The kitchen is empty, the cakes are gone; yesterday we carted the last of them to the post office, where the cost of stamps turned our purse inside out. We're broke. That rather depresses me, but my friend insists on celebrating—with two inches of whiskey left in Haha's bottle. Queenie has a spoonful in a bowl of coffee (she likes her coffee chicory-flavored and strong). The rest we divide between a pair of jelly glasses. We're both quite awed at the prospect of drinking straight whiskey; the taste of it brings screwed-up expressions and sour shudders. But by and by we begin to sing, the two of us singing different songs simultaneously. I don't know the words to mine, just: *Come on along, come on along, to the dark-town strutters' ball.* But I can dance: that's what I mean to be, a tap dancer in the movies. My dancing shadow rollicks on the walls; our voices rock the chinaware; we giggle: as if unseen hands were tickling us. Queenie rolls on her back, her paws plow the air, something like a grin stretches her black lips. Inside myself, I feel warm and sparky as those crumbling logs, carefree as the wind in the chimney. My friend waltzes round the stove, the hem of her poor calico skirt pinched between her fingers as though it were a party dress: *Show me the way to go home,* she sings, her tennis shoes squeaking on the floor. *Show me the way to go home.*

Enter: two relatives. Very angry. Potent with eyes that scold, tongues that scald. Listen to what they have to say, the words tumbling together into a wrathful tune: "A child of seven! whiskey on his breath! are you out of your mind? feeding a child of seven! must be loony! road to ruination! remember Cousin Kate? Uncle Charlie? Uncle Charlie's brother-in-law? shame! scandal! humiliation! kneel, pray, beg the Lord!"

Queenie sneaks under the stove. My friend gazes at her shoes, her chin quivers, she lifts her skirt and blows her nose and runs to her room. Long after the town has gone to sleep and the house is silent except for the chimings of clocks and the sputter of fading fires, she is weeping into a pillow already as wet as a widow's handkerchief.

"Don't cry," I say, sitting at the bottom of her bed and shivering despite my flannel nightgown that smells of last winter's cough syrup, "don't cry," I beg, teasing her toes, tickling her feet, "you're too old for that."

"It's because," she hiccups, "I *am* too old. Old and funny."

"Not funny. Fun. More fun than anybody. Listen. If you don't stop crying you'll be so tired tomorrow we can't go cut a tree."

She straightens up. Queenie jumps on the bed (where Queenie is not allowed) to lick her cheeks. "I know where we'll find real pretty trees, Buddy. And holly, too. With berries big as your eyes. It's way off in the woods. Farther than we've ever been. Papa used to bring us Christmas trees from there: carry them on his shoulder. That's fifty years ago. Well, now: I can't wait for morning."

Morning. Frozen rime[4] lusters the grass; the sun, round as an orange and orange as hot-weather moons, balances on the horizon, burnishes the silvered winter woods. A wild turkey calls. A renegade hog grunts in the undergrowth. Soon, by the edge of knee-deep, rapid-running water, we have to abandon the buggy. Queenie wades the stream first, paddles across barking complaints at the swiftness of the current, the pneumonia-making coldness of it. We follow, holding our shoes and equipment (a hatchet, a burlap sack) above our heads. A mile more: of chastising thorns, burs and briers that catch at our clothes; of rusty pine needles brilliant with gaudy fungus and molted feathers. Here, there, a flash, a flutter, an ecstasy of shrillings remind us that not all the birds have flown south. Always, the path unwinds through lemony sun pools and pitch-black vine tunnels. Another creek to cross: a disturbed armada of speckled trout froths the water round us, and frogs the size of plates practice belly flops; beaver workmen are building a dam. On the farther shore, Queenie shakes herself and trembles. My friend shivers, too: not with cold but enthusiasm. One of her hat's ragged roses sheds a petal as she lifts her head and inhales the pine-heavy air. "We're almost there; can you smell it, Buddy?" she says, as though we were approaching an ocean.

And, indeed, it is a kind of ocean. Scented acres of holiday trees, prickly-leafed holly. Red berries shiny as Chinese bells: black crows swoop upon them screaming. Having stuffed our burlap sacks with enough greenery and crimson to garland a dozen windows, we set about choosing a tree. "It should be," muses my friend, "twice as tall as a boy. So a boy can't steal the star." The one we pick is twice as tall as me. A brave handsome brute that survives thirty hatchet strokes before it keels with a creaking rending cry. Lugging it like a kill, we commence the long

---

[4] *rime:* granular coating of frost.

trek out. Every few yards we abandon the struggle, sit down and pant. But we have the strength of triumphant huntsmen; that and the tree's virile, icy perfume revive us, goad us on. Many compliments accompany our sunset return along the red clay road to town; but my friend is sly and noncommittal when passers-by praise the treasure perched in our buggy: what a fine tree and where did it come from? "Yonderways," she murmurs vaguely. Once a car stops and the rich mill owner's lazy wife leans out and whines: "Giveya two bits cash for that ol tree." Ordinarily my friend is afraid of saying no; but on this occasion she promptly shakes her head: "We wouldn't take a dollar." The mill owner's wife persists. "A dollar, my foot! Fifty cents. That's my last offer. Goodness, woman, you can get another one." In answer, my friend gently reflects: "I doubt it. There's never two of anything."

Home: Queenie slumps by the fire and sleeps till tomorrow, snoring loud as a human.

A trunk in the attic contains: a shoebox of ermine tails (off the opera cape of a curious lady who once rented a room in the house), coils of frazzled tinsel gone gold with age, one silver star, a brief rope of dilapidated, undoubtedly dangerous candylike light bulbs. Excellent decorations, as far as they go, which isn't far enough: my friend wants our tree to blaze "like a Baptist window," droop with weighty snows of ornament. But we can't afford the made-in-Japan splendors at the five-and-dime. So we do what we've always done: sit for days at the kitchen table with scissors and crayons and stacks of colored paper. I make sketches and my friend cuts them out: lots of cats, fish too (because they're easy to draw), some apples, some watermelons, a few winged angels devised from saved-up sheets of Hershey-bar tin foil. We use safety pins to attach these creations to the tree; as a final touch, we sprinkle the branches with shredded cotton (picked in August for this purpose). My friend, surveying the effect, clasps her hands together. "Now honest, Buddy. Doesn't it look good enough to eat?" Queenie tries to eat an angel.

After weaving and ribboning holly wreaths for all the front windows, our next project is the fashioning of family gifts. Tie-dye scarves for the ladies, for the men a home-brewed lemon and licorice and aspirin syrup to be taken "at the first Symptoms of a Cold and after Hunting." But when it comes time for making each other's gift, my friend and I separate to work secretly. I would like to buy her a pearl-handled knife, a radio, a whole pound of chocolate-covered cherries (we tasted some once, and she always swears: "I could live on them, Buddy, Lord yes I could—and that's not taking His name in vain"). Instead, I am building her a kite. She would like to give me a bicycle (she's said so on several million occasions: "If only I could, Buddy. It's bad enough in life to do without something *you* want; but confound it, what gets my goat is not being able to give somebody something you want *them* to have. Only one of these days I will, Buddy. Locate you a bike. Don't ask how. Steal it, maybe"). Instead, I'm fairly certain that she is building me a kite—the same as last year, and the year before: the year before that we exchanged slingshots. All of which is fine by me. For we are champion kite-fliers who study the wind like sailors; my friend, more accomplished than I, can get a kite aloft when there isn't enough breeze to carry clouds.

Christmas Eve afternoon we scrape together a nickel and go to the butcher's to buy Queenie's traditional gift, a good gnawable beef bone. The bone, wrapped in funny paper, is placed high in the tree near the silver star. Queenie knows it's there. She squats at the foot of the tree staring up in a trance of greed: when bedtime arrives she refuses to budge. Her excitement is equaled by my own. I kick the covers and turn my pillow as though it were a scorching summer's night. Somewhere a rooster crows: falsely, for the sun is still on the other side of the world.

"Buddy, are you awake?" It is my friend, calling from her room, which is next to mine; and an instant later she is sitting on my bed holding a candle. "Well, I can't sleep a hoot," she declares. "My mind's jumping like a jack rabbit. Buddy, do you think Mrs. Roosevelt will serve our cake at dinner?" We huddle in the bed, and she squeezes my hand I-love-you. "Seems like your hand used to be so much smaller. I guess I hate to see you grow up. When you're grown up, will we still be friends?" I say always. "But I feel so bad, Buddy. I wanted so bad to give you a bike. I tried to sell my cameo Papa gave me. Buddy"—she hesitates, as though embarrassed—"I made you another kite." Then I confess that I made her one, too; and we laugh. The candle burns too short to hold. Out it goes, exposing the starlight, the stars spinning at the window like a visible caroling that slowly, slowly daybreak silences. Possibly we doze; but the beginnings of dawn splash us like cold water: we're up, wide-eyed and wandering while we wait for others to waken. Quite deliberately my friend drops a kettle on the kitchen floor. I tap-dance in front of closed doors. One by one the household emerges, looking as though they'd like to kill us both; but it's Christmas, so they can't. First, a gorgeous breakfast: just everything you can imagine—from flapjacks and fried squirrel to hominy grits and honey-in-the-comb. Which puts everyone in a good humor except my friend and me. Frankly, we're so impatient to get at the presents we can't eat a mouthful.

Well, I'm disappointed. Who wouldn't be? With socks, a Sunday school shirt, some handkerchiefs, a hand-me-down sweater and a year's subscription to a religious magazine for children. *The Little Shepherd.* It makes me boil. It really does.

My friend has a better haul. A sack of Satsumas,[5] that's her best present. She is proudest, however, of a white wool shawl knitted by her married sister. But she *says* her favorite gift is the kite I built her. And it *is* very beautiful; though not as beautiful as the one she made me, which is blue and scattered with gold and green Good Conduct stars; moreover, my name is painted on it, "Buddy."

"Buddy, the wind is blowing."

The wind is blowing, and nothing will do till we've run to a pasture below the house where Queenie has scooted to bury her bone (and where, a winter hence, Queenie will be buried, too). There, plunging through the healthy waist-high grass, we unreel our kites, feel them twitching at the string like sky fish as they swim into the wind. Satisfied, sun-warmed, we sprawl in the grass and peel Satsumas and watch our kites cavort. Soon I forget the socks and hand-me-down sweater. I'm as happy as if we'd already won the fifty-thousand-dollar Grand Prize in that coffee-naming contest.

"My, how foolish I am!" my friend cries, suddenly alert, like a woman remembering too late she has biscuits in the oven. "You know what I've always thought?" she asks in a tone of discovery, and not smiling at me but a point beyond. "I've always thought a body would have to be sick and dying before they saw the Lord. And I imagined that when He came it would be like looking at the Baptist window: pretty as colored glass with the sun pouring through, such a shine you don't know it's getting dark. And it's been a comfort: to think of that shine taking away all the spooky feeling. But I'll wager it never happens. I'll wager at the very end a body realizes the Lord has already shown Himself. That things as they are"—her hand circles in a gesture that gathers clouds and kites and grass and Queenie pawing earth over her bone—"just what they've always seen, was seeing Him. As for me, I could leave the world with today in my eyes."

This is our last Christmas together.

Life separates us. Those who Know Best decide that I belong in a military school. And so follows a miserable succession of bugle-blowing prisons, grim reveille-ridden summer camps. I have a new home too. But it doesn't count. Home is where my friend is, and there I never go.

And there she remains, puttering around the kitchen. Alone with Queenie. Then alone. ("Buddy dear," she writes in her wild hard-to-read script, "yesterday Jim Macy's horse kicked Queenie bad. Be thankful she didn't feel much. I wrapped her in a Fine Linen sheet and rode her in the

---

[5] *Satsumas:* medium-sized, seedless fruits with thin, smooth skins.

buggy down to Simpson's pasture where she can be with all her Bones . . ."). For a few Novembers she continues to bake her fruitcakes single-handed; not as many, but some: and, of course, she always sends me "the best of the batch." Also, in every letter she encloses a dime wadded in toilet paper: "See a picture show and write me the story." But gradually in her letters she tends to confuse me with her other friend, the Buddy who died in the 1880s; more and more thirteenths are not the only days she stays in bed: a morning arrives in November, a leafless birdless coming of winter morning, when she cannot rouse herself to exclaim: "Oh my, it's fruitcake weather!"

And when that happens, I know it. A message saying so merely confirms a piece of news some secret vein had already received, severing from me an irreplaceable part of myself, letting it loose like a kite on a broken string. That is why, walking across a school campus on this particular December morning, I keep searching the sky. As if I expected to see, rather like hearts, a lost pair of kites hurrying toward heaven.

DISCUSSION

1. All of us are affected by the people we love. Slowly, as a result of such relationships, we learn different attitudes toward life. What has Buddy learned from his experiences with his old cousin?

2. Because he wants you to experience this memory with him, Truman Capote takes you back into that time by describing in detail the sights, smells, and sounds of "fruitcake weather." What are they?

3. The author tells us how a sixty-something-year-old woman and a seven-year-old boy are bound together as "each other's best friend." What draws them together? How are they similar?

4. Through *characterization* (see page 100) an author makes us see a character as a real person. Capote never tells us his best friend's name. But he tells us so much more about her. What lines best help you to see and to know her?

5. A writer's choice of words is called *diction*. Through a precise choice of precise words, writers can make us hear, feel, see, and understand, what they wish us to. Depending on her or his purpose, a writer may choose *tired* rather than *weary*, or *sizzling* rather than *hot*. Truman Capote's diction is vivid and precise. On page 170 he calls his cousin's hat a straw cartwheel instead of a straw hat, and by so doing, he has made that hat real to his readers. What examples of Capote's diction do you find especially effective?

For further activities, see page 214.

In December, 1955, Mrs. Rosa Parks was told to give up her seat on a Montgomery, Alabama, bus to a white passenger, as the law required. Mrs. Parks refused. She was arrested. That arrest led to the Montgomery bus boycott.

The Day of Days, December 5

MARTIN LUTHER KING, JR.

My wife and I awoke earlier than usual on Monday morning. We were up and fully dressed by five-thirty. The day for the protest had arrived, and we were determined to see the first act of this unfolding drama. I was still saying that if we could get 60 percent cooperation the venture would be a success.

Fortunately, a bus stop was just five feet from our house. This meant that we could observe the opening stages from our front window. The first bus was to pass around six o'clock. And so we waited through an interminable half hour. I was in the kitchen drinking my coffee when I heard Coretta cry, "Martin, Martin, come quickly!" I put down my cup and ran toward the living room. As I approached the front window Coretta pointed joyfully to a slowly moving bus: "Darling, it's empty!" I could hardly believe what I saw. I knew that the South Jackson line, which ran past our house, carried more Negro passengers than any other line in Montgomery, and that this first bus was usually filled with domestic workers going to their jobs. Would all of the other buses follow the pattern that had been set by the first? Eagerly we waited for the next bus. In fifteen minutes it rolled down the street, and, like the first, it was empty. A third bus appeared, and it too was empty of all but two white passengers.

I jumped in my car and for almost an hour I cruised down every major street and examined every passing bus. During this hour, at the

peak of the morning traffic, I saw no more than eight Negro passengers riding the buses. By this time I was jubilant. Instead of the 60 percent cooperation we had hoped for, it was becoming apparent that we had reached almost 100 percent. A miracle had taken place. The once dormant and quiescent Negro community was now fully awake.

All day long it continued. At the afternoon peak the buses were still as empty of Negro passengers as they had been in the morning. Students of Alabama State College, who usually kept the South Jackson bus crowded, were cheerfully walking or thumbing rides. Job holders had either found other means of transportation or made their way on foot. While some rode in cabs or private cars, others used less conventional means. Men were seen riding mules to work, and more than one horsedrawn buggy drove the streets of Montgomery that day.

During the rush hours the sidewalks were crowded with laborers and domestic workers, many of them well past middle age, trudging patiently to their jobs and home again, sometimes as much as twelve miles. They knew why they walked, and the knowledge was evident in the way they carried themselves. And as I watched them I knew that there is nothing more majestic than the determined courage of individuals willing to suffer and sacrifice for their freedom and dignity.

Many spectators had gathered at the bus stops to watch what was happening. At first they stood quietly, but as the day progressed they began to cheer the empty buses and laugh and make jokes. Noisy youngsters could be heard singing out, "No rider today." Trailing each bus through the Negro section were two policemen on motorcycles, assigned by the city commissioners, who claimed that Negro "goon squads" had been organized to keep other Negroes from riding the buses. In the course of the day the police succeeded in making one arrest. A college student who was helping an elderly woman across the street was charged with "intimidating passengers." But the "goon squads" existed only in the commission's imagination. No one was threatened or intimidated for riding the buses; the only harassment anyone faced was that of his own conscience.

Around nine-thirty in the morning I tore myself from the action of the city streets and headed for the crowded police court. Here Mrs. Parks was being tried for disobeying the city segregation ordinance. Her attorney, Fred D. Gray—the brilliant young Negro who later became the chief counsel for the protest movement—was on hand to defend her. After the judge heard the arguments, he found Mrs. Parks guilty and fined her ten dollars and court costs (a total of fourteen dollars). She appealed the case. This was one of the first clear-cut instances in which a Negro had been convicted for disobeying the

segregation law. In the past, either cases like this had been dismissed
or the people involved had been charged with disorderly conduct. So in
a real sense the arrest and conviction of Mrs. Parks had a two-fold impact: it was a precipitating factor to arouse the Negroes to positive action; and it was a test of the validity of the segregation law itself. I am
sure that supporters of such prosecutions would have acted otherwise
if they had had the prescience[1] to look beyond the moment. . . .

Meanwhile Roy Bennett had called several people together at
three o'clock to make plans for the evening mass meeting. Everyone
present was elated by the tremendous success that had already attended the protest. But beneath this feeling was the question, where
do we go from here? When E. D. Nixon reported on his discussion
with Abernathy and French earlier in the day, and their suggestions
for an *ad hoc*[2] organization, the group responded enthusiastically. The
next job was to elect the officers for the new organization.

As soon as Bennett had opened the nominations for president,
Rufus Lewis spoke from the far corner of the room: "Mr. Chairman, I
would like to nominate Reverend M. L. King for president." The motion was seconded and carried, and in a matter of minutes I was
unanimously elected. . . .

With the organizational matters behind us, we turned to a discussion of the evening meeting. Several people, not wanting the reporters
to know our future moves, suggested that we just sing and pray; if
there were specific recommendations to be made to the people, these
could be mimeographed and passed out secretly during the meeting.
This, they felt, would leave the reporters in the dark. Others urged
that something should be done to conceal the true identity of the leaders, feeling that if no particular name was revealed it would be safer
for all involved. After a rather lengthy discussion, E. D. Nixon rose
impatiently:

"We are acting like little boys," he said. "Somebody's name will
have to be known, and if we are afraid we might just as well fold up
right now. We must also be men enough to discuss our recommendations in the open; this idea of secretly passing something around on
paper is a lot of bunk. The white folks are eventually going to find it
out anyway. We'd better decide now if we are going to be fearless men
or scared boys."

With this forthright statement the air was cleared. Nobody would

---

[1] *prescience:* foreknowledge, foresight.
[2] *ad hoc:* for a specific purpose, case, or situation.

again suggest that we try to conceal our identity or avoid facing the issue head on. Nixon's courageous affirmation had given new heart to those who were about to be crippled by fear. . . .

Immediately the resolution committee set to drafting its statement. Despite our satisfaction at the success of the protest so far, we were still concerned. Would the evening meeting be well attended? Could we hope that the fortitude and enthusiasm of the Negro community would survive more than one such day of hardship? Someone suggested that perhaps we should reconsider our decision to continue the protest. "Would it not be better," said the speaker, "to call off the protest while it is still a success rather than let it go on a few more days and fizzle out? We have already proved our united strength to the white community. If we stop now we can get anything we want from the bus company, simply because they will have the feeling that we can do it again. But if we continue, and most of the people return to the buses tomorrow or the next day, the white people will laugh at us, and we will end up getting nothing." This argument was so convincing that we almost resolved to end the protest. But we finally agreed to let the mass meeting—which was only about an hour off—be our guide. If the meeting was well attended and the people were enthusiastic, we would continue; otherwise we would call off the protest that night.

Within five blocks of the church I noticed a traffic jam. Cars were lined up as far as I could see on both sides of the street. It was a moment before it occured to me that all of these cars were headed for the mass meeting. I had to park at least four blocks from the church, and as I started walking I noticed that hundreds of people were standing outside. In the dark night, police cars circled slowly around the area, surveying the orderly, patient, and good-humored crowd. The three or four thousand people who could not get into the church were to stand cheerfully throughout the evening listening to the proceedings on the loud-speakers that had been set up outside for their benefit. And when, near the end of the meeting, these speakers were silenced at the request of the white people in surrounding neighborhoods, the crowd would still remain quietly, content simply to be present.

It took fully fifteen minutes to push my way through to the pastor's study, where Dr. Wilson told me that the church had been packed since five o'clock. By now my doubts concerning the continued success of our venture were dispelled. The question of calling off the protest was now academic. The enthusiasm of these thousands of people swept everything along like an onrushing tidal wave.

It was some time before the remaining speakers could push their way to the rostrum through the tightly packed church. When the meeting began it was almost half an hour late. The opening hymn was the old familiar "Onward Christian Soldiers," and when that mammoth audience stood to sing, the voices outside swelling the chorus in the church, there was a mighty ring like the glad echo of heaven itself.

Rev. W. F. Alford, minister of the Beulah Baptist Church, led the congregation in prayer, followed by a reading of the Scripture by Rev. U. J. Fields, minister of the Bell Street Baptist Church. Then the chairman introduced me. As the audience applauded, I rose and stood before the pulpit. Television cameras began to shoot from all sides. The crowd grew quiet.

Without manuscript or notes, I told the story of what had happened to Mrs. Parks. Then I reviewed the long history of abuses and insults that Negro citizens had experienced on the city buses. "But there comes a time," I said, "that people get tired. We are here this evening to say to those who have mistreated us so long that we are tired—tired of being segregated and humiliated; tired of being kicked about by the brutal feet of oppression." The congregation met this statement with fervent applause. "We had no alternative but to protest," I continued. "For many years, we have shown amazing patience. We have sometimes given our white brothers the feeling that we liked the way we were being treated. But we come here tonight to be saved from that patience that makes us patient with anything less than freedom and justice." Again the audience interrupted with applause.

Briefly I justified our actions, both morally and legally. "One of the great glories of democracy is the right to protest for right." Comparing our methods with those of the White Citizens Councils and the Ku Klux Klan, I pointed out that while "these organizations are protesting for the perpetuation of injustice in the community, we are protesting for the birth of justice in the community. Their methods lead to violence and lawlessness. But in our protest there will be no cross burnings. No white person will be taken from his home by a hooded Negro mob and brutally murdered. There will be no threats and intimidation. We will be guided by the highest principles of law and order."

With this groundwork for militant action, I moved on to words of caution. I urged the people not to force anybody to refrain from riding the buses. "Our method will be that of persuasion, not coercion. We will only say to the people, 'Let your conscience be your guide.' " Emphasizing the Christian doctrine of love, "our actions must be guided by the deepest principles of our Christian faith. Love must be our regulating ideal. Once again we must hear the words of Jesus echoing across the centuries: 'Love your enemies, bless them that curse you, and pray for them that despitefully use you.' If we fail to do this our protest will end up as a meaningless drama on the stage of history, and its memory will be shrouded with ugly garments of shame. In spite of the mistreatment that we have confronted we must not become bitter, and end up by hating our white brothers. As Booker T. Washington said, 'Let no man pull you so low as to make you hate him.' " Once more the audience responded enthusiastically.

Then came my closing statement. "If you will protest courageously, and yet with dignity and Christian love, when the history books are written in future generations, the historians will have to pause and say, 'There lived a great people—a black people—who injected new meaning and dignity into the veins of civilization.' This is our challenge and our overwhelming responsibility." As I took my seat the people rose to their feet and applauded. I was thankful to God that the message had gotten over and that the task of combining the militant and the moderate had been at least partially accomplished. The people had been as enthusiastic when I urged them to love as they were when I urged them to protest.

As I sat listening to the continued applause I realized that this speech had evoked more response than any speech or sermon I had ever delivered, and yet it was virtually unprepared. I came to see for the first time what the older preachers meant when they said, "Open your mouth and God will speak for you." While I would not let this experience tempt me to overlook the need for continued preparation, it would always remind me that God can transform man's weakness into his glorious opportunity.

When Mrs. Parks was introduced from the rostrum by E. N. French, the audience responded by giving her a standing ovation. She was their heroine. They saw in her courageous person the symbol of their hopes and aspirations.

Now the time had come for the all-important resolution. Ralph Abernathy read the words slowly and forcefully. The main substance of the resolution called upon the Negroes not to resume riding the buses until (1) courteous treatment by the bus operators was guaranteed; (2) passengers were seated on a first-come, first-served basis—Negroes seated from the back of the bus toward the front while whites seated from the front toward the back; (3) Negro bus operators were employed on predominantly Negro routes. At the words "All in favor of the motion stand," every person to a man stood up, and those who were already standing raised their hands. Cheers began to ring out from both inside and outside. The motion was carried unanimously. The people had expressed their determination not to ride the buses until conditions were changed.

At this point I had to leave the meeting and rush to the other side of town to speak at a YMCA banquet. As I drove away my heart was full. I had never seen such enthusiasm for freedom. And yet this enthusiasm was tempered by amazing self-discipline. The unity of purpose and *esprit de corps*[3] of these people had been indescribably moving. No historian would ever be able fully to describe this meeting and no sociologist would ever be able to interpret it adequately. One had to be a part of the experience really to understand it.

At the Ben Moore Hotel, as the elevator slowly moved up to the roof garden where the banquet was being held, I said to myself, victory is already won, no matter how long we struggle to attain the three points of the resolution. It is a victory infinitely larger than the bus situation. The real victory was in the mass meeting, where thousands of black people stood revealed with a new sense of dignity and destiny. . . .

That night we were starting a movement that would gain national recognition; whose echoes would ring in the ears of people of every nation; a movement that would astound the oppressor, and bring new hope to the oppressed. That night was Montgomery's moment in history.

[3] *esprit de corps* (ĕ-sprē′ də kôr′): feeling of enthusiasm and devotion among members of a group.

DISCUSSION

1. "And as I watched them I knew that there is nothing more majestic than the determined courage of individuals willing to suffer and sacrifice for their freedom and dignity" (page 184). What issue, more important than simply where one may sit on a bus, is at stake here? What does the boycott have to do with that issue?

2. During his speech, Dr. King quoted Booker T. Washington: "Let no man pull you so low as to make you hate him." What does that mean? Why do you suppose Dr. King's audience reacted so enthusiastically to it?

3. To whom was December 5, 1955, in Montgomery, Alabama, the "day of days"? What was the unfolding drama begun that day that would continue for decades?

For further activities, see page 214.

The Way to Rainy Mountain

N. SCOTT MOMADAY

A single knoll rises out of the plain in Oklahoma, north and west of the
Wichita Range. For my people, the Kiowas, it is an old landmark, and
they gave it the name Rainy Mountain. The hardest weather in the world
is there. Winter brings blizzards, hot tornadic winds arise in the spring,
and in summer the prairie is an anvil's edge. The grass turns brittle
brown, and it cracks beneath your feet. There are green belts along the
rivers and creeks, linear groves of hickory and pecan, willow and witch
hazel. At a distance in July or August the steaming foliage seems almost
to writhe in fire. Great green and yellow grasshoppers are everywhere in
the tall grass, popping up like corn to sting the flesh, and tortoises crawl
about on the red earth, going nowhere in the plenty of time. Loneliness
is an aspect of the land. All things in the plain are isolate; there is no

confusion of objects in the eye, but *one* hill or *one* tree or *one* man. To look upon that landscape in the early morning, with the sun at your back, is to lose the sense of proportion. Your imagination comes to life, and this, you think, is where Creation was begun.

I returned to Rainy Mountain in July. My grandmother had died in the spring, and I wanted to be at her grave. She had lived to be very old and at last infirm. Her only living daughter was with her when she died, and I was told that in death her face was that of a child.

I like to think of her as a child. When she was born, the Kiowas were living that last great moment of their history. For more than a hundred years they had controlled the open range from the Smoky Hill River to the Red, from the headwaters of the Canadian to the fork of the Arkansas and Cimarron. In alliance with the Comanches, they had ruled the whole of the southern Plains. War was their sacred business, and they were among the finest horsemen the world has ever known. But warfare for the Kiowas was preeminently a matter of disposition rather than of survival, and they never understood the grim, unrelenting advance of the U.S. Cavalry. When at last, divided and ill-provisioned, they were driven onto the Staked Plains in the cold rains of autumn, they fell into panic. In Palo Duro Canyon they abandoned their crucial stores to pillage and had nothing then but their lives. In order to save themselves, they surrendered to the soldiers at Fort Sill and were imprisoned in the old stone corral that now stands as a military museum. My grandmother was spared the humiliation of those high gray walls by eight or ten years, but she must have known from birth the affliction of defeat, the dark brooding of old warriors.

Her name was Aho, and she belonged to the last culture to evolve in North America. Her forebears came down from the high country in western Montana nearly three centuries ago. They were a mountain people, a mysterious tribe of hunters whose language has never been positively classified in any major group. In the late seventeenth century they began a long migration to the south and east. It was a journey toward the dawn, and it led to a golden age. Along the way the Kiowas were befriended by the Crows, who gave them the culture and religion of the Plains. They acquired horses, and their ancient nomadic spirit was suddenly free of the ground. They acquired Tai-me, the sacred Sun Dance doll, from that moment the object and symbol of their worship, and so shared in the divinity of the sun. Not least, they acquired the sense of destiny, therefore courage and pride. When they entered upon the southern Plains they had been transformed. No longer were they slaves to the simple necessity of survival; they were a lordly and dangerous society of fighters and thieves, hunters, and priests of the sun. According to their origin myth, they entered the world through a hollow log. From one point of view, their migration was the fruit of an old prophecy, for indeed they emerged from a sunless world.

Although my grandmother lived out her long life in the shadow of Rainy Mountain, the immense landscape of the continental interior lay like memory in her blood. She could tell of the Crows, whom she had never seen, and of the Black Hills, where she had never been. I wanted to see in reality what she had seen more perfectly in the mind's eye, and traveled fifteen hundred miles to begin my pilgrimage.

Yellowstone, it seemed to me, was the top of the world, a region of deep lakes and dark timber, canyons and waterfalls. But, beautiful as it is, one might have the sense of confinement there. The skyline in all directions is close at hand, the high wall of the woods and deep cleavages of shade. There is a perfect freedom in the mountains, but it belongs to the eagle and the elk, the badger and the bear. The Kiowas reckoned their stature by the distance they could see, and they were bent and blind in the wilderness.

Descending eastward, the highland meadows are a stairway to the plain. In July the inland slope of the Rockies is luxuriant with flax and buckwheat, stonecrop and larkspur. The earth unfolds and the limit of the land recedes. Clusters of trees, and animals grazing far in the distance, cause the vision to reach away and wonder to build upon the mind. The sun follows a longer course in the day and the sky is immense beyond all comparison. The great billowing clouds that sail upon it are shadows that move upon the grain like water, dividing light. Farther down, in the land of the Crows and Blackfeet, the plain is yellow. Sweet clover takes hold of the hills and bends upon itself to cover and seal the soil. There the Kiowas paused on their way; they had come to the place where they must change their lives. The sun is at home on the plains. Precisely there does it have the certain character of a god. When the Kiowas came to the land of the Crows, they could see the dark lees of the hills at dawn across the Bighorn River, the profusion of light on the grain shelves, the oldest deity ranging after the solstices. Not yet would they veer southward to the caldron of the land that lay below; they must wean their blood from the northern winter and hold the mountains a while longer in their view. They bore Tai-me in procession to the east.

A dark mist lay over the Black Hills, and the land was like iron. At the top of a ridge I caught sight of Devil's Tower upthrust against the gray sky as if in the birth of time the core of the earth had broken through its crust and the motion of the world was begun. There are things in nature that engender an awful quiet in the heart of man; Devil's Tower is one of them. Two centuries ago, because they could not do otherwise, the Kiowas made a legend at the base of the rock. My grandmother said:

Eight children were there at play, seven sisters and their brother. Suddenly the boy was struck dumb; he trembled and began to run upon his hands and feet. His fingers became claws, and his body was covered with fur. Directly there was a bear where the boy had been. The sisters were terrified; they ran, and the bear after them. They came to the stump of a great tree, and the tree spoke to them. It bade them climb upon it, and as they did so it began to rise into the air. The bear came to kill them, but they were just beyond its reach. It reared against the tree and scored the bark all around with its claws. The seven sisters were borne into the sky, and they became the stars of the Big Dipper.

From that moment, and so long as the legend lives, the Kiowas have kinsmen in the night sky. Whatever they were in the mountains, they could be no more. However tenuous their well-being, however much they had suffered and would suffer again, they had found a way out of the wilderness.

My grandmother had a reverence for the sun, a holy regard that now is all but gone out of mankind. There was a wariness in her, and an ancient awe. She was Christian in her later years, but she had come a long way about, and she never forgot her birthright. As a child she had been to the Sun Dances; she had taken part in those annual rites, and by them she had learned the restoration of her people in the presence of Tai-me. She was about seven when the last Kiowa Sun Dance was held in 1887 on the Washita River above Rainy Mountain Creek. The buffalo were gone. In order to consummate the ancient sacrifice—to impale the head of a buffalo bull upon the medicine tree—a delegation of old men journeyed into Texas, there to beg and barter for an animal from the Goodnight herd. She was ten when the Kiowas came together for the last time as a living Sun Dance culture. They could find no buffalo; they had to hang an old hide from the sacred tree. Before the dance could begin, a company of soldiers rode out from Fort Sill under orders to disperse the tribe. Forbidden without cause the essential act of their faith, having seen the wild herds slaughtered and left to rot upon the ground, the Kiowas backed away forever from the medicine tree. That was July 20, 1890, at the great bend of the Washita. My grandmother was there. Without bitterness, and for as long as she lived, she bore a vision of deicide.

Now that I can have her only in memory, I see my grandmother in the several postures that were peculiar to her: standing at the wood stove on a winter morning and turning meat in a great iron skillet; sitting at the south window, bent above her beadwork, and afterwards, when her vision failed, looking down for a long time into the fold of her hands;

going out upon a cane, very slowly as she did when the weight of age came upon her; praying. I remember her most often at prayer. She made long, rambling prayers out of suffering and hope, having seen many things. I was never sure that I had the right to hear, so exclusive were they of all mere custom and company. The last time I saw her she prayed standing by the side of her bed at night, . . . the light of a kerosene lamp moving upon her dark skin. Her long, black hair, always drawn and braided in the day, lay upon her shoulders . . . like a shawl. I do not speak Kiowa, and I never understood her prayers, but there was something inherently sad in the sound, some merest hesitation upon the syllables of sorrow. She began in a high and descending pitch, exhausting her breath to silence; then again and again—and always the same intensity of effort, of something that is, and is not, like urgency in the human voice. Transported so in the dancing light among the shadows of her room, she seemed beyond the reach of time. But that was illusion; I think I knew then that I should not see her again.

Houses are like sentinels in the plain, old keepers of the weather watch. There, in a very little while, wood takes on the appearance of great age. All colors wear soon away in the wind and rain, and then the wood is burned gray and the grain appears and the nails turn red with rust. The windowpanes are black and opaque; you imagine there is nothing within, and indeed there are many ghosts, bones given up to the land. They stand here and there against the sky, and you approach them for a longer time than you expect. They belong in the distance; it is their domain.

Once there was a lot of sound in my grandmother's house, a lot of coming and going, feasting and talk. The summers there were full of excitement and reunion. The Kiowas are a summer people; they abide the cold and keep to themselves, but when the season turns and the land becomes warm and vital they cannot hold still; an old love of going returns upon them. The aged visitors who came to my grandmother's house when I was a child were made of lean and leather, and they bore themselves upright. They wore great black hats and bright ample shirts that shook in the wind. They rubbed fat upon their hair and wound their braids with strips of colored cloth. Some of them painted their faces and carried the scars of old and cherished enmities. They were an old council of warlords, come to remind and be reminded of who they were. Their wives and daughters served them well. The women might indulge themselves; gossip was at once the mark and compensation of their servitude. They made loud and elaborate talk among themselves, full of jest and gesture, fright and false alarm. They went abroad in fringed and flowered shawls, bright beadwork and German silver. They were at home in the kitchen, and they prepared meals that were banquets.

There were frequent prayer meetings, and great nocturnal feasts. When I was a child I played with my cousins outside, where the lamplight fell upon the ground and the singing of the old people rose up around us and carried away into the darkness. There were a lot of good things to eat, a lot of laughter and surprise. And afterwards, when the quiet returned, I lay down with my grandmother and could hear the frogs away by the river and feel the motion of the air.

Now there is a funeral silence in the rooms, the endless wake of some final word. The walls have closed in upon my grandmother's house. When I returned to it in mourning, I saw for the first time in my life how small it was. It was late at night, and there was a white moon, nearly full. I sat for a long time on the stone steps by the kitchen door. From there I could see out across the land; I could see the long row of trees by the creek, the low light upon the rolling plains, and the stars of the Big Dipper. Once I looked at the moon and caught sight of a strange thing. A cricket had perched upon the handrail, only a few inches away from me. My line of vision was such that the creature filled the moon like a fossil. It had gone there, I thought, to live and die, for there, of all places, was its small definition made whole and eternal. A warm wind rose up and purled like the longing within me.

The next morning I awoke at dawn and went out on the dirt road to Rainy Mountain. It was already hot, and the grasshoppers began to fill the air. Still, it was early in the morning, and the birds sang out of the shadows. The long yellow grass on the mountain shone in the bright light, and a scissortail hied above the land. There, where it ought to be, at the end of a long and legendary way, was my grandmother's grave. Here and there on the dark stones were ancestral names. Looking back once, I saw the mountain and came away.

DISCUSSION

1. Momaday states, "My grandmother had a reverence for the sun, a holy regard that now is all but gone out of mankind." What do you think he means?

2. The author also says that war was the Kiowas' "sacred business." What does he mean? Why then were the Kiowas defeated by the United States Cavalry?

3. How does Rainy Mountain reflect and symbolize the fate of American Indians? Do you think that either the author or his grandmother were bitter about what happened to the Indians? Should they be?

A Puerto Rican Pilgrimage

JACK AGÜEROS

I was born in Harlem in 1934. We lived on 111th Street off Fifth Avenue. It was a block of mainly three-story buildings—with brick fronts, or brownstone, or limestone imitations of brownstone. Our apartment was a three-room first-floor walk-up. It faced north and had three windows on the street, none in back. There was a master bedroom, a living room, a kitchen-dining room, a foyer with a short hall, and a bathroom. In the kitchen there was an air shaft to evacuate cooking odors and grease—we converted it to a chimney for Santa Claus.

The kitchen was dominated by a large Victorian china closet, and the built-in wall shelves were lined with oilcloth, trimmed with ruffle, both decorated by brilliant and miniature fruits. Prominent on a wall of the kitchen was a large reproduction of a still life, a harvest table full of produce, framed and under glass. From it, I learned to identify apples, pumpkins, bananas, pears, grapes, and melons, and "peaches without worms." A joke between my mother and me. (A peach we had bought in the city market, under the New Haven's elevated tracks, bore, like the trains above, passengers.)

On one shelf of the kitchen, over the stove, there was a lineup of ceramic canisters that carried words like "nutmeg," "ginger," and "basil." I did not know what those words meant and I don't know if my mother did either. "Spices," she would say, and that was that. They were of a yellow color that was not unlike the yellow of the stove. The kitchen was itself painted yellow, I think, very pale. But I am sure of one thing, it was not "Mickey Moused." "Mickey Mousing" was a technique used by house painters to decorate the areas of the walls that were contained by wood molding. Outside the molding they might paint a solid green. Inside the wood mold, the same solid green. Then with a twisted-up rag dipped in a lighter green they would trace random patterns.

We never used wallpaper or rugs. Our floors were covered with linoleum in every room. My father painted the apartment every year before Christmas, and in addition, he did all the maintenance, doing his own plastering and plumbing. No sooner would we move into an apartment than my father would repair holes or cracks, and if there were bulges in the plaster, he would break them open and redo the area—sometimes a whole wall. He would immediately modify the bathrooms to add a shower with separate valves, and usually as a routine matter, he cleaned out all the elbow traps, and changed all the washers on faucets. This was true of the other families in the buildings where I lived. Not a December came without a painting of the apartment.

We had Louis XIV furniture in the living room, reflected in the curved glass door and curved glass sides of the china closet. On the walls of the living room hung two prints that I loved. I would spend hours playing games with my mother based on the pictures, making up stories, etc. One day at Brooklyn College, a slide projector slammed, and I awoke after having dozed off during a dull lecture to see Van Gogh's "The Gleaners" on the screen. I almost cried. Another time I came across the other print in a book. A scene of Venice by Canaletto.

The important pieces of the living room, for me, were a Detrola radio with magic-eye tuning and the nightingale, Keero. The nightingale and the radio went back before my recollection. The bird could not stop singing, and people listened on the sidewalk below and came upstairs offering to buy Keero. . . .

Puppy, a white Spitz, was my constant companion. Puppy slept at the foot of my bed from the first day he came to our house till the day he died, when I was eleven or twelve and he was seven or eight.

My *madrina* lived on the third floor of our building, and for all practical purposes, her apartment and ours formed a duplex. My godmother really was my second mother. Rocking me to sleep, playing her guitar, and singing me little songs, she used to say, "I'm your real mother, 'cause I love you more." But I knew that wasn't so.

Carmen Diaz, my mother, came to New York in 1931. Her brother, a career soldier, had sent for her with the intention of taking her up to Plattsburg, where he was stationed. Like my father, she arrived in New York on a steamer. My uncle had planned to show his kid sister the big city before leaving for Plattsburg,

but during a week in New York my mother was convinced to stay. More opportunities, and other Spanish-speaking people, were the reasons that changed her mind.

Carmen had big plans for her life in America, intending to go to school and study interior decorating. But the Puerto Ricans who came to New York at that time found life in the city tough. It was the Depression, and work was hard to come by. My mother went from job to job for about six months and finally landed a job in the garment district as a seamstress. Twenty years later, she retired from the ILGWU,[1] her dream of becoming a decorator waylaid by bumping into my father on a Manhattan street and reviving their old romance. My father had been back in America since the mid-twenties. In America he remembers working a long day to earn $1.25. After a time, he found a job in a restaurant that paid nine dollars a week and provided two meals a day. That was a good deal, even at a six-day week, twelve to fifteen hours a day.

I am an only child. My parents and I always talked about my becoming a doctor. . . . A doctor helped everybody, rich and poor, white and black. If I became a doctor, I could study hay fever and find a cure for it, my godmother would say. Also, I could take care of my parents when they were old. I like the idea of helping, and for nineteen years my sole ambition was to study medicine.

My house had books, not many, but my parents encouraged me to read. As I became a good reader they bought books

---

[1] *ILGWU:* International Ladies Garment Workers Union.

for me and never refused me money for their purchase. My father once built a bookcase for me. It was an important moment, for I had always believed that my father was not too happy about my being a bookworm.

The atmosphere at home was always warm. We seemed to be a popular family. We entertained frequently, with two standing parties a year—at Christmas and for my birthday. Parties were always large. My father would dismantle the beds and move all the furniture so that the full two rooms could be used for dancing. My mother would cook up a storm, particularly at Christmas. *Pasteles, lechon asado, arroz con gandules,* and a lot of *coquito* to drink (meat-stuffed plantain, roast pork, rice with pigeon peas, and coconut nog). My father always brought in a band. They played without compensation and were guests at the party. They ate and drank and danced while a victrola covered the intermissions. One year my father brought home a whole pig and hung it in the foyer doorway. He and mother prepared it by rubbing it down with oil, oregano, and garlic. After preparation, the pig was taken down and carried over to a local bakery where it was cooked and returned home. Parties always went on till daybreak, and in addition to the band, there were always volunteers to sing and declaim poetry.

My mother kept an immaculate household. Bedspreads (chenille seemed to be very in) and lace curtains, washed at home like everything else, were hung up on huge racks with rows of tight nails. The racks were assembled in the living room, and the moisture from the wet bedspreads would fill the apartment. In a

sense, that seems to be the lasting image of that period of my life. The house was clean. The neighbors were clean. The streets, with few cars, were clean. The buildings were clean and uncluttered with people on the stoops. The park was clean. The visitors to my house were clean, and the relationships that my family had with other Puerto Rican families, and the Italian families that my father had met through baseball and my mother through the garment center, were clean. Second Avenue was clean and most of the apartment windows had awnings.

There was always music, there seemed to be no rain, and snow did not become slush. School was fun, we wrote essays about how grand America was, we put up hunchbacked cats at Halloween, we believed Santa Claus visited everyone. I believed everyone was Catholic. I grew up with dogs, nightingales, my godmother's guitar, rocking chair, cat, guppies, my father's occasional roosters, kept in a cage on the fire escape. Laundry delivered and collected by horse and wagon, fruits and vegetables sold the same way, windowsill refrigeration in winter, iceman and box in summer. The police my friends, likewise the teachers. . . .

My family moved in 1941 to Lexington Avenue into a larger apartment where I could have my own room. It was a light, sunny, railroad flat on the top floor of a well-kept building. I transferred to a new school, and whereas before my classmates had been mostly black, the new school had few blacks. The classes were made up of Italians, Irish, Jews, and a sprinkling of Puerto Ricans. My block was populated by Jews, Italians, and Puerto Ricans.

And then a whole series of different events began. I went to junior high school. We played in the backyards, where we tore down fences to build fires to cook stolen potatoes. We tore up whole hedges, because the green tender limbs would not burn when they were peeled, and thus made perfect skewers for our stolen "mickies." We played tag in the abandoned buildings, tearing the plaster off the walls, tearing the wire lath off the wooden slats, tearing the wooden slats themselves, good for fires, for kites, for sword fighting. We ran up and down the fire escapes playing tag and over and across many rooftops. The war ended and the heavy Puerto Rican migration began. The Irish and the Jews disappeared from the neighborhood. The Italians tried to consolidate east of Third Avenue.

What caused the clean and open world to end? Many things. Into an ancient neighborhood came pouring four to five times more people than it had been designed to hold. . . . The sudden surge in numbers caused new resentments, and prejudice was intensified. Some were forced to live in cellars, and were then characterized as cave dwellers.

Kids came who were confused by the new surroundings; their Puerto Ricanness forced us against a mirror asking, "If they are Puerto Ricans, what are we?" and thus they confused us. In our confusion we were sometimes pathetically reaching out, sometimes pathologically striking out. Gangs. Drugs. Wine. Smoking. Girls. Dances and slow-drag music. . . . Territories, brother gangs, and war councils establishing rules for right of way on blocks and avenues and for seating in the local theater. Pegged pants and zip guns. Slang.

. . . Education collapsed. Every classroom had ten kids who spoke no English. Black, Italian, Puerto Rican relations in the classroom were good, but we all knew we couldn't visit one another's neighborhoods. Sometimes we could not move too freely within our own blocks. On 109th, from the lamp post west, the Latin Aces, and from the lamp post east, the Senecas, the "club" I belonged to. The kids who spoke no English became known as Marine Tigers, picked up from a popular Spanish song. (The *Marine Tiger* and the *Marine Shark* were two ships that sailed from San Juan to New York and brought over many, many migrants from the island.)

The neighborhood had its boundaries. Third Avenue and east, Italian. Fifth Avenue and west, black. South, there was a hill on 103rd Street known locally as Cooney's Hill. When you got to the top of the hill, something strange happened: America began, because from the hill south was where the "Americans" lived . . . in a better neighborhood.

When, as a group of Puerto Rican kids, we decided to go swimming to Jefferson Park Pool, we knew we risked a fight and a beating from the Italians. And when we went to La Milagrosa Church in Harlem, we knew we risked a fight and a beating from the blacks. But when we went over Cooney's Hill, we risked dirty looks, disapproving looks, and questions from the police like, "What are you doing in this neighborhood?" and "Why don't you kids go back where you belong?"

Where we belonged! Man, I had written compositions about America. Didn't I belong on the Central Park tennis courts, even if I didn't know how to play? . . .

Weren't these policemen working for me too?

My mother leads me by the hand and carries a plain brown shopping bag. We enter an immense airplane hangar. Structural steel crisscrosses on the ceiling and walls: large round and square rivets look like buttons or bubbles of air trapped in the girders. There are long metallic counters with people bustling behind them. It smells of C.N. disinfectant. Many people stand on many lines up to these counters; there are many conversations going on simultaneously. The huge space plays tricks with voices and a very eerie combination of sounds results. A white cabbage is rolled down a counter at us. We retaliate by throwing down stamps.

For years I thought that sequence happened in a dream. The rolling cabbage rolled in my head, and little unrelated incidents seemed to bring it to the surface of my mind. I could not understand why I remembered a once-dreamt dream so vividly. . . . One day I asked my mother if she knew anything about it.

"That was home relief, 1937 or 1938. You were no more than four years old then. Your father had been working at a restaurant and I had a job downtown. I used to take you every morning to Dona Eduvije who cared for you all day. She loved you very much, and she was very clean and neat, but I used to cry on my way to work, wishing I could stay home with my son and bring him up like a proper mother would. But I guess I was fated to be a workhorse. When I was pregnant, I would get on the crowded subway and go to work. I would get on a crowded elevator up. Then down. Then back on the subway. Every day I was afraid that the crowd would hurt me, that I would lose my baby. But I had to work. I worked for the WPA [2] right into my ninth month."

My mother was telling it "like it was," and I sat stupefied, for I could not believe that what she said applied to the time I thought of as open and clean. I had been existing in my life like a small plant in a bell jar, my parents defining my awareness. There were things all around me I could not see.

"When you were born we had been living as boarders. It was hard to find an apartment, even in Harlem. You saw signs that said 'No Renting to Colored or Spanish.' That meant Puerto Ricans. We used to say, 'This is supposed to be such a great country?' But with a new baby we were determined not to be boarders and we took an apartment on 111th Street. Soon after we moved, I lost my job because my factory closed down. Your father was making seven or eight dollars a week in a terrible job in a carpet factory. They used to clean rugs, and your father's hands were always in strong chemicals. You know how funny some of his fingernails are? It was from that factory. He came home one night and he was looking at his fingers, and he started saying that he didn't come to this country to lose his hands. He wanted to hold a bat and play ball and he wanted to work—but he didn't want to lose his hands. So he quit the job and went to a restaurant for less pay. With me out of work, a new apartment and therefore

[2] *WPA:* Works Project Administration.

higher rent, we couldn't manage. Your father was furious when I mentioned home relief. He said he would rather starve than go on relief.

"But I went and filled out the papers and answered all the questions and swallowed my pride when they treated me like an intruder. I used to say to them, 'Find me a job—get my husband a better job—we don't want home relief.' But we had to take it. And all that mess with the stamps in exchange for food. And they used to have weekly 'specials' sort of— but a lot of things were useless—because they were American food. I don't remember if we went once a week or once every two weeks. You were so small I don't know how you remember that place and the long lines. It didn't last long because your father had everybody trying to find him a better job and finally somebody did. Pretty soon I went into the WPA and thank God, we never had to deal with those people again. I don't know how you remember that place, but I wish you didn't. I wish I could forget that home relief thing myself. It was the worst time for your father and me. He still hates it.

"You don't know how hard it was being married to your father then. He was young and very strong and very active and he wanted to work. Welfare deeply disturbed him, and I was afraid that he would actually get very violent if an investigator came to the house. They had a terrible way with people, like throwing that cabbage, that was the way they gave you everything, the way we used to throw the kitchen slop to the pigs in Puerto Rico. Some giving! Your father was, is, *muy macho,* and I used to worry

if anybody says anything or gives him that why-do-you-people-come-here-to-ruin-things look he'll be in jail for thirty years. He almost got arrested once when you were just a baby. We went to a hospital clinic—I don't remember now if it was Sydenham or Harlem Hospital—you had a swelling around your throat—and the doctor told me, 'Put on cold compresses.' I said I did that and it didn't help. The doctor said, 'Then put hot compresses.' Your father blew up. In his broken English, he asked the doctor . . . to transfer over to the stable on 104th Street. 'You do better with horses— maybe they don't care what kind of compresses they get.'

"One morning your father tells me, 'I got a new job. I start today driving a truck delivering soft drinks.' That night I ask him about the job—he says, 'I quit— bunch of Mafia—I went to the first four places on my list and each storeowner said, "I didn't order any soda." So I got the idea real fast. The Mafia was going to leave soda in each place and then make the guys buy from them only. As soon as I figured it out, I took the truck back, left it parked where I got it, and didn't even say good-bye.' The restaurant took him back. They liked him. The chef used to give him eggs and meats; it was very important to us. Your father never could keep still (still can't), so he was loved wherever he worked. I feel sorry for people on welfare—forget about the cabbage—I never should have taken you there."

When a Puerto Rican comes to America, he comes looking for a job. He takes the cold as one of a negative series of givens. The mad hustle, the filthy city, filthy air, filthy housing, sardine transportation, are in the series. He knows life will be tough and dangerous. But he thinks he can make a buck. And in his mind, there is only one tableau: himself retired, owner of his home in Puerto Rico, chickens cackling in the back yard.

It startles me still, though it has been five years since my parents went back to the island. I never believed them. My father, driving around New York for the Housing Authority, knowing more streets in more boroughs than I do, and my mother, curious in her later years about museums and theaters, and reading my books as fast as I would put them down, then giving me cryptic reviews. Salinger is really silly (*Catcher in the Rye*), but entertaining. That evil man deserved to die (*Moby Dick*). He's too much (Dostoevski in *Crime and Punishment*). I read this when I was a little girl in school (*Hamlet* and *Macbeth*). It's too sad for me (*Cry, the Beloved Country*).

My father, intrigued by the thought of passing the foreman's exam, sitting down with a couple of arithmetic books, and teaching himself at age fifty-five to do work problems and mixture problems and fractions and decimals, and going into the civil service exam and scoring a seventy-four and waiting up one night for me to show me three poems he had writ-

ten. These two cosmopolites, gladiators without skills or language, battling hostile environments and prejudiced people and systems, had graduated from Harlem to the Bronx, had risen into America's dream-cherished lower middle class, and then put it down for Puerto Rico after thirty plus years.

What is a migration, when is it not just a long visit?

I was born in Harlem, and I live downtown. And I am a migrant, for if a migration is anything, it is a state of mind. I have known those . . . who lived in America twenty and thirty years and never voted, never attended a community meeting, never filed a complaint against a landlord, never informed the police when they were robbed or swindled. . . . Never appeared at the State or City Commission on Human Rights, never reported a business fraud. . . .

And I am very much a migrant because I am still not quite at home in America. Always there are . . . people inclined to throwing cabbages. I cannot "earn and return." . . . However, I approach the future with optimism: . . . a larger number of leaders like myself, trained in the university, tempered in the ghetto, and with a vision of America moving . . . to a society open and clean, accessible to anyone.

DISCUSSION

1. Agüeros and his mother remember the old days differently. How are their recollections different? What is the significance of the white cabbage?

2. "I cannot earn and return," the author says. What does he mean? Why can't he?

Later, Armstrong would say, "That first hour on the moon was hardly the time for long thoughts; we had specific jobs to do. Of course the sights were simply magnificent, beyond any visual experience that I had ever been exposed to," and Aldrin would describe it as "a unique, almost mystical environment." In fact, there is an edge of the unexplained to their reactions. Their characteristic matter-of-fact response is overcome occasionally by swoops of hyperbole. And to everyone's slight surprise, they were almost two hours late for their EVA.[1] Their estimate of time was off by close to fifty percent. For astronauts that was an error comparable to a carpenter mistaking an eight-foot stud for a twelve-foot piece. If a carpenter can look at a piece of wood and guess its length to the nearest quarter-inch, it is because he has been working with lengths all his life. Equally, people in some occupations have a close ability to estimate time.

With astronauts, whose every day in a simulator was a day laid out on the measure of a time-line, the estimate of time elapsed had to become acute. Armstrong and Aldrin had consistently fulfilled their tasks in less time than was allotted. Now, curiously, they fell behind, then further behind. There were unexpected problems of course—it took longer to bleed the pressure out of the Lunar Module than had been anticipated, and the cooling units in the backpacks were sluggish at first in operation, but whether from natural excitement and natural anxiety, or an unconscious preoccupation with lunar phenomena so subtle that it is just at the edge of their senses, any extract from the transcript at this point where they are helping to adjust the Portable Life Support System on each others' backs shows real lack of enunciation. Nowhere else do the NASA stenographers have as much difficulty with where one voice ends and another begins.

> Tranquility:[2] *Got it (garbled) prime rows in.*
> Tranquility: *Okay.*
> Tranquility: *(garbled)*
> Tranquility: *Let me do that for you.*
> Tranquility: *(Inaudible)*
> Tranquility: *Mark I*
> Tranquility: *(garbled) valves*

---

[1] *EVA:* extravehicular activity.
[2] *Tranquility:* the astronauts' radio code name, after the Sea of Tranquility, the portion of the moon on which they landed.

Tranquility: *(garbled)*
Tranquility: *Okay*
Tranquility: *All of the (garbled)*
Tranquility *(garbled) locked and lock locked.*
Tranquility: *Did you put it—*
Tranquility: *Oh, wait a minute*
Tranquility: *Should be (garbled)*
Tranquility: *(garbled)*
Tranquility: *Roger. (garbled)*
Tranquility: *I'll try it on the middle*
Tranquility: *All right, check my (garbled) valves vertical*
Tranquility: *Both vertical*
Tranquility: *That's two vertical*
Tranquility: *Okay*
Tranquility: *(garbled)*
Tranquility: *Locked and double-locked*
Tranquility: *Okay*
Tranquility: *Miss marked*
Tranquility: *Sure wish I would have shaved last night.*
PAO:[3] *That was a Buzz Aldrin comment.*

The hint is faint enough, but the hint exists—something was conceivably interfering with their sense of order. Could it have been the lunar gravity? Clock-time was a measure which derived from pendulums and spiral springs, clock-time was anchored right into the tooth of earth gravity—so a time might yet be coming when psychologists, not geologists, would be conducting experiments on the moon. Did lunar gravity have power like a drug to shift the sense of time?

Armstrong was connected at last to his PLSS. He was drawing oxygen from the pack he carried on his back. But the hatch door would not open. The pressure would not go low enough in the Lem.[4] Down near a level of one pound per square inch, the last bit of man-created atmosphere in Eagle seemed to cling to its constituency, reluctant to enter the vacuums of the moon. But they did not know if they could get the hatch door open with a vacuum on one side and even a small pressure on the other. It was taking longer than they thought. While it was not a large concern since there would be other means to open it—redundancies pervaded throughout—nonetheless, a concern must have intruded: how intolerably comic they would appear if they came

---

[3] *PAO:* public affairs officer, who provided commentary.
[4] *LEM:* lunar module, craft in which the astronauts landed.

all the way and then were blocked before a door they could not crack. That thought had to put one drop of perspiration on the back of the neck. Besides, it must have been embarrassing to begin so late. The world of television was watching, and the astronauts had exhibited as much sensitivity to an audience as any bride on her way down the aisle.

It was not until nine-forty at night, Houston time, that they got the hatch open at last. In the heat of running almost two hours late, ensconced in the armor of a man-sized spaceship, could they still have felt an instant of awe as they looked out that open hatch at a panorama of theater: the sky is black, but the ground is brightly lit, bright as footlights on the floor of a dark theater. A black and midnight sky, yet on the moon ground, "you could almost go out in your shirt-sleeves and get a suntan," Aldrin would say. "I remember thinking, 'Gee, if I didn't know where I was, I could believe that somebody had created this environment somewhere out in the West and given us another simulation to work in.'" Everywhere on that pitted flat were shadows dark as the sky above, shadows dark as mine shafts.

What a struggle to push out from that congested cabin, now twice congested in their bulky-wham suits, no feeling of obstacle against their flesh, their sense of touch dead and numb, spaceman body manipulated out into the moon world like an upright piano turned by movers on the corner of the stairs.

"You're lined up on the platform. Put your left foot to the right a little bit. Okay, that's good. Roll left."

Armstrong was finally on the porch. Could it be with any sense of an alien atmosphere receiving the fifteen-layer encapsulations of the pack and suit on his back? Slowly, he climbed down the ladder. Archetypal, he must have felt, a boy descending the rungs in the wall of an abandoned well, or was it Jack down the stalk? And there he was on the bottom, on the footpad of the leg of the Lem, a metal plate perhaps three feet across. Inches away was the soil of the moon. But first he jumped up again to the lowest rung of the ladder. A couple of hours later, at the end of the EVA, conceivably exhausted, the jump from the ground to the rung, three feet up, might be difficult in that stiff and heavy space suit, so he tested it now. "It takes," said Armstrong, "a pretty good little jump."

Now, with television working, and some fraction of the world peering at the murky image of this instant, poised between the end of one history and the beginning of another, he said quietly, "I'm at the foot of the ladder. The Lem footpads are only depressed in the surface about one or two inches, although the surface appears to be very very fine-grained as you get close to it. It's almost like a powder." One of Armstrong's rare confessions of uneasiness is focused later on this moment. "I don't recall any particular emotion or feeling other than a little caution, a desire to be sure it was safe to put my weight on that surface outside Eagle's footpad."

Did his foot tingle in the heavy lunar overshoe? "I'm going to step off the Lem now."

Did something in him shudder at the touch of the new ground? Or did he draw a sweet strength from the balls of his feet? Nobody was necessarily going ever to know.

"That's one small step for a man," said Armstrong, "one giant leap for mankind." He had joined the ranks of the forever quoted. Patrick Henry, Henry Stanley, and Admiral Dewey moved over for him.

Now he was out there, one foot on the moon, then the other foot on the moon, the powder like velvet underfoot. With one hand still on the ladder, he comments, "The surface is fine and powdery. I can . . . I can pick it up loosely with my toe." And as he releases his catch, the grains fall back slowly to the soil, a fan of feathers gliding to the floor. "It does adhere in fine layers like powdered charcoal to the sole and sides of my boots. I only go in a small fraction of an inch. Maybe an eighth of an inch. But I can see the footprints of my boots and the treads in the fine sand particles."

Capcom: "Neil, this is Houston. We're copying."

Yes, they would copy. He was like a man who goes into a wrecked building to defuse a new kind of bomb. He talks into a microphone as he works, for if a mistake is made, and the bomb goes off, it will be easier for the next man if every detail of his activities has been mentioned as he performed them. Now, he released his grip on the ladder and pushed off for a few steps on the moon, odd loping steps, almost thrust into motion like a horse trotting up a steep slope. It could have been a moment equivalent to the first steps he took as an infant for there was nothing to hold onto and he did not dare to fall—the ground was too hot, the rocks might tear his suit. Yet if he stumbled, he could easily go over for he could not raise his arms above his head nor reach to his knees, his arms in the pressure bladder stood out before him like sausages; so, if he tottered, the weight of the pack could twist him around, or drop him. They had tried to shape up simulations of lunar gravity while weighted in scuba suits at the bottom of a pool, but water was not a vacuum through which to move; so they had also flown in planes carrying two hundred pounds of equipment on their backs. The pilot would take the plane through a parabolic trajectory. There would be a period of twenty-two seconds at the top of the curve when a simulation of one-sixth gravity would be present, and the two hundred pounds of equipment would weigh no more than on the moon, no more than thirty-plus pounds, and one could take loping steps down the aisle of the plane, staggering through unforeseen wobbles or turbulence. Then the parabolic trajectory was done, the plane was diving, and it would have to pull out of the dive. That created the reverse of one-sixth gravity—it multiplied gravity by two and a half times. The two hundred pounds of equipment now weighed five hundred pounds and the astronauts had to be supported by other men straining to help them bear the weight. So simulations gave them time for hardly more than a clue before heavy punishment was upon them. But now he was out in the open endless lunar gravity, his body and the reflexes of his life obliged to adopt a new rhythm and schedule of effort, a new disclosure of grace.

Still, he seemed pleased after the first few steps. "There seems to be no difficulty in moving around as we suspected. It's even perhaps easier than the simulations. . . ." He would run a few steps and stop, run a few steps and stop. Perhaps it was not unlike directing the Lem when it hovered over the ground. One moved faster than on earth and with less effort, but it was harder to stop—one had to pick the place to halt from several yards ahead. Yes, it was easier once moving, but awkward at the beginning and the end because of the obdurate plastic bendings of the suit. And once standing at rest, the sense of the vertical was sly. One could be leaning further forward than one knew. Or leaning backward. Like a needle on a dial one would have to oscillate from side to side of the vertical to find position. Conceivably the sensation was not unlike skiing with a child on one's back.

It was time for Aldrin to descend the ladder from the Lem to the ground, and Armstrong's turn to give directions: "The shoes are about to come over the sill. Okay, now drop your PLSS down. There you go. You're clear. . . . About an inch clearance on top of your PLSS."

Aldrin spoke for future astronauts: "Okay, you need a little bit of arching of the back to come down. . . ."

When he reached the ground, Aldrin took a big and exuberant leap up the ladder again, as if to taste the pleasures of one-sixth gravity all at once. "Beautiful, beautiful," he exclaimed.

Armstrong: "Isn't that something. Magnificent sight out here."

Aldrin: "Magnificent desolation."

They were looking at a terrain which lived in a clarity of focus unlike anything they had ever seen on earth. There was no air, of course, and so no wind, nor clouds, nor dust, nor even the finest scattering of light from the smallest dispersal of microscopic particles on a clear day on earth, no, nothing visible or invisible moved in the vacuum before them. All light was pure. No haze was present, not even the invisible haze of the finest day—therefore objects did not go out of focus as they receded into the distance. If one's eyes were good enough, an object at a hundred yards was as distinct as a rock at a few feet. And their eyes were good enough. Just as one could not determine one's altitude above the moon, not from fifty miles up nor five, so now along the ground before them no distance was real, for all distances had the faculty to appear equally near if one peered at them through blinders and could not see the intervening details. Again the sense of being on a stage or on the lighted floor of a room so large one could not see where the dark ceiling began must have come upon them, for there were no hints of gathering evanescence in ridge beyond ridge; rather each outline was as severe as the one in front of it, and since the ground was filled with small craters of every size, from antholes to potholes to empty pools, and the horizon was near, four times nearer than on earth and sharp as the line drawn by a pencil, the moon ground seemed to slope and drop in all directions "like swimming in an ocean with six-foot or eight-foot swells and waves," Armstrong said later. "In that condition, you never can see very far away from where you are." But what they could see, they could see entirely—to the depth of their field of view at any instant their focus was complete. And as they swayed from side to side, so a sense of the vertical kept eluding them, the slopes of the craters about them seeming to tilt a few degrees to one side of the horizontal, then the other. On earth, one had only to incline one's body an inch or two and a sense of the vertical was gone, but on the moon they could lean over, then further over, lean considerably further over without beginning to fall. So verticals slid and oscillated. Rolling from side to side, they could as well have been on water, indeed their sense of the vertical was probably equal to the subtle uncertainty of the body when a ship is rolling on a quiet sea. "I say," said Aldrin, "the rocks are rather slippery."

They were discovering the powder of the moon soil was curious indeed, comparable in firmness and traction to some matter between sand and snow. While the Lem looked light as a kite, for its pads hardly rested on the ground and it appeared ready to lift off and blow away, yet their own feet sometimes sank for two or three inches into the soft powder on the slope of very small craters, and their soles would slip as the powder gave way under their boots. In other places the ground was firm and harder than sand, yet all of these variations were to be found in an area not a hundred feet out from the legs of the Lem. As he explored his footing, Aldrin sent back comments to Mission Control, reporting in the rapt professional tones of a coach instructing his team on the conditions of the turf in a new plastic football field.

Meanwhile Armstrong was transporting the television camera away from the Lem to a position where it could cover most of their activities. Once properly installed, he revolved it through a full panorama of their view in order that audiences on earth might have a clue to what he saw. But in fact the transmission was too rudimentary to give any sense of what was about them, that desert sea of rocks, rubble, small boulders, and crater lips.

Aldrin was now working to set up the solar wind experiment, a sheet of aluminum foil hung on a stand. For the next hour and a half, the foil would be exposed to the solar wind, an invisible, unfelt, but high-velocity flow of noble gases from the sun like argon, krypton, neon, and helium. For the astronauts, it was the simplest of procedures, no more difficult than setting up a piece of sheet music on a music stand. At the end of the EVA, however, the aluminum foil would be rolled up, inserted in the rock box, and delivered eventually to a laboratory in Switzerland uniquely equipped for the purpose. There any noble gases which had been trapped in the atomic lattice of the aluminum would be baked out in virtuoso procedures of quantitative analysis, and a closer knowledge of the components of the solar wind would be gained. Since the solar wind, it may be recalled, was diverted by the magnetosphere away from the earth it had not hitherto been available for casual study.

That was the simplest experiment to set up; the other two would be deployed about an hour later. One was a passive seismometer to measure erratic disturbances and any periodic vibrations, as well as moonquakes, and the impact of meteors in the weeks and months to follow; it was equipped to radio this information to earth, the energy for transmission derived from solar panels which extended out to either side, and thereby gave it the look of one of those spaceships of the future with thin extended paperlike wings which one sees in science fiction drawings. In any case it was so sensitive that the steps of the astronauts were recorded as they walked by. Finally there was a Laser Ranging Retro-Reflector, an LRRR (or LRQ for L R-cubed), and that was a mirror whose face was a hundred quartz crystals, black as coal, cut to a precision never obtained before in glass—one-third of an arc/sec. Since each quartz crystal was a corner of a rectangle, any ray of light striking one of the three faces in each crystal would bounce off the other two in such a way that the light would return in exactly the same direction it had been received. A laser beam sent up from earth would therefore reflect back to the place from which it was sent. The time it required to travel this half-million miles from earth to moon round trip, a journey of less than three seconds, could be measured so accurately that physicists might then discern whether the moon was drifting away from the earth a few centimeters a year, or (by using two lasers) whether Europe and America might be drifting apart some comparable distance, or even if the Pacific Ocean were contracting. These measurements could then be entered into the caverns of Einstein's General Theory of Relativity, and new proof or disproof of the great thesis could be obtained.

We may be certain the equipment was remarkable. Still, its packaging and its ease of deployment had probably done as much to advance its presence on the ship as any clear priority over other scientific equipment; the beauty of these items from the point of view of NASA was that the astronauts could set them up in a few minutes while working in their space suits, even set them up with inflated gloves so insensitive that special silicone pads had to be inserted at the fingertips in order to leave the astronauts not altogether numb-fingered in their manipulations. Yet these marvels of measurement would soon be installed on the moon with less effort than it takes to remove a vacuum cleaner from its carton and get it operating.

It was at this point that patriotism, the corporation, and the national taste all came to occupy the same head of a pin, for the astronauts next proceeded to set up the flag. But that operation, as always, presented its exquisite problems. There was, we remind ourselves, no atmosphere for the flag to wave in. Any flag made of cloth would droop, indeed it would dangle. Therefore, a species of starched plastic flag had to be employed, a flag which would stand out, there, out to the nonexistent breeze, flat as a slab of plywood. No, that would not do either. The flag was better crinkled and curled. Waves and billows were bent into it, and a full corkscrew of a curl at the end. There it stands for posterity, photographed in the twists of a high gale on the windless moon, curled up tin flag, numb as a pickled pepper.

Aldrin would hardly agree. "Being able to salute that flag was one of the more humble yet proud experiences I've ever had. To be able to look at the American flag and know how much so many people had put of themselves and their work into getting it where it was. We sensed—we really did—this almost mystical identification of all the people in the world at that instant."

Two minutes after the flag was up, the President of the United States put in his phone call. Let us listen one more time:

"Because of what you have done," said Nixon, "the heavens have become a part of man's world. And as you talk to us from the Sea of Tranquility, it inspires us to redouble our efforts to bring peace and tranquility to earth. . . ."

"Thank you, Mr. President. It's a great honor and privilege for us to be here representing not only the United States, but men of peace of all nations. . . ."

In such piety is the schizophrenia of the ages.

Immediately afterward, Aldrin practiced kicking moon dust, but he was somewhat broken up. Either reception was garbled, or Aldrin was temporarily incoherent. "They seem to leave," he said to the Capcom, referring to the particles, "and most of them have about the same angle of departure and velocity. From where I stand, a large portion of them will impact at a certain distance out. Several—the percentage is, of course, that will impact. . . ."

Capcom: "Buzz, this is Houston. You're cutting out on the end of your transmissions. Can you speak a little more forward into your microphone. Over."

Aldrin: "Roger. I'll try that."

Capcom: "Beautiful."

Aldrin: "Now I had that one inside my mouth that time."

Capcom: "It sounded a little wet."

And on earth, a handful of young scientists were screaming, "Stop wasting time with flags and presidents—collect some rocks!"

DISCUSSION

1. From what Mailer says, what effect, both physical and mental, do you think this experience had on astronauts Armstrong and Aldrin?

2. What did the astronauts think when they first stood on the moon? What exactly did they see? What was the moon like?

3. Mailer does not simply tell us that the moonwalk was a very difficult undertaking; he shows us. Find sentences in the text that show how difficult the mission was.

4. Norman Mailer frequently uses comparisons to help us see or understand something that is unfamiliar in terms of something that is familiar. Mailer says ". . . the sky is black, but the ground is brightly lit, bright as footlights on the floor of a dark theater." Also, ". . . shadows dark as the sky above, shadows dark as mine shafts." What other examples of this kind of comparison can you find?

For further activities, see page 214.

VOCABULARY

My Life (page 152)

1.   Isadora Duncan was American, but she spent a lot of time in Europe and England. The British and Americans both speak English, of course, but with slight differences. When Isadora referred to one of her brothers hiding in a cupboard, what mental image did you form? In England, a cupboard is a closet. Below are British English words for items that we call by other names. What do they mean?

lift	biscuit	bonnet	chemist
braces	jersey	torch	flat
lorry	spanner	boot	petrol

2.   You probably noticed also that the British spelling of some words is different from American spelling. How do Americans spell these words?

parlour	theatre	neighbourhood
harbour	realise	civilised

First Hour on the Moon (page 204)

English is an ever-growing, ever-changing language. It grows because new inventions and discoveries require new words. By the same process, older words are constantly outdated. Look at the words and expressions listed here. Some are from industry; some are from space-age technology. What do they mean? Which ones are no longer in general use?

rumble seat	launch pad	ice box
caboose	AOK	jet lag
countdown	lift off	bucket seats
flash bulb	hubcap	running board

COMPOSITION

My Life (page 152)

In this selection, Isadora Duncan wrote about events in her childhood. They were events that turned out to have a far-reaching, positive effect upon her as an adult. None of us can know for certain what events and incidents will have that kind of effect upon us as we grow older. But we can speculate. What events or incidents from your life so far do you feel

will have positive benefits when you are older? Choose one or several and explain why you think so.

The Other Lady (page 159)

1. On page 166 Virginia Sorensen refers to the last time she saw her grandfather alive. Read again the section describing the meeting on the porch between her father and her grandfather. "It seems to me I knew what was said between them, every syllable, though it isn't possible that I really heard," the author writes. What do you think was said? Write the dialogue you think might have been spoken between the two men.

2. Have you ever wanted anything the way Virginia Sorensen wanted that pink hat? Has there been anything you wanted badly when you were younger, only to discover later that it wasn't so important after all? What was it? Write a few paragraphs in which you explain, as best you can recall, how you felt then and how your feelings have changed (if they have).

A Christmas Memory (page 170)

When Truman Capote wrote "A Christmas Memory," he was no longer a small boy living in rural Louisiana. But years later, he still remembered his elderly cousin. Is there some older person you feel you will always remember? If so, describe that person as clearly and warmly as Capote describes his cousin. And, like Capote, see if you can write that description without giving the person's name.

The Day of Days (page 182)

Martin Luther King states that some of the people who participated in the bus boycott had to walk as far as twelve miles to get to and from work. How do you suppose a person walking that distance would have explained her or his participation to a friend or relative in another city who did not understand it? Write the explanation you think that person would give.

First Hour on the Moon (page 204)

To the people who watched on television, the moonwalk of July 20, 1969, was an exciting event. But perhaps the people most excited were the astronauts themselves. Look again at the remarks made by the astronauts in this selection. Then write a brief speech that you think one of them might deliver to a group of high school students too young to have seen or to remember the moonwalk.

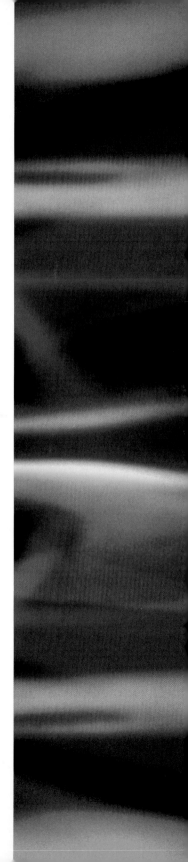

COMPOSITION

Outlines are hints, reminders of the order in which you intend to develop the ideas you want to express. These hints are useful in helping each thought in your paper prepare for the next thought, and then the next, and so on. In that way, your writing will guide the reader logically, *coherently,* over the material presented. It will avoid offering ideas haphazardly, as they might have occurred at random in your mind.

Outlines come first; writing comes afterward. But in order to examine how an outline works, we will look at a finished piece in this section to detect what hints, what reminders, the author may have jotted down before starting to write.

Considering the Montgomery bus boycott, Dr. King might have thought of a dozen ideas at once—the name of the woman who actually started the boycott, his anxiety about possible retaliation against the boycotters, how many people would participate, his own leadership role. But his mind had to *re*-order this jumbled material. Dr. King decided to let the reader experience the day chronologically, as he had. His notes might have looked something like this:

**USING AN
OUTLINE**

> morning
>> discovering the buses are empty
>> observing the people's reactions
>> attending Mrs. Parks's trial
> afternoon—planning meeting
>> electing officers
>> overcoming hesitations and fears
> evening
>> enormous turnout
>> speech
>> crowd's reactions
> afterthoughts— significance of the day

Having this kind of informal outline beside you to glance at can keep you on the track. You will not be as likely to leave out something important or to go off on a tangent. You will move more easily from one thing to the next, and you will be much less likely to get "stuck" halfway through a piece of writing.

ABOUT THE SELECTIONS

1. Nonfiction may seek to achieve two different purposes. One is to *explain*—what life was like in the past, how to write a poem, what really happened. Nonfiction may also seek to *persuade*—to persuade people to fight for a cause, or to see a movie, or to hire an applicant for a job. Choose a selection in this unit that persuades the reader to act or think in a certain manner. Examine, in a short composition, how the author goes about that task. Are examples included? Are consequences mentioned? How does the author's choice of words help persuade the reader? Your composition will be organized as an *analysis*—an explanation of the parts that make a single unit function.

2. Choose any four successive paragraphs from one selection in the unit. Around what central idea is each paragraph organized? What additional ideas does the paragraph include? How are those ideas related to the central one? Construct an outline that might have been used by the author to write the four paragraphs.

ON YOUR OWN

1. Pick a holiday that you have feelings about—Valentine's Day, Independence Day, Halloween, Thanksgiving, Christmas. In a paper convey your memories of how you have spent that holiday. By including details that made it special, try—as Capote does (page 170)—to convey what the day has meant to you. Use sensory words to help your reader experience the emotions you felt.

2. Think of a subject about which you can write with confidence: school lunches, driving a car, rights of—and restrictions on—students in your school, the most exasperating person you know. Let your ideas flow, jotting down brief reminders on a piece of paper as they occur to you. Now arrange the ideas in some logical sequence to form an outline, so that related but less important matters are subordinated to more important ones, and successive thoughts are prepared for by what has come before, and lead to what will follow.

3. Expand the outline you developed in the preceding topic into a completed composition. Be sure to include examples to make your thoughts clear and specific.

4. Gather material by finding someone willing to be interviewed who has special knowledge in a field—sports, animal training, computers, teaching, housework, general repair, etc. Interview that person and find out as much as you can about her or his special field. You will probably have far too much material for a brief paper. Decide how you will approach your subject. Then reorganize the material to remove repetitions, make relationships clear, and stress what is most important. The paper you will now write about the field is what matters, but you have your notes and outline available as well.

POETRY

WILLIAM CULLEN BRYANT

THANATOPSIS

To him who in the love of Nature holds
Communion with her visible forms, she speaks
A various language; for his gayer hours
She has a voice of gladness, and a smile
And eloquence of beauty, and she glides   5
Into his darker musings, with a mild
And healing sympathy, that steals away
Their sharpness, ere he is aware. When thoughts
Of the last bitter hour come like a blight
Over thy spirit, and sad images   10
Of the stern agony, and shroud, and pall,
And breathless darkness, and the narrow house,
Make thee to shudder and grow sick at heart,
Go forth, under the open sky, and list
To Nature's teachings, while from all around—   15
Earth and her waters, and the depths of air—
Comes a still voice. Yet a few days, and thee
The all-beholding sun shall see no more
In all his course; nor yet in the cold ground,
Where thy pale form was laid, with many tears,   20

Thanatopsis: Greek for "a view of death."   11. *pall:* cloth that covers a coffin.
14. *list:* listen.

Nor in the embrace of ocean, shall exist
Thy image. Earth, that nourished thee, shall claim
Thy growth, to be resolved to earth again,
And, lost each human trace, surrendering up
Thine individual being, shalt thou go   25
To mix forever with the elements,
To be a brother to the insensible rock
And to the sluggish clod, which the rude swain
Turns with his share, and treads upon. The oak
Shall send his roots abroad, and pierce thy mould.   30

    Yet not to thine eternal resting-place
Shalt thou retire alone, nor couldst thou wish
Couch more magnificent. Thou shalt lie down
With patriarchs of the infant world—with kings,
The powerful of the earth—the wise, the good,   35
Fair forms, and hoary seers of ages past,
All in one mighty sepulcher. The hills
Rock-ribbed and ancient as the sun—the vales
Stretching in pensive quietness between;
The venerable woods—rivers that move   40
In majesty, and the complaining brooks
That make the meadows green; and, poured round all,
Old Ocean's gray and melancholy waste—
Are but the solemn decorations all
Of the great tomb of man. The golden sun,   45
The planets, all the infinite host of heaven,
Are shining on the sad abodes of death,
Through the still lapse of ages. All that tread
The globe are but a handful to the tribes
That slumber in its bosom.—Take the wings   50
Of morning, pierce the Barcan wilderness,
Or lose thyself in the continuous woods
Where rolls the Oregon, and hears no sound,
Save his own dashings—yet the dead are there:

28–29. *the sluggish clod . . . his share:* the lazy lump of earth, which the rough
peasant turns over with his plowshare.　　30. *mould:* earthly remains.　　34.
patriarchs . . . world: founders of early civilizations.　　51. *Barcan:* Barca was
the ancient name for a desert region now included in Libya.　　53. *Oregon:* the
Columbia River.

And millions in those solitudes, since first   55
The flight of years began, have laid them down
In their last sleep—the dead reign there alone.
So shalt thou rest, and what if thou withdraw
In silence from the living, and no friend
Take note of thy departure? All that breathe   60
Will share thy destiny. The gay will laugh
When thou art gone, the solemn brood of care
Plod on, and each one as before will chase
His favorite phantom; yet all these shall leave
Their mirth and their employments, and shall come,   65
And make their bed with thee. As the long train
Of ages glide away, the sons of men,
The youth in life's green spring, and he who goes
In the full strength of years, matron and maid,
The speechless babe, and the gray-headed man—   70
Shall one by one be gathered to thy side,
By those, who in their turn shall follow them.

    So live, that when thy summons comes to join
The innumerable caravan which moves
To that mysterious realm where each shall take   75
His chamber in the silent halls of death,
Thou go not like the quarry-slave at night,
Scourged to his dungeon, but, sustained and soothed
By an unfaltering trust, approach thy grave,
Like one who wraps the drapery of his couch   80
About him, and lies down to pleasant dreams.

DISCUSSION

1. Whose is the "still voice" in line 17? What does that voice say (lines 17–30)?

2. What is Bryant saying about death? What lines from the poem sum this up?

3. When Bryant calls the earth "the great tomb of man," he is creating an *image*. An image can be simply a word picture that appeals to the senses—precise words that make you suddenly able to see or hear or smell or taste what the writer is describing—or an image can help make an idea clear and real. How does the earth-tomb image sum up what Bryant is saying about death?

For further activities, see page 276.

RALPH WALDO EMERSON

FORBEARANCE

Hast thou named all the birds without a gun?
Loved the wood rose, and left it on its stalk?
At rich men's tables eaten bread and pulse?
Unarmed, faced danger with a heart of trust?

And loved so well a high behavior,
In man or maid, that thou from speech refrained,
Nobility more nobly to repay?
O, be my friend, and teach me to be thine!

3. *pulse:* the seeds of peas, beans, or similar vegetables.

DISCUSSION
1.   Through his five questions, Emerson implies the qualities he would like any friend of his to possess. What are
those qualities? How do you interpret line 7?

2.   Why is "Forbearance" a good title for this poem?

HENRY WADSWORTH LONGFELLOW

The Fire of Drift-Wood

We sat within the farm-house old,
   Whose windows, looking o'er the bay,
Gave to the sea-breeze, damp and cold,
   An easy entrance, night and day.

Not far away we saw the port,   5
   The strange, old-fashioned, silent town,
The light-house, the dismantled fort,
   The wooden houses, quaint and brown.

We sat and talked until the night,
   Descending, filled the little room;   10
Our faces faded from the sight,
   Our voices only broke the gloom.

We spake of many a vanished scene,
   Of what we once had thought and said,
Of what had been, and might have been,   15
   And who was changed, and who was dead;

And all that fills the hearts of friends,
   When first they feel, with secret pain,
Their lives thenceforth have separate ends,
   And never can be one again;   20

The first slight swerving of the heart,
   That words are powerless to express,
And leave it still unsaid in part,
   Or say it in too great excess.

The very tones in which we spake   25
   Had something strange, I could but mark;
The leaves of memory seemed to make
   A mournful rustling in the dark.

26. *could but mark:* could not help noticing.

Oft died the words upon our lips,
    As suddenly, from out the fire   30
Built of the wreck of stranded ships,
    The flames would leap and then expire.

And, as their splendor flashed and failed,
    We thought of wrecks upon the main,
Of ships dismasted, that were hailed   35
    And sent no answer back again.

The windows, rattling in their frames,
    The ocean, roaring up the beach,
The gusty blast, the bickering flames,
    All mingled vaguely in our speech;   40

Until they made themselves a part
    Of fancies floating through the brain,
The long-lost ventures of the heart,
    That send no answers back again.

O flames that glowed! O hearts that yearned!   45
    They were indeed too much akin,
The drift-wood fire without that burned,
    The thoughts that burned and glowed within.

39. *bickering:* flickering.   47. *without:* outside.

DISCUSSION

1. Contrast the scene outside the old farmhouse with that on the inside.

2. What is the poet describing in lines 21–22: "The first slight swerving of the heart, / That words are powerless to express"?

3. *Meter,* the regular recurrence of stressed and unstressed syllables to give a rhythmical sound, makes this poem pleasant to the ear. Longfellow uses the *iambic foot,* a pattern with an unstressed syllable followed by a stressed syllable. In this poem there are four feet per line. On paper, meter is shown like this: "We sát withín the fárm-house óld." The accent marks, of course, show the stressed syllables. Mark two or three other lines to show that you have the feel of the rhythm.

EDGAR ALLAN POE

Alone

From childhood's hour I have not been
As others were—I have not seen
As others saw—I could not bring
My passions from a common spring—
From the same source I have not taken   5
My sorrow—I could not awaken
My heart to joy at the same tone—
And all I lov'd—I lov'd alone.
Then—in my childhood—in the dawn
Of a most stormy life—was drawn   10
From ev'ry depth of good and ill
The mystery which binds me still—
From the torrent, or the fountain—
From the red cliff of the mountain—
From the sun that round me roll'd   15
In its autumn tint of gold—
From the lightning in the sky
As it pass'd me flying by—
From the thunder, and the storm—
And the cloud that took the form   20
(When the rest of Heaven was blue)
Of a demon in my view.

To Helen

Helen, thy beauty is to me
    Like those Nicéan barks of yore
That gently, o'er a perfumed sea,
    The weary, way-worn wanderer bore
    To his own native shore.   5

On desperate seas long wont to roam,
    Thy hyacinth hair, thy classic face,
Thy Naiad airs have brought me home
    To the glory that was Greece,
    And the grandeur that was Rome.   10

Lo, in yon brilliant window-niche
    How statue-like I see thee stand,
The agate lamp within thy hand!
    Ah, Psyche, from the regions which
    Are holy-land!   15

2. *Nicéan barks:* boats from Nice, a French city on
the Mediterranean.   7. *Hyacinth:* suggests the
bluish color reflected from black hair.   8. *Naiad*
(nã'əd): In Greek mythology, the Naiads were beautiful maidens living in fountains and rivers.
13. *agate:* made from bluish-gray translucent stone.
14. *Psyche:* in Greek mythology, a mortal maiden
who personified Soul and Inspiration.

DISCUSSION   1.   In "Alone" the speaker sees himself as unique. Does he feel sorry for himself or pride himself on his difference from "others"? Discuss.

2.   "To Helen" was written to a woman named Jane. Poe called her Helen here,
after Helen of Troy, who was famous for her beauty. Rather than attempting to
describe Helen's beauty, Poe wrote about its *effect* on him. What does each
stanza tell you about this effect?

The CITY IN The SEA

Lo! Death has reared himself a throne
In a strange city lying alone
Far down within the dim West,
Where the good and the bad and the worst and the best
Have gone to their eternal rest.   5
There shrines and palaces and towers
(Time-eaten towers that tremble not!)
Resemble nothing that is ours.
Around, by lifting winds forgot,
Resignedly beneath the sky   10
The melancholy waters lie.

No rays from the holy heaven come down
On the long night-time of that town;
But light from out the lurid sea
Streams up the turrets silently—   15
Gleams up the pinnacles far and free—
Up domes—up spires—up kingly halls—
Up fanes—up Babylon-like walls—
Up shadowy long-forgotten bowers
Of sculptured ivy and stone flowers—   20
Up many and many a marvelous shrine
Whose wreathèd friezes intertwine
The viol, the violet, and the vine.
Resignedly beneath the sky
The melancholy waters lie.   25
So blend the turrets and shadows there
That all seem pendulous in air,
While from a proud tower in the town
Death looks gigantically down.

18. *fanes:* temples; *Babylon-like:* Babylon was one of the most
splendid cities in the ancient world.   22. *friezes:* bands of orna-
mental carving.

There open fanes and gaping graves   30
Yawn level with the luminous waves;
But not the riches there that lie
In each idol's diamond eye—
Not the gaily-jeweled dead
Tempt the waters from their bed;   35
For no ripples curl, alas!
Along that wilderness of glass—
No swellings tell that winds may be
Upon some far-off happier sea—
No heavings hint that winds have been   40
On seas less hideously serene.

But lo, a stir is in the air!
The wave—there is a movement there!
As if the towers had thrust aside,
In slightly sinking, the dull tide—   45
As if their tops had feebly given
A void within the filmy Heaven.
The waves have now a redder glow—
The hours are breathing faint and low—
And when, amid no earthly moans,   50
Down, down that town shall settle hence,
Hell, rising from a thousand thrones,
Shall do it reverence.

DISCUSSION

1. This poem is a series of visual images of a city that "Resemble[s] nothing that is ours." Where is the city? Why does light stream *up* the turrets? What do you consider the strongest images? What is the effect of the complete absence of sound imagery?

2. In the first line, death is *personified*; that is, it is given human qualities. How does this contribute to the poem's emotional effect?

3. The sound of a poem is an important part of its total effect. Lines can move quickly or slowly; words can flow together smoothly or be difficult to say. *Alliteration* (two or more words beginning with the same consonant sound, like "**d**own within the **d**im West") is one of the things to look for when you are thinking about the sound of a poem. So is the sound of the vowels—are they light and open, as in the word *easy*, or dark and monotonous, as in the word *dull*? Poe uses sound skillfully to reinforce meaning or imagery. Find some places in this poem where the sound adds to the effect.

OLIVER WENDELL HOLMES

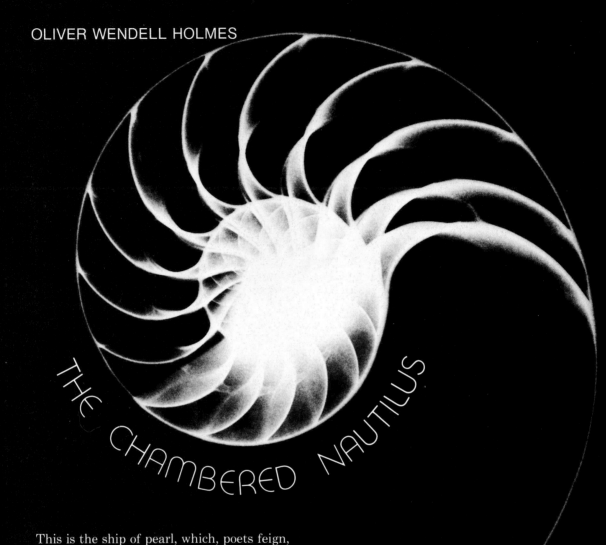

THE CHAMBERED NAUTILUS

This is the ship of pearl, which, poets feign,
　Sails the unshadowed main,—
　The venturous bark that flings
On the sweet summer wind its purpled wings
In gulfs enchanted, where the Siren sings,　　　　　　　5
　And coral reefs lie bare,
Where the cold sea-maids rise to sun their streaming hair.

1. *feign:* pretend, invent.　　5. *Siren:* in Greek mythology, a
nymph whose singing lures sailors onto the rocks.

Its webs of living gauze no more unfurl;
   Wrecked is the ship of pearl!
   And every chambered cell,   10
Where its dim dreaming life was wont to dwell,
As the frail tenant shaped his growing shell,
   Before thee lies revealed,—
Its irised ceiling rent, its sunless crypt unsealed!

Year after year beheld the silent toil   15
   That spread his lustrous coil;
   Still, as the spiral grew,
He left the past year's dwelling for the new,
Stole with soft step its shining archway through,
   Built up its idle door,   20
Stretched in his last-found home, and knew the old no more.

Thanks for the heavenly message brought by thee,
   Child of the wandering sea,
   Cast from her lap, forlorn!
From thy dead lips a clearer note is born   25
Than ever Triton blew from wreathèd horn!
   While on mine ear it rings,
Through the deep caves of thought I hear a voice that sings:—

Build thee more stately mansions, O my soul,
   As the swift seasons roll!   30
   Leave thy low-vaulted past!
Let each new temple, nobler than the last,
Shut thee from heaven with a dome more vast,
   Till thou at length art free,
Leaving thine outgrown shell by life's unresting sea!   35

8. *living gauze:* live tissue.   14. *irised:* rainbow-colored.

DISCUSSION   Holmes describes the shell of a nautilus and finds a lesson
for humans. What is that lesson? How do you interpret
"more stately mansions" (line 29)?

For further activities, see page 276.

WALT WHITMAN

FROM Song of Myself

1

I celebrate myself, and sing myself,
And what I assume you shall assume,
For every atom belonging to me as good belongs to you.
I loafe and invite my soul,
I lean and loafe at my ease observing a spear of summer grass.   5

My tongue, every atom of my blood, form'd from this soil, this air,
Born here of parents born here from parents the same, and their parents
    the same,
I, now thirty-seven years old in perfect health begin,
Hoping to cease not till death.

Creeds and schools in abeyance,   10
Retiring back a while sufficed at what they are, but never forgotten,
I harbor for good or bad, I permit to speak at every hazard,
Nature without check with original energy.

2

Houses and rooms are full of perfumes, the shelves are crowded with
    perfumes,
I breathe the fragrance myself and know it and like it,   15
The distillation would intoxicate me also, but I shall not let it.

The atmosphere is not a perfume, it has no taste of the distillation, it is
    odorless,
It is for my mouth forever, I am in love with it,
I will go to the bank by the wood and become undisguised and naked,
I am mad for it to be in contact with me.   20

The smoke of my own breath,

Echoes, ripples, buzz'd whispers, love-root, silk-thread, crotch and vine,

My respiration and inspiration, the beating of my heart, the passing of
blood and air through my lungs,

The sniff of green leaves and dry leaves, and the shore and dark-color'd
sea-rocks, and of hay in the barn,

The sound of the belch'd words of my voice loos'd to the eddies of the
wind,   25

A few light kisses, a few embraces, a reaching around of arms,

The play of shine and shade on the trees as the supple boughs wag,

The delight alone or in the rush of the streets, or along the fields and
hill-sides,

The feeling of health, the full-noon trill, the song of me rising from bed
and meeting the sun.

Have you reckon'd a thousand acres much? have you reckon'd the earth
much?   30

Have you practis'd so long to learn to read?

Have you felt so proud to get at the meaning of poems?

Stop this day and night with me and you shall possess the origin of all
poems,

You shall possess the good of the earth and sun (there are millions of
suns left),

You shall no longer take things at second or third hand, nor look
through the eyes of the dead, nor feed on the spectres in books,   35

You shall not look through my eyes either, nor take things from me,

You shall listen to all sides and filter them from your self.

6

A child said *What is the grass?* fetching it to me with full hands,

How could I answer the child? I do not know what it is any more
than he.

I guess it must be the flag of my disposition, out of hopeful green stuff
woven.   40

Or I guess it is the handkerchief of the Lord,

A scented gift and remembrancer designedly dropt,

Bearing the owner's name someway in the corners, that we may see and
remark, and say *Whose?*

Or I guess the grass is itself a child, the produced babe of the
    vegetation.

Or I guess it is a uniform hieroglyphic,   45
And it means, Sprouting alike in broad zones and narrow zones,
Growing among black folks as among white,
Kanuck, Tuckahoe, Congressman, Cuff, I give them the same, I receive
    them the same.

And now it seems to me the beautiful uncut hair of graves.
Tenderly will I use you curling grass,   50
It may be you transpire from the breasts of young men,
It may be if I had known them I would have loved them,
It may be you are from old people, or from offspring taken soon out of
    their mothers' laps.
And here you are the mothers' laps.
This grass is very dark to be from the white heads of old mothers,   55
Darker than the colorless beards of old men,
Dark to come from under the faint red roofs of mouths.

O I perceive after all so many uttering tongues,
And I perceive they do not come from the roofs of mouths for nothing.

I wish I could translate the hints about the dead young men and
    women,   60
And the hints about old men and mothers, and the offspring taken soon
    out of their laps.

What do you think has become of the young and old men?
And what do you think has become of the women and children?

They are alive and well somewhere,
The smallest sprout shows there is really no death,   65
And if ever there was it led forward life, and does not wait at the end to
    arrest it,
And ceas'd the moment life appear'd.

All goes onward and outward, nothing collapses,
And to die is different from what any one supposed, and luckier.

45. *hieroglyphic:* system of writing that uses pictures to represent words.   48. *Kanuck,*
Tuckahoe: French Canadian, Virginian.

7

Has any one supposed it lucky to be born?   70
I hasten to inform him or her it is just as lucky to die, and I know it.

I pass death with the dying and birth with the new-wash'd babe, and am
        not contain'd between my hat and boots,
And peruse manifold objects, no two alike and every one good,
The earth good and the stars good, and their adjuncts all good.

I am not an earth nor an adjunct of an earth,   75
I am the mate and companion of people, all just as immortal and fathom-
        less as myself,
(They do not know how immortal, but I know.)

Every kind for itself and its own, for me mine male and female,
For me those that have been boys and that love women,
For me the man that is proud and feels how it stings to be slighted,   80
For me the sweetheart and the old maid, for me mothers and the mothers
        of mothers,
For me lips that have smiled, eyes that have shed tears,
For me children and the begetters of children.

Undrape! you are not guilty to me, nor stale nor discarded,
I see through the broadcloth and gingham whether or no,   85
And am around, tenacious, acquisitive, tireless, and cannot be shaken
        away.

Patriarchs sit at supper with sons and grandsons and great grandsons
        around them,
In walls of adobie, in canvas tents, rest hunters and trappers after their
        day's sport,
The city sleeps and the country sleeps,
The living sleep for their time, the dead sleep for their time,   90
The old husband sleeps by his wife and the young husband sleeps by
        his wife;
And these tend inward to me, and I tend outward to them,
And such as it is to be of these more or less I am,
And of these one and all I weave the song of myself.

16

I am of old and young, of the foolish as much as the wise,   95
Regardless of others, ever regardful of others,
Maternal as well as paternal, a child as well as a man,
Stuff'd with the stuff that is coarse and stuff'd with the stuff that is fine,
One of the Nation of many nations, the smallest the same and the largest
    the same,
A Southerner soon as a Northerner, a planter nonchalant and hospitable
    down by the Oconee I live,   100
A Yankee bound my own way ready for trade, my joints the limberest
    joints on earth and the sternest joints on earth,
A Kentuckian walking the vale of the Elkhorn in my deerskin leggings, a
    Louisianian or Georgian,
A boatman over lakes or bays or along coasts, a Hoosier, Badger,
    Buckeye;
At home on Kanadian snowshoes or up in the bush, or with fishermen
    off Newfoundland,
At home in the fleet of iceboats, sailing with the rest and tacking,   105
At home on the hills of Vermont or in the woods of Maine, or the Texan
    ranch,
Comrade of Californians, comrade of free Northwesterners (loving their
    big proportions),
Comrade of raftsmen and coalmen, comrade of all who shake hands and
    welcome to drink and meat,
A learner with the simplest, a teacher of the thoughtfullest,
A novice beginning yet experient of myriads of seasons,   110
Of every hue and caste am I, of every rank and religion,
A farmer, mechanic, artist, gentleman, sailor, quaker,
Prisoner, fancy man, rowdy, lawyer, physician, priest.

I resist any thing better than my own diversity,
Breathe the air but leave plenty after me,   115
And am not stuck up, and am in my place.

(The moth and the fish eggs are in their place,
The bright suns I see and the dark suns I cannot see are in their place,
The palpable is in its place and the impalpable in its place.)

---

103. *Hoosier, Badger, Buckeye:* persons from Indiana, Wisconsin, Ohio.

19

. . . Do you take it I would astonish? 120
Does the daylight astonish? does the early redstart twittering through the
    woods?
Do I astonish more than they?

This hour I tell things in confidence,
I might not tell everybody, but I will tell you.

20

Who goes there? hankering, gross, mystical, nude; 125
How is it I extract strength from the beef I eat?

What is a man anyhow? what am I? what are you?

All I mark as my own you shall offset it with your own,
Else it were time lost listening to me.

I do not snivel that snivel the world over, 130
The months are vacuums and the ground but wallow and filth.

Whimpering and truckling fold with powders for invalids, conformity
    goes to the fourth-remov'd,
I wear my hat as I please indoors or out.

Why should I pray? why should I venerate and be ceremonious?

Having pried through the strata, analyzed to a hair, counsel'd with doc-
    tors and calculated close, 135
I find no sweeter fat than sticks to my own bones.

In all people I see myself, none more and not one a barleycorn less,
And the good or bad I say of myself I say of them.

I know I am solid and sound,
To me the converging objects of the universe perpetually flow, 140
All are written to me, and I must get what the writing means.

I know I am deathless,
I know this orbit of mine cannot be swept by a carpenter's compass,
I know I shall not pass like a child's carlacue cut with a burnt stick at
    night.

I know I am august,   145
I do not trouble my spirit to vindicate itself or be understood,
I see that the elementary laws never apologize,
(I reckon I behave no prouder than the level I plant my house by,
    after all.)

I exist as I am, that is enough,
If no other in the world be aware I sit content,   150
And if each and all be aware I sit content.

One world is aware and by far the largest to me, and that is myself,
And whether I come to my own today or in ten thousand or ten million
    years,
I can cheerfully take it now, or with equal cheerfulness I can wait.

My foothold is tenon'd and mortis'd in granite,   155
I laugh at what you call dissolution,
And I know the amplitude of time.

    30
All truths wait in all things,
They neither hasten their own delivery nor resist it,
They do not need the obstetric forceps of the surgeon,   160
The insignificant is as big to me as any,
(What is less or more than touch?)

Logic and sermons never convince,
The damp of the night drives deeper into my soul.

(Only what proves itself to every man and woman is so,   165
Only what nobody denies is so.)

---

155. *tenon'd and mortis'd:* fitted together to form a close joint.

A minute and a drop of me settle my brain,
I believe the soggy clods shall become lovers and lamps,
And a compend of compends is the meat of a man or woman,
And a summit and flower there is the feeling they have for each
    other,   170
And they are to branch boundlessly out of that lesson until it becomes
    omnific,
And until one and all shall delight us, and we them.

31
I believe a leaf of grass is no less than the journeywork of the stars,
And the pismire is equally perfect, and a grain of sand, and the egg of
    the wren,
And the tree-toad is a chef-d'œuvre for the highest,   175
And the running blackberry would adorn the parlors of heaven,
And the narrowest hinge in my hand puts to scorn all machinery,
And the cow crunching with depress'd head surpasses any statue,
And a mouse is miracle enough to stagger sextillions of infidels. . . .

169. *compend:* compendium, summary.   171. *omnific:* making all things; all-creating.
174. *pismire:* ant.   175. *chef-d'oeuvre:* French for ''masterpiece.''

32

I think I could turn and live with animals, they're so placid and
    self-contain'd,   180
I stand and look at them long and long.

They do not sweat and whine about their condition,
They do not lie awake in the dark and weep for their sins,
They do not make me sick discussing their duty to God,
Not one is dissatisfied, not one is demented with the mania of owning
    things,   185
Not one kneels to another, nor to his kind that lived thousands
    of years ago,
Not one is respectable or unhappy over the whole earth.

So they show their relations to me and I accept them,
They bring me tokens of myself, they evince them plainly
    in their possession.

I wonder where they get those tokens,   190
Did I pass that way huge times ago and negligently drop them?

Myself moving forward then and now and forever,
Gathering and showing more always and with velocity,
Infinite and omnigenous, and the like of these among them,
Not too exclusive toward the reachers of my remembrancers,   195
Picking out here one that I love, and now go with him on brotherly
    terms.

A gigantic beauty of a stallion, fresh and responsive to my caresses,
Head high in the forehead, wide between the ears,
Limbs glossy and supple, tail dusting the ground,
Eyes full of sparkling wickedness, ears finely cut, flexibly moving.   200

His nostrils dilate as my heels embrace him,
His well-built limbs tremble with pleasure as we race around and return.

I but use you a minute, then I resign you, stallion,
Why do I need your paces when I myself out-gallop them?
Even as I stand or sit passing faster than you.   205

194. *omnigenous:* of all kinds.

52

The spotted hawk swoops by and accuses me, he complains of my gab
    and my loitering.
I too am not a bit tamed, I too am untranslatable,
I sound my barbaric yawp over the roofs of the world.

The last scud of day holds back for me,
It flings my likeness after the rest and true as any on the shadow'd
    wilds,   210
It coaxes me to the vapor and the dusk.

I depart as air, I shake my white locks at the runaway sun,
I effuse my flesh in eddies, and drift it in lacy jags.

I bequeath myself to the dirt to grow from the grass I love,
If you want me again look for me under your boot-soles.   215

You will hardly know who I am or what I mean,
But I shall be good health to you nevertheless,
And filter and fibre your blood.

Failing to fetch me at first keep encouraged,
Missing me one place search another,   220
I stop somewhere waiting for you.

208. *yawp:* loud cry or yell.   209. *scud:* thin, wind-driven clouds.

DISCUSSION

1. The speaker in this poem seems to be Whitman himself. How would you characterize him? What is his attitude toward you, the listener-reader?

2. What is Whitman's view of life? Of nature and the relationship between it and humans? Of death? Point out lines in the poem that support your conclusions.

3. "Song of Myself" is written in *free verse*, poetry that does not rhyme and has no regular rhythm. Like actual speech, it is natural and unrestrained in its flow. Lines may vary in length, and the stanzas have little or no recurring pattern. Why is free verse a good form for a poem in which the speaker reaches out to the whole of human experience and the physical world—a poem in which the speaker says, "Every atom belonging to me as good as belongs to you," and "All goes onward and outward"?

WALT WHITMAN

O Captain! My Captain!

O Captain! my Captain! our fearful trip is done,
The ship has weathered every rack, the prize we sought is won,
The port is near, the bells I hear, the people all exulting,
While follow eyes the steady keel, the vessel grim and daring;
    But O heart! heart! heart!   5
      O the bleeding drops of red,
        Where on the deck my Captain lies,
        Fallen cold and dead.

O Captain! my Captain! rise up and hear the bells;
Rise up—for you the flag is flung—for you the bugle trills,   10
For you bouquets and ribboned wreaths—for you the shores a-crowding,
For you they call, the swaying mass, their eager faces turning;
    Here Captain! dear father!
      This arm beneath your head!
        It is some dream that on the deck,   15
        You've fallen cold and dead.

My Captain does not answer, his lips are pale and still,
My father does not feel my arm, he has no pulse nor will,
The ship is anchored safe and sound, its voyage closed and done,
From fearful trip the victor ship comes in with object won;   20
    Exult O shores, and ring O bells!
    But I with mournful tread,
      Walk the deck my Captain lies,
      Fallen cold and dead.

DISCUSSION

1. Whitman wrote this poem after the assassination of Abraham Lincoln. Because it addresses someone who is absent—in this case dead—it is called an *apostrophe*. If the captain in this poem is Lincoln, what is the ship? The trip?

2. The short lines that end each stanza are different from the rest—they show the personal reaction of the speaker. Read aloud the four lines that end stanzas one and two. How does their sound and rhythm reflect the way a griefstricken person would speak?

EMILY DICKINSON

If you were coming in the Fall

If you were coming in the Fall,
I'd brush the Summer by
With half a smile, and half a spurn,
As Housewives do, a Fly.

If I could see you in a year,   5
I'd wind the months in balls—
And put them each in separate Drawers,
For fear the numbers fuse—

If only Centuries, delayed,
I'd count them on my Hand,   10
Subtracting, till my fingers dropped
Into Van Dieman's Land.

If certain, when this life was out—
That yours and mine, should be
I'd toss it yonder, like a Rind,   15
And take Eternity—

But, now, uncertain of the length
Of this, that is between,
It goads me, like the Goblin Bee—
That will not state—its sting.   20

12. *Van Dieman's Land:* former name of Tasmania,
an island that is part of Australia; in other words, on
the other side of the globe.

DISCUSSION

How would the speaker react if she knew her
loved one was coming in the fall? In a year? In
"only" centuries? What is her greatest uncertainty?

A narrow Fellow in the Grass

A narrow Fellow in the Grass
Occasionally rides—
You may have met Him—did you not
His notice sudden is—

The Grass divides as with a Comb—   5
A spotted shaft is seen—
And then it closes at your feet
And opens further on—

He likes a Boggy Acre
A Floor too cool for Corn—   10
Yet when a Boy, and Barefoot—
I more than once at Noon
Have passed, I thought, a Whip lash
Unbraiding in the Sun
When stooping to secure it   15
It wrinkled, and was gone—

Several of Nature's People
I know, and they know me—
I feel for them a transport
Of cordiality—   20

But never met this Fellow
Attended, or alone
Without a tighter breathing
And Zero at the Bone—

DISCUSSION

1. When did you first realize that the poem
was about a snake?

2. Compare line 4 with this version: "His notice is sudden—"

A Charm invests a face

A Charm invests a face
Imperfectly beheld—
The Lady dare not lift her Veil
For fear it be dispelled—

But peers beyond her mesh—
And wishes—and denies—
Lest Interview—annul a want
That Image—satisfies—

The Bustle in a House

The Bustle in a House
The Morning after Death
Is solemnest of industries
Enacted upon Earth—

The Sweeping up the Heart
And putting Love away
We shall not want to use again
Until Eternity.

The Soul selects her own Society

The Soul selects her own Society—
Then—shuts the Door—
To her divine Majority—
Present no more—

Unmoved—she notes the Chariots—pausing—   5
At her low Gate—
Unmoved—an Emperor be kneeling
Upon her Mat—

I've known her—from an ample nation—
Choose One—
Then—close the Valves of her attention—   10
Like Stone—

DISCUSSION

1.   In "A Charm invests a face," why does the lady deny an interview? To what extent does her reason suggest a valid idea about people?

2.   In "The Bustle in a House," what makes the bustle the "solemnest of industries"? According to the last stanza, what is the person really doing?

3.   How is the soul portrayed in "The Soul selects her own Society"? What is the impact of the final line, "Like Stone—"?

Because I could not stop for Death

Because I could not stop for Death—
He kindly stopped for me—
The Carriage held but just Ourselves—
And Immortality.

We slowly drove—He knew no haste   5
And I had put away
My labor and my leisure too,
For His Civility—

We passed the School, where Children strove
At Recess—in the Ring—   10
We passed the Fields of Gazing Grain—
We passed the Setting Sun—

Or rather—He passed Us—
The Dews drew quivering and chill—
For only Gossamer, my Gown—   15
My Tippet—only Tulle—

We paused before a House that seemed
A Swelling of the Ground—
The Roof was scarcely visible—
The Cornice—in the Ground—   20

Since then—'tis Centuries—and yet
Feels shorter than the Day
I first surmised the Horses' Heads
Were toward Eternity—

16. *Tippet:* stole, scarf.   20. *Cornice:* molding that
tops a wall.

DISCUSSION   1.   What general truth about human experience do the first two lines suggest?

2.   What successive scenes does the carriage pass? Why do you think they are
in this order?

EDWIN ARLINGTON ROBINSON

Miniver Cheevy

Miniver Cheevy, child of scorn,
    Grew lean while he assailed the seasons;
He wept that he was ever born,
    And he had reasons.

Miniver loved the days of old   5
    When swords were bright and steeds were prancing;
The vision of a warrior bold
    Would set him dancing.

Miniver sighed for what was not,
    And dreamed, and rested from his labors;   10
He dreamed of Thebes and Camelot,
    And Priam's neighbors.

Miniver mourned the ripe renown
    That made so many a name so fragrant;
He mourned Romance, now on the town,   15
    And Art, a vagrant.

Miniver loved the Medici,
    Albeit he had never seen one;
He would have sinned incessantly
    Could he have been one.   20

Miniver cursed the commonplace
    And eyed a khaki suit with loathing;
He missed the medieval grace
    Of iron clothing.

Miniver scorned the gold he sought,   25
    But sore annoyed was he without it;
Miniver thought, and thought, and thought,
    And thought about it.

Miniver Cheevy, born too late,
    Scratched his head and kept on thinking;   30
Miniver coughed, and called it fate,
    And kept on drinking.

Richard Cory

Whenever Richard Cory went down town,
We people on the pavement looked at him:
He was a gentleman from sole to crown,
Clean favored, and imperially slim.

And he was always quietly arrayed,   5
And he was always human when he talked;
But still he fluttered pulses when he said,
"Good-morning," and he glittered when he walked.

And he was rich—yes, richer than a king—
And admirably schooled in every grace: 10
In fine, we thought that he was everything
To make us wish that we were in his place.

So on we worked, and waited for the light,
And went without the meat, and cursed the bread;
And Richard Cory, one calm summer night,   15
Went home and put a bullet through his head.

DISCUSSION   1. Do you think Miniver would have been happy if he had lived "When swords
were bright and steeds were prancing"? Explain.

2. What lines show that Miniver did not see the past realistically?

3. From whose point of view do we see Richard Cory? How does this point of
view help account for the impact of the final line?

4. Cory and the townspeople are characterized in part by *connotations,* those
meanings which certain words suggest in addition to their literal meanings. For
example, the people in the town live on the "pavement," go without "meat," and
eat "bread." The connotations of these words, when they are taken all together,
are of extreme simplicity, perhaps even poverty. What are the connotations of
"crown," "imperially," "glittered," and "king"—the words that characterize
Cory?

For further activities, see page 276.

EDGAR LEE MASTERS

Lucinda Matlock

I went to the dances at Chandlerville,
And played snap-out at Winchester.
One time we changed partners,
Driving home in the moonlight of middle June,
And then I found Davis.   5

We were married and lived together for seventy years,
Enjoying, working, raising the twelve children,
Eight of whom we lost
Ere I had reached the age of sixty.
I spun, I wove, I kept the house, I nursed the sick,   10
I made the garden, and for holiday
Rambled over the fields where sang the larks,
And by Spoon River gathering many a shell,
And many a flower and medicinal weed—
Shouting to the wooded hills, singing to the green valleys.   15
At ninety-six I had lived enough, that is all,
And passed to a sweet repose.
What is this I hear of sorrow and weariness,
Anger, discontent and drooping hopes?
Degenerate sons and daughters,   20
Life is too strong for you—
It takes life to love Life.

George Gray

I have studied many times
The marble which was chiseled for me—
A boat with a furled sail at rest in a harbor.
In truth it pictures not my destination
But my life.   5
For love was offered me and I shrank from its disillusionment;
Sorrow knocked at my door, but I was afraid;
Ambition called to me, but I dreaded the chances.
Yet all the while I hungered for meaning in my life.
And now I know that we must lift the sail   10
And catch the winds of destiny
Wherever they drive the boat.
To put meaning in one's life may end in madness,
But life without meaning is the torture
Of restlessness and vague desire—   15
It is a boat longing for the sea and yet afraid.

DISCUSSION   1.   From the details given in "Lucinda Matlock," what do you think is her evaluation of her own life? How does she feel toward her sons and daughters who express "Anger, discontent and drooping hopes"? To what extent do you agree with her final statement?

2.   In "George Gray," what was chiseled on Gray's tombstone? Why is this *ironic* (see page 84)? What risk, according to the speaker, may there be in putting meaning into one's life? What is the alternative?

EDGAR LEE MASTERS  SILENCE

I have known the silence of the stars and of the sea,
And the silence of the city when it pauses,
And the silence of a man and a maid,
And the silence for which music alone finds the word,
And the silence of the woods before the winds of spring begin,   5
And the silence of the sick
When their eyes roam about the room.
And I ask: For the depths,
Of what use is language?
A beast of the field moans a few times   10
When death takes its young:
And we are voiceless in the presence of realities—
We cannot speak.

A curious boy asks an old soldier
Sitting in front of the grocery store,   15
"How did you lose your leg?"
And the old soldier is struck with silence,
Or his mind flies away
Because he cannot concentrate it on Gettysburg.
It comes back jocosely   20
And he says, "A bear bit it off."
And the boy wonders, while the old soldier
Dumbly, feebly, lives over
The flashes of guns, the thunder of cannon,
The shrieks of the slain,   25
And himself lying on the ground,
And the hospital surgeons, the knives,
And the long days in bed.
But if he could describe it all
He would be an artist.   30
But if he were an artist there would be deeper wounds
Which he could not describe.

There is the silence of a great hatred,
And the silence of a great love,
And the silence of a deep peace of mind,   35

And the silence of an embittered friendship.
There is the silence of a spiritual crisis,
Through which your soul, exquisitely tortured,
Comes with visions not to be uttered
Into a realm of higher life,   40
And the silence of the gods who understand each other without speech.
There is the silence of defeat.
There is the silence of those unjustly punished;
And the silence of the dying whose hand
Suddenly grips yours.   45
There is the silence between father and son,
When the father cannot explain his life,
Even though he be misunderstood for it.

There is the silence that comes between husband and wife,
There is the silence of those who have failed;   50
And the vast silence that covers
Broken nations and vanquished leaders.
There is the silence of Lincoln,
Thinking of the poverty of his youth.
And the silence of Napoleon   55
After Waterloo.
And the silence of Jeanne d'Arc
Saying amid the flames, "Blessèd Jesus"—
Revealing in two words all sorrow, all hope.
And there is the silence of age,   60
Too full of wisdom for the tongue to utter it
In words intelligible to those who have not lived
The great range of life.

And there is the silence of the dead.
If we who are in life cannot speak   65
Of profound experiences,
Why do you marvel that the dead
Do not tell you of death?
Their silence shall be interpreted
As we approach them.   70

DISCUSSION   Do you agree with the poet's feeling that the most heartfelt moments, the deepest wisdom, or the greatest hurts are inexpressible? Explain. How would you answer the question in lines 8 and 9? What do the last two lines mean?

STEPHEN CRANE

A man said to the universe

A man said to the universe:
"Sir, I exist!"
"However," replied the universe,
"The fact has not created in me
A sense of obligation."

In the desert

In the desert
I saw a creature, naked, bestial,
Who, squatting upon the ground,
Held his heart in his hands,
And ate of it.   5
I said, "Is it good, friend?"
"It is bitter—bitter," he answered;
"But I like it
"Because it is bitter,
"And because it is my heart."   10

DISCUSSION   1.   Read aloud line 2 of "A man said to the universe" as you think the man
              would have said it. What, do you think, is his reaction to the reply of the uni-
              verse?

              2.   Why do you think the speaker of "In the desert" addresses the bestial crea-
              ture as "friend"? How do you interpret lines 7–10?

Do not weep

Do not weep, maiden, for war is kind.
Because your lover threw wild hands toward the sky
And the affrighted steed ran on alone,
Do not weep.
War is kind.   5

       Hoarse, booming drums of the regiment,
       Little souls who thirst for fight,
       These men were born to drill and die.
       The unexplained glory flies above them,
       Great is the battle-god, great, and his kingdom—   10
       A field where a thousand corpses lie.

Do not weep, babe, for war is kind.
Because your father tumbled in the yellow trenches,
Raged at his breast, gulped and died,
Do not weep.   15
War is kind.

       Swift blazing flag of the regiment,
       Eagle with crest of red and gold,
       These men were born to drill and die.
       Point for them the virtue of slaughter,   20
       Make plain to them the excellence of killing
       And a field where a thousand corpses lie.

Mother whose heart hung humble as a button
On the bright splendid shroud of your son,
Do not weep.   25
War is kind.

DISCUSSION

1. What is the speaker's attitude toward those who choose to be warriors? Cite lines that will support your answer.

2. What contrast is drawn between the appearance of the regiment and its function?

3. How does the repetition of "do not weep" and "war is kind" create *irony* (see page 84)? What statement about war is Crane really making?

For further activities, see page 276.

JAMES WELDON JOHNSON

THE CREATION

And God stepped out on space,
And he looked around and said:
I'm lonely—
I'll make me a world.

And far as the eye of God could see   5
Darkness covered everything,
Blacker than a hundred midnights
Down in a cypress swamp.

Then God smiled,
And the light broke,   10
And the darkness rolled up on one side,
And the light stood shining on the other,
And God said: That's good!

Then God reached out and took the light in his hands,
And God rolled the light around in his hands   15
Until he made the sun;
And he set that sun a-blazing in the heavens.
And the light that was left from making the sun
God gathered it up in a shining ball
And flung it against the darkness,   20
Spangling the night with the moon and stars.
Then down between
The darkness and the light
He hurled the world;
And God said: That's good!   25

Then God himself stepped down—
And the sun was on his right hand,
And the moon was on his left;
The stars were clustered about his head,
And the earth was under his feet.   30
And God walked, and where he trod
His footsteps hollowed the valleys out
And bulged the mountains up.

ROBERT FROST

BIRCHES

When I see birches bend to left and right
Across the lines of straighter darker trees,
I like to think some boy's been swinging them.
But swinging doesn't bend them down to stay
As ice-storms do. Often you must have seen them   5
Loaded with ice a sunny winter morning
After a rain. They click upon themselves
As the breeze rises, and turn many-colored
As the stir cracks and crazes their enamel.
Soon the sun's warmth makes them shed crystal shells   10
Shattering and avalanching on the snow-crust—
Such heaps of broken glass to sweep away
You'd think the inner dome of heaven had fallen.
They are dragged to the withered bracken by the load,
And they seem not to break though once they are bowed
So low for long, they never right themselves:
You may see their trunks arching in the woods
Years afterwards, trailing their leaves on the ground
Like girls on hands and knees that throw their hair
Before them over their heads to dry in the sun.   20
But I was going to say when Truth broke in
With all her matter-of-fact about the ice-storm
I should prefer to have some boy bend them
As he went out and in to fetch the cows—
Some boy too far from town to learn baseball,   25
Whose only play was what he found himself,
Summer or winter, and could play alone.
One by one he subdued his father's trees
By riding them down over and over again
Until he took the stiffness out of them,   30
And not one but hung limp, not one was left
For him to conquer. He learned all there was
To learn about not launching out too soon

And so not carrying the tree away
Clear to the ground. He always kept his poise   35
To the top branches, climbing carefully
With the same pains you use to fill a cup
Up to the brim, and even above the brim.
Then he flung outward, feet first, with a swish,
Kicking his way down through the air to the ground. 40
So was I once myself a swinger of birches.
And so I dream of going back to be.
It's when I'm weary of considerations,
And life is too much like a pathless wood
Where your face burns and tickles with the cobwebs 45
Broken across it, and one eye is weeping
From a twig's having lashed across it open.
I'd like to get away from earth awhile
And then come back to it and begin over.
May no fate willfully misunderstand me   50
And half grant what I wish and snatch me away
Not to return. Earth's the right place for love:
I don't know where it's likely to go better.
I'd like to go by climbing a birch tree,
And climb black branches up a snow-white trunk 55
Toward heaven, till the tree could bear no more,
But dipped its top and set me down again.
That would be good both going and coming back.
One could do worse than be a swinger of birches.

DISCUSSION

1. The speaker notes that birches in a woods may be bent from two causes. What are they? Which is more destructive?

2. What is the speaker's feeling for the boy in this poem who is unable to compete in social games like baseball or hockey?

3. What conditions in life make the speaker wish that he could again be "a swinger of birches"? Why would he be unwilling to leave the earth completely?

4. *Blank verse*, the form in which this poem is written, is often used for longer works or those where a conversational tone is wanted. Blank verse has no rhyme, and each line contains five *iambic feet* (see page 225). Read the poem aloud as though you were just talking with someone. How would rhyme change the effect of the poem?

ROBERT FROST

Nothing Gold Can Stay

Nature's first green is gold,
Her hardest hue to hold.
Her early leaf's a flower;
But only so an hour.
Then leaf subsides to leaf.
So Eden sank to grief,
So dawn goes down to day.
Nothing gold can stay.

6. *Eden:* in the biblical account, the first home of
Adam and Eve; Paradise.

DISCUSSION

1.   What is the meaning of "gold" in the first and last lines?

2.   How would you state the *theme* (see page 84)? Discuss
its truth as an observation of life.

FIRE AND ICE

SOME SAY THE WORLD WILL END IN FIRE,
SOME SAY IN ICE.
FROM WHAT I'VE TASTED OF DESIRE
I HOLD WITH THOSE WHO FAVOR FIRE.
BUT IF IT HAD TO PERISH TWICE,
I THINK I KNOW ENOUGH OF HATE
TO SAY THAT FOR DESTRUCTION ICE
IS ALSO GREAT
AND WOULD SUFFICE.

The Death of the Hired Man

Mary sat musing on the lamp-flame at the table,
Waiting for Warren. When she heard his step,
She ran on tip-toe down the darkened passage
To meet him in the doorway with the news
And put him on his guard. "Silas is back." 5
She pushed him outward with her through the door
And shut it after her. "Be kind," she said.
She took the market things from Warren's arms
And set them on the porch, then drew him down
To sit beside her on the wooden steps. 10

"When was I ever anything but kind to him?
But I'll not have the fellow back," he said.
"I told him so last haying, didn't I?
If he left then, I said, that ended it.
What good is he? Who else will harbor him 15
At his age for the little he can do?
What help he is there's no depending on.
Off he goes always when I need him most.
He thinks he ought to earn a little pay,
Enough at least to buy tobacco with, 20
So he won't have to beg and be beholden.
'All right,' I say, 'I can't afford to pay
Any fixed wages, though I wish I could.'
'Someone else can.' 'Then someone else will have to.'
I shouldn't mind his bettering himself 25
If that was what it was. You can be certain,
When he begins like that, there's someone at him
Trying to coax him off with pocket money—
In haying time, when any help is scarce.
In winter he comes back to us. I'm done." 30

"Sh! not so loud: he'll hear you," Mary said.

"I want him to: he'll have to soon or late."

"He's worn out. He's asleep beside the stove.
When I came up from Rowe's I found him here,
Huddled against the barn door fast asleep, 35

A miserable sight, and frightening, too—
You needn't smile—I didn't recognize him—
I wasn't looking for him—and he's changed.
Wait till you see."

        "Where did you say he'd been?"

"He didn't say. I dragged him to the house,   40
And gave him tea and tried to make him smoke.
I tried to make him talk about his travels.
Nothing would do: he just kept nodding off."

"What did he say? Did he say anything?"

"But little."

        "Anything? Mary, confess   45
He said he'd come to ditch the meadow for me."

"Warren!"

      "But did he? I just want to know."

"Of course he did. What would you have him say?
Surely you wouldn't grudge the poor old man
Some humble way to save his self-respect.   50
He added, if you really care to know,
He meant to clear the upper pasture, too.
That sounds like something you have heard before?
Warren, I wish you could have heard the way
He jumbled everything. I stopped to look   55
Two or three times—he made me feel so queer—
To see if he was talking in his sleep.
He ran on Harold Wilson—you remember—
The boy you had in haying four years since.
He's finished school, and teaching in his college.   60
Silas declares you'll have to get him back.
He says they two will make a team for work:
Between them they will lay this farm as smooth!
The way he mixed that in with other things.
He thinks young Wilson a likely lad, though daft   65
On education—you know how they fought
All through July under the blazing sun,
Silas up on the cart to build the load,
Harold along beside to pitch it on."

"Yes, I took care to keep well out of earshot."   70

"Well, those days trouble Silas like a dream.
You wouldn't think they would. How some things linger!
Harold's young college boy's assurance piqued him.
After so many years he still keeps finding
Good arguments he sees he might have used.   75
I sympathize. I know just how it feels
To think of the right thing to say too late.
Harold's associated in his mind with Latin.
He asked me what I thought of Harold's saying
He studied Latin, like the violin,   80
Because he liked it—that an argument!
He said he couldn't make the boy believe
He could find water with a hazel prong—
Which showed how much good school had ever done him.
He wanted to go over that. But most of all   85
He thinks if he could have another chance
To teach him how to build a load of hay——"

"I know, that's Silas' one accomplishment.
He bundles every forkful in its place,
And tags and numbers it for future reference,   90
So he can find and easily dislodge it
In the unloading. Silas does that well.
He takes it out in bunches like big birds' nests.
You never see him standing on the hay
He's trying to lift, straining to lift himself."   95

"He thinks if he could teach him that, he'd be
Some good perhaps to someone in the world.
He hates to see a boy the fool of books.
Poor Silas, so concerned for other folk,
And nothing to look backward to with pride,   100
And nothing to look forward to with hope,
So now and never any different."

Part of a moon was falling down the west,
Dragging the whole sky with it to the hills.
Its light poured softly in her lap. She saw it   105
And spread her apron to it. She put out her hand
Among the harp-like morning-glory strings,
Taut with the dew from garden bed to eaves,

As if she played unheard some tenderness
That wrought on him beside her in the night.   110
"Warren," she said, "he has come home to die:
You needn't be afraid he'll leave you this time."

"Home," he mocked gently.

       "Yes, what else but home?
It all depends on what you mean by home.
Of course he's nothing to us, any more   115
Than was the hound that came a stranger to us
Out of the woods, worn out upon the trail."

"Home is the place where, when you have to go there,
They have to take you in."

       "I should have called it
Something you somehow haven't to deserve."   120

Warren leaned out and took a step or two,
Picked up a little stick, and brought it back
And broke it in his hand and tossed it by.
"Silas has better claim on us you think
Than on his brother? Thirteen little miles   125
As the road winds would bring him to his door.
Silas has walked that far no doubt today.
Why doesn't he go there? His brother's rich,
A somebody—director in the bank."

"He never told us that."

       "We know it, though."   130

"I think his brother ought to help, of course.
I'll see to that if there is need. He ought of right
To take him in, and might be willing to—
He may be better than appearances.
But have some pity on Silas. Do you think   135
If he had any pride in claiming kin
Or anything he looked for from his brother,
He'd keep so still about him all this time?"

"I wonder what's between them."

       "I can tell you.
Silas is what he is—we wouldn't mind him—   140
But just the kind that kinsfolk can't abide.

He never did a thing so very bad.
He don't know why he isn't quite as good
As anybody. Worthless though he is,
He won't be made ashamed to please his brother."   145

"I can't think Si ever hurt anyone."

"No, but he hurt my heart the way he lay
And rolled his old head on that sharp-edged chair-back.
He wouldn't let me put him on the lounge.
You must go in and see what you can do.   150
I made the bed up for him there tonight.
You'll be surprised at him—how much he's broken.
His working days are done; I'm sure of it."

"I'd not be in a hurry to say that."

"I haven't been. Go, look, see for yourself.   155
But, Warren, please remember how it is:
He's come to help you ditch the meadow.
He has a plan. You mustn't laugh at him.
He may not speak of it, and then he may.
I'll sit and see if that small sailing cloud   160
Will hit or miss the moon."

                It hit the moon.
Then there were three there, making a dim row,
The moon, the little silver cloud, and she.

Warren returned—too soon, it seemed to her—
Slipped to her side, caught up her hand and waited.   165

"Warren?" she questioned.

                "Dead," was all he answered.

DISCUSSION

1. How do lines 100–101 summarize the tragic story of Silas's life? Why do you think he came to Mary and Warren rather than to his brother who lived nearby?

2. Characterize Mary and Warren. In making your judgments, take into consideration their definitions of "home" (lines 118–120).

3. A *narrative poem* is one that tells a story. What story elements does this poem have? How much of the story is told in dialogue?

For further activities, see page 276.

CARL SANDBURG

Chicago

Hog Butcher for the World,
Tool Maker, Stacker of Wheat,
Player with Railroads and the Nation's Freight Handler;
Stormy, husky, brawling,
City of the big Shoulders: 5

They tell me you are wicked and I believe them, for I have seen your
    painted women under the gas lamps luring the farm boys.
And they tell me you are crooked and I answer: Yes, it is true I have
    seen the gunman kill and go free to kill again.
And they tell me you are brutal and my reply is: On the faces of
    women and children I have seen the marks of wanton hunger.
And having answered so I turn once more to those who sneer at this
    my city, and I give them back the sneer and say to them:
Come and show me another city with lifted head singing so proud to
    be alive and coarse and strong and cunning.   10
Flinging magnetic curses amid the toil of piling job on job, here is a
    tall bold slugger set vivid against the little soft cities;
Fierce as a dog with tongue lapping for action, cunning as a savage
    pitted against the wilderness,
        Bareheaded,
        Shoveling,
        Wrecking,   15
        Planning,
        Building, breaking, rebuilding,
Under the smoke, dust all over his mouth, laughing with white teeth,
Under the terrible burden of destiny laughing as a young man laughs,
Laughing even as an ignorant fighter laughs who has never lost a
    battle,   20
Bragging and laughing that under his wrist is the pulse, and under his
    ribs the heart of the people,
        Laughing!
Laughing the stormy, husky, brawling laughter of Youth, half-naked,
    sweating, proud to be Hog Butcher, Tool Maker, Stacker of Wheat,
    Player with Railroads and Freight Handler to the Nation.

Limited

I am riding on a limited express, one of the crack trains of the nation.
Hurtling across the prairie into blue haze and dark air go fifteen all-
    steel coaches holding a thousand people.
(All the coaches shall be scrap and rust and all the men and women
    laughing in the diners and sleepers shall pass to ashes.)
I ask a man in the smoker where he is going and he answers:
    "Omaha."

DISCUSSION

1.   "Chicago," written over sixty years ago, captures the spirit of the Chicago that Sandburg knew. What elements are still characteristic of American cities?

2.   In lines 6–9 what accusations do "they" make? How does Sandburg answer these accusations?

3.   How does Sandburg's *personification* of the city add force and vitality to the poem? What characteristics tell you that the poem is *free verse* (see page 242)?

4.   The word *limited* has more than one meaning. Which meaning or meanings do you think Sandburg intended in his title "Limited"?

5.   Suggest a reason for the third line being in parentheses.

6.   What is *ironic* (see page 84) about the man's answer of "Omaha"?

For further activities, see page 276.

CARL SANDBURG

Four Preludes on Playthings of the Wind

"The past is a bucket of ashes"

1

The woman named Tomorrow
sits with a hairpin in her teeth
and takes her time
and does her hair the way she wants it
and fastens at last the last braid and coil   5
and puts the hairpin where it belongs
and turns and drawls: Well, what of it?
My grandmother, Yesterday, is gone.
What of it? Let the dead be dead.

2

The doors were cedar   10
and the panels strips of gold
and the girls were golden girls
and the panels read and the girls chanted:
    We are the greatest city,
    the greatest nation: 15
    nothing like us ever was.
The doors are twisted on broken hinges.
Sheets of rain swish through on the wind
    where the golden girls ran and the panels read:
    We are the greatest city,   20
    the greatest nation,
    nothing like us ever was.

3
It has happened before.
Strong men put up a city and got
    a nation together,   25
And paid singers to sing and women
    to warble: We are the greatest city,
        the greatest nation,
        nothing like us ever was.

And while the singers sang   30
and the strong men listened
and paid the singers well
and felt good about it all,
    there were rats and lizards who listened
    . . . and the only listeners left now   35
    . . . are . . . the rats . . . and the lizards.

And there are black crows
crying, "Caw, caw,"
bringing mud and sticks
building a nest   40
over the words carved
on the doors where the panels were cedar
and the strips on the panels were gold
and the golden girls came singing:
    We are the greatest city,   45
    the greatest nation:
    nothing like us ever was.
The only singers now are crows crying, "Caw, caw,"
And the sheets of rain whine in the wind and doorways.
And the only listeners now are . . . the rats   50
    . . . and the lizards.

4

The feet of the rats
scribble on the doorsills;
the hieroglyphs of the rat footprints
chatter the pedigrees of the rats   55
and babble of the blood
and gabble of the breed
of the grandfathers and the great-grandfathers
of the rats.

And the wind shifts   60
and the dust on a doorsill shifts
and even the writing of the rat footprints
tells us nothing, nothing at all
about the greatest city, the greatest nation
where the strong men listened   65
and the women warbled: Nothing like us ever was.

DISCUSSION

1. How does the poet feel about the claims of any group to be the greatest city or nation?

2. Why are rats, crows, and lizards effective *images* for this poem?

3. How do you interpret the title in relation to the meaning of the poem?

4. *Onomatopoeia* denotes words whose sounds suggest their meanings—like *hiss, bark,* or *crash.* Find several onomatopoetic words in this poem and tell why they are effective.

VOCABULARY

Thanatopsis (page 220)

Bryant's title is only one of many words in English that originated in Greek roots or prefixes. Be your own wordsmith and see how many words you can make using each of these Greek forms.

auto	graph	phos, phot	phil	phobia
log	psych	anthrop	therm	path

Richard Cory (page 249)

Synonyms may be very close in denotation but have marked differences in connotation. For example, *credulous* and *gullible* both describe one who is too readily inclined to believe, but *credulous,* perhaps because of its Latin root, has a more favorable connotation. The following words have a generally favorable connotation when they describe people. Give at least one synonym for each with a less favorable connotation.

proud	childlike	curious	daring	slender
firm	enthusiastic	acquisitive	aggressive	flexible

Limited (page 271)

Words with multiple meanings do much to enrich the language. Sandburg used "limited" to suggest both the kind of train and the response of the man in the smoker. Here are some words with more than one meaning. On separate paper, use each of them at least twice, in sentences, to suggest at least two different meanings.

senseless	road	cry	silver	adamantine

COMPOSITION

The Chambered Nautilus (page 230)

Holmes, like many other poets and philosophers, finds that creatures from the natural world can teach humans an important lesson. Think of such a creature you have observed or read about. In a short composition describe its behavior and explain why it is instructive.

Because I could not stop for Death (page 247)

This poem and "Thanatopsis" (page 220) present the poets' ideas about death. What similarities do you find? What differences? Which agrees more nearly with your own ideas? In a well-organized composition, compare the attitudes expressed in these two poems and indicate which you find more satisfactory.

Miniver Cheevy (page 248)

Do you know someone like Miniver Cheevy? Choose a character from real life or fiction whose negative attitude creates personal problems or makes life unpleasant for others. Write a story that gives a portrait of such a person, or write an essay about this kind of person and use details from your observations of human behavior to lend credence to your ideas.

Richard Cory (page 249)

As an exercise in creating a word portrait, write a prose sketch of a person, real or imagined, concentrating on details that help to distinguish character. Then, using your prose sketch as a rough draft, translate your sketch into a poetic portrait.

Do not weep (page 255)

Crane uses the statement "war is kind," but through irony he makes the reader feel that war is really senseless, cruel, and savage. Think of an idea you believe in strongly. Phrase it to say the opposite of what you mean. Then in two or three paragraphs develop the statement through the use of irony so that your real meaning is clear, in spite of the wording of the original statement.

The Death of the Hired Man (page 264)

Write a story that delves into the relationship between Silas and Harold when they worked together. Work from the clues you find in the poem regarding their respective characters. You will need to add incidents and dialogue, but be careful that you do not contradict Frost's characterization.

WALLACE STEVENS

A Postcard from the Volcano

Children picking up our bones
Will never know that these were once
As quick as foxes on the hill;

And that in autumn, when the grapes
Made sharp air sharper by their smell   5
These had a being, breathing frost;

And least will guess that with our bones
We left much more, left what still is
The look of things, left what we felt

At what we saw. The spring clouds blow   10
Above the shuttered mansion-house,
Beyond our gate and the windy sky

Cries out a literate despair.
We knew for long the mansion's look
And what we said of it became   15

A part of what it is . . . Children,
Still weaving budded aureoles,
Will speak our speech and never know,

Will say of the mansion that it seems
As if he that lived there left behind   20
A spirit storming in blank walls,

A dirty house in a gutted world,
A tatter of shadows peaked to white,
Smeared with the gold of the opulent sun.

17. *budded aureoles:* halos made of flowers.

DISCUSSION

1. The speaker states that "with our bones / We left much more." What have they left behind?

2. "Children . . . will speak our speech and never know." What does "speak our speech" mean? The speaker says several times that the children will "never know." What is it that they will never know?

3. Look carefully at the last stanza. How is the mansion described? What might it stand for?

4. What do you think "a postcard from the volcano" means? (Who sends the postcard? What is the volcano?)

For further activities, see page 320.

SARA TEASDALE

Advice to a Girl

No one worth possessing
Can be quite possessed;
Lay that on your heart,
My young angry dear;
This truth, this hard and precious stone,   5
Lay it on your hot cheek,
Let it hide your tear.
Hold it like a crystal
When you are alone
And gaze in the depths of the icy stone.   10
Long, look long and you will be blessed:
No one worth possessing
Can be quite possessed.

Lessons

Unless I learn to ask no help
    From any other soul but mine,
To seek no strength in waving reeds
    Nor shade beneath a straggling pine;
Unless I learn to look at Grief   5
    Unshrinking from her tear-blind eyes,
And take from Pleasure fearlessly
    Whatever gifts will make me wise—
Unless I learn these things on earth,
Why was I ever given birth?

DISCUSSION

1. "No one worth possessing / Can be quite possessed," the speaker says twice in "Advice to a Girl." What does she mean? Do you agree?

2. In line 5 the poet begins an extended comparison between "this truth" and a "stone." What four words are used to describe the stone? What does the speaker advise be done with the stone? Describe how "this truth" and the "stone" are alike.

3. In "Lessons" the poet *personifies* grief and pleasure, giving them human qualities. How, according to the poem, should one deal with grief and pleasure? Tell in your own words what other lessons the speaker feels must be learned.

ROBINSON JEFFERS

HURT HAWKS

I

The broken pillar of the wing jags from the clotted shoulder,
The wing trails like a banner in defeat,
No more to use the sky forever but live with famine
And pain a few days: cat nor coyote
Will shorten the week of waiting for death, there is game without
    talons.   5
He stands under the oak-bush and waits
The lame feet of salvation; at night he remembers freedom
And flies in a dream, the dawns ruin it.

He is strong and pain is worse to the strong, incapacity is worse.
The curs of the day come and torment him   10
At distance, no one but death the redeemer will humble that head,
The intrepid readiness, the terrible eyes.
The wild God of the world is sometimes merciful to those
That ask mercy, not often to the arrogant.
You do not know him, you communal people, or you have forgotten
    him;   15
Intemperate and savage, the hawk remembers him;
Beautiful and wild, the hawks, and men that are dying, remember him.

    II
I'd sooner, except the penalties, kill a man than a hawk; but the great
    redtail
Had nothing left but unable misery
From the bone too shattered for mending, the wing that trailed under his
    talons when he moved.   20
We had fed him six weeks, I gave him freedom,
He wandered over the foreland hill and returned in the evening, asking
    for death,
Not like a beggar, still eyed with the old
Implacable arrogance. I gave him the lead gift in the twilight. What fell
    was relaxed,
Owl-downy, soft feminine feathers; but what   25
Soared: the fierce rush: the night-herons by the flooded river cried fear at
    its rising
Before it was quite unsheathed from reality.

DISCUSSION   1. Tell in your own words what happens in parts I and II of the poem. What is "the lead gift" referred to in line 24?

2. How would you describe the poet's attitude toward the hawk? Mention specific words and phrases that reveal that attitude. How do other animals regard the wounded hawk (part I)? How do you interpret the last two lines of the poem?

3. What contrast is being made between the hawk and "you communal people" (line 15)? The poem tells of one hurt hawk. Why, then, do you think it is called "Hurt Hawks"?

EDNA ST. VINCENT MILLAY

Dirge Without Music

I am not resigned to the shutting away of loving hearts in the hard ground.
So it is, and so it will be, for so it has been, time out of mind:
Into the darkness they go, the wise and the lovely. Crowned
With lilies and with laurel they go; but I am not resigned.

Lovers and thinkers, into the earth with you.   5
Be one with the dull, the indiscriminate dust.
A fragment of what you felt, or what you knew,
A formula, a phrase remains,—but the best is lost.

The answers quick & keen, the honest look, the laughter, the love,
They are gone. They have gone to feed the roses. Elegant and curled   10
Is the blossom. Fragrant is the blossom. I know. But I do not approve.
More precious was the light in your eyes than all the roses in the world.

Down, down, down into the darkness of the grave
Gently they go, the beautiful, the tender, the kind;
Quietly they go, the intelligent, the witty, the brave.   15
I know. But I do not approve. And I am not resigned.

Dirge: funeral hymn; lament.   6. *indiscriminate:* not capable of making distinctions between more or less valuable things.

DISCUSSION   1.   For the most part this poem seems to be about death in general. What is it
the speaker laments most about death? Which line in the poem suggests that the
speaker is thinking of a specific person?

2.   Read the poem aloud, listening carefully to the way it sounds. Notice the
sound of the vowels, as in line 13: "Down, down, down into the darkness of the
grave." The line *sounds* dark and dull and mournful. Contrast it with the sound of
"quick & keen," in line 9. What other instances can you find of sound echoing
meaning? (Look for the pacing of the lines, too, and consonant sounds.)

Childhood Is the Kingdom Where Nobody Dies

Childhood is not from birth to a certain age and at a certain age
The child is grown, and puts away childish things.
Childhood is the kingdom where nobody dies.

Nobody that matters, that is. Distant relatives of course
Die, whom one never has seen or has seen for an hour,   5
And they gave one candy in a pink-and-green striped bag, or a jack-
    knife,
And went away, and cannot really be said to have lived at all.

And cats die. They die on the floor and lash their tails,
And their reticent fur is suddenly all in motion
With fleas that one never knew were there,   10
Polished and brown, knowing all there is to know,
Trekking off into the living world.
You fetch a shoe-box, but it's much too small, because she won't curl
    up now:
So you find a bigger box, and bury her in the yard, and weep.

But you do not wake up a month from then, two months,   15
A year from then, two years, in the middle of the night
And weep, with your knuckles in your mouth, and say Oh, God! Oh,
    God!
Childhood is the kingdom where nobody dies that matters,—mothers
    and fathers don't die.

And if you have said, "For heaven's sake, must you always be kissing
    a person?"
Or, "I do wish to gracious you'd stop tapping on the window with your
    thimble!"   20
Tomorrow, or even the day after tomorrow if you're busy having fun,
Is plenty of time to say, "I'm sorry, mother."

To be grown up is to sit at the table with people who have died, who
    neither listen nor speak;
Who do not drink their tea, though they always said
Tea was such a comfort.   25

Run down into the cellar and bring up the last jar of raspberries; they
    are not tempted.
Flatter them, ask them what was it they said exactly
That time, to the bishop, or to the overseer, or to Mrs. Mason;
They are not taken in.
Shout at them, get red in the face, rise,   30
Drag them up out of their chairs by their stiff shoulders and shake
    them and yell at them;
They are not startled, they are not even embarrassed; they slide back
    into their chairs.

Your tea is cold now.
You drink it standing up,
And leave the house.   35

DISCUSSION   1.   According to the poem, what is the difference between the death of a pet and of someone "that matters"?

2.   Childhood, says the speaker, is when tomorrow is plenty of time to say "I'm sorry, mother." What happens to that time when childhood is over? What sort of things does one regret afterwards?

3.   The tea table scene described in the last three stanzas is not meant to be taken literally—it is a dramatic enactment of the finality of death. What feelings is the speaker describing in the next-to-last stanza? What change occurs in the last stanza? What do you think "the house" refers to?

For further activities, see page 320.

ARCHIBALD MacLEISH

ARS POETICA

A poem should be palpable and mute
As a globed fruit,

Dumb
As old medallions to the thumb,

Silent as the sleeve-worn stone   5
Of casement ledges where the moss has grown—

- A poem should be wordless
As the flight of birds.

*

A poem should be motionless in time
As the moon climbs,   10

Leaving, as the moon releases
Twig by twig the night-entangled trees,

Leaving, as the moon behind the winter leaves,
Memory by memory the mind—

A poem should be motionless in time   15
As the moon climbs.

*

A poem should be equal to:
Not true.

For all the history of grief
An empty doorway and a maple leaf.   20

For love
The leaning grasses and two lights above the sea—

A poem should not mean
But be.

Ars Poetica: the art of poetry.

DISCUSSION

1. "Ars Poetica" is a series of images, or vivid mental pictures. These images are *metaphors*—they imply a comparison between two things. An unknown—what the poet is describing—is referred to in terms of the known—something that the reader can visualize. (When the comparison is stated directly, using *like* or *as,* it is called a *simile.*)

"Ars Poetica" begins with four similes that describe how a poem should be silent and wordless. Since a poem is made up of words, this seems like a contradiction. But look at the similes carefully. What do they tell you about what MacLeish means by the "silent" and "wordless" quality of a poem?

2. In lines 19–20, "all the history of grief" is referred to in terms of "an empty doorway and a maple leaf." Why is that image effective in conveying grief?

3. All of the images in the poem lead up to the statement in the last two lines. How do you interpret that statement? How does MacLeish's use of images in "Ars Poetica" illustrate the statement in the last two lines?

For further activities, see page 320.

E. E. CUMMINGS

anyone lived in a pretty how town

anyone lived in a pretty how town
(with up so floating many bells down)
spring summer autumn winter
he sang his didn't he danced his did.

Women and men (both little and small)   5
cared for anyone not at all
they sowed their isn't they reaped their same
sun moon stars rain

children guessed (but only a few
and down they forgot as up they grew   10
autumn winter spring summer)
that noone loved him more by more

when by now and tree by leaf
she laughed his joy she cried his grief
bird by snow and stir by still   15
anyone's any was all to her

someones married their everyones
laughed their cryings and did their dance
(sleep wake hope and then) they
said their nevers they slept their dream   20

stars rain sun moon
(and only the snow can begin to explain
how children are apt to forget to remember
with up so floating many bells down)

one day anyone died i guess   25
(and noone stooped to kiss his face)
busy folk buried them side by side
little by little and was by was

all by all and deep by deep
and more by more they dream their sleep 30
noone and anyone earth by april
wish by spirit and if by yes.

Women and men (both dong and ding)
summer autumn winter spring
reaped their sowing and went their came 35
sun moon stars rain

DISCUSSION

1. This poem tells a story. Who are the main characters? What is their relationship to the other people in the town?

2. Certain groups of words are used over and over like a refrain. What is the effect of the repetition? What point is Cummings making about the nature of human life?

3. Cummings often uses verbs as nouns: "he sang his didn't he danced his did." Point out other places where Cummings uses words in a way that makes them a different part of speech from what they usually are. What other unusual things does he do with words and meaning? How does Cummings's unusual choice and arrangement of words contribute to the poem's meaning?

4. *Rhythm* refers to the flowing sound of words together, the pace and beat, the rise and fall, the feeling and tone, that come through when a poem is read aloud. Read this poem aloud at least once. How does its rhythm fit the theme of the poem?

E. E. CUMMINGS

i thank You God for most this amazing

i thank You God for most this amazing
day:for the leaping greenly spirits of trees
and a blue true dream of sky;and for everything
which is natural which is infinite which is yes

(i who have died am alive again today,   5
and this is the sun's birthday;this is the birth
day of life and of love and wings:and of the gay
great happening illimitably earth)

how should tasting touching hearing seeing
breathing any—lifted from the no   10
of all nothing—human merely being
doubt unimaginable You?

(now the ears of my ears awake and
now the eyes of my eyes are opened)

DISCUSSION   1. How would you describe the mood of the speaker?
Point out words and phrases that express that mood. The
second and fourth stanzas are enclosed in parentheses.
Why are they set off from the other stanzas?

2. Cummings often reverses the usual order of words. For
example, he says ''most this amazing day'' rather than ''this
most amazing day.'' Find other examples of reversed word
order. What is the effect of this reversal?

MARIANNE MOORE

The Fox and the Grapes

A fox of Gascon, though some say of Norman descent,
When starved till faint gazed up at a trellis to which grapes
                                   were tied—
    Matured till they glowed with a purplish tint
    As though there were gems inside.   5
Now grapes were what our adventurer on strained haunches
                               chanced to crave
    But because he could not reach the vine
He said, "These grapes are sour; I'll leave them for some knave."

Better, I think, than an embittered whine.   10

                              (Book Three, XI)

DISCUSSION

1. When the fox can't reach the grapes, he rationalizes that they are sour and he doesn't want them anyway. Do you agree that his rationalization might be better than "an embittered whine"? Explain.

2. The usual moral at the end of this Aesop fable is something like, "It's easy to despise what you cannot get." Do you prefer the poet's "moral"? Explain.

For further activities, see page 320.

SILENCE

My father used to say,
"Superior people never make long visits,
have to be shown Longfellow's grave
or the glass flowers at Harvard.
Self-reliant like the cat—   5
that takes its prey to privacy,
the mouse's limp tail hanging like a shoelace from its mouth—
they sometimes enjoy solitude,
and can be robbed of speech
by speech which has delighted them.   10
The deepest feeling always shows itself in silence;
not in silence, but restraint."
Nor was he insincere in saying, "Make my house your inn."
Inns are not residences.

DISCUSSION

1.   According to the speaker's father, how do "superior
people" act when they are guests? Why don't they "have to
be shown Longfellow's grave / or the glass flowers at Harvard"? What is good about the kind of people who "can be
robbed of speech / by speech which has delighted them"?
What would this show about a person?

2.   The speaker's father believes that superior people do
not make long visits, yet he says, "Make my house your
inn." Why is this statement not insincere? What statement
would be insincere?

For further activities, see page 320.

THEODORE ROETHKE

Night Journey

Now as the train bears west,
Its rhythm rocks the earth,
And from my Pullman berth
I stare into the night
While others take their rest.   5
Bridges of iron lace,
A suddenness of trees,
A lap of mountain mist
All cross my line of sight,
Then a bleak wasted place,   10
And a lake below my knees.
Full on my neck I feel
The straining at a curve;
My muscles move with steel,
I wake in every nerve.   15
I watch a beacon swing
From dark to blazing bright;
We thunder through ravines
And gullies washed with light.
Beyond the mountain pass   20
Mist deepens on the pane;
We rush into a rain
That rattles double glass.
Wheels shake the roadbed stone,
The pistons jerk and shove,   25
I stay up half the night
To see the land I love.

DISCUSSION

1. Which lines emphasize the train's speed? Which words in these lines would you single out for creating the effect?

2. Read the poem aloud. How does the poem's *rhythm* (see page 290) suggest a train trip?

3. Although the poet completes this poem by saying, "To see the land I love," what case could you make that the speaker stays up because he enjoys feeling and hearing the train's movement?

The Waking

I wake to sleep, and take my waking slow.
I feel my fate in what I cannot fear.
I learn by going where I have to go.

We think by feeling. What is there to know?
I hear my being dance from ear to ear.   5
I wake to sleep, and take my waking slow.

Of those so close beside me, which are you?
God bless the Ground! I shall walk softly there,
And learn by going where I have to go.

Light takes the Tree; but who can tell us how?   10
The lowly worm climbs up a winding stair·
I wake to sleep, and take my waking slow.

Great Nature has another thing to do
To you and me; so take the lively air,
And, lovely, learn by going where to go.   15

This shaking keeps me steady. I should know.
What falls away is always. And is near.
I wake to sleep, and take my waking slow.
I learn by going where I have to go.

DISCUSSION

1. What does the line, "I learn by going where I have to go" mean? It is repeated with slight variation four times. Why? What does the poet mean when he says, "We think by feeling"?

2. Rather than attempting to interpret this poem in one or two silent readings, read the poem aloud several times. Notice the rhyme scheme and the sound of the lines. How do these increase your understanding of "The Waking"?

I

Runs falls rises stumbles on from darkness into darkness
and the darkness thicketed with shapes of terror
and the hunters pursuing and the hounds pursuing
and the night cold and the night long and the river
to cross and the jack-muh-lanterns beckoning beckoning   5
and blackness ahead and when shall I reach that somewhere
morning and keep on going and never turn back and keep on going

       Runagate
           Runagate
                Runagate   10

Many thousands rise and go
many thousands crossing over

                     O mythic North
                O star-shaped yonder Bible city

Some go weeping and some rejoicing   15
some in coffins and some in carriages
some in silks and some in shackles

       Rise and go or fare you well

No more auction block for me
no more driver's lash for me   20

     If you see my Pompey, 30 yrs of age,
     new breeches, plain stockings, negro shoes;
     if you see my Anna, likely young mulatto
     branded E on the right cheek, R on the left,
     catch them if you can and notify subscriber.   25
     Catch them if you can, but it won't be easy.
     They'll dart underground when you try to catch them,
     plunge into quicksand, whirlpools, mazes,
     turn into scorpions when you try to catch them.

And before I'll be a slave   30
I'll be buried in my grave

Runagate: renegade or deserter; here, a runaway slave.   5. *jack-muh-lanterns:* swamp gas.

North star and bonanza gold
I'm bound for the freedom, freedom-bound
and oh Susyanna don't you cry for me

Runagate   35

Runagate

II
Rises from their anguish and their power,

Harriet Tubman,

woman of earth, whipscarred,
a summoning, a shining   40

Mean to be free

And this was the way of it, brethren brethren,
way we journeyed from Can't to Can.
Moon so bright and no place to hide,
the cry up and the patterollers riding,   45
hound dogs belling in bladed air.
And fear starts a-murbling, Never make it,
we'll never make it. *Hush that now,*
and she's turned upon us, levelled pistol
glinting in the moonlight: 50
Dead folks can't jaybird-talk, she says;
you keep on going now or die, she says.

Wanted   Harriet Tubman   alias The General
alias Moses   Stealer of Slaves

In league with Garrison   Alcott   Emerson   55
Garrett   Douglas   Thoreau   John Brown

38. *Harriet Tubman:* an escaped slave who returned to the South
many times to lead other slaves to freedom. She carried a pistol to
prevent anyone from turning back, and thus endangering the lives
of the others.   45. *patterollers:* night guards over slaves.
55–56. *Garrison . . . John Brown:* leaders of the movement to abolish slavery.

Armed and known to be Dangerous

Wanted   Reward   Dead or Alive

Tell me, Ezekiel, oh tell me do you see
mailed Jehovah coming to deliver me?   60

Hoot-owl calling in the ghosted air,
five times calling to the hants in the air.
Shadow of a face in the scary leaves,
shadow of a voice in the talking leaves:

Come ride-a my train   65

Oh that train, ghost-story train
through swamp and savanna movering movering,
over trestles of dew, through caves of the wish,
Midnight Special on a sabre track movering movering,
first stop Mercy and the last Hallelujah.   70

Come ride-a my train

Mean mean mean to be free.

DISCUSSION   1.   Read aloud the first ten lines of the poem. What is the pace of your voice?
What emotion is being expressed? How is that pace and emotion appropriate for
the situation being described?

2.   The poem alternates between several different speakers. Who speaks in lines
21–29? Point out other voices in the poem. Which lines seem to be spoken by a
narrator or chorus?

3.   What were the slaves "crossing over" (line 12)? What other exodus do the
biblical references refer to?

4.   In lines 66–70 the poet uses an extended *metaphor* (see page 287), comparing the slaves' escape north to a ride on a train. (The Underground Railroad was
the name given the secret network of cooperation aiding fugitive slaves to escape
north to freedom.) What "tunnels" does this "train" go through? Why is its first
stop called "Mercy" and its last stop "Hallelujah"?

ROBERT HAYDEN

Those Winter Sundays

Sundays too my father got up early
and put his clothes on in the blueblack cold,
then with cracked hands that ached
from labor in the weekday weather made
banked fires blaze. No one ever thanked him.   5

I'd wake and hear the cold splintering, breaking.
When the rooms were warm, he'd call,
and slowly I would rise and dress,
fearing the chronic angers of that house,

Speaking indifferently to him,   10
who had driven out the cold
and polished my good shoes as well.
What did I know, what did I know
of love's austere and lonely offices?

DISCUSSION

1. What kind of man was the speaker's father? Did the son appreciate his father when he was a child? Does he now? Explain.

2. "Offices" as used in this poem means "an act performed for another or a religious service." It comes from a Latin word meaning "performance of duty." "Austere" means severe, stern, or plain, and it is often used to describe a person who is self-denying and restrained. What do you think "love's austere and lonely offices" (line 14) means? What is the emotional effect of the speaker's repeating the phrase "What did I know" (line 13)?

GWENDOLYN BROOKS

The Crazy Woman

I shall not sing a May song.
A May song should be gay.
I'll wait until November
And sing a song of gray.

I'll wait until November.   5
That is the time for me.
I'll go out in the frosty dark
And sing most terribly.

And all the little people
Will stare at me and say,   10
"That is the Crazy Woman
Who would not sing in May."

DISCUSSION Why does the speaker sing in November rather than in May? Do you think she is "crazy"? Explain.

GWENDOLYN BROOKS

BEVERLY HILLS, CHICAGO

("and the people live till they have white hair")
E. M. Price

The dry brown coughing beneath their feet,
(Only a while, for the handyman is on his way)
These people walk their golden gardens.
We say ourselves fortunate to be driving by today.

That we may look at them, in their gardens where   5
The summer ripeness rots. But not raggedly.
Even the leaves fall down in lovelier patterns here.
And the refuse, the refuse is a neat brilliancy.

When they flow sweetly into their houses
With softness and slowness touched by that everlasting gold,   10
We know what they go to. To tea. But that does not mean
They will throw some little black dots into some water and
    add sugar and the juice of the cheapest lemons that are sold,

While downstairs that woman's vague phonograph bleats, "Knock me a kiss."
And the living all to be made again in the sweatingest physical manner
Tomorrow. . . . Not that anybody is saying that these people have no trouble.   15
Merely that it is trouble with a gold-flecked beautiful banner.

Nobody is saying that these people do not ultimately cease to be. And
Sometimes their passings are even more painful than ours.
It is just that so often they live till their hair is white.
They make excellent corpses, among the expensive flowers. . . .   20

Nobody is furious. Nobody hates these people.
At least, nobody driving by in this car.
It is only natural, however, that it should occur to us
How much more fortunate they are than we are.

It is only natural that we should look and look   25
At their wood and brick and stone
And think, while a breath of pine blows,
How different these are from our own.

We do not want them to have less.
But it is only natural that we should think we have not enough.   30
We drive on, we drive on.
When we speak to each other our voices are a little gruff.

DISCUSSION

1. How does life in the Beverly Hills neighborhood contrast with the life of the speaker and her family? What is the significance of "they live till their hair is white" (line 19)?

2. Describe the attitude of the people in the car toward the people in Beverly Hills. Why are their voices "a little gruff" when they drive on?

3. The color gold is mentioned three times in connection with the Beverly Hills neighborhood. What are the *connotations* (see page 249) of the word *gold?*

ROBERT LOWELL

WATER

It was a Maine lobster town—
each morning boatloads of hands
pushed off for granite
quarries on the islands,

and left dozens of bleak   5
white frame houses stuck
like oyster shells
on a hill of rock,

and below us, the sea lapped
the raw little match-stick   10
mazes of a weir,
where the fish for bait were trapped.

Remember? We sat on a slab of rock.
From this distance in time,
it seems the color   15
of iris, rotting and turning purpler,

but it was only
the usual gray rock
turning the usual green
when drenched by the sea.   20

The sea drenched the rock
at our feet all day,
and kept tearing away
flake after flake.

One night you dreamed   25
You were a mermaid clinging
    to a wharf-pile,
and trying to pull
off the barnacles with your hands.
We wished our two souls
might return like gulls   30
to the rock. In the end,
the water was too cold for us.

11. *weir* (wîr): a fence placed in water to trap fish.

DISCUSSION

1. On one level this poem (up to the last two stanzas) is about two people spending a day together beside the ocean. On another level it is about their relationship. Pick out some of the images and words that describe the scene. What is their general effect? Is there anything bright about the poem?

2. If you look at the poem as a *metaphor* (see page 287), what is being compared to the slab of rock? What is being compared to the water? "In the end," the speaker says, "the water was too cold for us." What do you think he means?

3. The "slab of rock" is remembered as "the color / of iris" although "it was only / the usual gray rock." Why do you think the speaker remembers the rock differently from what it was?

JAMES DICKEY

The Heaven of Animals

Here they are. The soft eyes open.
If they have lived in a wood
It is a wood.
If they have lived on plains
It is grass rolling   5
Under their feet forever.

Having no souls, they have come,
Anyway, beyond their knowing.
Their instincts wholly bloom
And they rise.   10
The soft eyes open.

To match them, the landscape flowers,
Outdoing, desperately
Outdoing what is required:
The richest wood,   15
The deepest field.

For some of these,
It could not be the place
It is, without blood.
These hunt, as they have done,   20
But with claws and teeth grown perfect,

More deadly than they can believe.
They stalk more silently,
And crouch on the limbs of trees,
And their descent   25
Upon the bright backs of their prey

May take years
In a sovereign floating of joy.
And those that are hunted
Know this as their life,   30
Their reward: to walk

Under such trees in full knowledge
Of what is in glory above them,
And to feel no fear,
But acceptance, compliance.   35
Fulfilling themselves without pain

At the cycle's center,
They tremble, they walk
Under the tree,
They fall, they are torn,   40
They rise, they walk again.

DISCUSSION   1. How is "heaven" different from earth for the animals that hunt? For those that are hunted? How is life for both the same as on earth?

2. The hunted animals are "at the cycle's center" (line 37). What is the cycle?

3. How is the "heaven of animals" different from usual ideas about heaven? Do you think Dickey is making a point about the relationship between the strong and the weak? About human beings? Explain.

JAMES DICKEY

The

Lifeguard

In a stable of boats I lie still,
From all sleeping children hidden.
The leap of a fish from its shadow
Makes the whole lake instantly tremble.
With my foot on the water, I feel   5
The moon outside

Take the utmost of its power.
I rise and go out through the boats.
I set my broad sole upon silver,
On the skin of the sky, on the moonlight,   10
Stepping outward from earth onto water
In quest of the miracle

This village of children believed
That I could perform as I dived
For one who had sunk from my sight.   15
I saw his cropped haircut go under.
I leapt, and my steep body flashed
Once, in the sun.

Dark drew all the light from my eyes.
Like a man who explores his death   20
By the pull of his slow-moving shoulders,
I hung head down in the cold,
Wide-eyed, contained, and alone
Among the weeds,

And my fingertips turned into stone   25
From clutching immovable blackness.
Time after time I leapt upward
Exploding in breath, and fell back
From the change in the children's faces
At my defeat.   30

Beneath them, I swam to the boathouse
With only my life in my arms
To wait for the lake to shine back
At the risen moon with such power
That my steps on the light of the ripples   35
Might be sustained.

Beneath me is nothing but brightness
Like the ghost of a snow field in summer.
As I move toward the center of the lake,
Which is also the center of the moon,   40
I am thinking of how I may be
The savior of one

Who has already died in my care.
The dark trees fade from around me.
The moon's dust hovers together.   45
I call softly out, and the child's
Voice answers through blinding water.
Patiently, slowly,

He rises, dilating to break
The surface of stone with his forehead.   50
He is one I do not remember
Having ever seen in his life.
The ground that I stand on is trembling
Upon his smile.

I wash the black mud from my hands.   55
On a light given off by the grave
I kneel in the quick of the moon
At the heart of a distant forest
And hold in my arms a child
Of water, water, water.

DISCUSSION   1. The poem alternates between the lifeguard's memory of the child's drowning
and his fantasy of performing a "miracle." What miracle is he seeking? Which
lines in the poem tell of the actual drowning? Which describe the fantasy?

2. What images in the poem describe the lifeguard's failure to rescue the child?
Why is his failure so devastating to him?

3. There are several references to the lifeguard's stepping on the surface of the
lake. How is the surface of the lake described at various places in the poem?
What connection is there between the lifeguard's "walking on water" and his
fantasy of being the "savior of one / Who has already died in my care" (lines
42–43)?

4. The poem ends with the lifeguard holding in his arms "a child / Of water,
water, water." What is the effect of repeating "water" three times?

DENISE LEVERTOV

Laying the Dust

What a sweet smell rises
    when you lay the dust—
bucket after bucket of water thrown
on the yellow grass.
                The water   5
flashes
each time you
make it leap—
      arching its glittering back.
The sound of   10
       more water
pouring into the pail
almost quenches my thirst.
Surely when flowers
grow here, they'll not   15
smell sweeter than this
       wet ground, suddenly black.

DISCUSSION   What senses does the poet appeal to in "Laying the Dust"?
Describe how the water looks as it is thrown from the
bucket. How can the sound and the smell of the water be
"sweet"?

ANNE SEXTON

YOUNG

A thousand doors ago
when I was a lonely kid
in a big house with four
garages and it was summer
as long as I could remember,   5
I lay on the lawn at night,
clover wrinkling under me,
the wise stars bedding over me,
my mother's window a funnel
of yellow heat running out,   10
my father's window, half shut,
an eye where sleepers pass,
and the boards of the house
were smooth and white as wax
and probably a million leaves   15
sailed on their strange stalks
as the crickets ticked together
and I, in my brand new body,
which was not a woman's yet,
told the stars my questions   20
and thought God could really see
the heat and the painted light,
elbows, knees, dreams, goodnight.

DISCUSSION

1.   The speaker sets the time of her memory as "a thousand doors ago." What do you think she means by that? How can doors mark the passage of time?

2.   There are many vivid images in this poem. How does the poet use *metaphor* and *simile* (see page 287) to convey the experience of lying outside on a summer night?

TERESA PALOMA ACOSTA

My Mother Pieced Quilts

they were just meant as covers
in winters
as weapons
against pounding january winds

but it was just that every morning I awoke to these   5
october ripened canvases
passed my hand across their cloth faces
and began to wonder how you pieced
all these together
these strips of gentle communion cotton and flannel nightgowns   10
wedding organdies
dime store velvets

how you shaped patterns square and oblong and round
positioned
balanced   15
then cemented them
with your thread
a steel needle
a thimble

how the thread darted in and out   20
galloping along the frayed edges, tucking them in
as you did us at night
oh how you stretched and turned and re-arranged
your michigan spring faded curtain pieces

my father's santa fe work shirt   25
the summer denims, the tweeds of fall

in the evening you sat at your canvas
—our cracked linoleum floor the drawing board
me lounging on your arm
and you staking out the plan: 30
whether to put the lilac purple of easter against the red plaid of winter-going-
into-spring
whether to mix a yellow with blue and white and paint the
corpus christi noon when my father held your hand
whether to shape a five-point star from the   35
somber black silk you wore to grandmother's funeral

you were the river current
carrying the roaring notes
forming them into pictures of a little boy reclining
a swallow flying   40
you were the caravan master at the reins
driving your threaded needle artillery across the mosaic cloth bridges
delivering yourself in separate testimonies.

oh mother you plunged me sobbing and laughing
into our past   45
into the river crossing at five
into the spinach fields
into the plainview cotton rows
into tuberculosis wards
into braids and muslin dresses   50
sewn hard and taut to withstand the thrashings of twenty-five years

stretched out they lay
armed/ready/shouting/celebrating

knotted with love
the quilts sing on

DISCUSSION   1. The quilts the mother made were "just meant as covers / in winters," as protection against the cold. Why do you think she took such care to make them beautiful? What do lines 37–43 tell you? What were the quilts made of? Why do they mean so much to the daughter?

2. In the last line the speaker says "the quilts sing on." In what way do the quilts "sing"?

Second Nature

DIANA CHANG

How do I feel
Fine wrist to small feet?
I cough Chinese.

To me, it occurs that Cézanne
Is not a Sung painter.   5

(My condition is no less gratuitous
    than this remark.)

The old China muses through me.
I am foreign to the new.
I sleep upon dead years.

Sometimes I dream in Chinese.   10
I dream my father's dreams.

I wake, grown up
And someone else.

I am the thin edge I sit on.
I begin to gray —white and black
    and in between.   15
My hair is America.

New England moonlights in me.

I attend what is Chinese
In everyone.

We are in the air.   20

I shuttle passportless within myself,
My eyes slant around both hemispheres,
Gaze through walls

And long still to be
Accustomed,   25
At home here,

Strange to say.

DISCUSSION

1. The speaker has a dual heritage, Chinese and American. Which heritage seems to be her "first nature" and which her "second nature"? How can you tell?

2. The speaker says, "I shuttle passportless within myself" (line 21). (To shuttle is to make short, frequent trips between two points; a passport is a document that allows one to go from one country to another.) Why is this travel image an appropriate description of her dual nature? How does she feel about "traveling" between two hemispheres?

DIANE WAKOSKI

Inside Out

I walk the purple carpet into your eye
carrying the silver butter server
but a truck rumbles by,
                leaving its black tire prints on my foot
and old images   the sound of banging screen doors on hot   5
                                      afternoons
        and a fly buzzing over the Kool-Aid spilled on the sink
flicker, as reflections on the metal surface.

Come in, you said,
inside your paintings, inside the blood factory, inside the   10
old songs that line your hands, inside
eyes that change like a snowflake every second,
inside spinach leaves holding that one piece of gravel,
inside the whiskers of a cat,
inside your old hat, and most of all inside your mouth where   15
                                        you
grind the pigments with your teeth, painting
with a broken bottle on the floor, and painting
with an ostrich feather on the moon that rolls out of my
                                      mouth.   20

You cannot let me walk inside you too long inside
the veins where my small feet touch
bottom.
You must reach inside and pull me
like a silver bullet   25
from your arm.

NIKKI GIOVANNI

Revolutionary Dreams

i used to dream militant
dreams of taking
over america to show
these white folks how it should be
done   5
i used to dream radical dreams
of blowing everyone away with my perceptive
powers
of correct analysis
i even used to think i'd be the one   10
to stop the riot and negotiate the peace
then i awoke and dug
that if i dreamed natural
dreams of being a natural
woman doing what a woman   15
does when she's natural
i would have a revolution

DISCUSSION   What dreams did the speaker used to have? "Then I
awoke," she says. What realization does she come to? Do
you think her new revolutionary dreams are personal or political? Both? Explain.

For further activities, see page 320.

NIKKI GIOVANNI

POETRY

poetry is motion graceful
as a fawn
gentle as a teardrop
strong like the eye
finding peace in a crowded room   5

we poets tend to think
our words are golden
though emotion speaks too
loudly to be defined
by silence   10

sometimes after midnight or just before
the dawn
we sit typewriter in hand
pulling loneliness around us
forgetting our lovers or children   15
who are sleeping
ignoring the weary wariness
of our own logic
to compose a poem
      no one understands it   20
it never says "love me" for poets are
beyond love
it never says "accept me" for poems seek not
acceptance but controversy
it only says "i am" and therefore   25
i concede that you are too

a poem is pure energy
horizontally contained
between the mind
of the poet and the ear of the reader   30
if it does not sing discard the ear
for poetry is song
if it does not delight discard
the heart for poetry is joy
if it does not inform then close   35
off the brain for it is dead
if it cannot heed the insistent message
that life is precious

which is all we poets
wrapped in our loneliness   40
are trying to say

For activities, see page 320.

VOCABULARY

A Postcard from the Volcano (page 278)

Notice the vivid image Stevens uses to describe autumn:

> And that in autumn, when the grapes
> Made sharp air sharper by their smell
> These had a being, breathing frost.

Here, three senses are appealed to: smell, touch (the feeling of the air), and sight. Through this image one can almost feel and smell an autumn day so chilly that you can see your breath.

For your favorite season, try to create two or three images that appeal to sight, smell, and touch and that convey the feeling of the season as vividly as Stevens's images do.

The Fox and the Grapes (page 292)

This fable is the source of the expression "sour grapes," which you have probably heard before. There are many sayings from Aesop's fables that are so familiar they are part of everyday language. Look at the following expressions which originated from Aesop's fables and tell what each means. Then use each expression in an appropriate sentence or two.

1. familiarity breeds contempt
2. look before you leap
3. actions speak louder than words
4. don't kill the goose that lays the golden eggs
5. a wolf in sheep's clothing
6. don't count your chickens before they're hatched
7. the boy who cried "wolf"
8. put your shoulder to the wheel

COMPOSITION

Childhood Is the Kingdom Where Nobody Dies (page 283)

This poem defines childhood in an unusual way. Think of your own definition of childhood. Beginning with Millay's phrase "Childhood is the kingdom where . . .," give your own definition, either in a short essay or in a poem.

Ars Poetica (page 286)

The poem ends with the statement, "A poem should not mean / But be." In a short composition give your interpretation of this statement and tell how it compares to your own ideas about poetry.

The Fox and the Grapes (page 292)

Look at the expressions in the vocabulary exercise for this poem. Choose one of them to use as a moral and create your own fable. Remember that a fable uses animal characters to express a truth about human nature.

Silence (page 293)

The speaker's father describes the characteristics he thinks belong to "superior people." What characteristics do *you* think "superior people" have? Choose one or two characteristics, and in a poem or essay, explain them further.

Revolutionary Dreams (page 317)

The speaker talks of "a natural woman doing what a woman does when she's natural." In a short essay give your own definition of a "natural" woman.

Ars Poetica (page 286), Poetry (page 318)

Both of these poems give a definition of poetry. Which definition comes closest to your own definition of poetry? Using that poem as a model, try to create your own images to convey what you think poetry is.

COMPOSITION

There is a *before* and an *after* to almost everything you read—an outline before and a revision after. Simply jotting down some kind of rough outline before getting started helps a writer make sure that he or she does not get sidetracked and that nothing important is left out. Revising is just as vital. A writer allows time to go back over what he or she has initially put down on paper, spotting obvious mistakes and changing words and phrases to make the meaning clearer.

Even poets are seldom able to dash off a poem. Far more frequently, what they write is the result of long labor, testing each word, considering alternative phrasings, until they have arrived at what seems the most effective—the perfect!—expression of their thoughts. Whitman's manuscripts, for example, show a poet crossing out one line, adding another, inserting a fresh image here, replacing a word there with one that seems more accurate.

You might well discover that revising is one of the most interesting and important parts of the writing process. What should you look for when you have finished your first draft? Look first for the kinds of mistakes that you know you are most likely to make. Spelling errors, punctuation errors, statements that are not complete sentences, errors of agreement (a singular subject and a plural verb, for example, or a plural pronoun with a singular noun)—these are the kinds of errors writers often commit. If you know that you are prone to make them too, watch for those in particular.

But go beyond the obvious. Are your thoughts clearly expressed? Would more (or better) examples make them even clearer? Can you substitute more specific language for some general terms? Have you omitted any steps in your argument, or put the steps in the wrong order?

In short, don't simply reread what you have written. Rather, read with a purpose, your eyes alert and on the lookout for specific kinds of flaws. Some of the best writing is done, in fact, after the first draft is finished.

**MAKING
REVISIONS**

ABOUT THE SELECTIONS

1. Of the many poems in this unit, which is your favorite? In a page or so, account for your choice as precisely as you can. Is it the subject matter, the thought expressed, the imagery, the melody, the relevance to your own life, or some other characteristic that appeals to you most? Quote passages from the poem to make your reasons clear, and be sure to revise to correct errors and make your sentences more precise.

2. Choose one of the shorter poems in the section and read it aloud, alone, several times. Look up any words you don't know. What words should be stressed? In what different tones of voice should different lines be read? Where should pauses be introduced? In two or three paragraphs offer specific advice on how to read the poem aloud effectively.

3. Several poems—by Robinson, Masters, Frost, Hayden, and others—describe particular people. Choose one character portrayed in verse and write a prose sketch of her or him. Be sure you understand all that the poet tells you about the person. Use your imagination, but don't introduce contradictory facts. For example, Richard Cory did kill himself. Your sketch must not change his fate, but it may help us understand it better.

4. A number of these poems describe regions that never existed: "The City in the Sea," and "The Heaven of Animals," among others. Imagine yourself propelled into one such region. Give a first-person account of your visit there. Exactly what did you see, hear, smell, taste, feel?

ON YOUR OWN

1. A *parody* is an imitation of a particular writer's work. A caricature cartoons a person's features amusingly; similarly, a parody exaggerates a writer's characteristics in ways that may make us smile. Try your hand at parodying one of the poets in this section. That is, write like her or him. What makes the poet distinctive? Is there a typical subject matter? A typical verse form? A fondness for certain kinds of words or rhythms? Remember: a good parody exaggerates, but it also reveals a sound knowledge of the poet being parodied.

2. Several poems in this unit develop comparisons: between the earth and a tomb (page 220), between a woman's beauty and a lovely ship (page 226), between a certain truth and a hard precious stone (page 279). Devise a comparison of your own to help your reader see something in a fresh way. Start with a thing, a person, an idea, an impression, or whatever.

3. Write a six-line stanza of *blank verse* on any appropriate subject of your choosing. Be sure you understand what blank verse is. (Rereading a few lines of "Thanatopsis" or "Birches" aloud will set the meter re-echoing in your mind. Ta-TUM, ta-TUM, ta-TUM, ta-TUM, ta-TUM: and now it's time for you to try your hand.) The first draft that you write you must revise; but every poet has to do the same.

4. Now recast the subject of the preceding assignment into the form of a four-line poem in *free verse*. Use line lengths appropriately, to emphasize what is important.

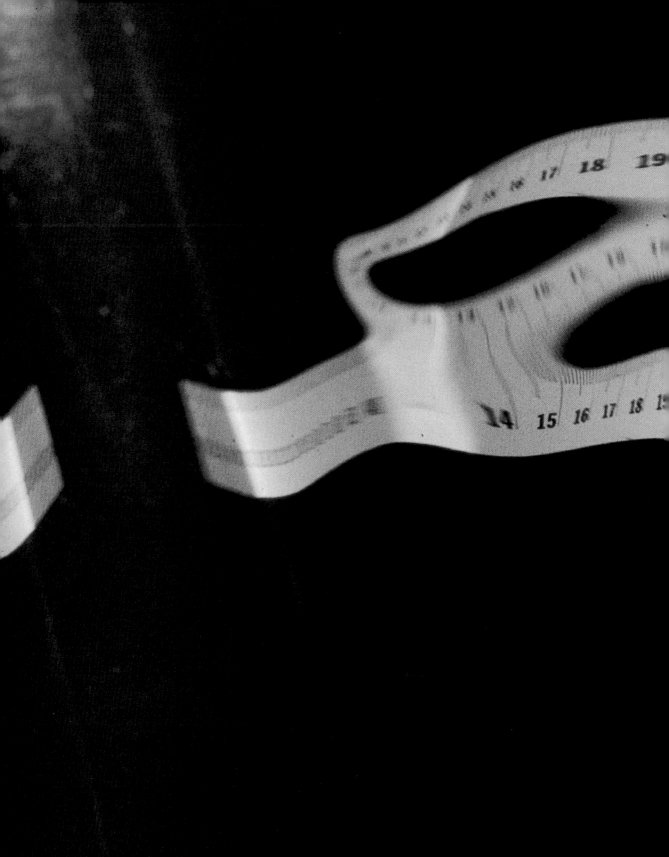

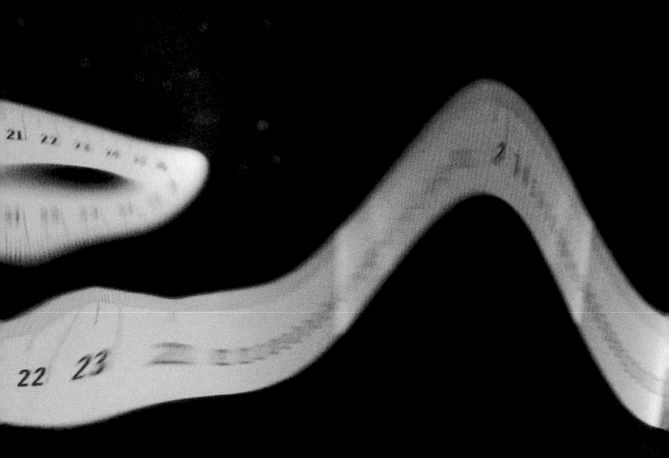

DRAMA

OUR TOWN

THORNTON WILDER

CHARACTERS

STAGE MANAGER	WOMAN IN THE BALCONY
DR. GIBBS	TALL MAN AT BACK OF AUDITORIUM
JOE CROWELL, JR.	LADY IN A BOX
HOWIE NEWSOME	SIMON STIMSON
MRS. GIBBS	MRS. SOAMES
MRS. WEBB	CONSTABLE WARREN
GEORGE GIBBS	THREE BASEBALL PLAYERS
REBECCA GIBBS	SI CROWELL
WALLY WEBB	SAM CRAIG
EMILY WEBB	JOE STODDARD
PROFESSOR WILLARD	PEOPLE OF THE TOWN
MR. WEBB	

The entire play takes place in Grover's Corners, New Hampshire, 1901 to 1913.

Act 1

No curtain. No scenery. The audience, arriving, sees an empty stage in half-light. Presently the Stage Manager, hat on and pipe in mouth, enters and begins placing a table and three chairs downstage left, and a table and three chairs downstage right. He also places a low bench at the corner of what will be the Webb house, left. "Left" and "right" are from the point of view of the actor facing the audience. "Up" is toward the back wall. As the house lights go down he has finished setting the stage and, leaning against the right proscenium[1] pillar, watches the late arrivals in the audience. When the auditorium is in complete darkness he speaks:

[1] *proscenium* (prō-sē′nē-əm): small area on a stage in front of the curtain; where action takes place when curtain is closed.

STAGE MANAGER: This play is called "Our Town." It was written by Thornton Wilder; produced and directed by A—— (or: produced by A——; directed by B——). In it you will see Miss C——; Miss D——; Miss E——; and Mr. F——; Mr. G——; Mr. H——; and many others. The name of the town is Grover's Corners, New Hampshire—just across the Massachusetts line: latitude 42 degrees 40 minutes; longitude 70 degrees 37 minutes. The First Act shows a day in our town. The day is May 7, 1901. The time is just before dawn. [A rooster crows.] The sky is beginning to show some streaks of light over in the East there, behind our mount'in. The morning star always gets wonderful bright the minute before it has to go,—doesn't it? [He stares at it for a moment, then goes upstage.] Well, I'd better show you how our town lies. Up here—[that is: parallel with the back wall] is Main Street. Way back there is the railway station; tracks go that way. Polish Town's across the tracks, and some Canuck[2] families. [toward the left] Over there is the Congregational Church; across the street's the Presbyterian. Methodist and Unitarian are over there. Baptist is down in the holla' by the river. Catholic Church is over beyond the tracks. Here's the Town Hall and Post Office combined; jail's in the basement. Bryan[3] once made a speech from these very steps here. Along here's a row of stores. Hitching posts and horse blocks in front of them. First automobile's going to come along in about five years—belonged to Banker Cartwright, our richest citizen . . . lives in the big white house up on the hill. Here's the grocery store and here's Mr. Morgan's drugstore. Most everybody in town manages to look into those two stores once a day. Public School's over yonder. High School's still farther over. Quarter of nine mornings, noontimes, and three o'clock afternoons, the hull town can hear the yelling and screaming from those schoolyards. [He approaches the table and chairs downstage right.] This is our doctor's house,—Doc Gibbs'. This is the back door. [Two arched trellises, covered with vines and flowers, are pushed out, one by each proscenium pillar.] There's some scenery for those who think they have to have scenery. This is Mrs. Gibbs' garden. Corn . . . peas . . . beans . . . hollyhocks . . . heliotrope . . . and a lot of burdock. [Crosses the stage] In those days our newspaper come out twice a week—the Grover's Corners *Sentinel*— and this is Editor Webb's house. And this is Mrs. Webb's garden. Just like Mrs. Gibbs', only it's got a lot of sunflowers, too. [He looks upward, center stage.] Right here . . .'s a big butternut tree. [He returns to his place by the right proscenium pillar and looks at the audience for a minute.] Nice town, y'know what I mean? Nobody very remarkable ever come out of it, s'far as we know. The earliest tombstones in the cemetery up there on the mountain say 1670–1680—they're Grovers and Cart-

[2] *Canuck:* slang term for French-Canadian.
[3] *Bryan:* William Jennings Bryan (1860–1925), American statesman and lawyer; three-time presidential candidate.

wrights and Gibbses and Herseys—
same names as are around here now.
Well, as I said: it's about dawn. The
only lights on in town are in a cottage
over by the tracks where a Polish
mother's just had twins. And in the
Joe Crowell house, where Joe Junior's
getting up so as to deliver the paper.
And in the depot, where Shorty Hawkins is gettin' ready to flag the 5:45 for
Boston. [A train whistle is heard. The
Stage Manager takes out his watch and
nods.] Naturally, out in the country—
all around—there've been lights on for
some time, what with milkin's and so
on. But town people sleep late. So—
another day's begun. There's Doc
Gibbs comin' down Main Street now,
comin' back from that baby case. And
here's his wife comin' downstairs to
get breakfast. [Mrs. Gibbs, a plump,
pleasant woman in the middle thirties,
comes "downstairs" right. She pulls up an
imaginary window shade in her kitchen
and starts to make a fire in her stove.]
Doc Gibbs died in 1930. The new hospital's named after him. Mrs. Gibbs
died first—long time ago, in fact. She
went out to visit her daughter,
Rebecca, who married an insurance
man in Canton, Ohio, and died
there—pneumonia—but her body was
brought back here. She's up in the
cemetery there now—in with a whole
mess of Gibbses and Herseys—she
was Julia Hersey 'fore she married Doc
Gibbs in the Congregational Church
over there. In our town we like to
know the facts about everybody.
There's Mrs. Webb, coming downstairs to get her breakfast, too.—That's
Doc Gibbs. Got that call at half past

one this morning. And there comes Joe
Crowell, Jr., delivering Mr. Webb's
Sentinel.

Dr. Gibbs has been coming along Main Street
from the left. At the point where he would turn
to approach his house, he stops, sets down
his—imaginary—black bag, takes off his hat,
and rubs his face with fatigue, using an enormous handkerchief. Mrs. Webb, a thin, serious,
crisp woman, has entered her kitchen, left, tying
on an apron. She goes through the motions of
putting wood into a stove, lighting it, and preparing breakfast. Suddenly, Joe Crowell, Jr.,
eleven, starts down Main Street from the right,
hurling imaginary newspapers into doorways.

JOE CROWELL, JR: Morning, Doc Gibbs.

DR. GIBBS: Morning, Joe.

JOE CROWELL, JR: Somebody been sick, Doc?

DR. GIBBS: No. Just some twins born over in
Polish Town.

JOE CROWELL, JR: Do you want your paper
now?

DR. GIBBS: Yes, I'll take it.—Anything serious goin' on in the world since
Wednesday?

JOE CROWELL, JR: Yessir. My schoolteacher,
Miss Foster, 's getting married to a
fella over in Concord.

DR. GIBBS: I declare.—How do you boys feel
about that?

JOE CROWELL, JR: Well, of course, it's none
of my business—but I think if a person starts out to be a teacher, she
ought to stay one.

DR. GIBBS: How's your knee, Joe?

JOE CROWELL, JR: Fine, Doc, I never think
about it at all. Only like you said, it
always tells me when it's going to rain.

DR. GIBBS: What's it telling you today?
Goin' to rain?

JOE CROWELL, JR: No, sir.

DR. GIBBS: Sure?

JOE CROWELL, JR; Yessir.

DR. GIBBS: Knee ever make a mistake?

JOE CROWELL, JR: No, sir. [Joe goes off. Dr. Gibbs stands reading his paper.]

STAGE MANAGER: Want to tell you something about that boy Joe Crowell there. Joe was awful bright—graduated from high school here, head of his class. So he got a scholarship to Massachusetts Tech. Graduated head of his class there, too. It was all wrote up in the Boston paper at the time. Goin' to be a great engineer, Joe was. But the war broke out and he died in France.—All that education for nothing.

HOWIE NEWSOME [off left]: Giddap, Bessie! What's the matter with you today?

STAGE MANAGER: Here comes Howie Newsome, deliverin' the milk.

Howie Newsome, about thirty, in overalls, comes along Main Street from the left, walking beside an invisible horse and wagon and carrying an imaginary rack with milk bottles. The sound of clinking milk bottles is heard. He leaves some bottles at Mrs. Webb's trellis, then, crossing the stage to Mrs. Gibbs's, he stops center to talk to Dr. Gibbs.

HOWIE NEWSOME: Morning, Doc.

DR. GIBBS: Morning, Howie.

HOWIE NEWSOME: Somebody sick?

DR. GIBBS: Pair of twins over to Mrs. Goruslawski's.

HOWIE NEWSOME: Twins, eh? This town's gettin' bigger every year.

DR. GIBBS: Goin' to rain, Howie?

HOWIE NEWSOME: No, no. Fine day—that'll burn through. Come on, Bessie.

DR. GIBBS: Hello Bessie. [He strokes the horse, which has remained up center.] How old is she, Howie?

HOWIE NEWSOME: Going on seventeen.

Bessie's all mixed up about the route ever since the Lockharts stopped takin' their quart of milk every day. She wants to leave 'em a quart just the same—keeps scolding me the hull trip. [He reaches Mrs. Gibbs's back door. She is waiting for him.]

MRS. GIBBS: Good morning, Howie.

HOWIE NEWSOME: Morning, Mrs. Gibbs. Doc's just comin' down the street.

MRS. GIBBS: Is he? Seems like you're late today.

HOWIE NEWSOME: Yes. Somep'n went wrong with the separator. Don't know what 'twas. [He passes Dr. Gibbs up center.] Doc!

DR. GIBBS: Howie!

MRS. GIBBS [calling upstairs]: Children! Children! Time to get up.

HOWIE NEWSOME: Come on, Bessie! [He goes off right.]

MRS. GIBBS: George! Rebecca! [Dr. Gibbs arrives at his back door and passes through the trellis into his house.] Everything all right, Frank?

DR. GIBBS: Yes. I declare—easy as kittens.

MRS. GIBBS: Bacon'll be ready in a minute. Set down and drink your coffee. You can catch a couple hours' sleep this morning, can't you?

DR. GIBBS: Hm! . . . Mrs. Wentworth's coming at eleven. Guess I know what it's about, too. Her stummick ain't what it ought to be.

MRS. GIBBS: All told, you won't get more'n three hours' sleep. Frank Gibbs, I don't know what's goin' to become of you. I do wish I could get you to go away someplace and take a rest. I think it would do you good.

MRS. WEBB: Emileeee! Time to get up! Wally! Seven o'clock!

MRS. GIBBS: I declare, you got to speak to George. Seems like something's come over him lately. He's no help to me at all. I can't even get him to cut me some wood.

DR. GIBBS [washing and drying his hands at the sink. Mrs. Gibbs is busy at the stove]: Is he sassy to you?

MRS. GIBBS: No. He just whines! All he thinks about is that baseball—George! Rebecca! You'll be late for school.

DR. GIBBS: M-m-m. . . .

MRS. GIBBS: George!

DR. GIBBS: George, look sharp!

GEORGE'S VOICE: Yes, Pa!

DR. GIBBS [as he goes off the stage]: Don't you hear your mother calling you? I guess I'll go upstairs and get forty winks.

MRS. WEBB: Walleee! Emileee! You'll be late for school! Walleee! You wash yourself good or I'll come up and do it myself.

REBECCA GIBBS' VOICE: Ma! What dress shall I wear?

MRS. GIBBS: Don't make a noise. Your father's been out all night and needs his sleep. I washed and ironed the blue gingham for you special.

REBECCA: Ma, I hate that dress.

MRS. GIBBS: Oh, hush-up-with-you.

REBECCA: Every day I go to school dressed like a sick turkey.

MRS. GIBBS: Now, Rebecca, you always look *very* nice.

REBECCA: Mama, George's throwing soap at me.

MRS. GIBBS: I'll come and slap the both of you,—that's what I'll do.

A factory whistle sounds. The children dash in and take their places at the tables. Right, George, about sixteen, and Rebecca, eleven.

Left, Emily and Wally, same ages. They carry strapped schoolbooks.

STAGE MANAGER: We've got a factory in our town too—hear it? Makes blankets. Cartwrights own it and it brung 'em a fortune.

MRS. WEBB: Children! Now I won't have it. Breakfast is just as good as any other meal and I won't have you gobbling like wolves. It'll stunt your growth,—that's a fact. Put away your book, Wally.

WALLY: Aw, Ma! By ten o'clock I got to know all about Canada.

MRS. WEBB: You know the rule 's well as I do—no books at table. As for me, I'd rather have my children healthy than bright.

EMILY: I'm both, Mama: you know I am. I'm the brightest girl in school for my age. I have a wonderful memory.

MRS. WEBB: Eat your breakfast.

WALLY: I'm bright, too, when I'm looking at my stamp collection.

MRS. GIBBS: I'll speak to your father about it when he's rested. Seems to me twenty-five cents a week's enough for a boy your age. I declare I don't know how you spend it all.

GEORGE: Aw, Ma,—I gotta lotta things to buy.

MRS. GIBBS: Strawberry phosphates—that's what you spend it on.

GEORGE: I don't see how Rebecca comes to have so much money. She has more'n a dollar.

REBECCA [spoon in mouth, dreamily]: I've been saving it up gradual.

MRS. GIBBS: Well, dear, I think it's a good thing to spend some every now and then.

REBECCA: Mama, do you know what I love most in the world—do you?—Money.

MRS. GIBBS: Eat your breakfast.

THE CHILDREN: Mama, there's first bell.—I gotta hurry.—I don't want any more.—I gotta hurry.

The children rise, seize their books, and dash out through the trellises. They meet, down center, and chattering, walk to Main Street, then turn left. The Stage Manager goes off, unobtrusively, right.

MRS. WEBB: Walk fast, but you don't have to run. Wally, pull up your pants at the knee. Stand up straight, Emily.

MRS. GIBBS: Tell Miss Foster I send her my best congratulations—can you remember that?

REBECCA: Yes, Ma.

MRS. GIBBS: You look real nice, Rebecca. Pick up your feet.

ALL: Good-by.

Mrs. Gibbs fills her apron with food for the chickens and comes down to the footlights.

MRS. GIBBS: Here, chick, chick, chick. No, go away, you. Go away. Here, chick, chick, chick. What's the matter with *you?* Fight, fight, fight,—that's all you do. Hm . . . *you* don't belong to me. Where'd you come from? [She shakes her apron.] Oh, don't be so scared. Nobody's going to hurt you.

Mrs. Webb is sitting on the bench by her trellis, stringing beans.

Good morning, Myrtle. How's your cold?

MRS. WEBB: Well, I still get that tickling feeling in my throat. I told Charles I didn't know as I'd go to choir practice tonight. Wouldn't be any use.

MRS. GIBBS: Have you tried singing over your voice?

MRS. WEBB: Yes, but somehow I can't do that and stay on the key. While I'm resting myself I thought I'd string some of these beans.

MRS. GIBBS [rolling up her sleeves as she crosses the stage for a chat]: Let me help you. Beans have been good this year.

MRS. WEBB: I've decided to put up forty quarts if it kills me. The children say they hate 'em, but I notice they're able to get 'em down all winter. [Pause. Brief sound of chickens cackling.]

MRS. GIBBS: Now, Myrtle. I've got to tell you something, because if I don't tell somebody I'll burst.

MRS. WEBB: Why, Julia Gibbs!

MRS. GIBBS: Here, give me some more of those beans. Myrtle, did one of those secondhand-furniture men from Boston come to see you last Friday?

MRS. WEBB: No-o.

MRS. GIBBS: Well, he called on me. First I thought he was a patient wantin' to see Dr. Gibbs. 'N he wormed his way into my parlor, and, Myrtle Webb, he offered me three hundred and fifty dollars for Grandmother Wentworth's highboy, as I'm sitting here!

MRS. WEBB: Why, Julia Gibbs!

MRS. GIBBS: He did! That old thing! Why, it was so big I didn't know where to put it and I almost give it to Cousin Hester Wilcox.

MRS. WEBB: Well, you're going to take it, aren't you?

MRS. GIBBS: I don't know.

MRS. WEBB: You don't know—three hundred and fifty dollars! What's come over you?

MRS. GIBBS: Well, if I could get the Doctor to take the money and go away someplace on a real trip, I'd sell it like that.—Y'know, Myrtle, it's been the dream of my life to see Paris, France.—Oh, I don't know. It sounds crazy, I suppose, but for years I've been promising myself that if we ever had the chance——

MRS. WEBB: How does the Doctor feel about it?

MRS. GIBBS: Well, I did beat about the bush a little and said that if I got a legacy—that's the way I put it—I'd make him take me somewhere.

MRS. WEBB: M-m-m. . . . What did he say?

MRS. GIBBS: You know how he is. I haven't heard a serious word out of him since I've known him. No, he said, it might make him discontented with Grover's Corners to go traipsin' about Europe; better let well enough alone, he says. Every two years he makes a trip to the battlefields of the Civil War and that's enough treat for anybody, he says.

MRS. WEBB: Well, Mr. Webb just *admires* the way Dr. Gibbs knows everything about the Civil War. Mr. Webb's a good mind to give up Napoleon and move over to the Civil War, only Dr. Gibbs being one of the greatest experts in the country just makes him despair.

MRS. GIBBS: It's a fact! Dr. Gibbs is never so happy as when he's at Antietam or Gettysburg. The times I've walked over those hills, Myrtle, stopping at every bush and pacing it all out, like we were going to buy it.

MRS. WEBB: Well, if that secondhand man's really serious about buyin' it, Julia, you sell it. And then you'll get to see Paris, all right. Just keep droppin' hints from time to time—that's how I got to see the Atlantic Ocean, y'know.

MRS. GIBBS: Oh, I'm sorry I mentioned it. Only it seems to me that once in your life before you die you ought to see a country where they don't talk in English and don't even want to.

The Stage Manager enters briskly from the right. He tips his hat to the ladies, who nod their heads.

STAGE MANAGER: Thank you, ladies. Thank you very much. [Mrs. Gibbs and Mrs. Webb gather up their things, return into their homes and disappear.] Now we're going to skip a few hours. But first we want a little more information about the town, kind of a scientific account, you might say. So I've asked Professor Willard of our State University to sketch in a few details of our past history here. Is Professor Willard here? [Professor Willard, a rural savant, pince-nez[4] on a wide satin ribbon, enters from the right with some notes in his hand.] May I introduce Professor Willard of our State University. A few brief notes, thank you, Professor,—unfortunately our time is limited.

PROFESSOR WILLARD: Grover's Corners . . . let me see . . . Grover's Corners lies on the old Pleistocene granite of the Appalachian range. I may say it's some of the oldest land in the world. We're very proud of that. A shelf of Devonian basalt crosses it with vestiges of Mesozoic shale, and some sandstone

---

[4] *pince-nez* (păns′nā): eyeglasses that are clipped to the bridge of the nose.

outcroppings; but that's all more recent: two hundred, three hundred million years old. Some highly interesting fossils have been found . . . I may say: unique fossils . . . two miles out of town, in Silas Peckham's cow pasture. They can be seen at the museum in our University at any time—that is, at any reasonable time. Shall I read some of Professor Gruber's notes on the meteorological situation—mean precipitation, et cetera?

STAGE MANAGER: Afraid we won't have time for that, Professor. We might have a few words on the history of man here.

PROFESSOR WILLARD: Yes . . . anthropological data: Early Amerindian stock. Cotahatchee tribes . . . no evidence before the tenth century of this era . . . hm . . . now entirely disappeared . . . possible traces in three families. Migration toward the end of the seventeenth century of English brachycephalic [5] blue-eyed stock . . . for the most part. Since then some Slav and Mediterranean——

STAGE MANAGER: And the population, Professor Willard?

PROFESSOR WILLARD: Within the town limits: 2,640.

STAGE MANAGER: Just a moment, Professor. [He whispers into the professor's ear.]

PROFESSOR WILLARD: Oh, yes, indeed?—The population, *at the moment*, is 2,642. The Postal District brings in 507 more, making a total of 3,149.—Mortality and birth rates: constant.—By MacPherson's gauge: 6,032.

STAGE MANAGER: Thank you very much, Professor. We're all very much obliged to you, I'm sure.

PROFESSOR WILLARD: Not at all, sir, not at all.

STAGE MANAGER: This way, Professor, and thank you again. [Exit Professor Willard] Now the political and social report: Editor Webb.—Oh, Mr. Webb? [Mrs. Webb appears at her back door.]

MRS. WEBB: He'll be here in a minute. . . . He just cut his hand while he was eatin' an apple.

STAGE MANAGER: Thank you, Mrs. Webb.

MRS. WEBB: Charles! Everybody's waitin'. [Exit Mrs. Webb]

STAGE MANAGER: Mr. Webb is Publisher and Editor of the Grover's Corners *Sentinel*. That's our local paper, y'know.

Mr. Webb enters from his house, pulling on his coat. His finger is bound in a handkerchief.

MR. WEBB: Well . . . I don't have to tell you that we're run here by a Board of Selectmen.—All males vote at the age of twenty-one. Women vote indirect. We're lower middle class: sprinkling of professional men . . . ten percent illiterate laborers. Politically, we're eighty-six percent Republicans; six percent Democrats; four percent Socialists; rest, indifferent. Religiously, we're eighty-five percent Protestants; twelve percent Catholics; rest, indifferent.

STAGE MANAGER: Have you any comments, Mr. Webb?

MR. WEBB: Very ordinary town, if you ask me. Little better behaved than most. Probably a lot duller. But our young people here seem to like it well enough. Ninety percent of 'em gradu-

---

[5] *brachycephalic* (brăk-ē-sə-făl′ĭk): having a short, almost round head.

ating from high school settle down right here to live—even when they've been away to college.

STAGE MANAGER: Now, is there anyone in the audience who would like to ask Editor Webb anything about the town?

WOMAN IN THE BALCONY: Is there much drinking in Grover's Corners?

MR. WEBB: Well, ma'am, I wouldn't know what you'd call *much*. Satiddy nights the farmhands meet down in Ellery Greenough's stable and holler some. We've got one or two town drunks, but they're always having remorses every time an evangelist comes to town. No, ma'am, I'd say likker ain't a regular thing in the home here, except in the medicine chest. Right good for snake bite, y'know—always was.

BELLIGERENT MAN AT BACK OF AUDITORIUM: Is there no one in town aware of——

STAGE MANAGER: Come forward, will you, where we can all hear you—— What were you saying?

BELLIGERENT MAN: Is there no one in town aware of social injustice and industrial inequality?

MR. WEBB: Oh, yes, everybody is—somethin' terrible. Seems like they spend most of their time talking about who's rich and who's poor.

BELLIGERENT MAN: Then why don't they do something about it? [He withdraws without waiting for an answer.]

MR. WEBB: Well, I dunno. . . . I guess we're all hunting like everybody else for a way the diligent and sensible can rise to the top and the lazy and quarrelsome can sink to the bottom. But it ain't easy to find. Meanwhile, we do all we can to help those that can't help

themselves and those that can we leave alone.—Are there any other questions?

LADY IN A BOX: Oh, Mr. Webb? Mr. Webb, is there any culture or love of beauty in Grover's Corners?

MR. WEBB: Well, ma'am, there ain't much— not in the sense you mean. Come to think of it, there's some girls that play the piano at High School Commencement; but they ain't happy about it. No, ma'am, there isn't much culture; but maybe this is the place to tell you that we've got a lot of pleasures of a kind here: we like the sun comin' up over the mountain in the morning, and we all notice a good deal about the birds. We pay a lot of attention to them. And we watch the change of the seasons; yes, everybody knows about them. But those other things—you're right, ma'am,—there ain't much.—*Robinson Crusoe* and the Bible; and Handel's "Largo," we all know that; and Whistler's "Mother"—those are just about as far as we go.

LADY IN A BOX: So I thought. Thank you, Mr. Webb.

STAGE MANAGER: Thank you, Mr. Webb. [Mr. Webb retires.] Now, we'll go back to the town. It's early afternoon. All 2,642 have had their dinners and all the dishes have been washed. [Mr. Webb, having removed his coat, returns and starts pushing a lawn mower to and fro beside his house.] There's an early-afternoon calm in our town: a buzzin' and a hummin' from the school buildings; only a few buggies on Main Street—the horses dozing at the hitching posts; you all remember what it's like. Doc Gibbs is in his office, tapping people and making them say "ah." Mr. Webb's cuttin' his lawn over there; one man in ten thinks it's a privilege to push his own lawn mower. No, sir. It's later than I thought. There are the children coming home from school already.

Shrill girls' voices are heard, off left. Emily comes along Main Street, carrying some books. There are some signs that she is imagining herself to be a lady of startling elegance.

EMILY: I *can't,* Lois. I've got to go home and help my mother. I *promised.*

MR. WEBB: Emily, walk simply. Who do you think you are today?

EMILY: Papa, you're terrible. One minute you tell me to stand up straight and the next minute you call me names. I just don't listen to you. [She gives him an abrupt kiss.]

MR. WEBB: Golly, I never got a kiss from such a great lady before.

He goes out of sight. Emily leans over and picks some flowers by the gate of her house. George Gibbs comes careening down Main Street. He is throwing a ball up to dizzying heights, and waiting to catch it again. This sometimes requires taking six steps backward. He bumps into an old lady invisible to us.

GEORGE: Excuse me, Mrs. Forrest.

STAGE MANAGER [as Mrs. Forrest]: Go out and play in the fields, young man. You got no business playing baseball on Main Street.

GEORGE: Awfully sorry, Mrs. Forrest.—Hello, Emily.

EMILY: H'lo.

GEORGE: You made a fine speech in class.

EMILY: Well . . . I was really ready to make a speech about the Monroe Doctrine, but at the last minute Miss Corcoran made me talk about the Louisiana Purchase instead. I worked an awful long time on both of them.

GEORGE: Gee, it's funny, Emily. From my window up there I can just see your head nights when you're doing your homework over in your room.

EMILY: Why, can you?

GEORGE: You certainly do stick to it, Emily. I don't see how you can sit still that long. I guess you like school.

EMILY: Well, I always feel it's something you have to go through.

GEORGE: Yeah.

EMILY: I don't mind it really. It passes the time.

GEORGE: Yeah.—Emily, what do you think? We might work out a kinda telegraph from your window to mine; and once in a while you could give me a kinda hint or two about one of those algebra problems. I don't mean the answers, Emily, of course not . . . just some little hint. . . .

EMILY: Oh, I think *hints* are allowed.—So—ah—if you get stuck, George, you whistle to me; and I'll give you some hints.

GEORGE: Emily, you're just naturally bright, I guess.

EMILY: I figure that it's just the way a person's born.

GEORGE: Yeah. But, you see, I want to be a farmer, and my Uncle Luke says whenever I'm ready I can come over and work on his farm and if I'm any good I can just gradually have it.

EMILY: You mean the house and everything?

Enter Mrs. Webb with a large bowl and sits on the bench by her trellis.

GEORGE: Yeah. Well, thanks . . . I better be getting out to the baseball field. Thanks for the talk, Emily.—Good afternoon, Mrs. Webb.

MRS. WEBB: Good afternoon, George.

GEORGE: So long, Emily.

EMILY: So long, George.

MRS. WEBB: Emily, come and help me string these beans for the winter. George Gibbs let himself have a real conversation, didn't he? Why, he's growing up. How old would George be?

EMILY: I don't know.

MRS. WEBB: Let's see. He must be almost sixteen.

EMILY: Mama, I made a speech in class today and I was very good.

MRS. WEBB: You must recite it to your father at supper. What was it about?

EMILY: The Louisiana Purchase. It was like silk off a spool. I'm going to make speeches all my life.—Mama, are these big enough?

MRS. WEBB: Try and get them a little bigger if you can.

EMILY: Mama, will you answer me a question, serious?

MRS. WEBB: Seriously, dear—not serious.

EMILY: Seriously,—will you?

MRS. WEBB: Of course, I will.

EMILY: Mama, am I good looking?

MRS. WEBB: Yes, of course you are. All my children have got good features; I'd be ashamed if they hadn't.

EMILY: Oh, Mama, that's not what I mean. What I mean is: am I *pretty*?

MRS. WEBB: I've already told you, yes. Now that's enough of that. You have a nice young pretty face. I never heard of such foolishness.

EMILY: Oh, Mama, you never tell us the truth about anything.

MRS. WEBB: I *am* telling you the truth.

EMILY: Mama, were *you* pretty?

MRS. WEBB: Yes, I was, if I do say it. I was the prettiest girl in town next to Mamie Cartwright.

EMILY: But, Mama, you've got to say *something* about me. Am I pretty enough . . . to get anybody . . . to get people interested in me?

MRS. WEBB: Emily, you make me tired. Now stop it. You're pretty enough for all normal purposes.—Come along now and bring that bowl with you.

EMILY: Oh, Mama, you're no help at all.

STAGE MANAGER: Thank you. Thank you! That'll do. We'll have to interrupt again here. Thank you, Mrs. Webb; thank you, Emily. [Mrs. Webb and Emily withdraw.] There are some more things we want to explore about this town. [He comes to the center of the stage. During the following speech the lights gradually dim to darkness, leaving only a spot on him.] I think this is a good time to tell you that the Cartwright interests have just begun building a new bank in Grover's Corners—had to go to Vermont for the marble, sorry to say. And they've asked a friend of mine what they should put in the cornerstone for people to dig up . . . a thousand years from now. . . . Of course, they've put in a copy of the *New York Times* and a copy of Mr. Webb's *Sentinel*. . . . We're kind of interested in this because some scientific fellas have found a way of painting all that reading matter with a

glue—a silicate glue—that'll make it keep a thousand—two thousand years. We're putting in a Bible . . . and the Constitution of the United States—and a copy of William Shakespeare's plays. What do you say, folks? What do you think? Y'know—Babylon once had two million people in it, and all we know about 'em is the names of the kings and some copies of wheat contracts . . . and contracts for the sale of slaves. Yet every night all those families sat down to supper, and the father came home from his work, and the smoke went up the chimney,—same as here. And even in Greece and Rome, all we know about the *real* life of the people is what we can piece together out of the joking poems and the comedies they wrote for the theater back then. So I'm going to have a copy of this play put in the cornerstone and the people a thousand years from now'll know a few simple facts about us— more than the Treaty of Versailles and the Lindbergh flight. See what I mean? So—people a thousand years from now—this is the way we were in the provinces north of New York at the beginning of the twentieth century.— This is the way we were: in our growing up and in our marrying and in our living and in our dying.

A choir partially concealed in the orchestra pit has begun singing "Blest Be the Tie That Binds." Simon Stimson stands directing them. Two ladders have been pushed onto the stage; they serve as indication of the second story in the Gibbs and Webb houses. George and Emily mount them, and apply themselves to their schoolwork. Dr. Gibbs has entered and is seated in his kitchen reading.

Well!—good deal of time's gone by. It's evening. You can hear choir practice going on in the Congregational Church. The children are at home doing their schoolwork. The day's running down like a tired clock.

SIMON STIMSON: Now look here, everybody. Music come into the world to give pleasure.—Softer! Softer! Get it out of your heads that music's only good when it's loud. You leave loudness to the Methodists. You couldn't beat 'em, even if you wanted to. Now again. Tenors!

GEORGE: Hssst! Emily!

EMILY: Hello.

GEORGE: Hello!

EMILY: I can't work at all. The moonlight's so *terrible.*

GEORGE: Emily, did you get the third problem?

EMILY: Which?

GEORGE: The *third?*

EMILY: Why, yes, George—that's the easiest of them all.

GEORGE: I don't see it. Emily, can you give me a hint?

EMILY: I'll tell you one thing: the answer's in yards.

GEORGE: ! ! ! In yards? How do you mean?

EMILY: In *square* yards.

GEORGE: Oh . . . in square yards.

EMILY: Yes, George, don't you see?

GEORGE: Yeah.

EMILY: In square yards of *wallpaper.*

GEORGE: Wallpaper,—oh, I see. Thanks a lot, Emily.

EMILY: You're welcome. My, isn't the moonlight *terrible?* And choir practice going on.—I think if you hold your breath you can hear the train all the way to Contoocook. Hear it?

GEORGE: M-m-m—What do you know!

EMILY: Well, I guess I better go back and try to work.

GEORGE: Good night, Emily. And thanks.

EMILY: Good night, George.

SIMON STIMSON: Before I forget it: how many of you will be able to come in Tuesday afternoon and sing at Fred Hersey's wedding?—show your hands. That'll be fine; that'll be right nice. We'll do the same music we did for Jane Trowbridge's last month.—Now we'll do: "Art Thou Weary; Art Thou Languid?" It's a question, ladies and gentlemen, make it talk. Ready.

DR. GIBBS: Oh, George, can you come down a minute?

GEORGE: Yes, Pa. [He descends the ladder.]

DR. GIBBS: Make yourself comfortable, George; I'll only keep you a minute. George, how old are you?

GEORGE: I? I'm sixteen, almost seventeen.

DR. GIBBS: What do you want to do after school's over?

GEORGE: Why, you know, Pa. I want to be a farmer on Uncle Luke's farm.

DR. GIBBS: You'll be willing, will you, to get up early and milk and feed the stock . . . and you'll be able to hoe and hay all day?

GEORGE: Sure, I will. What are you . . . what do you mean, Pa?

DR. GIBBS: Well, George, while I was in my office today I heard a funny sound . . . and what do you think it was? It was your mother chopping wood. There you see your mother—getting up early; cooking meals all day long; washing and ironing;—and still she has to go out in the back yard and chop wood. I suppose she just got tired of asking you. She just gave up and decided it was easier to do it herself. And you eat her meals, and put on the clothes she keeps nice for you, and you run off and play baseball,—like she's some hired girl we keep around the house but that we don't like very much. Well, I knew all I had to do was call your attention to it. Here's a handkerchief, son. George, I've decided to raise your spending money twenty-five cents a week. Not, of course, for chopping wood for your mother, because that's a present you give her, but because you're getting older—and I imagine there are lots of things you must find to do with it.

GEORGE: Thanks, Pa.

DR. GIBBS: Let's see—tomorrow's your payday. You can count on it—— Hmm. Probably Rebecca'll feel she ought to have some more too. Wonder what could have happened to your mother. Choir practice never was as late as this before.

GEORGE: It's only half past eight, Pa.

DR. GIBBS: I don't know why she's in that old choir. She hasn't any more voice than an old crow. . . . Traipsin' around the streets at this hour of the night. . . . Just about time you retired, don't you think?

GEORGE: Yes, Pa. [George mounts to his place on the ladder.]

Laughter and good nights can be heard on stage left and presently Mrs. Gibbs, Mrs. Soames and Mrs. Webb come down Main Street. When they arrive at the corner of the stage they stop.

MRS. SOAMES: Good night, Martha. Good night, Mr. Foster.

MRS. WEBB: I'll tell Mr. Webb; I *know* he'll want to put it in the paper.

MRS. GIBBS: My, it's late!

MRS. SOAMES: Good night, Irma.

MRS. GIBBS: Real nice choir practice, wa'n't it? Myrtle Webb! Look at that moon, will you! Tsk-tsk-tsk. Potato weather, for sure. [They are silent a moment, gazing up at the moon.]

MRS. SOAMES: Naturally I didn't want to say a word about it in front of those others, but now we're alone—really, it's the worst scandal that ever was in this town!

MRS. GIBBS: What?

MRS. SOAMES: Simon Stimson!

MRS. GIBBS: Now, Louella!

MRS. SOAMES: But, Julia! To have the organist of a church *drink* and *drunk* year after year. You know he was drunk tonight.

MRS. GIBBS: Now, Louella! We all know about Mr. Stimson, and we all know about the troubles he's been through, and Dr. Ferguson knows too, and if Dr. Ferguson keeps him on there in his job the only thing the rest of us can do is just not to notice it.

MRS. SOAMES: *Not to notice it!* But it's getting worse.

MRS. WEBB: No, it isn't, Louella. It's getting better. I've been in that choir twice as long as you have. It doesn't happen anywhere near so often. . . . My, I hate to go to bed on a night like this.—I better hurry. Those children'll be sitting up till all hours. Good night, Louella. [They all exchange good nights. She hurries downstage, enters her house and disappears.]

MRS. GIBBS: Can you get home safe, Louella?

MRS. SOAMES: It's as bright as day. I can see Mr. Soames scowling at the window now. You'd think we'd been to a dance the way the menfolk carry on.

More good nights. Mrs. Gibbs arrives at her home and passes through the trellis into the kitchen.

MRS. GIBBS: Well, we had a real good time.

DR. GIBBS: You're late enough.

MRS. GIBBS: Why, Frank, it ain't any later 'n usual.

DR. GIBBS: And you stopping at the corner to gossip with a lot of hens.

MRS. GIBBS: Now, Frank, don't be grouchy. Come out and smell the heliotrope in the moonlight. [They stroll out arm in arm along the footlights.] Isn't that wonderful? What did you do all the time I was away?

DR. GIBBS: Oh, I read—as usual. What were the girls gossiping about tonight?

MRS. GIBBS: Well, believe me, Frank—there is something to gossip about.

DR. GIBBS: Hmm! Simon Stimson far gone, was he?

MRS. GIBBS: Worst I've ever seen him. How'll that end, Frank? Dr. Ferguson can't forgive him forever.

DR. GIBBS: I guess I know more about Simon Stimson's affairs than anybody in this town. Some people ain't made for small-town life. I don't know how that'll end; but there's nothing we can do but just leave it alone. Come, get in.

MRS. GIBBS: No, not yet. . . . Frank, I'm worried about you.

DR. GIBBS: What are you worried about?

MRS. GIBBS: I think it's my duty to make plans for you to get a real rest and change. And if I get that legacy, well, I'm going to insist on it.

DR. GIBBS: Now, Julia, there's no sense in going over that again.

MRS. GIBBS: Frank, you're just *unreasonable!*

DR. GIBBS [starting into the house]: Come on, Julia, it's getting late. First thing you know you'll catch cold. I gave George a piece of my mind tonight. I reckon you'll have your wood chopped for a while anyway. No, no, start getting upstairs.

MRS. GIBBS: Oh, dear. There's always so many things to pick up, seems like. You know, Frank, Mrs. Fairchild always locks her front door every night. All those people up that part of town do.

DR. GIBBS [blowing out the lamp]: They're all getting citified, that's the trouble with them. They haven't got nothing fit to burgle and everybody knows it.

They disappear. Rebecca climbs up the ladder beside George.

GEORGE: Get out, Rebecca. There's only room for one at this window. You're always spoiling everything.

REBECCA: Well, let me look just a minute.

GEORGE: Use your own window.

REBECCA: I did; but there's no moon there. . . . George, do you know what I think, do you? I think maybe the moon's getting nearer and nearer and there'll be a big 'splosion.

GEORGE: Rebecca, you don't know anything. If the moon were getting nearer, the guys that sit up all night with telescopes would see it first and they'd tell about it, and it'd be in all the newspapers.

REBECCA: George, is the moon shining on South America, Canada and half the whole world?

GEORGE: Well—prob'ly is.

The Stage Manager strolls on. Pause. The sound of crickets is heard.

STAGE MANAGER: Nine thirty. Most of the lights are out. No, there's Constable Warren trying a few doors on Main Street. And here comes Editor Webb, after putting his newspaper to bed.

Mr. Warren, an elderly policeman, comes along Main Street from the right, Mr. Webb from the left.

MR. WEBB: Good evening, Bill.

CONSTABLE WARREN: Evenin', Mr. Webb.

MR. WEBB: Quite a moon!

CONSTABLE WARREN: Yepp.

MR. WEBB: All quiet tonight?

CONSTABLE WARREN: Simon Stimson is rollin' around a little. Just saw his wife movin' out to hunt for him so I looked the other way—there he is now.

Simon Stimson comes down Main Street from the left, only a trace of unsteadiness in his walk.

MR. WEBB: Good evening, Simon. . . . Town seems to have settled down for the night pretty well. . . . [Simon Stimson comes up to him and pauses a moment and stares at him, swaying slightly.] Good evening. . . . Yes, most of the town's settled down for the night, Simon. . . . I guess we better do the same. Can I walk along a ways with you? [Simon Stimson continues on his way without a word and disappears at the right.] Good night.

CONSTABLE WARREN: I don't know how that's goin' to end, Mr. Webb.

MR. WEBB: Well, he's seen a peck of trouble, one thing after another. . . . Oh, Bill . . . if you see my boy smoking cigarettes, just give him a word, will you? He thinks a lot of you, Bill.

CONSTABLE WARREN: I don't think he smokes no cigarettes, Mr. Webb. Leastways, not more'n two or three a year.

MR. WEBB: Hm . . . I hope not.—Well, good night, Bill.

CONSTABLE WARREN: Good night, Mr. Webb. [Exit.]

MR. WEBB: Who's that up there? Is that you, Myrtle?

EMILY: No, it's me, Papa.

MR. WEBB: Why aren't you in bed?

EMILY: I don't know. I just can't sleep yet, Papa. The moonlight's so *won*-derful. And the smell of Mrs. Gibbs's heliotrope. Can you smell it?

MR. WEBB: Hm. . . . Yes. Haven't any troubles on your mind, have you, Emily?

EMILY: *Troubles,* Papa? No.

MR. WEBB: Well, enjoy yourself, but don't let your mother catch you. Good night, Emily.

EMILY: Good night, Papa.

Mr. Webb crosses into the house, whistling "Blest Be the Tie That Binds," and disappears.

REBECCA: I never told you about that letter Jane Crofut got from her minister when she was sick. He wrote Jane a letter and on the envelope the address was like this: It said: Jane Crofut; The Crofut Farm; Grover's Corners; Sutton County; New Hampshire; United States of America.

GEORGE: What's funny about it?

REBECCA: But listen, it's not finished: the United States of America; Continent of North America; Western Hemisphere; the Earth; the Solar System; the Universe; the Mind of God—that's what it said on the envelope.

GEORGE: What do you know!

REBECCA: And the postman brought it just the same.

GEORGE: What do you know!

STAGE MANAGER: That's the end of the First Act, friends. You can go and smoke now, those that smoke.

DISCUSSION

1. How would you describe the role of the Stage Manager? What purposes does he serve?

2. In Act I you learn several things about life in small-town America in 1901. What do you learn about (a) medical care, (b) voting rights, (c) attitudes about the arts, and (d) law enforcement? What else do you learn? What attitudes and conditions described in the play are the same today?

3. Who are the characters you meet in Act I? Describe their various relationships or situations.

4. Do you receive any hints about what may happen later in the play? If so, what are the hints and what do they suggest?

Act 2

The tables and chairs of the two kitchens are still on the stage. The ladders and the small bench have been withdrawn. The Stage Manager has been at his accustomed place watching the audience return to its seats.

STAGE MANAGER: Three years have gone by. Yes, the sun's come up over a thousand times. Summers and winters have cracked the mountains a little bit more and the rains have brought down some of the dirt. Some babies that weren't even born before have begun talking regular sentences already; and a number of people who thought they were right young and spry have noticed that they can't bound up a flight of stairs like they used to, without their heart fluttering a little. All that can happen in a thousand days. Nature's been pushing and contriving in other ways, too: a number of young people fell in love and got married. Yes, the mountain got bit away a few fractions of an inch; millions of gallons of water went by the mill; and here and there a new home was set up under a roof. Almost everybody in the world gets married,—you know what I mean? In our town there aren't hardly any exceptions. Most everybody in the world climbs into their graves married. The First Act was called the Daily Life. This act is called Love and Marriage. There's another act coming after this: I reckon you can guess what that's about. So: It's three years later. It's 1904. It's July 7th, just after High School Commencement. That's the time most of our young people jump up and get married. Soon as they've passed their last examinations in solid geometry and Cicero's Orations, looks like they suddenly feel themselves fit to be married. It's early morning. Only this time it's been raining. It's been pouring and thundering. Mrs. Gibbs's garden, and Mrs. Webb's here: drenched. All those bean poles and pea vines: drenched. All yesterday over there on Main Street, the rain looked like curtains being blown along. Hm . . . it may begin again any minute. There! You can hear the 5:45 for Boston. [Mrs. Gibbs and Mrs. Webb enter their kitchens and start the day as in the First Act.] And there's Mrs. Gibbs and Mrs. Webb come down to make breakfast, just as though it were an ordinary day. I don't have to point out to the women in my audience that those ladies they see before them, both of those ladies cooked three meals a day—one of 'em for twenty years, the other for forty—and no summer vacation. They brought up two children apiece, washed, cleaned the house,— and *never a nervous breakdown.*

It's like what one of those Middle West poets said: You've got to love life to have life,[6] and you've got to have life to love life. . . . It's what they call a vicious circle.

[6] *You've . . . life:* an approximate quotation from ''Lucinda Matlock''; see page 250.

HOWIE NEWSOME [off stage left]: Giddap, Bessie!

STAGE MANAGER: Here comes Howie Newsome delivering the milk. And there's Si Crowell delivering the papers like his brother before him.

Si Crowell has entered hurling imaginary newspapers into doorways; Howie Newsome has come along Main Street with Bessie.

SI CROWELL: Morning, Howie.

HOWIE NEWSOME: Morning, Si.—Anything in the papers I ought to know?

SI CROWELL: Nothing much, except we're losing about the best baseball pitcher Grover's Corners ever had—George Gibbs.

HOWIE NEWSOME: Reckon he is.

SI CROWELL: He could hit and run bases, too.

HOWIE NEWSOME: Yep. Mighty fine ball player.—Whoa! Bessie! I guess I can stop and talk if I've a mind to!

SI CROWELL: I don't see how he could give up a thing like that just to get married. Would you, Howie?

HOWIE NEWSOME: Can't tell, Si. Never had no talent that way. [Constable Warren enters. They exchange good mornings.] You're up early, Bill.

CONSTABLE WARREN: Seein' if there's anything I can do to prevent a flood. River's been risin' all night.

HOWIE NEWSOME: Si Crowell's all worked up here about George Gibbs' retiring from baseball.

CONSTABLE WARREN: Yes, sir; that's the way it goes. Back in '84 we had a player, Si—even George Gibbs couldn't touch him. Name of Hank Todd. Went down to Maine and become a parson. Wonderful ball player.—Howie, how does the weather look to you?

HOWIE NEWSOME: Oh, 'tain't bad. Think maybe it'll clear up for good.

Constable Warren and Si Crowell continue on their way. Howie Newsome brings the milk first to Mrs. Gibbs's house. She meets him by the trellis.

MRS. GIBBS: Good morning, Howie. Do you think it's going to rain again?

HOWIE NEWSOME: Morning, Mrs. Gibbs. It rained so heavy, I think maybe it'll clear up.

MRS. GIBBS: Certainly hope it will.

HOWIE NEWSOME: How much did you want today?

MRS. GIBBS: I'm going to have a houseful of relations, Howie. Looks to me like I'll need three-a-milk and two-a-cream.

HOWIE NEWSOME: My wife says to tell you we both hope they'll be very happy, Mrs. Gibbs. Know they *will*.

MRS. GIBBS: Thanks a lot, Howie. Tell your wife I hope she gits there to the wedding.

HOWIE NEWSOME: Yes, she'll be there; she'll be there if she kin. [Howie Newsome crosses to Mrs. Webb's house.] Morning, Mrs. Webb.

MRS. WEBB: Oh, good morning, Mr. Newsome. I told you four quarts of milk, but I hope you can spare me another.

HOWIE NEWSOME: Yes'm . . . and the two of cream.

MRS. WEBB: Will it start raining again, Mr. Newsome?

HOWIE NEWSOME: Well. Just sayin' to Mrs. Gibbs as how it may lighten up. Mrs. Newsome told me to tell you as how we hope they'll both be very happy, Mrs. Webb. Know they *will*.

MRS. WEBB: Thank you, and thank Mrs. Newsome and we're counting on seeing you at the wedding.

HOWIE NEWSOME: Yes, Mrs. Webb. We hope to git there. Couldn't miss that. Come on, Bessie.

Exit Howie Newsome. Dr. Gibbs descends in shirt sleeves, and sits down at his breakfast table.

DR. GIBBS: Well, Ma, the day has come. You're losin' one of your chicks.

MRS. GIBBS: Frank Gibbs, don't you say another word. I feel like crying every minute. Sit down and drink your coffee.

DR. GIBBS: The groom's up shaving himself—only there ain't an awful lot to shave. Whistling and singing, like he's glad to leave us.—Every now and then he says "I do" to the mirror, but it don't sound convincing to me.

MRS. GIBBS: I declare, Frank, I don't know how he'll get along. I've arranged his clothes and seen to it he's put warm things on,—Frank! they're too *young.* Emily won't think of such things. He'll catch his death of cold within a week.

DR. GIBBS: I was remembering my wedding morning, Julia.

MRS. GIBBS: Now don't start that, Frank Gibbs.

DR. GIBBS: I was the scaredest young fella in the State of New Hampshire. I thought I'd make a mistake for sure. And when I saw you comin' down that aisle I thought you were the prettiest girl I'd ever seen, but the only trouble was that I'd never seen you before. There I was in the Congregational Church marryin' a total stranger.

MRS. GIBBS: And how do you think I felt!—Frank, weddings are perfectly awful things. Farces,—that's what they are! [She puts a plate before him.] Here, I've made something for you.

DR. GIBBS: Why, Julia Hersey—French toast!

MRS. GIBBS: 'Tain't hard to make and I had to do *something.* [Pause. Dr. Gibbs pours on the syrup.]

DR. GIBBS: How'd you sleep last night, Julia?

MRS. GIBBS: Well, I heard a lot of the hours struck off.

DR. GIBBS: Ye-e-s! I get a shock every time I think of George setting out to be a family man—that great gangling thing!—I tell you Julia, there's nothing so terrifying in the world as a *son.* The relation of father and son is the darndest, awkwardest——

MRS. GIBBS: Well, mother and daughter's no picnic, let me tell you.

DR. GIBBS: They'll have a lot of troubles, I suppose, but that's none of our business. Everybody has a right to their own troubles.

MRS. GIBBS [at the table, drinking her coffee, meditatively]: Yes . . . people are meant to go through life two by two. 'Tain't natural to be lonesome. [Pause. Dr. Gibbs starts laughing.]

DR. GIBBS: Julia, do you know one of the things I was scared of when I married you?

MRS. GIBBS: Oh, go along with you!

DR. GIBBS: I was afraid we wouldn't have material for conversation more'n'd last us a few weeks. [Both laugh.] I was afraid we'd run out and eat our meals in silence, that's a fact.—Well, you and I been conversing for twenty years now without any noticeable barren spells.

MRS. GIBBS: Well,—good weather, bad weather—'tain't very choice, but I always find something to say. [She goes to the foot of the stairs.] Did you hear Rebecca stirring around upstairs?

DR. GIBBS: No. Only day of the year Rebecca hasn't been managing everybody's business up there. She's hiding in her room.—I got the impression she's crying.

MRS. GIBBS: Lord's sakes!—This has got to stop.—Rebecca! Rebecca! Come and get your breakfast.

George comes rattling down the stairs, very brisk.

GEORGE: Good morning, everybody. Only five more hours to live. [Makes the gesture of cutting his throat, and a loud "k-k-k," and starts through the trellis.]

MRS. GIBBS: George Gibbs, where are you going?

GEORGE: Just stepping across the grass to see my girl.

MRS. GIBBS: Now, George! You put on your overshoes. It's raining torrents. You don't go out of this house without you're prepared for it.

GEORGE: Aw, Ma. It's just a *step!*

MRS. GIBBS: George! You'll catch your death of cold and cough all through the service.

DR. GIBBS: George, do as your mother tells you!

Dr. Gibbs goes upstairs. George returns reluctantly to the kitchen and pantomimes putting on overshoes.

MRS. GIBBS: From tomorrow on you can kill yourself in all weathers, but while you're in my house you'll live wisely, thank you.—Maybe Mrs. Webb isn't

used to callers at seven in the morning.—Here, take a cup of coffee first.

GEORGE: Be back in a minute. [He crosses the stage, leaping over the puddles.] Good morning, Mother Webb.

MRS. WEBB: Goodness! You frightened me!—Now, George, you can come in a minute out of the wet, but you know I can't ask you in.

GEORGE: Why not—?

MRS. WEBB: George, you know 's well as I do: the groom can't see his bride on his wedding day, not until he sees her in church.

GEORGE: Aw!—that's just a superstition.—Good morning, Mr. Webb.

Enter Mr. Webb.

MR. WEBB: Good morning, George.

GEORGE: Mr. Webb, you don't believe in that superstition, do you?

MR. WEBB: There's a lot of common sense in some superstitions, George. [He sits at the table, facing right.]

MRS. WEBB: Millions have folla'd it, George, and you don't want to be the first to fly in the face of custom.

GEORGE: How is Emily?

MRS. WEBB: She hasn't waked up yet. I haven't heard a sound out of her.

GEORGE: Emily's *asleep!!!*

MRS. WEBB: No wonder! We were up 'til all hours, sewing and packing. Now I'll tell you what I'll do; you set down here a minute with Mr. Webb and drink this cup of coffee; and I'll go upstairs and see she doesn't come down and surprise you. There's some bacon, too; but don't be long about it.

Exit Mrs. Webb. Embarrassed silence. Mr. Webb dunks doughnuts in his coffee. More silence.

MR. WEBB [suddenly and loudly]: Well, George, how are you?

GEORGE [startled, choking over his coffee]: Oh, fine, I'm fine. [Pause] Mr. Webb, what sense could there be in a superstition like that?

MR. WEBB: Well, you see,—on her wedding morning a girl's head's apt to be full of . . . clothes and one thing and another. Don't you think that's probably it?

GEORGE: Ye-e-s. I never thought of that.

MR. WEBB: A girl's apt to be a mite nervous on her wedding day. [Pause]

GEORGE: I wish a fellow could get married without all that marching up and down.

MR. WEBB: Every man that's ever lived has felt that way about it, George; but it hasn't been any use. It's the women-folk who've built up weddings, my boy. For a while now the women have it all their own. A man looks pretty small at a wedding, George. All those good women standing shoulder to shoulder making sure that the knot's tied in a mighty public way.

GEORGE: But . . . you *believe* in it, don't you, Mr. Webb?

MR. WEBB [with alacrity]: Oh, yes; *oh, yes.* Don't you misunderstand me, my boy. Marriage is a wonderful thing,—wonderful thing. And don't you forget that, George.

GEORGE: No, sir.—Mr. Webb, how old were you when you got married?

MR. WEBB: Well, you see: I'd been to college and I'd taken a little time to get settled. But Mrs. Webb—she wasn't much older than what Emily is. Oh, age hasn't much to do with it, George,—not compared with . . . uh . . . other things.

GEORGE: What were you going to say, Mr. Webb?

MR. WEBB: Oh, I don't know.—Was I going to say something? [Pause] George, I was thinking the other night of some advice my father gave me when I got married. Charles, he said, Charles, start out early showing who's boss, he said. Best thing to do is to give an order, even if it don't make sense; just so she'll learn to obey. And he said: if anything about your wife irritates you—her conversation, or anything—just get up and leave the house. That'll make it clear to her, he said. And, oh, yes! he said never, *never* let your wife know how much money you have, never.

GEORGE: Well, Mr. Webb . . . I don't think I could. . . .

MR. WEBB: So I took the opposite of my father's advice and I've been happy ever since. And let that be a lesson to you, George, never to ask advice on personal matters.—George, are you going to raise chickens on your farm?

GEORGE: What?

MR. WEBB: Are you going to raise chickens on your farm?

GEORGE: Uncle Luke's never been much interested, but I thought——

MR. WEBB: A book came into my office the other day, George, on the Philo System of raising chickens. I want you to read it. I'm thinking of beginning in a small way in the back yard, and I'm going to put an incubator in the cellar——

Enter Mrs. Webb.

MRS. WEBB: Charles, are you talking about that old incubator again? I thought you two'd be talking about things worth while.

MR. WEBB [bitingly]: Well, Myrtle, if you want to give the boy some good advice, I'll go upstairs and leave you alone with him.

MRS. WEBB [pulling George up]: George, Emily's got to come downstairs and eat her breakfast. She sends you her love but she doesn't want to lay eyes on you. Good-by.

GEORGE: Good-by.

George crosses the stage to his own home, bewildered and crestfallen. He slowly dodges a puddle and disappears into his house.

MR. WEBB: Myrtle, I guess you don't know that older superstition.

MRS. WEBB: What do you mean, Charles?

MR. WEBB: Since the cave men: no bridegroom should see his father-in-law on the day of the wedding, or near it. Now remember that. [Both leave the stage.]

STAGE MANAGER: Thank you very much, Mr. and Mrs. Webb.—Now I have to interrupt again here. You see, we want to know how all this began—this wedding, this plan to spend a lifetime together. I'm awfully interested in how big things like that begin. You know how it is: you're twenty-one or twenty-two and you make some decisions; then whisssh! you're seventy: you've been a lawyer for fifty years, and that white-haired lady at your side has eaten over fifty thousand meals with you. How do such things begin? George and Emily are going to show you now the conversation they had when they first knew that . . . that . . . as the saying goes . . . they were

meant for one another. But before they do it I want you to try and remember what it was like to have been very young. And particularly the days when you were first in love; when you were like a person sleepwalking, and you didn't quite see the street you were in, and didn't quite hear everything that was said to you. You're just a little bit crazy. Will you remember that, please? Now they'll be coming out of high school at three o'clock. George has just been elected President of the Junior Class, and as it's June, that means he'll be President of the Senior Class all next year. And Emily's just been elected Secretary and Treasurer. I don't have to tell you how important that is. [He places a board across the backs of two chairs, which he takes from those at the Gibbs family's table. He brings two high stools from the wings and places them behind the board. Persons sitting on the stools will be facing the audience. This is the counter of Mr. Morgan's drugstore. The sounds of young people's voices are heard off left.] Yepp,—there they are coming down Main Street now.

Emily, carrying an armful of—imaginary—schoolbooks, comes along Main Street from the left.

EMILY: I can't, Louise. I've got to go home. Good-by. Oh, Ernestine! Ernestine! Can you come over tonight and do Latin? Isn't that Cicero the worst thing—! Tell your mother you *have* to. G'by. G'by, Helen. G'by, Fred.

George, also carrying books, catches up with her.

GEORGE: Can I carry your books home for you, Emily?

EMILY [coolly]: Why . . . uh. . . . Thank you. It isn't far. [She gives them to him.]

GEORGE: Excuse me a minute, Emily.—Say, Bob, if I'm a little late, start practice anyway. And give Herb some long high ones.

EMILY: Good-by, Lizzy.

GEORGE: Good-by, Lizzy.—I'm awfully glad you were elected, too, Emily.

EMILY: Thank you.

They have been standing on Main Street, almost against the back wall. They take the first steps toward the audience when George stops and says:

GEORGE: Emily, why are you mad at me?

EMILY: I'm not mad at you.

GEORGE: You've been treating me so funny lately.

EMILY: Well, since you ask me, I might as well say it right out, George,—[She catches sight of a teacher passing.] Good-by, Miss Corcoran.

GEORGE: Good-by, Miss Corcoran.— Wha—— what is it?

EMILY [not scoldingly; finding it difficult to say]: I don't like the whole change that's come over you in the last year. I'm sorry if that hurts your feelings, but I've got to—tell the truth and shame the devil.

GEORGE: A *change*?—Wha—— what do you mean?

EMILY: Well, up to a year ago I used to like you a lot. And I used to watch you as you did everything . . . because we'd been friends so long . . . and then you began spending all your time at *baseball* . . . and you never stopped to speak to anybody any more. Not even to your own family you didn't . . . and, George, it's a fact, you've got awful conceited and stuck-up, and all the girls say so. They may not say so to your face, but that's what they say about you behind your back, and it hurts me to hear them say it, but I've got to agree with them a little. I'm sorry if it hurts your feelings . . . but I can't be sorry I said it.

GEORGE: I . . . I'm glad you said it, Emily. I never thought that such a thing was happening to me. I guess it's hard for a fella not to have faults creep into his character.

They take a step or two in silence, then stand still in misery.

EMILY: I always expect a man to be perfect and I think he should be.

GEORGE: Oh . . . I don't think it's possible to be perfect, Emily.

EMILY: Well, my *father* is, and as far as I can see *your* father is. There's no reason on earth why you shouldn't be, too.

GEORGE: Well, I feel it's the other way round. That men aren't naturally good; but girls are.

EMILY: Well, you might as well know right now that I'm not perfect. It's not as easy for a girl to be perfect as a man, because we girls are more—more— nervous.—Now I'm sorry I said all that about you. I don't know what made me say it.

GEORGE: Emily,—

EMILY: Now I can see it's not the truth at all. And I suddenly feel that it isn't important, anyway.

GEORGE: Emily . . . would you like an ice-cream soda, or something, before you go home?

EMILY: Well, thank you. . . . I would.

They advance toward the audience and make an abupt right turn, opening the door of Morgan's drugstore. Under strong emotion, Emily keeps her face down. George speaks to some passersby.

GEORGE: Hello, Stew,—how are you?— Good afternoon, Mrs. Slocum.

The Stage Manager, wearing spectacles and assuming the role of Mr. Morgan, enters abruptly from the right and stands between the audience and the counter of his soda fountain.

STAGE MANAGER: Hello, George. Hello, Emily.—What'll you have?—Why, Emily Webb,—what you been crying about?

GEORGE [he gropes for an explanation]: She . . . she just got an awful scare, Mr. Morgan. She almost got run over by that hardware-store wagon. Everybody says that Tom Huckins drives like a crazy man.

STAGE MANAGER [drawing a drink of water]: Well, now! You take a drink of water, Emily. You look all shook up. I tell you, you've got to look both ways before you cross Main Street these days. Gets worse every year.—What'll you have?

EMILY: I'll have a strawberry phosphate, thank you, Mr. Morgan.

GEORGE: No, no, Emily. Have an ice-cream soda with me. Two strawberry ice-cream sodas, Mr. Morgan.

STAGE MANAGER [working the faucets]: Two strawberry ice-cream sodas, yes sir. Yes, sir. There are a hundred and twenty-five horses in Grover's Corners this minute I'm talking to you. State Inspector was in here yesterday. And now they're bringing in these automo-biles, the best thing to do is to just

stay home. Why, I can remember when a dog could go to sleep all day in the middle of Main Street and nothing come along to disturb him. [He sets the imaginary glasses before them.] There they are. Enjoy 'em. [He sees a customer, right.] Yes, Mrs. Ellis. What can I do for you? [He goes out right.]

EMILY: They're so expensive.

GEORGE: No, no,—don't you think of that. We're celebrating our election. And then do you know what else I'm celebrating?

EMILY: N-no.

GEORGE: I'm celebrating because I've got a friend who tells me all the things that ought to be told me.

EMILY: George, *please* don't think of that. I don't know why I said it. It's not true. You're——

GEORGE: No, Emily, you stick to it. I'm glad you spoke to me like you did. But you'll *see*: I'm going to change so quick—you bet I'm going to change. And, Emily, I want to ask you a favor.

EMILY: What?

GEORGE: Emily, if I go away to State Agriculture College next year, will you write me a letter once in a while?

EMILY: I certainly will. I certainly will, George. . . . [Pause. They start sipping the sodas through the straws.] It certainly seems like being away three years you'd get out of touch with things. Maybe letters from Grover's Corners wouldn't be so interesting after a while. Grover's Corners isn't a very important place when you think of all—New Hampshire; but I think it's a very nice town.

GEORGE: The day wouldn't come when I wouldn't want to know everything that's happening here. I know *that's* true, Emily.

EMILY: Well, I'll try to make my letters interesting. [Pause.]

GEORGE: Y'know, Emily, whenever I meet a farmer I ask him if he thinks it's important to go to Agriculture School to be a good farmer.

EMILY: Why, George——

GEORGE: Yeah, and some of them say that it's even a waste of time. You can get all those things, anyway, out of the pamphlets the government sends out. And Uncle Luke's getting old,—he's about ready for me to start in taking over his farm tomorrow, if I could.

EMILY: My!

GEORGE: And, like you say, being gone all the time . . . in other places and meeting other people. . . . Gosh, if anything like that can happen I don't want to go away. I guess new people aren't any better than old ones. I'll bet they almost never are. Emily . . . I feel that you're as good a friend as I've got. I don't need to go and meet the people in other towns.

EMILY: But, George, maybe it's very important for you to go and learn all that about—cattle judging and soils and those things. . . . Of course, I don't know.

GEORGE [after a pause, very seriously]: Emily, I'm going to make up my mind right now. I won't go. I'll tell Pa about it tonight.

EMILY: Why, George, I don't see why you have to decide right now. It's a whole year away.

GEORGE: Emily, I'm glad you spoke to me about that . . . that fault in my character. What you said was right; but there was *one* thing wrong in it, and that was when you said that for a year I wasn't noticing people, and . . . you, for instance. Why, you say you were watching me when I did everything . . . I was doing the same about you all the time. Why, sure,—I always thought about you as one of the chief people I thought about. I always made sure where you were sitting on the bleachers, and who you were with, and for three days now I've been trying to walk home with you; but something's always got in the way. Yesterday I was standing over against the wall waiting for you, and you walked home with *Miss Corcoran.*

EMILY: George! . . . Life's awful funny! How could I have known that? Why, I thought——

GEORGE: Listen, Emily, I'm going to tell you why I'm not going to Agriculture School. I think that once you've found a person that you're very fond of . . . I mean a person who's fond of you, too, and likes you enough to be interested in your character. . . . Well, I think that's just as important as college is, and even more so. That's what I think.

EMILY: I think it's awfully important, too.

GEORGE: Emily.

EMILY: Y-yes, George.

GEORGE: Emily, if I *do* improve and make a big change . . . would you be . . . I mean: *could* you be. . . .

EMILY: I . . . I am now; I always have been.

GEORGE [pause]: So I guess this is an important talk we've been having.

EMILY: Yes . . . yes.

GEORGE [takes a deep breath and straightens his back]: Wait just a minute and I'll walk you home. [With mounting alarm he digs into his pockets for the money. The Stage Manager enters, right. George, deeply embarrassed, but direct, says to him:] Mr. Morgan, I'll have to go home and get the money to pay you for this. It'll only take me a minute.

STAGE MANAGER [pretending to be affronted]: What's that? George Gibbs, do you mean to tell me——!

GEORGE: Yes, but I had reasons, Mr. Morgan.—Look, here's my gold watch to keep until I come back with the money.

STAGE MANAGER: That's all right. Keep your watch. I'll trust you.

GEORGE: I'll be back in five minutes.

STAGE MANAGER: I'll trust you ten years, George,—not a day over.—Got all over your shock, Emily?

EMILY: Yes, thank you, Mr. Morgan. It was nothing.

GEORGE [taking up the books from the counter]: I'm ready.

They walk in grave silence across the stage and pass through the trellis at the Webbs' back door and disappear. The Stage Manager watches them go out, then turns to the audience, removing his spectacles.

STAGE MANAGER: Well,—[He claps his hands as a signal.] Now we're ready to get on with the wedding. [He stands waiting while the set is prepared for the next scene. Stagehands remove the chairs, tables, and trellises from the Gibbs and Webb houses. They arrange the pews for the church in the center of the stage. The congregation will sit facing the back wall. The aisle of the church starts at the center of the back wall and comes toward the audience. A small platform is placed against the back wall on which the Stage Manager will stand later, playing the minister. The image of a stained-glass window is cast from a lantern slide upon the back wall. When all is ready the Stage Manager strolls to the center of the stage, down front, and, musingly, addresses the audience.] There are a lot of things to be said about a wedding; there are a lot of thoughts that go on during a wedding. We can't get them all into one wedding, naturally, and especially not into a wedding at Grover's Corners, where they're awfully plain and short. In this wedding I play the minister. That gives me the right to say a few more things about it.

For a while now, the play gets pretty serious. Y'see, some churches say that marriage is a sacrament. I don't quite know what this means, but I can guess. Like Mrs. Gibbs said a few minutes ago: People were made to live two-by-two. This is a good wedding, but people are so put together that even at a good wedding there's a lot of confusion way down deep in people's minds and we thought that that ought to be in our play, too.

The real hero of this scene isn't on the stage at all, and you know who that is. It's like what one of those European fellas said: every child born into the world is nature's attempt to make a perfect human being. Well, we've seen nature pushing and contriving for some time now. We all know that nature's interested in quantity; but I think she's interested in quality, too,—that's why I'm in the ministry. And don't forget all the other witnesses at this wedding,—the ancestors. Millions of them. Most of them set out to live two-by-two, also. Millions of them. Well, that's all my sermon. 'Twan't very long, anyway.

The organ starts playing Handel's "Largo." The congregation streams into the church and sits in silence. Church bells are heard. Mrs. Gibbs sits in the front row, the first seat on the aisle, the right section; next to her are Rebecca and Dr. Gibbs. Across the aisle Mrs. Webb, Wally and Mr. Webb. A small choir takes its place, facing the audience under the stained-glass window. Mrs. Webb, on the way to her place, turns back and speaks to the audience.

MRS. WEBB: I don't know why on earth I should be crying. I suppose there's nothing to cry about. It came over me at breakfast this morning; there was Emily eating her breakfast as she's done for seventeen years and now she's going off to eat it in someone else's house. I suppose that's it. And Emily! She suddenly said: I can't eat another mouthful, and she put her head down on the table and *she* cried. [She starts toward her seat in the church, but turns back and adds:] Oh, I've got to say it: you know, there's something downright cruel about sending our girls out into marriage this way. I hope some of her girl friends have told her a thing or two. It's cruel, I know, but I couldn't bring myself to say anything. I went into it blind as a bat myself. [In half-amused exasperation.] The whole world's wrong, that's what's the matter. There they come.

She hurries to her place in the pew. George starts to come down the right aisle of the theater, through the audience. Suddenly three members of his baseball team appear by the right proscenium pillar and start whistling and catcalling to him. They are dressed for the ball field.

THE BASEBALL PLAYERS: Eh, George, George! Hast—Yaow! Look at him, fellas—he looks scared to death. Yaow! George, don't look so innocent, you old geezer. We know what you're thinking. Don't disgrace the team, big boy. Whoo-oo-oo.

STAGE MANAGER: All right! All right! That'll do. That's enough of that. [Smiling, he pushes them off the stage. They lean back to shout a few more catcalls.] There used to be an awful lot of that kind of thing at weddings in the old days,—Rome, and later. We're more civilized now,—so they say.

The choir starts singing "Love Divine, All Love Excelling—." George has reached the stage. He stares at the congregation a moment, then takes a few steps of withdrawal, toward the right proscenium pillar. His mother, from the front row, seems to have felt his confusion. She leaves her seat and comes down the aisle quickly to him.

MRS. GIBBS: George! George! What's the matter?

GEORGE: Ma, I don't want to grow old. Why's everybody pushing me so?

MRS. GIBBS: Why, George . . . you wanted it.

GEORGE: No, Ma, listen to me——

MRS. GIBBS: No, no, George,—you're a man now.

GEORGE: Listen, Ma,—for the last time I ask you. . . . All I want to do is to be a fella——

MRS. GIBBS: George! If anyone should hear you! Now stop. Why, I'm ashamed of you!

GEORGE [he comes to himself and looks over the scene] What? Where's Emily?

MRS. GIBBS [relieved]: George! You gave me such a turn.

GEORGE: Cheer up, Ma. I'm getting married.

MRS. GIBBS: Let me catch my breath a minute.

GEORGE [comforting her]: Now, Ma, you save Thursday nights. Emily and I are coming over to dinner every Thursday night . . . you'll see. Ma, what are you crying for? Come on; we've got to get ready for this.

Mrs. Gibbs, mastering her emotion, fixes his tie and whispers to him. In the meantime, Emily, in white and wearing her wedding veil, has come through the audience and mounted onto the stage. She too draws back, frightened, when she sees the congregation in the church. The choir begins: "Blest Be the Tie That Binds."

EMILY: I never felt so alone in my whole life. And George over there, looking so . . .! I *hate* him. I wish I were dead. Papa! Papa!

MR. WEBB [leaves his seat in the pews and comes toward her anxiously]: Emily! Emily! Now don't get upset. . . .

EMILY: But, Papa,—I don't want to get married. . . .

MR. WEBB: Sh—sh—Emily. Everything's all right.

EMILY: Why can't I stay for a while just as I am? Let's go away,—

MR. WEBB: No, no, Emily. Now stop and think a minute.

EMILY: Don't you remember that you used to say,—all the time you used to say—all the time: that I was *your* girl! There must be lots of places we can go to. I'll work for you. I could keep house.

MR. WEBB: Sh. . . . You mustn't think of such things. You're just nervous,

Emily. [He turns and calls:] George! George! Will you come here a minute? [He leads her toward George.] Why you're marrying the best young fellow in the world. George is a fine fellow.

EMILY: But Papa,—

Mrs. Gibbs returns unobtrusively to her seat. Mr. Webb has one arm around his daughter. He places his hand on George's shoulder.

MR. WEBB: I'm giving away my daughter, George. Do you think you can take care of her?

GEORGE: Mr. Webb, I want to . . . I want to try. Emily, I'm going to do my best. I love you, Emily. I need you.

EMILY: Well, if you love me, help me. All I want is someone to love me.

GEORGE: I will, Emily. Emily, I'll try.

EMILY: And I mean for *ever*. Do you hear? For ever and ever.

They fall into each other's arms. The March from Lohengrin is heard. The Stage Manager, as clergyman, stands on the box, up center.

MR. WEBB: Come, they're waiting for us. Now you know it'll be all right. Come, quick.

George slips away and takes his place beside the Stage Manager–Clergyman. Emily proceeds up the aisle on her father's arm.

STAGE MANAGER: Do you, George, take this woman, Emily, to be your wedded wife, to have. . . .

Mrs. Soames has been sitting in the last row of the congregation. She now turns to her neighbors and speaks in a shrill voice. Her chatter drowns out the rest of the clergyman's words.

MRS. SOAMES: Perfectly lovely wedding! Loveliest wedding I ever saw. Oh, I do

love a good wedding, don't you?
Doesn't she make a lovely bride?

GEORGE: I do.

STAGE MANAGER: Do you, Emily, take this man, George, to be your wedded husband,— [Again his further words are covered by those of Mrs. Soames.]

MRS. SOAMES: Don't know *when* I've seen such a lovely wedding. But I always cry. Don't know why it is, but I always cry. I just like to see young people happy, don't you? Oh, I think it's lovely.

The ring. The kiss. The stage is suddenly arrested into silent tableau. The Stage Manager, his eyes on the distance, as though to himself:

STAGE MANAGER: I've married over two hundred couples in my day. Do I believe in it? I don't know.

M—— marries N—— millions of them. The cottage, the go-cart, the Sunday-afternoon drives in the Ford, the first rheumatism, the grandchildren, the second rheumatism, the deathbed, the reading of the will,— [He now looks at the audience for the first time, with a warm smile that removes any sense of cynicism from the next line.] Once in a thousand times it's interesting.—Well, let's have Mendelssohn's "Wedding March"!

The organ picks up the March. The bride and groom come down the aisle, radiant, but trying to be very dignified.

MRS. SOAMES: Aren't they a lovely couple? Oh, I've never been to such a nice wedding. I'm sure they'll be happy. I always say: *happiness*, that's the great thing! The important thing is to be happy.

The bride and groom reach the steps leading into the audience. A bright light is thrown upon them. They descend into the auditorium and run up the aisle joyously.

STAGE MANAGER: That's all the Second Act, folks. Ten minutes' intermission.

DISCUSSION   1.   Why, do you think, does the playwright begin Act II with the wedding day of George and Emily instead of building suspense about the outcome of their romance?

2.   What advice had Mr. Webb's father given him about "showing who's boss" and dealing with irritation? Did Mr. Webb take the advice? Would you? Explain.

3.   What do you think of Emily's remarks about being "perfect" (page 351)? Why might she feel that it is easier for a man to be "perfect"?

Act 3

During the intermission the audience has seen the stagehands arranging the stage. On the right-hand side, a little right of the center, ten or twelve ordinary chairs have been placed in three openly spaced rows facing the audience. These are graves in the cemetery. Toward the end of the intermission the actors enter and take their places. The front row contains: toward the center of the stage, an empty chair; then Mrs. Gibbs; Simon Stimson. The second row contains, among others, Mrs. Soames. The third row has Wally Webb. The dead do not turn their heads or their eyes to right or left, but they sit in a quiet without stiffness. When they speak their tone is matter-of-fact, without sentimentality and, above all, without lugubriousness. The Stage Manager takes his accustomed place and waits for the house lights to go down.

STAGE MANAGER: This time nine years have gone by, friends—summer, 1913. Gradual changes in Grover's Corners. Horses are getting rarer. Farmers coming into town in Fords. Everybody locks their house doors now at night. Ain't been any burglars in town yet, but everybody's heard about 'em. You'd be surprised, though—on the whole, things don't change much around here.

This is certainly an important part of Grover's Corners. It's on a hilltop— a windy hilltop—lots of sky, lots of clouds,—often lots of sun and moon and stars. You come up here on a fine afternoon and you can see range on range of hills—awful blue they are— up there by Lake Sunapee and Lake Winnipesaukee . . . and way up, if you've got a glass, you can see the White Mountains and Mt. Washington—where North Conway and Conway is. And, of course, our favorite mountain, Mt. Monadnock, 's right here—and all these towns that lie around it: Jaffrey, 'n East Jaffrey, 'n Peterborough, 'n Dublin; and [then pointing down in the audience] there, quite a ways down, is Grover's Corners. Yes, beautiful spot up here. Mountain laurel and li-lacks. I often wonder why people like to be buried in Woodlawn and Brooklyn when they might pass the same time up here in New Hampshire. Over there—[pointing to stage left] are the old stones,—1670, 1680. Strongminded people that come a long way to be independent. Summer people walk around there laughing at the funny words on the tombstones . . . it don't do any harm. And genealogists come up from Boston—get paid by city people for looking up their ancestors. They want to make sure they're Daughters of the American Revolution and of the *Mayflower*. . . . Well, I guess that don't do any harm, either. Wherever you come near the human race, there's layers and layers of nonsense. . . . Over there are some Civil War veterans. Iron flags on their graves . . . New Hampshire boys . . . had a notion that the Union ought to be kept together, though they'd never seen more than fifty miles of it themselves. All they knew was the name, friends—the United States of America. The United States of America. And they went and died about it.

This here is the new part of the cemetery. Here's your friend Mrs. Gibbs. 'N let me see—— Here's Mr. Stimson, organist at the Congregational Church. And Mrs. Soames who enjoyed the wedding so—you remember? Oh, and a lot of others. And Editor Webb's boy, Wallace, whose appendix burst while he was on a Boy Scout trip to Crawford Notch. Yes, an awful lot of sorrow has sort of quieted down up here. People just wild with grief have brought their relatives up to this hill. We all know how it is . . . and then time . . . and sunny days . . . and rainy days . . . 'n snow. . . . We're all glad they're in a beautiful place and we're coming up here ourselves when our fit's over.

Now there are some things we all know, but we don't take'm out and look at'm very often. We all know that *something* is eternal. And it ain't houses and it ain't names, and it ain't earth, and it ain't even the stars . . . everybody knows in their bones that *something* is eternal, and that something has to do with human beings. All the greatest people ever lived have been telling us that for five thousand years and yet you'd be surprised how people are always losing hold of it. There's something way down deep that's eternal about every human being. [Pause.] You know as well as I do that the dead don't stay interested in us living people for very long. Gradually, gradu-

ally, they lose hold of the earth . . . and the ambitions they had . . . and the pleasures they had . . . and the things they suffered . . . and the people they loved. They get weaned away from earth—that's the way I put it,—weaned away. And they stay here while the earth part of 'em burns away, burns out; and all that time they slowly get indifferent to what's goin' on in Grover's Corners. They're waitin'. They're waitin' for something that they feel is comin'. Something important, and great. Aren't they waitin' for the eternal part in them to come out clear? Some of the things they're going to say maybe'll hurt your feelings—but that's the way it is: mother 'n daughter . . . husband 'n wife . . . enemy 'n enemy . . . money 'n miser . . . all those terribly important things kind of grow pale around here. And what's left when memory's gone, and your identity, Mrs. Smith? [He looks at the audience a minute, then turns to the stage.] Well! There are some *living* people. There's Joe Stoddard, our undertaker, supervising a new-made grave. And here comes a Grover's Corners boy, that left town to go out West.

Joe Stoddard has hovered about in the background. Sam Craig enters left, wiping his forehead from the exertion. He carries an umbrella and strolls front.

SAM CRAIG: Good afternoon, Joe Stoddard.
JOE STODDARD: Good afternoon, good afternoon. Let me see now: do I know you?
SAM CRAIG: I'm Sam Craig.
JOE STODDARD: Gracious sakes' alive! Of all

people! I should'a knowed you'd be back for the funeral. You've been away a long time, Sam.

SAM CRAIG: Yes, I've been away over twelve years. I'm in business out in Buffalo now, Joe. But I was in the East when I got news of my cousin's death, so I thought I'd combine things a little and come and see the old home. You look well.

JOE STODDARD: Yes, yes, can't complain. Very sad, our journey today, Samuel.

SAM CRAIG: Yes.

JOE STODDARD: Yes, yes. I always say I hate to supervise when a young person is taken. They'll be here in a few minutes now. I had to come here early today—my son's supervisin' at the home.

SAM CRAIG [reading stones]: Old Farmer McCarty, I used to do chores for him—after school. He had the lumbago.

JOE STODDARD: Yes, we brought Farmer McCarty here a number of years ago now.

SAM CRAIG [staring at Mrs. Gibbs's knees]: Why, this is my Aunt Julia . . . I'd forgotten that she'd . . . of course, of course.

JOE STODDARD: Yes, Doc Gibbs lost his wife two-three years ago . . . about this time. And today's another pretty bad blow for him, too.

MRS. GIBBS [to Simon Stimson: in an even voice]: That's my sister Carey's boy, Sam . . . Sam Craig.

SIMON STIMSON: I'm always uncomfortable when *they're* around.

MRS. GIBBS: Simon.

SAM CRAIG: Do they choose their own verses much, Joe?

JOE STODDARD: No . . . not usual. Mostly the bereaved pick a verse.

SAM CRAIG: Doesn't sound like Aunt Julia. There aren't many of those Hersey sisters left now. Let me see: where are . . . I wanted to look at my father's and mother's. . . .

JOE STODDARD: Over there with the Craigs . . . Avenue F.

SAM CRAIG [reading Simon Stimson's epitaph]: He was organist at church, wasn't he?—Hm, drank a lot, we used to say.

JOE STODDARD: Nobody was supposed to know about it. He'd seen a peck of trouble. [Behind his hand] Took his own life, y'know?

SAM CRAIG: Oh, did he?

JOE STODDARD: Hung himself in the attic. They tried to hush it up, but of course it got around. He chose his own epytaph.[7] You can see it there. It ain't a verse exactly.

SAM CRAIG: Why, it's just some notes of music—what is it?

JOE STODDARD: Oh, I wouldn't know. It was wrote up in the Boston papers at the time.

SAM CRAIG: Joe, what did she die of?

JOE STODDARD: Who?

SAM CRAIG: My cousin.

JOE STODDARD: Oh, didn't you know? Had some trouble bringing a baby into the world. 'Twas her second, though. There's a little boy 'bout four years old.

SAM CRAIG [opening his umbrella]: The grave's going to be over there?

JOE STODDARD: Yes, there ain't much more room over here among the Gibbses, so

---

[7] *epytaph*: epitaph; inscription on a tombstone.

they're opening up a whole new Gibbs section over by Avenue B. You'll excuse me now. I see they're comin'.

From left to center, at the back of the stage, comes a procession. Four men carry a casket, invisible to us. All the rest are under umbrellas. One can vaguely see: Dr. Gibbs, George, the Webbs, etc. They gather about a grave in the back center of the stage, a little to the left of center.

MRS. SOAMES: Who is it, Julia?

MRS. GIBBS [without raising her eyes]: My daughter-in-law, Emily Webb.

MRS. SOAMES [a little surprised, but no emotion]: Well, I declare! The road up here must have been awful muddy. What did she die of, Julia?

MRS. GIBBS: In childbirth.

MRS. SOAMES: Childbirth. [Almost with a laugh] I'd forgotten all about that. My, wasn't life awful—[with a sigh] and wonderful.

SIMON STIMSON [with a sideways glance]: Wonderful, was it?

MRS. GIBBS: Simon! Now, remember!

MRS. SOAMES: I remember Emily's wedding. Wasn't it a lovely wedding! And I remember her reading the class poem at Graduation Exercises. Emily was one of the brightest girls ever graduated from High School. I've heard Principal Wilkins say so time after time. I called on them at their new farm, just before I died. Perfectly beautiful farm.

A WOMAN FROM AMONG THE DEAD: It's on the same road we lived on.

A MAN AMONG THE DEAD: Yepp, right smart farm.

They subside. The group by the grave starts singing "Blest Be the Tie That Binds."

A WOMAN AMONG THE DEAD: I always liked that hymn. I was hopin' they'd sing a hymn.

Pause. Suddenly Emily appears from among the umbrellas. She is wearing a white dress. Her hair is down her back and tied by a white ribbon like a little girl. She comes slowly, gazing wonderingly at the dead, a little dazed. She stops halfway and smiles faintly. After looking at the mourners for a moment, she walks slowly to the vacant chair beside Mrs. Gibbs and sits down.

EMILY [to them all, quietly, smiling]: Hello.

MRS. SOAMES: Hello, Emily.

A MAN AMONG THE DEAD: Hello, M's Gibbs.

EMILY [warmly]: Hello, Mother Gibbs.

MRS. GIBBS: Emily.

EMILY: Hello. [With surprise] It's raining. [Her eyes drift back to the funeral company.]

MRS. GIBBS: Yes. . . . They'll be gone soon, dear. Just rest yourself.

EMILY: It seems thousands and thousands of years since I . . . Papa remembered that that was my favorite hymn.
Oh, I wish I'd been here a long time. I don't like being new here.—How do you do, Mr. Stimson?

SIMON STIMSON: How do you do, Emily.

Emily continues to look about her with a wondering smile; as though to shut out from her mind the thought of the funeral company she starts speaking to Mrs. Gibbs with a touch of nervousness.

EMILY: Mother Gibbs, George and I have made that farm into just the best place you ever saw. We thought of you all the time. We wanted to show you the new barn and a great long ce-ment drinking fountain for the stock. We bought that out of the money you left us.

MRS. GIBBS: I did?

EMILY: Don't you remember, Mother Gibbs—the legacy you left us? Why, it was over three hundred and fifty dollars.

MRS. GIBBS: Yes, yes, Emily.

EMILY: Well, there's a patent device on the drinking fountain so that it never overflows, Mother Gibbs, and it never sinks below a certain mark they have there. It's fine. [Her voice trails off and her eyes return to the funeral group.] It won't be the same to George without me, but it's a lovely farm. [Suddenly she looks directly at Mrs. Gibbs.] Live people don't understand, do they?

MRS. GIBBS: No, dear—not very much.

EMILY: They're sort of shut up in little boxes, aren't they? I feel as though I knew them last a thousand years ago. . . . My boy is spending the day at Mrs. Carter's. [She sees Mr. Carter among the dead.] Oh, Mr. Carter, my little boy is spending the day at your house.

MR. CARTER: Is he?

EMILY: Yes, he loves it there.—Mother Gibbs, we have a Ford, too. Never gives any trouble. I don't drive, though. Mother Gibbs, when does this feeling go away?—Of being . . . one of *them?* How long does it . . .?

MRS. GIBBS: Sh! dear. Just wait and be patient.

EMILY [with a sigh]: I know.—Look, they're finished. They're going.

MRS. GIBBS: Sh—.

The umbrellas leave the stage. Dr. Gibbs has come over to his wife's grave and stands before it a moment. Emily looks up at his face. Mrs. Gibbs does not raise her eyes.

EMILY: Look! Father Gibbs is bringing some of my flowers to you. He looks just like George, doesn't he? Oh, Mother Gibbs, I never realized before how troubled and how . . . how in the dark live persons are. Look at him. I loved him so. From morning till night, that's all they are—troubled. [Dr. Gibbs goes off.]

THE DEAD: Little cooler than it was.—Yes, that rain's cooled it off a little. Those northeast winds always do the same thing, don't they? If it isn't a rain, it's a three-day blow.—

A patient calm falls on the stage. The Stage Manager appears at his proscenium pillar, smoking. Emily sits up abruptly with an idea.

EMILY: But, Mother Gibbs, one can go back; one can go back there again . . . into living. I feel it. I know it. Why just then for a moment I was thinking about . . . about the farm . . . and for a minute I *was* there, and my baby was on my lap as plain as day.

MRS. GIBBS: Yes, of course you can.

EMILY: I can go back there and live all those days over again . . . why not?

MRS. GIBBS: All I can say is, Emily, don't.

EMILY [she appeals urgently to the Stage Manager]: But it's true, isn't it? I can go and live . . . back there . . . again.

STAGE MANAGER: Yes, some have tried—but they soon come back here.

MRS. GIBBS: Don't do it, Emily.

MRS. SOAMES: Emily, don't. It's not what you think it'd be.

EMILY: But I won't live over a sad day. I'll choose a happy one—I'll choose the day I first knew that I loved George. Why should that be painful?

They are silent. Her question turns to the Stage Manager.

STAGE MANAGER: You not only live it; but you watch yourself living it.

EMILY: Yes?

STAGE MANAGER: And as you watch it; you see the thing that they—down there—never know. You see the future. You know what's going to happen afterwards.

EMILY: But is that—painful? Why?

MRS. GIBBS: That's not the only reason why you shouldn't do it, Emily. When you've been here longer you'll see that our life here is to forget all that, and think only of what's ahead, and be ready for what's ahead. When you've been here longer you'll understand.

EMILY [softly]: But, Mother Gibbs, how can I *ever* forget that life? It's all I know. It's all I had.

MRS. SOAMES: Oh, Emily. It isn't wise. Really, it isn't.

EMILY: But it's a thing I must know for myself. I'll choose a happy day, anyway.

MRS. GIBBS: *No!*—At least choose an unimportant day. Choose the least important day in your life. It will be important enough.

EMILY [to herself]: Then it can't be since I was married; or since the baby was born. [To the Stage Manager, eagerly] I can choose a birthday at least, can't I?—I choose my twelfth birthday.

STAGE MANAGER: All right. February 11th, 1899. A Tuesday.—Do you want any special time of day?

EMILY: Oh, I want the whole day.

STAGE MANAGER: We'll begin at dawn. You remember it had been snowing for several days; but it had stopped the night before, and they had begun clearing the roads. The sun's coming up.

EMILY [with a cry; rising]: There's Main Street . . . why, that's Mr. Morgan's drugstore before he changed it! . . . And there's the livery stable.

The stage at no time in this act has been very dark; but now the left half of the stage gradually becomes very bright—the brightness of a crisp winter morning. Emily walks toward Main Street.

STAGE MANAGER: Yes, it's 1899. This is fourteen years ago.

EMILY: Oh, that's the town I knew as a little girl. And, *look,* there's the old white fence that used to be around our house. Oh, I'd forgotten that! Oh, I love it so! Are they inside?

STAGE MANAGER: Yes, your mother'll be coming downstairs in a minute to make breakfast.

EMILY [softly]: Will she?

STAGE MANAGER: And you remember: your father had been away for several days; he came back on the early-morning train.

EMILY: No . . .?

STAGE MANAGER: He'd been back to his college to make a speech—in western New York, at Clinton.

EMILY: Look! There's Howie Newsome. There's our policeman. But he's *dead;* he *died.*

The voices of Howie Newsome, Constable Warren and Joe Crowell, Jr., are heard at the left of the stage. Emily listens in delight.

HOWIE NEWSOME: Whoa, Bessie!—Bessie! 'Morning, Bill.

CONSTABLE WARREN: Morning, Howie.

HOWIE NEWSOME: You're up early.

CONSTABLE WARREN: Been rescuin' a party; darn near froze to death, down by Polish Town thar. Got drunk and lay out in the snowdrifts. Thought he was in bed when I shook'm.

EMILY: Why, there's Joe Crowell. . . .

JOE CROWELL: Good morning, Mr. Warren. Morning, Howie.

Mrs. Webb has appeared in her kitchen, but Emily does not see her until she calls.

MRS. WEBB: Chil-*dren!* Wally! Emily! . . . Time to get up.

EMILY: Mama, I'm here! Oh! how young Mama looks! I didn't know Mama was ever that young.

MRS. WEBB: You can come and dress by the kitchen fire, if you like; but hurry. [Howie Newsome has entered along Main Street and brings the milk to Mrs. Webb's door.] Good morning, Mr. Newsome. Whhhh—it's cold.

HOWIE NEWSOME: Ten below by my barn, Mrs. Webb.

MRS. WEBB: Think of it! Keep yourself wrapped up. [She takes her bottles in, shuddering.]

EMILY [with an effort]: Mama, I can't find my blue hair ribbon anywhere.

MRS. WEBB: Just open your eyes, dear, that's all. I laid it out for you special—on the dresser, there. If it were a snake it would bite you.

EMILY: Yes, yes. . . .

She puts her hand on her heart. Mr. Webb comes along Main Street, where he meets Constable Warren. Their movements and voices are increasingly lively in the sharp air.

MR. WEBB: Good morning, Bill.

CONSTABLE WARREN: Good morning, Mr. Webb. You're up early.

MR. WEBB: Yes, just been back to my old college in New York State. Been any trouble here?

CONSTABLE WARREN: Well, I was called up this mornin' to rescue a Polish fella— darn near froze to death he was.

MR. WEBB: We must get it in the paper.

CONSTABLE WARREN: 'Twan't much.

EMILY [whispers]: Papa.

Mr. Webb shakes the snow off his feet and enters his house. Constable Warren goes off, right.

MR. WEBB: Good morning, Mother.

MRS. WEBB: How did it go, Charles?

MR. WEBB: Oh, fine, I guess. I told'm a few things.—Everything all right here?

MRS. WEBB: Yes—can't think of anything that's happened, special. Been right cold. Howie Newsome says it's ten below over to his barn.

MR. WEBB: Yes, well, it's colder than that at Hamilton College. Students' ears are falling off. It ain't Christian.—Paper have any mistakes in it?

MRS. WEBB: None that I noticed. Coffee's ready when you want it. [He starts upstairs.] Charles! Don't forget; it's Emily's birthday. Did you remember to get her something?

MR. WEBB [patting his pocket]: Yes, I've got something here. [Calling up the stair] Where's my girl? Where's my birthday girl? [He goes off left.]

MRS. WEBB: Don't interrupt her now, Charles. You can see her at breakfast. She's slow enough as it is. Hurry up, children! It's seven o'clock. Now, I don't want to call you again.

EMILY [softly, more in wonder than in grief]: I can't bear it. They're so young and beautiful. Why did they ever have to get old? Mama, I'm here. I'm grown up. I love you all, everything.—I can't look at everything hard enough. [She looks questioningly at the Stage Manager, saying or suggesting: "Can I go in?" He nods briefly. She crosses to the inner door to the kitchen, left of her mother, and as though entering the room, says, suggesting the voice of a girl of twelve:] Good morning, Mama.

MRS. WEBB [crossing to embrace and kiss her; in her characteristic matter-of-fact manner]: Well, now, dear, a very happy birthday to my girl and many happy returns. There are some surprises waiting for you on the kitchen table.

EMILY: Oh, Mama, you *shouldn't* have. [She throws an anguished glance at the Stage Manager.] I can't—I can't.

MRS. WEBB [facing the audience, over her stove]: But birthday or no birthday, I want you to eat your breakfast good and slow. I want you to grow up and be a good strong girl. That in the blue paper is from your Aunt Carrie; and I reckon you can guess who brought the post-card album. I found it on the doorstep when I brought in the milk—George Gibbs . . . must have come over in the cold pretty early . . . right nice of him.

EMILY [to herself]: Oh, George! I'd forgotten that. . . .

MRS. WEBB: Chew that bacon good and slow. It'll help keep you warm on a cold day.

EMILY [with mounting urgency]: Oh, Mama, just look at me one minute as though you really saw me. Mama, fourteen years have gone by. I'm dead. You're a grandmother, Mama. I married George Gibbs, Mama. Wally's dead, too.

Mama, his appendix burst on a camping trip to North Conway. We felt just terrible about it—don't you remember? But, just for a moment now we're all together. Mama, just for a moment we're happy. *Let's look at one another.*

MRS. WEBB: That in the yellow paper is something I found in the attic among your grandmother's things. You're old enough to wear it now, and I thought you'd like it.

EMILY: And this is from you. Why, Mama, it's just lovely and it's just what I wanted. It's beautiful! [She flings her arms around her mother's neck. Her mother goes on with her cooking, but is pleased.]

MRS. WEBB: Well, I hoped you'd like it. Hunted all over. Your Aunt Norah couldn't find one in Concord, so I had to send all the way to Boston. [Laughing] Wally has something for you, too. He made it at manual-training class and he's very proud of it. Be sure you make a big fuss about it.—Your father has a surprise for you, too; don't know what it is myself. Sh—here he comes.

MR. WEBB [off stage]: Where's my girl? Where's my birthday girl?

EMILY [in a loud voice to the Stage Manager]: I can't. I can't go on. It goes so fast. We don't have time to look at one another. [She breaks down sobbing. The lights dim on the left half of the stage. Mrs. Webb disappears.] I didn't realize. So all that was going on and we never noticed. Take me back—up the hill—to my grave. But first: Wait! One more look. Good-by, Good-by, world. Good-by, Grover's Corners . . . Mama and Papa. Good-by to clocks ticking . . . and Mama's sunflowers. And food and coffee.

And new-ironed dresses and hot baths . . . and sleeping and waking up. Oh, earth, you're too wonderful for anybody to realize you. [She looks toward the Stage Manager and asks abruptly, through her tears:] Do any human beings ever realize while they live it?—every, every minute.

STAGE MANAGER: No. [Pause] The saints and poets, maybe—they do some.

EMILY: I'm ready to go back. [She returns to her chair beside Mrs. Gibbs. Pause.]

MRS. GIBBS: Were you happy?

EMILY: No . . . I should have listened to you. That's all human beings are! Just blind people.

MRS. GIBBS: Look, it's clearing up. The stars are coming out.

EMILY: Oh, Mr. Stimson, I should have listened to them.

SIMON STIMSON [with mounting violence; bitingly]: Yes, now you know. Now you know! That's what it was to be alive. To move about in a cloud of ignorance; to go up and down trampling on the feelings of those . . . of those about you. To spend and waste time as though you had a million years. To be always at the mercy of one self-centered passion, or another. Now you know—that's the happy existence you wanted to go back to. Ignorance and blindness.

MRS. GIBBS [spiritedly]: Simon Stimson, that ain't the whole truth and you know it. Emily, look at that star. I forget its name.

A MAN AMONG THE DEAD: My boy Joel was a sailor,—knew 'em all. He'd set on the porch evenings and tell 'em all by name. Yes, sir, wonderful!

ANOTHER MAN AMONG THE DEAD: A star's mighty good company.

A WOMAN AMONG THE DEAD: Yes. Yes, 'tis.

SIMON STIMSON: Here's one of *them* coming.

THE DEAD: That's funny. 'Tain't no time for one of them to be here.—Goodness sakes.

EMILY: Mother Gibbs, it's George.

MRS. GIBBS: Sh, dear. Just rest yourself.

EMILY: It's George.

George enters from the left, and slowly comes toward them.

A MAN FROM AMONG THE DEAD: And my boy, Joel, who knew the stars—he used to say it took millions of years for that speck o' light to git to the earth. Don't seem like a body could believe it, but that's what he used to say—millions of years.

George sinks to his knees, then falls full length at Emily's feet.

A WOMAN AMONG THE DEAD: Goodness! That ain't no way to behave!

MRS. SOAMES: He ought to be home.

EMILY: Mother Gibbs?

MRS. GIBBS: Yes, Emily?

EMILY: They don't understand, do they?

MRS. GIBBS: No, dear. They don't understand.

The Stage Manager appears at the right, one hand on a dark curtain which he slowly draws across the scene. In the distance a clock is heard striking the hour very faintly.

STAGE MANAGER: Most everybody's asleep in Grover's Corners. There are a few lights on: Shorty Hawkins, down at the depot, has just watched the Albany train go by. And at the livery stable somebody's setting up late and talking.—Yes, it's clearing up. There are the stars—doing their old, old criss-cross journeys in the sky. Scholars haven't settled the matter yet, but they seem to think there are no living be-ings up there. Just chalk . . . or fire. Only this one is straining away, strain-ing away all the time to make some-thing of itself. The strain's so bad that every sixteen hours everybody lies down and gets a rest. [He winds his watch.] Hm. . . . Eleven o'clock in Grover's Corners.—You get a good rest, too. Good night.

THE END

DISCUSSION

1. Why do the dead urge Emily not to "go back" (pages 364–365)? Explain why she later regrets her decision to go back.

2. Mrs. Gibbs advises Emily, "At least choose an unimportant day. Choose the least important day in your life." Why do you think she offers this advice?

3. In what way does the cemetery scene express a view about death? What is that view?

The Play as a Whole

1. In all three acts of the play, the hymn "Blest Be the Tie That Binds" is sung. Why is it a particularly appropriate choice?

2. How does the passage of time figure in the overall meaning of the play? In what way is the title of the play itself appropriate?

3. Who in your opinion is the most important character in the play? Why do you think so?

4. The *structure* of a play is the way in which the play is put together. And how the play is put together depends on the playwright's purpose. This play has three acts. What are the first two called, according to the Stage Manager? What would you call the third? What do these titles tell you about the theme or underlying meaning of the play?

Exposition explains the situation at the beginning of a play. It is usually pre-sented through the dialogue of the characters at the beginning of the play. But in *Our Town* the playwright uses exposition just a bit differently. First, the exposition appears not just at the beginning of the play, but at the beginning of each act. Second, the exposition is presented through the Stage Manager, a character in the play, but one who has little interaction with the other characters. How is the theme of the play developed in the Stage Manager's exposition?

The cast of characters is not given here; we meet them as they appear on the scene. The scene is an old-time western town, and some of the characters will seem very familiar.

THE BRIDE COMES TO YELLOW SKY

A FILM SCRIPT / SLIGHTLY ADAPTED FOR THIS USE

JAMES AGEE

FADE IN——EXT. MAIN STREET OF YELLOW SKY—DUSK. Late summer dusk; SOUND of church bell O.S. PULL DOWN onto Potter's little home, of which the second story is a jail—barred windows. Jack Potter comes out his door, dressed for travel, carrying a bag. He walks a few steps, then glances back around at his house.

PRISONER [in upper window]: So long, Marshal. Don't do nothing I
    wouldn't do.
POTTER: Don't you do nothing I wouldn't, s'more like it. You lock
    yourself in right after mealtimes.
PRISONER: You can trust me, Marshal.
POTTER: I don't need to. I done tole Laura Lee to keep an eye on you.
    [Pause; shyly] Well, so long. I'll be back in a couple of days.

He walks away.

PRISONER [calling after]: Give my howdy to the gals in San Antone!
POTTER: You do that when you git out. I ain't no hand fer it.
PRISONER: Oh, I doan know, Marshal. They tell me still waters run
    deep.

Potter doesn't answer. He walks on away.

DOLLY SHOT—POTTER AND DEACON SMEED. Deacon Smeed falls in with him. CAMERA DOLLIES along with them. The following dialogue interrupted two or three times by eminently respectable people converging on the church. All treat Potter respectfully but a little remotely.

SMEED: Evening, Mr. Potter.
POTTER: Evening, Deacon.
SMEED: Leaving town so soon again?

POTTER: It's been most two months.

SMEED: Oh *has* it indeed, indeed. Hm. And what's going to happen to
your prisoner, if I may ask?

POTTER: Laura Lee's gonna take care of him.

SMEED: Mrs. Bates? [Potter nods.] She'll bring him his meals?

POTTER: He'll let himself out for 'em.

SMEED: Do you think that—ah—looks right?

POTTER [quietly]: Afraid I ain't worrying *how* it looks, Deacon. It's the
easiest way, and you know as well as I do, he ain't gonna make
no trouble.

SMEED: I'm afraid you don't care how *anything* looks, Mr. Potter.

POTTER: Oh now, Deacon, don't start on that church business again!

SMEED: I'm sorry, Marshal, but every respectable person in Yellow Sky
agrees with me. If only for appearance' sake, you ought to come
to church.

POTTER: Looky here, Deacon. We never did get nowheres with that argument, and we never will. I ain't got nothin' against church-
goin'; I just don't hold with it fer myself.

SMEED: And then all these mysterious trips to San Antonio lately——

They pause in front of church.

POTTER: Now looky here, Deacon—if you mean light women and such,
you know I ain't a man to fool around with them.

SMEED: Oh, you *misconstrue me,* Marshal, *indeed* you do. But . . .
Caesar's wife, you know. . . .

The church bell stops ringing.

POTTER: How's that?

SMEED: She must be *above* suspicion.

POTTER: Well, who's suspicious? You?

SMEED: Of course not, Marshal. Perish the thought. Only you never *say*
why you're going to San Antonio.

POTTER [after a pause]: Just business. Goodnight Deacon.

SMEED: Goodnight, Mr. Potter.

Potter walks ahead; he blows out his cheeks; his eyes focus gratefully on: VIEW-
POINT SHOT—"THE WEARY GENTLEMAN" SALOON   CUT TO

POTTER AS BEFORE. He checks his watch and speeds up out of shot.   CUT TO
MEDIUM SHOT—DEACON. He pauses at the church door, sees Potter enter the
"Weary Gentleman," and goes into church, over SOUND of first hymn.   CUT TO

INTERIOR. "WEARY GENTLEMAN"—DUSK. There is a typical western bar, behind which Laura Lee, a woman in her fifties, is presiding as bartender. CAMERA
PANS Potter to bar. He leaves his bag on a table near the door.

POTTER: Evenin', Laura Lee.

LAURA LEE [behind bar]: Hi, Jack.

JASPER: Jack.

ED: Howdy, Marshal.

POTTER: Jasper, Ed.

ED: Leavin' town again?

POTTER: That's right.

ED: San Antone?

POTTER [nods; drinks]: Laura Lee, you tell Frank no drinks, no foolin'
    around. Just come right straight here and eat and get right back
    again. 'Cause it's got the Deacon bothered, him goin' out at all.

LAURA LEE: Aw, Smeed. I tell you, Jack, when you waded in here and
    cleaned the town up, it wasn't just a favor you done us. Every-
    thing's gettin' too blame respectable.

POTTER: It was my job.

LAURA LEE: I don't hold it agin you. But if things get too tame around
    here, you'll up an' quit town fer good.

POTTER: Uh, uh. I aim to be buried here. Besides, long as ole Scratchy
    busts loose now an' then, things won't never get *too* tame.

OVER mention of Scratchy, Laura Lee's eyes focus on something O.S.

LAURA LEE [a little absently]: Here's *to* 'im.

Potter's eyes follow hers. MEDIUM SHOT—ALONG BAR—FROM THEIR ANGLE
a half-finished glass of beer, no customer. CLOSE SHOT—POTTER. A glance
from the beer to Laura Lee, a look of slightly concerned inquiry, meaning, "Is
that Scratchy's?" CLOSE SHOT—LAURA LEE nodding.

LAURA LEE: It don't work holding him to nothing, Jack. I figured maybe
    beer, on 'lowance. . . .

POTTER: Don't hear me hollerin', do you? It's worth tryin'. Only thing
    bothers me is if I'm out of town.

LAURA LEE: He ain't due for another tear yet.

POTTER: Ain't sure we can count on him hittin' 'em regular, no more.
    He's gettin' rouncier all the time.

JASPER [breaking a pause]: What ye doin' in San Antone, Jack?

Laura Lee gives him a cold glance.

POTTER: Just a business trip.

OVER this last, Scratchy comes in through a side door and up to bar, to a half-finished glass of beer.

POTTER: Howdy, Scratchy.

Scratchy doesn't answer. Potter and others are quietly amused.

LAURA LEE: What's wrong with ye, Scratchy? Cat got yer tongue?

Scratchy drinks glass down.

LAURA LEE [continuing]: Yer last one tonight. Rather wait fer it?
SCRATCHY: Just draw me my beer.
POTTER: Ain't still sore, are ye, Scratchy?
SCRATCHY: You know it was all in fun. What d'ye go an' plug me fer?
POTTER: 'Tain't fun, Scratchy. Not skeerin' the daylights out o' folks that
    ain't used to gun-play.
SCRATCHY: You're a fine one to talk about gun-play. Mean, sneakin'
    skunk!
POTTER: Sneakin'? It was fair and above board, like it always is.
LAURA LEE: He just beat ye to the draw, an' you know it.
SCRATCHY: That don't make my leg no happier.
POTTER: Mendin' a'right, Scratchy?
SCRATCHY: Oh, I git around.
POTTER: Just mind where ye git to, that's all I ask.
SCRATCHY: Next time, I'll make you dance.
POTTER: Better not be no next time. 'Cause next time, instead o' the
    meat o' the leg, I might have to pop you in the kneecap.
SCRATCHY: You wouldn't do that.
POTTER: I wouldn't want to. But I might have to, Scratchy, just to learn
    you. You don't know it but you're gettin' dangersome when you
    drink, lately.
SCRATCHY: Me—dangersome? A good man with a gun's a safe man
    with a gun, an' I'm the best they is.
LAURA LEE: When you're in yer likker, yeah. But you don't drink fer fun
    no more, Scratchy. You kinda go out o' yer head.
POTTER: That's right, Scratchy. One o' these days you're gonna shoot to
    kill, an' swing fer it, an' then all of us'll be sorry.
SCRATCHY: I don't need to kill nobody more—I got my notches, an' to
    spare—— [He pats his gun.]
POTTER: That was all right, agin the kind o' varmints that used to be
    around here in the old days—— You come in right handy. Sort of
    a scavenger, like a turkey-buzzard. But you can't go shootin' up
    law-abidin' citizens an' git away with it.

SCRATCHY [with extreme contempt]: Who wants to shoot a law-abidin'
 citizen!

UNDER the above, Potter finishes his drink, pays, starts out.

POTTER: Well. . . .
SCRATCHY: You leavin' town again?
POTTER: 'Bye, Laura Lee. See you day after tomorrow. [To Scratchy] You
 watch yer drinkin' while I'm gone.
SCRATCHY: I'll save it all up fer you, Jack. 'Tain't nobody else is wuth
 the hangover.

Potter exits.

JASPER: Reckon what he's up to, all these trips to San Antone?
LAURA LEE: Never you mind, it's his business.
ED: You ain't sweet on Jack, are ye, Laura Lee?
LAURA LEE [a cold look at him]: Only man I ever was, he's in his grave ten
 year.

SHE HEARS the train draw out, pours and drinks.

LAURA LEE [continuing]: But if I was, that's the only one *man* enough
 since.   CUT TO

INT. DAY COACH—CLOSE SHOT—POTTER—NIGHT. He finishes rolling a cigarette, lights it and, elbow on windowsill, settles into the tired posture of night
travel, gazing out of window. CAMERA SLOWLY PANS, losing his face, then his
reflected face, squaring on the dark land flooding past.   FADE OUT

FADE IN——INT. PARLOR CAR——CAMERA LOOKS SQUARELY through win-
dow at fast-moving daylit land, reversing direction of preceding shot; then in a
SLOW PAN picks up the reflection of Bride's face in window; then the face itself;
then PULLS AWAY into: TWO-SHOT—POTTER AND BRIDE. For a few moments
we merely HOLD on them, as though this were a provincial wedding portrait of
the period. (Circa 1895) He has an outdoor clumsiness in his new suit, which is
a shade tight and small for him. Her very new-looking hat and dress are in
touchingly ambitious, naive taste.
    Between their heads, in the seat just behind theirs, the head of a "sophisti-
cated" man turns slowly, slyly watching, filled with patronizing amusement.
Potter, gradually aware, turns and looks him in the eye; the guy shrivels and
turns away fast. HOLD on Bride and Potter a moment. Bride looks at something
O.S.

MEDIUM SHOT—TWO WOMEN watch her, whispering and giggling. MEDIUM
SHOT—CENTERING POTTER AND BRIDE—FROM VIEWPOINT OF WOMEN.
The Bride smiles very sweetly, looking straight in the CAMERA, and we HEAR
O.S. a more intense giggling and whispering and a few inaudible words.

The Bride looks a little puzzled, her smile fading; then she smiles again, sure there can be no malice toward her; then looks straight ahead of her. Both are glowing and intensely shy. His large, spread hands englobe his knees; hers are discreet in her lap. He stares straight ahead, his eyes a little unfocused. She keeps looking around. With almost the manner of a little girl, she draws a deep breath and utters a quiet sigh of joy, at the same time slightly raising, then relaxing, the hands on her lap. He hears her happy sigh; he looks at her; he watches her shyly and with a certain awe. He slowly shakes his head in the manner of one who can scarcely believe his good fortune. He lifts his own hands from his knees; decides they were where they belong; carefully replaces them. When he finally speaks he tries to be light and tender and it is clear that the loudness of his voice startles and embarrasses him, and in the b.g. heads flinch slightly.

POTTER: WELL, MRS. POTTER!
BRIDE [by reflex]: Shh!

Both are terribly embarrassed.

POTTER [quick and low]: Sorry! Frog in my throat.
BRIDE [ditto]: I'm sorry, I didn't mean to shush you. It just made me
     jump's all.
POTTER: You shush me any time yer a mind to.
BRIDE [after a pause; with shy daring]: You *call* me that, any time yer a
     mind to. 'Cause I like to hear you say it. Only not so loud.
POTTER [after a pause, whispering it, very shy]: Mrs. Potter. . . .

Overwhelmed by his daring, he blushes and looks away. She shivers with quiet delight; she glances up at him, then all around, with shy pride; then, as delicately as if it were asleep, she moves her hands in her lap as to uncover her wedding ring, and slowly, almost unbelievingly, lowers her eyes and looks at it. Then she looks around again speculatively.

BRIDE: Think they can tell we just got m——[she speaks the word almost
     sacredly] married?
POTTER: Don't see how they would. We ain't treatin' 'em to no lovey
     dovey stuff or none o' that monkey business.
BRIDE [whisper]: Jack!
POTTER: 'Scuse me.
BRIDE: It's all right.
POTTER: No it ain't neither. It ain't fittin' I talk to you like that.
BRIDE: Yes it is, Jack. I reckon it just kinda crep up on me from behind.

Silent, they look out the window. They have run out of talk. They have plenty to think about, but soon he feels he has to make conversation.

POTTER: This-yer train sure does gobble up the miles, don't it?
BRIDE: My yes. Just goes like the wind.

POTTER: It's a thousand mile from one end o' Texas to the other, and it
   don't only stop but four times.

BRIDE: My land!

POTTER: It only stops for water at Yaller Sky.

BRIDE: Oh.

POTTER: Hope you ain't gonna mind. What I mean, it's a good town,
   but it might look awful puny, side o' San Antone.

BRIDE: Oh *no*. I never did like a big town. I like it where ever'body
   knows ever'body else.

POTTER: You'll like it there then.

They run out of talk again. She looks around with more and more appreciation of
the opulence and splendor of the car. CAMERA PANS around Pullman car.

BRIDE'S VOICE [O.S.]: I just can't get over it! [Pause] It's all so handsome
   and rich-lookin'!

POTTER'S VOICE [O.S.]: Yeah. They do it in style, sure enough, don't
   they?

BRIDE'S VOICE [O.S.]: It's just like it was a palace or sumpin'. Even the
   ceilin'!

MEDIUM SHOT—A FANCY CEILING OIL PAINTING—CUPIDS, ETC.

POTTER'S VOICE [O.S.]: Gee. You sure do notice things. I never even seen
   it.

CLOSE SHOT—POTTER who has been looking up.

POTTER [continuing]: Ever rode a parlor car before?

BRIDE: No.

POTTER: Me neither. One of these days we'll go a trip overnight.

Both are quietly aghast with embarrassment.

POTTER [struggling]: I mean, I always did have a hankerin' to see what
   them Pullman berths are like.

BRIDE [helping him]: This is wonderful enough.

POTTER: Shucks. This ain't *nothing*. After a while we'll go forward to
   the diner and get a big layout. Ever et in a diner?

BRIDE: No. I always took me along some lunch.

POTTER: Finest meal in the world. Charge a dollar.

CLOSE THREE SHOT—POTTER, BRIDE AND SOPHISTICATED MAN. Sophisticated man registers, "What rubes!"

BRIDE: A dollar? Why that's too much—for us—ain't it, Jack?

POTTER: Not this trip, anyhow. We're gonna do the whole thing.

He swells up, a little like a nabob, and looks away so she can look at him admiringly.   DISSOLVE TO

INSERT: INT. SCRATCHY'S HOUSE (ADOBE)—DAY——EXTREME CLOSE
SHOT. Sighting above the bore of a long-barreled, blue-black revolver, against a
raggedly curtained window. INSERT: The smoothly spinning cylinder of the revolver. Scratchy's other hand, with a rag, wipes the weapon clear of cleaning oil;
the weapon is turned this way and that, lovingly, catching the light; then is
sighted along, aiming it at a picture on a calendar; and is dry fired, with a click of
the tongue and a whispered, "Got ye that time, ye dog!"; then it is laid delicately
down on a patchwork quilt. CAMERA PANS with Scratchy's hand to a pint whiskey bottle on the floor by the bed. (Next to it is another bottle, empty.) Hand and
bottle move out of shot; SOUND of drinking; bottle is returned, a good inch lower; hand unwraps a second revolver from a worn, fine old napkin. Then a rag,
then a little can of cleaning oil and a little rod. The hands start cleaning revolver.

    OVER THIS ENTIRE SCENE, Scratchy Wilson's voice is HEARD, deeply and
still tranquilly drunk, humming as much as singing, "Brighten the Corner." The
singing is of course interrupted; by his muttered line; by occasional shortness of
breath; by his drinking and a sharp cough afterward; and just as it resumes after
the drinking, the voice is raw. But in overall mood it is as happy and innocent as
a baby talking to itself in its crib. Over hand cleaning revolver,   CUT TO

INT. PARLOR CAR—DAY——MEDIUM SHOT—CENTERING POTTER AND
BRIDE. The dining steward walks through SHOT fast, hitting chimes.

STEWARD: Fust call for dinnah! Fust call!

Only Potter and Bride react. A quick exchange of glances and they get up and
follow steward out of shot.

INT. DINING CAR—DAY——MEDIUM SHOT. Shooting past waiters ranked ready
beside empty tables as Potter and Bride enter the car, registering abrupt dismay
at all the service, whiteness, glitter and loneliness.

VIEWPOINT SHOT—THREE WAITERS solicit them, with knowing glances. ME-
DIUM SHOT—DOLLY. The waiter nearest them tries to steer them toward a two-
some table. Potter, in a replying spasm of independence, steers Bride to a four-
chair table opposite. The two sit down side by side as CAMERA DOLLIES sidelong into a TWO SHOT.

POTTER [low]: Looks like we're the only customers.

Instantly a hand plants a large menu in Potter's hand, blocking off his face, and
then the same to the Bride.

WAITER'S VOICE [juicy, O.S.]: There you are sir! An' how're *you*-all today!

Potter slowly lowers menu, looks to waiter. Bride, ditto, looks to Potter.

POTTER: Gone up on yer prices, ain't ye?

WAITER'S VOICE [O.S.]: Things are costin' more all ovah, these days. [Oily] Matter o' fact, though, we can 'commodate folks of more moderate means. [His finger reaches down and points out on menu.] There's a nice gumbo, good sandwiches. . . .

POTTER [across him]: We'll have the dollar and a quarter dinner.

The Bride watches him with admiration.

WAITER: Yes indeed, sir. The chicken or the ham, sir? The ham is *mighty* delicious today, sir.

POTTER: Chicken.

WAITER: Yes, *sir!*

They unfold their napkins. Potter glances about. VIEWPOINT UP-SHOT. Several waiters pretend not to watch. BRIDE AND POTTER AS BEFORE. As Bride settles her napkin in lap, he starts tucking his high into his vest.   DISSOLVE TO

EXT. "WEARY GENTLEMAN" SALOON—DAY DOLLY SHOT. Following the nattily dressed Drummer through swinging doors into INT. "WEARY GENTLEMAN" SALOON, we pause and shoot past him as he hesitates and looks around at Jasper, Laura Lee, and Frank. All glance at him casually and resume talking.

FRANK: Not even a small beer?

LAURA LEE [sliding a tall one toward Jasper]: Not even that, Frank. What's more, it's high time you locked yourself back in. 'Cause Jack Potter's treatin' you white, an' it's up to you to treat him the same. Now git along with ye.

CLOSE SHOT—DRUMMER. Over "lock yourself back in," he registers sharp interest, glancing keenly back and forth between Frank and Laura Lee.

FRANK'S VOICE [O.S.]: He'd treat me a whole lot whiter if he'd get back when he said he would.

LAURA LEE'S VOICE [O.S.]: He ain't but a day late.

FRANK'S VOICE [O.S.]: A day's a long time when you spend it in jail.

Drummer registers curiosity and consternation and looks exclusively at Frank. NEW ANGLE—LAURA LEE AND FRANK.

LAURA LEE: Read them magazines he give ye.

CAMERA PANS with Frank as he starts toward door, HOLDING on Drummer.

FRANK: Done read 'em four or five times. Git tired of it, all that bang-bang stuff. [To Drummer] Howdy, stranger.

He walks on out.

DRUMMER [belated and odd]: Howdy.

CAMERA PANS with his walk up to the bar.

DRUMMER [to Laura Lee]: Did I hear that man correctly, ma'am? Is he a
      jail-bird?
LAURA LEE: If you want to put it that way.
DRUMMER [looks to Jasper who is wholly neutral]: Well! [He looks to both; both
      are neutral.] Well!
LAURA LEE: What'll ye have, mister?
DRUMMER: Beer, please, a big head on it.

Laura Lee draws and hands it to him, sizing him up.

LAURA LEE: Big head.
DRUMMER: Nice little town.
LAURA LEE: It'll pass.
DRUMMER: Oh, I've had quite a profitable morning's work. [He sips.]
LAURA LEE: That'll be a nickel, mister.

He pays and sips again.

DRUMMER: Matter of fact, I'm a Drummer.
LAURA LEE: I can see that.
DRUMMER: That's right. I travel in stockings. "Ex*quis*ite" stockings. [Hust-
      ling his sample case to bar] Paris to your doorstep, that's our slogan.
      Now if you're willing to spare a moment of your time, I can
      promise you, a lady of your taste and refinement, you just won't
      be able to *resist!*
LAURA LEE [across him]: Don't trouble yourself, mister, I don't——

But the drummer is already lifting the lid of the case. She leans her arms on it,
nipping his fingers.

LAURA LEE [continuing]:—Now, looky here, young feller; I ain't even
      a'goin' to *look* at them fool stockin's, let alone *resist* 'em.

OVER THIS, two Mexican sheepherders enter quietly by the rear door and sit at a
table.

LAURA LEE [to Mexicans]: What's yours, Narciso Gulliermo Diorisio
      Mario?
1ST MEXICAN: Cervezas.

The second Mexican nods.

DRUMMER [sucking his fingers]: That hurt, ma'am.
LAURA LEE [drawing beer]: Wouldn't be surprised.
JASPER: Seen Scratchy around, Laura Lee?

LAURA LEE: Not since t'other night.

JASPER: Gittin' so ye can't count on him fer nothin'. He was 'sposed to clair out my cess-pool yesterday. Never showed up.

LAURA LEE [pause—quietly]: Can't say as I blame him, Jasper, that's a job ye do yourself—nobody ought to have to do it for him.

JASPER: Well—sometimes ye gotta take what ye can git.

She is silent.

JASPER [continuing]: All I hope is, he ain't a-tyin' one on.

CLOSE SHOT—LAURA LEE.

LAURA LEE: If I had to do a job like that fer you, I might tie on a few myself.

CAMERA PANS as she takes beer to end of bar. First Mexican pays and takes them. She sits on her stool, looking at nobody. A NEW ANGLE—JASPER. He watches her, nettled, and a little malicious.

JASPER: Hey, Laura Lee.

LAURA LEE: Yeah.

JASPER: Reckon what Jack Potter's *up* to in San Antone.

LAURA LEE: Reckon what business 'tis o' yourn.

JASPER: Just figured he might of *told you.*

LAURA LEE [quiet and stern]: Jack Potter ain't tied to *my* apron strings, nor nobody's.   FAST WIPE TO

INT. DINING CAR—DAY. Potter and Bride are finishing their desserts opposite a wooden, middle-aged married couple (the car is now full of people). We INTER-CUT CLOSE SHOT as Potter and the man meet glances; Bride and woman do same. Potter glances secretively down at his lapel and, privately as he can, scratches with his thumbnail at a food stain. Their voices are low:

BRIDE: Don't worry. I can get that off in a jiffy.

POTTER: Ain't likely I'll wear it much, nohow.

BRIDE: Why, you'll wear it a-Sundays, church an' all.

POTTER [uneasy]: I ain't never been much of a hand for church.

BRIDE: You don't ever go?

Potter uneasily shakes his head.

BRIDE [continuing; uneasy]: I don't know what I'd do, for lonesomeness, without no church to go to.

WAITER'S VOICE [O.S.]: Look what I done brung yah both! An extra pot of nice fresh coffee.

VIEWPOINT UP-SHOT cuts into his line. He leans over, setting down pot, beaming, proprietary, working for a big tip. NEW ANGLE—POTTER AND BRIDE. Mild embarrassment reactions; they murmur appreciation ad lib.

BRIDE: Want some more?
POTTER: No thanks.

She pours for herself. The sugar is not in easy reach.

POTTER [formally, to other man]: Pass the sugar, please.
MAN [glumly]: Certainly.
POTTER: Thank you.
MAN: Certainly.
POTTER [to Bride]: Sugar?
BRIDE: Sure you won't have some more coffee?
POTTER: All right. Thanks. Thank you.
BRIDE: Certainly.

She leans to pour for him, much enjoying serving him, and knocks her napkin from the edge of the table to the floor between them. Both quickly stoop to reach for it. INSERT: Their hands touch accidentally and fly apart as if they had struck a spark.

BOTH: *'Scuse* me!

TWO SHOT—POTTER AND BRIDE AS BEFORE. As they straighten up quickly, Potter bumps the table making a clatter and the Bride slops a little of the coffee from the pot in her other hand onto their clothes.

TOGETHER: POTTER [to everyone]: *'Scuse me.* BRIDE [to him]: Gee, I'm sorry.

REVERSE ANGLE. The two older people exchange unsmiling glances and pretend nothing is happening. POTTER AND BRIDE AS BEFORE. He with his handkerchief, she with his napkin, they gently dab coffee off each other; they are embarrassed but not at all at odds.

As the waiter's arm presents the check to Potter, the CAMERA LIFTS AND TILTS, DOLLYING gently in to center his right hand near his trousers pocket. The hand makes the odd, helpless gesture of putting aside a holster which isn't there.

BRIDE'S VOICE [O.S.]: What's the matter?
POTTER'S VOICE [O.S.]: Just habit I reckon. Fust time in years I ain't totin'
    a gun.

CAMERA ZOOMS, centering.   FAST DISSOLVE TO

INT. SCRATCHY'S—DAY—CLOSE VIEWPOINT SHOT. Scratchy's loaded cartridge belt lies heavy and lethal across his knees. He thumbs in the last cartridge

and lays aside the belt. The CAMERA, as Scratchy rises to his feet, goes into a short SPINNING BLUR IN AND OUT OF FOCUS.

SCRATCHY'S VOICE [O.S.]: Whoa there.

CAMERA proceeds into a slow, wobbly DOLLYING PAN, past window and bureau to pegs where Scratchy's hand fumbles among his few clothes. Most of them are old and poor but his hands select and get off the hook a violently fancy pseudowestern shirt on which CAMERA comes into ULTRA SHARP FOCUS. Then one hand, as CAMERA CREEPS IN, FOCUS DITTO, reaches for a real shocker of a necktie, muffs it, and as CAMERA comes into EXTREME CLOSE SHOT, drags it drunkenly, snakily, slithering from its hook. All this time Scratchy is muttering and humming. OVER the slithering tie we   IRIS OUT

IRIS IN——INT. PARLOR CAR—DAY. Center CAMERA on Potter's more conservative tie. Tense and uneasy, he adjusts it. TWO SHOT—POTTER AND BRIDE. He is tense; she is content. He takes out and looks at a thick hunter watch. Watching him, she realizes his uneasiness. She checks her own watch with his.

BRIDE: Mine's slow.
POTTER: Nope: I trust yourn. She's a seventeen jeweller.

Behind them, the "sophisticated" man slopes an amused eye.

BRIDE: Gracious.

Potter corrects his watch, pockets it and avoids her eyes. She watches him. An uneasy silence. He looks at his watch again.

BRIDE [continuing]: Jack.
POTTER: Hmm.
BRIDE: Somethin's eatin' at you.
POTTER: Me?

She nods—a pause.

POTTER: Nuthin' much. Only I wisht I'd sent a telegram.
BRIDE: Thought you did, there at the depot.
POTTER: I just tore it up.

Silence.

BRIDE [shyly]: Was it—about us—gittin' married this morning?
POTTER: I oughta told 'um, back in Yaller Sky. That's all. You see,
    they're so used to me bein' a bachelor an' all. They ain't gonna
    take it no way good, me never tellin' 'em—an' all of a sudden I
    come home married—[an articulate pause; ashamed]—Reckon I'm
    just plain bashful.

BRIDE [very shy]: Reckon I feel the same.

He looks at her, unbelieving. She corroborates her statement with a little nod. They are so relieved they awkwardly resist an impulse to join hands and both face rigidly front, their tension growing.   FAST DISSOLVE TO

INT. SCRATCHY'S HOUSE—DAY. A lurching CLOSE PAN to a broken, distorting mirror. The CAMERA is on Scratchy, and the reflection is his. He is wearing a fancy shirt, both revolvers and the cartridge belt and he has to stoop to see himself. He is in a reeling slouch, glaring, stinking drunk. He draws closer, making savage faces which are still more savagely distorted in the mirror. He becomes momentarily fascinated by these distortions. He draws both guns and lurches into EXTREME CLOSEUP, growling low:

SCRATCHY: All right, Jack Potter. Yore time has come!

CAMERA PULLS BACK centering hands getting, from his dresser drawer, a newish hat as phony as the shirt. The hands lift this through the shot as valuably as the Holy Grail and CAMERA again LEANS for mirror reflection as he preens the hat on his head.   DISSOLVE TO

INT. "WEARY GENTLEMAN"—DAY——CLOSE SHOT—THE DRUMMER. His eyes fixed almost on the lens in the cold manner of a snake charming a bird. CAMERA PULLS AWAY along his fully extended, shirt-sleeved, and fancily sleeve-gartered arm. It is clothed to the armpit in a super-sheer, elaborately clocked dark stocking.

DRUMMER [soft and almost lascivious]: Speaks louder than words, doesn't
      it! [He shifts his eye O.S.] *You* tell her, gentlemen; in *all your experi-
      ence,* did you ever meet a lady that wouldn't *swoon* just to look
      at it? [Eyes back to center] Sheer as twilight air. And just look at that
      clocking! [He points it out, then his subtle hand impersonates a demi-
      mondaine foot.] Nothing like it ever contrived before, by the most
      inspired continental designers, to give style to the ankle and
      moulding to the calf. [He runs fingers up his arm to the armpit, his eyes
      follow.] And they run all the way up—opera length. [He casts his
      eyes down, then returns to off-center and gives his eyes all he's got. With a
      trace of hoarseness, almost whispering.] How about it, madam? [He
      gives her an homme-fatale smile. A grand pause.]

TWO SHOT—JASPER AND ED. They look toward him with quiet disgust. TWO SHOT—TWO MEXICANS. They glance at each other and toward Laura Lee. CLOSE SHOT—LAURA LEE. She gives the merchandise one more cold, fascinated once-over, then looks the Drummer in the eye.

LAURA LEE: All right son. I'm still resistin'. So, fork over that dollar.
DRUMMER: But madam, you haven't given the Exquizzit——

LAURA LEE [across him]: Save yer breath young feller. Why, if my hus-
   band had caught me in a pair o' them things, he'd broke my jaw.
   You're in the *wrong territory,* son. 'Cause this is a man's country.
   It's hard country.

A young man comes in quickly.

YOUNG MAN: Scratchy Wilson's drunk an' he's turned loose with both
   hands.

Both Mexicans set down their unfinished beers and fade out the rear door. The
Drummer views with mystification; nobody pays any attention to him. They're as
quick and efficient as a well-rehearsed fire-drill. Jasper and Ed go out the front
door and close the window shutters. The young man bolts the rear door. Laura
Lee bars the window on her side and goes center, swinging shut one leaf of the
plank door. As Jasper and Ed return, Jasper swings the other shut and bars his
window and Ed brings from the corner the bar for the main door and helps Laura
Lee put it in place. Laura Lee returns to her place behind the bar. In the sudden,
solemn, chapel-like gloom, the Drummer is transfixed; his eyes glitter.

DRUMMER: Say, what *is* this?

A silent reaction from the men.

DRUMMER [continuing]: Is there going to be a gun-fight?
JASPER [grimly]: Dunno if there'll be a fight or not, but there'll be some
   shootin'—some good shootin'.
YOUNG MAN: Oh, there's a fight just *waitin'* out there in the street, if
   anyone wants it.

Jasper and Ed nod solemnly.

DRUMMER [to young man]: What'd ye say his name was?
ALL: Scratchy Wilson.

The Drummer does a fast multiple take, person-to-person.

DRUMMER: What're you goin' to do?

Grim silence.

DRUMMER [continuing]: Does he do this often?

More silence.

DRUMMER [continuing]: Can he break down that door?
LAURA LEE: No: he's give that up. But when he comes you'd better lay
   down on the floor, stranger. He'd dead sure to *shoot* at that door,
   an' there's no tellin' what a stray bullet might do.

The Drummer, keeping a strict eye on the door, begins carefully removing the stocking from his arm.

DRUMMER: Will he kill anybody?

The men laugh low and scornfully.

JASPER: He's out to shoot, an' he's out fer trouble. Don't see no good
    experimentin' with him.
DRUMMER: But what do you *do* in a case like this? What do you do?
YOUNG MAN: Why, he an' Jack Potter——
JASPER AND ED [across him]: Jack ain't back yet.
YOUNG MAN [suddenly frightened]: *Lordy!*
DRUMMER: Well who's he? What's *he* got to do with it?
YOUNG MAN: He's Marshal.
LAURA LEE: Comes to shootin', he's the only one in town can go up
    agin him.

Far off, O.S. we HEAR a wild Texas yell, a shot, another yell. Everyone becomes very still and tense.

DRUMMER [half-whispered]: That must be him comin', hey?

The men look at him in irritation and look away again. They wait, their eyes shining in the gloom. Jasper holds up three fingers. Moving like a ghost, Laura Lee gets out three glasses and the bottle. The Drummer lifts one forlorn finger; she adds another glass. They pour. In unison they snap the drinks down at a gulp and walk to windows to look through chinks. The Drummer quietly puts a coin on the bar. Laura Lee just looks at it, at him, and away. He shamefacedly takes back his coin. She silently takes a Winchester from beneath the bar and breaks it.

DRUMMER [whispered]: You goin' to *shoot* him?

Silence; everyone looks at him bleakly.

LAURA LEE [low]: Not if I can help it. I ain't a good enough shot. Might
    kill him.
DRUMMER: Well, it'd be pure self-defense if you did, wouldn't it?

No answer.

DRUMMER [continuing]: Well, *wouldn't* it? Good riddance *too, I'd* say.

LAURA LEE closes the breech.

LAURA LEE [low]: Mister, Scratchy Wilson's an old friend. Nobody'd
    harm a hair of his head if they's any way out—let alone kill him.
    You see, trouble is, he's a wonder with a gun. Just a wonder. An'

he's a terror when he's drunk. So when he goes on the war trail, we hunt our holes—naturally.

DRUMMER: But—why do they allow him—what's he doin' in a town like this?

LAURA LEE: He's the last of the old gang that used to hang out along the river here.

A silence. Then nearer, but distant, a howl is HEARD. The Drummer reacts, jittery.

LAURA LEE [continuing]: You better come back o' the bar. I kinda fixed it up.

DRUMMER [ashamed]: No thanks, I'll——

LAURA LEE [with a peremptory gesture]: Come on.

He does. He squats low in the front angle of the bar and examines, with some relief, the various plates of scrap metal with which she has armored it. O.S., nearer, we HEAR another shot and three yowls. There's a shuffling of feet. They look at each other.

MEN [quietly]: Here he comes!

PAN SHOT. We DOLLY with Laura Lee, carrying her gun, to look through a chink in the shutter, and through the chink see Scratchy round the corner at the far end of the empty street, yelling, a long heavy blue-black revolver in either hand. We HEAR his words, distant, but preternaturally powerful, as he strides to the middle of the street and stops dead, both guns alert, threatening and at bay.

SCRATCHY: *Yaller Sky, hyar I come!*

MEDIUM SHOT—SCRATCHY: He holsters a revolver, extracts a pint bottle from his belt, cocks it vertically and drains it, and tosses it high and glittering into the sunlight, in mid-air; then shoots it into splinters, left-handed, and does a quick 360-degree whirl, drawing both guns, as if against enemies ambushing him from the rear. He raises a small tornado of dust. CUT to a HEAD CLOSEUP into which he finishes his pivot, glaring. His eyes glittering, drunk, mad, frightening. He is eaten up with some kind of interior bitter wildness.

SCRATCHY [a low growl!]: Got ye, ye yaller-bellies!

PULL DOWN AND AWAY. He gives a lonely Texas yowl; the echoes die. He glares all about him; his eyes, focusing on something O.S., take on sudden purpose.

SCRATCHY [loud]: Jack Potter!

MEDIUM SHOT—WITH STILL CAMERA—POTTER'S HOUSE—FREEZE CLOSER SHOT—SCRATCHY trying to adjust his eyes to this oddity.

SCRATCHY [louder]: Jack Potter!

MEDIUM SHOT POTTER'S HOUSE—AS BEFORE.

SCRATCHY'S VOICE [O.S.]: You heared me, Jack Potter. Come on out an' face the music. 'Caze it's time to dance.

CLOSE SHOT—SCRATCHY. Dead silence. He is puzzled.

SCRATCHY: 'Tain't no ways like you Potter, asullin' there in yer house. You ain't no possum. I treated ye fair an' square. I saved it all up for ye, like I told ye. Now you play square with me.
FRANK'S VOICE [O.S., scared]: Hey, Scratchy.
SCRATCHY [puzzled, looking around]: How's that? Who is that?

POTTER'S HOUSE—PAST SCRATCHY.

FRANK'S VOICE: Hit's me. Frank.
SCRATCHY: Why don't ye say so. Whar ye at?
FRANK'S VOICE: I'm up yere in the jail.
SCRATCHY: Well *show* yerself! What ye skeered of?
FRANK'S VOICE: You.
SCRATCHY: Me? Shucks. Only man needs to be skeered o' me is Jack Potter, the yaller hound.
FRANK'S VOICE: Jack ain't here, Scratchy.
SCRATCHY: What ye mean he ain't here?
FRANK'S VOICE: He ain't got back yet, that's what I mean. That's what I was tryin' to tell you.
SCRATCHY: Ain't back! Don't gimme none o' that. He come back yesterday when he promised he would.
FRANK'S VOICE: No he didn't.
SCRATCHY: You lie to *me*. Frank Gudger, I'll give ye what *fer*.

He shoots, striking a bar and ringing a musical note.

FRANK'S VOICE: Scratchy! Don't do that! Hit's dangersome.
SCRATCHY: Not if ye keep yer head low it ain't.
FRANK'S VOICE: 'Tis too. Ye can't tell *whar* them bullets'll *rebound*.
SCRATCHY: Don't you dast tell me how to shoot, ye pore wall-eyed woods colt. *Is* Jack Potter back or *ain't* he?
FRANK'S VOICE: No he ain't and that's the honest truth.
SCRATCHY: Don't you *sass* me.

CLOSE SHOT. Scratchy shoots another bar, ringing a different musical note, which is followed by a shattering of glass.

SCRATCHY [continuing]: Is he back?

FRANK'S VOICE: Quit it, Scratchy. Ye done busted my lamp chimbley.

SCRATCHY: *Is* he back or *ain't* he?

FRANK'S VOICE: All right, have it yer own way. He's back if you say so.

SCRATCHY: Well, why didn't you tell me so straight off?

No answer.

SCRATCHY [continuing]: Why don't he come on out then?

FRANK'S VOICE: Reckon he would if he was inside.

SCRATCHY: Oh, he ain't inside, huh?

FRANK'S VOICE: Not that I know of.

SCRATCHY: Well, that leaves just one other place for him to be.

He turns toward the "Weary Gentleman," hikes his trousers, reaches for the bottle which is no longer there.

SCRATCHY [growling and starting]: Dad burn it. Never seed it yet I didn't run out just at the wrong time!

He walks fast past the respectable houses, the churches and so on, and DOLLY-ING, SHOOTING PAST HIM, we see they all have an unearthly quietness. As he walks, he talks, now to himself, now shouting.

SCRATCHY [continuing]: But that's all right. Just lay low. 'Caze quick as I wet my whistle, I'm gonna show ye some shootin'!

He stops in front of Morgan's house.

SCRATCHY [continuing]: You Jasper Morgan. Yeah, and that snivellin' woman o' yourn, too! Too dainty to do like ordinary folks. Too high an' mighty! Git yerself a lot o' fancy plumbing, an' ye ain't man enough to clean out yer own cess-pool. "Let Scratchy do it." Ain't nuthin' so low but Scratchy'll do it for the price of a pint.

He glares around for a target. He spies a potted fern suspended from the porch ceiling. He shoots the suspension chain and the whole thing drops to the porch floor with a foomp. There! Clean that up! He turns, Deacon's house is opposite.

SCRATCHY [continuing; a horrible travesty of a sissy voice]: *Deacon! Oh Deacon Smee-eed!* [He makes two syllables of Smeed.] You home, Deacon? Kin I pay ye a little call? *Most* places in town, ye just *knock* an' walk *in,* but that ain't *good* enough for a *good* man, *is* it, Deacon? Oh *no!* No—*no!* Pay a little call on the Deacon, ye got to shove a 'lectric bell, real special. [A hard shift of tone] All right. Smeed, start singin' them psalms o' yourn. You'll be whangin' 'em on a harp, few mo' minutes, you an' yer missuz, too. Can't stop in right now, I'm a mite too thirsty. But I'll be back, Deacon. Oh, I'll be back. [He studies the house.] Here's my callin' card.

He takes careful aim, and INSERT: Hits the doorbell, so fusing it that it rings continuously. We HEAR a woman scream hysterically.

CLOSE SHOT OF SCRATCHY.

SCRATCHY: Ah, quit it. Don't holler 'til yer hurt.

INT. DEACON'S HOUSE—DEACON AND WIFE. Past Deacon and his wife, through the curtained window, we see Scratchy pass. The Deacon has an arm around his wife. He is trying pathetically to resemble an intrepid doomed frontiersman.

DEACON: He'll pay for this. By the Almighty, he'll pay dearly. I'm not
    going to stand for it, I'm simply not going——
MRS. SMEED: Oh hush. For goodness sake, stop that horrid *bell!*

He looks at her, goes into the hallway with wounded dignity, and jerks a wire loose. Just as the bell stops, there is a shot and the stinging SOUND O.S. of the church bell being shot at. The Deacon reacts to this latest outrage.

MEDIUM SHOT—UPWARD—CHURCH BELL—FROM SCRATCHY'S VIEW-POINT——CLOSE SHOT—SHOOTING DOWN—SCRATCHY looking up at bell, both pleased and angry, and shooting again at the church bell.

SCRATCHY [he bellows]: Come on out and fight if you dast—only you
    don't dast.

He starts glancing all around; the revolvers in each hand are as sensitive as snakes; the little fingers play in a musician-like way; INTER-CUT with still facades of details of greater stillness; a motionless curtain of machine-made lace with a head dimly silhouetted behind; a drawn shade, with an eye and fingertips visible at the edge.

SCRATCHY [continuing]: O no! You know who's *boss* in *this* town. Mar-
    cellus T. Wilson, that's who. He ain't fittin' to wipe yer boots on,
    no-sirree, he's the lowest of low, but he's boss all the same. 'Caze
    this is a boss [gesturing with a revolver], an' *this* is a boss [another],
    an' this is the feller that can boss the both of 'em better'n any
    other man that's left in this woreout womanizin' country. An'
    there ain't hardly a man of ye dast *touch* a gun, let alone come
    up again a *man* with one. Oh no! Got lil' ole honeybunch to
    worry about, lil' old wifey-pifey, all the young 'uns, make ye some
    easy money runnin' a store, doctorin', psalm-singing, fix ye a
    purty lawn so Scratchy kin cut it for ye. Oh, I—- [he searches help-
    lessly, then half-says]—hate—I could wipe every one of ye offen the
    face o' the earth, a-hidin' behind yore women's skirts, ever' re-
    spectable last one of ye! Come out an' fight! Come on! Come on!
    Dad *blast* ye!

He glares all around again. There is no kind of response at all. His attention shifts; his eyes focus on something O.S.; he becomes purposeful.

EXT. "WEARY GENTLEMAN" SALOON—BARRICADED—DAY—— DOLLY SHOT over Scratchy's shoulder as he advances on door.   CUT TO

MEDIUM CLOSE SHOT—SCRATCHY. He comes to door and hammers on it with gun butt.

SCRATCHY: Laura Lee. [Pause] Laura Lee. [Pause]

Now he hammers with both revolvers.

SCRATCHY [continuing; yelling]: *Laura Lee!* [No answer] You can't fool me. I know you're there. Open up. I want a drink. [No answer] All I want's a little drink.

Now he hammers harder than ever. Over SOUND of hammering,
                                                          CUT INSIDE

TO CLOSE SHOTS IN THIS ORDER: CLOSE SHOT—LAURA LEE low behind bar, her rifle ready if need be, thumb on safety. CLOSE SHOT—THREE LOCAL MEN on floor, watching the door fixedly. CLOSE SHOT—THE DRUMMER behind the bar, plenty scared.

CLOSE SHOT—BACK TO SCRATCHY finishing his hammering. He is rather tired. He glares at the door a moment, then:

SCRATCHY: All right then. All right.

He looks around him, sore. He sights a scrap of paper in the dirt, picks it up, and with a vicious and cruel thrust, nails it to the door with a knife. Then he turns his back contemptuously on the saloon, walks to the far side of the street and, spinning quickly and lithely, fires at the sheet of paper. INSERT: The bullet misses by half an inch. SCRATCHY AS BEFORE.

SCRATCHY: Well, I, Gah . . . gittin' old in yer old age, Scratchy.

He takes careful aim and fires. INSERT: The bullet splits the haft of the knife; the blade clatters down; the paper follows, fluttering; a hole appears in the door.

CLOSE SHOT—INT. "WEARY GENTLEMAN." Jasper is on floor, between a chair and a spittoon. Bullet flicks wood from chair, ricochets with appropriate SOUNDS, puncturing spittoon from which dark liquid oozes. Jasper, with slow horror, looks at it.

FROM SCRATCHY'S VIEWPOINT the paper finishes settling. CLOSE SHOT—SCRATCHY. He is satisfied; he turns and starts walking grandly away. Suddenly he cries out:

SCRATCHY: Hey! [And stops and faces the saloon again] Hey, tell Jack Potter to come on out o' there like a man!

REVERSE ANGLE—OVER SCRATCHY. No answer.

SCRATCHY [continuing; yelling]: *Jack!* JACK POTTER?

CLOSE SHOT—INT. SALOON.

LAURA LEE: Jack Potter ain't here, Scratchy, an' *you know it!* 'Cause if he was, he'd be out thar arter ye.

CLOSE SHOT—SCRATCHY. He hesitates, thinks it over.

SCRATCHY [uncertainly]: You wouldn't fool me, would ye, Laura Lee?
LAURA LEE'S VOICE [O.S.]: I never did, did I?
SCRATCHY: Well don't never you try it. 'Caze I ain' the man'll stand fer it. [Suddenly sore] That lyin' no-'count Frank! I'll fix *him!* I'll cook *his* goose!

HE STARTS OUT FAST UP THE STREET—there is the SOUND of a distant train whistle O.S. Over it   DISSOLVE TO

INT. PARLOR CAR—DAY——SOUND of dying wail of whistle O.S. Throughout scene, SOUND of slowing train. TWO SHOT—POTTER AND BRIDE. Tension and emotion increase in their faces.

POTTER [with desperate finality]: Well——

She looks to him anxiously—he meets her eyes briefly and both smile, then lower their eyes pathetically. He gratefully thinks of *something* to do.

POTTER: [continuing]: Better git down our truck.

With day-coach reflex, he stands up, reaching for the nonexistent baggage rack, realizes his mistake, and pretends he is only tidying his clothes.

PORTER'S VOICE [O.S., loud and glad]: Don't you bother, mister——
                                                              CUT TO

CLOSE SHOT—PORTER grinning.

PORTER [continuing]:—I got it all ready an' waitin'!

FULL SHOT. Some amused heads turn. BRIDE AND POTTER AS BEFORE. He sits abashed. Train SOUND is much slower. Their time is short.

POTTER [smiling and wretched]: Home at last.
BRIDE [uneasy]: Mm-hmm.

A silence. CLOSE SHOT—POTTER in real desperation. O.S. SOUND of train bell.

POTTER [sweating; rapidly]: Say listen. You ain't goana like me for this an' I don't blame ye, but I just can't face 'em if we can help it, not right yet. What I want, I want to sorta *sneak* in, if we can git away with it, an' make home without nobody seein' us, an' then study what to do about 'em. I figure we got a chance if we kinda skin along the hind side o' Main Street. We got cover 'til about sixty foot from my door. Would ye do it?

CAMERA PULLS AND PANS into TWO SHOT—POTTER AND BRIDE.

BRIDE [fervent]: Oh gee, if only they don't ketch us!
POTTER [incredulously grateful]: You don't hate me fer it?
BRIDE [with all her heart]: *Hate* you?

They look at each other with entirely new love. The train is stopping. They get up fast and leave the shot.   CUT TO

EXT. STATION YELLOW SKY—DAY. As train pulls to a stop, PAN AND DOLLY into CLOSEUP-SHOT of train steps. The Porter descends first and leaves the shot. Potter, with Bride behind and above him, peers anxiously forward along the station platform. LONG SHOT—HIS VIEWPOINT. The empty platform. MEDIUM SHOT—PANNING.

POTTER [over shoulder]: Come on girl. Hurry.

He steps to platform, she follows unassisted. He grabs up both bags and, looking back to her, collides with the untipped, dismayed Porter.

POTTER: Oh.

He sets down bags. A fumbling rush for change. He hands out a coin.

POTTER [continuing]: Much obliged.

He picks up bags and starts walking, the Bride alongside.

POTTER: Let's git outa here.
PORTER [across him]: Much obliged to *you,* sir.

Potter walks away so fast that she has to hustle to keep alongside. Both are eagle-eyed—he with anxiety, she with that and with simple interest. REVERSE ANGLE SHOT. We glimpse an empty segment of street.

BRIDE'S VOICE [O.S.]: Gee, I don't see *nobody.*

BRIDE AND POTTER AS BEFORE

POTTER: Just the hot time o' day, let's not risk it.

They walk still faster around rear corner of station and out of sight.   CUT TO

CLOSE SHOT—CELL WINDOW IN POTTER'S HOUSE. It is empty; very, very slowly a little mirror rises to eye level above the sill—and jerks down fast.

CLOSE SHOT between the rear of two buildings toward the vacant Main Street. Potter's head comes CLOSE INTO SHOT, then the Bride's.

POTTER [whispering]: All right.

They dart noiselessly across the gap.

POTTER [continuing]: Good girl.

They laugh, low and sheepish, and steal ahead. CAMERA PANS WITH THEM l. to r.

POTTER [still whispering]: Next corner, dear, an' I can show you our
    home.
BRIDE [same]: Oh, Jack.

She stops. Her eyes are damp. He stops.

POTTER [whispering]: Sumpin' the matter?

VERY CLOSE SHOT—BRIDE.

BRIDE: The way you said that!
POTTER'S VOICE [O.S.]: Said what?
BRIDE [moved]: Our home!

She smiles very shyly. He is moved and says, in a most embarrassed voice:

POTTER: Come on then, girl.—Let's *get* there.

ANOTHER ANGLE. They start walking fast and quiet; we PAN with them, approaching the frame corner of a house.

POTTER [continuing]: Now right the next second, you can see it!

They continue, WE LEAD THEM slightly as they circle the corner and come face to face with a CLOSE SHOT of SCRATCHY. He is leaning against the wall, just around the corner, reloading. Instantly he drops this revolver, whips the other from its holster, and aims it at Potter's chest. A deadly silence.

REVERSE ANGLE—OVER SCRATCHY ONTO POTTER AND BRIDE. The Bride grabs Potter's right arm. He drops both bags and exhibits the desperate reflex of a man whose fighting arm has never before been encumbered. He reaches for the gun that is not there. He sweeps her behind him.

CLOSEUP—SCRATCHY.

CLOSE SHOT—THE BRIDE: Her face looks crumpled with terror; she gazes at the gun as at an apparitional snake.

CLOSE SHOT—POTTER. He looks up from the gun into Scratchy's eyes.

CLOSE SHOT—THE REVOLVER——CAMERA RISES SLOWLY TO BRING IN SCRATCHY IN EXTREME CLOSEUP. His eyes are cold and mad; his face is almost solemn.

SCRATCHY [almost reproachfully]: Tried to sneak up on me. Tried to sneak up on me!

TWO SHOTS OF THE MEN—THE BRIDE BEHIND POTTER. Potter makes a slight movement; Scratchy thrusts his revolver venomously forward; CAMERA LUNGES FORWARD CORRESPONDINGLY.

CLOSE SHOT OF SCRATCHY.

SCRATCHY [he smiles with a new and quiet ferocity]: No, don't ye do it, Jack Potter. Don't you move a finger towards a gun just yet. Don't you bat an eyelash. The time has come fer me to settle with you, so I aim to do it my own way, an' loaf along without no interferin'. So if ye don't want a gun bent on ye, or a third eye right now, just mind what I tell ye.

He slowly raises his revolver to eye level, so that it is pointing a little upward, DEAD INTO THE LENS.

CLOSE SHOT—POTTER—PAST GUN. He is looking directly down the barrel. He is not at all a cowardly man but he is looking directly into the eye of death. Sweat breaks out on his face.

EXTREME CLOSE SHOT looking down the pistol barrel.

EXTREME CLOSE SHOT—POTTER then, THE BRIDE'S FACE, saying ''our home'' (without sound) and smiling. RETURN TO POTTER. His eyes, a little dizzily out of focus, restore to normal.

POTTER [quietly]: I ain't got a gun, Scratchy. Honest I ain't. You'll have to do all the shootin' yerself.

CLOSE SHOT—SCRATCHY—PAST POTTER. He goes livid and steps forward and lashes his weapon to and fro.

SCRATCHY: Don't you tell me you ain't got no gun on you, you whelp. Don't tell me no lie like that. There ain't a man in Texas ever seen you without no gun. Don't take me fer no kid.

His eyes blaze with light; his throat works like a pump.

CLOSE SHOT—POTTER—PAST SCRATCHY.

POTTER: I ain't takin' you fer no kid. I'm takin' you fer a fool. I tell you I ain't got a gun an' I ain't. If you're gonna shoot me up, ya better do it now; you'll never get a chance like this again.

PULL AWAY INTO TWO SHOT—Scratchy calms a little.

SCRATCHY [sneering]: If you ain't got a gun, why ain't you got a gun?
　　Been to Sunday school?
POTTER: You know where I been. I been in San Antone. An' I ain't got
　　a gun because I just got married. An' if I'd thought there was
　　goin' to be any galoots like you prowlin' around, when I brought
　　my wife home, I'd a had a gun, an' don't you fergit it.
SCRATCHY [says the word with total, uncomprehending vacancy]: Married?
POTTER: Yes, married, I'm married.
SCRATCHY [a little more comprehension]: Married? You mean, *you?* [He
　　backs off a pace; the arm and pistol drop.] No. [He studies Potter cagily
　　and shakes his head.]

Then literally for the first time, he sees the Bride.

SCRATCHY [continuing]: What's that ye got there? Is this the lady?
POTTER: Yes, this is the lady.

A silence.

SCRATCHY: Well, I'spose it's all off now.
POTTER: It's all off if you say so, Scratchy. You know I didn't make the
　　trouble.

He picks up both valises.

NEW SHOT—SCRATCHY—OVER POTTER. He studies Potter up and down,
slowly, incredulously. Then he looks at the ground.

SCRATCHY: Well, I 'low it's off, Jack. [He shakes his head.] *Married!*

He looks up with infinite reproach, sadness and solitude. He picks up his fallen
revolver. He hefts it and turns both revolvers in his hands, looking at them, then
puts them with finality into their holsters. Then he again meets Potter's eyes.

SCRATCHY [continuing; almost inaudibly]: G'bye, Jack.

CLOSE SHOT—POTTER. He begins to comprehend; he is moved.

POTTER: 'Bye, Scratchy.

REVERSE ANGLE—SCRATCHY. He looks at Potter a moment, then turns around
and walks heavily away.

TWO SHOT—POTTER AND BRIDE. She emerges from behind him, whimpering,
glancing from man to man, hugging his arm. His eyes on Scratchy O.S., he is
hardly aware of her.

INSERT: A lace curtain is plucked aside and Deacon's wife looks out.

CLOSE SHOT. A front door opens cautiously, squeakily; and cautiously, a man we don't know emerges.   CUT TO

INT. "WEARY GENTLEMAN"—DAY. The doors open; Jasper, Ed, the Young Man, and finally Laura Lee, followed by the Drummer, emerge onto the porch, looking up the street. LONG SHOT—POTTER, BRIDE AND SCRATCHY through this group as a few people timidly venture into the space between.

REVERSE ANGLE—GROUP SHOT—FAVORING LAURA LEE AND DRUMMER.

DRUMMER [smug]: You were saying, ma'am—this is a *hard* country?

She gives him a look and looks again toward Scratchy and company.

LONG SHOT—PAST ED AND DRUMMER. The Deacon trots out to Potter, frantically effusive. PANTOMIME introductions.

ED: Drummer, looks like ye got ye a new customer.

Drummer registers certainty and anticipation.

DRUMMER [to Laura Lee]: And how about you, ma'am?

CLOSE SHOT—LAURA LEE. She turns on him, colder than ever.

LAURA LEE [in measured tones]: I wouldn't wear them things if it killed
    me.

Then she realizes she is dead. Her eyes fall, tragic and defiant, to a neutral angle. In b.g., Jasper, watching her, realizes a little of the meaning. He is sympathetic.

ED'S VOICE [O.S.]: Well look at that!

LONG SHOT—PAST ALL OF THEM. Potter is walking toward home with Deacon and the Bride as if between custodians. They stop. The Deacon, extra effusive, peels off and toddles for home.

CLOSE MOVING SHOT—POTTER AND BRIDE WALKING. She glances back toward the filling, watchful street, which we see past them. Potter is looking toward Scratchy O.S.

BRIDE: Sure looks like the cat's outa the bag.
POTTER: More like a wild-cat.

He stops. So do Bride and CAMERA.

POTTER [continuing]: You know? There's somethin' I always wanted to
    do.

He sets down the suitcases and looks her up and down, business-like. She is willing but mystified. He picks her up.

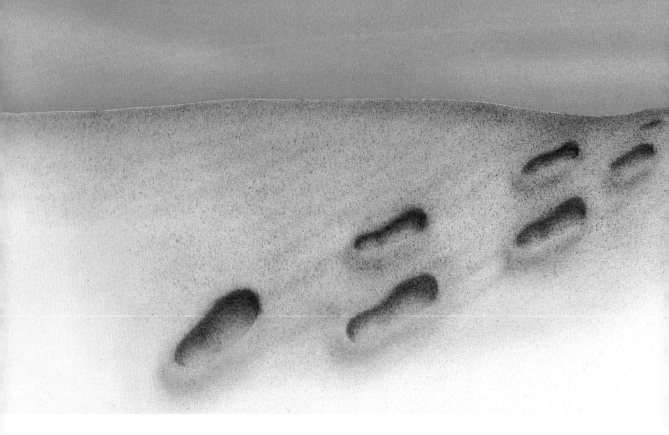

BRIDE [surprised and grateful]: Oh, Jack. . . .

As he carries her forward out of the shot, he looks sadly again toward Scratchy O.S. while she, loving and puzzled, looks at him.

MEDIUM SHOT—FRANK at the window.

FRANK: Howdy Marshal! Proud to know ye Miz Potter! Welcome home!

With the attempted velocity of a fast baseball, he slams down handfuls of improvised confetti. PULL CAMERA DOWN. Potter and Bride walk to door amid showering confetti. CONTINUE PULLING DOWN as Potter shoves door open with his shoe, enters, Bride in arms, and shoves door shut. DOLLY IN—STILL PULLING DOWN TO CLOSE SHOT showing that Scratchy has shot the lock to pieces. END PULL DOWN—vertical to the doorstep as last confetti flutters down. Salient are the torn pictures of the murderous faces and weapons of early western fiction.

VERY LONG SHOT—SCRATCHY. Very small, he walks heavily away toward a solitary, still more distant hovel; empty earth and sky all around. A LONG HOLD; then CAMERA PULLS DOWN TO CLOSE SHOT—the funnel-shaped tracks of his feet in heavy sand.

THE END

DISCUSSION

1. As Potter carries his Bride into the house, Frank showers them with "confetti" torn from magazine pictures of early western fiction; Scratchy goes slowly homeward, leaving only his departing footprints in the sand. What do these scenes help us to understand? What has changed in Yellow Sky?

2. Marshal Potter speaks and acts with assurance in Yellow Sky; on the train with the Bride, he is like a fish out of water. How does he appear to others on the train? How does he try to hide his lack of confidence?

3. *Complications,* in a play or a story, are developments that interfere with the main characters' plans. What is the chief complication in this story?

4. Describe the ways in which tension is gradually heightened as the play develops.

5. The action intensifies until the *climax* of the play is reached. What is the climax of this story—the "moment of truth" that is reached by characters and audience alike? Which characters are involved in this moment?

6. All that is left after the climax is the *denouement*—a final "unravelling" of the plot's different strands. What questions are answered in these final scenes? Are there any "loose ends" left that you wonder about?

VOCABULARY

The Bride Comes to Yellow Sky

1.   To make sure you understood the camera instructions in this script, write a brief definition of each of the following. Some of them may be defined from their obvious meaning, some from the context in which they are used in the play. A few you may need to look for in the dictionary.

O.S.	viewpoint shot	dolly	pull down
b.g.	medium shot	iris	long hold
fade in	close shot	insert	ultra sharp focus
slow pan	from their angle	freeze	pull away
fast wipe	reverse angle	two shot	inter-cut

COMPOSITION

Our Town

1.   On page 347 Mr. Webb says "There's a lot of common sense in some superstitions, George." You may or may not agree with him. But for a moment try to take Mr. Webb's point of view. Write the dialogue you think he would use in explaining what superstitions he means and why he believes them.

2.   *Our Town* shows a cross section of the citizens of Grover's Corners. In a brief composition, show a cross section of the people in your town or neighborhood. Or, if you prefer, present several people in the form of a dramatic sketch in which the people speak for themselves. Have a stage manager introduce them, if you wish.

3.   The Grover's Corners that Thornton Wilder shows is a small town of many decades ago. How would that town appear today? The same? Different? How so? Write a brief description of a modern Grover's Corners, including some of its citizens.

4.   Before the wedding ceremony George and Emily are both feeling nervous and doubtful. Look back at the comments they make. Why are they feeling apprehensive? Assume that George and Emily are both friends of yours. What advice would you give them at this important time in their lives?

5. Look again at Emily's lines on page 367 beginning "I didn't realize. . . ." She concludes her speech by saying good-bye to her mother and father and to many often unnoticed and taken-for-granted parts of everyday life. What would *you* miss? Using Emily's list as a guide, make your own list of good-byes.

The Bride Comes to Yellow Sky

1. James Agee created this film play from a short story by Stephen Crane. When a writer takes a story from one medium and uses it in another, many changes must be made; each medium makes its own demands. Choose one of the following sections of the play, and rewrite it as you imagine the original short story may have been written. Keep in mind those things you must describe, that the camera and stage directions will no longer communicate.

    a. On Main Street: Potter, departing, talks first with the prisoner, Frank, and then with the Deacon (pages 370–372).
    b. In the "Weary Gentleman" (pages 372–375).
    c. In the Parlor Car (pages 375–378).
    d. In the "Weary Gentleman": waiting for Scratchy (pages 386–394).
    e. The confrontation between Potter and Scratchy (pages 396–398).

2. Take a scene from one of the short stories you have read and write it as a film script, indicating angles, freezes, closeups, inserts, cuts, and so forth. Remember that how your audience sees the scene now depends on you—you can add meaning, emphasize certain things, call attention to a detail—all by the kind of camera shots you choose. Be sure to look at one or two scenes from *The Bride Comes to Yellow Sky* before you begin to see how Agee uses the camera to *interpret* the action.

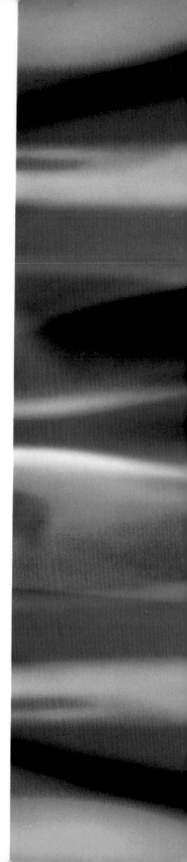

COMPOSITION

When you are writing about literature, you will interest your reader and persuade her or him more readily if you *cite* from the work under consideration. These *citations,* or quotations from poem or play or story or novel, are the specific lines that support your general remarks. But the citations must be appropriate. They must be efficient. And they must be acknowledged.

An *appropriate* citation quotes only that material from the work that bears directly on the point you are making. Suppose the point concerns the complex situation of Scratchy Wilson in "The Bride Comes to Yellow Sky." Scratchy can shoot up a whole town, and yet nobody in that same town would "harm a hair of his head if they's any way out—let alone kill him" (page 387). The citation here—the lines quoted from Agee's play—brings the very language of the characters themselves to bear on the general point. And that language confirms the complexity of the situation beyond doubt. Thus the citation is appropriate.

It is also *efficient.* In other words, it is no longer than it needs to be to make the point. Don't quote whole speeches from the source when a single phrase—or even one vivid word—will do. It is better to quote briefly and frequently than occasionally and at length. The former method results in a paper that shows that you are thoroughly familiar with the play or poem or story you're discussing. And a paper containing frequent brief quotations reveals your willingness to test each opinion against the literature itself.

But the citations that result from such testing must be *acknowledged.* The page reference in parentheses after the citation above provides such an acknowledgment. It tells the reader: on page 381 (or wherever) you will find the source of the quotation—and so may check what I have written.

A final point: if all quotations throughout a paper come from one source—from "The Bride Comes to Yellow Sky," for instance—put each acknowledgment immediately after the quotation. (In the case of a short poem, the acknowledgment will refer the reader to a line rather than a page.) Only if you are including quotations from several different articles or books or other sources should you resort to footnotes at the bottom of the page.

**CITATIONS
AND
FOOTNOTES**

ABOUT THE SELECTIONS

1.   For this evening's entertainment you have a choice. You may go to a local movie where the film of "The Bride Comes to Yellow Sky" is showing. Or you may go to a theater in town where a group of actors will be performing *Our Town*. Which of the two will you choose to see? Why? In a thoughtful paper, explain your choice as specifically as you can.

2.   Cast well-known actors and actresses in the major roles of one of these two plays. Who, for example, would make a good Potter? Or, in Wilder's play, who might best play Emily? Explain in detail the reasons you cast the leading roles as you did. Specific references to other roles your stars have played will help make your reasoning persuasive.

3.   *Our Town* concerns abiding truths about life. People in all times and places have fallen in love, agonized about the future, grieved over friends and family who have died. Yet though the underlying truths remain, the surfaces of life change. People do dress differently now, and speak differently from the way they did in Grover's Corners. Update a scene from Wilder's play. The basic truths of the scene will be the same as in *Our Town,* but the surfaces will reflect *your* town, your world that you know firsthand, with the language, dress, and customs of the present.

4.   Look up Stephen Crane's famous short story "The Bride Comes to Yellow Sky," on which James Agee has based the play in this unit. What liberties has Agee taken with Crane's story? When he does change the story, why does he do so? Compare and contrast the two versions, citing appropriately and efficiently from each to make your points clear. Try to use citations in your discussion, but avoid simply writing a generalization, then tacking on a quotation under it, then writing another generalization, and so on.

ON YOUR OWN

1.   Like Emily, choose an *ordinary* day in your past to revisit. As vividly as you can, describe a single moment of that day. Think hard. What sights, sounds, smells, tastes, and touches can you recover?

2.   Wilder, Agee, and Stephen Crane all lived interesting lives. Choose one to research. Make sure you consult at least three sources—encyclopedias, magazine articles, obituaries, biographical dictionaries. Then write an account, a page or two long, that describes the writer's life and clarifies his achievement. Try to capture the qualities that distinguished that life. Use footnotes to acknowledge your indebtedness to other biographers' opinions and evaluations. (You need not, of course, footnote facts that are undisputed, such as proper names, book titles, and dates of birth or death.)

VALUES

Blues Ain't No Mockin Bird

TONI CADE BAMBARA

The puddle had frozen over and me and Cathy went stompin in it.
The twins from next door—Tyrone and Terry—were swingin so high
out of sight, we forgot we were waitin our turn on the tire. Cathy
jumped up and came down hard on her heels and started tap-dancin.
And the frozen patch splinterin every which way underneath kinda
spooky.

"Looks like a plastic spider web," she said. "A sort of weird spider, I guess, with many mental problems."

But really it looked like the crystal paper-weight Granny kept in
the parlor. She was on the back porch, Granny was, making the cakes
drunk. The old ladle dripping rum into the Christmas tins, like it used
to drip maple syrup into the pails when we lived in the Judson's
woods, like it poured cider into the vats when we were on the
Cooper place, like it used to scoop buttermilk and soft cheese when
we lived at the dairy.

"Go tell that man we ain't a bunch of trees."

"Ma'm?"

"I said to tell that man to get away from here with that camera."

Me and Cathy look over toward the meadow where the men with
the station wagon'd been roamin around all mornin. The tall man
with a huge camera lassoed to his shoulder was buzzin our way.

"They're makin movie pictures," yelled Tyrone, stiffenin his legs
and twistin so the tire'd come down slow so they could see.

"They're makin movie pictures," sang out Terry.

"That boy don't never have anything original to say," say Cathy
grown-up.

By the time the man with the camera had cut across our neighbor's yard, the twins were out of the trees swingin low and Granny
was onto the steps, the screen door bammin soft and scratchy against
her palms.

"We thought we'd get a shot or two of the house and everything
and then——"

"Good mornin," Granny cut him off. And smiled that smile.

"Good mornin," he said, head all down the way Bingo does when

you yell at him about the bones on the kitchen floor. "Nice place you got here, aunty. We thought we'd take a——"

"Did you?" said Granny with her eyebrows. Cathy pulled up her socks and giggled.

"Nice things here," said the man buzzin his camera over the yard. The pecan barrels, the sled, me and Cathy, the flowers, the painted stones along the driveway, the trees, the twins, the toolshed.

"I don't know about the thing, the it, and the stuff," said Granny still talkin with her eyebrows. "Just people here is what I tend to consider."

Camera man stopped buzzin. Cathy giggled into her collar.

"Mornin, ladies," a new man said. He had come up behind us when we weren't lookin. "And gents," discoverin the twins givin him a nasty look. "We're filmin for the county," he said with a smile. "Mind if we shoot a bit around here?"

"I do indeed," said Granny with no smile.

Smilin man was smilin up a storm. So was Cathy. But he didn't seem to have another word to say, so he and the camera man backed on out the yard, but you could hear the camera buzzin still.

"Suppose you just shut that machine off," said Granny real low through her teeth and took a step down off the porch and then another.

"Now, aunty," Camera said pointin the thing straight at her.

"Your mama and I are not related."

Smilin man got his notebook out and a chewed-up pencil. "Listen," he said movin back into our yard, "We'd like to have a statement from you . . . for the film. We're filmin for the county, see. Part of the food-stamp campaign. You know about the food stamps?"

Granny said nuthin.

"Maybe there's somethin you want to say for the film. I see you grow your own vegetables," he smiled real nice. "If more folks did that, see, there'd be no need——"

Granny wasn't sayin nuthin. So they backed on out, buzzin at our clothesline and the twins' bicycles, then back on down to the meadow.

The twins were danglin in the tire lookin at Granny. Me and Cathy were waitin, too, cause Granny always got somethin to say. She teaches steady with no let-up.

"I was on this bridge one time," she started off. "Was a crowd cause this man was goin to jump, you understand. And a minister was there and the police and some other folks. His woman was there, too."

"What was they doin?" asked Tyrone.

"Tryin to talk him out of it was what they was doin. The minister talkin about how it was a mortal sin, suicide. His woman takin bites out of her own hand and not even knowin it, so nervous and cryin and talkin fast."

"So what happened?" asked Tyrone.

"So here comes . . . this person . . . with a camera, takin pictures of the man and the minister and the woman. Takin pictures of the man in his misery about to jump cause life so bad and people been messin with him so bad. This person takin up the whole roll of film practically. But savin a few, of course."

"Of course," said Cathy hatin the person. Me standin there wonderin how Cathy knew it was "of course" when I didn't and it was my grandmother.

After a while Tyrone say, "Did he jump?"

"Yeh, did he jump?" say Terry all eager.

And Granny just stared at the twins till their faces swallow up the eager and they don't even care any more about the man jumping. Then she goes back onto the porch and lets the screen door go for itself.

I'm lookin to Cathy to finish the story cause she knows Granny's whole story before me even. Like she knew how come we move so much and Cathy ain't but a third cousin we picked up on the way last Thanksgivin visitin. But she knew it was on account of people drivin Granny crazy till she'd get up in the night and start packin. Mumblin and packin and wakin everybody up sayin, "Let's get on away from here before I kill me somebody." Like people wouldn't pay her for things like they said they would. Or Mr. Judson bringin us boxes of old clothes and raggedy magazines. Or Mrs. Cooper comin in our kitchen and touchin everything and sayin how clean it all was. Granny goin crazy, and Grandaddy Cain pullin her off the people sayin, "Now now, Cora." But next day loadin up the truck, with rocks all in his jaw, madder than Granny in the first place.

"I read a story once," said Cathy soundin like Granny teacher. "About this lady Goldilocks who barged into a house that wasn't even hers. And not invited, you understand. Messed over the people's groceries and broke up the people's furniture. Had the nerve to sleep in the folks' bed."

"Then what happened?" asked Tyrone. "What they do, the folks, when they come in to all this mess?"

"Did they make her pay for it?" asked Terry makin a fist. "I'd've made her pay me."

I didn't even ask. I could see Cathy actress was very likely to just walk away and leave us in mystery about this story which I heard was about some bears.

"Did they throw her out?" asked Tyrone, like his father sounds when he's bein extra nasty plus to the washin machine man.

"Woulda," said Terry. "I woulda gone up side her head with my fist and——"

"You woulda done whatcha always do—go cry to Mama, you big baby," said Tyrone. So naturally Terry starts hittin on Tyrone, and next thing you know they tumblin out the tire and rollin on the ground. But Granny didn't say a thing or send the twins home or step out on the steps to tell us about how we can't afford to be fightin amongst ourselves. She didn't say nuthin. So I get into the tire to take my turn. And I could see her leanin up against the pantry table starin at the cakes she was puttin up for the Christmas sale, mumblin real low and grumpy and holdin her forehead like it wanted to fall off and mess up the rum cakes.

Behind me I hear before I can see Grandaddy Cain comin through the woods in his field boots. Then I twist around to see the shiny black oilskin cuttin through what little left there was of yellows, reds, and oranges. His great white head not quite round cause of this bloody thing high on his shoulder, like he was wearin a cap on side-ways. He takes the short cut through the pecan grove, and the sound of twigs snappin overhead and underfoot travels clear and cold all the way up to us. And here comes Smilin and Camera up behind him like they was goin to do somethin. Folks like to go for him sometimes. Cathy say it's because he's so tall and quiet and like a king. And people just can't stand it. But Smilin and Camera don't hit him in the head or nuthin. They just buzz on him as he stalks by with the chicken hawk slung over his shoulder, squawkin, drippin red down the back of the oilskin.

He passes the porch and stops a second for Granny to see he's caught the hawk at last, but she's just starin and mumblin and not at the hawk. So he nails the bird to the toolshed door, the hammerin crackin through the eardrums. And the bird flappin himself to death and droolin down the door to paint the gravel in the driveway red, then brown, then black. And the two men movin up on tiptoe like they was invisible or we were blind.

"Get them persons out of my flower bed, Mister Cain," say Granny moanin real low like at a funeral.

"How come your grandmother calls her husband 'Mister Cain' all the time?" Tyrone whispers all loud and nosey and from the city and don't know no better. Like his mama, Miss Myrtle, tell us never mind the formality as if we had no better breeding than to call her Myrtle plain. And then this awful thing—a giant hawk—come wailin up over the meadow, flyin low and tilted and screamin, zigzaggin through the pecan grove, breakin branches and hollerin, snappin past the clothes-line, flyin every which way, flyin into things reckless with crazy.

"He's come to claim his mate," say Cathy fast and ducks down.

We all fall quick and flat into the gravel driveway, stones scrapin my face. I squinch my eyes open again at the hawk on the door tryin to fly up out of her death like it was just a sack flown into by mistake. Her body holdin her there on that nail, though. The mate beatin the air overhead and clutchin for hair, for heads, for landin space.

The camera man duckin and bendin and runnin and fallin, jigglin the camera and scared. And Smilin jumpin up and down swipin at the huge bird, tryin to bring the hawk down with just his raggedy ole cap. Grandaddy Cain straight up and silent, watchin the circles of the hawk, then aimin the hammer off his wrist. The giant bird fallin, silent and slow.

Then here comes Camera and Smilin all big and bad now that the awful screechin thing is on its back and broken, here they come. And Grandaddy Cain looks up at them like it was the first time noticin, but not payin them too much mind cause he's listenin, we all listenin, to that low groanin music comin from the porch. And we figure any minute, somethin in my back tells me any minute now, Granny gonna bust through that screen with somethin in her hand and murder on her mind.

So Grandaddy say above the buzzin but quiet, "Good day, gentle-men." Just like that. Like he'd invited them in to play cards and they'd stayed too long and all the sandwiches were gone and Reverend Webb was droppin by and it was time to go.

They didn't know what to do. But like Cathy say, folks can't stand Grandaddy tall and silent and like a king. They can't neither. The smile the men smilin is pullin the mouth back and showin the teeth. Lookin like the wolf man, both of them. Then Grandaddy holds his hand out—this huge hand I used to sit in when I was a baby and he'd carry me through the house to my mother like I was a gift on a tray. Like he used to on the trains. They called the other men just waiters. But they spoke of Grandaddy separate and said The Waiter. And said he had engines in his feet and motors in his hands and couldn't no train throw him off and couldn't nobody turn him round. They were big enough for motors, his hands were. He held that one hand out all still and it gettin to be not at all a hand but a person in itself.

"He wants you to hand him the camera," Smilin whispers to Camera, tiltin his head to talk secret like they was in the jungle or somethin and come upon a native that don't speak the language. The men start untyin the straps, and they put the camera into that great hand speckled with the hawk's blood all black and crackly now. And the hand don't even drop with the weight, just the fingers move, curl up around the machine. But Grandaddy lookin straight at the men. They lookin at each other and everywhere but at Grandaddy's face.

"We filmin for the county, see," say Smilin. "We puttin together a movie for the food stamp program . . . filmin all around these parts. Uhh, filmin for the county."

"Can I have my camera back?" say the tall man with no machine on his shoulder but still keepin it high like the camera was still there or needed to be. "Please, Sir."

Then Grandaddy's other hand flies up like a sudden and gentle bird, slaps down fast on top of the camera and lifts off half like it was a calabash cut for sharing.

"Hey," Camera jumps forward. He gathers up the parts into his chest and everythin unrollin and fallin all over. "Whatcha trying to do? You'll ruin the film." He looks down into his chest of metal reels and things like he's protectin a kitten from the cold.

"You standin in the misses' flower bed," say Grandaddy. "This is our own place."

The two men look at him, then at each other, then back at the mess in the camera man's chest, and they just back off. One sayin over and over all the way down to the meadow, "Watch it, Bruno. Keep ya fingers off the film."

Then Grandaddy picks up the hammer and jams it into the oilskin pocket, scrapes his boots, and goes into the house. And you can hear the squish of his boots headin through the house. And you can see the funny shadow he throws from the parlor window onto the ground by the string bean patch. The hammer draggin the pocket of the oilskin out so Grandaddy looked even wider. Granny was hummin now—high, not low and grumbly. And she was doin the cakes again, you could smell the molasses from the rum.

"There's this story I'm goin to write one day," say Cathy dreamer. "About the proper use of the hammer."

"Can I be in it?" Tyrone say, with his hand up like it was a matter of first come first served.

"Perhaps," say Cathy climbin onto the tire to pump us up. "If you there and you ready."

DISCUSSION

1. "Your mama and I are not related," Granny says, when Camera calls her "aunty." Explain her reaction.

2. Granny "teaches steady with no let-up." What does her story about the man's attempt to commit suicide have to do with the visit of Camera and Smilin? Why does Granny just stare at the twins and then slam the screen door when they ask her if the man jumped?

3. The dying chicken hawk and its mate are a dramatic backdrop for the action of the story. Think of two or three reasons the writer may have included them in the story.

For further activities, see page 450.

One Perfect Rose

DOROTHY PARKER

A single flow'r he sent me, since we met.
All tenderly his messenger he chose;
Deep-hearted, pure, with scented dew still wet—
One perfect rose.

I knew the language of the floweret;   5
"My fragile leaves," it said, "his heart enclose."
Love long has taken for his amulet
One perfect rose.

Why is it no one ever sent me yet
One perfect limousine, do you suppose?   10
Ah no, it's always just my luck to get
One perfect rose.

An Immorality

EZRA POUND

Sing we for love and idleness,
Naught else is worth the having.

Though I have been in many a land,
There is naught else in living.

And I would rather have my sweet,
Though rose-leaves die of grieving,

Than do high deeds in Hungary
To pass all men's believing.

DISCUSSION

1. What attitudes toward life does Pound present in this poem?

2. Do you think the title of the poem is appropriate? Explain.

A Tree
A Rock
A Cloud

CARSON McCULLERS

It was raining that morning, and still very dark. When the boy reached the streetcar café he had almost finished his route and he went in for a cup of coffee. The place was an all-night café owned by a bitter and stingy man called Leo. After the raw, empty street the café seemed friendly and bright: along the counter there were a couple of soldiers, three spinners from the cotton mill, and in a corner a man who sat hunched over with his nose and half his face down in a beer mug. The boy wore a helmet such as aviators wear. When he went into the café he unbuckled the chin strap and raised the right flap up over his pink little ear; often as he drank his coffee someone would speak to him in a friendly way. But this morning Leo did not look into his face and none of the men were talking. He paid and was leaving the café when a voice called out to him:

"Son! Hey Son!"

He turned back and the man in the corner was crooking his finger and nodding to him. He had brought his face out of the beer mug and he seemed suddenly very happy. The man was long and pale, with a big nose and faded orange hair.

"Hey Son!"

The boy went toward him. He was an undersized boy of about twelve, with one shoulder drawn higher than the other because of the weight of the paper sack. His face was shallow, freckled, and his eyes were round child eyes.

"Yeah Mister?"

The man laid one hand on the paper boy's shoulders, then grasped the boy's chin and turned his face slowly from one side to the other. The boy shrank back uneasily.

"Say! What's the big idea?"

The boy's voice was shrill; inside the café it was suddenly very quiet.

The man said slowly: "I love you."

All along the counter the men laughed. The boy, who had scowled and sidled away, did not know what to do. He looked over the counter at Leo, and Leo watched him with a weary, brittle jeer. The boy tried to laugh also. But the man was serious and sad.

"I did not mean to tease you, Son," he said. "Sit down and have a beer with me. There is something I have to explain."

Cautiously, out of the corner of his eye, the paper boy questioned the men along the counter to see what he should do. But they had gone back to their beer or their breakfast and did not notice him. Leo put a cup of coffee on the counter and a little jug of cream.

"He is a minor," Leo said.

The paper boy slid himself up onto the stool. His ear beneath the upturned flap of the helmet was very small and red. The man was nodding at him soberly. "It is important," he said. Then he reached in his hip pocket and brought out something which he held up in the palm of his hand for the boy to see.

"Look very carefully," he said.

The boy stared, but there was nothing to look at very carefully. The man held in his big, grimy palm a photograph. It was the face of a woman, but blurred, so that only the hat and the dress she was wearing stood out clearly.

"See?" the man asked.

The boy nodded and the man placed another picture in his palm. The woman was standing on a beach in a bathing suit. The suit made her stomach very big, and that was the main thing you noticed.

"Got a good look?" He leaned over closer and finally asked: "You ever seen her before?"

The boy sat motionless, staring slantwise at the man. "Not so I know of."

"Very well." The man blew on the photographs and put them back into his pocket. "That was my wife."

"Dead?" the boy asked.

Slowly the man shook his head. He pursed his lips as though about to whistle and answered in a long-drawn way: "Nuuu——" he said. "I will explain."

The beer on the counter before the man was in a large brown mug. He did not pick it up to drink. Instead he bent down and, putting his face over the rim, he rested there for a moment. Then with both hands he tilted the mug and sipped.

"Some night you'll go to sleep with your big nose in a mug and drown," said Leo. "Prominent transient drowns in beer. That would be a cute death."

The paper boy tried to signal to Leo. While the man was not looking he screwed up his face and worked his mouth to question soundlessly: "Drunk?" But Leo only raised his eyebrows and turned away to put some pink strips of bacon on the grill. The man pushed the mug away from him, straightened himself, and folded his loose crooked hands on the counter. His face was sad as he looked at the paper boy. He did not blink, but from time to time the lids closed down with delicate gravity over his pale green eyes. It was nearing dawn and the boy shifted the weight of the paper sack.

"I am talking about love," the man said. "With me it is a science."

The boy half slid down from the stool. But the man raised his forefinger, and there was something about him that held the boy and would not let him go away.

"Twelve years ago I married the woman in the photograph. She was my wife for one year, nine months, three days, and two nights. I loved her. Yes. . . ." He tightened his blurred, rambling voice and said again: "I loved her. I thought also that she loved me. I was a railroad engineer. She had all home comforts and luxuries. It never crept into my brain that she was not satisfied. But do you know what happened?"

"Mgneeow!" said Leo.

The man did not take his eyes from the boy's face. "She left me. I came in one night and the house was empty and she was gone. She left me."

"With a fellow?" the boy asked.

Gently the man placed his palm down on the counter. "Why naturally, Son. A woman does not run off like that alone."

The café was quiet, the soft rain black and endless in the street outside. Leo pressed down the frying bacon with the prongs of his long fork. "So you have been chasing the floozie for eleven years. You frazzled old rascal!"

For the first time the man glanced at Leo. "Please don't be vulgar. Besides, I was not speaking to you." He turned back to the boy and said in a trusting and secretive undertone: "Let's not pay any attention to him. O.K.?"

The paper boy nodded doubtfully.

"It was like this," the man continued. "I am a person who feels many things. All my life one thing after another has impressed me. Moonlight. The leg of a pretty girl. One thing after another. But the point is that when I had enjoyed anything there was a peculiar sensation as though it was laying around loose in me. Nothing seemed to finish itself up or fit in with the other things. Women? I had my portion of them. The same. Afterwards laying around loose in me. I was a man who had never loved."

Very slowly he closed his eyelids, and the gesture was like a curtain drawn at the end of a scene in a play. When he spoke again his voice was excited and the words came fast—the lobes of his large, loose ears seemed to tremble.

"Then I met this woman. I was fifty-one years old and she always said she was thirty. I met her at a filling station and we were married within three days. And do you know what it was like? I just can't tell you. All I had ever felt was gathered together around this woman. Nothing lay around loose in me any more but was finished up by her."

The man stopped suddenly and stroked his long nose. His voice sank down to a steady and reproachful undertone: "I'm not explaining this right. What happened was this. There were these beautiful feelings and loose little pleasures inside me. And this woman was something like an assembly line for my soul. I run these little pieces of myself through her and I come out complete. Now do you follow me?"

"What was her name?" the boy asked.

"Oh," he said. "I called her Dodo. But that is immaterial."

"Did you try to make her come back?"

The man did not seem to hear. "Under the circumstances you can imagine how I felt when she left me."

Leo took the bacon from the grill and folded two strips of it between a bun. He had a gray face, with slitted eyes, and a pinched nose saddled by faint blue shadows. One of the mill workers signaled for more coffee and Leo poured it. He did not give refills on coffee free. The spinner ate breakfast there every morning, but the better Leo knew his customers the stingier he treated them. He nibbled his own bun as though he grudged it to himself.

"And you never got hold of her again?"

The boy did not know what to think of the man, and his child's face was uncertain with mingled curiosity and doubt. He was new on the paper route; it was still strange to him to be out in the town in the black, queer, early morning.

"Yes," the man said. "I took a number of steps to get her back. I went around trying to locate her. I went to Tulsa where she had folks. And to Mobile. I went to every town she had ever mentioned to me, and I hunted down every man she had formerly been connected with. Tulsa, Atlanta, Chicago, Cheehaw, Memphis. . . . For the better part of two years I chased around the country trying to lay hold of her."

"But the pair of them had vanished from the face of the earth!" said Leo.

"Don't listen to him," the man said confidentially. "And also just forget those

two years. They are not important. What matters is that around the third year a curious thing begun to happen to me."

"What?" the boy asked.

The man leaned down and tilted his mug to take a sip of beer. But as he hovered over the mug his nostrils fluttered slightly; he sniffed the staleness of the beer and did not drink. "Love is a curious thing to begin with. At first I thought only of getting her back. It was a kind of mania. But then as time went on I tried to remember her. But do you know what happened?"

"No," the boy said.

"When I laid myself down on a bed and tried to think about her my mind became a blank. I couldn't see her. I would take out her pictures and look. No good. Nothing doing. A blank. Can you imagine it?"

"Say Mac!" Leo called down the counter. "Can you imagine this bozo's mind a blank!"

Slowly, as though fanning away flies, the man waved his hand. His green eyes were concentrated and fixed on the shallow little face of the paper boy.

"But a sudden piece of glass on a sidewalk. Or a nickel tune in a music box. A shadow on a wall at night. And I would remember. It might happen in a street and I would cry or bang my head against a lamppost. You follow me?"

"A piece of glass . . ." the boy said.

"Anything. I would walk around and I had no power of how and when to remember her. You think you can put up a kind of shield. But remembering don't come to a man face forward—it corners around sideways. I was at the mercy of everything I saw and heard. Suddenly instead of me combing the countryside to find her she begun to chase me around in my very soul. *She* chasing *me,* mind you! in my soul."

The boy asked finally: "What part of the country were you in then?"

"Ooh," the man groaned. "I was a sick mortal. It was like smallpox. I confess, Son, that I boozed. I committed any sin that suddenly appealed to me. I am loath to confess it but I will do so. When I recall that period it is all curdled in my mind, it was so terrible."

The man leaned his head down and tapped his forehead on the counter. For a few seconds he stayed bowed over in this position, the back of his stringy neck covered with orange furze, his hands with their long warped fingers held palm to palm in an attitude of prayer. Then the man straightened himself; he was smiling and suddenly his face was bright and tremulous and old.

"It was in the fifth year that it happened," he said. "And with it I started my science."

Leo's mouth jerked with a pale, quick grin. "Well none of we boys are getting any younger," he said. Then with sudden anger he balled up a dishcloth he was holding and threw it down hard on the floor. "You draggle-tailed old Romeo!"

"What happened?" the boy asked.

The old man's voice was high and clear: "Peace," he answered.

"Huh?"

"It is hard to explain scientifically, Son," he said. "I guess the logical explanation is that she and I had fleed around

from each other for so long that finally we just got tangled up together and lay down and quit. Peace. A queer and beautiful blankness. It was spring in Portland and the rain came every afternoon. All evening I just stayed there on my bed in the dark. And that is how the science come to me."

The windows in the streetcar were pale blue with light. The two soldiers paid for their beers and opened the door—one of the soldiers combed his hair and wiped off his muddy puttees before they went outside. The three mill workers bent silently over their breakfasts. Leo's clock was ticking on the wall.

"It is this. And listen carefully. I meditated on love and reasoned it out. I realized what is wrong with us. Men fall in love for the first time. And what do they fall in love with?"

The boy's soft mouth was partly open and he did not answer.

"A woman," the old man said. "Without science, with nothing to go by, they undertake the most dangerous and sacred experience in God's earth. They fall in love with a woman. Is that correct, Son?"

"Yeah," the boy said faintly.

"They start at the wrong end of love. They begin at the climax. Can you wonder it is so miserable? Do you know how men should love?"

The old man reached over and grasped the boy by the collar of his leather jacket. He gave him a gentle little shake and his green eyes gazed down unblinking and grave.

"Son, do you know how love should be begun?"

The boy sat small and listening and still. Slowly he shook his head. The old man leaned closer and whispered:

"A tree. A rock. A cloud."

It was still raining outside in the street: a mild, gray, endless rain. The mill whistle blew for the six o'clock shift and the three spinners paid and went away. There was no one in the café but Leo, the old man, and the little paper boy.

"The weather was like this in Portland," he said. "At the time my science was begun. I meditated and I started very cautious. I would pick up something from the street and take it home with me. I bought a goldfish and I concentrated on the goldfish and I loved it. I graduated from one thing to another. Day by day I was getting this technique. On the road from Portland to San Diego——"

"Aw shut up!" screamed Leo suddenly. "Shut up! Shut up!"

The old man still held the collar of the boy's jacket; he was trembling and his face was earnest and bright and wild. "For six years now I have gone around by myself and built up my science. And now I am a master. Son. I can love anything. No longer do I have to think about it even. I see a street full of people and a beautiful light comes in me. I watch a bird in the sky. Or I meet a traveler on the road. Everything, Son. And anybody. All stranger and all loved! Do you realize what a science like mine can mean?"

The boy held himself stiffly, his hands curled tight around the counter edge. Finally he asked: "Did you ever really find that lady?"

"What? What say, Son?"

"I mean," the boy asked timidly. "Have you fallen in love with a woman again?"

The old man loosened his grasp on the boy's collar. He turned away and for the first time his green eyes had a vague and scattered look. He lifted the mug from the counter, drank down the yellow beer. His head was shaking slowly from side to side. Then finally he answered: "No, Son. You see that is the last step in my science. I go cautious. And I am not quite ready yet."

"Well!" said Leo. "Well well well!"

The old man stood in the open doorway. "Remember," he said. Framed there in the gray damp light of the early morning he looked shrunken and seedy and frail. But his smile was bright. "Remember I love you," he said with a last nod. And the door closed quietly behind him.

The boy did not speak for a long time. He pulled down the bangs on his forehead and slid his grimy little forefinger around the rim of his empty cup. Then without looking at Leo he finally asked:

"Was he drunk?"

"No," said Leo shortly.

The boy raised his clear voice higher.

"Then was he a dope fiend?"

"No."

The boy looked up at Leo, and his flat little face was desperate, his voice urgent and shrill. "Was he crazy? Do you think he was a lunatic?" The paper boy's voice dropped suddenly with doubt. "Leo? Or not?"

But Leo would not answer him. Leo had run a night café for fourteen years, and he held himself to be a critic of craziness. There were the town characters and also the transients who roamed in from the night. He knew the manias of all of them. But he did not want to satisfy the questions of the waiting child. He tightened his pale face and was silent.

So the boy pulled down the right flap of his helmet and as he turned to leave he made the only comment that seemed safe to him, the only remark that could not be laughed down and despised:

"He sure has done a lot of traveling."

DISCUSSION

1. How does the boy respond when the man says "I love you"? Why is his response quite understandable?

2. What do you think Leo's attitude toward the man is? What lines in the story tell you?

3. How does the title of the story reflect the man's view of the world and his attitude toward love?

Father's Voice

WILLIAM STAFFORD

"No need to get home early;
the car can see in the dark."
    He wanted me to be rich
    the only way we could,
    easy with what we had.   5

And always that was his gift,
given for me ever since,
    easy gift, a wind
    that keeps on blowing for flowers
    or birds wherever I look.   10

World, I am your slow guest,
one of the common things
    that move in the sun and have
    close, reliable friends
    in the earth, in the air, in the rock.

DISCUSSION

1. What is the gift the speaker inherits from his father?

2. How do the views in "Father's Voice" compare with those of the man in Carson McCullers's story "A Tree A Rock A Cloud"?

CHINOOK DANCE

TED PALMANTEER

"Enter. . . . Please come in. It is only beginning to become good. The goods are piled high, for each person who dances will receive his gift of thanks. Let us dance and call the chinook winds. We will pray that this long winter shall end. Here, let me take your coats and hats."

This is the beginning of a strange way. Yet it is essential in my country, the Pacific Northwest, where we still thank each season for its blessings. Each has to be thanked, including the harsh winter from the Northlands, as without him, how could we appreciate what life he leaves us when he is gone? For only then can we renew our cherished old ways of summer life. It's like having a fresh plate of hot food after a long cold starvation period. So now we thank winter, and ask for our brothers the chinook winds to blow once again across the lands. They will take the cold of death and renew it with the warm life of spring.

Let there be friendship, dance around the pole, sing and dance. That song is through, now we await another singer. As soon as anyone has a song hit him, he will sing for us and we will again sing and dance until exhaustion.

An old lady slowly rises. She pulls her violet winddress away from her black shawl and leaves an empty space where she was sitting. Now she reaches inside her beaded bag and pulls out a green scarf with many knots. It holds whatever is her Indian power; she is an Indian doctor. With great strain, she shuffles onto the floor; her feet scraping the rough boards, she steps up to the pole. She grasps it with one hand and begins to speak. A translator interprets, for she comes from a different language. Now she turns to her translator; she tells him to tell who she is, where she's from, why she's here, and what she will do.

Here, she releases the pole and begins untying the knots in her green scarf. The translator tells us this woman's name, Lively Chickadee, and she comes from the northlands of British Columbia in Canada. He goes on to say that the old one is here to tell us, and show us how the real old chinook dances were, for we had lost the true way of doing them, as she had observed. He said she had been here visiting him, a relative, and he had brought her to the chinook dance. He said when the old one was young, the dances lasted all night and they used only one singer, an Indian doctor of great powers.

Respect is shown on every face; the people are willing to listen, and all are waiting for the old lady. In all patience they wait, watching her untie the knots in her scarf. Her parched skin is sunk between the bones of her fingers, and her fingernails haven't been cut and they curve awkwardly under. They are yellow on the edges and cracked with age.

Yet we sit and watch, for it is forbidden to help an old person. She would only scorn us, and tell us she is not yet dead, to be helped.

Finally, she draws out of her scarf a slender strand of buckskin with knots tied in, in certain places—some close, some far, some in groups. This she ties on the pole about even with the top of her head. Next she pulls out buckskin sewed together in many layers, with long fringes, and on each end of fringe is a deer hoof, tied a hand length below the deer hide thong. She pulls more of these deer-hoof rattles out and ties them onto the pole until she has four rows tied firmly about a hand length apart.

This pole is slender and stretches from the floor to the ceiling. It is sacred and only Indian doctors of power dare to touch it, and here she is tying things onto it. Still she ties more; she takes the green scarf and ties it firmly a hand's length above the buckskin thong.

Here she tells us that the knotted thong is a message; it is knotted in certain places in a code. This message is to her power, and through her power, she will continue with the Mighty Changer. Next she says the green scarf above the whole of her possessions on the pole stands for spring. Next she says that when the spirits come into the room, the deer hooves will lead us in our dance.

Now she calls for the little children, for they are the easiest to be taught, and will dance in the true spirit. Shyly, they sidle onto the floor, not knowing what to do. Then she takes her red scarf off her head, and she ties it another hand length below all the hooves. She explains this, saying that the red stands for her blood, which is old, and she must pass it on before she dies. She says that the ancient ones dwell in her blood waiting to be released and she is going to do that tonight, here, in the chinook dance.

She shakes her thin grey braids, telling of when she was young like these children. She tells of how her hair was long and black and beautiful. She tells of how good the old ways were. Next she explains to the children why they are to dance, saying they are asking for the chinook winds and the warmth of summer again. They nod their heads awkwardly, really not knowing what she wants, yet willing to do it, for it is expected of them.

She takes one hand, grabs the pole, and closes her eyes, squeezing tears of old memories back. From deep within her comes a cry, a song, a prayer, a soul, filling to massive proportions. She starts to dance, one arm upraised calling her spirit, and her other hand tightly grasping the pole. She lunges into life, her face beams with youth, and her body dances into the far unknown past.

Yet this very old lady had staggered and shuffled up to the pole, and here she dances in jarring jumps. The children shuffle, waiting for one to start; then they begin to step, to dance, to sing, and so complete in everything they seem to go into a trance. Smiles of appreciation cross the faces of the people; this is good, this woman has strong medicine. We are as one, we feel the ancient one stirring in our dusty bodies.

On, the children dance. They are the buds of spring; they are the ancient ones. They are the chinook winds. The room becomes wet with war pride, tears pour over old faces, and the people smile.

Then the spirits enter. The room senses this and seems to have become numb. People are there yet, they are all over, they are not people at all, but images.

Then the red scarf begins to float around the pole, flicking, moving, striking, snapping. The spirits are testing the pole. The old lady sees this. Now she grabs the pole with both hands, she wails, she screams, still in her song, and the children dance. The leather thong jerks into life, wrapping and unwrapping her wrists, the knots leaving welts on her parched hands. The second scarf moves like a snake; it encircles the pole, floats out again, reaching at the dancers. Still, she holds the pole, her feet firmly implanted. Her sweaty skin shows complete exhaustion. Yet she sings, and one would think she would collapse any minute.

Slowly . . . easily, a hoof moves; it shakes itself awake, it starts to jump out, rattling it awakens the others, then more, until one row is all moving, rattling. Row after row, now all four rows are shaking, rattling. Now they begin to keep time with the song. Here again, the old lady begins to jump, both hands encircling the pole. The deer hooves extend out like living fingers, then contracting, striking in time.

The old lady calls for all to join, and everyone rises. Into the lines they go, dancing around and around the pole. The deer hooves are trying to escape their leather thongs; they jump hard to their very ends, still

filling the room with more power. This song is sung on every tongue, feet tramp the floor to a thunder, and the whole room goes into the spirit world. The floor is covered with sweat, yet they dance on. On they dance, on they dance, on they dance.

All night they dance, while that little old lady jumps in the center holding on to the spirit pole. The children are still seemingly in a trance. Tears still pour across ancient faces. The song still wails and the feet thunder.

At the abrupt break of dawn, all stop, for the spirits have vanished into the other world. The door is opened. People emerge steaming, red with heat, soaked with work yet they walk with open shirts in the January cold. Here it is morning, truly the coldest part of all, and here the men walk about telling sly jokes, jesting, and kidding each other with open shirts.

The women have gone to the long kitchen where the hot food will be brought into the dining room. Everyone goes back inside, a ritual is carried out, then bowls are passed to everyone. The first food is a kind of stew. This is in thanks once again to the powers for keeping the people fed and healthy all winter.

Slowly, a warm breeze stirs across the snow, and the chinook winds begin to blow. Now begins the melting of winter, the beginning of spring, another life, ending another dance.

DISCUSSION

1. Why do the Native Americans give thanks to "the harsh winter from the Northlands"?

2. Why does Lively Chickadee feel that she must perform the "real old Chinook dances"?

3. Why does Lively Chickadee teach the old dances to children? Why is it important that the children learn the dances?

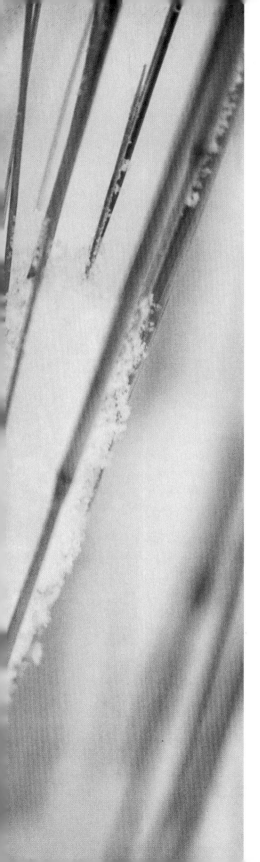

WINTER SPRING

RICHARD WILBUR

A script of trees before the hill
Spells cold, with laden serifs; all the walls
Are battlemented still;
But winter spring is winnowing the air
Of chill, and crawls   5
Wet-sparkling on the gutters;
Everywhere
Walls wince, and there's the steal of waters.

Now all this proud royaume
Is Veniced. Through the drift's mined dome   10
One sees the rowdy rusted grass,
And we're amazed as windows stricken bright.
This too-soon spring will pass
Perhaps tonight,
And doubtless it is dangerous to love   15
This somersault of seasons;
But I am weary of
The winter way of loving things for reasons.

2. *serifs:* fine lines added to the main strokes of letters. (This type has no serifs, but the type in the poem does.)   4–5. *winnowing . . . chill:* blowing the cold away, as chaff is blown from grain in winnowing.   9. *royaume:* kingdom.

DISCUSSION

1. Wilbur is describing the way a day late in winter suddenly contains a hint of spring. To do this he uses *metaphor* (see page 287) very strikingly. Look back at the poem line by line— what aspect of "winter spring" is he describing with each metaphor?

2. Why might it be "dangerous" to love winter spring?

For further activities, see page 450.

A Young Puritan's Code   JONATHAN EDWARDS

Being sensible that I am unable to do anything without God's help, I do humbly entreat him by his grace to enable me to keep these resolutions so far as they are agreeable to his will, for Christ's sake.

REMEMBER TO READ OVER THESE RESOLUTIONS ONCE A WEEK.

Resolved, *never to* DO, BE, *or* SUFFER anything in soul or body, less or more, but what tends to the glory of God.

Resolved, never to lose one moment of *time;* but improve it in the most profitable way I possibly can.

Resolved, to live with all my might while I do live.

Resolved, never to do anything which I should be afraid to do if it were the last hour of my life.

Resolved, to think much, on all occasions, of my own dying and of the common circumstances which attend death.

Resolved, to be endeavoring to find out fit objects of charity and liberality.

Resolved, never to do anything out of revenge.

Resolved, never to suffer the least motions of anger to irrational beings.

Resolved, never to speak evil of any person except some particular good call for it.

Resolved, to maintain the strictest temperance in eating and drinking.

Resolved, never to do anything which if I should see in another, I should count a just occasion to despise him for or to think any way the more meanly of him.

Resolved, to study the Scriptures so steadily, constantly, and frequently as that I may find and plainly perceive myself to grow in the knowledge of the same.

Resolved, never to speak anything that is ridiculous or matter of laughter on the Lord's day.

Whenever I hear anything spoken in conversation of any person, if I think it would be praiseworthy in me, resolved to endeavor to imitate it.

Resolved, after afflictions, to inquire what I am the better for them; what good I *have* got, and what I *might* have got by them.

DISCUSSION   Which resolution do you think would be the most difficult to keep? Which resolutions do you find relevant and worth striving for?

For further activities, see page 450.

the minister's black veil

NATHANIEL HAWTHORNE

The sexton stood in the porch of Milford meeting house, pulling lustily at the bell rope. The old people of the village came stooping along the street. Children with bright faces tripped merrily beside their parents, or mimicked a graver gait in the conscious dignity of their Sunday clothes. Spruce bachelors looked sidelong at the pretty maidens and fancied that the Sabbath sunshine made them prettier than on weekdays. When the throng had mostly streamed into the porch, the sexton began to toll the bell, keeping his eye on the Reverend Mr. Hooper's door. The first glimpse of the clergyman's figure was the signal for the bell to cease its summons.

"But what has good Parson Hooper got upon his face?" cried the sexton in astonishment.

All within hearing immediately turned about and beheld the semblance of Mr. Hooper, pacing slowly his meditative way towards the meetinghouse. With one accord they started, expressing more wonder than if some strange minister were coming to dust the cushions of Mr. Hooper's pulpit.

"Are you sure it is our parson?" inquired Goodman Gray of the sexton.

"Of a certainty it is good Mr. Hooper," replied the sexton. "He was to have exchanged pulpits with Parson Shute, of Westbury; but Parson Shute sent to excuse himself yesterday, being to preach a funeral sermon."

The cause of so much amazement may appear sufficiently slight. Mr. Hooper, a gentlemanly person of about thirty, though still a bachelor was dressed with due clerical neatness, as if a careful wife had starched his band and brushed the weekly dust from his Sunday's garb. There was but one thing remarkable in his appearance. Swathed about his forehead and hanging down over his face, so low as to be shaken by his breath, Mr. Hooper had on a black veil. On a nearer view, it seemed to consist of two folds of crepe, which entirely concealed his features except the mouth and chin, but probably did not intercept his sight farther than to give a darkened aspect to all living and inanimate things. With this gloomy shade before him, good Mr. Hooper walked onward at a slow and quiet pace, stooping somewhat and looking on the ground, as is customary with abstracted men, yet nodding kindly to those of his parishioners who still waited on the meetinghouse steps. But so wonder-struck were they that his greeting hardly met with a return.

"I can't really feel as if good Mr. Hooper's face was behind that piece of crepe," said the sexton.

"I don't like it," muttered an old woman as she hobbled into the meetinghouse. "He has changed himself into something awful, only by hiding his face."

"Our parson has gone mad!" cried Goodman Gray, following him across the threshold.

A rumor of some unaccountable phenomenon had preceded Mr. Hooper into the meetinghouse and set all the congregation astir. Few could refrain from twisting their heads towards the door; many stood upright and turned directly about; while several little boys clambered upon the seats and came down again with a terrible racket. There was a general bustle, a rustling of women's gowns and shuffling of the men's feet, greatly at variance with that hushed repose which should attend the entrance of the minister. But Mr. Hooper appeared not to notice the perturbation of his people. He entered with an almost noiseless step, bent his head mildly to the pews on each side, and bowed as he passed his oldest parishioner, a white-haired great-grandsire, who occupied an armchair in the center of the aisle. It was strange to observe how slowly this venerable man became conscious of something singular in the appearance of his pastor. He seemed not fully to partake of the prevailing wonder till Mr. Hooper had ascended the stairs and showed himself in the pulpit, face to face with his congregation except for the black veil. That mysterious emblem was never once withdrawn. It shook with his measured breath as he gave out the psalm; it threw its obscurity between him and the holy page as he read the Scriptures; and while he prayed, the veil lay heavily on his uplifted countenance. Did he seek to hide it from the dread Being whom he was addressing?

Such was the effect of this simple piece of crepe that more than one woman of delicate nerves was forced to leave the meetinghouse. Yet perhaps the pale-faced congregation was almost as fearful a sight to the minister, as his black veil to them.

Mr. Hooper had the reputation of a good preacher, but not an energetic one: he strove to win his people heavenward by mild, persuasive influences, rather than to drive them thither by the thunders of the Word. The sermon which he now delivered was marked by the same characteristics of style and manner as the general series of his pulpit oratory. But there was something, either in the sentiment of the discourse itself or in the imagination of the auditors, which made it greatly the most powerful effort that they had ever heard from their pastor's lips. It was tinged, rather more darkly than usual, with the gentle gloom of Mr. Hooper's temperament. The subject had reference to secret sin, and those sad mysteries which we hide from our nearest and dearest, and would fain conceal from our own consciousness, even forgetting that the Omniscient[1] can detect them. A subtle power was breathed into his words. Each member of the congregation, the most innocent girl, and the man of hardened breast, felt as if the preacher had crept upon them, behind his awful veil, and discovered their hoarded iniquity of deed or thought. Many spread their clasped hands on their bosoms. There was nothing terrible in what Mr. Hooper said; at least, no violence; and yet, with every tremor of his melancholy voice, the hearers quaked. An unsought pathos came hand in hand with awe. So sensible were the audience of some unwonted attribute in their minister that they longed for a breath of wind to blow aside the veil, almost believing that a stranger's visage would be discovered, though the form, gesture, and voice were those of Mr. Hooper.

At the close of the services, the people hurried out with indecorous confusion, eager to communicate their pent-up amazement, and conscious of lighter spirits, the moment they lost sight of the black veil. Some gathered in little circles, huddled closely together, with their mouths all whispering in the center; some went homeward alone, wrapped in silent meditation; some talked loudly and profaned the Sabbath day with ostentatious laughter. A few shook their sagacious heads, intimating that they could penetrate the mystery; while one or two affirmed that there was no mystery at all, but only that Mr. Hooper's eyes were so weakened by the midnight lamp as to require a shade. After a brief interval, forth came good Mr. Hooper also, in the rear of his flock. Turning his veiled face from one group to another, he paid due reverence to the hoary heads, saluted the middle-aged with kind dignity as their friend and spiritual guide, greeted the young with mingled authority and love, and laid his hands on the little children's heads to bless them. Such was always his custom on the Sabbath day. Strange and bewildered looks repaid him for his courtesy. None, as on former occasions, aspired to the honor of walking by their pastor's side. Old Squire Saunders, doubtless by an accidental lapse of memory, neglected to invite Mr. Hooper to his table, where the good clergyman had been wont to bless the food almost every Sunday since his settlement. He returned, therefore, to the parsonage, and at the moment of closing the door, was observed to look back

---

[1] *Omniscient* (ŏm-nĭsh′ənt): all-knowing; that is, God.

upon the people, all of whom had their eyes fixed upon the minister. A sad smile gleamed faintly from beneath the black veil and flickered about his mouth, glimmering as he disappeared.

"How strange," said a lady, "that a simple black veil, such as any woman might wear on her bonnet, should become such a terrible thing on Mr. Hooper's face!"

"Something must surely be amiss with Mr. Hooper's intellects," observed her husband, the physician of the village. "But the strangest part of the affair is the effect of this vagary,[2] even on a sober-minded man like myself. The black veil, though it covers only our pastor's face, throws its influence over his whole person, and makes him ghostlike from head to foot. Do you not feel it so?"

"Truly do I," replied the lady; "and I would not be alone with him for the world. I wonder he is not afraid to be alone with himself!"

"Men sometimes are so," said her husband.

The afternoon service was attended with similar circumstances. At its conclusion, the bell tolled for the funeral of a young lady. The relatives and friends were assembled in the house, and the more distant acquaintances stood about the door, speaking of the good qualities of the deceased, when their talk was interrupted by the appearance of Mr. Hooper, still covered with his black veil. It was now an appropriate emblem. The clergyman stepped into the room where the corpse was laid, and bent over the coffin to take a last farewell of his deceased parishioner. As he stooped, the veil hung straight down from his forehead, so that if her eyelids had not been closed for ever, the dead maiden might have seen his face. Could Mr. Hooper be fearful of her glance that he so hastily caught back the black veil? A person who watched the interview between the dead and living scrupled not[3] to affirm that at the instant when the clergyman's features were disclosed, the corpse had slightly shuddered, rustling the shroud and muslin cap, though the countenance retained the composure of death. A superstitious old woman was the only witness of this prodigy.[4] From the coffin, Mr. Hooper passed into the chamber of the mourners, and thence to the head of the staircase, to make the funeral prayer. It was a tender and heart-dissolving prayer, full of sorrow, yet so imbued with celestial hopes that the music of a heavenly harp, swept by the fingers of the dead, seemed faintly to be heard among the saddest accents of the minister. The people trembled, though they but darkly understood him when he prayed that they, and himself,

[2] *vagary:* erratic notion.
[3] *scrupled not:* did not hesitate.
[4] *prodigy:* marvel.

and all of mortal race, might be ready, as he trusted this young maiden had been, for the dreadful hour that should snatch the veil from their faces. The bearers went heavily forth, and the mourners followed, saddening all the street, with the dead before them, and Mr. Hooper in his black veil behind.

"Why do you look back?" said one in the procession to his partner.

"I had a fancy," replied she, "that the minister and the maiden's spirit were walking hand in hand."

"And so had I, at the same moment," said the other.

That night the handsomest couple in Milford village were to be joined in wedlock. Though reckoned a melancholy man, Mr. Hooper had a placid cheerfulness for such occasions, which often excited a sympathetic smile, where livelier merriment would have been thrown away. There was no quality of his disposition which made him more beloved than this. The company at the wedding awaited his arrival with impatience, trusting that the strange awe which had gathered over him throughout the day would now be dispelled. But such was not the result. When Mr. Hooper came, the first thing that their eyes rested on was the same horrible black veil which had added deeper gloom to the funeral and could portend nothing but evil to the wedding. Such was its immediate effect on the guests that a cloud seemed to have rolled duskily from beneath the black crepe and dimmed the light of the candles. The bridal pair stood up before the minister. But the bride's cold fingers quivered in the tremulous hand of the bridegroom, and her deathlike paleness caused a whisper that the maiden who had been buried a few hours before was come from her grave to be married. If ever another wedding were so dismal, it was that famous one, where they tolled the wedding knell.[5] After performing the ceremony, Mr. Hooper raised a glass of wine to his lips, wishing happiness to the new married couple, in a strain of mild pleasantry that ought to have brightened the features of the guests, like a cheerful gleam from the hearth. At that instant, catching a glimpse of his figure in the looking glass, the black veil involved his own spirit in the horror with which it overwhelmed all others. His frame shuddered—his lips grew white—he spilt the untasted wine upon the carpet—and rushed forth into the darkness. For the Earth, too, had on her Black Veil.

The next day, the whole village of Milford talked of little else than Parson Hooper's black veil. That, and the mystery concealed behind it, supplied a topic for discussion between acquaintances meeting in the street, and good women gossiping at their open windows. It was the first

---

[5] *knell:* sounding of a bell, especially for a funeral.

item of news that the tavern keeper told to his guests. The children bab-
bled of it on their way to school. One imitative little imp covered his face
with an old black handkerchief, thereby so affrighting his playmates that
the panic seized himself, and he well nigh lost his wits by his own waggery. [6]

It was remarkable that of all the busy-bodies and impertinent people
in the parish, not one ventured to put the plain question to Mr. Hooper,
wherefore he did this thing. Hitherto, whenever there appeared the
slightest call for such interference, he had never lacked advisers, nor
shown himself averse to be guided by their judgment. If he erred at all, it
was by so painful a degree of self-distrust that even the mildest censure
would lead him to consider an indifferent action as a crime. Yet, though
so well acquainted with this amiable weakness, no individual among his
parishioners chose to make the black veil a subject of friendly remon-
strance. There was a feeling of dread, neither plainly confessed nor carefully concealed, which caused each to shift the responsibility upon
another, till at length it was found expedient to send a deputation of the
church in order to deal with Mr. Hooper about the mystery before it
should grow into a scandal. Never did an embassy so ill discharge its duties. The minister received them with friendly courtesy, but became silent
after they were seated, leaving to his visitors the whole burden of intro-
ducing their important business. The topic, it might be supposed, was obvious enough. There was the black veil, swathed round Mr. Hooper's
forehead and concealing every feature above his placid mouth, on which
at times they could perceive the glimmering of a melancholy smile. But
that piece of crepe, to their imagination, seemed to hang down before his
heart, the symbol of a fearful secret between him and them. Were the
veil but cast aside, they might speak freely of it, but not till then. Thus
they sat a considerable time, speechless, confused, and shrinking uneasily
from Mr. Hooper's eye, which they felt to be fixed upon them with an
invisible glance. Finally the deputies returned abashed to their constitu-
ents, pronouncing the matter too weighty to be handled except by a
council of the churches if, indeed, it might not require a general synod. [7]

But there was one person in the village, unappalled by the awe with
which the black veil had impressed all beside herself. When the deputies
returned without an explanation, or even venturing to demand one, she,
with the calm energy of her character, determined to chase away the
strange cloud that appeared to be settling round Mr. Hooper, every mo-

---

[6] *waggery:* wittiness.
[7] *synod:* assembly of church officials.

ment more darkly than before. As his plighted wife, it should be her privilege to know what the black veil concealed. At the minister's first visit, therefore, she entered upon the subject with a direct simplicity which made the task easier both for him and her. After he had seated himself, she fixed her eyes steadfastly upon the veil but could discern nothing of the dreadful gloom that had so overawed the multitude: it was but a double fold of crepe, hanging down from his forehead to his mouth and slightly stirring with his breath.

"No," said she aloud, and smiling, "there is nothing terrible in this piece of crepe except that it hides a face which I am always glad to look upon. Come, good sir, let the sun shine from behind the cloud. First lay aside your black veil: then tell me why you put it on."

Mr. Hooper's smile glimmered faintly.

"There is an hour to come," said he, "when all of us shall cast aside our veils. Take it not amiss, beloved friend, if I wear this piece of crepe till then."

"Your words are a mystery too," returned the young lady. "Take away the veil from them, at least."

"Elizabeth, I will," said he, "so far as my vow may suffer me. Know, then, this veil is a type and a symbol, and I am bound to wear it ever, both in light and darkness, in solitude and before the gaze of multitudes, and as with strangers, so with my familiar friends. No mortal eye will see it withdrawn. This dismal shade must separate me from the world: even you, Elizabeth, can never come behind it!"

"What grievous affliction hath befallen you," she earnestly inquired, "that you should thus darken your eyes for ever?"

"If it be a sign of mourning," replied Mr. Hooper, "I, perhaps, like most other mortals, have sorrows dark enough to be typified by a black veil."

"But what if the world will not believe that it is the type of an innocent sorrow?" urged Elizabeth. "Beloved and respected as you are, there may be whispers that you hide your face under the consciousness of secret sin. For the sake of your holy office, do away this scandal!"

The color rose into her cheeks as she intimated the nature of the rumors that were already abroad in the village. But Mr. Hooper's mildness did not forsake him. He even smiled again—that same sad smile, which always appeared like a faint glimmering of light, proceeding from the obscurity beneath the veil.

"If I hide my face for sorrow, there is cause enough," he merely replied; "and if I cover it for secret sin, what mortal might not do the same?"

And with this gentle, but unconquerable obstinacy did he resist all her entreaties. At length Elizabeth sat silent. For a few moments she appeared lost in thought, considering, probably, what new methods might be tried to withdraw her lover from so dark a fantasy, which, if it had no other meaning, was perhaps a symptom of mental disease. Though of a firmer character than his own, the tears rolled down her cheeks. But in an instant as it were, a new feeling took the place of sorrow: her eyes were fixed insensibly on the black veil, when like a sudden twilight in the air, its terrors fell around her. She arose and stood trembling before him.

"And do you feel it then at last?" said he mournfully.

She made no reply, but covered her eyes with her hand, and turned to leave the room. He rushed forward and caught her arm.

"Have patience with me, Elizabeth!" cried he passionately. "Do not desert me, though this veil must be between us here on earth. Be mine, and hereafter there shall be no veil over my face, no darkness between our souls! It is but a mortal veil—it is not for eternity! Oh! you know not how lonely I am, and how frightened, to be alone behind my black veil. Do not leave me in this miserable obscurity for ever!"

"Lift the veil but once, and look me in the face," said she.

"Never! It cannot be!" replied Mr. Hooper.

"Then, farewell!" said Elizabeth.

She withdrew her arm from his grasp and slowly departed, pausing at the door to give one long, shuddering gaze that seemed almost to penetrate the mystery of the black veil. But even amid his grief, Mr. Hooper smiled to think that only a material emblem had separated him from happiness, though the horrors which it shadowed forth must be drawn darkly between the fondest of lovers.

From that time no attempts were made to remove Mr. Hooper's black veil or by a direct appeal to discover the secret which it was supposed to hide. By persons who claimed a superiority to popular prejudice, it was reckoned merely an eccentric whim, such as often mingles with the sober actions of men otherwise rational, and tinges them all with its own semblance of insanity. But with the multitude, good Mr. Hooper was irreparably a bugbear. He could not walk the street with any peace of mind, so conscious was he that the gentle and timid would turn aside to avoid him, and that others would make it a point of hardihood to throw themselves in his way. The impertinence of the latter class compelled him to give up his customary walk at sunset to the burial ground; for when he leaned pensively over the gate, there would always be faces behind the gravestones, peeping at his black veil. A fable went the rounds that the stare of the dead people drove him thence. It grieved him to the very depth of his kind heart to observe how the children fled from his approach, breaking up their merriest sports, while his melancholy figure was yet afar off. Their instinctive dread caused him to feel more strongly than aught else that a preternatural[8] horror was interwoven with the threads of the black crepe. In truth, his own antipathy to the veil was known to be so great that he never willingly passed before a mirror, nor stooped to drink at a still fountain, lest in its peaceful bosom he should be affrighted by himself. This was what gave plausibility to the whispers that Mr. Hooper's conscience tortured him for some great crime too horrible to be entirely concealed, or otherwise than so obscurely intimated. Thus, from beneath the black veil, there rolled a cloud into the sunshine, an ambiguity of sin or sorrow, which enveloped the poor minister, so that love or sympathy could never reach him. It was said that ghost and fiend consorted with him there. With self-shudderings and outward terrors, he walked continually in its shadow, groping darkly within his own soul, or gazing through a medium that saddened the whole world. Even the lawless wind, it was believed, respected his dreadful secret and never blew aside the veil. But still good Mr. Hooper sadly smiled at the pale visages of the worldly throng as he passed by.

Among all its bad influences, the black veil had the one desirable effect of making its wearer a very efficient clergyman. By the aid of his mysterious emblem—for there was no other apparent cause—he became a man of awful power over souls that were in agony for sin. His converts always regarded him with a dread peculiar to themselves, affirming, though but figuratively, that before he brought them to celestial light, they had been with him behind the black veil. Its gloom, indeed, enabled him to sympathize with all dark affections. Dying sinners cried aloud for Mr. Hooper and would not yield their breath till he appeared; though ever, as he stooped to whisper consolation, they shuddered at the veiled face so near their own. Such were the terrors of the black veil even when Death had bared his visage! Strangers came long distances to attend service at his church, with the mere idle purpose of gazing at his figure, because it was forbidden them to behold his face. But many were made to quake ere they departed! Once, during Governor Belcher's administration, Mr. Hooper was appointed to preach the election sermon. Covered with his black veil, he stood before the chief magistrate, the council, and the representatives, and wrought so deep an impression that the legislative measures of that year were characterized by all the gloom and piety of our earliest ancestral sway.

[8] *preternatural:* abnormal.

In this manner Mr. Hooper spent a long life, irreproachable in outward act, yet shrouded in dismal suspicions; kind and loving, though unloved, and dimly feared; a man apart from men, shunned in their health and joy, but ever summoned to their aid in mortal anguish. As years wore on, shedding their snows above his sable veil, he acquired a name throughout the New England churches, and they called him Father Hooper. Nearly all his parishioners who were of mature age when he was settled had been borne away by many a funeral; he had one congregation in the church, and a more crowded one in the churchyard; and having wrought so late into the evening and done his work so well, it was now good Father Hooper's turn to rest.

Several persons were visible by the shaded candlelight in the death chamber of the old clergyman. Natural connections he had none. But there was the decorously grave, though unmoved physician, seeking only to mitigate the last pangs of the patient whom he could not save. There were the deacons and other eminently pious members of his church. There, also, was the Reverend Mr. Clark of Westbury, a young and zealous divine, who had ridden in haste to pray by the bedside of the expiring minister. There was the nurse, no hired handmaiden of death, but one whose calm affection had endured thus long in secrecy, in solitude, amid the chill of age, and would not perish, even at the dying hour. Who, but Elizabeth? And there lay the hoary head of good Father Hooper upon the death pillow, with the black veil still swathed about his brow and reaching down over his face, so that each more difficult gasp of his faint breath caused it to stir. All through life that piece of crepe had hung between him and the world: it had separated him from cheerful brotherhood and woman's love, and kept him in that saddest of all prisons, his own heart; and still it lay upon his face, as if to deepen the gloom of his darksome chamber and shade him from the sunshine of eternity.

For some time previous his mind had been confused, wavering doubtfully between the past and the present, and hovering forward as it were, at intervals, into the indistinctness of the world to come. There had been feverish turns, which tossed him from side to side and wore away what little strength he had. But in his most convulsive struggles, and in the wildest vagaries of his intellect, when no other thought retained its sober influence, he still showed an awful solicitude lest the black veil should slip aside. Even if his bewildered soul could have forgotten, there was a faithful woman at his pillow, who, with averted eyes, would have covered that aged face, which she had last beheld in the comeliness of manhood. At length the death-stricken old man lay quietly in the torpor of mental and bodily exhaustion, with an imperceptible pulse, and breath that grew fainter and fainter except when a long, deep, and irregular inspiration[9] seemed to prelude the flight of his spirit.

The minister of Westbury approached the bedside.

"Venerable Father Hooper," said he, "the moment of your release is at hand. Are you ready for the lifting of the veil, that shuts in time from eternity?"

Father Hooper at first replied merely by a feeble motion of his head; then, apprehensive, perhaps that his meaning might be doubtful, he exerted himself to speak.

"Yea," said he, in faint accents, "my soul hath a patient weariness until that veil be lifted."

"And is it fitting," resumed the Reverend Mr. Clark, "that a man so given to prayer, of such a blameless example, holy in deed and thought, so far as mortal judgment may pronounce; is it fitting that a father in the church should leave a shadow on his memory that may seem to blacken a life so pure? I pray you, my venerable brother, let not this thing be! Suffer us to be gladdened by your triumphant aspect as you go to your reward. Before the veil of eternity be lifted, let me cast aside this black veil from your face!"

And thus speaking the Reverend Mr. Clark bent forward to reveal the mystery of so many years. But exerting a sudden energy that made all the beholders stand aghast, Father Hooper snatched both his hands from beneath the bedclothes and pressed them strongly on the black veil, resolute to struggle if the minister of Westbury would contend with a dying man.

"Never!" cried the veiled clergyman. "On earth, never!"

"Dark old man!" exclaimed the affrighted minister, "with what horrible crime upon your soul are you now passing to the judgment?"

Father Hooper's breath heaved; it rattled in his throat; but with a mighty effort grasping forward with his hands, he caught hold of life and held it back till he should speak. He even raised himself in bed; and there he sat, shivering with the arms of death around him, while the black veil hung down, awful, at that last moment, in the gathered terrors of a lifetime. And yet the faint, sad smile, so often there, now seemed to glimmer from its obscurity and linger on Father Hooper's lips.

"Why do you tremble at me alone?" cried he, turning his veiled face round the circle of pale spectators. "Tremble also at each other! Have men avoided me, and women shown no pity, and children screamed and

---

[9] *inspiration:* breathing.

fled, only for my black veil? What, but the mystery which it obscurely typifies, has made this piece of crepe so awful? When the friend shows his inmost heart to his friend; the lover to his best beloved; when man does not vainly shrink from the eye of his Creator, loathsomely treasuring up the secret of his sin; then deem me a monster, for the symbol beneath which I have lived, and die! I look around me, and lo! on every visage a Black Veil!"

While his auditors shrank from one another in mutual affright, Father Hooper fell back upon his pillow, a veiled corpse, with a faint smile lingering on the lips. Still veiled, they laid him in his coffin, and a veiled corpse they bore him to the grave. The grass of many years has sprung up and withered on that grave, the burial stone is moss grown, and good Mr. Hooper's face is dust; but awful is still the thought that it moldered beneath the Black Veil!

DISCUSSION

1.   Lying on his deathbed, Father Hooper says, "I look around me, and lo! on every visage a Black Veil!" What does he mean?

2.   Strangely enough, Mr. Hooper becomes an even more effective minister after assuming the black veil. How do you account for this change?

3.   Hawthorne's stories often contain *symbols*—objects that stand for something larger than themselves. Mr. Hooper said that his veil was a symbol. What does it symbolize to the people of the village? What does Mr. Hooper say it symbolizes for him?

4.   Why do *you* think Mr. Hooper wore the black veil?

For further activities, see page 450.

PATTERNS

AMY LOWELL

I walk down the garden paths,
And all the daffodils
Are blowing, and the bright blue squills.

I walk down the patterned garden paths
In my stiff, brocaded gown.   5
With my powdered hair and jeweled fan,
I too am a rare
Pattern. As I wander down
The garden paths.

My dress is richly figured,   10
And the train
Makes a pink and silver stain
On the gravel, and the thrift

Of the borders.
Just a plate of current fashion,   15
Tripping by in high-heeled, ribboned shoes.
Not a softness anywhere about me,
Only whalebone and brocade.
And I sink on a seat in the shade
Of a lime tree. For my passion   20
Wars against the stiff brocade.
The daffodils and squills
Flutter in the breeze
As they please.
And I weep;   25
For the lime tree is in blossom
And one small flower has dropped upon my bosom

And the plashing of waterdrops
In the marble fountain
Comes down the garden paths.   30
The dripping never stops.
Underneath my stiffened gown
Is the softness of a woman bathing in a marble basin,
A basin in the midst of hedges grown
So thick, she cannot see her lover hiding,   35

3. *squills:* narrow leaved plants bearing bell shaped flowers.
13. *thrift:* tufted plants with pink or white flowers.

But she guesses he is near,
And the sliding of the water
Seems the stroking of a dear
Hand upon her.
What is Summer in a fine brocaded gown!
I should like to see it lying in a heap upon the ground.
All the pink and silver crumpled up on the ground.

I would be the pink and silver as I ran along the paths,
And he would stumble after,
Bewildered by my laughter. 45
I should see the sun flashing from his sword hilt and the buckles on his shoes.
I would choose
To lead him in a maze along the patterned paths,
A bright and laughing maze for my heavy-booted lover.
Till he caught me in the shade, 50
And the buttons of his waistcoat bruised my body as he clasped me,
Aching, melting, unafraid.
With the shadows of the leaves and the sundrops,
And the plopping of the waterdrops,
All about us in the open afternoon— 55
I am very like to swoon
With the weight of this brocade,
For the sun sifts through the shade.

Underneath the fallen blossom
In my bosom, 60
Is a letter I have hid.
It was brought to me this morning by a rider from the Duke.
"Madam, we regret to inform you that Lord Hartwell
Died in action Thursday se'nnight."
As I read it in the white, morning sunlight, 65
The letters squirmed like snakes.
"Any answer, Madam," said my footman.
"No," I told him.
"See that the messenger takes some refreshment.
No, no answer." 70
And I walked into the garden,
Up and down the patterned paths,
In my stiff, correct brocade.
The blue and yellow flowers stood up proudly in the sun,
Each one. 75
I stood upright too,
Held rigid to the pattern
By the stiffness of my gown.
Up and down I walked,
Up and down. 80

---

64. *se'nnight:* period of seven days and nights.

In a month he would have been my husband.
In a month, here, underneath this lime,
We would have broke the pattern;
He for me, and I for him,
He as Colonel, I as Lady,   85
On this shady seat.
He had a whim
That sunlight carried blessing.
And I answered, "It shall be as you have said."
Now he is dead.   90

In Summer and in Winter I shall walk
Up and down
The patterned garden paths
In my stiff, brocaded gown.
The squills and daffodils   95
Will give place to pillared roses, and to asters, and to snow.
I shall go
Up and down
In my gown.

Gorgeously arrayed,   100
Boned and stayed.
And the softness of my body will be guarded from embrace
By each button, hook, and lace.
For the man who should loose me is dead,
Fighting with the Duke in Flanders,   105
In a pattern called a war.
Christ! What are patterns for?

DISCUSSION   1.   As used by Lowell, patterns include the garden path, herself, her gown, and war. What do these "patterns" have in common?

2.   A certain musical effect is acquired in this poem by the use of *assonance*— the repetition of vowel sounds close together. In lines 11–12 the words "train," "makes," and "stain" are examples of assonance. Do not confuse rhyme and assonance. "Lake" and "make" are examples of rhyme (and assonance); "lake" and "fate" are examples of assonance only. What other examples of assonance can you find in the poem?

For further activities, see page 450.

VOCABULARY

Blues Ain't No Mockin Bird (page 408)

When Grandaddy says "Good day, gentlemen" to the camera men, the narrator says it was as if "he'd invited them in to play cards and they'd stayed too long and all the sandwiches were gone . . ." (page 413). The origin of the word *sandwich* is quite appropriate to this sentence. The word comes from the Fourth Earl of Sandwich (1718–1792), for whom sandwiches were invented so that he could stay at the gambling table without having to stop for meals.

You may not realize how many words in our language come from the names of real people. Check each of the following words in a good dictionary and tell what person's name it comes from and who that person was.

1. begonia
2. boycott
3. braille
4. camellia
5. cardigan
6. chauvinism
7. derrick
8. doily
9. leotard
10. maverick
11. Melba toast
12. sequoia
13. teddy bear
14. titian

Winter Spring (page 431)

A. A pun is a play on words based on the similarity of sound between two words with different meanings. In "Winter Spring" Wilbur uses a pun with the word "Veniced" which connotes both the canals of Venice and the similar sound of *finished*. What is the pun on the word "steal" (line 8)?

B. Read the following sentences. "I'm glad I passed my electrocardiogram," said Tom wholeheartedly. "I'm very thirsty," said Tom dryly. "I won't touch that apple," said Tom adamantly.

These sentences are Tom Swifties, or adverbial puns. See how swift you are. On separate paper, write sentences that have these endings.

1. ———said Tom gravely.
2. ———said Tom weakly.
3. ———said Tom sternly.
4. ———said Tom intently.
5. ———said Tom hoarsely.
6. ———said Tom hospitably.

The Minister's Black Veil (page 433)

The minister's black veil sets "all the congregation astir." The word *congregation* comes from the Latin prefix *com-*, "together," plus the root *greg*, which means "herd, flock." The word literally means "to flock together."

The following four words all contain the root *greg*. Look up each word in a good dictionary and tell what the prefix means and what the literal meaning of the word is. Then use each word in a sentence.

egregious   gregarious   segregate   aggregate

COMPOSITION

Blues Ain't No Mockin Bird (page 408)

Modern technology increases the possibilities of invading a person's privacy. Write an essay outlining your views of the right to privacy and the steps government should take to insure the right.

A Young Puritan's Code (page 432)

Although codes of behavior tend to be somewhat rigid, we all have certain standards that we adhere to, or try to, in our lives. In several paragraphs write your own code of behavior, and explain why the things you list are important to you.

The Minister's Black Veil (page 433)

1. Describe a situation from your own experience in which a change in your appearance has caused other people to view you differently.

2. Imagine that you are Mr. Hooper, and that you have decided to explain the black veil to the congregation. In a paragraph or two try to convince your parishioners that they need not fear you and your veil.

Patterns (page 446)

Lowell ends the poem with the question "What are patterns for?" Answer this question in an essay which includes the advantages and disadvantages of "patterns."

The Tropics in New York

CLAUDE McKAY

Bananas ripe and green, and ginger-root,
  Cocoa in pods and alligator pears,
And tangerines and mangoes and grape fruit,
  Fit for the highest prize at parish fairs,

Set in the window, bringing memories   5
  Of fruit-trees laden by low-singing rills,
And dewy dawns, and mystical blue skies
  In benediction over nun-like hills.

My eyes grew dim, and I could no more gaze;
  A wave of longing through my body swept,   10
And, hungry for the old, familiar ways,
  I turned aside and bowed my head and wept.

To a Young Girl
Leaving the Hill Country

ARNA BONTEMPS

The hills are wroth; the stones have scored you bitterly
because you looked upon the naked sun
oblivious of them, because you did not see
the trees you touched or mountains that you walked upon.

But there will come a day of darkness in the land,   5
a day wherein remembered sun alone comes through
to mark the hills; then perhaps you'll understand
just how it was you drew from them and they from you.

For there will be a bent old woman in that day
who, feeling something of this country in her bones,   10
will leave her house tapping with a stick, who will (they say)
come back to seek the girl she was in these familiar stones.

DISCUSSION

Both of these poems deal with the relationship between a
person and the land of her or his youth. How is that relationship the same in each poem? How is it different?

The Tall Men

WILLIAM FAULKNER

They passed the dark bulk of the cotton gin. Then they saw the lamplit house and the other car, the doctor's coupé, just stopping at the gate, and they could hear the hound baying.

"Here we are," the old deputy marshal said.

"What's that other car?" the younger man said, the stranger, the state draft investigator.

"Doctor Schofield's," the marshal said. "Lee McCallum asked me to send him out when I telephoned we were coming."

"You mean you warned them?" the investigator said. "You telephoned ahead that I was coming out with a warrant for these two evaders? Is this how you carry out the orders of the United States Government?"

The marshal was a lean, clean old man who chewed tobacco, who had been born and lived in the county all his life.

"I understood all you wanted was to arrest these two McCallum boys and bring them back to town," he said.

"It was!" the investigator said. "And now you have warned them, given them a chance to run. Possibly put the Government to the expense of hunting them down with troops. Have you forgotten that you are under a bond yourself?"

"I ain't forgot it," the marshal said. "And ever since we left Jefferson I been trying to tell you something for you not to forget. But I reckon it will take these McCallums to impress that on you. . . . Pull in behind the other car. We'll try to find out first just how sick whoever it is that is sick is."

The investigator drew up behind the other car and switched off and blacked out his lights. "These people," he said. Then he thought, *But this doddering, tobacco-chewing old man is one of them, too, despite the honor and pride of his office, which should have made him different.* So he didn't speak it aloud, removing the keys and getting out of the car, and then locking the car itself, rolling the windows up first, thinking, *These people who lie about and conceal the ownership of land and property in order to hold relief jobs which they have no intention of performing, standing on their constitutional rights against having to work, who jeopardize the very job itself through petty and transparent subterfuge to acquire a free mattress which they intend to attempt to sell; who would relinquish even the job, if by so doing they could receive free food and a place, any rathole, in town to sleep in; who, as farmers, make false statements to get seed loans*

which they will later misuse, and then react in loud vituperative outrage and aston-
ishment when caught at it. And then, when at long last a suffering and threatened
Government asks one thing of them in return, one thing simply, which is to put their
names down on a selective-service list, they refuse to do it.

The old marshal had gone on. The investigator followed, through a
stout paintless gate in a picket fence, up a broad brick walk between two
rows of old shabby cedars, toward the rambling and likewise paintless
sprawl of the two-story house in the open hall of which the soft lamplight glowed and the lower story of which, as the investigator now perceived, was of logs.

He saw a hall full of soft lamplight beyond a stout paintless gallery
running across the log front, from beneath which the same dog which
they had heard, a big hound, came booming again, to stand four-square
facing them in the walk, bellowing, until a man's voice spoke to it from
the house. He followed the marshal up the steps onto the gallery. Then
he saw the man standing in the door, waiting for them to approach—a
man of about forty-five, not tall, but blocky, with a brown, still face and
horseman's hands, who looked at him once, brief and hard, and then no
more, speaking to the marshal, "Howdy, Mr. Gombault. Come in."

"Howdy, Rafe," the marshal said. "Who's sick?"

"Buddy," the other said. "Slipped and caught his leg in the hammer
mill this afternoon."

"Is it bad?" the marshal said.

"It looks bad to me," the other said. "That's why we sent for the
doctor instead of bringing him in to town. We couldn't get the bleeding
stopped."

"I'm sorry to hear that," the marshal said. "This is Mr. Pearson."
Once more the investigator found the other looking at him, the brown
eyes still, courteous enough in the brown face, the hand he offered hard
enough, but the clasp quite limp, quite cold. The marshal was still speaking. "From Jackson. From the draft board." Then he said, and the investigator could discern no change whatever in his tone: "He's got a warrant
for the boys."

The investigator could discern no change whatever anywhere. The
limp hard hand merely withdrew from his, the still face now looking at
the marshal. "You mean we have declared war?"

"No," the marshal said.

"That's not the question, Mr. McCallum," the investigator said. "All
required of them was to register. Their numbers might not even be
drawn this time; under the law of averages, they probably would not be.
But they refused—failed, anyway—to register."

"I see," the other said. He was not looking at the investigator. The investigator couldn't tell certainly if he was even looking at the marshal, although he spoke to him, "You want to see Buddy? The doctor's with him now."

"Wait," the investigator said. "I'm sorry about your brother's accident, but I——" The marshal glanced back at him for a moment, his shaggy gray brows beetling, with something at once courteous yet a little impatient about the glance, so that during the instant the investigator sensed from the old marshal the same quality which had been in the other's brief look. The investigator was a man of better than average intelligence; he was already becoming aware of something a little different here from what he had expected. But he had been in relief work in the state several years, dealing almost exclusively with country people, so he still believed he knew them. So he looked at the old marshal, thinking, *Yes. The same sort of people, despite the office, the authority and responsibility which should have changed him.* Thinking again, *These people. These people.* "I intend to take the night train back to Jackson," he said. "My reservation is already made. Serve the warrant and we will——"

"Come along," the old marshal said. "We are going to have plenty of time."

So he followed—there was nothing else to do—fuming and seething, attempting in the short length of the hall to regain control of himself in order to control the situation, because he realized now that if the situation were controlled, it would devolve upon him to control it; that if their departure with their prisoners were expedited, it must be himself and not the old marshal who would expedite it. He had been right. The doddering old officer was not only at bottom one of these people, he had apparently been corrupted anew to his old, inherent, shiftless sloth and unreliability merely by entering the house. So he followed in turn, down the hall and into a bedroom; whereupon he looked about him not only with amazement but with something very like terror. The room was a big room, with a bare unpainted floor, and besides the bed, it contained only a chair or two and one other piece of old-fashioned furniture. Yet to the investigator it seemed so filled with tremendous men cast in the same mold as the man who had met them that the very walls themselves must bulge. Yet they were not big, not tall, and it was not vitality, exuberance, because they made no sound, merely looking quietly at him where he stood in the door, with faces bearing an almost identical stamp of kinship—a thin, almost frail old man of about seventy, slightly taller than the others; a second one, white-haired, too, but otherwise identical with the man who had met them at the door; a third one about the same age as the man who had met them, but with something delicate in his face and something tragic and dark and wild in the same dark eyes; the two

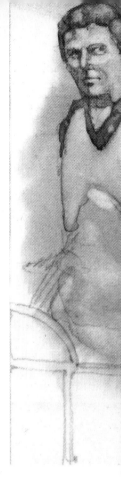

absolutely identical blue-eyed youths; and lastly the blue-eyed man on
the bed over which the doctor, who might have been any city doctor, in
his neat city suit, leaned—all of them turning to look quietly at him and
the marshal as they entered. And he saw, past the doctor, the slit trousers
of the man on the bed and the exposed, bloody, mangled leg, and he
turned sick, stopping just inside the door under that quiet, steady regard
while the marshal went up to the man who lay on the bed, smoking a
cob pipe, a big, old-fashioned, wicker-covered demijohn, such as the investigator's grandfather had kept whisky in, on the table beside him.

"Well, Buddy," the marshal said, "this is bad."

"Ah, it was my own fault," the man on the bed said. "Stuart kept
warning me about that frame I was using."

"That's correct," the second old one said.

Still the others said nothing. They just looked steadily and quietly at
the investigator until the marshal turned slightly and said, "This is Mr.
Pearson. From Jackson. He's got a warrant for the boys."

Then the man on the bed said, "What for?"

"That draft business, Buddy," the marshal said.

"We're not at war now," the man on the bed said.

"No," the marshal said, "It's that new law. They didn't register."

"What are you going to do with them?"

"It's a warrant, Buddy. Swore out."

"That means jail."

"It's a warrant," the old marshal said. Then the investigator saw that the man on the bed was watching him, puffing steadily at the pipe.

"Pour me some whisky, Jackson," he said.

"No," the doctor said. "He's had too much already."

"Pour me some whisky, Jackson," the man on the bed said. He puffed steadily at the pipe, looking at the investigator. "You come from the Government?" he said.

"Yes," the investigator said. "They should have registered. That's all required of them yet. They did not——" His voice ceased, while the seven pairs of eyes contemplated him, and the man on the bed puffed steadily.

"We would have still been here," the man on the bed said. "We wasn't going to run." He turned his head. The two youths were standing side by side at the foot of the bed. "Anse, Lucius," he said.

To the investigator it sounded as if they answered as one, "Yes, father."

"This gentleman has come all the way from Jackson to say the Government is ready for you. I reckon the quickest place to enlist will be Memphis. Go upstairs and pack."

The investigator started, moved forward. "Wait!" he cried.

But Jackson, the eldest, had forestalled him. He said, "Wait," also, and now they were not looking at the investigator. They were looking at the doctor.

"What about his leg?" Jackson said.

"Look at it," the doctor said. "He almost amputated it himself. It won't wait. And he can't be moved now. I'll need my nurse to help me, and some ether, provided he hasn't had too much whisky to stand the anesthetic too. One of you can drive to town in my car. I'll telephone——"

"Ether?" the man on the bed said. "What for? You just said yourself it's pretty near off now. I could whet up one of Jackson's butcher knives and finish it myself, with another drink or two. Go on. Finish it."

"You couldn't stand any more shock," the doctor said. "This is whisky talking now."

"Shucks," the other said. "One day in France we was running through a wheat field and I saw the machine gun, coming across the wheat, and I tried to jump it like you would jump a fence rail somebody was swinging at your middle, only I never made it. And I was on the ground then, and along toward dark that begun to hurt, only about that time something went whang on the back of my helmet, like when you hit a anvil, so I never knowed nothing else until I woke up. There was a heap of us racked up along a bank outside a field dressing station, only it took a long time for the doctor to get around to all of us, and by that time it was hurting bad. This here ain't hurt none to speak of since I got a-holt of this johnny-jug. You go on and finish it. If it's help you need, Stuart and Rafe will help you. . . . Pour me a drink, Jackson."

This time the doctor raised the demijohn and examined the level of the liquor. "There's a good quart gone," he said. "If you've drunk a quart of whisky since four o'clock, I doubt if you could stand the anesthetic. Do you think you could stand it if I finished it now?"

"Yes, finish it. I've ruined it; I want to get shut of it."

The doctor looked about at the others, at the still, identical faces watching him. "If I had him in town, in the hospital, with a nurse to watch him, I'd probably wait until he got over this first shock and got the whisky out of his system. But he can't be moved now, and I can't stop the bleeding like this, and even if I had ether or a local anesthetic——"

"Shucks," the man on the bed said. "God never made no better local nor general comfort or anesthetic neither than what's in this johnny-jug. And this ain't Jackson's leg nor Stuart's nor Rafe's nor Lee's. It's mine. I done started it; I reckon I can finish cutting it off any way I want to."

But the doctor was still looking at Jackson. "Well, Mr. McCallum?" he said. "You're the oldest."

But it was Stuart who answered. "Yes," he said. "Finish it. What do you want? Hot water, I reckon."

"Yes," the doctor said. "Some clean sheets. Have you got a big table you can move in here?"

"The kitchen table," the man who had met them at the door said. "Me and the boys——"

"Wait," the man on the bed said. "The boys won't have time to help you." He looked at them again. "Anse, Lucius," he said.

Again it seemed to the investigator that they answered as one. "Yes, father."

"This gentleman yonder is beginning to look impatient. You better start. Come to think of it, you won't need to pack. You will have uniforms in a day or two. Take the truck. There won't be nobody to drive you to Memphis and bring the truck back, so you can leave it at the Gayoso Feed Company until we can send for it. I'd like for you to enlist into the old Sixth Infantry, where I used to be. But I reckon that's too much to hope, and you'll just have to chance where they send you. But it likely won't matter, once you are in. The Government done right by me in my day, and it will do right by you. You just enlist wherever they want to send you, need you, and obey your sergeants and officers until you find out how to be soldiers. Obey them, but remember your name and don't take nothing from no man. You can go now."

"Wait!" the investigator cried again; again he started, moved forward into the center of the room. "I protest this! I'm sorry about Mr. McCallum's accident. I'm sorry about the whole business. But it's out of my hands and out of his hands now. This charge, failure to register according to law, has been made and the warrant issued. It cannot be evaded this way. The course of the action must be completed before any other step can be taken. They should have thought of this when these boys failed to register. If Mr. Gombault refuses to serve this warrant, I will serve it myself and take these men back to Jefferson with me to answer this charge as made. And I must warn Mr. Gombault that he will be cited for contempt!"

The old marshal turned, his shaggy eyebrows beetling again, speaking down to the investigator as if he were a child, "Ain't you found out yet that me or you neither ain't going nowhere for a while?"

"What?" the investigator cried. He looked about at the grave faces once more contemplating him with that remote and speculative regard. "Am I being threatened?" he cried.

"Ain't anybody paying any attention to you at all," the marshal said. "Now you just be quiet for a while, and you will be all right, and after a while we can go back to town."

So he stopped again and stood while the grave, contemplative faces freed him once more of that impersonal and unbearable regard, and saw the two youths approach the bed and bend down in turn and kiss their father on the mouth, and then turn as one and leave the room, passing him without even looking at him. And sitting in the lamplit hall beside the old marshal, the bedroom door closed now, he heard the truck start up and back and turn and go down the road, the sound of it dying away, ceasing, leaving the still, hot night—the Mississippi Indian summer, which had already outlasted half of November—filled with the loud last shrilling of the summer's cicadas, as though they, too, were aware of the imminent season of cold weather and of death.

"I remember old Anse," the marshal said pleasantly, chattily, in that tone in which an adult addresses a strange child. "He's been dead fifteen-sixteen years now. He was about sixteen when the old war broke out, and he walked all the way to Virginia to get into it. He could have enlisted and fought right here at home, but his ma was a Carter, so wouldn't nothing do him but to go all the way back to Virginia to do his fighting, even though he hadn't never seen Virginia before himself; walked all the way back to a land he hadn't never even seen before and enlisted in Stonewall Jackson's army and stayed in it all through the Valley, and right up to Chancellorsville, where them Carolina boys shot Jackson by mistake, and right on up to that morning in 'Sixty-five when Sheridan's cavalry blocked the road from Appomattox to the Valley, where they might have got away again. And he walked back to Mississippi with just about what he had carried away with him when he left, and he got married and built the first story of this house—this here log story we're in right now—and started getting them boys—Jackson and Stuart and Raphael and Lee and Buddy.

"Buddy come along late, late enough to be in the other war, in France in it. You heard him in there. He brought back two medals, an American medal and a French one, and no man knows till yet how he got them, just what he done. I don't believe he even told Jackson and Stuart and them. He hadn't hardly got back home, with them numbers on his uniform and the wound stripes and them two medals, before he had found him a girl, found her right off, and a year later them twin boys was born, the livin', spittin' image of old Anse McCallum. If old Anse had just been about seventy-five years younger, the three of them might have been thriblets. I remember them—two little critters exactly alike, and wild as spikehorn bucks, running around here day and night both with a pack of coon dogs until they got big enough to help Buddy and Stuart and Lee with the farm and the gin, and Rafe with the horses and mules, when he would breed and raise and train them and take them to Memphis to sell, right on up to three, four years back, when they went to the agricultural college for a year to learn more about whiteface cattle.

"That was after Buddy and them had quit raising cotton. I remember that too. It was when the Government first begun to interfere with how a man farmed his own land, raised his cotton. Stabilizing the price, using up the surplus, they called it, giving a man advice and help, whether he wanted it or not. You may have noticed them boys in yonder tonight; curious folks almost, you might call them. That first year, when county agents was trying to explain the new system to farmers, the agent come out here and tried to explain it to Buddy and Lee and Stuart, explaining how they would cut down the crop, but that the Government would pay farmers the difference, and so they would actually be better off than trying to farm by themselves.

" 'Why, we're much obliged,' Buddy says. 'But we don't need no help. We'll just make the cotton like we always done; if we can't make a crop of it, that will just be our lookout and our loss, and we'll try again.

"So they wouldn't sign no papers nor no cards nor nothing. They just went on and made the cotton like old Anse had taught them to; it was like they just couldn't believe that the Government aimed to help a man whether he wanted help or not, aimed to interfere with how much of anything he could make by hard work on his own land, making the crop and ginning it right here in their own gin, like they had always done, and hauling it to town to sell, hauling it all the way into Jefferson before they found out they couldn't sell it because, in the first place, they had made too much of it and, in the second place, they never had no card to sell what they would have been allowed. So they hauled it back. The gin wouldn't hold all of it, so they put some of it under Rafe's mule shed and they put the rest of it right here in the hall where we are setting now, where they would have to walk around it all winter and keep themselves reminded to be sho and fill out that card next time.

"Only next year they didn't fill out no papers neither. It was like they still couldn't believe it, still believed in the freedom and liberty to make or break according to a man's fitness and will to work, guaranteed by the Government that old Anse had tried to tear in two once and failed, and admitted in good faith he had failed and taken the consequences, and that had give Buddy a medal and taken care of him when he was far away from home in a strange land and hurt.

"So they made their second crop. And they couldn't sell it to nobody neither because they never had no cards. This time they built a special shed to put it under, and I remember how in that second winter Buddy come to town one day to see Lawyer Gavin Stevens. Not for legal advice how to sue the Government or somebody into buying the cotton, even if they never had no card for it, but just to find out why. 'I was for going ahead and signing up for it,' Buddy says. 'If that's going to be the new rule. But we talked it over, and Jackson ain't no farmer, but he knowed father longer than the rest of us, and he said father would have said no, and I reckon now he would have been right.'

"So they didn't raise any more cotton; they had a plenty of it to last a while—twenty-two bales, I think it was. That was when they went into whiteface cattle, putting old Anse's cotton land into pasture, because that's what he would have wanted them to do if the only way they could raise cotton was by the Government telling them how much they could raise and how much they could sell it for, and where, and when, and then pay them for not doing the work they didn't do. Only even when they didn't raise cotton, every year the county agent's young fellow would come out to measure the pasture crops they planted so he could pay them for that, even if they never had no not-cotton to be paid for. Except that he never measured no crop on this place. 'You're welcome to look at what we are doing,' Buddy says. 'But don't draw it down on your map.'

" 'But you can get money for this,' the young fellow says. 'The Government wants to pay you for planting all this.'

" 'We are aiming to get money for it,' Buddy says. 'When we can't we will try something else. But not from the Government. Give that to them that want to take it. We can make out.'

"And that's about all. Them twenty-two bales of orphan cotton are down yonder in the gin right now, because there's room for it in the gin now because they ain't using the gin no more. And them boys grew up and went off a year to the agricultural college to learn right about white-face cattle, and then come back to the rest of them—these here curious folks living off here to themselves, with the rest of the world all full of pretty neon lights burning night and day both, and easy, quick money scattering itself around everywhere for any man to grab a little, and every man with a shiny new automobile already wore out and throwed away and the new one delivered before the first one was even paid for, and everywhere a fine loud grabble and snatch of AAA and WPA[1] and a dozen other three-letter reasons for a man not to work. Then this here draft comes along, and these curious folks ain't got around to signing that neither, and you come all the way from Jackson with your paper all signed and regular, and we come out here, and after a while we can go back to town. A man gets around, don't he?"

"Yes," the investigator said. "Do you suppose we can go back to town now?"

"No," the marshal told him in that same kindly tone, "not just yet. But we can leave after a while. Of course you will miss your train. But there will be another one tomorrow."

He rose, though the investigator had heard nothing. The investigator watched him go down the hall and open the bedroom door and enter and close it behind him. The investigator sat quietly, listening to the night sounds and looking at the closed door until it opened presently and the marshal came back, carrying something in a bloody sheet, carrying it gingerly.

"Here," he said. "Hold it a minute."

"It's bloody," the investigator said.

"That's all right," the marshal said. "We can wash when we get through." So the investigator took the bundle and stood holding it while he watched the old marshal go back down the hall and on through it and

---

[1] *AAA, WPA:* The Agricultural Adjustment Association and the Works Project Administration were agencies created during the Depression to provide jobs and relief for farmers and workers.

vanish and return presently with a lighted lantern and a shovel. "Come along," he said. "We're pretty near through now."

The investigator followed him out of the house and across the yard, carrying gingerly the bloody, shattered, heavy bundle in which it still seemed to him he could feel some warmth of life, the marshal striding on ahead, the lantern swinging against his leg, the shadow of his striding scissoring and enormous along the earth, his voice still coming back over his shoulder, chatty and cheerful, "Yes, sir. A man gets around and sees a heap; a heap of folks in a heap of situations. The trouble is, we done got into the habit of confusing the situations with the folks. Take yourself, now," he said in that same kindly tone, chatty and easy; "you mean all right. You just went and got yourself all fogged up with rules and regulations. That's our trouble. We done invented ourselves so many alphabets and rules and recipes that we can't see anything else; if what we see can't be fitted to an alphabet or a rule, we are lost. We have come to be like critters doctor folks might have created in laboratories, that have learned how to slip off their bones and guts and still live, still be kept alive indefinite and forever maybe even without even knowing the bones and the guts are gone. We have slipped our backbone; we have about decided a man don't need a backbone any more; to have one is old-fashioned. But the groove where the backbone used to be is still there, and the backbone has been kept alive, too, and someday we're going to slip back onto it. I don't know just when nor just how much of a wrench it will take to teach us, but someday."

They had left the yard now. They were mounting a slope; ahead of them the investigator could see another clump of cedars, a small clump, somehow shaggily formal against the starred sky. The marshal entered it and stopped and set the lantern down and, following with the bundle, the investigator saw a small rectangle of earth enclosed by a low brick coping. Then he saw the two graves, or the headstones—two plain granite slabs set upright in the earth.

"Old Anse and Mrs. Anse," the marshal said. "Buddy's wife wanted to be buried with her folks. I reckon she would have been right lonesome up here with just McCallums. Now, let's see." He stood for a moment, his chin in his hand; to the investigator he looked exactly like an old lady trying to decide where to set out a shrub. "They was to run from left to right, beginning with Jackson. But after the boys was born, Jackson and Stuart was to come up here by their pa and ma, so Buddy could move up some and make room. So he will be about here." He moved the lantern nearer and took up the shovel. Then he saw the investigator still holding the bundle. "Set it down," he said "I got to dig first."

"I'll hold it," the investigator said.

"Nonsense, put it down," the marshal said. "Buddy won't mind."

So the investigator put the bundle down on the brick coping and the marshal began to dig, skillfully and rapidly, still talking in that cheerful, interminable voice, "Yes, sir. We done forget about folks. Life has done got cheap, and life ain't cheap. Life's a pretty durn valuable thing. I don't mean just getting along from one WPA relief check to the next one, but honor and pride and discipline that make a man worth preserving, make him of any value. That's what we got to learn again. Maybe it takes trouble, bad trouble, to teach it back to us; maybe it was the walking to Virginia because that's where his ma come from, and losing a war and then walking back, that taught it to old Anse. Anyway, he seems to learned it, and to learned it good enough to bequeath it to his boys. Did you notice how all Buddy had to do was to tell them boys of his it was time to go, because the Government had sent them word? And how they told him good-bye? Growned men kissing one another without hiding and without shame. Maybe that's what I am trying to say. . . . There," he said. "That's big enough."

He moved quickly, easily; before the investigator could stir, he had lifted the bundle into the narrow trench and was covering it, covering it as rapidly as he had dug, smoothing the earth over it with the shovel. Then he stood up and raised the lantern—a tall, lean old man, breathing easily and lightly.

"I reckon we can go back to town now," he said.

DISCUSSION

1. The old marshal says to the investigator, "You . . . got yourself all fogged up with rules and regulations," and the basic conflict in the story comes from differing attitudes toward rules and regulations. How would you describe the McCallums' attitude toward government rules and regulations? What is the attitude of the investigator? Of the marshal?

2. Discuss the significance of Buddy's instructions to his sons: "Obey them, but remember your name and don't take nothing from no man." How do these instructions reflect the basic beliefs of the McCallum family?'

3. What impressions does the investigator have about "these people"? How has he gained these impressions? The marshal says, "We done got into the habit of confusing situations with the folks." Is this what has happened to the investigator? Explain. Are there any indications that his attitude changes?

4. The McCallums were "not big, not tall." How, then, do you explain the title of the story?

For further activities, see page 490.

A Work of Artifice

MARGE PIERCY

The bonsai tree
in the attractive pot
could have grown eighty feet tall
on the side of a mountain
till split by lightning.   5
But a gardener
carefully pruned it.
It is nine inches high.
Every day as he
whittles back the branches   10
the gardener croons,
It is your nature
to be small and cozy,
domestic and weak;
how lucky, little tree,   15
to have a pot to grow in.
With living creatures
one must begin very early
to dwarf their growth:
the bound feet,   20
the crippled brain,
the hair in curlers,
the hands you
love to touch.

DISCUSSION

1. This poem is an extended *metaphor* (see page 287). It compares a bonsai tree to a woman whose growth as a person has been restricted. What is the attitude of this gardener toward his bonsai tree, and how is that attitude similar to an attitude taken toward women? Who or what might the gardener be who "dwarfs" the growth of "living creatures"?

2. Look at the four images in lines 20–24. How does each image represent stunted growth for a woman?

For further activities, see page 490.

Turning

LUCILLE CLIFTON

turning into my own
turning on in
to my own self
at last
turning out of the   5
white cage, turning out of the
lady cage
turning at last
on a stem like a black fruit
in my own season   10
at last

THE DEVIL AND DANIEL WEBSTER

STEPHEN VINCENT BENÉT

It's a story they tell in the border country, where Massachusetts joins Vermont and New Hampshire.

Yes, Dan'l Webster's dead—or at least they buried him. But every time there's a thunderstorm around Marshfield, they say you can hear his rolling voice in the hollows of the sky. And they say that if you go to his grave and speak loud and clear, "Dan'l Webster—Dan'l Webster!" the ground'll begin to shiver and the trees begin to shake. And after a while you'll hear a deep voice saying, "Neighbor, how stands the Union?" Then you'd better answer the Union stands as she stood, rock-bottomed and copper-sheathed, one and indivisible, or he's liable to rear right out of the ground. At least, that's what I was told when I was a youngster.

You see, for a while, he was the biggest man in the country. He never got to be President, but he was the biggest man. There were thousands that trusted in him right next to God Almighty, and they told stories about him that were like the stories of patriarchs and such. They said,

when he stood up to speak, stars and stripes came right out in the sky, and once he spoke against a river and made it sink into the ground. They said, when he walked the woods with his fishing rod, Killall, the trout would jump out of the streams right into his pockets, for they knew it was no use putting up a fight against him; and, when he argued a case, he could turn on the harps of the blessed and the shaking of the earth underground. That was the kind of man he was, and his big farm up at Marshfield was suitable to him. The chickens he raised were all white meat down through the drumsticks, the cows were tended like children, and the big ram he called Goliath had horns with a curl like a morning-glory vine and could butt through an iron door. But Dan'l wasn't one of your gentlemen farmers, he knew all the ways of the land, and he'd be up by candlelight to see that the chores got done. A man with a mouth like a mastiff, a brow like a mountain, and eyes like burning anthracite—that was Dan'l Webster in his prime. And the biggest case he argued never got written down in the books, for he argued it against the devil, nip and tuck and no holds barred. And this is the way I used to hear it told.

There was a man named Jabez Stone, lived at Cross Corners, New Hampshire. He wasn't a bad man to start with, but he was an unlucky man. If he planted corn, he got borers; if he planted potatoes, he got blight. He had good-enough land, but it didn't prosper him; he had a decent wife and children, but the more children he had, the less there was to feed them. If stones cropped up in his neighbor's field, boulders boiled up in his; if he had a horse with the spavins, he'd trade it for one with the staggers and give something extra. There's some folks bound to be like that, apparently. But one day Jabez Stone got sick of the whole business.

He'd been plowing that morning, and he'd just broke the plowshare on a rock that he could have sworn hadn't been there yesterday. And, as he stood looking at the plowshare, the off horse began to cough—that ropy kind of cough that means sickness and horse doctors. There were two children down with the measles, his wife was ailing, and he had a whitlow on his thumb. It was about the last straw for Jabez Stone. "I vow," he said, and he looked around him kind of desperate—"I vow it's enough to make a man want to sell his soul to the devil! And I would, too, for two cents!"

Then he felt a kind of queerness come over him at having said what he'd said; though, naturally, being a New Hampshireman, he wouldn't take it back. But, all the same, when it got to be evening and, as far as he could see, no notice had been taken, he felt relieved in his mind, for he was a religious man. But notice is always taken, sooner or later, just like the Good Book says. And, sure enough, next day, about suppertime, a soft-spoken, dark-dressed stranger drove up in a handsome buggy and asked for Jabez Stone.

Well, Jabez told his family it was a lawyer, come to see him about a legacy. But he knew who it was. He didn't like the looks of the stranger, nor the way he smiled with his teeth. They were white teeth, and plentiful—some say they were filed to a point, but I wouldn't vouch for that. And he didn't like it when the dog took one look at the stranger and ran away howling, with his tail between his legs. But having passed his word, more or less, he stuck to it, and they went out behind the barn and made their bargain. Jabez Stone had to prick his finger to sign, and the stranger lent him a silver pin. The wound healed clean, but it left a little white scar.

After that, all of a sudden, things began to pick up and prosper for Jabez Stone. His cows got fat and his horses sleek, his crops were the envy of the neighborhood, and lightning might strike all over the valley, but it wouldn't strike his barn. Pretty soon, he was one of the prosperous people of the county; they asked him to stand for selectman, and he stood for it; there began to be talk of running him for state senate. All in all, you might say the Stone family was as happy and contented as cats in a dairy. And so they were except for Jabez Stone.

He'd been contented enough, the first few years. It's a great thing when bad luck turns; it drives most other things out of your head. True, every now and then, esepcially in rainy weather, the little white scar on his finger would give him a twinge. And once a year, punctual as clockwork, the stranger with the handsome buggy would come driving by. But the sixth year, the stranger lighted, and, after that, his peace was over for Jabez Stone.

The stranger came up through the lower field, switching his boots with a cane—they were handsome black boots, but Jabez Stone never liked the look of them, particularly the toes. And after he'd passed the time of day, he said, "Well, Mr. Stone, you're a hummer! It's a very pretty property you've got here, Mr. Stone."

"Well, some might favor it and others might not," said Jabez Stone, for he was a New Hampshireman.

"Oh, no need to decry your industry!" said the stranger, very easy, showing his teeth in a smile. "After all, we know what's been done, and it's been according to specifications. So when— ahem—the mortgage falls due next year, you shouldn't have any regrets."

"Speaking of that mortgage, mister," said Jabez Stone, and he looked around for help to the earth and sky, "I'm beginning to have one or two doubts about it."

"Doubts?" said the stranger, not quite so pleasantly.

"Why, yes," said Jabez Stone. "This being the U.S.A. and me having always been a religious man." He cleared his throat and got bolder. "Yes, sir," he said, "I'm beginning to have considerable doubts as to that mortgage holding in court."

"There's courts and courts," said the stranger, clicking his teeth. "Still, we might as well have a look at the original document," And he hauled out a big black pocketbook, full of papers. "Sherwin, Slater, Stevens, Stone," he muttered. "I, Jabez Stone, for a term of seven years——Oh, it's quite in order, I think."

But Jabez Stone wasn't listening, for he saw something else flutter out of the black pocketbook. It was something that looked like a moth, but it wasn't a moth. And as Jabez Stone stared at it, it seemed to speak to him in a small sort of piping voice, terrible small and thin, but terrible human. "Neighbor Stone!" it squeaked. "Neighbor Stone! Help Me! For God's sake, help me!"

But before Jabez Stone could stir hand or foot, the stranger whipped out a big bandanna handkerchief, caught the creature in it, just like a butterfly, and started tying up the ends of the bandanna.

"Sorry for the interruption," he said, "As I was saying——"

But Jabez Stone was shaking all over like a scared horse.

"That's Miser Stevens' voice!" he said, in a croak. "And you've got him in your handkerchief!"

The stranger looked a little embarrassed.

"Yes, I really should have transferred him to the collecting box," he said with a simper, "but there were some rather unusual specimens there and I didn't want them crowded. Well, well, these little contretemps[1] will occur."

"I don't know what you mean by contertan," said Jabez Stone, "but that

---

[1] *contretemps:* embarrassing accidents.

was Miser Stevens' voice! And he ain't dead! You can't tell me he is! He was just as spry and mean as a woodchuck, Tuesday!"

"In the midst of life——" said the stranger, kind of pious. "Listen!" Then a bell began to toll in the valley and Jabez Stone listened, with the sweat running down his face. For he knew it was tolled for Miser Stevens and that he was dead.

"These long-standing accounts," said the stranger with a sigh; "one really hates to close them. But business is business."

He still had the bandanna in his hand, and Jabez Stone felt sick as he saw the cloth struggle and flutter.

"Are they all as small as that?" he asked hoarsely.

"Small?" said the stranger. "Oh, I see what you mean. Why, they vary." He measured Jabez Stone with his eyes, and his teeth showed. "Don't worry, Mr. Stone," he said. "You'll go with a very good grade. I wouldn't trust you outside the collecting box. Now, a man like Dan'l Webster, of course,—well, we'd have to build a special box for him, and even at that, I imagine the wing spread would astonish you. But, in your case, as I was saying——"

"Put that handkerchief away!" said Jabez Stone, and he began to beg and to pray. But the best he could get at the end was a three years' extension, with conditions.

But till you make a bargain like that, you've got no idea of how fast four years can run. By the last months of those years, Jabez Stone's known all over the state and there's talk of running him for governor—and it's dust and ashes in his mouth. For every day, when he gets up, he thinks, "There's one more night gone," and every night when he lies down, he thinks of the black pocketbook and the soul of Miser Stevens, and it makes him sick at heart. Till, finally, he can't bear it any longer, and, in the last days of the last year, he hitches up his horse and drives off to seek Dan'l Webster. For Dan'l was born in New Hampshire, only a few miles from Cross Corners, and it's well known that he has a particular soft spot for old neighbors.

It was early in the morning when he got to Marshfield, but Dan'l was up already, talking Latin to the farm hands and wrestling with the ram, Goliath, and trying out a new trotter, and working up speeches to make against John C. Calhoun. But when he heard a New Hampshireman had come to see him, he dropped everything else he was doing, for that was Dan'l's way. He gave Jabez Stone a breakfast that five men couldn't eat, went into the living history of every man and woman in Cross Corners, and finally asked him how he could serve him.

Jabez Stone allowed that it was a kind of mortgage case.

"Well, I haven't pleaded a mortgage case in a long time, and I don't generally plead now, except before the Supreme Court," said Dan'l, "but if I can, I'll help you."

"Then I've got hope for the first time in ten years," said Jabez Stone, and told him the details.

Dan'l walked up and down as he listened, hands behind his back, now and then asking a question, now and then plunging his eyes at the floor, as if they'd bore through it like gimlets. When Jabez

Stone had finished, Dan'l puffed out his cheeks and blew. Then he turned to Jabez Stone and a smile broke over his face like the sunrise over Monadnock.

"You'll take it?" said Jabez Stone, hardly daring to believe.

"Yes," said Dan'l Webster, "I've got about seventy-five other things to do and the Missouri Compromise to straighten out, but I'll take your case. For if two New Hampshiremen aren't a match for the devil, we might as well give the country back to the Indians."

Then he shook Jabez Stone by the hand and said, "Did you come down here in a hurry?"

"Well, I admit I made time," said Jabez Stone.

"You'll go back faster," said Dan'l Webster, and he told 'em to hitch up Constitution and Constellation to the carriage. They were matched grays with one white forefoot, and they stepped like greased lightning.

Well, I won't describe how excited and pleased the whole Stone family was to have the great Dan'l Webster for a guest, when they finally got there. Jabez Stone had lost his hat on the way, blown off when they overtook a wind, but he didn't take much account of that. But after supper he sent the family off to bed, for he had most particular business with Mr. Webster. Mrs. Stone wanted them to sit in the front parlor, but Dan'l Webster knew front parlors and said he preferred the kitchen. So it was there they sat, waiting for the stranger, with a jug on the table between them and a bright fire on the hearth—the stranger being scheduled to show up on the stroke of midnight, according to specifications.

Well, most men wouldn't have asked for better company than Dan'l Webster and a jug. But with every tick of the clock Jabez Stone got sadder and sadder. His eyes roved round, and though he sampled the jug you could see he didn't taste it. Finally, on the stroke of 11:30 he reached over and grabbed Dan'l Webster by the arm.

"Mr. Webster, Mr. Webster!" he said, and his voice was shaking with fear and a desperate courage. "For God's sake, Mr. Webster, harness your horses and get away from this place while you can!"

"You've brought me a long way, neighbor, to tell me you don't like my company," said Dan'l Webster, quite peaceable, pulling at the jug.

"Miserable wretch that I am!" groaned Jabez Stone. "I've brought you a devilish way, and now I see my folly. Let him take me if he wills. I don't hanker after it, I must say, but I can stand it. But you're the Union's stay and New Hampshire's pride! He mustn't get you, Mr. Webster! He mustn't get you!"

Dan'l Webster looked at the distracted man, all gray and shaking in the firelight, and laid a hand on his shoulder.

"I'm obliged to you, Neighbor Stone," he said gently. "It's kindly thought of. But there's a jug on the table and a case in hand. And I never left a jug or a case half finished in my life."

And just at that moment there was a sharp rap on the door.

"Ah," said Dan'l Webster, very cooly, "I thought your clock was a trifle slow, Neighbor Stone." He stepped to the door and opened it. "Come in!" he said.

The stranger came in—very dark and tall he looked in the firelight. He was carrying a box under his arm—a black japanned box with little air holes in the lid. At the sight of the box, Jabez Stone gave a low cry and shrank into a corner of the room.

"Mr. Webster, I presume," said the stranger, very polite, but with his eyes glowing like a fox's deep in the woods.

"Attorney of record for Jabez Stone," said Dan'l Webster, but his eyes were glowing too. "Might I ask your name?"

"I've gone by a good many," said the stranger carelessly. "Perhaps Scratch will do for the evening. I'm often called that in these regions."

Then he sat down at the table and poured himself a drink from the jug. The liquor was cold in the jug, but it came steaming into the glass.

"And now," said the stranger, smiling and showing his teeth, "I shall call upon you, as a law-abiding citizen, to assist me in taking possession of my property."

Well, with that the argument began—and it went hot and heavy. At first Jabez Stone had a flicker of hope, but when he saw Dan'l Webster being forced back at point after point, he just scrunched in his corner, with his eyes on that japanned box. For there wasn't any doubt as to the deed or the signature— that was the worst of it. Dan'l Webster twisted and turned and thumped his fist on the table, but he couldn't get away from that. He offered to compromise the case; the stranger wouldn't hear of it. He pointed out the property had increased in value, and state senators ought to be

worth more; the stranger stuck to the letter of the law. He was a great lawyer, Dan'l Webster, but we know who's the King of Lawyers, as the Good Book tells us, and it seemed as if, for the first time, Dan'l Webster had met his match.

Finally the stranger yawned a little. "Your spirited efforts on behalf of your client do you credit, Mr. Webster," he said, "but if you have no more arguments to adduce, I'm rather pressed for time"— and Jabez Stone shuddered.

Dan'l Webster's brow looked dark as a thundercloud.

"Pressed or not, you shall not have this man!" he thundered. "Mr. Stone is an American citizen, and no American citizen may be forced into the service of a foreign prince. We fought England for that in '12 and we'll fight all hell for it again!"

"Foreign?" said the stranger. "And who calls me a foreigner?"

"Well, I never yet heard of the dev— of your claiming American citizenship," said Dan'l Webster with surprise.

"And who with better right?" said the stranger, with one of his terrible smiles. "When the first wrong was done to the first Indian, I was there. When the first slaver put out for the Congo, I stood on her deck. Am I not in your books and stories and beliefs, from the first settlements on? Am I not spoken of, still, in every church in New England? 'Tis true the North claims me for a Southerner and the South for a Northerner, but I am neither. I am merely an honest American like yourself—and of the best descent— for, to tell the truth, Mr. Webster, though I don't like to boast of it, my name is

older in this country than yours."

"Aha!" said Dan'l Webster, with the veins standing out in his forehead, "then I stand on the Constitution! I demand a trial for my client."

"The case is hardly one for an ordinary court," said the stranger, his eyes flickering. "And, indeed, the lateness of the hour——"

"Let it be any court you choose, so it is an American judge and an American jury!" said Dan'l Webster in his pride. "Let it be the quick or the dead; I'll abide the issue!"

"You have said it," said the stranger, and pointed his finger at the door. And with that, and all of a sudden, there was a rushing of wind outside and a noise of footsteps. They came, clear and distinct, through the night. And yet, they were not like the footsteps of living men.

"In God's name, who comes by so late?" cried Jabez Stone, in an ague of fear.

"The jury Mr. Webster demands," said the stranger, sipping at his boiling glass. "You must pardon the rough appearance of one or two; they will have come a long way."

And with that the fire burned blue· and the door blew open and twelve men entered, one by one.

If Jabez Stone had been sick with terror before, he was blind with terror now. For there was Walter Butler, the loyalist, who spread fire and horror through the Mohawk Valley in the times of the Revolution; and there was Simon Girty, the renegade, who saw white men burned at the stake and whooped with the Indians to see them burn. His eyes were green, like a catamount's, and the stains on his hunting shirt did not come from the blood of the deer. King Philip was there, wild and proud as he had been in life, with the great gash in his head that gave him his death wound, and cruel Governor Dale, who broke men on the wheel. There was Morton of Merry Mount, who so vexed the Plymouth Colony, with his flushed, loose, handsome face and his hate of the godly. There was Teach, the bloody pirate, with his black beard curling on his breast. The Reverend John Smeet, with his strangler's hands and his Geneva gown, walked as daintily as he had to the gallows. The red print of the rope was still around his neck, but he carried a perfumed handkerchief, in one hand. One and all, they came into the room with the fires of hell still upon them, and the stranger named their names and their deeds as they came, till the tale of twelve was told. Yet the stranger had told the truth—they had all played a part in America.

"Are you satisfied with the jury?" said the stranger mockingly, when they had taken their places.

The sweat stood upon Dan'l Webster's brow, but his voice was clear.

"Quite satisfied," he said. "Though I miss General Arnold from the company."

"Benedict Arnold is engaged upon other business," said the stranger, with a glower. "Ah, you asked for a justice, I believe."

He pointed his finger once more, and a tall man, soberly clad in Puritan garb, with the burning gaze of the fanatic, stalked into the room and took his judge's place.

"Justice Hathorne is a jurist of experience," said the stranger. "He presided at

certain witch trials held in Salem. There were others who repented of the business later, but not he."

"Repent of such notable wonders and undertakings?" said the stern old justice, "Nay, hang them—hang them all!" And he muttered to himself in a way that struck ice into the soul of Jabez Stone.

Then the trial began, and, as you might expect, it didn't look anyways good for the defense. And Jabez Stone didn't make much of a witness in his own behalf. He took one look at Simon Girty and screeched, and they had to put him back in his corner in a kind of swoon.

It didn't halt the trial, though; the trial went on, as trials do. Dan'l Webster had faced some hard juries and hanging judges in his time, but this was the hardest he'd ever faced, and he knew it. They sat there with a kind of glitter in their eyes, and the stranger's smooth voice went on and on. Every time he'd raise an objection, it'd be "Objection sustained," but whenever Dan'l objected, it'd be "Objection denied." Well, you couldn't expect fair play from a fellow like this Mr. Scratch.

It got to Dan'l in the end, and he began to heat, like iron in the forge. When he got up to speak he was going to flay that stranger with every trick known to the law, and the judge and jury, too. He didn't care if it was contempt of court or what would happen to him for it. He didn't care any more what happened to Jabez Stone. He just got madder and madder, thinking of what he'd say. And yet, curiously enough, the more he thought about it, the less he was able to arrange his speech in his mind.

Till, finally, it was time for him to

get up on his feet, and he did so, all ready to bust out with lightnings and denunciations. But before he started he looked over the judge and jury for a moment, such being his custom. And he noticed the glitter in their eyes was twice as strong as before, and they all leaned forward. Like hounds just before they get the fox, they looked, and the blue mist of evil in the room thickened as he watched them. Then he saw what he'd been about to do, and he wiped his forehead, as a man might who's just escaped falling into a pit in the dark.

For it was him they'd come for, not only Jabez Stone. He read it in the glitter of their eyes and in the way the stranger hid his mouth with one hand. And if he fought them with their own weapons, he'd fall into their power; he knew that, though he couldn't have told you how. It was his own anger and horror that burned in their eyes; and he'd have to wipe that out or the case was lost. He stood there for a moment, his black eyes burning like anthracite. And then he began to speak.

He started off in a low voice, though you could hear every word. They say he could call on the harps of the blessed when he chose. And this was just as simple and easy as a man could talk. But he didn't start out by condemning or reviling. He was talking about the things that make a country a country, and a man a man.

And he began with the simple things that everybody's known and felt—the freshness of a fine morning when you're young, and the taste of food when you're hungry, and the new day that's every day when you're a child. He took them up and he turned them in his hands. They were good things for any man. But without freedom, they sickened. And when he talked of those enslaved, and the sorrows of slavery, his voice got like a big bell. He talked of the early days of America and the men who had made those days. It wasn't a spread-eagle[2] speech, but he made you see it. He admitted all the wrong that had ever been done. But he showed how, out of the wrong and the right, the suffering and the starvations, something new had come. And everybody had played a part in it, even the traitors.

Then he turned to Jabez Stone and showed him as he was—an ordinary man who'd had hard luck and wanted to change it. And, because he'd wanted to change it, now he was going to be punished for all eternity. And yet there was good in Jabez Stone, and he showed that good. He was hard and mean, in some ways, but he was a man. There was sadness in being a man, but it was a proud thing too. And he showed what the pride of it was till you couldn't help feeling it. Yes, even in hell, if a man was a man, you'd know it. And he wasn't pleading for any one person any more, though his voice rang like an organ. He was telling the story and the failures and the endless journeys of mankind. They got tricked and trapped and bamboozled, but it was a great journey. And no demon that was ever foaled could know the inwardness of it—it took a man to do that.

The fire began to die on the hearth and the wind before morning to blow. The light was getting gray in the room when Dan'l Webster finished. And his words came back at the end to New Hampshire ground, and the one spot of land that each man loves and clings to. He painted a picture of that, and to each one of that jury he spoke of things long forgotten. For his voice could search the heart, and that was his gift and his strength. And to one, his voice was like the forest and its secret and to another like the sea and the storms of the sea; and one heard the cry of his lost nation in it, and another saw a little harmless scene he hadn't remembered for years. But each saw something. And when Dan'l Webster finished he didn't know whether or not he'd saved Jabez Stone. But he knew he'd done a miracle. For the glitter was gone from the eyes of judge and jury, and, for the moment, they were men again, and knew they were men.

"The defense rests," said Dan'l Webster, and stood there like a mountain. His ears were still ringing with his speech, and he didn't hear anything else till he heard Judge Hathorne say, "The jury will retire to consider its verdict."

Walter Butler rose in his place and his face had a dark, gay pride on it.

"The jury has considered its verdict," he said, and looked the stranger full in the eye. "We find for the defendant, Jabez Stone."

With that, the smile left the stranger's face, but Walter Butler did not flinch.

"Perhaps 'tis not strictly in accordance with the evidence," he said, "but even the damned may salute the eloquence of Mr. Webster."

With that, the long crow of a rooster split the gray morning sky, and judge and jury were gone from the room like a puff of smoke and as if they had never

---

[2] *spread-eagle:* elaborately exaggerated.

been there. The stranger turned to Dan'l Webster, smiling wryly.

"Major Butler was always a bold man," he said. "I had not thought him quite so bold. Nevertheless, my congratulations, as between two gentlemen."

"I'll have that paper first, if you please," said Dan'l Webster, and he took it and tore it into four pieces. It was queerly warm to the touch. "And now," he said, "I'll have you!" and his hand come down like a bear trap on the stranger's arm. For he knew that once you bested anybody like Mr. Scratch in fair fight, his power on you was gone. And he could see that Mr. Scratch knew it too.

The stranger twisted and wriggled, but he couldn't get out of that grip. "Come, come, Mr. Webster," he said, smiling palely. "This sort of thing is ridic—ouch!—is ridiculous. If you're worried about the costs of the case, naturally, I'd be glad to pay——"

"And so you shall!" said Dan'l Webster, shaking him till his teeth rattled. "For you'll sit right down at that table and draw up a document, promising never to bother Jabez Stone nor his heirs or assigns nor any other New Hampshireman till doomsday! For any hades we want to raise in this state, we can raise ourselves, without assistance from strangers."

"Ouch!" said the stranger. "Ouch! Well, they never did run very big to the barrel, but—ouch!—I agree!"

So he sat down and drew up the document. But Dan'l Webster kept his hand on his coat collar all the time.

"And, now, may I go?" said the stranger, quite humble, when Dan'l'd

seen the document was in proper and legal form.

"Go?" said Dan'l, giving him another shake. "I'm still trying to figure out what I'll do with you. For you've settled the costs of the case, but you haven't settled with me. I think I'll take you back to Marshfield," he said, kind of reflective. "I've got a ram there named Goliath, that can butt through an iron door. I'd kind of like to turn you loose in his field and see what he'd do."

Well, with that, the stranger began to beg and to plead. And he begged and he pled so humble that finally Dan'l, who was naturally kindhearted, agreed to let him go. The stranger seemed terrible grateful for that and said, just to show they were friends, he'd tell Dan'l's fortune before leaving. So Dan'l agreed to that, though he didn't take much stock in fortune-tellers ordinarily. But, naturally, the stranger was a little different.

Well, he pried and he peered at the lines in Dan'l's hands. And he told him one thing and another that was quite remarkable. But they were all in the past.

"Yes, all that's true, and it happened," said Dan'l Webster. "But what's to come in the future?"

The stranger grinned, kind of happily, and shook his head.

"The future's not as you think it," he said. "It's dark. You have a great ambition, Mr. Webster."

"I have," said Dan'l firmly, for everybody knew he wanted to be President.

"It seems almost within your grasp," said the stranger, "but you will not attain it. Lesser men will be made President and you will be passed over."

"And, if I am, I'll still be Daniel Webster," said Dan'l. "Say on."

"You have two strong sons," said the stranger, shaking his head. "You look to found a line. But each will die in war and neither reach greatness."

"Live or die, they are still my sons," said Dan'l Webster. "Say on."

"You have made great speeches," said the stranger. "You will make more."

"Ah," said Dan'l Webster.

"But the last great speech you make will turn many of your own against you," said the stranger. "They will call you Ichabod; they will call you by other names. Even in New England, some will say you have turned your coat and sold your country, and their voices will be loud against you till you die."

"So it is an honest speech, it does not matter what men say," said Dan'l Webster. Then he looked at the stranger and their glances locked.

"One question," he said. "I have fought for the Union all my life. Will I see that fight won against those who would tear it apart?"

"Not while you live," said the stranger, grimly, "but it will be won. And after you are dead, there are thousands who will fight for your cause, because of words that you spoke."

"Why, then, you long-barreled, slab-sided, lantern-jawed, fortune-telling note-shaver!" said Dan'l Webster, with a great roar of laughter, "be off with you to your own place before I put my mark on you! For, by the thirteen original colonies, I'd go to the Pit myself to save the Union!"

And with that he drew back his foot for a kick that would have stunned a horse. It was only the tip of his shoe that caught the stranger, but he went flying out of the door with his collecting box under his arm.

"And now," said Dan'l Webster, seeing Jabez Stone beginning to rouse from his swoon, "let's see what's left in the jug, for it's dry work talking all night. I hope there's pie for breakfast, Neighbor Stone."

But they say that whenever the devil comes near Marshfield, even now, he gives it a wide berth. And he hasn't been seen in the state of New Hampshire from that day to this. I'm not talking about Massachusetts or Vermont.

DISCUSSION

1. What do Webster's answers to the stranger's predictions reveal about his character?

2. "When the first wrong was done to the first Indian, I was there. When the first slaver put out for the Congo, I stood on her deck" (page 413). What does the stranger mean by these remarks?

3. How does the first description of Webster prepare you for the kind of events that follow?

For further activities, see page 490.

Get Up, Blues

JAMES A. EMANUEL

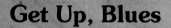

Blues
Never climb a hill
Or sit on a roof
In starlight.

Blues   5
Just bend low
And moan in the street
And shake a borrowed cup.

Blues
Just sit around   10
Sipping,
Hatching yesterdays.

Get up, Blues.
Fly.
Learn what it means   15
To be up high.

DISCUSSION

1. What are the blues? How are they described here?

2. What do you think "hatching yesterdays" (line 12)
means?

3. How do you interpret the poem's message?

Karma Repair Kit: Items 1–4

RICHARD BRAUTIGAN

1. Get enough food to eat,
    and eat it.

2. Find a place to sleep where it is quiet,
    and sleep there.

3. Reduce intellectual and emotional noise
        until you arrive at the silence of yourself,
            and listen to it.

4.

Karma: In Hinduism and Buddhism, the sum and the consequences of a person's actions during the successive phases of existence. These in turn help determine one's destiny.

Frank Chin has written several works of fiction, including the television drama *The Year of the Dragon*. In this interview he talks about the special experience of being a Chinese-American.

Interview with Frank Chin

VICTOR G. AND BRETT DE BARY NEE

I went to Cal for a while and then I went to Iowa.[1] I was there on a fellowship and all I was required to do was write some stuff, turn it in, and go in for a conference. That's all I did. The sessions would go, well, "This is a fine story, but we've all read Joyce Cary," you know. "This theme is already pretty hackneyed," and so on. I didn't want to go in there to cut people's stuff up, compare it, and try to decide who and where it came from. If the influence was really obvious there was something wrong, but most of these people had some skill, and well, there was just nothing in that for me. So I just did my thing. Most of the stuff I got was the point of view trip. "You haven't used enough of the local color of Chinatown." I would say, "But it isn't local color. I don't want to talk about neon lights and chop suey and funny music." R. V. Cassill was one of my teachers. He told me, "You know, you're writing about the Chinese in a way that I don't think American people would be interested in." Because they were just like people, right? My people, I mean they're common to me. "But don't you think you should make them interesting to the audience?" And this kind of stunned me, you know, because I thought I was just writing. But now I was being told in a backhanded way that I had a point of view and my point of view wasn't white. . . .

In Iowa no one—the only Chinese there were foreign-born, most of them students. Everyone there treated me like a foreigner including the Chinese students, because I was a foreigner to them, and that got very depressing. The only place I could get a job was in the Chinese restaurant in this town. Getting a place to live, well, this professor befriended me, found me a room, and took me over to see the landlady.

---

[1] *Cal . . . Iowa:* references to the University of California at Berkeley and the State University of Iowa.

The landlady came out and I was smoking. The guy said, "You better put your cigarette out, she might not approve." I'd just started the cigarette so I bent over, pinched it out, and I was putting it back in my pocket, kind of hunched over, and I look up, this lady is bowing to me. I look at the professor, he kind of shrugs, so I bow, and he bows, and she says, "Is this him?" "Yes, this is Frank Chin and this is Mrs. So and So." I say, "How do you do, Mrs. So and So." She says, "Oh, he speaks English!" "Yes, I do, Mrs. So and So." She says, "What's his name?" "My name is Frank, ma'am." "Oh, well that's only your American name." And I had to admit that's probably all it was, you know. "Yeah, it's only my American name." And I'm getting really tired of this. Then she says, "You speak very fluent English!" "Thank you, ma'am." "Oh, what part of China are you from?"

"I'm from San Francisco, ma'am." Rather than put her down. . . . But she goes on, "How long have you been in this country?" You know, that was her mental set: all Chinese are foreigners, therefore San Francisco is in China. I said, "Well, I've been here twenty years or so." And she said, "You should speak good English, then!" And I said, "Yes, I should, shouldn't I?"

She took me to one end of the room. "Do you like this rug?" "No, I don't like this rug." "That rug okay?" "Yeah, that rug's okay." She said, "Are you going to do any cooking?" I said, "Yeah, I've been known to do a little cooking so I can eat every now and again." She said, "Alright, I'll bring you some things. I know, Chinese like to make a mess when they cook, don't they?" I said no, I didn't know that. She said, "Oh, yes, I've been to the Philippines and I know that when Chinese cook they like to have a big mess. I'll just bring you some cloth to wipe off the stove each time you cook." I said, "OK. You bring me the cloth and I'll wipe the stove with it. Gladly, gladly." She says, "Well, here we call it 'rags.' " "Oh, 'rags.' Cu-lean-ing rrrrags." "Excuse me. Cu-lean-ing rrrrags." I'm looking at her and she's staring me in the face, mouthing the words "cleaning rags" and I realize I'm being given a lesson in English.

Well, that was Iowa. After a while I had to get out. . . . The Chinese restaurant just wasn't doing it for me. This is where the Chinese students from China are, you know, and they laugh at me because my Chinese is so bad. . . .

But the thing taught me something, you know. That I was Chinese-American, whatever that meant. That I was not an individual, not just a human being. Just a human being in this culture, in this society, is a white man, he can disappear. I couldn't disappear, no matter how enlightened I was, no matter how straight my English was. Someone, just because they saw my skin color, would detect an accent. Someone would always correct me. And well, then I began to look at my writing, what I'd been writing about in my letters and everything was just to this point. The Chinese-American, well, schizophrenia. That I'd been playing a kind of Ping Pong game, you know. Now I'm Chinese, now I'm American. But up against real Chinese in this isolated setting I saw that I had nothing in common with them. That they didn't understand me, and I didn't understand them. We both used chopsticks, okay, that's recognizable. But that's mechanics, not culture. On a personal gut level that doesn't make us brothers.

So if you're Chinese-American, this is where you come back to. This is your home, your spiritual home, whether you know it or not. But one thing, if you write, period, you're exploiting Chinatown. It's very complex. Writing and art to the Chinese-American is white. I get this when I go out and say, "More Chinese-Americans should write. We should tell them who we are, we should express our sensibility in our own terms instead of letting guys like Tom Wolfe come in and write about us." You know, we should be speaking for ourselves. "Aren't you asking us to ape the whites when you say that?" I'm asked this by Chinese suburbanites who've been college educated. They look on the writing as white, as if there's no such thing as writing and individuality in Chinese culture itself. This is how sick we've become. And the either-or thing. The either-or thing is right in that scientific name we go by, "Chinese," hyphen, "American." At San Francisco State, just as an experiment in a few classes, without giving them my bias and my own trip, I asked the students if they could divide themselves into what they thought were their American and Chinese qualities. Fold a piece of paper in half, the right half would be American, the left half Chinese. Everything that was interesting, adventurous, original, creative, fun, daring, artistic, was American. Everything old-fashioned, inhibiting, restraining, dull, repressive, uncreative, stultifying, was Chinese. That isn't so, you know, these are gross oversimplifications. . . . But these kids believe it, and it's what they've been because the title "Chinese-American," the cliché "blending East and West," encourages you to say, "Well, what are my Chinese parts? What are my American parts?" And what you break down, you break down according to the lines of the stereotype. It's something conditioned into you that you don't even realize. It's self-contempt. The Chinese are dumb, the Chinese are inhibited. The Chinese are restrained.

No American-born Chinese-American writer has ever published and become even slightly known and still lives in Chinatown. They don't identify with it any more, they see Chinatown as backward. In fact, the Chinese-Americans who have written come from a generation which strongly believed in the stereotypes as being real. They looked on writing as the proof that they were not of the stereotype, that they were assimilated, nearing white. They bought their way into second-class white status by humiliating their whole race and people and history. . . .

So many of us pat ourselves on the back, "Look, look! Look what we're not doing!" We're not doing this, we're not doing that, we're really great. We've made it. Well, we haven't.

If I had had to write something like that in order to sell, I would have said it of the Chinese as if I weren't one. And that would have linked me up with that first generation of Chinese-American writers, buying my way out of bondage by the rejection of my race. Well, I can't do that any more because I see that if I were to do that it's a price I have to continue to pay, and I'm not willing to do that. In my writing the ills, you know, everything that's terrible about Chinatown, I love them because they were mine. I know they have to be corrected because I lived them. I feel that I have a certain authority to say that they're no good, but in my terms they're no good. I say they're no good, but at the same time I kind of cherish the memory of these things. It breaks my heart that my grandmother lived in this country her whole life, she was born here, and she couldn't speak a word of English. You know, I was in her house when she died. It was a terrible experience and her old friends, some of them are still alive, I remember I was able to talk to them somehow. They couldn't speak English at all. And it breaks my heart that I can't even go up to them now and have the confidence to say in Chinese, "Remember me?" And somehow my Chinese name is even foreign to me. But no white

American can claim that misery, that's mine. That's what I write about, that makes my experience unique and that somehow makes me fine and defines my commonality with a lot of Chinese-Americans. And I'm not going to cast that aside to praise chop suey.

What I value most I guess is what I'm doing, trying to legitimize the Chinese-American sensibility. Call it my accident in time and space and that all the talent, everything I have is good only for this. Nothing else is any good until I get this done or started. And if I can't legitimize it, or if Chinese-American sensibility isn't legitimized, then my writing is no good.

DISCUSSION

1. During his stay in Iowa, Chin encounters Chinese students from China. What does the experience make him realize about himself?

2. As an experiment Chin has his college students list their Chinese qualities and their American qualities. What "gross simplifications" are revealed in their answers?

3. This piece is taken from an interview with Frank Chin. Find some places in the selection that indicate that Chin is speaking and not writing. How is this indicated by his *diction,* or choice of words? Find specific words or phrases that would probably not appear in a formal piece of writing.

4. Chin says that his goal as a writer is "to legitimize the Chinese-American sensibility" (page 486). From this interview, how would you describe his concept of Chinese-American sensibility?

THOMAS IRON-EYES

Born Circa 1840, Died 1919
Rosebud Agency
So. Dak.

MARNIE WALSH

1

I woke before the day, when the night bird
Knocked three times upon my door
To warn the Other Sleep was coming.
By candlelight I painted the two broad stripes
Of white across my forehead, the three scarlet spots   5
Upon my cheek. I greased well my braids
With sour fat from the cooking pan, then tied them
With a bit of bright string
Saved for this occasion.
From the trunk I took the dress of ceremony: 10
The breechclout and the elkskin shirt,
The smoke of their breath strong in my nose;
The smoke not of this time, this life or place
But of my youth, of many lodges I dwelt within,
The pony raids, the counting coup,   15
The chase and kill of buffalo;
The smell of grass when it was green,
The smell of coming snows
When food was plentiful within the camp
And ice crept over the rivers.   20
I put on the dress; then the leggings with scalps,
Now thin and colorless as the hair
Of sickly animals, sinew tied along the seams;
And on my feet the red-beaded moccasins
Worn by none but the bravest of warriors.   25
I lie here, my dry bones and ancient skin
Holding my old heart.
The daystar finds me ready for the journey.

15. *counting coup:* doing brave deeds.

2

Another time, another life, another place,
My people would have wrapped me   30
In deerskin, sewed me in the finest hides;
Borne me in honor to the cottonwood bier,
Laying at my right hand the sacred pipe
And at my left the arrows and bow, the lance
I bound with thongs and hung   35
With the feathers from the eagle's breast.
Below the scaffold of the dead
My pony of the speckled skin and fierce heart
Would be led, and with a blow of the stone axe
Lie down to wait my needs.   40
Far above in the sacred hoop of the sky
Long-sighted hawks hanging on silent wings
Would mark my passing.

3

When the Life-Giver hid from the night
The dark wind would speak to my spirit   45
And I would arise, taking up my weapons.
Mounting my horse I would follow
The great path over the earth, beyond the stars.
I would see the glow of cooking fires
As bright as arrow tips across the northern sky;   50
Waiting for me, old friends would dance and feast
And play the games of gambling.
Behind me drums would beat and willow whistles cry
Like the doves of spring who nested
In the berry bushes near the river of my village.   55
I would pause to hear my sons in council,
Speaking of my deeds in war, my strength and wisdom.
My woman in her sorrow would tear her clothing,
Bloody her face marked with ashes,
And with a knife cut off her plaited hair.   60

4

But I am Thomas, here, where no grass grows,
Where no clear rivers run;
Where dirt and despair abound,
Where heat and rain alike rust out
The souls of my people, the roofs of tin;   65
Where disease like a serpent slips from house to house
And hunger sits in the dooryard.
I am Thomas. I wait for the wagon
To bring the government box of pine;
I wait for the journey to the burying ground   70
Below the sandy butte where rattlesnakes
Stink in burrows, and the white man's wooden trinities
Stand in crooked rows.
There I will be put beneath the earth.
They will seal in my spirit.   75
I will not hear the dark wind's cry
To come and take the starry road
Across the circle of the sky.

DISCUSSION

1. In stanza 1 the speaker prepares for his death ("the
Other Sleep"). What preparations does he make? What is
being described in stanza 2? In stanza 3?

2. Look at the first line of stanza four: "But I am Thomas,
here, where no grass grows." What transition has been
made between stanza 3 and stanza 4? The speaker feels
that even his life after death will be changed. Why? Explain
as thoroughly as you can.

3. The phrase "I am Thomas" occurs twice in stanza four.
What is the effect of the repetition?

4. What is this poem saying about the plight of Native
Americans?

FOCUS

VOCABULARY

The Tall Men (page 454)

The words *expedited* and *evaded* from this story contain a prefix that is very useful for you to know: *ex-* or *e-*, meaning "out, beyond." *Expedite* combines *ex-* with a Latin word meaning "feet," and it literally means "to free the feet." Its dictionary meaning is "to speed up the progress of; help along."

Knowing the meaning of a word's parts can often help you to remember its definition because you will have a concrete mental picture to reinforce it. Whenever you look up a word in the dictionary, check its root meaning.

Each word in List A is followed by the meaning of its root. See if you can match each word with its correct dictionary meaning in List B.

List A
1. excavate—to hollow out
2. excerpt—to pick out
3. egregious—standing out from the herd
4. ebullient—to boil over
5. eccentric—out of center
6. exorbitant—out of orbit
7. efface—to remove the face
8. egress—to step out
9. explicate—to fold out
10. extenuate—to thin out

List B
1. exit
2. extravagant, immoderate
3. overflowing with excitement or enthusiasm
4. passage or scene selected from a speech, book, film, play, or the like
5. to make a hole in
6. departing from the established norm or rule
7. outstandingly bad; flagrant
8. to make clear the meaning of
9. to lessen or attempt to lessen the magnitude of an offense or guilt by providing partial excuses
10. to rub or wipe out

A Work of Artifice (page 466)

The phrase "the hands you love to touch" comes from an advertising slogan, and the implication is that a woman's hands exist primarily to be touched and should be absolutely smooth. (You can see why the phrase is appropriate to Piercy's poem.) This kind of implication is a form of sexism, assigning certain qualities or roles to a person solely on the basis of sex. Advertising can often be sexist, showing men and women in stereotyped roles. Here are some examples from ads that were used in the past.

> Is it true blondes have more fun?
> My wife, I think I'll keep her.
> So simple to repair even a woman can do it.
> Protect yourself like a man.
> Would he like you to look younger?

See how many examples you can collect from present-day TV commercials and magazine ads. Share your findings with other members of the class. You might want to discuss in class why sexism in advertising is undesirable.

The Devil and Daniel Webster (page 468)

A. The sense of New England is captured in this story in part by the use of regional language. For example, Daniel Webster is referred to as "Dan'l" and it is said that he may "rear up" out of the ground. On separate paper, write another regional name for the items below.

1. hotcakes
2. soda pop
3. bubbler
4. rotary
5. sack
6. baby buggy
7. bucket
8. skillet
9. grinder
10. teeter-totter

B. Many words we use are the result of blending two words together. *Scratch* is a blend of two Middle English words *scrat* and *catch,* both of which meant to scrape with the fingernails. *Scrunched* is another blend, combining *squeezed* and *crunched.* Below are some words that you use or hear frequently. Every one of them is a blend. On separate paper, write the meaning of each, as well as the words that form the blend. Use your dictionary if you need help.

1. blimp
2. brunch
3. chortle
4. chump
5. happenstance
6. motel
7. smog

COMPOSITION

TOPIC SENTENCES

"You see, for a while, he was the biggest man in the country," begins the third paragraph of "The Devil and Daniel Webster" (page 468). The rest of the paragraph illustrates that topic sentence: when he stood up to speak, stars and stripes appeared in the sky; when he went fishing, trout would jump into his pockets; his chickens were all white meat; his forehead was like a mountain. The next-to-last sentence mentions the biggest case Daniel ever argued. The last sentence, "And this is the way I used to hear it told," both concludes this paragraph and leads into the next.

The topic sentence in the next paragraph is the second one: "He wasn't a bad man to start with, but he was an unlucky man." The rest of the paragraph tells how Jabez Stone was unlucky, concluding with the sentence: "But one day Jabez Stone got sick of the whole business," which leads to the next paragraph. That paragraph elaborates on the central idea "It was about the last straw for Jabez Stone." This time the topic sentence is the next-to-last sentence in the paragraph.

To be sure, the particular pattern that Benét uses is less important than the fact that he uses a pattern. All good prose writers follow some underlying plan as they write, moving purposefully to fulfill a design. Thus, each paragraph is like a piece of a pattern, or like a building block in the larger structure.

The *topic sentence* within a paragraph states the central idea, which other sentences within the paragraph will exemplify, modify, or elaborate on. Often (but as you have seen, by no means always) a topic sentence comes first in the paragraph. It can come at the end of a paragraph, or in the middle. A topic sentence placed at the end generally summarizes the idea developed in the preceding sentences. But regardless of its position, the topic sentence expresses an idea or thought which connects the other sentences in the paragraph. In your own writing, make sure each of your paragraphs has a central idea and that each paragraph leads logically and smoothly to the next.

ABOUT THE SELECTIONS

1.   We all live by our own set of values.
Some, for example, find privacy almost as
vital for life as breathing. Others may enjoy
privacy, but not miss it when it is absent
from their lives. Similarly, some people gain
vital nourishment from nature, whereas
others could happily spend their lives in
the city, far from woods and fields. Which
selection in the section comes closest to
expressing your own set of values? What
values emerged through the selection?
Why do they matter to you?

2.   In the opening paragraph of "Chinook
Dance" (page 426) the first sentence is the
topic sentence. Which sentence states the
topic of the second paragraph? of the
third? of the fourth? In each case, how are
the other sentences in the paragraph related to the topic sentence?

3.   In his play *The Crucible*, Arthur Miller
says, "It is still impossible for man to organize his social life without repressions, and
the banner has yet to be struck between
order and freedom." How does that statement relate to "The Tall Men"?

ON YOUR OWN

1.   A *cynic* is someone who values nothing. It is in her or his skeptical nature to
mistrust every motive and ridicule almost
every goal. To the cynic love is merely
selfishness or simple-mindedness. Patriotism is what a few people in power extol to
get you to behave as they want you to.
Teachers don't really care anything about
you; they're just in it for the money. To the
cynic, it's every person for herself or himself, and you might as well get all you can.
How would you respond to a cynic? In a
thoughtful paper that mentions specific examples and incidents, refute the cynic's attitude toward life.

2.   Carson McCullers's story (page 417)
concerns an encounter. Nothing sensa-
tional happens. Yet the encounter, quiet as
it is, contains a great deal of meaning.
Write about an encounter in your own life
that was low-keyed but significant. Make
sure that the reader experiences the meeting between two people clearly. Where did
it take place? What did the other person
look like? Why was it significant? Revise
what you have written to sharpen the language and focus the imagery.

3.   Devise a single sentence that might be
used as the basis for an entire paper. You
might model your sentence after one of the
statements from "A Young Puritan's
Code." Your sentence may be a generalization that calls for examples to make the
generalization clear. Or it may indicate a
classification to be made, or an analysis to
be conducted. Or the sentence may propose a comparison and contrast that the
remainder of the paper will develop.

4.   Using the sentence of the preceding
assignment as your opening statement,
write a paper of no more than two pages.
Follow the pattern you decide upon, and let
your topic sentences within pargraphs
make the pattern clear.

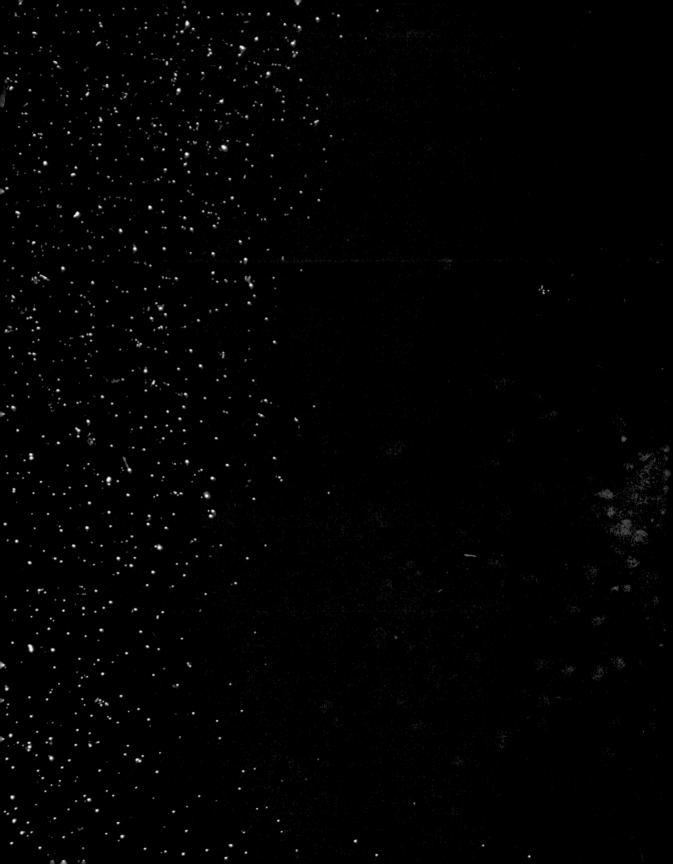

VISIONS

The Story of an Hour

KATE CHOPIN

Knowing that Mrs. Mallard was afflicted with a heart trouble, great care was taken to break to her as gently as possible the news of her husband's death.

It was her sister Josephine who told her, in broken sentences; veiled hints that revealed in half concealing. Her husband's friend Richards was there, too, near her. It was he who had been in the newspaper office when intelligence of the railroad disaster was received, with Brently Mallard's name leading the list of "killed." He had only taken the time to assure himself of its truth by a second telegram, and had hastened to forestall any less careful, less tender friend in bearing the sad message.

She did not hear the story as many women have heard the same, with a paralyzed inability to accept its significance. She wept at once, with sudden, wild abandonment, in her sister's arms. When the storm of grief had spent itself she went away to her room alone. She would have no one follow her.

There stood, facing the open window, a comfortable, roomy armchair. Into this she sank, pressed down by a physical exhaustion that haunted her body and seemed to reach into her soul.

She could see in the open square before her house the tops of trees that were all aquiver with the new spring life. The delicious breath of rain was in the air. In the street below a peddler was crying his wares. The notes of a distant song which some one was singing reached her faintly, and countless sparrows were twittering in the eaves.

There were patches of blue sky showing here and there through the clouds that had met and piled one above the other in the west facing her window.

She sat with her head thrown back upon the cushion of the chair, quite motionless, except when a sob came up into her throat and shook her, as a child who has cried itself to sleep continues to sob in its dreams.

She was young, with a fair, calm face, whose lines bespoke repression and even a certain strength. But now there was a dull stare in her eyes, whose gaze was fixed away off yonder on one of those patches of blue sky. It was not a glance of reflection, but rather indicated a suspension of intelligent thought.

There was something coming to her and she was waiting for it, fearfully. What was it? She did not know; it was too subtle and elusive to name. But she felt it, creeping out of the sky, reaching toward her through the sounds, the scents, the color that filled the air.

Now her bosom rose and fell tumultuously. She was beginning to recognize this thing that was approaching to possess her, and she was striving to beat it back with her will—as powerless as her two white slender hands would have been.

When she abandoned herself a little whispered word escaped her slightly parted lips. She said it over and over under her breath: "Free, free, free!" The vacant stare and the look of terror that had followed it went from her eyes. They stayed keen and bright. Her pulses beat fast, and the coursing blood warmed and relaxed every inch of her body.

She did not stop to ask if it were or were not a monstrous joy that held her. A clear and exalted perception enabled her to dismiss the suggestion as trivial.

She knew that she would weep again when she saw the kind, tender hands folded in death; the face that had never looked save with love upon her, fixed and gray and dead. But she saw beyond that bitter moment a long procession of years to come that would belong to her absolutely. And she opened and spread her arms out to them in welcome.

There would be no one to live for her during those coming years; she would live for herself. There would be no powerful will bending hers in that blind persistence with which men and women believe they have a right to impose a private will upon a fellow-creature. A kind intention or a cruel intention made the act seem no less a crime as she looked upon it in that brief moment of illumination.

And yet she had loved him—sometimes. Often she had not. What did it matter! What could love, the unsolved mystery, count for in the face of this possession of self-assertion which she suddenly recognized as the strongest impulse of her being!

"Free! Body and soul free!" she kept whispering.

Josephine was kneeling before the closed door with her lips to the keyhole, imploring for admission. "Louise, open the door! I beg; open the door—you will make yourself ill. What are you doing, Louise? For heaven's sake open the door."

"Go away. I am not making myself ill." No; she was drinking in a very elixir of life through that open window.

Her fancy was running riot along those days ahead of her. Spring days, and summer days, and all sorts of days that would be her own. She breathed a quick prayer that life might be long. It was only yesterday she had thought with a shudder that life might be long.

She arose at length and opened the door to her sister's importunities. There was a feverish triumph in her eyes, and she carried herself unwittingly like a goddess of Victory. She clasped her sister's waist, and together they descended the stairs. Richards stood waiting for them at the bottom.

Some one was opening the front door with a latchkey. It was Brently Mallard who entered, a little travel-stained, composedly carrying his gripsack and umbrella. He had been far from the scene of accident, and did not even know there had been one. He stood amazed at Josephine's piercing cry; at Richards' quick motion to screen him from the view of his wife.

But Richards was too late.

When the doctors came they said she had died of heart disease—of joy that kills.

DISCUSSION

1. What does the news of her husband's death cause Mrs. Mallard to feel, to learn about herself? Are you surprised at her reaction? Explain.

2. *Irony* arises from the difference between what appears to be and what really is. One form of irony is verbal irony— saying one thing and meaning another. On a deeper level there is irony of situation—the difference between what is expected and what actually happens, between what appears to be true and what is true. What is ironic in this story?

For further activities, see page 536.

THE INSIDE SEARCH

ZORA NEALE HURSTON

I do not know when the visions began. Certainly I was not more than seven years old, but I remember the first coming very distinctly. My brother Joel and I had made a hen take an egg back and been caught as we turned the hen loose. We knew we were in for it and decided to scatter until things cooled off a bit. He hid out in the barn, but I combined discretion with pleasure, and ran clear off the place. Mr. Linsay's house was vacant for a spell. He was a neighbor who was off working somewhere at the time. I had not thought of stopping there when I set out, but I saw a big raisin lying on the porch and stopped to eat it. There was some cool shade on the porch, so I sat down, and soon I was asleep in a strange way. Like clearcut stereopticon slides, I saw twelve scenes flash before me, each one held until I had seen it well in every detail, and then be replaced by another. There was no continuity as in an average dream. Just disconnected scene after scene with blank spaces in between. I knew that they were all true, a preview of things to come, and my soul writhed in agony and shrunk away. But I knew that there was no shrinking. These things had to be. I did not wake up when the last one flickered and vanished, I merely sat up and saw the Methodist Church, the line of moss-draped oaks, and our strawberry patch stretching off to the left.

So when I left the porch, I left a great deal behind me. I was weighed down with a power I did not want. I had knowledge before its time. I knew my fate. I knew that I would be an orphan and homeless. I knew that while I was still helpless, that the comforting circle of my family would be broken, and that I would have to wander cold and friendless until I had served my time. I would stand beside a dark pool of water and see a huge fish move slowly away at a time when I would be somehow in the depth of despair. I would hurry to catch a train, with doubts and fears driving me and seek solace in a place and fail to find it when I arrived, then cross many tracks to board the train

again. I knew that a house, a shotgun-built house[1] that needed a new coat of white paint, held torture for me, but I must go. I saw deep love betrayed, but I must feel and know it. There was no turning back. And last of all, I would come to a big house. Two women waited there for me. I could not see their faces, but I knew one to be young and one to be old. One of them was arranging some queer-shaped flowers such as I had never seen. When I had come to these women, then I would be at the end of my pilgrimage, but not the end of my life. Then I would know peace and love and what goes with those things, and not before.

These visions would return at irregular intervals. Sometimes two or three nights running. Sometimes weeks and months apart. I had no warning. I went to bed and they came. The details were always the same, except in the last picture. Once or twice I saw the old faceless woman standing outdoors beside a tall plant with that same off-shape white flower. She turned suddenly from it to welcome me. I knew what was going on in the house without going in, it was all so familiar to me.

I never told anyone around me about these strange things. It was too different. They would laugh me off as a story-teller. Besides, I had a feeling of difference from my fellow men, and I did not want it to be found out. Oh, how I cried out to be just as everybody else! But the voice said No. I must go where I was sent. The weight of the commandment laid heavy and made me moody at times. When I was an ordinary child, with no knowledge of things but the life about me, I was reasonably happy. I would hope that the call would never come again. But even as I hoped I knew that the cup meant for my lips would not pass. I must drink the bitter drink. I studied people all around me, searching for someone to fend it off. But I was told inside myself that there was no one. It gave me a feeling of terrible aloneness. I stood in a world of vanished communion with my kind, which is worse than if it had never been. Nothing is so desolate as a place where life has been and gone. I stood on a soundless island in a tideless sea.

Time was to prove the truth of my visions, for one by one they came to pass. As soon as one was fulfilled, it ceased to come. As this happened, I counted them off one by one and took consolation in the fact that one more station was past, thus bringing me nearer the end of my trials, and nearer to the big house, with the kind women and the strange white flowers.

---

[1] *shotgun-built house:* small, rectangular building.

Years later, after the last one had come and gone, I read a sentence or a paragraph now and then in the columns of O. O. McIntyre which perhaps held no special meaning for the millions who read him, but in which I could see through those slight revelations that he had had similar experiences. Kipling knew the feeling for himself, for he wrote of it very definitely in his *Plain Tales from the Hills.* So I took comfort in knowing that they were fellow pilgrims on my strange road.

I consider that my real childhood ended with the coming of the pronouncements. True, I played, fought, and studied with other children, but always I stood apart within. Often I was in some lonesome wilderness, suffering strange things and agonies while other children in the same yard played without a care. I asked myself why me? Why? Why? A cosmic loneliness was my shadow. Nothing and nobody around me really touched me. It is one of the blessings of this world that few people see visions and dream dreams.

DISCUSSION

1. Why did the author tell no one about the visions?

2. Look again at the author's last sentence: "It is one of the blessings of this world that few people see visions and dream dreams." What does she mean? Do you agree? Explain.

For further activities, see page 536.

poem at thirty

SONIA SANCHEZ

it is midnight
no magical bewitching
hour for me
i know only that
i am here waiting   5
remembering that
once as a child
i walked two
miles in my sleep.
did i know   10
then where i
was going?
traveling. i'm
always traveling.
i want to tell   15
you about me
about nights on a
brown couch when
i wrapped my
bones in lint and   20
refused to move.
no one touches
me anymore.
father do not
send me out   25
among strangers.
you you black man
stretching scraping
the mold from your body.
here is my hand.   30
i am not afraid
of the night.

DISCUSSION

1. "i wrapped my / bones in lint," and "scraping / the mold from your body" are both very strong images used to describe mental and emotional states. What kind of feelings is the poet describing?

2. From the title we know that the poem describes a time in the speaker's life. Which of these statements seems to best describe what she is feeling? (a) She is sorry that she is no longer a child. (b) She is falling in love. (c) She has isolated herself in the past and now she wants to reach out to the world. Explain your choice, or sum up her feelings in your own words.

The Centaur

MAY SWENSON

The summer that I was ten—
Can it be there was only one
summer that I was ten? It must

have been a long one then—
each day I'd go out to choose   5
a fresh horse from my stable

which was a willow grove
down by the old canal.
I'd go on my two bare feet.

But when, with my brother's jack-knife,
I had cut me a long limber horse
with a good thick knob for a head,

and peeled him slick and clean
except a few leaves for the tail,
and cinched my brother's belt   15

around his head for a rein,
I'd straddle and canter him fast
up the grass bank to the path,

trot along in the lovely dust
that talcumed over his hoofs,   20
hiding my toes, and turning

his feet to swift half-moons.
The willow knob with the strap
jouncing between my thighs

was the pommel and yet the poll   25
of my nickering pony's head.
My head and my neck were mine,

yet they were shaped like a horse.
My hair flopped to the side
like the mane of a horse in the wind.   30

My forelock swung in my eyes,
my neck arched and I snorted.
I shied and skittered and reared,

stopped and raised my knees,
pawed at the ground and quivered.   35
My teeth bared as we wheeled

and swished through the dust again.
I was the horse and the rider,
and the leather I slapped to his rump

spanked my own behind.   40
Doubled, my two hoofs beat
a gallop along the bank,

the wind twanged in my mane,
my mouth squared to the bit.
And yet I sat on my steed   45

quiet, negligent riding,
my toes standing the stirrups,
my thighs hugging his ribs.

At a walk we drew up to the porch.
I tethered him to a paling.   50
Dismounting, I smoothed my skirt

and entered the dusky hall.
My feet on the clean linoleum
left ghostly toes in the hall.

25. *pommel:* upper part of a saddle.
poll: top of the head.

31. *forelock:* lock of hair that grows or falls
on the forehead.

Where have you been? said my mother.   55
Been riding, I said from the sink,
and filled me a glass of water.

What's that in your pocket? she said.
Just my knife. It weighted my pocket
and stretched my dress awry.   60

Go tie back your hair, said my mother,
and *Why is your mouth all green?*
*Rob Roy, he pulled some clover
as we crossed the field,* I told her.

DISCUSSION

1.   How does the title fit the poem? How
doesn't it? Why do you think the poem is called
"The Centaur"?

2.   What caused the "ghostly toes in the hall"?
What previous image does this refer to?

Jugábamos/We Played

TINO VILLANUEVA

en el barrio
—en las tardes de fuego
when the dusk prowls
    en la calle desierta
pues los jefes y jefas
    trabajan
      —often late hours
after school
    we play canicas. . . .

           Alurista

The memories of childhood
have no order, and no end.

        Dylan Thomas

we would play/we would jump/
we would play at everything.
ritual and recreation it was, in the patio of my barrio
in the just-awakening week: kneeling there
in sunnybronzed delight   5
when my kingdom was a pocketful of
golden marbles.
how in wide-eyed wonder i sought winning
two agates for my eyes/& so,
not knowing what it meant, i played for keeps.   10

we would play/we would put our lives on the line—

    my posse always got its man/
    i was the Chicano Lone Ranger/i was Tarzan
    of backyard pecan trees/time-tall trees blooming
    with the color of adventure/trees that ripened   15
    with my age through rain-ruined days.

en el barrio . . . canicas: in the barrio/—in the afternoons full of
fire/when the dusk prowls/in the deserted street/for our fathers
and mothers/work/—often late hours/after school/we play at marbles. . . .

running/gamboling i played oblivious to
fine earth shifting in the cuffs of my fading jeans/
crawling/leaping always reaching/
reaching/reaching even the delicacies of the indomitable   20
void/
running about the nooks and corners of my patio
where grandma had tulips and carnations planted/
running between the sun and its reverberant glare
in those afternoons of that fire.   25

we would play/we would leap/
we would play at everything.
myth and sensation it was, when the tree-house wind blew
in simultaneous weathers: it was a green wind
tasting of fig, of mint, of peaches at times—   30

    our garden's aromas.

and in my Cracker-Jack-joy of late saturday afternoons
my red wagon was full of dog/& my tricycle traveled
one last time every turnpike of my yard.

now the fun running to soothe the dry sun on my tongue/   35
now the tireless striding toward stilled water of
buoyant ice cubes in a glass transparent dripping
in the gripping of my mother's hand.

we would play/we would run/
we would play at everything.   40
shouting and emotion it was, in my chosen pastime:

    thirteen years out of the womb i was
    pubescent Walter Mitty fleet as Mickey Mantle
    at the Stadium:

    tok! . . . there's a long drive to center . . . Villanueva   45
    is back/back/back/the ball is up against the wall . . .

    as i banged my back against our dilapidated
    picket fence. grandpa repaired it twelve times over.
    yes, i dreamed of spikes and baseball diamonds/

---

17. *oblivious to:* unaware of.   20–21. *indomitable void:* unconquerable nothingness.   43. *Walter Mitty:* the daydreaming character in a story by James Thurber (page 522).

meantime   50
barefooted i played in narrow dusty streets
(a dust decreed by the City Council, i know now.)
my buddies in bubble-gum smiles chose up sides/
so batter up 'cause i'm a portsider like
Whitey Ford/i've the eagle eye of Ted Williams.   55
i tugged the bill of my sea-blue cap for luck/
had NY on it:

time out! let the dust settle/as it must/
traffic should slow down on gravel streets—

especially Coca-Cola trucks.   60

but the game goes on/dust mixing with perspiration.
inning after inning this game becomes a night game too/
this 100-watt bulb lights the narrow playing field.

such were the times of year-rounded yearnings
when at the end of light's flight i listened in   65
reflective boyhood silence.
then the day-done sun glistened, burned deeply,
disappearing into my eyes blinking: innocently
i blinked toward the towering twilight.

we would play/we would jump/   70
we would play at everything.

DISCUSSION   1.   The poet characterizes early play as "ritual and recreation"; find the two other sets of paired words that describe the games of later childhood and of the early teen years. In what way are these descriptions appropriate? What one characteristic do all the games and play seem to have in common?

2.   "innocently / i blinked toward the towering twilight," the poet says in lines 68–69. Yet earlier he speaks of "sunnybronzed delight," suggesting the feeling of early morning. What might the twilight symbolize, or represent? Find other words and phrases that suggest the passing, and even the running out, of time.

3.   By what means—typographical and other—has Villanueva given his poem its unusual vitality? What are some of the words that convey images of color and light?

THE BEDQUILT

DOROTHY CANFIELD FISHER

Of all the Elwell family Aunt Mehetabel was certainly the most unimportant member. It was in the old-time New England days, when an unmarried woman was an old maid at twenty, at forty was everyone's servant, and at sixty had gone through so much discipline that she could need no more in the next world. Aunt Mehetabel was sixty-eight.

She had never for a moment known the pleasure of being important to anyone. Not that she was useless in her brother's family; she was expected, as a matter of course, to take upon herself the most tedious and uninteresting part of the household labors. On Mondays she accepted as her share the washing of the men's shirts, heavy with sweat and stiff with dirt from the fields and from their own hardworking bodies. Tuesdays she never dreamed of being allowed to iron anything pretty or even interesting, like the baby's white dresses or the fancy aprons of her young lady nieces. She stood all day pressing out a monotonous succession of dish-cloths and towels and sheets.

In preserving-time she was allowed to have none of the pleasant responsibility of deciding when the fruit had cooked long enough, nor did she share in the little excitement of pouring the sweet-smelling stuff into the stone jars. She sat in a corner with the children and stoned cherries incessantly, or hulled strawberries until her fingers were dyed red.

The Elwells were not consciously unkind to their aunt, they were even in a vague way fond of her; but she was so insignificant a figure in their lives that she was almost invisible to them. Aunt Mehetabel did not resent this treatment; she took it quite as unconsciously as they gave it. It was to be expected when one was an old-maid dependent in a busy family. She gathered what crumbs of comfort she could from their occasional careless kindnesses and tried to hide the hurt which even yet pierced her at her brother's rough joking. In the winter when they all sat before the big hearth, roasted apples, drank mulled cider, and teased the girls about their beaux and the boys about their sweethearts, she shrank into a dusky corner with her knitting, happy if the evening passed without her brother saying, with a crude sarcasm, "Ask your Aunt Mehetabel about the beaux that used to come a-sparkin' her!" or, "Mehetabel, how was't when you was in love with Abel Cummings?" As a matter of fact, she had been the same at twenty as at sixty, a mouselike little creature, too shy for anyone to notice, or to raise her eyes for a moment and wish for a life of her own.

Her sister-in-law, a big hearty housewife, who ruled indoors with as autocratic a sway as did her husband on the farm, was rather kind in an absent, offhand way to the shrunken little old woman, and it was through her that Mehetabel was able to enjoy the one pleasure of her life. Even as a girl she had been clever with her needle in the way of patching bedquilts.[1] More than that she could never learn to do. The garments which she made for herself were lamentable affairs, and she was humbly grateful of any help in the bewildering business of putting them together. But in patchwork she enjoyed a tepid importance. She could really do that as well as anyone else. During years of devotion to this one art she had accumulated a considerable store of quilting patterns. Sometimes the neighbors would send over and ask "Miss Mehetabel" for the loan of her sheaf-of-wheat design, or the double-star pattern. It was with an agreeable flutter at being able to help someone that she went to the dresser, in her bare little room under the eaves, and drew out from her crowded portfolio the pattern desired.

She never knew how her great idea came to her. Sometimes she thought she

[1] *patching bedquilts:* making a bedquilt by piecing and sewing together small bits of cloth into a design.

must have dreamed it, sometimes she even wondered reverently, in the phraseology of the weekly prayer-meeting, if it had not been "sent" to her. She never admitted to herself that she could have thought of it without other help. It was too great, too ambitious, too lofty a project for her humble mind to have conceived. Even when she finished drawing the design with her own fingers, she gazed at it incredulously, not daring to believe that it could indeed be her handiwork. At first it seemed to her only like a lovely but unreal dream. For a long time she did not once think of putting an actual quilt together following that pattern, even though she herself had invented it. It was not that she feared the prodigious effort that would be needed to get those tiny, oddly shaped pieces of bright-colored material sewed together with the perfection of fine workmanship needed. No, she thought zestfully and eagerly of such endless effort, her heart uplifted by her vision of the mosaic-beauty of the whole creation as she saw it, when she shut her eyes to dream of it—that complicated, splendidly difficult pattern— good enough for the angels in heaven to quilt.

But as she dreamed, her nimble old fingers reached out longingly to turn her dream into reality. She began to think adventurously of trying it out—it would perhaps not be too selfish to make one square—just one unit of her design to see how it would look. She dared do nothing in the household where she was a dependent, without asking permission. With a heart full of hope and fear thumping furiously against her old ribs, she approached the mistress of the house on churning-day, knowing with the innocent guile of a child that the country woman was apt to be in a good temper while working over the fragrant butter in the cool cellar.

Sophia listened absently to her sister-in-law's halting petition. "Why, yes, Mehetabel," she said, leaning far down into the huge churn for the last golden morsels—"why, yes, start another quilt if you want to. I've got a lot of pieces from the spring sewing that will work in real good." Mehetabel tried honestly to make her see that this would be no common quilt, but her limited vocabulary and her emotion stood between her and expression. At last Sophia said, with a kindly impatience: "Oh, there! Don't bother me. I never could keep track of your quiltin' patterns, anyhow. I don't care what pattern you go by."

Mehetabel rushed back up the steep attic stairs to her room, and in a joyful agitation began preparations for the work of her life. Her very first stitches showed her that it was even better than she hoped. By some heaven-sent inspiration she had invented a pattern beyond which no patchwork quilt could go.

She had but little time during the daylight hours filled with the incessant household drudgery. After dark she did not dare to sit up late at night lest she burn too much candle. It was weeks before the little square began to show the pattern. Then Mehetabel was in a fever to finish it. She was too conscientious to shirk even the smallest part of her share of the housework, but she rushed through it now so fast that she was panting as she climbed the stairs to her little room.

Every time she opened the door, no matter what weather hung outside the one small window, she always saw the little room flooded with sunshine. She smiled to herself as she bent over the innumerable scraps of cotton cloth on her work table. Already—to her—they were ranged in orderly, complex, mosaic-beauty.

Finally she could wait no longer, and one evening ventured to bring her work down beside the fire where the family sat, hoping that good fortune would give her a place near the tallow candles on the mantelpiece. She had reached the last corner of that first square and her needle flew in and out, in and out, with nervous speed. To her relief no one noticed her. By bedtime she had only a few more stitches to add.

As she stood up with the others, the square fell from her trembling old hands and fluttered to the table. Sophia glanced at it carelessly. "Is that the new quilt you said you wanted to start?" she asked, yawning. "Looks like a real pretty pattern. Let's see it."

Up to that moment Mehetabel had labored in the purest spirit of selfless adoration of an ideal. The emotional shock given her by Sophia's cry of admiration as she held the work towards the candle to examine it, was as much astonishment as joy to Mehetabel.

"Land's sakes!" cried her sister-in-law. "Why, Mehetabel Elwell, where did you git that pattern?"

"I made it up," said Mehetabel. She spoke quietly but she was trembling.

"No!" exclaimed Sophia. "Did you! Why, I never see such a pattern in my life. Girls, come here and see what your Aunt Mehetabel is doing."

The three tall daughters turned back reluctantly from the stairs. "I never could seem to take much interest in patchwork quilts," said one. Already the old-time skill born of early pioneer privation and the craving for beauty had gone out of style.

"No, nor I neither!" answered Sophia. "But a stone image would take an interest in this pattern. Honest, Mehetabel, did you really think of it yourself?" She held it up closer to her eyes and went on, "And how under the sun and stars did you ever git your courage up to start in a-making it? Land! Look at all those tiny squinchy little seams! Why, the wrong side ain't a thing *but* seams! Yet the good side's just like a picture, so smooth you'd think 'twas woven that way. Only nobody could."

The girls looked at it right side, wrong side, and echoed their mother's exclamations. Mr. Elwell himself came over to see what they were discussing. "Well, I declare!" he said, looking at his sister with eyes more approving than she could ever remember. "I don't know a thing about patchwork quilts, but to my eye that beats old Mis' Andrew's quilt that got the blue ribbon so many times at the County Fair."

As she lay that night in her narrow hard bed, too proud, too excited to sleep, Mehetabel's heart swelled and tears of joy ran down from her old eyes.

The next day her sister-in-law astonished her by taking the huge pan of potatoes out of her lap and setting one of the younger children to peeling them. "Don't you want to go on with that quiltin' pattern?" she said. "I'd kind o' like to see how you're goin' to make the grapevine design come out on the corner."

For the first time in her life the dependent old maid contradicted her powerful sister-in-law. Quickly and jealously she said, "It's not a grapevine. It's a sort of curlicue I made up."

"Well, it's nice-looking anyhow," said Sophia pacifyingly. "I never could have made it up."

By the end of the summer the family interest had risen so high that Mehetabel was given for herself a little round table in the sitting room, for *her,* where she could keep her pieces and use odd minutes for her work. She almost wept over such kindness and resolved firmly not to take advantage of it. She went on faithfully with her monotonous housework, not neglecting a corner. But the atmosphere of her world was changed. Now things had a meaning. Through the longest task of washing milk-pans, there rose a rainbow of promise. She took her place by the little table and put the thimble on her knotted, hard finger with the solemnity of a priestess performing a rite.

She was even able to bear with some degree of dignity the honor of having the minister and the minister's wife comment admiringly on her great project. The family felt quite proud of Aunt Mehetabel as Minister Bowman had said it was work as fine as any he had ever seen, "and he didn't know but finer!" The remark was repeated verbatim to the neighbors in the following weeks when they dropped in and examined in a perverse Vermontish silence some astonishingly difficult tour de force[2] which Mehetabel had just finished.

The Elwells especially plumed themselves on the slow progress of the quilt. "Mehetabel has been to work on that corner for six weeks, come Tuesday, and she ain't half done yet," they explained to visitors. They fell out of the way of always expecting her to be the one to run on errands, even for the children. "Don't bother your Aunt Mehetabel," Sophia would call. "Can't you see she's got to a ticklish place on the quilt?" The old woman sat straighter in her chair, held up her head. She was a part of the world at last. She joined in the conversation and her remarks were listened to. The children were even told to mind her when she asked them to do some service for her, although this she ventured to do but seldom.

One day some people from the next town, total strangers, drove up to the Elwell house and asked if they could inspect the wonderful quilt which they had heard about even down in their end of the valley. After that, Mehetabel's quilt came little by little to be one of the local sights. No visitor to town, whether he knew the Elwells or not, went away without having been to look at it. To make her presentable to strangers, the Elwells saw to it that their aunt was better

[2] *tour de force:* an accomplishment of strength, skill, or artistic merit.

dressed than she had ever been before. One of the girls made her a pretty little cap to wear on her thin white hair.

A year went by and a quarter of the quilt was finished. A second year passed and half was done. The third year Mehetabel had pneumonia and lay ill for weeks and weeks, horrified by the idea that she might die before her work was completed. A fourth year and one could really see the grandeur of the whole design. In September of the fifth year, the entire family gathered around her to watch eagerly, as Mehetabel quilted the last stitches. The girls held it up by the four corners and they all looked at it in hushed silence.

Then Mr. Elwell cried as one speaking with authority, "By ginger! That's goin' to the County Fair!"

Mehetabel blushed a deep red. She had thought of this herself, but never would have spoken aloud of it.

"Yes indeed!" cried the family. One of the boys was dispatched to the house of a neighbor who was Chairman of the Fair Committee for their village. He came back beaming, "Of course he'll take it. Like's not it may git a prize, he says. But he's got to have it right off because all the things from our town are going tomorrow morning."

Even in her pride Mehetabel felt a pang as the bulky package was carried out of the house. As the days went on she felt lost. For years it had been her one thought. The little round stand had been heaped with a litter of bright-colored scraps. Now it was desolately bare. One of the neighbors who took the long journey to the Fair reported when he came back that the quilt was hung in a good place in a glass case in "Agricultural Hall." But that meant little to Mehetabel's ignorance of everything outside her brother's home. She drooped. The family noticed it. One day Sophia said kindly, "You feel sort o' lost without the quilt, don't you, Mehetabel?"

"They took it away so quick!" she said wistfully. "I hadn't hardly had one good look at it myself."

The Fair was to last a fortnight. At the beginning of the second week Mr. Elwell asked his sister how early she could get up in the morning.

"I dunno. Why?" she asked.

"Well, Thomas Ralston has got to drive to West Oldton to see a lawyer. That's four miles beyond the Fair. He says if you can git up so's to leave here at four in the morning he'll drive you to the Fair, leave you there for the day, and bring you back again at night." Mehetabel's face turned very white. Her eyes filled with tears. It was as though someone had offered her a ride in a golden chariot up to the gates of heaven. "Why, you can't *mean* it!" she cried wildly. Her brother laughed. He could not meet her eyes. Even to his easy-going unimaginative indifference to his sister this was a revelation of the narrowness of her life in his home. "Oh, 'tain't so much— just to go to the Fair," he told her in some confusion, and then "Yes, sure I mean it. Go git your things ready, for it's tomorrow morning he wants to start."

A trembling, excited old woman stared all that night at the rafters. She who had never been more than six miles from home—it was to her like going into another world. She who had never seen anything more exciting than a church supper was to see the County Fair. She had never dreamed of doing it. She could not at all imagine what it would be like.

The next morning all the family rose early to see her off. Perhaps her brother had not been the only one to be shocked by her happiness. As she tried to eat her breakfast they called out conflicting advice to her about what to see. Her brother said not to miss inspecting the stock, her nieces said the fancywork was the only thing worth looking at, Sophia told her to be sure to look at the display of preserves. Her nephews asked her to bring home an account of the trotting races.

The buggy drove up to the door, and she was helped in. The family ran to and fro with blankets, woolen tippet,[3] a hot soapstone from the kitchen range. Her wraps were tucked about her. They all stood together and waved good-bye as she drove out of the yard. She waved back, but she scarcely saw them. On her return home that evening she was ashy pale, and so stiff that her brother had to lift her out bodily. But her lips were set in a blissful smile. They crowded around her with questions until Sophia pushed them all aside. She told them Aunt Mehetabel was too tired to speak until she had had her supper. The young people held their tongues while she drank her tea, and

---

[3] *tippet:* a covering for the shoulders, sometimes made of fur, with long ends that hang in front.

absent-mindedly ate a scrap of toast with an egg. Then the old woman was helped into an easy chair before the fire. They gathered about her, eager for news of the great world, and Sophia said, "Now, come, Mehetabel, tell us all about it!"

Mehetabel drew a long breath. "It was just perfect!" she said. "Finer even than I thought. They've got it hanging up in the very middle of a sort o' closet made of glass, and one of the lower corners is ripped and turned back so's to show the seams on the wrong side."

"What?" asked Sophia, a little blankly.

"Why, the quilt!" said Mehetabel in surprise. "There are a whole lot of other ones in that room, but not one that can hold a candle to it, if I do say it who shouldn't. I heard lots of people say the same thing. You ought to have heard what the women said about that corner, Sophia. They said—well, I'd be ashamed to *tell* you what they said. I declare if I wouldn't!"

Mr. Elwell asked, "What did you think of that big ox we've heard so much about?"

"I didn't look at the stock," returned his sister indifferently. She turned to one of her nieces. "That set of pieces you gave me, Maria, from your red waist, come out just lovely! I heard one woman say you could 'most smell the red roses."

"How did Jed Burgess' bay horse place in the mile trot?" asked Thomas.

"I didn't see the races."

"How about the preserves?" asked Sophia.

"I didn't see the preserves," said Mehetabel calmly.

Seeing that they were gazing at her with astonished faces she went on, to give them a reasonable explanation, "You see I went right to the room where the quilt was, and then I didn't want to leave it. It had been so long since I'd seen it. I had to look at it first real good myself, and then I looked at the others to see if there was any that could come up to it. Then the people begun comin' in and I got so interested in hearin' what they had to say I couldn't think of goin' anywheres else. I ate my lunch right there too, and I'm glad as can be I did, too; for what do you think?"—she gazed about her with kindling eyes. "While I stood there with a sandwich in one hand, didn't the head of the hull concern come in and open the glass door and pin a big bow of blue ribbon right in the middle of the quilt with a label on it, 'First Prize.'"

There was a stir of proud congratulation. Then Sophia returned to questioning, "Didn't you go to see anything else?"

"Why, no," said Mehetabel. "Only the quilt. Why should I?"

She fell into a reverie. As if it hung again before her eyes she saw the glory that shone around the creation of her hand and brain. She longed to make her listeners share the golden vision with her. She struggled for words. She fumbled blindly for unknown superlatives. "I tell you it looked like——" she began, and paused.

Vague recollections of hymnbook phrases came into her mind. They were the only kind of poetic expression she knew. But they were dismissed as being sacrilegious to use for something in real life. Also as not being nearly striking enough.

Finally, "I tell you it looked real *good*," she assured them and sat staring into the fire, on her tired old face the supreme content of an artist who has realized his ideal.

DISCUSSION

1. The bedquilt causes changes in the family's attitude toward Aunt Mehetabel. How do their attitudes change? How is the quilt responsible for these changes?

2. A character's *motivation,* or reasons for her or his actions, must be presented in such a way that the reader can understand the character's behavior. Aunt Mehetabel spends five years making the bedquilt. Why? What is her motivation?

3. How do you think Aunt Mehetabel's life will be different now? How will she be different? Why do you think so?

For further activities, see page 536.

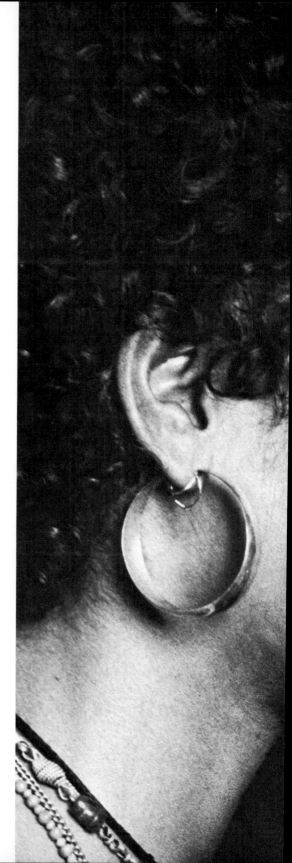

OYE MUNDO / sometimes

JESÚS PAPOLETO MELÉNDEZ

sometimes(
      when the night air feels *chevere*
)when i can hear the real sound
of *el barrio*
on *la conga*   *y timbales*   5
coke bottles
& garbage can tops

      when i can feel
      & reallyreally touch
      la música latina/   *africana*   10

& the fingerpoppin soul
emergin from tears/   sweet tears of laughter

      & i can feel
      a conglomeration of vibrations/
      heat waves   15
      body waves
      people waves
      of real *gente*
      /& i feel gooooooood

when i can taste the rare culture   20
of *cuchifritos*   *y lechón*
chitterlins   & black-eyed peas
& corn bread

      & *la pompa* is open
      & coooooooools the hot tar   25
      of summer heated streets
      where children play
      kick-the-can (
& sirens
cannot be heard)   30

      /sometimes

2. *chevere:* great.   18. *gente:* people.
21. *lechón:* pig.   24. *la pompa:* the pump (here, hydrant).

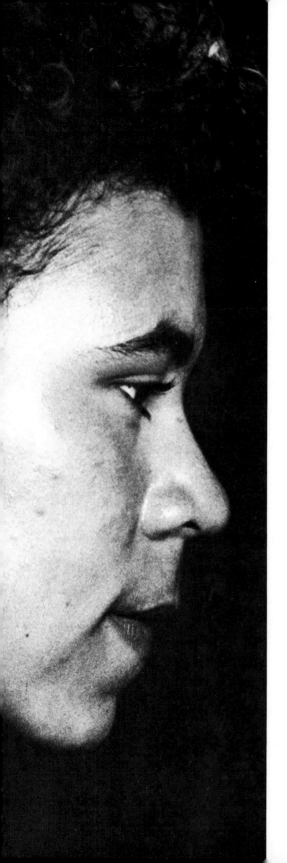

sometimes
when the last of the ghetto poets
writes of flowers
growin in gutters   /& i know it's real   35

          /sometimes

sometimes/   sometimes
when i can almost hear   /being echoed back
an answer
to my ghetto cry   40
sometimes/   sometimes
i run up the fire escape/   not to escape
& climb on the roof
& stand on the ledge
& look down   45
& yell out
to the midnight world
below
above
around   50
within:

OYE MUNDO TÚ ERES BONITO!!!

& i forget about the junkies
on the stoop.

52. *Oye mundo tú eres bonito:* Listen, world, you are
good.

DISCUSSION

1. Why do you think the speaker hears the
real sounds of the barrio only at night?

2. How does the stressing and repetition of
the word ''sometimes'' emphasize what is left
unsaid in the poem? What might be some other
things the speaker would like to forget?

3. In line 52 the speaker says (in Spanish),
''Listen, world, you are good.'' How does he
mean this?

PEDRO

Pedro Infante—Mexican Singer, Actor,
Genius, who died piloting his own
plane, April 1957, at the age of 37

LUÍS OMAR SALINAS

You took the world and embraced
    it as a child
        your arms
           your voice
                your heart   5
    touched the sea

    you had many loves
        among them Mexico

when you died
            it rose to its feet   10
            to pay homage to you

mountains of snow
                were singing
    your songs

Pedro I remember you   15
        when I was a child
        and how you brought
                        tears

    silence within silence

DISCUSSION

1. "Pedro" makes five separate statements. What is each of them saying about Pedro Infante?

2. Why does the last line, "silence within silence," stand alone? What two things could the line mean? How does the lack of punctuation add to the effect of this line?

I Have a Rendezvous with Death

ALAN SEEGER

I have a rendezvous with Death
At some disputed barricade,
When Spring comes back with rustling shade
And apple blossoms fill the air—
I have a rendezvous with Death   5
When Spring brings back blue days and fair.

It may be he shall take my hand
And lead me into his dark land
And close my eyes and quench my breath—
It may be I shall pass him still.   10
I have a rendezvous with Death
On some scarred slope of battered hill,
When Spring comes round again this year
And the first meadow flowers appear.

God knows 'twere better to be deep   15
Pillowed in silk and scented down,
Where Love throbs out in blissful sleep,
Pulse nigh to pulse and breath to breath,
Where hushed awakenings are dear. . . .
But I've a rendezvous with Death   20
At midnight in some flaming town,
When Spring trips north again this year,
And I to my pledged word am true,
I shall not fail that rendezvous.

1. *rendezvous* (rän'dā-vōō): a prearranged meeting.
16. *down:* fine, soft feathers forming the first plumage of a young
bird; used for making pillows.

DISCUSSION

1. This poem was written by a soldier. If you did not know that, would you be able to tell just from reading the poem? If so, how?

2. Why has the speaker chosen spring as the season to be associated with his death? What other season or seasons might he have used? How would they change the tone and imagery of the poem?

THE SECRET LIFE OF WALTER MITTY

JAMES THURBER

"We're going through!" The Commander's voice was like thin ice breaking. He wore his full-dress uniform, with the heavily braided white cap pulled down rakishly over one cold gray eye. "We can't make it, sir. It's spoiling for a hurricane, if you ask me." "I'm not asking you, Lieutenant Berg," said the Commander. "Throw on the power lights! Rev her up to 8,500! We're going through!" The pounding of the cylinders increased: ta-pocketa-pocketa-pocketa-*pocketa-pocketa*. The Commander stared at the ice forming on the pilot window. He walked over and twisted a row of complicated dials. "Switch on No. 8 auxiliary!" he shouted. "Switch on No. 8 auxiliary!" repeated Lieutenant Berg. "Full strength in No. 3 turret!" shouted the Commander. "Full strength in No. 3 turret!" The crew, bending to their various tasks in the huge, hurtling eight-engined Navy hydroplane looked at each other and grinned. "The Old Man'll get us through," they said to one another. "The Old Man ain't afraid of nothing!" . . .

"Not so fast! You're driving too fast!" said Mrs. Mitty. "What are you driving so fast for?"

"Hmm?" said Walter Mitty. He looked at his wife, in the seat beside him, with shocked astonishment. She seemed grossly unfamiliar, like a strange woman who had yelled at him in a crowd. "You were up to fifty-five," she said. "You know I don't like to go more than forty. You were up to fifty-five." Walter Mitty drove on toward Waterbury in silence, the roaring of the SN202 through the worst storm in twenty years of Navy flying fading in the remote, intimate airways of his mind. "You're tensed up again," said Mrs. Mitty. "It's one of your days. I wish you'd let Dr. Renshaw look you over."

Walter Mitty stopped the car in front of the building where his wife went to have her hair done. "Remember to get those overshoes while I'm having my hair done," she said. "I don't need overshoes," said Mitty. She put her mirror back into her bag. "We've been all through that," she said, getting out of the car. "You're not a young man any longer." He raced the engine a little. "Why don't you wear your gloves? Have you lost your gloves?" Walter Mitty reached in a pocket and brought out the gloves. He put them on, but after she had turned and gone into the building and he had driven on to a red light, he took them off again. "Pick it up, brother!" snapped a cop as the light changed, and Mitty hastily pulled on his gloves and lurched ahead. He drove around the streets aimlessly for a time, and then he drove past the hospital on his way to the parking lot.

. . . "It's the millionaire banker, Wellington McMillan," said the pretty nurse. "Yes?" said Walter Mitty, removing his gloves slowly. "Who has the case?" "Dr. Renshaw and Dr. Benbow, but there are two specialists here, Dr. Remington from New York and Dr. Pritchard-Mitford from London. He flew over." A door opened down a long, cool corridor and Dr. Renshaw came out. He looked distraught and haggard. "Hello, Mitty," he said. "We're having a tough time with McMillan, the millionaire banker and close personal friend of Roosevelt. Obstreosis of the ductal tract. Tertiary. Wish you'd take a look at him." "Glad to," said Mitty.

In the operating room there were whispered introductions: "Dr. Remington. Dr. Mitty. Dr. Pritchard-Mitford, Dr. Mitty." "I've read your book on streptothricosis," said Pritchard-Mitford, shaking hands. "A brilliant performance, sir." "Thank you," said Walter Mitty. "Didn't know you were in the States, Mitty," grumbled Remington. "Coals to Newcastle,[1] bringing Mitford and me up here for a tertiary." "You are very kind," said Mitty. A huge, compli-

cated machine, connected to the operating table, with many tubes and wires, began at this moment to go pocketa-pocketa-pocketa. "The new anaesthetizer is giving way!" shouted an intern. "There is no one in the East who knows how to fix it!" "Quiet, man!" said Mitty, in a low, cool voice. He sprang to the machine, which was now going pocketa-pocketa-queep-pocketa-queep. He began fingering delicately a row of glistening dials. "Give me a fountain pen!" he snapped. Someone handed him a fountain pen. He pulled a faulty piston out of the machine and inserted the pen in its place. "That will hold for ten minutes," he said. "Get on with the operation." A nurse hurried over and whispered to Renshaw, and Mitty saw the man turn pale. "Coreopsis has set in," said Renshaw nervously. "If you would take over, Mitty?" Mitty looked at him and at the craven[2] figure of Benbow, who drank, and at the grave, uncertain faces of the two great specialists. "If you wish," he said. They slipped a white gown on him; he adjusted a mask and drew on thin gloves; nurses handed him shining. . . .

"Back it up, Mac! Look out for that Buick!" Walter Mitty jammed on the brakes. "Wrong lane, Mac," said the parking lot attendant, looking at Mitty closely. "Gee. Yeh," muttered Mitty. He began cautiously to back out of the lane marked "Exit Only." "Leave her sit there," said the attendant. "I'll put her away." Mitty got out of the car. "Hey, better leave the key."

"Oh," said Mitty, handing the man the ignition key. The attendant vaulted

---

[1] *Coals to Newcastle:* Newcastle is an important coal port. The expression bringing coals to Newcastle means to make a wasted effort.

[2] *craven:* cowardly.

into the car, backed it up with insolent skill, and put it where it belonged.

They're so cocky, thought Walter Mitty, walking along Main Street; they think they know everything. Once he had tried to take his chains off, outside New Milford, and he had got them wound around the axles. A man had had to come out in a wrecking car and unwind them, a young, grinning garageman. Since then Mrs. Mitty always made him drive to a garage to have the chains taken off. The next time, he thought, I'll wear my right arm in a sling; they won't grin at me then. I'll have my right arm in a sling and they'll see I couldn't possibly take the chains off myself. He kicked at the slush on the sidewalk. "Overshoes," he said to himself, and he began looking for a shoe store.

When he came out into the street again, with the overshoes in a box under his arm, Walter Mitty began to wonder what the other thing was his wife had told him to get. She had told him twice before they set out from their house for Waterbury. In a way he hated these weekly trips to town—he was always getting something wrong. Kleenex, he thought, Squibb's, razor blades? No. Toothpaste, toothbrush, bicarbonate, carborundum, initiative and referendum? He gave it up. But she would remember it. "Where's the what's-its-name?" she would ask. "Don't tell me you forgot the what's-its-name." A newsboy went by shouting something about the Waterbury trial.

. . . "Perhaps this will refresh your memory." The District Attorney suddenly thrust a heavy automatic at the quiet figure on the witness stand. "Have you ever seen this before?" Walter Mitty took the gun and examined it expertly. "This is my Webley-Vickers 50.80," he said calmly. An excited buzz ran around the courtroom. The Judge rapped for order. "You are a crack shot with any sort of firearms, I believe?" said the District Attorney, insinuatingly. "Objection!" shouted Mitty's attorney. "We have shown that the defendant could not have fired the shot. We have shown that he wore his right arm in a sling on the night of the fourteenth of July." Walter Mitty raised his hand briefly and the bickering attorneys were stilled. "With any known make of gun," he said evenly, "I could have killed Gregory Fitzhurst at three hundred feet *with my left hand.*" Pandemonium broke loose in the courtroom. A woman's scream rose above the bedlam and suddenly a lovely, dark-haired girl was in Walter Mitty's arms. The District Attorney struck at her savagely. Without rising from his chair, Mitty let the man have it on the point of the chin. "You miserable cur!" . . .

"Puppy biscuit," said Walter Mitty. He stopped walking and the buildings of Waterbury rose up out of the misty courtroom and surrounded him again. A woman who was passing laughed. "He said 'Puppy biscuit,'" she said to her companion. "That man said 'Puppy biscuit' to himself." Walter Mitty hurried on. He went into an A. & P., not the first one he came to but a smaller one farther up the street. "I want some biscuit for small, young dogs," he said to the clerk. "Any special brand, sir?" The greatest pistol shot in the world thought a moment. "It says 'Puppies Bark for It' on the box," said Walter Mitty.

His wife would be through at the hairdresser's in fifteen minutes, Mitty saw in looking at his watch, unless they had trouble drying it; sometimes they had trouble drying it. She didn't like to get to the hotel first; she would want him to be there waiting for her as usual. He found a big leather chair in the lobby, facing a window, and he put the overshoes and the puppy biscuit on the floor beside it. He picked up an old copy of *Liberty* and sank down into the chair. "Can Germany Conquer the World Through the Air?" Walter Mitty looked at the pictures of bombing planes and of ruined streets.

. . . "The cannonading has got the wind up[3] in young Raleigh, sir," said the sergeant. Captain Mitty looked up at him through tousled hair. "Get him to bed," he said wearily. "With the others. I'll fly alone." "But you can't, sir," said the sergeant anxiously. "It takes two men to handle that bomber and the Archies[4] are pounding the air. Von Richtman's circus[5] is between here and Saulier." "Somebody's got to get that ammunition dump," said Mitty. "I'm going over. Spot of brandy?" He poured a drink for the sergeant and one for himself. War thundered and whined around the dugout and battered at the door. There was a rending of wood, and splinters flew through the room. "A bit of a near thing," said Captain Mitty carelessly. "The box barrage is closing in," said the sergeant. "We only live once, Sergeant," said Mitty, with his faint, fleeting smile.

"Or do we?" He poured another brandy and tossed it off. "I never see a man could hold his brandy like you, sir," said the sergeant. "Begging your pardon, sir." Captain Mitty stood up and strapped on his huge Webley-Vickers automatic. "It's forty kilometers through hell, sir," said the sergeant. Mitty finished one last brandy. "After all," he said softly, "what isn't?" The pounding of the cannon increased; there was the rat-tat-tatting of machine guns, and from somewhere came the menacing pocketa-pocketa-pocketa of the new flame-throwers. Walter Mitty walked to the door of the dugout humming "Auprès de Ma Blonde."[6] He turned and waved to the sergeant. "Cheerio!" he said. . . .

Something struck his shoulder. "I've been looking all over this hotel for you," said Mrs. Mitty. "Why do you have to hide in this old chair? How did you expect me to find you?" "Things close in," said Walter Mitty vaguely. "What?" Mrs. Mitty said. "Did you get the what's-its-name? The puppy biscuit? What's in that box?" "Overshoes," said Mitty. "Couldn't you have put them on in the store?" "I was thinking," said Walter Mitty. "Does it ever occur to you that I am sometimes thinking?" She looked at him. "I'm going to take your temperature when I get you home," she said.

They went out through the revolving doors that made a faintly derisive whistling sound when you pushed them. It was two blocks to the parking lot. At the drugstore on the corner she said,

---

[3] *got the wind up:* British expression meaning flustered or to make flustered.

[4] *Archies:* antiaircraft guns; a term from World War I.

[5] *Von Richtman's circus:* Von Richtofen's Flying Circus, German fighter planes during World War I.

[6] *Auprès de Ma Blonde:* French song popular during World War I.

"Wait here for me. I forgot something. I won't be a minute." She was more than a minute. Walter Mitty lighted a cigarette. It began to rain, rain with sleet in it. He stood up against the wall of the drugstore, smoking. . . . He put his shoulders back and his heels together. "Forget the handkerchief," said Walter Mitty scornfully. He took one last drag on his cigarette and snapped it away. Then, with that faint, fleeting smile playing about his lips, he faced the firing squad; erect and motionless, proud and disdainful, Walter Mitty the Undefeated, inscrutable[7] to the last.

---

[7] *inscrutable:* mysterious, not easily understood.

DISCUSSION

1. What character or personality traits do Commander Mitty, Doctor Mitty, Defendant Mitty, Captain Mitty, and condemned man Mitty have in common? In what ways is the real Walter Mitty different from them?

2. How would you describe Walter Mitty's wife? How would you describe the relationship between the Mittys?

3. When the story opens Walter Mitty is already deep into his first fantasy. We can only guess how he has happened to let his mind wander. But we do know what triggered the others. Find the statement or situation that causes each one.

4. A *type* character is one that can be classified into a general group: hero, lover, braggart, clown, villain, etc. Some characters can readily fit into one such group, but this does not prevent them from being fully developed characters. A *stereotyped* character, however, is one that is oversimplified and lacking in dimension. Stereotypes are easily spotted because they are characters who are without individuality and are therefore totally predictable: the strong, silent cowboy, the mad scientist, the harassed housewife, and so on.

Is Walter Mitty a type or a stereotype? Explain. His fantasy heroes are stereotypes. How would you label each of them?

For further activities, see page 536.

HUNCHBACK MADONNA

FRAY ANGÉLICO CHÁVEZ

Old and crumbling, the squat-built adobe mission of El Tordo sits in a hollow high up near the snow-capped Truchas. A few clay houses huddle close to it like tawny chicks about a ruffled old hen. On one of the steep slopes which has the peaks for a background, sleeps the ancient grave-yard with all its inhabitants, or what little is left of them. The town itself is quite as lifeless during the winter months, when the few folks that live there move down to warmer levels by the Rio Grande; but when the snows have gone, except for the white crusts on the peaks, they return to herd their sheep and goats and with them comes a stream of pious pil-grims and curious sightseers which lasts throughout the spring and sum-mer weather.

They come to see and pray before the stoop-shouldered Virgin, people from as far south as Belen who from some accident or some spi-nal or heart affliction are shoulder-bent and want to walk straight again. Others, whose faith is not so simple or who have no faith at all, have come from many parts of the country and asked the way to El Tordo, not only to see the curiously painted Madonna in which the natives put so much stock, but to visit a single grave in a corner of the *campo santo*[1] which, they have heard, is covered in spring with a profusion of wild flowers, whereas the other sunken ones are bare altogether, or at the most sprinkled only with sagebrush and tumbleweed. And, of course, they want to hear from the lips of some old inhabitant the history of the town and the church, the painting and the grave, and particularly of Mana Seda.

No one knows, or cares to know, when the village was born. It is more thrilling to say, with the natives, that the first settlers came up from the Santa Clara valley long before the railroad came to New Mexico, when the Indians of Nambé and Taos still used bows and arrows and obsidian clubs; when it took a week to go to Santa Fe, which looked no different from the other northern towns at the time, only somewhat big-ger. After the men had allotted the scant farming land among themselves, and each family raised its adobe hut of one or two rooms to begin with,

---

[1] *campo santo:* cemetery.

they set to making adobes for a church that would shoulder above their homes as a guardian parent. On a high, untillable slope they marked out as their God's acre a plot which was to be surrounded by an adobe wall. It was not long before large pines from the forest nearby had been carved into beams and corbels[2] and hoisted into their places on the thick walls. The women themselves mud-plastered the tall walls outside with their bare hands; within they made them a soft white with a lime mixture applied with the woolly side of sheepskins.

The Padre, whose name the people do not remember, was so pleased with the building, and with the crudely wrought reredos[3] behind the altar, that he promised to get at his own expense a large hand-painted *Nuestra Señora de Guadalupe*[4] to hang in the middle of the *retablo*.[5] But this had to wait until the next traders' ox-drawn caravan left Santa Fe for Chihuahua in Old Mexico and came back again. It would take years, perhaps, if there was no such painting ready and it must be made to order.

With these first settlers of El Tordo had come an old woman who had no relatives in the place they had left. For no apparent reason she had chosen to cast her lot with the emigrants, and they had willingly brought her along in one of their wooden-wheeled *carretas*,[6] had even built her a room in the protective shadow of the new church. For that had been her work before, sweeping the house of God, ringing the Angelus morning, noon and night, adorning the altar with lace cloths and flowers, when there were flowers. She even persuaded the Padre, when the first May came around, to start an ancient custom prevalent in her place of origin: that of having little girls dressed as queens and their maids-in-waiting present bunches of flowers to the Virgin Mary every evening in May. She could not wait for the day when the Guadalupe picture would arrive.

They called her *Mana Seda*, "Sister Silk." Nobody knew why; they had known her by no other name. The women thought she had got it long ago for being always so neat, or maybe because she embroidered so many altar-cloths. But the men said it was because she looked so much like a silk-spinning spider; for she was very much humpbacked—so bent forward that she could look up only sideways and with effort. She always wore black, a black shiny dress and black shawl with long leg-like fringes and, despite her age and deformity, she walked about quite swiftly and noiselessly. "Yes," they said, "like the black widow spider."

---

[2] *corbels:* brackets projecting from a wall, usually to support an arch or cornice.
[3] *reredos:* screen or partition behind an altar.
[4] *Nuestra Señora de Guadalupe:* Our Lady of Guadalupe.
[5] *retablo:* altar-piece.
[6] *carretas:* long, narrow carts.

Being the cause of the May devotions at El Tordo, she took it upon herself to provide the happy girls with flowers for the purpose. The geraniums which she grew in her window were used up the first day, as also those that other women had tended in their own homes. So she scoured the slopes around the village for wild daisies and Indian paintbrush, usually returning in the late afternoon with a shawlful to spill at the eager children's feet. Toward the end of May she had to push deeper into the forest, whence she came back with her tireless, short-stepped spider-run, her arms and shawl laden with wild iris and cosmos, verbenas and mariposa lilies from the pine shadows.

This she did year after year, even after the little "queens" of former Mays got married and new tots grew up to wear their veils. Mana Seda's one regret was that the image of the Virgin of Guadalupe had not come, had been lost on the way when the Comanches or Apaches attacked and destroyed the Chihuahua-Santa Fe ox-train.

One year in May (it was two days before the close of the month), when the people were already whispering among themselves that Mana Seda was so old she must die soon, or else last forever, she was seen hurrying into the forest early in the morning, to avail herself of all the daylight possible, for she had to go far into the wooded canyons this time. At the closing services of May there was to be, not one queen, but a number of them with their attendants. Many more flowers were needed for this, and the year had been a bad one for flowers, since little snow had fallen the winter before.

Mana Seda found few blooms in her old haunts, here and there an aster with half of its petals missing or drought-toasted, or a faded columbine fast wilting in the cool but moistureless shade. But she must find enough flowers; otherwise the good heavenly Mother would have a sad and colorless farewell this May. On and on she shuttled in between the trunks of spruce and fir, which grew thicker and taller and closer-set as the canyon grew narrower. Further up she heard the sound of trickling water; surely the purple iris and freckled lily flames would be rioting there, fresh and without number. She was not disappointed, and without pausing to recover her breath, began lustily to snap off the long, luscious stems and lay them on her shawl, spread out on the little meadow. Her haste was prompted by the darkness closing in through the evergreens, now turning blacker and blacker, not with approaching dusk, but with the smoky pall of thunderheads that had swallowed up the patches of blue among the tops of the forest giants.

Far away arose rumblings that grew swiftly louder and nearer. The great trees, which always whispered to her even on quiet, sunny days, began to hiss and whine angrily at the unseen wind that swayed them and swung their arms like maidens unwilling to be kissed or danced with. And then a deafening sound exploded nearby with a blinding bluish light. Others followed, now on the right or on the left, now before or behind, as Mana Seda, who had thrown her flower-weighted mantle on her arched back, started to run—in which direction she knew not, for the rain was slashing down in sheets that blurred the dark boles and boulders all around her.

At last she fell, whimpering prayers to the holy Virgin with a water-filled mouth that choked her. Of a sudden, sunlight began to fall instead between the towering trees, now quiet and dripping with emeralds and sapphires. The storm had passed by, the way spring rains in the Truchas Mountains do, as suddenly as it had come. In a clearing not far ahead, Mana Seda saw a little adobe hut. On its one chimney stood a wisp of smoke, like a white feather. Still clutching her heavy, rain-soaked shawl, she ran to it and knocked at the door, which was opened by an astonished young man with a short, sharp knife in his hand.

"I thought the mountain's bowels where the springs come from had burst," she was telling the youth, who meanwhile stirred a pot of brown beans that hung with a pail of coffee over the flames in the corner fireplace. "But our most holy Lady saved me when I prayed to her, *gracias a Dios*. The lightning and the water stopped, and I saw her flying above me. She had a piece of sky for a veil, and her skirt was like the beautiful red roses at her feet. She showed me your house."

Her host tried to hide his amusement by taking up his work again, a head he had been carving on the end of a small log. She saw that he was no different from the grown boys of El Tordo, dark and somewhat lean-bodied in his plain homespun. All about, against the wall and in niches, could be seen several other images, wooden and gaily colored *bultos*,[7] and more *santos*[8] painted on pieces of wood or hide. Mana Seda guessed that this must be the young stranger's trade, and grew more confident because of it. As she spread out her shawl to dry before the open fire, her load of flowers rolled out soggily on the bare earth floor. Catching his questioning stare, she told him what they were for, and about the church and the people of El Tordo.

"But that makes me think of the apparition of Our Lady of Guadalupe," he said. "Remember how the Indian Juan Diego filled his blanket with roses, as Mary most holy told him to do? And how, when he let

---

[7] *bultos:* carved image of the head and neck.
[8] *santos:* saints.

down his *tilma* before the Bishop, out fell the roses, and on it was the miraculous picture of the Mother of God?"

Yes, she knew the story well; and she told him about the painting of the Guadalupe which the priest of El Tordo had ordered brought from Mexico and which was lost on the way. Perhaps, if the Padre knew of this young man's ability, he would pay him for making one. Did he ever do work for churches? And what was his name?

"My name is Esquipula," he replied. "*Sí*, I have done work for the Church. I made the *retablo* of 'San Francisco' for his church in Ranchos de Taos, and also the 'Cristo' for Santa Cruz. The 'Guadalupe' at San Juan, I painted it. I will gladly paint another for your chapel." He stopped all of a sudden, shut his eyes tight, and then quickly leaned toward the bent old figure who was helping herself to some coffee. "Why do you not let me paint one right now—on your shawl!"

She could not answer at first. Such a thing was unheard of. Besides, she had no other *tápalo* to wear. And what would the people back home say when she returned wearing the Virgin on her back? What would She say?

"You can wear the picture turned inside where nobody can see it. Look! You will always have holy Mary with you, hovering over you, hugging your shoulders and your breast! Come," he continued, seeing her ready to yield, "it is too late for you to go back to El Tordo. I will paint it now, and tomorrow I and Mariquita will take you home."

"And who is Mariquita?" she wanted to know.

"Mariquita is my little donkey," was the reply.

Mana Seda's black shawl was duly hung and spread tight against a bare stretch of wall, and Esquipula lost no time in tracing with white chalk the outlines of the small wood-print which he held in his left hand as a model. The actual laying of the colors, however, went much slower because of the shawl's rough and unsized texture. Darkness came, and Esquipula lit an oil lamp, which he held in one hand as he applied the pigments with the other. He even declined joining his aged guest at her evening meal of beans and stale *tortillas*, because he was not hungry, he explained, and the picture must be done.

Once in a while the painter would turn from his work to look at Mana Seda, who had become quite talkative, something the people back at El Tordo would have marveled at greatly. She was recounting experiences of her girlhood which, she explained, were more vivid than many things that had happened recently.

Only once did he interrupt her, and that without thinking first. He said, almost too bluntly: "How did you become hunchbacked?"

Mana Seda hesitated, but did not seem to take the question amiss. Patting her shoulder as far as she could reach to her bulging back, she answered: "The woman who was nursing me dropped me on the hard dirt floor when I was a baby, and I grew up like a ball. But I do not remember, of course. My being bent out of shape did not hurt me until

the time when other little girls of my age were chosen to be flower-maids in May. When I was older, and other big girls rejoiced at being chosen May queens, I was filled with bitter envy. God forgive me, I even cursed. I at last made up my mind never to go to the May devotions, nor to Mass either. In the place of my birth, the shores of the Rio Grande are made up of wet sand which sucks in every living creature that goes in; I would go there and return no more. But something inside told me the Lord would be most pleased if I helped the other lucky girls with their flowers. That would make me a flower-bearer every day. Esquipula, my son, I have been doing this for seventy-four Mays!"

Mana Seda stopped and reflected in deep silence. The youth who had been painting absent-mindedly and looking at her, now noticed for the first time that he had made the Virgin's shoulders rather stooped, like Mana Seda's, though not quite so much. His first impulse was to run the yellow sun-rays into them and cover up the mistake, but for no reason he decided to let things stand as they were. By and by he put the last touches to his *oeuvre de caprice*, [9] offered the old lady his narrow cot in a corner, and went out to pass the night in Mariquita's humble shed.

The following morning saw a young man leading a grey burro through the forest, and on the patient animal's back swayed a round black shape, grasping her mantle with one hand while the other held tight to the small wooden saddle. Behind her, their bright heads bobbing from its wide mouth, rode a sack full of iris and tiger-lilies from the meadow where the storm had caught Mana Seda the day before. Every once in a while, Esquipula had to stop the beast and go after some new flower which the rider had spied from her perch; sometimes she made him climb up a steep rock for a crannied blossom he would have passed unnoticed.

The sun was going down when they at last trudged into El Tordo and halted before the church, where the priest stood surrounded by a bevy of inquiring, disappointed girls. He rushed forth immediately to help Mana Seda off the donkey, while the children pounced upon the flowers with shouts of glee. Asking questions and not waiting for answers, he led the stranger and his still stranger charge into his house, meanwhile giving orders that the burro be taken to his barn and fed.

Mana Seda dared not sit with the Padre at table and hied herself to the kitchen for her supper. Young Esquipula, however, felt very much at ease, answering all his host's questions intelligently, at which the pastor was agreeably surprised, but not quite so astonished as when he heard for the first time of Mana Seda's childhood disappointments.

---

[9] *oeuvre de caprice:* used here to mean improvised masterpiece.

"Young man," he said, hurriedly finishing his meal, "there is little time to lose. Tonight is the closing of May—and it will be done, although we are unworthy." Dragging his chair closer to the youth, he plotted out his plan in excited whispers which fired Esquipula with an equal enthusiasm.

The last bell was calling the folk of El Tordo in the cool of the evening. Six queens with their many white-veiled maids stood in a nervous, noisy line at the church door, a garden of flowers in their arms. The priest and the stranger stood on guard facing them, begging them to be quiet, looking anxiously at the people who streamed past them into the edifice. Mana Seda finally appeared and tried to slide quietly by, but the Padre barred her way and pressed a big basket filled with flowers and lighted candles into her brown, dry hands. At the same time Esquipula took off her black shawl and dropped over her grey head and hunched form a precious veil of Spanish lace.

In her amazement she could not protest, could not even move a step, until the Padre urged her on, whispering into her ear that it was the holy Virgin's express wish. And so Mana Seda led all the queens that evening, slowly and smoothly, not like a black widow now, folks observed, but like one of those little white moths moving over alfalfa fields in the moonlight. It was the happiest moment of her long life. She felt that she must die from pure joy, and many others observing her, thought so too.

She did not die then; for some years afterward, she wore the new black *tápalo* the Padre gave her in exchange for the old one, which Esquipula installed in the *retablo* above the altar. But toward the last she could not gather any more flowers on the slopes, much less in the forest. They buried her in a corner of the *campo santo,* and the following May disks of daisies and bunches of verbenas came up on her grave. It is said they have been doing it ever since, for curious travelers to ask about, while pious pilgrims come to pray before the hunchback Madonna.

DISCUSSION

1. Why does the Padre say to Esquipula "we are unworthy" of Mana Seda?

2. What led to Mana Seda's decision to become a flower bearer?

3. Chávez uses vivid images to describe the countryside of New Mexico. Find some that you think are particularly effective.

For further activities, see page 536.

536

VOCABULARY

The Secret Life of Walter Mitty (page 522)

1.   In the years since James Thurber wrote this famous story, the name Walter Mitty has become part of our language. We use it to refer to ourselves when we indulge in elaborate fantasies in which we are the heroes. We may use it also when we are in real situations that seem more like fantasy than reality. Literature has given us other names that we use as stereotypes to describe certain kinds of people. How many of the ones below can you explain?

Scrooge	Babbitt	Mrs. Malaprop
Pollyanna	Simon Legree	Cinderella
	Judas	

2.   James Thurber also made use of onomatopoeia, a term which you may think of only in terms of poetry. In three of Walter Mitty's fantasies, the term "pocketa pocketa" appears. It has no real meaning and yet it represents a sound familiar to us. Look at the words below. The first one is also a James Thurber creation. Since these are "sound" words, you should pronounce them, following the instructions in parentheses. What meaning do these words have? What things make these sounds?

chuffa chuffa (repeat several times, rapidly)
vroom (say once, slowly)
whoosh (say once, slowly)
kerplosh (say with accent on second syllable)

COMPOSITION

The Story of an Hour (page 496)

Write a letter that you think Mr. Mallard might write to a friend in which he informs that friend of Mrs. Mallard's death. In your letter, try to sustain the situational irony expressed in the last line of the story.

The Inside Search (page 499)

Zora Neale Hurston tells us what visions she saw as a child. She also says that over the years they came true. Choose one of the visions and write a story about how it came true.

The Bedquilt (page 509)

1. Imagine you are at the county fair and meet Aunt Mehetabel in front of her bedquilt. Aside from complimenting her on it and congratulating her on winning the blue ribbon, what would you say to her? Write a page or two of dialogue between yourself and Aunt Mehetabel. Write Aunt Mehetabel's conversation in the style used in "The Bedquilt."

2. Aunt Mehetabel's nieces are too young to appreciate many of the things that are important to Aunt Mehetabel. They have no appreciation for the past, for tradition. Write a brief composition, using the words you think Aunt Mehetabel would use, in which she tries to explain to her nieces why the past is important and what they can learn from it.

The Secret Life of Walter Mitty (page 522)

1. Walter Mitty has no difficulty imagining himself the hero in any number of situations. Try your hand at writing a fantasy starring Walter Mitty as the sheriff of a small Western town in the late 1800s. In order to do this effectively you will have to think of the sheriff and all the other characters as stereotypes.

2. Women too have fantasies in which they too are stereotyped heroines. Choose one of Walter Mitty's fantasies, the courtroom scene, for example, and rewrite it from a woman's point of view. Or, if you prefer, make up a new situation with a woman in the starring role as heroine.

Hunchback Madonna (page 527)

Think of a time in your life when you were discriminated against because of something you couldn't help. Write a brief essay describing the time, the place, and your feelings.

Carriers of the Dream Wheel

N. SCOTT MOMADAY

This is the Wheel of Dreams
Which is carried on their voices,
By means of which their voices turn
And center upon being.
It encircles the First World,   5
This powerful wheel.
They shape their songs upon the wheel
And spin the names of the earth and sky,
The aboriginal names.
They are old men, or men   10
Who are old in their voices,
And they carry the wheel among the camps,
Saying: Come, come,
Let us tell the old stories,
Let us sing the sacred songs.   15

DISCUSSION

1. What is this "Wheel of Dreams"? Where and how is it carried? Why is the wheel a good image or metaphor for what the poet is describing?

2. Our modern world still needs its dream wheels. Who are their carriers?

For further activities, see page 560.

FOR MY PEOPLE

MARGARET WALKER

For my people everywhere singing their slave songs repeatedly: their
    dirges and their ditties and their blues and jubilees, praying their
    prayers nightly to an unknown god, bending their knees humbly to
    an unseen power;

For my people lending their strength to the years, to the gone years and   5
    the now years and the maybe years, washing ironing cooking scrub-
    bing sewing mending hoeing plowing digging planting pruning
    patching dragging along never gaining never reaping never knowing
    and never understanding;

For my playmates in the clay and dust and sand of Alabama backyards   10
    playing baptizing and preaching and doctor and jail and soldier and
    school and mama and cooking and playhouse and concert and store
    and hair and Miss Choomby and company;

For the cramped bewildered years we went to school to learn to know
    the reasons why and the answers to and the people who and the   15
    places where and the days when, in memory of the bitter hours
    when we discovered we were black and poor and small and different
    and nobody cared and nobody wondered and nobody understood;

For the boys and girls who grew in spite of these things to be man and
    woman, to laugh and dance and sing and play and drink their wine   20
    and religion and success, to marry their playmates and bear children
    and then die of consumption and anemia and lynching;

For my people thronging 47th Street in Chicago and Lenox Avenue in
    New York and Rampart Street in New Orleans, lost disinherited dis-
    possessed and happy people filling the cabarets and taverns and oth-   25
    er people's pockets needing bread and shoes and milk and land and
    money and something—something all our own;

For my people walking blindly spreading joy, losing time being lazy,
sleeping when hungry, shouting when burdened, drinking when
hopeless, tied and shackled and tangled among ourselves by the un-   30
seen creatures who tower over us omnisciently and laugh;

For my people blundering and groping and floundering in the dark of
churches and schools and clubs and societies, associations and councils and committees and conventions, distressed and disturbed and
deceived and devoured by money-hungry glory-craving leeches,   35
preyed on by facile force of state and fad and novelty, by false
prophet and holy believer;

For my people standing staring trying to fashion a better way from confusion, from hypocrisy and misunderstanding, trying to fashion a
world that will hold all the people, all the faces, all the adams and   40
eves and their countless generations;

Let a new earth rise. Let another world be born. Let a bloody peace be
written in the sky. Let a second generation full of courage issue
forth; let a people loving freedom come to growth. Let a beauty full
of healing and a strength of final clenching be the pulsing in our   45
spirits and our blood. Let the martial songs be written, let the dirges
disappear. Let a race of men now rise and take control.

DISCUSSION

1. "Let a new earth rise. Let another world be born." Why does the author feel a new earth is necessary? How would it differ from the old earth?

2. Who are the "unseen creatures who tower over us omnisciently and laugh"?

3. What have been her people's expectations of life? How have they tried to live with these expectations?

4. How does the author think this "new earth" must come about? Do you agree, or do you think there is another way?

For further acitivities, see page 560.

it is said

ALURISTA

it is said

              that Motecuhzoma Ilhuicamina

sent**********

             an expedition

looking for the northern   5

             mythical land

wherefrom the Aztecs came

             la tierra

                 de

                    Aztlán   10

             mythical land for those

             who dream of roses and

swallow thorns

             or for those who swallow thorns

      in powdered milk   15

feeling guilty about smelling flowers

             about looking for Aztlán

---

2. *Motecuhzoma Ilhuicamina* (mō-tĕ-koo-sō'mä ĕl-hwē-kä-mē'nä): a reference to the Aztec emperor Moctezuma (Montezuma).
10. *Aztlán* (äst-län'): Used by some Chicanos to mean formerly Mexican states of Southwest U.S. Also used to describe a shared consciousness of Chicano heritage.

DISCUSSION

1. Who are those who "dream of roses and swallow thorns"? What are the thorns?

2. What is different "for those who swallow thorns / in powdered milk"? Why might they feel guilty?

For further activities, see page 560.

Let America Be America Again

LANGSTON HUGHES

Let America be America again.
Let it be the dream it used to be.
Let it be the pioneer on the plain
Seeking a home where he himself is free.

(America never was America to me.)   5

Let America be the dream the dreamers dreamed——
Let it be that great strong land of love
Where never kings connive nor tyrants scheme
That any man be crushed by one above.

(It never was America to me.)   10

O, let my land be a land where Liberty
Is crowned with no false patriotic wreath,
But opportunity is real, and life is free,
Equality is in the air we breathe.

(There's never been equality for me,   15
Nor freedom in this "homeland of the free.")

Say who are you that mumbles in the dark?
And who are you that draws your veil across the stars?

I am the poor white, fooled and pushed apart,
I am the Negro bearing slavery's scars.   20
I am the red man driven from the land,
I am the immigrant clutching the hope I seek——
And finding only the same old stupid plan
Of dog eat dog, of mighty crush the weak.

I am the young man, full of strength and hope,   25
Tangled in that ancient endless chain
Of profit, power, gain, of grab the land!
Of grab the gold! Of grab the ways of satisfying need!
Of work the men! Of take the pay!
Of owning everything for one's own greed!   30

I am the farmer, bondsman to the soil.
I am the worker, sold to the machine.
I am the Negro, servant to you all.
I am the people, worried, hungry, mean——
Hungry yet today despite the dream.   35
Beaten yet today——O, Pioneers!
I am the man who never got ahead,
The poorest worker bartered through the years.

Yet I'm the one who dreamt our basic dream
In that Old World while still a serf of kings,   40
Who dreamt a dream so strong, so brave, so true,
That even yet its mighty daring sings
In every brick and stone, in every furrow turned
That's made America the land it has become.
O, I'm the man who sailed those early seas   45
In search of what I meant to be my home——
For I'm the one who left dark Ireland's shore,
And Poland's plain, and England's grassy lea,
And torn from Black Africa's strand I came
To build a "homeland of the free."   50

The free?

A dream——
Still beckoning to me!

O, let America be America again——
The land that never has been yet——   55
And yet must be——
The land where *every* man is free.
The land that's mine——
The poor man's, Indian's, Negro's, ME——
Who made America,   60
Whose sweat and blood, whose faith and pain,

Whose hand at the foundry, whose plow in the rain,
Must bring back our mighty dream again.

Sure, call me any ugly name you choose——
The steel of freedom does not stain.   65
From those who live like leeches on the people's lives,
We must take back our land again,
America!

O, yes,
I say it plain,   70
America never was America to me,
And yet I swear this oath——
America will be!
An ever-living seed,
Its dream   75
Lies deep in the heart of me.

We, the people, must redeem
Our land, the mines, the plants, the rivers,
The mountains and the endless plain——
All, all the stretch of these great green states——   80
And make America again!

DISCUSSION

1. This poem was written forty years ago. In what ways do you think America today is closer to the poet's dream? Are there ways in which the dream has become further from realization? Explain your answer.

2. Look at the *structure,* or arrangement, of this poem. Why are some lines in parentheses? In lines 17–18 whose voice speaks? To whom? What lines answer the question this voice asks?

3. What change takes place in the poem after line 18? After line 53?

4. What does the poet mean when he says "we must *redeem* the land"? This word has several meanings; which meaning do you think was in the poet's mind?

For further activities, see page 560.

The Gettysburg Address

ABRAHAM LINCOLN

Four score and seven years ago our fathers brought forth on this continent, a new nation, conceived in Liberty, and dedicated to the proposition that all men are created equal.

Now we are engaged in a great civil war, testing whether that nation, or any nation so conceived and so dedicated, can long endure. We are met on a great battlefield of that war. We have come to dedicate a portion of that field, as a final resting place for those who here gave their lives that that nation might live. It is altogether fitting and proper that we should do this.

But, in a larger sense, we can not dedicate—we can not consecrate—we can not hallow—this ground. The brave men, living and dead, who struggled here, have consecrated it, far above our poor power to add or detract. The world will little note, nor long remember what we say here, but it can never forget what they did here. It is for us the living, rather, to be dedicated here to the unfinished work which they who fought here have thus far so nobly advanced. It is rather for us to be here dedicated to the great task remaining before us—that from these honored dead we take increased devotion to that cause for which they gave the last full measure of devotion—that we here highly resolve that these dead shall not have died in vain—that this nation, under God, shall have a new birth of freedom—and that government of the people, by the people, for the people, shall not perish from the earth.

DISCUSSION

1. Why do you think Lincoln's Gettysburg Address has become so famous?

2. Lincoln said that the world would "little note, nor long remember" what was said at Gettysburg that day. In what ways was he right? In what ways wrong?

For further activities, see page 560.

Harrison Bergeron

KURT VONNEGUT, JR.

The year was 2081, and everybody was finally equal. They weren't only equal before God and the law. They were equal every which way. Nobody was smarter than anybody else. Nobody was better looking than anybody else. Nobody was stronger or quicker than anybody else. All this equality was due to the 211th, 212th, and 213th Amendments to the Constitution, and to the unceasing vigilance of agents of the United States Handicapper General.

Some things about living still weren't quite right, though. April, for instance, still drove people crazy by not being springtime. And it was in that clammy month that the H-G men took George and Hazel Bergeron's fourteen-year-old son, Harrison, away.

It was tragic, all right, but George and Hazel couldn't think about it very hard. Hazel had a perfectly average intelligence, which meant she couldn't think about anything except in short bursts. And George, while his intelligence was way above normal, had a little mental handicap radio in his ear. He was required by law to wear it at all times. It was tuned to a government transmitter. Every twenty seconds or so, the transmitter would send out some sharp noise to keep people like George from taking unfair advantage of their brains.

George and Hazel were watching television. There were tears on Hazel's cheeks, but she'd forgotten for the moment what they were about.

On the television screen were ballerinas.

A buzzer sounded in George's head. His thoughts fled in a panic, like bandits from a burglar alarm.

"That was a real pretty dance, that dance they just did," said Hazel.

"Huh?" said George.

"That dance—it was nice," said Hazel.

"Yup," said George. He tried to think a little about the ballerinas. They weren't really very good—no better than anybody else would have been, anyway. They were burdened with sashweights and bags of birdshot, and their faces were masked, so that no one, seeing a free and graceful gesture or a pretty face, would feel like something the cat drug in. George was toying with the vague notion that maybe dancers shouldn't be handicapped. But he didn't get very far with it before another noise in his ear radio scattered his thoughts.

George winced. So did two out of the eight ballerinas.

Hazel saw him wince. Having no mental handicap herself, she had to ask George what the latest sound had been.

"Sounded like somebody hitting a milk bottle with a ball-peen hammer," said George.

"I'd think it would be real interesting, hearing all the different sounds," said Hazel, a little envious. "All the things they think up."

"Um," said George.

"Only, if I was Handicapper General, you know what I would do?" said Hazel. Hazel, as a matter of fact, bore a strong resemblance to the Handicapper General, a woman named Diana Moon Glampers. "If I was Diana Moon Glampers," said Hazel, "I'd have chimes on Sunday—just chimes. Kind of in honor of religion."

"I could think, if it was just chimes," said George.

"Well—maybe make 'em real loud," said Hazel. "I think I'd make a good Handicapper General."

"Good as anybody else," said George.

"Who knows better'n I do what normal is?" said Hazel.

"Right," said George. He began to think glimmeringly about his abnormal son who was now in jail, about Harrison, but a twenty-one-gun salute in his head stopped that.

"Boy!" said Hazel, "that was a doozy, wasn't it?"

It was such a doozy that George was white and trembling, and tears stood on the rims of his red eyes. Two of the eight ballerinas had collapsed to the studio floor, were holding their temples.

"All of a sudden you look so tired," said Hazel. "Why don't you stretch out on the sofa, so's you can rest your handicap bag on the pillows, honeybunch." She was referring to the forty-seven pounds of bird-shot in a canvas bag, which was padlocked around George's neck. "Go on and rest the bag for a little while," she said. "I don't care if you're not equal to me for a while."

George weighed the bag with his hands. "I don't mind it," he said. "I don't notice it any more. It's just a part of me."

"You been so tired lately—kind of wore out," said Hazel. "If there was just some way we could make a little hole in the bottom of the bag, and just take out a few of them lead balls. Just a few."

"Two years in prison and two thousand dollars fine for every ball I took out," said George. "I don't call that a bargain."

"If you could just take a few out when you came home from work," said Hazel. "I mean—you don't compete with anybody around here. You just set around."

"If I tried to get away with it," said George, "then other people'd get away with it—and pretty soon we'd be right back to the dark ages again, with everybody competing against everybody else. You wouldn't like that, would you?"

"I'd hate it," said Hazel.

"There you are," said George. "The minute people start cheating on laws, what do you think happens to society?"

If Hazel hadn't been able to come up with an answer to this question, George couldn't have supplied one. A siren was going off in his head.

"Reckon it'd fall all apart," said Hazel.

"What would?" said George blankly.

"Society," said Hazel uncertainly. "Wasn't that what you just said?"

"Who knows?" said George.

The television program was suddenly interrupted for a news bulletin. It wasn't clear at first as to what the bulletin was about, since the announcer, like all announcers, had a serious speech impediment. For about half a minute, and in a state of high excitement, the announcer tried to say, "Ladies and gentlemen—"

He finally gave up, handed the bulletin to a ballerina to read.

"That's all right—" Hazel said of the announcer, "he tried. That's the big thing. He tried to do the best he could with what God gave him. He should get a nice raise for trying so hard."

"Ladies and gentlemen—" said the ballerina, reading the bulletin. She must have been extraordinarily beautiful, because the mask she wore was hideous. And it was easy to see that she was the strongest and most graceful of all the dancers, for her handicap bags were as big as those worn by two-hundred-pound men.

And she had to apologize at once for her voice, which was a very unfair voice for a woman to use. Her voice was a warm, luminous, timeless melody. "Excuse me—" she said, and she began again, making her voice absolutely uncompetitive.

"Harrison Bergeron, age fourteen," she said in a grackle squawk, "has just escaped from jail, where he was held on suspicion of plotting to overthrow the government. He is a genius and an athlete, is underhandicapped, and should be regarded as extremely dangerous."

A police photograph of Harrison Bergeron was flashed on the screen upside down, then sideways, upside down again, then right side up. The picture showed the full length of Harrison against a background calibrated in feet and inches. He was exactly seven feet tall.

The rest of Harrison's appearance was Halloween and hardware. Nobody had ever borne heavier handicaps. He had outgrown hindrances faster than the H-G men could think them up. Instead of a little ear radio for a mental handicap, he wore a tremendous pair of earphones, and spectacles with thick wavy lenses. The spectacles were intended to make him not only half blind, but to give him whanging headaches besides.

Scrap metal was hung all over him. Ordinarily, there was a certain symmetry, a military neatness to the handicaps issued to strong people, but Harrison looked like a walking junkyard. In the race of life, Harrison carried three hundred pounds.

And to offset his good looks, the H-G men required that he wear at all times a red rubber ball for a nose, keep his eyebrows shaved off, and cover his even white teeth with black caps at snaggle-tooth random.

"If you see this boy," said the ballerina, "do not—I repeat, do not—try to reason with him."

There was the shriek of a door being torn from its hinges.

Screams and barking cries of consternation came from the television set. The photograph of Harrison Bergeron on the screen jumped again and again, as though dancing to the tune of an earthquake.

George Bergeron correctly identified the earthquake, and well he might have—for many was the time his own home had danced to the same crashing tune. "That must be Harrison!" said George.

The realization was blasted from his mind instantly by the sound of an automobile collision in his head.

When George could open his eyes

again, the photograph of Harrison was gone. A living, breathing Harrison filled the screen.

Clanking, clownish, and huge, Harrison stood in the center of the studio. The knob of the uprooted studio door was still in his hand. Ballerinas, technicians, musicians, and announcers cowered on their knees before him, expecting to die.

"I am the Emperor!" cried Harrison. "Do you hear? I am the Emperor! Everybody must do what I say at once!" He stamped his foot and the studio shook.

"Even as I stand here—" he bellowed, "crippled, hobbled, sickened—I am a greater ruler than any man who ever lived! Now watch me become what I *can* become!"

Harrison tore the straps of his handicap harness like wet tissue paper, tore straps guaranteed to support five thousand pounds.

Harrison's scrap-iron handicaps crashed to the floor.

Harrison thrust his thumbs under the bar of the padlock that secured his head harness. The bar snapped like celery. Harrison smashed his headphones and spectacles against the wall.

He flung away his rubber-ball nose, revealed a man that would have awed Thor, the god of thunder.

"I shall now select my Empress!" he said, looking down on the cowering people. "Let the first woman who dares rise to her feet claim her mate and her throne!"

A moment passed, and then a ballerina arose, swaying like a willow.

Harrison plucked the mental handicap from her ear, snapped off her physical handicaps with marvelous delicacy.

Last of all, he removed her mask.

She was blindingly beautiful.

"Now——" said Harrison, taking her hand, "shall we show the people the meaning of the word dance? Music!" he commanded.

The musicians scrambled back into their chairs, and Harrison stripped them of their handicaps, too. "Play your best," he told them, "and I'll make you barons and dukes and earls."

The music began. It was normal at first—cheap, silly, false. But Harrison snatched two musicians from their chairs, waved them like batons as he sang the music as he wanted it played. He slammed them back into their chairs.

The music began again and was much improved.

Harrison and his Empress merely listened to the music for a while—listened gravely, as though synchronizing their heartbeats with it.

They shifted their weights to their toes.

Harrison placed his big hands on the girl's tiny waist, letting her sense the weightlessness that would soon be hers.

And then, in an explosion of joy and grace, into the air they sprang!

Not only were the laws of the land abandoned, but the law of gravity and the laws of motion as well.

They reeled, whirled, swiveled, flounced, capered, gamboled, and spun.

They leaped like deer on the moon.

The studio ceiling was thirty feet high, but each leap brought the dancers nearer to it.

It became their obvious intention to kiss the ceiling.

They kissed it.

And then, neutralizing gravity with love and pure will, they remained suspended in air inches below the ceiling, and they kissed each other for a long, long time.

It was then that Diana Moon Glampers, the Handicapper General, came into the studio with a double-barreled ten-gauge shotgun. She fired twice, and the Emperor and the Empress were dead before they hit the floor.

Diana Moon Glampers loaded the gun again. She aimed it at the musicians and told them they had ten seconds to get their handicaps back on.

It was then that the Bergerons' television tube burned out.

Hazel turned to comment about the blackout to George. But George had gone out into the kitchen for a can of beer.

George came back in with the beer, paused while a handicap signal shook him up. And then he sat down again. "You been crying?" he said to Hazel.

"Yup," she said.

"What about?" he said.

"I forget," she said. "Something real sad on television."

"What was it?" he said.

"It's all kind of mixed up in my mind," said Hazel.

"Forget sad things," said George.

"I always do," said Hazel.

"That's my girl," said George. He winced. There was the sound of a riveting gun in his head.

"Gee—I could tell that one was a doozy," said Hazel.

"You can say that again," said George.

"Gee—" said Hazel, "I could tell that one was a doozy."

DISCUSSION

1. Handicaps are given the best or strongest players in some sports to give everyone a nearly equal chance of winning. Kurt Vonnegut carries this idea to a ridiculous extreme. In the world of "Harrison Bergeron," what has been lost by this practice? What do the dancers illustrate of this loss?

2. George and Hazel Bergeron find it almost impossible to have a connected conversation. George's thoughts are continually interrupted by his handicap. Hazel, however, is not handicapped, because she is "average." What has happened to the concept of "average" in their society?

3. A *satire* is a literary work that holds up human folly to ridicule and scorn. In this story, what "human folly" does Vonnegut ridicule?

For further activities, see page 560.

"When I wrote the following pages . . . I lived alone in the woods a mile from any neighbor, in a house which I had built myself on the shore of Walden Pond in Concord, Massachusetts, and earned my living by the labor of my hands only. I lived there two years and two months. At present I am a sojourner in civilized life again. . . ."

FROM

HENRY DAVID THOREAU

I went to the woods because I wished to live deliberately, to front only the essential facts of life, and see if I could not learn what it had to teach, and not, when I came to die, discover that I had not lived. I did not wish to live what was not life, living is so dear, nor did I wish to practise resignation, unless it was quite necessary. I wanted to live deep and suck out all the marrow of life, to live so sturdily and Spartan-like as to put to rout all that was not life, to cut a broad swath and shave close, to drive life into a corner, and reduce it to its lowest terms, and, if it proved to be mean, why then to get the whole and genuine meanness of it, and publish its meanness to the world; or if it were sublime, to know it by experience, and be able to give a true account of it in my next excursion. . . .

Our life is frittered away by detail. An honest man hardly need to count more than his ten fingers, or in extreme cases he may add his ten toes, and lump the rest. Simplicity, simplicity, simplicity! I say, let your affairs be as two or three, and not a hundred or a thousand; instead of a million count half a dozen, and keep your accounts on your thumb nail. In the midst of this chopping sea of civilized life, such are the clouds and storms and quicksands and thousand-and-one items to be allowed for, that a man has to live, if he would not founder and go to the bottom and not make his port at all, by dead reckoning, and he must be a great calculator indeed who succeeds. Simplify, simplify. Instead of three meals a day, if it be necessary eat but one; instead of a hundred dishes, five; and reduce other things in proportion. . . .

Why should we live with such hurry and waste of life? We are determined to be starved before we are hungry. Men say that a stitch in time saves nine, and so they take a thousand stitches today to save nine tomorrow. As for *work*, we haven't any of any consequence. We have the Saint Vitus' dance,[1] and cannot possibly keep our heads still. . . . After a night's sleep the news is as indispensable as the breakfast. "Pray tell me anything new that has happened to a man anywhere on this globe"—and he reads it over his coffee and rolls, that a man has had his eyes gouged out this morning on the Wachito River; never dreaming the while that he lives in the dark unfathomed mammoth cave of this world, and has but the rudiment of an eye himself.

For my part, I could easily do without the post-office. I think that there are very few important communications made through it. To speak critically, I never received more than one or two letters in my life—I wrote this some years ago—that were worth the postage. The penny-post is, commonly, an institution through which you seriously offer a man that penny for his thoughts which is so often safely offered in jest. And I am sure that I never read any memorable news in a newspaper. If we read of one man robbed, or murdered, or killed by accident, or one house burned, or one vessel wrecked, or one steamboat blown up, or one cow run over on the Western Railroad, or one mad dog killed, or one lot of grasshoppers in the winter, we never need read of another. One is enough. If you are acquainted with the principle, what do you care for a myriad instances and applications? To a philosopher all *news*, as it is called, is gossip, and they who edit and read it are old women over their tea. Yet not a few are greedy after this gossip. There was such a rush, as I hear, the other day at one of the offices to learn the foreign news by the last arrival, that several large squares of plate glass belonging to the establishment were broken by the pressure—news which I seriously think a ready wit might write a twelvemonth or twelve years beforehand with sufficient accuracy. As for Spain, for instance, if you know how to throw in Don Carlos and the Infanta, and Don Pedro and Seville and Granada, from time to time in the right proportions—they may have changed the names a little since I saw the papers—and serve up a bull-fight when other entertainments fail, it will be true to the letter, and give us as good an idea of the exact state of ruin of things in Spain as the most succinct and lucid reports under this head in the newspapers: and as for England, almost the last significant scrap of news from that quarter was the revolution of 1649; and if you have learned the history of her crops for an average year, you never need attend to that thing again, unless your speculations are of a merely pecuniary character. If one may judge who rarely looks into the newspapers, nothing new does ever happen in foreign parts, a French revolution not excepted.

---

[1] *St. Vitus' dance:* disease of nervous system, causing involuntary jerky movements.

Let us spend one day as deliberately as Nature, and not be thrown off the track by every nutshell and mosquito's wing that falls on the rails. Let us rise early and fast, or break fast, gently and without perturbation; let company come and let company go, let the bells ring and the children cry—determined to make a day of it. Why should we knock under and go with the stream? Let us not be upset and overwhelmed in that terrible rapid and whirlpool called a dinner, situated in the meridian shallows. Weather this danger and you are safe, for the rest of the way is down hill. With unrelaxed nerves, with morning vigor, sail by it, looking another way, tied to the mast like Ulysses.[2] If the engine whistles, let it whistle till it is hoarse for its pains. If the bell rings, why should we run? We will consider what kind of music they are like. Let us settle ourselves, and work and wedge our feet downward through the mud and slush of opinion, and prejudice, and tradition, and delusion, and appearance, that alluvion which covers the globe, through Paris and London, through New York and Boston and Concord, through church and state, through poetry and philosophy and religion, till we come to a hard bottom and rocks in place, which we can call reality. . . .

Time is but the stream I go a-fishing in. I drink at it; but while I drink I see the sandy bottom and detect how shallow it is. Its thin current slides away, but eternity remains. I would drink deeper; fish in the sky, whose bottom is pebbly with stars. I cannot count one. I know not the first letter of the alphabet. I have always been regretting that I was not as wise as the day I was born. The intellect is a cleaver; it discerns and rifts its way into the secret of things. I do not wish to be any more busy with my hands than is necessary. My head is hands and feet. I feel all my best faculties concentrated in it. My instinct tells me that my head is an organ for burrowing, as some creatures use their snout and forepaws, and with it I would mine and burrow my way through these hills. I think that the richest vein is somewhere hereabout; so by the divining rod and thin rising vapors I judge; and here I will begin to mine.

I had this advantage, at least, in my mode of life, over those who were obliged to look abroad for amusement, to society and the theatre, that my life itself was become my amusement and never ceased to be novel. It was a drama of many scenes and without an end. If we were always indeed getting our living, and regulating our lives according to the last and best mode we had learned, we should never be troubled with ennui. Follow your genius closely enough, and it will not fail to show you

2 *like Ulysses:* Ulysses tied himself to his ship's mast so that he could resist the Sirens' song calling him to change course and be dashed on the rocks.

a fresh prospect every hour. Housework was a pleasant pastime. When my floor was dirty, I rose early, and, setting all my furniture out of doors on the grass, bed and bedstead making but one budget, dashed water on the floor, and sprinkled white sand from the pond on it, and then with a broom scrubbed it clean and white; and by the time the villagers had broken their fast the morning sun had dried my house sufficiently to allow me to move in again, and my meditations were almost uninterrupted. It was pleasant to see my whole household effects out on the grass, making a little pile like a gypsy's pack, and my three-legged table, from which I did not remove the books and pen and ink, standing amid the pines and hickories. They seemed glad to get out themselves, and as if unwilling to be brought in. I was sometimes tempted to stretch an awning over them and take my seat there. It was worth the while to see the sun shine on these things, and hear the free wind blow on them; so much more interesting most familiar objects look out of doors than in the house. . . .

I find it wholesome to be alone the greater part of the time. To be in company, even with the best, is soon wearisome and dissipating. I love to be alone. I never found the companion that was so companionable as solitude. We are for the most part more lonely when we go abroad among men than when we stay in our chambers. A man thinking or working is always alone, let him be where he will. Solitude is not measured by the miles of space that intervene between a man and his fellows. The really diligent student in one of the crowded hives of Cambridge College is as solitary as a dervis in the desert. The farmer can work alone in the field or the woods all day long, hoeing or chopping, and not feel lonesome, because he is employed; but when he comes home at night he cannot sit down in a room alone, at the mercy of his thoughts, but must be where he can "see the folks," and recreate, and as he thinks remunerate, himself for his day's solitude; and hence he wonders how the student can sit alone in the house all night and most of the day without ennui and "the blues"; but he does not realize that the student, though in the house, is still at work in *his* field, and chopping in *his* woods, as the farmer in his, and in turn seeks the same recreation and society that the latter does, though it may be a more condensed form of it.

Society is commonly too cheap. We meet at very short intervals, not having had time to acquire any new value for each other. We meet at meals three times a day, and give each other a new taste of that old musty cheese that we are. We have had to agree on a certain set of rules, called etiquette and politeness, to make this frequent meeting tolerable and that we need not come to open war. We meet at the post-office, and at the sociable, and about the fireside every night; we live thick and are in each other's way, and stumble over one another, and think that we thus lose some respect for one another. Certainly less frequency would suffice for all important and hearty communications. Consider the girls in a factory—never alone, hardly in their dreams. It would be better if there were but one inhabitant to a square mile, as where I live. The value of a man is not in his skin, that we should touch him.

I left the woods for as good a reason as I went there. Perhaps it seemed to me that I had several more lives to live, and could not spare any more time for that one. It is remarkable how easily and insensibly we fall into a particular route, and make a beaten track for ourselves. I had not lived there a week before my feet wore a path from my door to the pond-side; and though it is five or six years since I trod it, it is still quite distinct. It is true, I fear that others may have fallen into it, and so helped to keep it open. The surface of the earth is soft and impressible by the feet of men; and so with the paths which the mind travels. How worn and dusty, then, must be the highways of the world, how deep the ruts of tradition and conformity! I did not wish to take a cabin passage, but rather to go before the mast and on the deck of the world, for there I could best see the moonlight amid the mountains. I do not wish to go below now.

I learned this, at least, by my experiment; that if one advances confidently in the direction of his dreams, and endeavors to live the life which he has imagined, he will meet with a success unexpected in common hours. He will put some things behind, will pass an invisible boundary; new, universal, and more liberal laws will begin to establish themselves around and within him; or the old laws be expanded and interpreted in his favor in a more liberal sense, and he will live with the license of a higher order of beings. In proportion as he simplifies his life, the laws of the universe will appear less complex, and solitude will not be solitude, nor poverty poverty, nor weakness weakness. If you have built castles in the air, your work need not be lost; that is where they should be. Now put the foundations under them.

DISCUSSION

1. "I left the woods for as good a reason as I went there," says Thoreau. What were his reasons for beginning and for ending this experience?

2. How would you go about living "one day as deliberately as Nature" (page 555)? What changes in your own life would be necessary?

3. Many people now, in all parts of the country, are trying to live as Thoreau lived in the mid-nineteenth century at Walden Pond. How do their attempts differ from his? What conditions unknown to Thoreau might make such experiments more difficult now?

4. If Thoreau had set up his cabin at the edge of your town, would his life have seemed successful to you? How do you think he would have been regarded by the people of your town? Would their opinion have disturbed him?

5. Thoreau had the ability to compress complex ideas into short, memorable sentences. His approach to life made him particularly aware of *paradox*—those things in life which seem to contradict themselves. What does Thoreau mean when he says, on page 557, "I never found the companion that was so companionable as solitude"?

For further activities, see page 560.

VOCABULARY

Harrison Bergeron (page 547)

New words are constantly being added to our language. Many of them are due to advances in technology; an encyclopedia of the early 1900s would have many listings under *A,* but *automobile* would not be among them. Below are four words found in this story. On separate paper, use each of these words in a sentence. Then write a definition for each word, as you understand it. Finally, find all four words in the dictionary, and check your definitions. Which of these words would have been found in a dictionary of 1900? How might they have been defined?

transmitter   calibrated   synchronizing   neutralizing

Walden (page 553)

Choosing the right word is one of the most important tasks in writing. Thoreau is a master of the precise word and phrase. Like any writer, however, he is at the mercy of the reader, upon whom falls the task of attaching the right meaning to that right word. If this does not happen, there is no chance for the writer to explain, as there would be in conversation. Below are four short quotations from *Walden;* each depends upon the meaning of one key word. Choose the definition that best replaces the word in bold type. Then look back at the full passage on the page indicated. Is your choice the one Thoreau had in mind? Be careful—the best meaning may seem the most unlikely!

1. "to live deep and suck out all the *marrow* of life" (page 553)
   a. vitality   b. material filling bone cavities   c. squash

2. "he . . . has but the *rudiment* of an eye" (p. 554)
   a. fundamental skill   b. undeveloped form   c. imperfectly developed form

3. "the mud and slush of opinion, . . . that *alluvion* which covers the globe" (p. 555)
   a. flood   b. flow of water against a shore   c. sediment deposited by water

4. "the intellect is a *cleaver*" (p. 555)
   a. sharp, heavy knife   b. plant with small, white flower   c. that which clings

COMPOSITION

For My People (page 539)

Music has always been an important expression of human vision. Margaret Walker speaks of "their dirges and their ditties and their blues and jubilees" when she writes of her people's endurance and her vision. Perhaps there is a song or a poem that expresses your vision of the way the world should be. Choose a line, or lines that are most meaningful to you, and write a brief paper explaining how these words speak of your vision.

Carriers of the Dream Wheel (page 538)
Let America Be America Again (page 539)
it is said (page 542)

How important is a knowledge of our histories as we dream of a better world? Do we need to know "the people who and the places where and the days when" (page 539) in order to avoid past mistakes, or could we build a better future if we had no knowledge of past prejudices? Write a short paper expressing your views.

The Gettysburg Address (page 546)

This short piece of prose is poetic in tone though not in form. Try rewriting it in poetic form. Do not change the words; only arrange the lines and space so that it looks and feels like a poem.

Harrison Bergeron (page 547)

Writing as if from a date in the future, choose some custom of our present society, and write a brief story or essay in which this custom becomes a legal requirement for all people and is enforced to the point of ridiculousness.

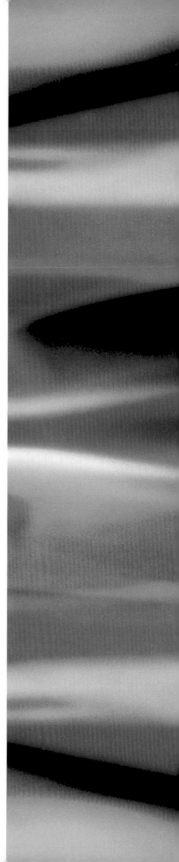

OPENINGS

COMPOSITION

How should you begin a paper? No single rule will apply in all cases, but if you pay attention to the following suggestions, your openings will be more effective.

1. *Know where your paper is headed when you start to write.* Your first sentence should sound firm, not hesitant.

2. *Don't crowd too much into the opening sentence.* Inexperienced writers often try to say too much at the start. Indeed, they sometimes give the whole paper away in the first paragraph, leaving the reader with little reason to read on. The best opening is clear, simple, and interesting. It arrests the reader's attention, and awakens the desire to know more.

3. *Vary your beginnings.* An effective beginning can take the form of a brief anecdote, a specific example, or an appropriate quotation that prepares the reader for what the paper will develop. Don't use any one device all the time; that kind of writing soon becomes mannered and predictable. But keep in mind the advantages of sometimes beginning with the specific rather than the general—and with the human rather than the impersonal. General and impersonal: "Inflation is a problem that affects everybody." Specific: "Mortarshell Bubblegum, that mainstay in many a student's diet, has more than doubled in price since making its debut here scarcely three years ago."

4. *Revise the opening.* Know what your paper is setting out to do and how it plans to do it. Then get started; get something down. Don't stop and polish the opening sentence. By the end of the paper, you may discover that the whole first paragraph is unnecessary. Time spent revising what is doomed eventually to be thrown out will have been time wasted.

On the other hand, *once the first draft is done,* do revise the opening. If you have time to revise only one part of the paper, the opening should be that part. It is the opening that will either discourage or excite the reader's interest; it introduces you, the writer. Read your revision as objectively as you can. Is it clear? Is it interesting? Does it promise something interesting to follow?

ABOUT THE SELECTIONS

1.   The selections in this section offer visions of life as it may seem at one special instant, or life as it might become. Some visions show a time better than the present, whether in the past or in the future. Of those, which envisages a world that you would most like to be a part of? In a paper, explore the characteristics of that world concretely and specifically.

2.   Which of the poems in this unit did you find most difficult to understand? Reread the poem several times, preferably aloud. Look up words you don't know. Try to track down any allusions with which you are not familiar. Then write a paper explaining the extent to which your understanding of the poem has been enlarged by this exploration.

3.   Consider the openings of the prose selections in this section. Which ones are particularly effective? How do you account for their effectiveness? Do any seem inadequate? In a paper that quotes from the selections, discuss your impressions of the various introductory sentences.

ON YOUR OWN

1.   Have you ever experienced anything approaching a vision—a sudden flash of awareness that casts reality into a different light? It may have been a dreamlike moment that revealed life to be indescribably beautiful—or just the opposite. Either report on or imagine such an experience in writing. When did it occur? What was seen? What effect did it have on you?

2.   Each of the following openings is weak. Suggest what is wrong with each one, then see if you can emend the opening to make it effective.

   a.   Henry David Thoreau was a citizen of Concord, Massachusetts, who moved to the woods at Walden Pond, near his home town, when a young man, and lived alone there in a hut, having a number of experiences during that time which formed the basis of his book *Walden,* published in the 1850s and ignored then, but now regarded as a major work.

   b.   I hope to show three things in this paper: that sailing is fun, that it requires skill, and that it is healthful.

   c.   This play is a hard one to read and write about, because the ideas it expresses are complicated, and the language it is written in is one that people no longer speak.

3.   Write two different openings for papers. First, write an opening sentence that is a generalization; make it clear and interesting. Indicate in broad terms what such a paper would concern and how it would be developed. Then, write an opening that is specific—a statement about a specific person in a specific place. Indicate in note form how the specific reference will be developed and what it has to do with the paper that would follow.

REALITIES

The Open Boat

STEPHEN CRANE

I

None of them knew the color of the sky. Their eyes glanced level, and were fastened upon the waves that swept toward them. These waves were of the hue of slate, save for the tops, which were of foaming white, and all of the men knew the colors of the sea. The horizon narrowed and widened, and dipped and rose, and at all times its edge was jagged with waves that seemed thrust up in points like rocks.

Many a man ought to have a bath-tub larger than the boat which here rode upon the sea. These waves were most wrongfully and barbarously abrupt and tall, and each froth-top was a problem in small-boat navigation.

The cook squatted in the bottom, and looked with both eyes at the six inches of gunwale which separated him from the ocean. His sleeves were rolled over his fat forearms, and the two flaps of his unbuttoned vest dangled as he bent to bail out the boat. Often he said, "That was a narrow clip." As he remarked it he invariably gazed eastward over the broken sea.

The oiler, steering with one of the two oars in the boat, sometimes raised himself suddenly to keep clear of water that swirled in over the stern. It was a thin little oar and it seemed often ready to snap.

The correspondent, pulling at the other oar, watched the waves and wondered why he was there.

The injured captain, lying in the bow, was at this time buried in that profound dejection and indifference which comes, temporarily at least, to even the bravest and most enduring when, willy-nilly, the firm fails, the army loses, the ship goes down. The mind of the master of a vessel is rooted deep in the timbers of her, though he has commanded for a day or a decade, and this captain had on him the stern impression of a scene in the grays of dawn of seven turned faces, and later a stump of a top-mast with a white ball on it that slashed to and fro at the waves, went low and lower, and down. Thereafter there was something strange in his voice. Although steady, it was deep with mourning, and of a quality beyond oration or tears.

"Keep 'er a little more south, Billie," said he.

"A little more south, sir," said the oiler in the stern.

A seat in this boat was not unlike a seat upon a bucking bronco, and by the same token, a bronco is not much smaller. The craft pranced and reared and plunged like an animal. As each wave came, and she rose for it, she seemed like a horse making at a fence outrageously high. The manner of her scramble over these walls of water is a mystic thing, and, moreover, at the top of them were ordinarily these problems in white water, the foam racing down from the summit of each wave, requiring a new leap, and a leap from the air. Then, after scornfully bumping a crest, she would slide and race and splash down a long incline, and arrive bobbing and nodding in front of the next menace.

A singular disadvantage of the sea lies in the fact that, after successfully surmounting one wave, you discover that there is another behind it, just as important and just as nervously anxious to do something effective in the way of swamping boats. In a ten-foot dinghy[1] one can get an idea of the resources of the sea in the line of waves that is not probable to the average experience, which is never at sea in a dinghy. As each slaty wall of water approached, it shut all else from the view of the men in the boat, and it was not difficult to imagine that this particular wave was the final outburst of the ocean, the last effort of the grim water. There was a terrible grace in the move of the waves, and they came in silence, save for the snarling of the crests.

In the wan light the faces of the men must have been gray. Their eyes must

[1] *dinghy:* a small rowboat, often carried on the deck of a ship.

have glinted in strange ways as they gazed steadily astern. Viewed from a balcony, the whole thing would, doubtless, have been weirdly picturesque. But the men in the boat had no time to see it, and if they had had leisure, there were other things to occupy their minds. The sun swung steadily up the sky, and they knew it was broad day because the color of the sea changed from slate to emerald-green streaked with amber lights, and the foam was like tumbling snow. The process of the breaking day was unknown to them. They were aware only of this effect upon the color of the waves that rolled toward them.

In disjointed sentences the cook and the correspondent argued as to the difference between a lifesaving station and a house of refuge. The cook had said: "There's a house of refuge just north of the Mosquito Inlet Light, and as soon as they see us they'll come off in their boat and pick us up."

"As soon as who see us?" said the correspondent.

"The crew," said the cook.

"Houses of refuge don't have crews," said the correspondent. "As I understand them, they are only places where clothes and grub are stored for the benefit of shipwrecked people. They don't carry crews."

"Oh, yes, they do," said the cook.

"No, they don't," said the correspondent.

"Well, we're not there yet, anyhow," said the oiler in the stern.

"Well," said the cook, "perhaps it's not a house of refuge that I'm thinking of as being near Mosquito Inlet Light; perhaps it's a lifesaving station."

"We're not there yet," said the oiler in the stern.

II

As the boat bounced from the top of each wave, the wind tore through the hair of the hatless men, and as the craft plopped her stern down again the spray splashed past them. The crest of each of these waves was a hill, from the top of which the men surveyed, for a moment, a broad tumultuous expanse, shining and wind-riven. It was probably splendid. It was probably glorious, this play of the free sea, wild with lights of emerald and white and amber.

"Bully good thing it's an onshore wind," said the cook. "If not, where would we be? Wouldn't have a show."

"That's right," said the correspondent.

The busy oiler nodded his assent.

Then the captain, in the bow, chuckled in a way that expressed humor, contempt, tragedy, all in one. "Do you think we've got much of a show now, boys?" said he.

Whereupon the three were silent, save for a trifle of hemming and hawing. To express any particular optimism at this time they felt to be childish and stupid, but they all doubtless possessed this sense of the situation in their mind. A young man thinks doggedly at such times. On the other hand, the ethics of their condition was decidedly against any open suggestion of hopelessness. So they were silent.

"Oh, well," said the captain, soothing his children, "we'll get ashore all right."

But there was that in his tone which made them think, so the oiler quoth:

"Yes! If this wind holds!"

The cook was bailing: "Yes! If we don't get pounded in the surf."

Canton flannel gulls flew near and far. Sometimes they sat down on the sea, near patches of brown seaweed that rolled on the waves with a movement like carpets on a line in a gale. The birds sat comfortably in groups, and they were envied by some of the dinghy, for the wrath of the sea was no more to them than it was to a covey of prairie chickens a thousand miles inland. Often they came very close and stared at the men with black beadlike eyes. At these times they were uncanny and sinister in their unblinking scrutiny, and the men hooted angrily at them, telling them to be gone. One came, and evidently decided to alight on the top of the captain's head. The bird flew parallel to the boat and did not circle, but made short sidelong jumps in the air in chicken-fashion. His black eyes were wistfully fixed upon the captain's head. "Ugly brute," said the oiler to the bird. "You look as if you were made with a jackknife." The cook and the correspondent swore darkly at the creature. The captain naturally wished to knock it away with the end of the heavy painter;[2] but he did not dare do it, because anything resembling an emphatic gesture would have capsized this freighted boat, and so with his open hand, the captain gently and carefully waved the gull away. After it had been discouraged from the pursuit the captain breathed easier on account of his hair, and others breathed easier because the bird struck their minds at this time as being somehow gruesome and ominous.

In the meantime the oiler and the correspondent rowed; and also they rowed. They sat together in the same seat, and each rowed an oar. Then the oiler took both oars; then the correspondent took both oars; then the oiler; then the correspondent. They rowed and they rowed. The very ticklish part of the business was when the time came for the reclining one in the stern to take his turn at the oars. By the very last star of truth, it is easier to steal eggs from under a hen than it was to change seats in the dinghy. First the man in the stern slid his hand along the thwart and moved with care, as if he were of Sèvres.[3] Then the man in the rowing seat slid his hand along the other thwart. It was all done with the most extraordinary care. As the two sidled past each other, the whole party kept watchful eyes on the coming wave, and the captain cried: "Look out, now! Steady, there!"

The brown mats of seaweed that appeared from time to time were like islands, bits of earth. They were traveling, apparently, neither one way nor the other. They were, to all intents, stationary. They informed the men in the boat that it was making progress slowly toward the land.

The captain, rearing cautiously in the bow after the dinghy soared on a great swell, said that he had seen the lighthouse at Mosquito Inlet. Presently the cook remarked that he had seen it. The correspondent was at the oars then, and

---

[2] *painter:* rope with which a ship is tied to dock.

[3] *Sevres* (sĕv'rə): delicate porcelain, easily broken.

for some reason he too wished to look at the lighthouse; but his back was toward the far shore, and the waves were important, and for some time he could not seize an opportunity to turn his head. But at last there came a wave more gentle than the others, and when at the crest of it he swiftly scoured the western horizon.

"See it?" said the captain.

"No," said the correspondent, slowly; "I didn't see anything."

"Look again," said the captain. He pointed. "It's exactly in that direction."

At the top of another wave the correspondent did as he was bid, and this time his eyes chanced on a small, still thing on the edge of the swaying horizon. It was precisely like the point of a pin. It took an anxious eye to find a lighthouse so tiny.

"Think we'll make it, Captain?"

"If this wind holds and the boat don't swamp, we can't do much else," said the captain.

The little boat, lifted by each towering sea and splashed viciously by the crests, made progress that in the absence of seaweed was not apparent to those in her. She seemed just a wee thing wallowing miraculously, top up, at the mercy of five oceans. Occasionally a great spread of water, like white flames, swarmed into her.

"Bail her, cook," said the captain, serenely.

"All right, Captain," said the cheerful cook.

III

It would be difficult to describe the subtle brotherhood of men that was here established on the seas. No one said that it was so. No one mentioned it. But it dwelt in the boat, and each man felt it warm him. They were a captain, an oiler, a cook, and a correspondent, and they were friends, friends in a more curiously iron-bound degree than may be common. The hurt captain, lying against the water jar in the bow, spoke always in a low voice and calmly, but he could never command a more ready and swiftly obedient crew than the motley three of the dinghy. It was more than a mere recognition of what was best for the common safety. There was surely in it a quality that was personal and heartfelt. And after this devotion to the commander of the boat there was this comradeship that the correspondent, for instance, who had been taught to be cynical of men, knew even at the time was the best experience of his life. But no one said that it was so. No one mentioned it.

"I wish we had a sail," remarked the captain. "We might try my overcoat on the end of an oar and give you two boys a chance to rest." So the cook and the correspondent held the mast and spread wide the overcoat. The oiler steered, and the little boat made good way with her new rig. Sometimes the oiler had to scull sharply to keep a sea from breaking into the boat, but otherwise sailing was a success.

Meanwhile the lighthouse had been growing slowly larger. It had now almost assumed color, and appeared like a little gray shadow on the sky. The man at the oars could not be prevented from turning his head rather often to try for a glimpse of this little gray shadow.

At last, from the top of each wave the men in the tossing boat could see land. Even as the lighthouse was an upright shadow on the sky, this land seemed but a long black shadow on the sea. It certainly was thinner than paper. "We must be about opposite New Smyrna," said the cook, who had coasted this shore often in schooners. "Captain, by the way, I believe they abandoned that lifesaving station there about a year ago."

"Did they?" said the captain.

The wind slowly died away. The cook and correspondent were not now obliged to slave in order to hold high the oar. But the waves continued their old impetuous swooping at the dinghy, and the little craft, no longer under way, struggled woundily over them. The oiler or the correspondent took the oars again.

Shipwrecks are apropos[4] of nothing. If men could only train for them and have them occur when the men had reached pink condition, there would be less drowning at sea. Of the four in the dinghy none had slept any time worth mentioning for two days and two nights previous to embarking in the dinghy, and in the excitement of clambering about the deck of a foundering ship they had also forgotten to eat heartily.

For these reasons, and for others, neither the oiler nor the correspondent was fond of rowing at this time. The correspondent wondered ingenuously how in the name of all that was sane could there be people who thought it amusing to row a boat. It was not an amusement; it was

a diabolical punishment, and even a genius of mental aberrations could never conclude that it was anything but a horror to the muscles and a crime against the back. He mentioned to the boat in general how the amusement of rowing struck him, and the weary-faced oiler smiled in full sympathy. Previously to the foundering, by the way, the oiler had worked double-watch in the engine room of the ship.

"Take her easy, now, boys," said the captain. "Don't spend yourselves. If we have to run a surf you'll need all your strength, because we'll sure have to swim for it. Take your time."

Slowly the land arose from the sea. From a black line it became a line of black and a line of white, trees and sand. Finally, the captain said that he could make out a house on the shore. "That's the house of refuge, sure," said the cook. "They'll see us before long, and come out after us."

The distant lighthouse reared high. "The keeper ought to be able to make us out now, if he's looking through a glass," said the captain. "He'll notify the lifesaving people."

"None of those other boats could have got ashore to give word of the wreck," said the oiler, in a low voice. "Else the lifeboat would be out hunting us."

Slowly and beautifully the land loomed out of the sea. The wind came again. It had veered from the northeast to the southeast. Finally, a new sound struck the ears of the men in the boat. It was the low thunder of the surf on the shore. "We'll never be able to make the

---

[4] *apropos* (ăp′rə-pō): relevant.

lighthouse now," said the captain. "Swing her head a little more north, Billie," said he.

"A little more north, sir," said the oiler.

Whereupon the little boat turned her nose once more down the wind, and all but the oarsman watched the shore grow. Under the influence of this expansion doubt and direful apprehension was leaving the minds of the men. The management of the boat was still most absorbing, but it could not prevent a quiet cheerfulness. In an hour, perhaps, they would be ashore.

Their backbones had become thoroughly used to balancing in the boat, and they now rode this wild colt of a dinghy like circus men. The correspondent thought that he had been drenched to the skin, but happening to feel in the top pocket of his coat, he found therein eight cigars. Four of them were soaked with sea water; four were perfectly scatheless. After a search, somebody produced three dry matches, and thereupon the four waifs rode impudently in their little boat, and with an assurance of an impending rescue shining in their eyes, puffed at the big cigars and judged well and ill of all men. Everbody took a drink of water.

IV

"Cook," remarked the captain, "there don't seem to be any signs of life about your house of refuge."

"No," replied the cook. "Funny they don't see us!"

A broad stretch of lowly coast lay before the eyes of the men. It was of dunes topped with dark vegetation. The roar of the surf was plain, and sometimes they could see the white lip of a wave as it spun up the beach. A tiny house was blocked out black upon the sky. Southward, the slim lighthouse lifted its little gray length.

Tide, wind, and waves were swinging the dinghy northward. "Funny they don't see us," said the men.

The surf's roar was here dulled, but its tone was nevertheless thunderous and mighty. As the boat swam over the great rollers, the men sat listening to this roar. "We'll swamp sure," said everybody.

It is fair to say here that there was not a lifesaving station within twenty miles in either direction; but the men did not know this fact, and in consequence they made dark and opprobrious remarks concerning the eyesight of the nation's lifesavers. Four scowling men sat in the dinghy, and surpassed records in the invention of epithets.

"Funny they don't see us."

The lightheartedness of a former time had completely faded. To their sharpened minds it was easy to conjure pictures of all kinds of incompetency and blindness, and, indeed, cowardice. There was the shore of the populous land, and it was bitter and bitter to them that from it came no sign.

"Well," said the captain, ultimately, "I suppose we'll have to make a try for ourselves. If we stay out here too long, we'll none of us have strength left to swim after the boat swamps."

And so the oiler, who was at the oars, turned the boat straight for the shore. There was a sudden tightening of muscles. There was some thinking.

"If we don't all get ashore," said the captain,—"if we don't all get ashore, I suppose you fellows know where to send news of my finish?"

They then briefly exchanged some addresses and admonitions. As for the reflections of the men, there was a great deal of rage in them. Perchance they might be formulated thus: "If I am going to be drowned—if I am going to be drowned—if I am going to be drowned, why, in the name of the seven mad gods who rule the sea, was I allowed to come thus far and contemplate sand and trees? Was I brought here merely to have my nose dragged away as I was about to nibble the sacred cheese of life? It is preposterous! If this old ninny-woman, Fate, cannot do better than this, she should be deprived of the management of men's fortunes. She is an old hen who knows not her intention. If she has decided to drown me, why did she not do it in the beginning, and save me all this trouble? The whole affair is absurd. . . . But no; she cannot mean to drown me. She dare not drown me. She cannot drown me. Not after all this work!" Afterward the man might have had an impulse to shake his fist at the clouds. "Just you drown me, now, and then hear what I call you!"

The billows that came at this time were more formidable. They seemed always just about to break and roll over the little boat in a turmoil of foam. There was a preparatory and long growl in the speech of them. No mind unused to the sea would have concluded that the dinghy could ascend these sheer heights in time. The shore was still afar. The oiler was a wily surfman. "Boys," he said swiftly, "she won't live three minutes more, and we're too far out to swim. Shall I take her to sea again, Captain?"

"Yes; go ahead!" said the captain.

This oiler, by a series of quick miracles and fast and steady oarsmanship, turned the boat in the middle of the surf and took her safely to sea again.

There was a considerable silence as the boat bumped over the furrowed sea to deeper water. Then somebody in gloom spoke: "Well, anyhow, they must have seen us from the shore by now."

The gulls went in slanting flight up the wind toward the gray, desolate east. A squall, marked by dingy clouds, and clouds brick-red, like smoke from a burning building, appeared from the southeast.

"What do you think of those lifesaving people? Ain't they peaches?"

"Funny they haven't seen us."

"Maybe they think we're out here for sport! Maybe they think we're fishin'. Maybe they think we're fools."

It was a long afternoon. A changed tide tried to force them southward, but wind and wave said northward. Far ahead, where coastline, sea, and sky formed their mighty angle, there were little dots which seemed to indicate a city on the shore.

"St. Augustine?"

The captain shook his head. "Too near Mosquito Inlet."

And the oiler rowed, and then the correspondent rowed; then the oiler rowed. It was a weary business. The human back can become the seat of more aches and pains than are registered in books for the composite anatomy of a regiment. It is a limited area, but it can become the theater of innumerable muscular conflicts, tangles, wrenches, knots, and other comforts.

"Did you ever like to row, Billie?" asked the correspondent.

"No," said the oiler; "hang it!"

When one exchanged the rowing seat for a place in the bottom of the boat, he suffered a bodily depression that caused him to be careless of everything save an obligation to wiggle one finger. There was the cold sea water swashing to and fro in the boat, and he lay in it. His head, pillowed on a thwart, was within an inch of the swirl of a wave-crest, and sometimes a particularly obstreperous sea came inboard and drenched him once more. But these matters did not annoy him. It is almost certain that if the boat capsized he would have tumbled comfortably out upon the ocean as if he felt sure that it was a great, soft mattress.

"Look! There's a man on the shore!"

"Where?"

"There! See 'im! See 'im!"

"Yes, sure! He's walking along."

"Now he's stopped. Look! He's facing us!"

"He's waving at us!"

"So he is! By thunder!"

"Ah, now we're all right! Now we're all right! There'll be a boat out here for us in half an hour."

"He's going on. He's running. He's going up to that house there."

The remote beach seemed lower than the sea, and it required a searching glance to discern the little black figure. The captain saw a floating stick and they rowed to it. A bath towel was by some weird

chance in the boat, and tying this on the stick, the captain waved it. The oarsman did not dare turn his head, so he was obliged to ask questions.

"What's he doing now?"

"He's standing still again. He's looking, I think. . . . There he goes again. Toward the house. . . . Now he's stopped again."

"Is he waving at us?"

"No, not now! He was, though."

"Look! There comes another man!"

"He's running."

"Look at him go, would you!"

"Why, he's on a bicycle. Now he's met the other man. They're both waving at us. Look!"

"There comes something up the beach."

"What is that thing?"

"Why, it looks like a boat."

"Why, certainly it's a boat."

"No, it's on wheels."

"Yes, so it is. Well, that must be the lifeboat. They drag them along shore on a wagon."

"That's the lifeboat, sure."

"No, it's—it's an omnibus."

"I tell you it's a lifeboat."

"It is not! It's an omnibus. I can see it plain. See? One of these big hotel omnibuses."

"By thunder, you're right. It's an omnibus, sure as fate. What do you suppose they are doing with an omnibus? Maybe they are going around collecting the life crew, hey?"

"That's it, likely. Look! There's a fellow waving a little black flag. He's standing on the steps of the omnibus. There come those other two fellows. Now they're all talking together. Look at the fellow with the flag. Maybe he ain't waving it!"

"That ain't a flag, is it? That's his coat. Why, certainly, that's his coat."

"So it is. It's his coat. He's taken it off and is waving it around his head. But would you look at him swing it!"

"Oh, say, there isn't any lifesaving station there. That's just a winter resort hotel omnibus that has brought over some of the boarders to see us drown."

"What's that idiot with the coat mean? What's he signaling, anyhow?"

"It looks as if he were trying to tell us to go north. There must be a lifesaving station up there."

"No! He thinks we're fishing. Just giving us a merry hand. See? Ah, there, Willie!"

"Well, I wish I could make something out of those signals. What do you suppose he means?"

"He don't mean anything. He's just playing."

"Well, if he'd just signal us to try the surf again, or to go to sea and wait, or go north, or go south, or go to the devil— there would be some reason in it. But look at him. He just stands there and keeps his coat revolving like a wheel!"

"There come more people."

"Now there's quite a mob. Look! Isn't that a boat?"

"Where? Oh, I see where you mean. No, that's no boat."

"That fellow is still waving his coat."

"He must think we like to see him do that. Why don't he quit it? It don't mean anything."

"I don't know. I think he is trying to make us go north. It must be that there's a lifesaving station there somewhere."

"Say, he ain't tired yet. Look at 'im wave!"

"Wonder how long he can keep that up. He's been revolving his coat ever since he caught sight of us. He's an idiot. Why aren't they getting men to bring a boat out? A fishing boat—one of those big yawls—could come out here all right. Why don't he do something?"

"Oh, it's all right now."

"They'll have a boat out here for us in less than no time, now that they've seen us."

A faint yellow tone came into the sky over the low land. The shadows on the sea slowly deepened. The wind bore coldness with it, and the men began to shiver.

"Holy smoke!" said one, allowing his voice to express his impious mood, "if we keep monkeying out here! If we've got to flounder out here all night!"

"Oh, we'll never have to stay here all night! Don't you worry. They've seen us now, and it won't be long before they'll come chasing out after us."

The shore grew dusky. The man waving a coat blended gradually into this gloom, and it swallowed in the same manner the omnibus and the group of people. The spray, when it dashed uproariously over the side, made the voyagers shrink and swear like men who were being branded.

"I'd like to catch the chump who waved the coat. I feel like soaking him one, just for luck."

"Why? What did he do?"

"Oh, nothing, but then he seemed too cheerful."

In the meantime the oiler rowed, and then the correspondent rowed, and then the oiler rowed. Gray-faced and bowed forward, they mechanically, turn by turn, plied the leaden oars. The form of the lighthouse had vanished from the southern horizon, but finally a pale star appeared, just lifting from the sea. The streaked saffron in the west passed before the all-merging darkness, and the sea to the east was black. The land had vanished, and was expressed only by the low and drear thunder of the surf.

"If I am going to be drowned—if I am going to be drowned—if I am going to be drowned, why, in the name of the seven mad gods who rule the sea, was I allowed to come thus far and contemplate sand and trees? Was I brought here merely to have my nose dragged away as I was about to nibble the sacred cheese of life?"

The patient captain, drooped over the water jar, was sometimes obliged to speak to the oarsman.

"Keep her head up! Keep her head up!"

"Keep her head up, sir." The voices were weary and low.

This was surely a quiet evening. All save the oarsman lay heavily and listlessly in the boat's bottom. As for him, his eyes were just capable of noting the tall black waves that swept forward in a most sinister silence, save for an occasional subdued growl of a crest.

The cook's head was on a thwart, and he looked without interest at the water under his nose. He was deep in other scenes. Finally he spoke. "Billie," he murmured, dreamfully, "what kind of pie do you like best?"

V

"Pie," said the oiler and the correspondent, agitatedly. "Don't talk about those things, blast you!"

"Well," said the cook, "I was just thinking about ham sandwiches, and——"

A night on the sea in an open boat is a long night. As darkness settled finally, the shine of the light, lifting from the sea in the south, changed to full gold. On the northern horizon a new light appeared, a small bluish gleam on the edge of the waters. These two lights were the furniture of the world. Otherwise there was nothing but waves.

Two men huddled in the stern, and distances were so magnificent in the dinghy that the rower was enabled to keep his feet partly warmed by thrusting them under his companions. Their legs indeed extended far under the rowing seat until they touched the feet of the captain forward. Sometimes, despite the efforts of the tired oarsman, a wave came piling into the boat, an icy wave of the night, and the chilling water soaked them anew. They would twist their bodies for a moment and groan, and sleep the dead sleep once more, while the water in the boat gurgled about them as the craft rocked.

The plan of the oiler and the correspondent was for one to row until he lost the ability, and then arouse the other from his sea-water couch in the bottom of the boat.

The oiler plied the oars until his head dropped forward, and the overpowering sleep blinded him, and he rowed yet afterward. Then he touched a man in the bottom of the boat, and called his name. "Will you spell me for a little while?" he said meekly.

"Sure, Billie," said the correspondent, awakening and dragging himself to a sitting position. They exchanged places carefully, and the oiler, cuddling down in the sea at the cook's side, seemed to go to sleep instantly.

The particular violence of the sea had ceased. The waves came without snarling. The obligation of the man at the oars was to keep the boat headed so that the tilt of the rollers would not capsize her, and to preserve her from filling when the crests rushed past. The black waves were silent and hard to be seen in the darkness. Often one was almost upon the boat before the oarsman was aware.

In a low voice the correspondent addressed the captain. He was not sure that the captain was awake, although this iron man seemed to be always awake. "Captain, shall I keep her making for that light north, sir?"

That same steady voice answered him. "Yes. Keep it about two points off the port bow."

The cook had tied a life belt around himself in order to get even the warmth which this clumsy cork contrivance could donate, and he seemed almost stovelike when a rower, whose teeth invariably chattered wildly as soon as he ceased his labor, dropped down to sleep.

The correspondent, as he rowed, looked down at the two men sleeping underfoot. The cook's arm was around the oiler's shoulders, and, with their fragmentary clothing and haggard faces, they were the babes of the sea, a grotesque rendering of the old babes in the wood.

Later he must have grown stupid at his work, for suddenly there was a growling of water, and a crest came with a roar and a swash into the boat, and it was a wonder that it did not set the cook afloat in his life belt. The cook continued to sleep, but the oiler sat up, blinking his eyes and shaking with the new cold.

"Oh, I'm awful sorry, Billie," said the correspondent contritely.

"That's all right, old boy," said the oiler, and lay down again and was asleep.

Presently it seemed that even the captain dozed, and the correspondent thought that he was the one man afloat on all the oceans. The wind had a voice as it came over the waves, and it was sadder than the end.

There was a long, loud swishing astern of the boat, and a gleaming trail of phosphorescence, like blue flame, was furrowed on the black waters. It might have been made by a monstrous knife.

Then there came a stillness, while the correspondent breathed with open mouth and looked at the sea.

Suddenly there was another swish and another long flash of bluish light, and this time it was alongside the boat, and might almost have been reached with an oar. The correspondent saw an enormous fin speed like a shadow through the water, hurling the crystalline spray and leaving the long glowing trail.

The correspondent looked over his shoulder at the captain. His face was hidden, and he seemed to be asleep. He looked at the babes of the sea. They certainly were asleep. So, being bereft of sympathy, he leaned a little way to one side and swore softly into the sea.

But the thing did not then leave the vicinity of the boat. Ahead or astern, on one side or the other, at intervals long or short, fled the long sparkling streak, and there was to be heard the whirroo of the dark fin. The speed and power of the thing was greatly to be admired. It cut the water like a gigantic and keen projectile.

The presence of this biding thing did not affect the man with the same horror that it would if he had been a picknicker. He simply looked at the sea dully and swore in an undertone.

Nevertheless, it is true that he did not wish to be alone with the thing. He wished one of his companions to awake by chance and keep him company with it. But the captain hung motionless over the water jar, and the oiler and the cook in the bottom of the boat were plunged in slumber.

VI

"If I am going to be drowned—if I am going to be drowned—if I am going to be drowned, why, in the name of the seven mad gods who rule the sea, was I allowed to come thus far and contemplate sand and trees?"

During this dismal night, it may be remarked that a man would conclude that it was really the intention of the seven mad gods to drown him, despite the abominable injustice of it. For it was certainly an abominable injustice to drown a man who had worked so hard, so hard. The man felt it would be a crime most unnatural. Other people had drowned at sea since galleys swarmed with painted sails, but still——

When it occurs to a man that nature does not regard him as important, and that she feels she would not maim the universe by disposing of him, he at first wishes to throw bricks at the temple, and he hates deeply the fact that there are no bricks and no temples. Any visible expression of nature would surely be pelleted with his jeers.

Then, if there be no tangible thing to hoot he feels, perhaps, the desire to confront a personification and indulge in pleas, bowed to one knee, and with hands supplicant, saying: "Yes, but I love myself."

A high cold star on a winter's night is the word he feels that she says to him. Thereafter he knows the pathos of his situation.

The men in the dinghy had not discussed these matters, but each had, no doubt, reflected upon them in silence and according to his mind. There was seldom any expression upon their faces save the general one of complete weariness. Speech was devoted to the business of the boat.

To chime the notes of his emotion, a verse mysteriously entered the correspondent's head. He had even forgotten that he had forgotten this verse, but it suddenly was in his mind.

A soldier of the Legion lay dying in
  Algiers,
There was a lack of woman's nursing,
  there was dearth of woman's
  tears;
But a comrade stood beside him, and
  he took that comrade's hand,
And he said: "I shall never see my
  own, my native land."

In his childhood, the correspondent had been made acquainted with the fact that a soldier of the Legion lay dying in Algiers, but he had never regarded the fact as important. Myriads of his school-fellows had informed him of the soldier's plight, but the dinning had naturally ended by making him perfectly indifferent. He had never considered it his affair that a soldier of the Legion lay dying in Algiers, nor had it appeared to him as a matter for sorrow. It was less to him than the breaking of a pencil's point.

Now, however, it quaintly came to him as a human, living thing. It was no longer merely a picture of a few throes in the breast of a poet, meanwhile drinking tea and warming his feet at the grate; it was an actuality—stern, mournful, and fine.

The correspondent plainly saw the soldier. He lay on the sand with his feet out straight and still. While his pale left hand was upon his chest in an attempt to thwart the going of his life, the blood came between his fingers. In the far Algerian distance, a city of low square forms was set against a sky that was faint with the last sunset hues. The correspondent, plying the oars and dreaming of the slow and slower movements of the lips of the soldier, was moved by a profound and perfectly impersonal comprehension. He was sorry for the soldier of the Legion who lay dying in Algiers.

The thing which had followed the boat and waited, had evidently grown bored at the delay. There was no longer to be heard the slash of the cutwater,[5]

and there was no longer the flame of the long trail. The light in the north still glimmered, but it was apparently no nearer to the boat. Sometimes the boom of the surf rang in the correspondent's ears, and he turned the craft seaward then and rowed harder. Southward, someone had evidently built a watch fire on the beach. It was too low and too far to be seen, but it made a shimmering, roseate reflection upon the bluff back of it, and this could be discerned from the boat. The wind came stronger, and sometimes a wave suddenly raged out like a mountain cat, and there was to be seen the sheen and sparkle of a broken crest.

The captain, in the bow, moved on his water jar and sat erect. "Pretty long night," he observed to the correspondent. He looked at the shore. "Those lifesaving people take their time."

"Did you see that shark playing around?"

"Yes, I saw him. He was a big fellow, all right."

"Wish I had known you were awake."

Later the correspondent spoke into the bottom of the boat.

"Billie!" There was a slow and gradual disentanglement. "Billie, will you spell me?"

"Sure," said the oiler.

As soon as the correspondent touched the cold, comfortable sea water in the bottom of the boat and had huddled close to the cook's life belt, he was deep in sleep, despite the fact that his teeth played all the popular airs. This sleep was so good to him that it was but a moment before he heard a voice call his name in a

---

[5] *cutwater:* front of a boat's prow.

tone that demonstrated the last stages of exhaustion. "Will you spell me?"

"Sure, Billie."

The light in the north had mysteriously vanished, but the correspondent took his course from the wide-awake captain.

Later in the night they took the boat farther out to sea, and the captain directed the cook to take one oar at the stern and keep the boat facing the seas. He was to call out if he should hear the thunder of the surf. This plan enabled the oiler and the correspondent to get respite together. "We'll give those boys a chance to get into shape again," said the captain. They curled down and, after a few preliminary chatterings and trembles, slept once more the dead sleep. Neither knew they had bequeathed to the cook the company of another shark, or perhaps the same shark.

As the boat caroused on the waves, spray occasionally bumped over the side and gave them a fresh soaking, but this had no power to break their repose. The ominous slash of the wind and the water affected them as it would have affected mummies.

"Boys," said the cook, with the notes of every reluctance in his voice, "she's drifted in pretty close. I guess one of you had better take her to sea again." The correspondent, aroused, heard the crash of the toppled crests.

As he was rowing, the captain gave him some whisky-and-water, and this steadied the chills out of him. "If I ever get ashore and anybody shows me even a photograph of an oar——"

At last there was a short conversation.

"Billie. . . . Billie, will you spell me?"

"Sure," said the oiler.

VII

When the correspondent again opened his eyes, the sea and the sky were each of the gray hue of the dawning. Later, carmine and gold was painted upon the waters. The morning appeared finally, in its splendor, with a sky of pure blue, and the sunlight flamed on the tips of the waves.

On the distant dunes were set many little black cottages, and a tall white windmill reared above them. No man, nor dog, nor bicycle appeared on the beach. The cottages might have formed a deserted village.

The voyagers scanned the shore. A conference was held in the boat. "Well," said the captain, "if no help is coming, we might better try a run through the surf right away. If we stay out here much longer we will be too weak to do anything for ourselves at all." The others silently acquiesced in this reasoning. The boat was headed for the beach. The correspondent wondered if none ever ascended the tall wind tower, and if then they never looked seaward. This tower was a giant, standing with its back to the plight of the ants. It represented in a degree, to the correspondent, the serenity of Nature amid the struggles of the individual— Nature in the wind, and Nature in the vision of men. She did not seem cruel to him then, nor beneficent, nor treacherous, nor wise. But she was indifferent, flatly indifferent. It is, perhaps, plausible that a man in this situation, impressed with the unconcern of the universe, should see the innumerable flaws of his life, and have them taste wickedly in his mind, and wish for another chance. A distinction between right and wrong seems absurdly clear to him then, in this new ignorance of the grave edge, and he understands that if he were given another opportunity he would mend his conduct and his words, and be better and brighter during an introduction or at a tea.

"Now, boys," said the captain, "she is going to swamp, sure. All we can do is to work her in as far as possible, and then, when she swamps, pile out and scramble for the beach. Keep cool now, and don't jump until she swamps sure."

The oiler took the oars. Over his shoulders he scanned the surf. "Captain," he said, "I think I'd better bring her about, and keep her head on to the seas and back her in."

"All right, Billie," said the captain. "Back her in." The oiler swung the boat then and, seated in the stern, the cook and the correspondent were obliged to look over their shoulders to contemplate the lonely and indifferent shore.

The monstrous inshore rollers heaved the boat high until the men were again enabled to see the white sheets of water scudding up the slanted beach. "We won't get in very close," said the captain. Each time a man could wrest his attention from the rollers, he turned his glance toward the shore, and in the expression of the eyes during this contemplation there was a singular quality. The correspon-

dent, observing the others, knew that they were not afraid, but the full meaning of their glances was shrouded.

As for himself, he was too tired to grapple fundamentally with the fact. He tried to coerce his mind into thinking of it, but the mind was dominated at this time by the muscles, and the muscles said they did not care. It merely occurred to him that if he should drown it would be a shame.

There were no hurried words, no pallor, no plain agitation. The men simply looked at the shore. "Now, remember to get well clear of the boat when you jump," said the captain.

Seaward the crest of a roller suddenly fell with a thunderous crash, and the long white comber came roaring down upon the boat.

"Steady now," said the captain. The men were silent. They turned their eyes from the shore to the comber and waited. The boat slid up the incline, leaped at the furious top, bounced over it, and swung down the long back of the wave. Some water had been shipped and the cook bailed it out.

But the next crest crashed also. The tumbling, boiling flood of white water caught the boat and whirled it almost perpendicular. Water swarmed in from all sides. The correspondent had his hands on the gunwale at this time, and when the water entered at that place he swiftly withdrew his fingers, as if he objected to wetting them.

The little boat, drunken with this weight of water, reeled and snuggled deeper into the sea.

"Bail her out, cook! Bail her out," said the captain.

"All right, Captain," said the cook.

"Now, boys, the next one will do for us, sure," said the oiler. "Mind to jump clear of the boat."

The third wave moved forward, huge, furious, implacable. It fairly swallowed the dinghy, and almost simultaneously the men tumbled into the sea. A piece of life belt had lain in the bottom of the boat, and as the correspondent went overboard he held this to his chest with his left hand.

The January water was icy, and he reflected immediately that it was colder than he had expected to find it on the coast of Florida. This appeared to his dazed mind as a fact important enough to be noted at the time. The coldness of the water was sad; it was tragic. This fact was somehow so mixed and confused with his opinion of his own situation that it seemed almost a proper reason for tears. The water was cold.

When he came to the surface he was conscious of little but the noisy water. Afterward he saw his companions in the sea. The oiler was ahead in the race. He was swimming strongly and rapidly. Off to the correspondent's left, the cook's great white and corked back bulged out of the water, and in the rear the captain was hanging with his one good hand to the keel of the overturned dinghy.

There is a certain immovable quality to a shore, and the correspondent wondered at it amid the confusion of the sea.

It seemed also very attractive, but the correspondent knew that it was a long journey, and he paddled leisurely. The piece of life preserver lay under him, and sometimes he whirled down the incline of a wave as if he were on a hand sled.

But finally he arrived at a place in the sea where travel was beset with difficulty. He did not pause swimming to inquire what manner of current had caught him, but there his progress ceased. The shore was set before him like a bit of scenery on a stage, and he looked at it and understood with his eyes each detail of it.

As the cook passed, much farther to the left, the captain was calling to him, "Turn over on your back, cook! Turn over on your back and use the oar."

"All right, sir." The cook turned on his back, and, paddling with an oar, went ahead as if he were a canoe.

Presently the boat also passed to the left of the correspondent, with the captain clinging with one hand to the keel. He would have appeared like a man raising himself to look over a board fence if it were not for the extraordinary gymnastics of the boat. The correspondent marveled that the captain could still hold to it.

They passed on nearer to shore,—the oiler, the cook, the captain,—and following them went the water jar, bouncing gaily over the seas.

The correspondent remained in the grip of this strange new enemy, a current. The shore, with its white slope of sand and its green bluff, topped with little silent cottages, was spread like a picture before him. It was very near to him then, but he was impressed as one who, in a gallery, looks at a scene from Brittany or Algiers.

He thought: "I am going to drown? Can it be possible? Can it be possible? Can it be possible?" Perhaps an individual must consider his own death to be the final phenomenon of nature.

But later a wave perhaps whirled him out of this small deadly current, for he found suddenly that he could again make progress toward the shore. Later still he was aware that the captain, clinging with one hand to the keel of the dinghy, had his face turned away from the shore and toward him, and was calling his name. "Come to the boat! Come to the boat!"

In his struggle to reach the captain and the boat, he reflected that when one gets properly wearied drowning must really be a comfortable arrangement—a cessation of hostilities accompanied by a large degree of relief; and he was glad of it, for the main thing in his mind for some moments had been horror of the temporary agony; he did not wish to be hurt.

Presently he saw a man running along the shore. He was undressing with most remarkable speed. Coat, trousers, shirt, everything flew magically off him.

"Come to the boat!" called the captain.

"All right, Captain." As the correspondent paddled, he saw the captain let himself down to bottom and leave the boat. Then the correspondent performed his one little marvel of the voyage. A large wave caught him and flung him with ease and supreme speed completely over the boat and far beyond it. It struck him even then as an event in gymnastics and a true miracle of the sea. An overturned boat in the surf is not a plaything to a swimming man.

The correspondent arrived in water that reached only to his waist, but his condition did not enable him to stand for more than a moment. Each wave knocked him into a heap, and the undertow pulled at him.

Then he saw the man who had been running and undressing, and undressing and running, come bounding into the water. He dragged ashore the cook, and then waded toward the captain; but the captain waved him away and sent him to the correspondent. He was naked—naked as a tree in winter; but a halo was about his head, and he shone like a saint. He gave a strong pull, and a long drag, and a bully heave at the correspondent's hand. The correspondent, schooled in the minor formulae, said, "Thanks, old man." But suddenly the man cried, "What's that?" He pointed a swift finger. The correspondent said, "Go."

In the shallows, face downward, lay the oiler. His forehead touched sand that was periodically, between each wave, clear of the sea.

The correspondent did not know all that transpired afterward. When he achieved safe ground he fell, striking the sand with each particular part of his body. It was as if he had dropped from a roof, but the thud was grateful to him.

It seemed that instantly the beach was populated with men with blankets, clothes, and flasks, and women with coffeepots and all the remedies sacred to their minds. The welcome of the land to the men from the sea was warm and generous; but a still and dripping shape was carried slowly up the beach, and the land's welcome for it could only be the different and sinister hospitality of the grave.

When it came night, the white waves paced to and fro in the moonlight, and the wind brought the sound of the great sea's voice to the men on shore, and they felt that they could then be interpreters.

DISCUSSION

1. In the first paragraph Crane says that the men "knew the color of the sea" but none of them "knew the color of the sky." This detail suggests the importance of the sea: they are surrounded by the sea; they must fight its strength to save themselves; and their existence is defined by the sea and its changing moods. How does Crane *show* this rather than say this?

2. Who are the four men in the boat? Why do you think Crane named only one of them? To what extent is each individualized?

3. When the "ugly brute" of a bird tries to perch on the captain's head, the others feel it is "somehow gruesome and ominous." What other ominous sign appears?

4. The hopes of the men go up and then down; they are about to be saved and then they lose hope. This movement is much like the movement of the waves— up and then down and then up again. Cite two or three examples of this movement.

5. Crane sees nature as indifferent to human life. The sea may well destroy the men, and the shore is indifferent. How do the men react to this indifference? How does Crane's poem "A man said to the universe" (page 254) relate to this story?

For further activities, see page 606.

Don't Cry, Darling, It's Blood All Right

OGDEN NASH

Whenever poets want to give you the idea that something is particularly
    meek and mild,
They compare it to a child,
Thereby proving that though poets with poetry may be rife
They don't know the facts of life.
If of compassion you desire either a tittle or a jot,   5
Don't try to get it from a tot.
Hard-boiled, sophisticated adults like me and you
May enjoy ourselves thoroughly with *Little Women* and *Winnie-the-Pooh,*
But innocent infants these titles from their reading course eliminate
As soon as they discover that it was honey and nuts and mashed potatoes
    instead of human flesh that Winnie-the-Pooh and Little Women
    ate.   10
Innocent infants have no use for fables about rabbits or donkeys or tor-
    toises or porpoises,
What they want is something with plenty of well mutilated corpoises.
Not on legends of how the rose came to be a rose instead of a petunia is
    their fancy fed,
But on the inside story of how somebody's bones got ground up to make
    somebody else's bread.
They'll go to sleep listening to the story of the little beggar-maid who got
    to be queen by being kind to the bees and the birds,   15
But they're all eyes and ears the minute they suspect a wolf or a giant is
    going to tear some poor woodcutter into quarters or thirds.
It really doesn't take much to fill their cup;
All they want is for somebody to be eaten up.
Therefore I say unto you, all you poets who are so crazy about meek and
    mild little children and their angelic air,
If you are sincere and really want to please them, why just go out and
    get yourselves devoured by a bear.   20

DISCUSSION

1. According to Nash, what puts children to sleep? What wakes them up?

2. Nash is known for his creative rhymes, such as "eliminate"–"Women ate" (lines 9 and 10). Find other examples. What is the effect of crowding so much into one line, as in line 15 or 16?

For further activities, see page 606.

This story is set in Spain during the civil war of the 1930s.

Old Man at the Bridge

ERNEST HEMINGWAY

An old man with steel rimmed spectacles and very dusty clothes sat by the side of the road. There was a pontoon bridge across the river and carts, trucks, and men, women and children were crossing it. The mule-drawn carts staggered up the steep bank from the bridge with soldiers helping push against the spokes of the wheels. The trucks ground up and away heading out of it all and the peasants plodded along in the ankle deep dust. But the old man sat there without moving. He was too tired to go any farther.

It was my business to cross the bridge, explore the bridgehead beyond and find out to what point the enemy had advanced. I did this and returned over the bridge. There were not so many carts now and very few people on foot, but the old man was still there.

"Where do you come from?" I asked him.

"From San Carlos," he said, and smiled.

That was his native town and so it gave him pleasure to mention it and he smiled.

"I was taking care of animals," he explained.

"Oh," I said, not quite understanding.

"Yes," he said, "I stayed, you see, taking care of animals. I was the last one to leave the town of San Carlos."

He did not look like a shepherd nor a herdsman and I looked at his dusty clothes and his gray dusty face and his steel rimmed spectacles and said, "What animals were they?"

"Various animals," he said, and shook his head. "I had to leave them."

I was watching the bridge and the African looking country of the Ebro Delta and wondering how long now it would be before we would see the enemy, and listening all the while for the first noises that would signal that ever mysterious event called contact, and the old man still sat there.

"What animals were they?" I asked.

"There were three animals altogether," he explained. "There were two goats and a cat and then there were four pairs of pigeons."

"And you had to leave them?" I asked.

"Yes. Because of the artillery. The captain told me to go because of the artillery."

"And you have no family?" I asked, watching the far end of the bridge where a few last carts were hurrying down the slope of the bank.

"No," he said, "only the animals I stated. The cat, of course, will be all right. A cat can look out for itself, but I cannot think what will become of the others."

"What politics have you?" I asked.

"I am without politics," he said. "I am seventy-six years old. I have come twelve kilometers now and I think now I can go no further."

"This is not a good place to stop," I said. "If you can make it, there are trucks up the road where it forks for Tortosa."

"I will wait a while," he said, "and then I will go. Where do the trucks go?"

"Towards Barcelona," I told him.

"I know no one in that direction," he said, "but thank you very much. Thank you again very much."

He looked at me very blankly and tiredly, then said, having to share his worry with some one, "The cat will be all right, I am sure. There is no need to be unquiet about the cat. But the others. Now what do you think about the others?"

"Why they'll probably come through it all right."

"You think so?"

"Why not," I said, watching the far bank where now there were no carts.

"But what will they do under the artillery when I was told to leave because of the artillery?"

"Did you leave the dove cage unlocked?" I asked.

"Yes."

"Then they'll fly."

"Yes, certainly they'll fly. But the others. It's better not to think about the others," he said.

"If you are rested I would go," I urged. "Get up and try to walk now."

"Thank you," he said and got to his feet, swayed from side to side and then sat down backwards in the dust.

"I was taking care of animals," he said dully, but no longer to me. "I was only taking care of animals."

There was nothing to do about him. It was Easter Sunday and the Fascists were advancing toward the Ebro.[1] It was a gray overcast day with a low ceiling so their planes were not up. That and the fact that cats know how to look after themselves was all the good luck that old man would ever have.

---

[1] *Easter . . . Ebro:* 1938. Franco's troops had reached the sea below the Ebro and were turning north toward the Loyalist capital at Barcelona. They would win the war within a year.

DISCUSSION

1. The old man, like the goats, is an innocent victim of war. What will become of the goats? Of the old man?

2. Who is the narrator? Why is he at the bridge at the moment of the story? When he says of the old man at the end, "There was nothing to do about him," what is he feeling?

3. Why does the old man not want to cross the bridge and go on to Barcelona? Of what is the bridge a *symbol* (see page 445)?

4. *Understatement,* the opposite of exaggeration, is a rhetorical device that makes something appear less significant than it really is. It is an effective way of emphasizing. In this story concern for the life of the old man is understated. Re-read the last paragraph. What powerful statement does it make?

The Jilting of Granny Weatherall

KATHERINE ANNE PORTER

She flicked her wrist neatly out of Doctor Harry's pudgy careful fingers and pulled the sheet up to her chin. The brat ought to be in knee breeches. Doctoring around the country with spectacles on his nose! "Get along now, take your schoolbooks and go. There's nothing wrong with me."

Doctor Harry spread a warm paw like a cushion on her forehead where the forked green vein danced and made her eyelids twitch. "Now, now, be a good girl, and we'll have you up in no time."

"That's no way to speak to a woman nearly eighty years old just because she's down. I'd have you respect your elders, young man."

"Well, Missy, excuse me." Doctor Harry patted her cheek. "But I've got to warn you, haven't I? You're a marvel, but you must be careful or you're going to be good and sorry."

"Don't tell me what I'm going to be. I'm on my feet now, morally speaking. It's Cornelia. I had to go to bed to get rid of her."

Her bones felt loose, and floated around in her skin, and Doctor Harry floated like a balloon around the foot of the bed. He floated and pulled down his waistcoat and swung his glasses on a cord. "Well, stay where you are, it certainly can't hurt you."

"Get along and doctor your sick," said Granny Weatherall. "Leave a well woman alone. I'll call for you when I want you. . . . Where were you forty years ago when I pulled through milk leg[1] and double pneumonia? You weren't even born. Don't let Cornelia lead you on," she shouted, because Doctor Harry appeared to float up to the ceiling and out. "I pay my own bills, and I don't throw my money away on nonsense!"

She meant to wave good-by, but it was too much trouble. Her eyes closed of themselves, it was like a dark curtain drawn around the bed. The pillow rose and floated under her, pleasant as a hammock in a light wind. She listened to the leaves rustling outside the window. No, somebody was swishing newspapers: no, Cornelia and Doctor Harry were whispering together. She leaped broad awake, thinking they whispered in her ear.

"She was never like this, *never* like this!" "Well, what can we expect?" "Yes, eighty years old. . . ."

Well, and what if she was? She still had ears. It was like Cornelia to whisper around doors. She always kept things secret in such a public way. She was always

---

[1] *milk leg:* swelling of the legs after childbirth.

being tactful and kind. Cornelia was dutiful; that was the trouble with her. Dutiful and good: "So good and dutiful," said Granny, "that I'd like to spank her." She saw herself spanking Cornelia and making a fine job of it.

"What'd you say, Mother?"

Granny felt her face tying up in hard knots.

"Can't a body think, I'd like to know?"

"I thought you might want something."

"I do. I want a lot of things. First off, go away and don't whisper."

She lay and drowsed, hoping in her sleep that the children would keep·out and let her rest a minute. It had been a long day. Not that she was tired. It was always pleasant to snatch a minute now and then. There was always so much to be done, let me see: tomorrow.

Tomorrow was far away and there was nothing to trouble about. Things were finished somehow when the time came; thank God there was always a little margin over for peace: then a person could spread out the plan of life and tuck in the edges orderly. It was good to have everything clean and folded away, with the hair brushes and tonic bottles sitting straight on the white embroidered linen: the day started without fuss and the pantry shelves laid out with rows of jelly glasses and brown jugs and white stone-china jars with blue whirligigs and words painted on them: coffee, tea, sugar, ginger, cinnamon, allspice: and the bronze clock with the lion on top nicely dusted off. The dust that lion could collect in twenty-four hours! The box in the attic with all those letters tied up, well, she'd have to go through that tomorrow. All those letters—George's letters and John's letters and her letters to them both—lying around for the children to find afterwards made her uneasy. Yes, that would be tomorrow's business. No use to let them know how silly she had been once.

While she was rummaging around she found death in her mind and it felt clammy and unfamiliar. She had spent so much time preparing for death there was no need for bringing it up again. Let it take care of itself now. When she was sixty she had felt very old, finished, and went around making farewell trips to see her children and grandchildren, with a secret in her mind: This is the very last of your mother, children! Then she made her will and came down with a long fever. That was all just a notion like a lot of other things, but it was lucky too, for she had once for all got over the idea of dying for a long time. Now she couldn't be worried. She hoped she had better sense now. Her father had lived to be one hundred and two years old and had drunk a noggin of strong hot toddy on his last birthday. He told the reporters it was his daily habit, and he owed his long life to that. He had made quite a scandal and was very pleased about it. She believed she'd just plague Cornelia a little.

"Cornelia! Cornelia!" No footsteps, but a sudden hand on her cheek. "Bless you, where have you been?"

"Here, Mother."

"Well, Cornelia, I want a noggin of hot toddy."

"Are you cold, darling?"

"I'm chilly, Cornelia. Lying in bed stops the circulation. I must have told you that a thousand times."

Well, she could just hear Cornelia telling her husband that Mother was getting a little childish and they'd have to humor her. The thing that most annoyed her was that Cornelia thought she was deaf, dumb, and blind. Little hasty glances and tiny gestures tossed around her and over her head saying, "Don't cross her, let her have her way, she's eighty years old," and she sitting there as if she lived in a thin glass cage. Sometimes Granny almost made up her mind to pack up and move back to her own house where nobody could remind her every minute that she was old. Wait, wait, Cornelia, till your own children whisper behind your back!

In her day she had kept a better house and had got more work done. She wasn't too old yet for Lydia to be driving eighty miles for advice when one of the children jumped the track, and Jimmy still dropped in and talked things over: "Now, Mammy, you've a good business head, I want to know what you think of this? . . ." Old. Cornelia couldn't change the furniture around without asking. Little things, little things! They had been so sweet when they were little. Granny wished the old days were back again with the children young and everything to be done over. It had been a hard pull, but not too much for her. When she thought of all the food she had cooked, and all the clothes she had cut and sewed, and all the gardens she had made—well, the children showed it. There they were, made out of her, and they couldn't get away

from that. Sometimes she wanted to see John again and point to them and say, Well, I didn't do so badly, did I? But that would have to wait. That was for tomorrow. She used to think of him as a man, but now all the children were older than their father, and he would be a child beside her if she saw him now. It seemed strange and there was something wrong in the idea. Why, he couldn't possibly recognize her. She had fenced in a hundred acres once, digging the post holes herself and clamping the wires with just a . . . boy to help. That changed a woman. John would be looking for a young woman with the peaked Spanish comb in her hair and the painted fan. Digging post holes changed a woman. Riding country roads in the winter when women had their babies was another thing: sitting up nights with sick horses . . . and sick children and hardly ever losing one. John, I hardly ever lost one of them! John would see that in a minute, that would be something he could understand, she wouldn't have to explain anything!

It made her feel like rolling up her sleeves and putting the whole place to rights again. No matter if Cornelia was determined to be everywhere at once, there were a great many things left undone on this place. She would start tomorrow and do them. It was good to be strong enough for everything, even if all you made melted and changed and slipped under your hands, so that by the time you finished you almost forgot what you were working for. What was it I set out to do? she asked herself intently, but she could not remember. A fog rose over the valley, she saw it marching across the

creek swallowing the trees and moving up the hill like an army of ghosts. Soon it would be at the near edge of the orchard, and then it was time to go in and light the lamps. Come in, children, don't stay out in the night air.

Lighting the lamps had been beautiful. The children huddled up to her and breathed like little calves waiting at the bars in the twilight. Their eyes followed the match and watched the flame rise and settle in a blue curve, then they moved away from her. The lamp was lit, they didn't have to be scared and hang on to mother any more. God, for all my life I thank Thee. Without Thee, my God, I could never have done it. Hail, Mary, full of grace.

I want you to pick all the fruit this year and see that nothing is wasted. There's always someone who can use it. Don't let good things rot for want of using. You waste life when you waste good food. Don't let things get lost. It's bitter to lose things. Now, don't let me get to thinking, not when I am tired and taking a little nap before supper. . . .

The pillow rose about her shoulders and pressed against her heart and the memory was being squeezed out of it: oh, push down the pillow, somebody: it would smother her if she tried to hold it. Such a fresh breeze blowing and such a green day with no threats in it. But he had not come, just the same. What does a woman do when she has put on the white veil and set out the white cake for a man and he doesn't come? She tried to remember. No, I swear he never harmed me but in that. He never harmed me but in that . . . and what if he did? There was

the day, the day, but a whirl of dark smoke rose and covered it, crept up and over into the bright field where everything was planted so carefully in orderly rows. That was hell, she knew hell when she saw it. For sixty years she had prayed against remembering him and against losing her soul in the deep pit of hell, and now the two things were mingled in one and the thought of him was a smoky cloud from hell that moved and crept in her head when she had just got rid of Doctor Harry and was trying to rest a minute. Wounded vanity, Ellen, said a sharp voice in the top of her mind. Don't let your wounded vanity get the upper hand of you. Plenty of girls get jilted. You were jilted, weren't you? Then stand up to it. Her eyelids wavered and let in streamers of blue-gray light like tissue paper over her eyes. She must get up and pull the shades down or she'd never sleep. She was in bed again and the shades were not down. How could that happen? Better turn over, hide from the light, sleeping in the light gave you nightmares. "Mother, how do you feel now?" and a stinging wetness on her forehead. But I don't like having my face washed in cold water!

Hapsy? George? Lydia? Jimmy? No, Cornelia, and her features were swollen and full of little puddles. "They're coming, darling, they'll all be here soon." Go wash your face, child, you look funny.

Instead of obeying, Cornelia knelt down and put her head on the pillow. She seemed to be talking but there was no sound. "Well, are you tongue-tied? Whose birthday is it? Are you going to give a party?"

Cornelia's mouth moved urgently in strange shapes. "Don't do that, you bother me, daughter."

"Oh, no, Mother. Oh, no. . . ."

Nonsense. It was strange about children. They disputed your every word. "No what, Cornelia?"

"Here's Doctor Harry."

"I won't see that boy again. He just left five minutes ago."

"That was this morning, Mother. It's night now. Here's the nurse."

"This is Doctor Harry, Mrs. Weatherall. I never saw you look so young and happy!"

"Ah, I'll never be young again—but I'd be happy if they'd let me lie in peace and get rested."

She thought she spoke up loudly, but no one answered. A warm weight on her forehead, a warm bracelet on her wrist, and a breeze went on whispering, trying to tell her something. A shuffle of leaves in the everlasting hand of God, He blew on them and they danced and rattled. "Mother, don't mind, we're going to give you a little hypodermic." "Look here, daughter, how do ants get in this bed? I saw sugar ants yesterday." Did you send for Hapsy too?

It was Hapsy she really wanted. She had to go a long way back through a great many rooms to find Hapsy standing with a baby on her arm. She seemed to herself to be Hapsy also, and the baby on Hapsy's arm was Hapsy and himself and herself, all at once, and there was no surprise in the meeting. Then Hapsy melted from within and turned flimsy as gray gauze and the baby was a gauzy shadow, and Hapsy came up close and said, "I thought you'd never come," and looked at her very searchingly and said, "You haven't changed a bit!" They leaned forward to kiss, when Cornelia began whispering from a long way off, "Oh, is there anything you want to tell me? Is there anything I can do for you?"

Yes, she had changed her mind after sixty years and she would like to see George. I want you to find George. Find him and be sure to tell him I forgot him. I want him to know I had my husband just the same and my children and my house like any other woman. A good house too and a good husband that I loved and fine children out of him. Better than I hoped for even. Tell him I was given back everything he took away and more. Oh, no, oh, God, no, there was something else besides the house and the man and the children. Oh, surely they were not all? What was it? Something not given back. . . . Her breath crowded down under her ribs and grew into a monstrous frightening shape with cutting edges; it bored up into her head, and the agony was unbelievable: Yes, John, get the Doctor now, no more talk, my time has come.

When this one was born it should be the last. The last. It should have been born first, for it was the one she had truly wanted. Everything came in good time. Nothing left out, left over. She was strong, in three days she would be as well as ever. Better. A woman needed milk in her to have her full health.

"Mother, do you hear me?"

"I've been telling you——"

"Mother, Father Connolly's here."

"I went to Holy Communion only last week. Tell him I'm not so sinful as all that."

"Father just wants to speak to you."

He could speak as much as he pleased. It was like him to drop in and inquire about her soul as if it were a teething baby, and then stay on for a cup of tea and a round of cards and gossip. He always had a funny story of some sort, usually about an Irishman who made his little mistakes and confessed them, and the point lay in some absurd thing he would blurt out in the confessional showing his struggles between native piety and original sin. Granny felt easy about her soul. Cornelia, where are your manners? Give Father Connolly a chair. She had her secret comfortable understanding with a few favorite saints who cleared a straight road to God for her. All as surely signed and sealed as the papers for the new Forty Acres. Forever . . . heirs and assigns forever. Since the day the wedding cake was not cut, but thrown out and wasted. The whole bottom dropped out of the world, and there she was blind and sweating with nothing under her feet and the walls falling away. His hand had caught her under the breast, she had not fallen, there was the freshly polished floor with the green rug on it, just as before. He had cursed like a sailor's parrot and said, "I'll kill him for you." Don't lay a hand on him, for my sake leave something to God. "Now, Ellen, you must believe what I tell you. . . ."

So there was nothing to worry about any more, except sometimes in the night one of the children screamed in a nightmare, and they both hustled out shaking and hunting for the matches and calling, "There, wait a minute, here we are!" John, get the doctor now, Hapsy's time

has come. But there was Hapsy standing by the bed in a white cap. "Cornelia, tell Hapsy to take off her cap. I can't see her plain."

Her eyes opened very wide and the room stood out like a picture she had seen somewhere. Dark colors with the shadows rising towards the ceiling in long angles. The tall black dresser gleamed with nothing on it but John's picture, enlarged from a little one, with John's eyes very black when they should have been blue. You never saw him, so how do you know how he looked? But the man insisted the copy was perfect, it was very rich and handsome. For a picture, yes, but it's not my husband. The table by the bed had a linen cover and a candle and a crucifix. The light was blue from Cornelia's silk lampshades. No sort of light at all, just frippery. You had to live forty years with kerosene lamps to appreciate honest electricity. She felt very strong and she saw Doctor Harry with a rosy nimbus around him.

"You look like a saint, Doctor Harry, and I vow that's as near as you'll ever come to it."

"She's saying something."

"I heard you, Cornelia. What's all this carrying-on?"

"Father Connolly's saying——"

Cornelia's voice staggered and bumped like a cart in a bad road. It rounded corners and turned back again and arrived nowhere. Granny stepped up in the cart very lightly and reached for the reins, but a man sat beside her and she knew him by his hands, driving the cart. She did not look in his face, for she knew without seeing, but looked instead down the road where the trees leaned over and bowed to each other and a thousand birds were singing a Mass. She felt like singing too, but she put her hand in the bosom of her dress and pulled out a rosary, and Father Connolly murmured Latin in a very solemn voice and tickled her feet. My God, will you stop that nonsense? I'm a married woman. What if he did run away and leave me to face the priest by myself? I found another a whole world better. I wouldn't have exchanged my husband for anybody except St. Michael himself, and you may tell him that for me with a thank you in the bargain.

Light flashed on her closed eyelids, and a deep roaring shook her. Cornelia, is that lightning? I hear thunder. There's going to be a storm. Close all the windows. Call the children in. . . . "Mother, here we are, all of us." "Is that you, Hapsy?" "Oh, no, I'm Lydia. We drove as fast as we could." Their faces drifted above her, drifted away. The rosary fell out of her hands and Lydia put it back. Jimmy tried to help, their hands fumbled together, and Granny closed two fingers around Jimmy's thumb. Beads wouldn't do, it must be something alive. She was so amazed her thoughts ran round and round. So, my dear Lord, this is my death and I wasn't even thinking about it. My children have come to see me die. But I can't, it's not time. Oh, I always hated surprises. I wanted to give Cornelia the amethyst set—Cornelia, you're to have the amethyst set, but Hapsy's to wear it when she wants, and, Doctor Harry, do shut up. Nobody sent for you. Oh, my dear Lord, do wait a minute. I meant to do something about the Forty Acres. Jim-

my doesn't need it and Lydia will later on, with that worthless husband of hers. I meant to finish the altar cloth and send six bottles of wine to Sister Borgia for her dyspepsia.[2] I want to send six bottles of wine to Sister Borgia, Father Connolly, now don't let me forget.

Cornelia's voice made short turns and tilted over and crashed. "Oh, Mother, oh, Mother, oh, Mother. . . ."

"I'm not going, Cornelia. I'm taken by surprise. I can't go."

You'll see Hapsy again. What about her? "I thought you'd never come." Granny made a long journey outward, looking for Hapsy. What if I don't find her? What then? Her heart sank down and down, there was no bottom to death, she couldn't come to the end of it. The blue light from Cornelia's lampshade drew into a tiny point in the center of her brain, it flickered and winked like an eye, quietly it fluttered and dwindled. Granny lay curled down within herself, amazed and watchful, staring at the point of light that was herself; her body was now only a deeper mass of shadow in an endless darkness and this darkness would curl around the light and swallow it up. God, give a sign!

For the second time there was no sign. Again no bridegroom and the priest in the house. She could not remember any other sorrow because this grief wiped them all away. Oh, no, there's nothing more cruel than this—I'll never forgive it. She stretched herself with a deep breath and blew out the light.

[2] *dyspepsia:* indigestion.

DISCUSSION

1.   At the end of the story Granny Weatherall feels that she has been jilted a second time. What did she expect as death approached? Why was the second one harder to bear?

2.   As Granny remembers events from her life, which seem most important to her? Of what is she proud? What things still undone bother her?

3.   Describe the relationship between Granny and her daughter Cornelia.

4.   Porter uses short, polished phrases in her descriptions of people. For example, Cornelia "always kept things secret in such a public way" (page 593); her voice, as it sounded to Granny, "staggered and bumped like a cart in a bad road" (p. 599). Find several other examples that are equally vivid and precise.

5.   How would you state the theme of this story?

For further activities, see page 606.

Song of a Woman Abandoned by the Tribe Because She Is Too Old To Keep Up with Their Migration

Translated from Southern Shoshone by MARY AUSTIN

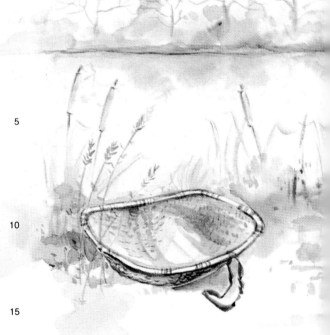

Alas, that I should die,
That I should die now,
I who know so much!

It will miss me,
The twirling fire stick;   5
The fire coal between the hearth stones,
It will miss me.

The medicine songs,
The songs of magic healing;
The medicine herbs by the water borders,   10
They will miss me;
The basket willow,
It will miss me;
All the wisdom of women,
It will miss me.   15

Alas, that I should die,
Who know so much.

DISCUSSION

1. The inevitability and imminence of death make humans seek out different forms of immortality. In what things does this woman think she will continue to live?

2. She does not mention people missing her. Why not, do you think? What collective mind does she feel a part of?

Bells for John Whiteside's Daughter

JOHN CROWE RANSOM

There was such speed in her little body,
And such lightness in her footfall,
It is no wonder her brown study
Astonishes us all.

Her wars were bruited in our high window. 5
We looked among orchard trees and beyond,
Where she took arms against her shadow,
Or harried unto the pond

The lazy geese, like a snow cloud
Dripping their snow on the green grass, 10
Tricking and stopping, sleepy and proud,
Who cried in goose, Alas,

For the tireless heart within the little
Lady with rod that made them rise
From their noon apple-dreams and scuttle 15
Goose-fashion under the skies!

But now go the bells, and we are ready,
In one house we are sternly stopped
To say we are vexed at her brown study,
Lying so primly propped. 20

3. *brown study:* state of being in deep thought.

DISCUSSION

1. In death the child is "primly propped." How does this contrast with her life?

2. Her brown study astonishes and vexes "us" (lines 3 and 19). Why do you think the poet used such understatements instead of words that express greater emotion?

3. What do the bells signify?

Where Have You Gone...?

MARI EVANS

where have you gone . . .

with your confident
walk . . . with
your crooked smile . . .

why did you leave   5
me
when you took your
laughter
and departed
Are you aware that   10
with you
went the sun
all light
and what few stars
there were . . . ?   15
where have you gone
with your confident
walk your
crooked smile the
rent money   20
in one pocket and
my heart
in
another . . .

FAREWELL

LIZ SOHAPPY BAHE

You sang round-dance songs.
I danced not to thundering drums
but to your voice singing.

You chiseled wood sculpture.
I watched not the tools or chips fly   5
but your strong hands carving.

You lived in a northern village.
I went there not to meet your people
but to walk where you had walked.

You followed calling drums.   10
I waited, willing the drums to stop.

DISCUSSION   In both of these poems the speaker is a woman addressing
an absent man; yet they are far apart in tone. How would
you describe the tone of each poem?

606

FOCUS

VOCABULARY

The Open Boat (page 566)

Language, like other living things, changes. New words come into use in a variety of ways. One consistent pattern of change in words is clipping, or the shortening of words. When Crane wrote "The Open Boat" in the latter part of the 1800s, the word *onmibus* was used for what we now call a bus. Listed below are other words that have been clipped. What short word has developed from each?

hobby horse   rattlesnake
brigantine   *mobile vulgus*
distillery   influenza
fanatic   periwig
photograph   memorandum

Try to think of several other words that have been similarly treated.
    A variation of clipping is back-formation, in which a new verb, for example, is made from an existing noun. What verb has been made from each of these nouns?

editor   beggar   pedlar   diagnosis   rover

Don't Cry, Darling, It's Blood All Right (page 588)

Rhyming can be a children's game or a sophisticated game that word lovers play for fun. Nash's unusual rhymes delight the reader. They may result from misspelling, coinage, transposition of words or syllables, or the grouping of two completely unrelated words. Here are some of his rhymes culled from other poems. First, see if you can outrhyme him; then compose a dozen or so outlandish rhymes of your own.

family—calamily   leopard—peppered
lipstick—hips stick   panther—anther ["answer"]
piazza—happy as a   language—orangutanguage
prodigality—waspitality   frigid—unabridged
foolishest—mulishest   coinage—joinage

The Jilting of Granny Weatherall (page 593)

Another process that increases English vocabulary is using one word in different functions, or as different parts of speech. Many words that entered the language as nouns make useful verbs and/or adjectives and become, in effect, new words. The word *plague* was originally a noun only, but Porter finds it an expressive verb: "She believed she'd just plague Cornelia a little." Following are words that may be used as more than one part of speech. Give sentences for each that illustrate this functional shift.

feature	elbow	hazard	doom
boomerang	process	sabotage	jet
camouflage	flock		

COMPOSITION

The Jilting of Granny Weatherall (page 593)

Imagine that you are in Granny Weatherall's place and are about to die. You are eighty years old and have lived a full life. You look back over your life and consider its pleasures and sorrows; its richness and poverty. Those you love come to see you. In a composition describe the scene and give the thoughts that pass through your mind. Include a dialogue between you and those who have come to see you.

Where Have You Gone . . . ? (page 604), Farewell (page 605)

Write your own "Where Have You Gone?" or "Farewell," a poem or a few paragraphs addressed to a real or an imaginary person in which you express your feelings about being left behind in some way. Make whatever you write sound glad, angry, resigned, sad, or however you feel now.

The Sentimentality of William Tavener

WILLA CATHER

It takes a strong woman to make any sort of success of living in the West, and Hester undoubtedly was that. When people spoke of William Tavener as the most prosperous farmer in McPherson County, they usually added that his wife was a "good manager." She was an executive woman, quick of tongue and something of an imperatrix.[1] The only reason her husband did not consult her about his business was that she did not wait to be consulted.

It would have been quite impossible for one man, within the limited sphere of human action, to follow all Hester's advice, but in the end William usually acted upon some of her suggestions. When she incessantly denounced the "shiftlessness" of letting a new threshing machine stand unprotected in the open, he eventually built a shed for it. When she sniffed contemptuously at his notion of fencing a hog corral with sod walls, he made a spiritless beginning on the structure—merely to "show his temper," as she put it—but in the end he went off quietly to town and bought enough barbed wire to complete the fence. When the first heavy rains came on, and the pigs rooted down the sod wall and made little paths all over it to facilitate their ascent, he heard his wife relate with relish the story of the little pig that built a mud house, to the minister at the dinner table, and William's gravity never relaxed for an instant. Silence, indeed, was William's refuge and his strength.

William set his boys a wholesome example to respect their mother. People who knew him very well suspected that he even admired her. He was a hard man towards his neighbors, and even towards his sons: grasping, determined and ambitious.

There was an occasional blue day about the house when William went over the store bills, but he never objected to items relating to his wife's gowns or bonnets. So it came about that many of the foolish, unnecessary little things that Hester bought for her boys, she had charged to her personal account.

One spring night Hester sat in a rocking chair by the sitting room window, darning socks. She rocked violently and sent her long needle vigorously back and forth over her gourd, and it took only a very casual glance to see that she was wrought up over something. William sat on the other side of the table reading his farm paper. If he had noticed his wife's agitation, his calm, clean-shaven face betrayed no sign of concern. He must have noticed the sarcastic turn of her remarks at the supper table, and he must have noticed the moody silence of the older boys as they ate. When supper was but half over little Billy, the youngest, had

[1] *imperatrix:* female emperor.

suddenly pushed back his plate and slipped away from the table, manfully trying to swallow a sob. But William Tavener never heeded ominous forecasts in the domestic horizon, and he never looked for a storm until it broke.

After supper the boys had gone to the pond under the willows in the big cattle corral, to get rid of the dust of plowing. Hester could hear an occasional splash and a laugh ringing clear through the stillness of the night, as she sat by the open window. She sat silent for almost an hour reviewing in her mind many plans of attack. But she was too vigorous a woman to be much of a strategist, and she usually came to her point with directness. At last she cut her thread and suddenly put her darning down, saying emphatically:

"William, I don't think it would hurt you to let the boys go to that circus in town tomorrow."

William continued to read his farm paper, but it was not Hester's custom to wait for an answer. She usually divined his arguments and assailed them one by one before he uttered them.

"You've been short of hands all summer, and you've worked the boys hard, and a man ought use his own flesh and blood as well as he does his hired hands. We're plenty able to afford it, and it's little enough our boys ever spend. I don't see how you can expect 'em to be steady and hard workin', unless you encourage 'em a little. I never could see much harm in circuses, and our boys have never been to one. Oh, I know Jim Howley's boys get drunk an' carry on when they go, but our boys ain't that sort, an' you know it, William. The animals are real instructive, an' our boys don't get to see much out here on the prairie. It was different where we were raised, but the boys have got no advantages here, an' if you don't take care, they'll grow up to be greenhorns."

Hester paused a moment, and William folded up his paper, but vouchsafed no remark. His sisters in Virginia had often said that only a quiet man like William could ever have lived with Hester Perkins. Secretly, William was rather proud of his wife's "gift of speech," and of the fact that she could talk in prayer meeting as fluently as a man. He confined his own efforts in that line to a brief prayer at Covenant meetings.

Hester shook out another sock and went on.

"Nobody was ever hurt by goin' to a circus. Why, law me! I remember I went to one myself once, when I was little. I had most forgot about it. It was over at Pewtown, an' I remember how I had set my heart on going. I don't think I'd ever forgiven my father if he hadn't taken me, though that red clay road was in a frightful way after the rain. I mind they had an elephant and six poll parrots, an' a Rocky Mountain lion, an' a cage of monkeys, an' two camels. My! but they were a sight to me then!"

Hester dropped the black sock and shook her head and smiled at the recollection. She was not expecting anything from William yet, and she was fairly startled when he said gravely, in much the same tone in which he announced the hymns in prayer meeting:

"No, there was only one camel. The other was a dromedary."

She peered around the lamp and looked at him keenly.

"Why, William, how come you to know?"

William folded his paper and answered with some hesitation, "I was there, too."

Hester's interest flashed up. "Well, I never, William! To think of my finding it out after all these years! Why, you couldn't have been much bigger'n our Billy then. It seems queer I never saw you when you was little, to remember about you. But then you Back Creek folks never have anything to do with us Gap people. But how come you to go? Your father was stricter with you than you are with your boys."

"I reckon I shouldn't 'a gone," he said slowly, "but boys will do foolish things. I had done a good deal of fox hunting the winter before, and father let me keep the bounty money. I hired Tom Smith's Tap to weed the corn for me, an' I slipped off unbeknownst to father an' went to the show."

Hester spoke up warmly: "Nonsense, William! It didn't do you no harm, I guess. You was always worked hard enough. It must have been a big sight for a little fellow. That clown must have just tickled you to death."

William crossed his knees and leaned back in his chair.

"I reckon I could tell all that fool's jokes now. Sometimes I can't help thinkin' about 'em in meetin' when the sermon's long. I mind I had on a pair of new boots that hurt me like the mischief, but I forgot all about 'em when that fellow rode the donkey. I recall I had to take them boots off as soon as I got out of sight o' town, and walked home in the mud barefoot."

"O poor little fellow!" Hester ejaculated, drawing her chin nearer and leaning her elbows on the table. "What cruel shoes they did use to make for children. I remember I went up to Back Creek to see the circus wagons go by. They came down from Romney, you know. The circus men stopped at the creek to water the animals, an' the elephant got stubborn an' broke a big limb off the yellow willow tree that grew there by the toll house porch, an' the Scribners were 'fraid as death he'd pull the house down. But this much I saw him do; he waded in the creek an' filled his trunk with water and squirted it in at the window and nearly ruined Ellen Scribner's pink lawn dress that she had just ironed an' laid out on the bed ready to wear to the circus."

"I reckon that must have been a trial to Ellen," chuckled William, "for she was mighty prim in them days."

Hester drew her chair still nearer William's. Since the children had begun growing up, her conversation with her husband had been almost wholly confined to questions of economy and expense. Their relationship had become purely a business one, like that between landlord and tenant. In her desire to indulge her boys she had unconsciously assumed a defensive and almost hostile attitude towards her husband. No debtor ever haggled with his usurer more doggedly than did Hester with her husband in behalf of her sons. The strategic contest had gone on so long that it had almost crowded out the memory of a closer relationship. This exchange of confidences tonight, when common recollections took them unawares and opened their hearts, had all the miracle of romance. They talked on and on; of old neighbors, of old familiar faces in the valley where they had grown up, of long forgotten incidents of their youth— weddings, picnics, sleighing parties and baptizings. For years they had talked of nothing else but butter and eggs and the prices of things, and now they had as much to say to each other as people who meet after a long separation.

When the clock struck ten, William rose and went over to his walnut secretary and unlocked it. From his red leather wallet he took out a ten-dollar bill and laid in on the table beside Hester.

"Tell the boys not to stay late, an' not to drive the horses hard," he said quietly, and went off to bed.

Hester blew out the lamp and sat still in the dark a long time. She left the bill lying on the table where William had placed it. She had a painful sense of having missed something, or lost something; she felt that somehow the years had cheated her.

The little locust trees that grew by the fence were white with blossoms. Their heavy odor floated in to her on the night wind and recalled a night long ago, when the first whippoorwill of the spring was heard, and the rough, buxom girls of Hawkins Gap had held her laughing and struggling under the locust trees, and searched in her bosom for a lock of her sweetheart's hair, which is supposed to be on every girl's breast when the first whippoorwill sings. Two of those same girls had been her bridesmaids. Hester had been a very happy bride. She rose and went softly into the room where William lay. He was sleeping heavily, but occasionally moved his hand before his face to ward off the flies. Hester went into the parlor and took the piece of mosquito net from the basket of wax apples and pears that her sister had made before she died. One of the boys had brought it all the way from Virginia, packed in a tin pail, since Hester would not risk shipping so precious an ornament by freight. She went back to the bedroom and spread the net over William's head. Then she sat down by the bed and listened to his deep, regular breathing until she heard the boys returning. She went out to meet them and warn them not to waken their father.

"I'll be up early to get your breakfast, boys. Your father says you can go to the show." As she handed the money to the eldest, she felt a sudden throb of allegiance to her husband and said sharply, "And you be careful of that, an' don't waste it. Your father works hard for his money."

The boys looked at each other in astonishment and felt that they had lost a powerful ally.

DISCUSSION

1. William Tavener was known as "the most prosperous farmer in McPherson County." How does William feel about money? How does Hester? What has money become in their relationship? At the end of the story the boys are astonished by Hester's sharp remarks about the ten dollars she gives them. What does this new attitude in Hester suggest about the future?

2. What does the circus mean, or symbolize, to William? To Hester? How does it bring them closer together?

3. Hester moves the mosquito net from the basket of apples and pears and spreads the net over William's head. What does this gesture mean? What new feeling does it show?

4. In a literary work *tone* is the attitude an author takes toward her or his subject. That attitude is revealed through choice of details, through diction and style, through the comments that are made, and through the emphasis placed upon characters and events. An author may write in any tone that a human uses in speaking—joyful, angry, detached, frank, mysterious. How does Cather feel about William and Hester? Does she show them as foolish humans or wise ones? Does she seem to care about what happens to them? How would you describe her tone?

For further activities, see page 652.

ALONE/december/night

VICTOR HERNÁNDEZ CRUZ

it's been so long
speaking to people
who think it all
too complex
stupidity in their eyes   5
&
it's been so long
so far from the truth
so far from a roof
to talk to   10
or a hand to touch
or anything to really
love

it's been so long
talking to myself   15
alone
in the night
listening to a music
that is me.

DISCUSSION According to the speaker, certain things or conditions have "been so long."
What are some of them? Which do you think are most important? What seems to
be the attitude or mood of the speaker? Explain.

Preface to a Twenty Volume Suicide Note

IMAMU AMIRI BARAKA

Lately, I've become accustomed to the way
The ground opens up and envelops me
Each time I go out to walk the dog.
Or the broad edged silly music the wind
Makes when I run for a bus—   5

Things have come to that.

And now, each night I count the stars,
And each night I get the same number.
And when they will not come to be counted
I count the holes they leave.   10

Nobody sings anymore.

And then last night, I tiptoed up
To my daughter's room and heard her
Talking to someone, and when I opened
The door, there was no one there . . .   15
Only she on her knees,
Peeking into her own clasped hands.

DISCUSSION

1. Instead of telling you his state of mind, the writer picks five things that describe it. What are these things?

2. Look at these experiences all together. What do they, or some of them, seem to have in common? Keep in mind the title of the poem. How would you describe the overall feeling the writer tries to convey?

3. How is the speaker's matter-of-fact tone appropriate to the theme of the poem?

Early January

W. S. MERWIN

A year has come to us as though out of hiding
It has arrived from an unknown distance
From beyond the visions of the old
Everyone waited for it by the wrong roads
And it is hard for us now to be sure it is here
A stranger to nothing
In our hiding places

DISCUSSION   The new year is described in *metaphor* as a traveler arriving
from a distance. What does the author mean by "everyone"
missed its coming and was later unsure that it had arrived?

For further activities, see page 652.

LULLABY

LESLIE SILKO

The sun had gone down but the snow in the wind gave off its own light. It came in thick tufts like new wool—washed before the weaver spins it. Ayah reached out for it like her own babies had, and she smiled when she remembered how she had laughed at them. She was an old woman now, and her life had become memories. She sat down with her back against the wide cottonwood tree, feeling the rough bark on her back bones; she faced east and listened to the wind and snow sing a high-pitched Yeibechei song. Out of the wind she felt warmer, and she could watch the wide fluffy snow fill in her tracks, steadily, until the direction she had come from was gone. By the light of the snow she could see the dark outline of the big arroyo a few feet away. She was sitting on the edge of Cebolleta Creek, where in the springtime the thin cows would graze on grass already chewed flat to the ground. In the wide deep creek bed where only a trickle of water flowed in the summer, the skinny cows would wander, looking for new grass along winding paths splashed with manure.

Ayah pulled the old Army blanket over her head like a shawl. Jimmie's blanket—the one he had sent to her. That was a long time ago and the green wool was faded, and it was unraveling on the edges. She did not want to think about Jimmie. So she thought about the weaving and the way her mother had done it. On the tall wooden loom set into the sand under a tamarack tree for shade. She could see it clearly. She had been only a little girl when her grandma gave her the wooden combs to pull the twigs and burrs from the raw, freshly washed wool. And while she combed the wool, her grandma sat beside her, spinning a silvery strand of yarn around the smooth cedar spindle. Her mother worked at the loom with yarns dyed bright yellow and red and gold. She watched them dye the yarn in boiling black pots full of beeweed petals, juniper berries, and sage. The blankets her mother made were soft and woven so tight that rain rolled off them like birds' feathers. Ayah remembered sleeping warm on cold windy nights, wrapped in her mother's blankets on the hogan's[1] sandy floor.

The snow drifted now, with the northwest wind hurling it in gusts. It drifted up around her black overshoes—old ones with little metal buckles. She smiled at the snow which was trying to cover her little by little. She could remember when they had no black rubber overshoes; only the high buckskin leggings that they wrapped over their elk-hide moccasins. If the snow was dry or frozen, a person could walk all day and not get wet; and in the evenings the beams of the ceiling would hang with lengths of pale buckskin leggings, drying out slowly.

She felt peaceful remembering. She didn't feel cold any more. Jimmie's blanket seemed warmer than it had ever been. And she could remember the morning he was born. She could remember whispering to her mother who was sleeping on the other side of the hogan, to tell her it was time now. She did not want to wake the others. The second time she called to her, her mother stood up and pulled on her shoes; she knew. They walked to the old stone hogan together, Ayah walking a step behind her mother.

She waited alone, learning the rhythms of the pains while her mother went to call the old woman to help them. The morning was already warm even before dawn and Ayah smelled the bee flowers blooming and the young willow growing at the springs. She could remember that so clearly, but his birth merged into the births of the other children and to her it became all the same birth. They named him for the summer morning and in English they called him Jimmie.

It wasn't like Jimmie died. He just never came back, and one day a dark blue sedan with white writing on its doors pulled up in front of the boxcar shack where the rancher let the Indians live. A man in a khaki uniform trimmed in gold gave them a yellow piece of paper and told them that Jimmie was dead. He said the Army would try to get the body back and then it would be shipped to them; but it wasn't likely because the helicopter had burned after it crashed. All of this was told to Chato because he could understand English. She stood inside the doorway holding the baby while Chato listened. Chato spoke English like a white man and he spoke Spanish too. He was taller than the white man and he stood straighter too. Chato didn't explain why; he just told the military man they could keep the body if they found it. The white man looked bewildered; he nodded his head and he left. Then Chato looked at her and shook his head, and then he told her, "Jimmie isn't coming home anymore," and when he spoke, he used the words to speak of the dead. She didn't cry then, but she hurt inside with anger.

[1] *hogan's* (hō´gänz): A hogan is the traditional cone-shaped Navajo dwelling.

And she mourned him as the years passed, when a horse fell with Chato and broke his leg, and the white rancher told them he wouldn't pay Chato until he could work again. She mourned Jimmie because he would have worked for his father then; he would have saddled the big bay horse and ridden the fence lines each day, with wire cutters and heavy gloves, fixing the breaks in the barbed wire and putting the stray cattle back inside again.

She mourned him after the white doctors came to take Danny and Ella away. She was at the shack alone that day when they came. It was back in the days before they hired Navajo women to go with them as interpreters. She recognized one of the doctors. She had seen him at the children's clinic at Cañoncito about a month ago. They were wearing khaki uniforms and they waved papers at her and a black ball point pen, trying to make her understand their English words. She was frightened by the way they looked at the children, like the lizard watches the fly. Danny was swinging on the tire swing on the elm tree behind the rancher's house, and Ella was toddling around the front door, dragging the broomstick horse Chato made for her. Ayah could see they wanted her to sign the papers, and Chato had taught her to sign her name. It was something she was proud of. She only wanted them to go, and to take their eyes away from her children.

She took the pen from the man without looking at his face and she signed the papers in three different places he pointed to. She stared at the ground by their feet and waited for them to leave. But they stood there and began to point and gesture at the children. Danny stopped swinging. Ayah could see his fear. She moved suddenly and grabbed Ella into her arms; the child squirmed, trying to get back to her toys. Ayah ran with the baby toward Danny; she screamed for him to run and then she grabbed him around his chest and carried him too. She ran south into the foothills of juniper trees and black lava rock. Behind her she heard the doctors running, but they had been taken by surprise, and as the hills became steeper and the cholla cactus were thicker, they stopped. When she reached the top of the hill, she stopped too to listen in case they were circling around her. But in a few minutes she heard a car engine start and they drove away. The children had been too surprised to cry while she ran with them. Danny was shaking and Ella's little fingers were gripping Ayah's blouse.

She stayed up in the hills for the rest of the day, sitting on a black lava boulder in the sunshine where she could see for miles all around her. The sky was light blue and cloudless, and it was warm for late April. The sun warmth relaxed her and took the fear and anger away. She lay back on the rock and watched the sky. It seemed to her that she could walk into the sky, stepping through clouds endlessly. Danny played with little pebbles and stones, pretending they were birds, eggs and then little rabbits. Ella sat at her feet and dropped fistfuls of dirt into the breeze, watching the dust and particles of sand intently. Ayah watched a hawk soar high above them, dark wings gliding; hunting or only watching, she did not know. The hawk was patient and he circled all afternoon before he disappeared around the high volcanic peak the Mexicans call Guadalupe.

Late in the afternoon, Ayah looked down at the gray boxcar shack with the paint all peeled from the wood; the stove pipe on the roof was rusted and crooked. The fire she had built that morning in the oil drum stove had burned out. Ella was asleep in her lap now and Danny sat close to her, complaining that he was hungry; he asked when they would go to the house. "We will stay up here until your father comes," she told him, "because those white men were chasing us." The boy remembered then and he nodded at her silently.

If Jimmie had been there he could have read those papers and explained to her what they said. Ayah would have known, then, never to sign them. The doctors came back the next day and they brought a BIA[2] policeman with them. They told Chato they had her signature and that was all they needed. Except for the kids. She listened to Chato sullenly; she hated him when he told her it was the old woman who died in the winter, spitting blood; it was her old grandma who had given the children this disease. "They don't spit blood" she said coldly. "The whites lie." She held Ella and Danny close to her, ready to run to the hills again. "I want a medicine man first," she said to Chato, not looking at him. He

shook his head. "It's too late now. The policeman is with them. You signed the paper." His voice was gentle.

It was worse than if they had died: to lose the children and to know that somewhere, in a place called Colorado, in a place full of sick and dying strangers, her children were without her. There had been babies that died soon after they were born, and one that died before he could walk. She had carried them herself, up to the boulders and great pieces of the cliff that long ago crashed down from Long Mesa; she laid them in the crevices of sandstone and buried them in fine brown sand with round quartz pebbles that washed down from the hills in the rain. She had endured it because they had been with her. But she could not bear this pain. She did not sleep for a long time after they took her children. She stayed on the hill where they had fled the first time, and she slept rolled up in the blanket Jimmie had sent her. She carried the pain in her belly and it was fed by everything she saw: the blue sky of their last day together and the dust and pebbles they played with; the swing in the elm tree and broomstick horse choked life from her. The pain filled her stomach and there was no room for food or for her lungs to fill with air. The air and the food would have been theirs.

She hated Chato, not because he let the policeman and doctors put the screaming children in the government car, but because he had taught her to sign her name. Because it was like the old ones always told her about learning their language or any of their ways: it endan-

[2] *BIA:* Bureau of Indian Affairs.

gered you. She slept alone on the hill until the middle of November when the first snows came. Then she made a bed for herself where the children had slept. She did not lie down beside Chato again until many years later, when he was sick and shivering and only her body could keep him warm. The illness came after the white rancher told Chato he was too old to work for him any more, and Chato and his old woman should be out of the shack by the next afternoon because the rancher had hired new people to work there. That had satisfied her. To see how the white man repaid Chato's years of loyalty and work. All of Chato's fine-sounding English talk didn't change things.

II

It snowed steadily and the luminous light from the snow gradually diminished into the darkness. Somewhere in Cebolleta a dog barked and other village dogs joined with it. Ayah looked in the direction she had come, from the bar where Chato was buying the wine. Sometimes he told her to go on ahead and wait; and then he never came. And when she finally went back looking for him, she would find him passed out at the bottom of the wooden steps to Azzie's Bar. All the wine would be gone and most of the money too, from the pale blue check that came to them once a month in a government envelope. It was then that she would look at his face and his hands, scarred by ropes and the barbed wire of all those years, and she would think, this man is a stranger; for forty years she had smiled at him and

cooked his food, but he remained a stranger. She stood up again, with the snow almost to her knees, and she walked back to find Chato.

It was hard to walk in the deep snow and she felt the air burn in her lungs. She stopped a short distance from the bar to rest and readjust the blanket. But this time he wasn't waiting for her on the bottom step with his old Stetson hat pulled down and his shoulders hunched up in his long wool overcoat.

She was careful not to slip on the wooden steps. When she pushed the door open, warm air and cigarette smoke hit her face. She looked around slowly and deliberately, in every corner, in every dark place that the old man might find to sleep. The bar owner didn't like Indians in there, especially Navajos, but he let Chato come in because he could talk Spanish like he was one of them. The men at the bar stared at her, and the bartender saw that she left the door open wide. Snow flakes were flying inside like moths and melting into a puddle on the oiled wood floor. He motioned to her to close the door, but she did not see him. She held herself straight and walked across the room slowly, searching the room with every step. The snow in her hair melted and she could feel it on her forehead. At the far corner of the room, she saw red flames at the mica window of the old stove door; she looked behind the stove just to make sure. The bar got quiet except for the Spanish polka music playing on the jukebox. She stood by the stove and shook the snow from her blanket and held it near the stove to dry. The wet wool smell reminded her of new-born goats in early March, brought inside to warm near the fire. She felt calm.

In past years they would have told her to get out. But her hair was white now and her face was wrinkled. They looked at her like she was a spider crawling slowly across the room. They were afraid; she could feel the fear. She looked at their faces steadily. They reminded her of the first time the white people brought her children back to her that winter. Danny had been shy and hid behind the thin white woman who brought them. And the baby had not known her until Ayah took her into her arms, and then Ella had nuzzled close to her as she had when she was nursing. The blonde woman was nervous and kept looking at a dainty gold watch on her wrist. She sat on the bench near the small window and watched the dark snow clouds gather around the mountains; she was worrying about the unpaved road. She was frightened by what she saw inside too: the strips of venison drying on a rope across the ceiling and the children jabbering excitedly in a language she did not know. So they stayed for only a few hours. Ayah watched the government car disappear down the road and she knew they were already being weaned from these lava hills and from this sky. The last time they came was in early June, and Ella stared at her the way the men in the bar were now staring. Ayah did not try to pick her up; she smiled at her instead and spoke cheerfully to Danny. When he tried to answer her, he could not seem to remember and he spoke English words

with the Navajo. But he gave her a scrap of paper that he had found somewhere and carried in his pocket; it was folded in half, and he shyly looked up at her and said it was a bird. She asked Chato if they were home for good this time. He spoke to the white woman and she shook her head. "How much longer," he asked, and she said she didn't know; but Chato saw how she stared at the boxcar shack. Ayah turned away then. She did not say good-bye.

III

She felt satisfied that the men in the bar feared her. Maybe it was her face and the way she held her mouth with teeth clenched tight, like there was nothing anyone could do to her now. She walked north down the road, searching for the old man. She did this because she had the blanket, and there would be no place for him except with her and the blanket in the old adobe barn near the arroyo. They always slept there when they came to Cebolleta. If the money and the wine were gone, she would be relieved because then they could go home again; back to the old hogan with a dirt roof and rock walls where she herself had been born. And the next day the old man could go back to the few sheep they still had, to follow along behind them, guiding them into dry sandy arroyos where sparse grass grew. She knew he did not like walking behind old ewes when for so many years he rode big quarter horses and worked with cattle. But she wasn't sorry for him; he should have known all along what would happen.

There had not been enough rain for their garden in five years; and that was when Chato finally hitched a ride into the town and brought back brown boxes of rice and sugar and big tin cans of welfare peaches. After that, at the first of the month they went to Cebolleta to ask the postmaster for the check; and then Chato would go to the bar and cash it. They did this as they planted the garden every May, not because anything would survive the summer dust, but because it was time to do this. And the journey passed the days that smelled silent and dry like the caves above the canyon with yellow painted buffaloes on their walls.

IV

He was walking along the pavement when she found him. He did not stop or turn around when he heard her behind him. She walked beside him and she noticed how slowly he moved now. He smelled strong of woodsmoke. Lately he had been forgetting. Sometimes he called her by his sister's name and she had been gone for a long time. Once she had found him wandering on the road to the white man's ranch, and she asked him why he was going that way; he laughed at her and said, "You know they can't run that ranch without me," and he walked on determined, limping on the leg that had been crushed many years before. Now he looked at her curiously, as if for the first time, but he kept shuffling along, moving slowly along the side of the highway. His gray hair had grown long and spread out on the shoulders of the long overcoat. He wore the old felt hat pulled down over his ears. His boots were worn out at the toes and he had stuffed pieces of an old red shirt in the holes. The rags made his feet look like little animals up to their ears in snow. She laughed at his feet; the snow muffled the sound of her laugh. He stopped and looked at her again. The wind had quit blowing and the snow was falling straight down; the southeast sky was beginning to clear and Ayah could see a star.

"Let's rest awhile," she said to him. They walked away from the road and up the slope to the giant boulders that had tumbled down from the red sandrock mesa throughout the centuries of rainstorms and earth tremors. In a place where the boulders shut out the wind, they sat down with their backs against the rock. She offered half of the blanket to him and they sat wrapped together.

The storm passed swiftly. The clouds moved east. They were massive and full, crowding together across the sky. She watched them with the feeling of horses—steely blue-gray horses startled across the sky. The powerful haunches pushed into the distances and the tail hairs streamed white mist behind them. The sky cleared. Ayah saw that there was nothing between her and the stars. The light was crystalline. There was no shimmer, no distortion through earth haze. She breathed the clarity of the night sky; she smelled the purity of the half moon and the stars. He was lying on his side with his knees pulled up near his belly for warmth. His eyes were closed now, and in the light from the stars and the moon, he looked young again.

She could see it descend out of the night sky: an icy stillness from the edge of the thin moon. She recognized the freezing. It came gradually, sinking snow flake by snow flake until the crust was heavy and deep. It had the strength of the stars in Orion, and its journey was endless. Ayah knew that with the wine he would sleep. He would not feel it. She tucked the blanket around him, remembering how it was when Ella had been with her; and she felt the rush so big inside her heart for the babies. And she sang the only song she knew to sing for babies. She could not remember if she had ever sung it to her children, but she knew that her grandmother had sung it and her mother had sung it:

The earth is your mother,
  she holds you.
The sky is your father,
  he protects you.
sleep,
sleep,
Rainbow is your sister,
  she loves you.
The winds are your brothers,
  they sing to you.
sleep,
sleep,
We are together always
We are together always
There never was a time
when this
was not so.

DISCUSSION

1. At the end, what is about to happen is fairly obvious. What is ironic in the words of Ayah's song?

2. What kind of person does Chato appear to be? (How do you know? Be specific.) How would you characterize Ayah? Chato and Ayah have sometimes had conflicting views. Which of the two seems to have valued more highly the traditional Navajo way of life? Explain.

3. Much of the story is told by *flashback,* scenes that show action that took place before the beginning of the story. What is the effect of the flashbacks in "Lullaby"—how dependent is the story on flashback?

AUTO WRECK

KARL SHAPIRO

Its quick soft silver bell beating, beating,
And down the dark one ruby flare
Pulsing out red light like an artery,
The ambulance at top speed floating down
Past beacons and illuminated clocks   5
Wings in a heavy curve, dips down,
And brakes speed, entering the crowd.
The doors leap open, emptying light;
Stretchers are laid out, the mangled lifted
And stowed into the little hospital.   10
Then the bell, breaking the hush, tolls once,
And the ambulance with its terrible cargo
Rocking, slightly rocking, moves away,
As the doors, an afterthought, are closed.

We are deranged, walking among the cops   15
Who sweep glass and are large and composed.
One is still making notes under the light.
One with a bucket douches ponds of blood
Into the street and gutter.
One hangs lanterns on the wrecks that cling,   20
Empty husks of locusts, to iron poles.

Our throats were tight as tourniquets,
Our feet were bound with splints, but now,
Like convalescents intimate and gauche,
We speak through sickly smiles and warn   25
With the stubborn saw of common sense,
The grim joke and the banal resolution.
The traffic moves around with care,
But we remain, touching a wound
That opens to our richest horror.   30
Already old, the question Who shall die?
Becomes unspoken Who is innocent?

For death in war is done by hands;
Suicide has cause and stillbirth, logic;
And cancer, simple as a flower, blooms.   35
But this invites the occult mind,
Cancels our physics with a sneer,
And spatters all we knew of denouement
Across the expedient and wicked stones.

DISCUSSION

1. The opening images suggest the emotional intensity of this poem. What is "beating, beating"? What is "pulsing out red"? What does the bell tolling in line 11 suggest?

2. Stanza 3 describes the bystanders in the language of hospitals. What metaphoric comparisons are made?

3. What "wound" is opened in the bystanders? How is death in war, suicide, stillbirth, and cancer different from that in an auto wreck? What is spattered "Across the expedient and wicked stones"?

In the 1770s a Frenchman living in
Orange County, New York, presented
the first clear picture of the American as
a unique being.

What Is an American?

ST. JEAN DE CRÈVECOEUR

I wish I could be acquainted with the feelings and thoughts which must
agitate the heart and present themselves to the mind of an enlightened
Englishman when he first lands on this continent. He must greatly rejoice
that he lived at a time to see this fair country discovered and settled; he
must necessarily feel a share of national pride when he views the chain
of settlement which embellishes these extended shores. . . . Here he be-
holds fair cities, substantial villages, extensive fields, an immense country
filled with decent houses, good roads, orchards, meadows, and bridges,
where an hundred years ago all was wild, woody, and uncultivated! What
a train of pleasing ideas this fair spectacle must suggest; it is a prospect
which must inspire a good citizen with the most heartfelt pleasure.

    The difficulty consists in the manner of viewing so extensive a scene.
He is arrived on a new continent; a modern society offers itself to his
contemplation, different from what he had hitherto seen. It is not composed, as in Europe, of great lords who possess everything, and of a herd
of people who have nothing. Here are no aristocratical families, no courts,
no kings, no bishops, no ecclesiastical[1] dominion, no invisible power giving to a few a very visible one; no great manufacturers employing thousands, no great refinements of luxury. The rich and the poor are not so
far removed from each other as they are in Europe. Some few towns excepted, we are all tillers of the earth, from Nova Scotia to West Florida.
We are a people of cultivators, scattered over an immense territory, com-
municating with each other by means of good roads and navigable rivers,
united by the silken bands of mild government, all respecting the laws

---

[1] *ecclesiastical* (ĭ-klē-zē-ăs′tĭ-kəl): of the church.

without dreading their power, because they are equitable. We are all animated with the spirit of an industry which is unfettered and unrestrained, because each person works for himself.

If he travels through our rural districts he views not the hostile castle, and the haughty mansion, contrasted with the claybuilt hut and miserable cabin, where cattle and men help to keep each other warm and dwell in meanness,[2] smoke, and indigence. A pleasing uniformity of decent competence appears throughout our habitations. The meanest of our log houses is a dry and comfortable habitation. Lawyer or merchant are the fairest titles our towns afford; that of a farmer is the only appellation[3] of the rural inhabitants of our country. It must take some time ere he can reconcile himself to our dictionary, which is but short in words of dignity and names of honor. There, on a Sunday, he sees a congregation of respectable farmers and their wives, all clad in neat homespun, well mounted, or riding in their own humble wagons. There is not among them an esquire,[4] saving[5] the unlettered magistrate. There he sees a parson as simple as his flock, a farmer who does not riot[6] on the labor of others. We have no princes, for whom we toil, starve, and bleed: we are the most perfect society now existing in the world. Here man is free as he ought to be; nor is this pleasing equality so transitory as many others are. Many ages will not see the shores of our great lakes replenished with inland nations, nor the unknown bounds of North America entirely peopled. Who can tell how far it extends? Who can tell the millions of men whom it will feed and contain? for no European foot has as yet traveled half the extent of this mighty continent!

The next wish of this traveler will be to know whence came all these people? They are a mixture of English, Scotch, Irish, French, Dutch, Germans, and Swedes. From this promiscuous breed,[7] that race now called Americans have arisen. . . .

In this great American asylum,[8] the poor of Europe have by some means met together, and in consequence of various causes; to what purpose should they ask one another what countrymen they are? Alas, two thirds of them had no country. Can a wretch who wanders about, who works and starves, whose life is a continual scene of sore affliction or pinching penury; can that man call England or any other kingdom his country? A country that had no bread for him, whose fields procured him

[2] *meanness:* squalor.
[3] *appellation:* name.
[4] *esquire:* in the English gentry, a man whose rank is next below a knight.
[5] *saving:* except.
[6] *riot:* feast; live excessively.
[7] *promiscuous breed:* group of differing kinds.
[8] *asylum:* here, sanctuary.

no harvest, who met with nothing but the frowns of the rich, the severity of the laws, with jails and punishments; who owned not a single foot of the extensive surface of this planet? No! urged by a variety of motives, here they came. Everything has tended to regenerate them; new laws, a new mode of living, a new social system; here they are become men: in Europe they were as so many useless plants, wanting vegetative mold,[9] and refreshing showers; they withered and were mowed down by want, hunger, and war; but now by the power of transplantation, like all other plants they have taken root and flourished! Formerly they were not numbered in any civil lists of their country except in those of the poor; here they rank as citizens. By what invisible power has this surprising metamorphosis[10] been performed? By that of the laws and that of their industry. . . .

What then is the American, this new man? He is either an European, or the descendant of an European, hence that strange mixture of blood which you will find in no other country. I could point out to you a family whose grandfather was an Englishman, whose wife was Dutch, whose son married a French woman, and whose present four sons have now four wives of different nations. *He* is an American, who, leaving behind him all his ancient prejudices and manners, receives new ones from the new mode of life he has embraced, the new government he obeys, and the new rank he holds. He becomes an American by being received in the broad lap of our great Alma Mater.[11] Here individuals of all nations are melted into a new race of men, whose labors and posterity will one day cause great changes in the world. Americans are the western pilgrims, who are carrying along with them that great mass of arts, sciences, vigor, and industry which began long since in the east; they will finish the great circle.

The Americans were once scattered all over Europe; here they are incorporated into one of the finest systems of population which has ever appeared, and which will hereafter become distinct by the power of the different climates they inhabit. The American ought therefore to love this country much better than that wherein either he or his forefathers were born. Here the rewards of his industry follow with equal steps the progress of his labor; his labor is founded on the basis of nature, *self-interest;* can it want a stronger allurement? Wives and children, who before in

---

[9] *wanting vegetative mold:* lacking rich soil.
[10] *metamorphosis* (mĕt-ə-môr′fə-sĭs): striking change in appearance or circumstances.
[11] *Alma Mater:* literally, fostering mother.

vain demanded of him a morsel of bread, now, fat and frolicsome, gladly help their father to clear those fields whence exuberant crops are to arise to feed and to clothe them all; without any part being claimed, either by a despotic prince, a rich abbot, or a mighty lord. Here religion demands but little of him; a small voluntary salary to the minister and gratitude to God; can he refuse these? The American is a new man, who acts upon new principles; he must therefore entertain new ideas and form new opinions. From involuntary idleness, servile dependence, penury, and useless labor, he has passed to toils of a very different nature, rewarded by ample subsistence. [12]—This is an American.

[12] *subsistence:* livelihood.

DISCUSSION

1. What important differences does Crèvecoeur find between America and the lands from which immigrants came?

2. To what extent have the author's predictions for the future of America proved accurate?

3. Is Crèvecoeur's definition of an American still valid? If not, what changes should be made?

4. What connotations have the italicized words in the following expressions?
a. "great lords who possess everything, and . . . a *herd* of people who have nothing" (page 628)
b. "the *silken* bands of mild government" (p. 628)
c. "individuals of all nations are *melted* into a new race" (p. 630)

For further activities, see page 652.

On December 7, 1941, Japanese planes bombed
the U. S. naval base at Pearl Harbor on the island
of Oahu in Hawaii, bringing America into World
War II.

What Is Pearl Harbor?

JEANNE WAKATSUKI HOUSTON and JAMES D. HOUSTON

On that first weekend in December there must have been twenty or twenty-five boats getting ready to leave. I had just turned seven. I remember it was Sunday because I was out of school, which meant I could go down to the wharf and watch. In those days—1941—there was no smog around Long Beach. The water was clean, the sky a sharp Sunday blue, with all the engines of that white sardine fleet puttering up into it, and a lot of yelling, especially around Papa's boat. Papa loved to give orders. He had attended military school in Japan until the age of seventeen, and part of him never got over that. My oldest brothers, Bill and Woody, were his crew. They would have to check the nets again, and check the fuel tanks again, and run back to the grocery store for some more cigarettes, and then somehow everything had been done, and they were easing away from the wharf, joining the line of boats heading out past the lighthouse, into the harbor.

Papa's boat was called *The Nereid*—long, white, lowslung, with a foredeck wheel cabin. He had another smaller boat, called *The Waka* (a short version of our name), which he kept in Santa Monica, where we lived. But *The Nereid* was

his pride. It was worth about $25,000 before the war, and the way he stood in the cabin steering toward open water you would think the whole fleet was under his command. Papa had a mustache then. He wore knee-high rubber boots, a rust-colored turtleneck Mama had knitted him, and a black skipper's hat. He liked to hear himself called "Skipper."

Through one of the big canneries he had made a deal to pay for *The Nereid* with percentages of each catch, and he was anxious to get it paid off. He didn't much like working for someone else if he could help it. A lot of fishermen around San Pedro Harbor had similar contracts with the canneries. In typical Japanese fashion, they all wanted to be independent commercial fishermen, yet they almost always fished together. They would take off from Terminal Island, help each other find the schools of sardine, share nets and radio equipment—competing and co-operating at the same time.

You never knew how long they'd be gone, a couple of days, sometimes a week, sometimes a month, depending on the fish. From the wharf we waved good-bye—my mother, Bill's wife, Woody's wife Chizu, and me. We yelled at them to have a good trip, and after they were out of earshot and the sea had swallowed their engine noises, we kept waving. Then we just stood there with the other women, watching. It was a kind of duty, perhaps a way of adding a little good luck to the voyage, or warding off the bad. It was also marvelously warm, almost summery, the way December days can be sometimes in southern California. When the boats came back, the women who lived on Terminal Island would be rushing to the canneries. But for the moment there wasn't much else to do. We watched until the boats became a row of tiny white gulls on the horizon. Our vigil would end when they slipped over the edge and disappeared. You had to squint against the glare to keep them sighted, and with every blink you expected the last white speck to be gone.

But this time they didn't disappear. They kept floating out there, suspended, as if the horizon had finally become what it always seemed to be from shore: the sea's limit, beyond which no man could sail. They floated a while, then they began to grow, tiny gulls becoming boats again, a white armada cruising toward us.

"They're coming back," my mother said.

"Why would they be coming back?" Chizu said.

"Something with the engine."

"Maybe somebody got hurt."

"But they wouldn't *all* come back," Mama said, bewildered.

Another woman said, "Maybe there's a storm coming."

They all glanced at the sky, scanning the unmarred horizon. Mama shook her head. There was no explanation. No one

had ever seen anything like this before. We watched and waited, and when the boats were still about half a mile off the lighthouse, a fellow from the cannery came running down to the wharf shouting that the Japanese had just bombed Pearl Harbor.

Chizu said to Mama, "What does he mean? What is Pearl Harbor?"

Mama yelled at him, "What is Pearl Harbor?"

But he was running along the docks, like Paul Revere, bringing the news, and didn't have time to explain.

That night Papa burned the flag he had brought with him from Hiroshima thirty-five years earlier. It was such a beautiful piece of material, I couldn't believe he was doing that. He burned a lot of papers too, documents, anything that might suggest he still had some connection with Japan. These precautions didn't do him much good. He was not only an alien; he held a commercial fishing license, and in the early days of the war the FBI was picking up all such men, for fear they were somehow making contact with enemy ships off the coast. Papa himself knew it would only be a matter of time.

They got him two weeks later, when we were staying overnight at Woody's place, on Terminal Island. Five hundred Japanese families lived there then, and FBI deputies had been questioning everyone, ransacking houses for anything that could conceivably be used for signaling planes or ships or that indicated loyalty to the Emperor. Most of the houses had radios with a short-wave band and a high aerial on the roof so that wives could make contact with the fishing boats during these long cruises. To the FBI every radio owner was a potential saboteur. The confiscators were often deputies sworn in hastily during the turbulent days right after Pearl Harbor, and these men seemed to be acting out the general panic, seeing sinister possibilities in the most ordinary household items: flashlights, kitchen knives, cameras, lanterns, toy swords.

If Papa were trying to avoid arrest, he wouldn't have gone near that island. But I think he knew it was futile to hide out or resist. The next morning two FBI men in fedora hats and trench coats—like out of a thirties movie—knocked on Woody's door, and when they left, Papa was between them. He didn't struggle. There was no point to it. He had become a man without a country. The land of his birth was at war with America; yet after thirty-five years here he was still prevented by law from becoming an American citizen. He was suddenly a man with no rights who looked exactly like the enemy.

About all he had left at this point was his tremendous dignity. He was tall for a Japanese man, nearly six feet, lean and hard and healthy-skinned from the sea. He was over fifty. Ten children and a lot of hard luck had worn him down, had worn away most of the arrogance he came to this country with. But he still had dignity, and he would not let those deputies push him out the door. He led them.

Mama knew they were taking all the alien men first to an interrogation center right there on the island. Some were simply being questioned and released. In the beginning she wasn't too worried; at least she wouldn't let herself be. But it grew dark and he wasn't back. Another day went by and we still had heard nothing. Then word came that he had been taken into custody and shipped out. Where to, or for how long? No one knew. All my brothers' attempts to find out were fruitless.

What had they charged him with? We didn't know that either, until an article appeared the next day in the Santa Monica paper, saying he had been arrested for delivering oil to Japanese submarines offshore.

My mother began to weep. It seems now that she wept for days. She was a small, plump woman who laughed easily and cried easily, but I had never seen her cry like this. I couldn't understand it. I remember clinging to her legs, wondering why everyone was crying. This was the beginning of a terrible, frantic time for all my family. But I myself didn't cry about Papa, or have any inkling of what was wrenching Mama's heart, until the next time I saw him, almost a year later.

In December of 1941 Papa's disappearance didn't bother me nearly so much as the world I soon found myself in.

He had been a jack-of-all-trades. When I was born he was farming near Inglewood. Later, when he started fishing, we moved to Ocean Park, near Santa Monica, and until they picked him up, that's where we lived, in a big frame house with a brick fireplace, a block back from the beach. We were the only Japanese family in the neighborhood. Papa liked it that way. He didn't want to be

labeled or grouped by anyone. But with him gone and no way of knowing what to expect, my mother moved all of us down to Terminal Island. Woody already lived there, and one of my older sisters had married a Terminal Island boy. Mama's first concern now was to keep the family together; and once the war began, she felt safer there than isolated racially in Ocean Park. But for me, at age seven, the island was a country as foreign as India or Arabia would have been. It was the first time I had lived among other Japanese, or gone to school with them, and I was terrified all the time.

This was partly Papa's fault. One of his threats to keep us younger kids in line was "I'm going to sell you to the Chinese man." When I had entered kindergarten two years earlier, I was the only Oriental in the class. They sat me next to a Caucasian girl who happened to have very slanted eyes. I looked at her and began to scream, certain Papa had sold me out at last. My fear of her ran so deep I could not speak of it, even to Mama, couldn't explain why I was screaming. For two weeks I had nightmares about this girl, until the teachers finally moved me to the other side of the room. And it was still with me, this fear of Oriental faces, when we moved to Terminal Island.

In those days it was a company town, a ghetto owned and controlled by the canneries. The men went after fish, and whenever the boats came back—day or night—the women would be called to process the catch while it was fresh. One in the afternoon or four in the morning, it made no difference. My mother had to go to work right after we moved there. I can still hear the whistle—two toots for French's, three for Van Camp's—and she and Chizu would be out of bed in the middle of the night, heading for the cannery.

The house we lived in was nothing more than a shack, a barracks with single plank walls and rough wooden floors, like the cheapest kind of migrant workers' housing. The people around us were hardworking, boisterous, a little proud of their nickname, *yo-go-re,* which meant literally *uncouth one,* or roughneck, or dead-end kid. They not only spoke Japanese exclusively, they spoke a dialect peculiar to Kyushu, where their familes had come from in Japan, a rough, fisherman's language, full of oaths and insults. Instead of saying *ba-ka-ta-re,* a common insult meaning *stupid,* Terminal Islanders would say *ba-ka-ya-ro,* a coarser and exclusively masculine use of the word, which implies gross stupidity. They would swagger and pick on outsiders and persecute anyone who didn't speak as they did. That was what made my own time there so hateful. I had never spoken anything but English, and the other kids in the second grade despised me for it. They were tough and mean. Each day after school I dreaded their ambush. My brother Kiyo, three years older, would wait for me at the door, where we would decide whether to run straight home together, or split up, or try a new and unexpected route.

None of these kids ever actually attacked. It was the threat that frightened us, their fearful looks, and the noises they would make, like miniature Samurai, in a language we couldn't understand.

At the time it seemed we had been living under this reign of fear for years. In fact, we lived there about two months. Late in February the navy decided to clear Terminal Island completely. Even though most of us were American-born, it was dangerous having that many Orientals so close to the Long Beach Naval Station, on the opposite end of the island. We had known something like this was coming. But, like Papa's arrest, not much could be done ahead of time. There were four of us kids still young enough to be living with Mama, plus Granny, her mother, sixty-five then, speaking no English, and nearly blind. Mama didn't know where else she could get work, and we had nowhere else to move *to.* On February 25 the choice was made for us. We were given forty-eight hours to clear out.

The secondhand dealers had been prowling around for weeks, like wolves, offering humiliating prices for goods and furniture they knew many of us would have to sell sooner or later. Mama had left all but her most valuable possessions in Ocean Park, simply because she had nowhere to put them. She had brought along her pottery, her silver, heirlooms like the kimonos Granny had brought from Japan, tea sets, lacquered tables, and one fine old set of china, blue and white porcelain, almost translucent. On the day we were leaving, Woody's car was so crammed with boxes and luggage and kids we had just run out of room. Mama had to sell this china.

One of the dealers offered her fifteen dollars for it. She said it was a full setting for twelve and worth at least two hundred. He said fifteen was his top price. Mama started to quiver. Her eyes blazed up at him. She had been packing all night and trying to calm down Granny, who didn't understand why we were moving again and what all the rush was about. Mama's nerves were shot, and now navy jeeps were patrolling the streets. She didn't say another word. She just glared at this man, all the rage and frustration channeled at him through her eyes.

He watched her for a moment and said he was sure he couldn't pay more than seventeen fifty for that china. She reached into the red velvet case, took out a dinner plate and hurled it at the floor right in front of his feet.

The man leaped back shouting, "Hey! Hey, don't do that! Those are valuable dishes!"

Mama took out another dinner plate and hurled it at the floor, then another and another, never moving, never opening her mouth, just quivering and glaring at the retreating dealer, with tears streaming down her cheeks. He finally turned and scuttled out the door, heading for the next house. When he was gone she stood there smashing cups and bowls and platters until the whole set lay in scattered blue and white fragments across the wooden floor.

The American Friends Service helped us find a small house in Boyle Heights, another minority ghetto, in downtown Los Angeles, now inhabited briefly by a few hundred Terminal Island refugees. Executive Order 9066 had been signed by President Roosevelt, giving the War Department authority to define military areas in the western states and to exclude from them anyone who might threaten the war effort. There was a lot of talk about internment, or moving inland, or something like that in store for all Japanese Americans. I remember my brothers sitting around the table talking very intently about what we were going to do, how we would keep the family together. They had seen how quickly Papa was removed, and they knew now that he would not be back for quite a while. Just before leaving Terminal Island Mama had received her first letter, from Bismarck, North Dakota. He had been imprisoned at Fort Lincoln, in an all-male camp for enemy aliens.

Papa had been the patriarch. He had always decided everything in the family. With him gone, my brothers, like councilors in the absence of a chief, worried about what should be done. The ironic thing is, there wasn't much left to decide. These were mainly days of quiet, desperate waiting for what seemed at the time to be inevitable. There is a phrase the Japanese use in such situations, when something difficult must be endured. You would hear the older heads, the Issei, telling others very quietly, *"Shikata ga nai"* (It cannot be helped). *"Shikata ga nai"* (It must be done).

Mama and Woody went to work packing celery for a Japanese produce dealer. Kiyo and my sister May and I enrolled in the local school, and what sticks in my memory from those few weeks is the teacher—not her looks, her remoteness. In Ocean Park my teacher had been a kind, grandmotherly woman who used to sail with us in Papa's boat from time to time and who wept the day we had to leave. In Boyle Heights the teacher felt cold and distant. I was confused by all

the moving and was having trouble with the classwork, but she would never help me out. She would have nothing to do with me.

This was the first time I had felt outright hostility from a Caucasian. Looking back, it is easy enough to explain. Public attitudes toward the Japanese in California were shifting rapidly. In the first few months of the Pacific war, America was on the run. Tolerance had turned to distrust and irrational fear. The hundred-year-old tradition of anti-Orientalism on the west coast soon resurfaced, more vicious than ever. Its result became clear about a month later, when we were told to make our third and final move.

The name Manzanar meant nothing to us when we left Boyle Heights. We didn't know where it was or what it was. We went because the government ordered us to. And, in the case of my older brothers and sisters, we went with a certain amount of relief. They had all heard stories of Japanese homes being attacked, of beatings in the streets of California towns. They were as frightened of the Caucasians as Caucasians were of us. Moving, under what appeared to be government protection, to an area less directly threatened by the war seemed not such a bad idea at all. For some it actually sounded like a fine adventure.

Our pickup point was a Buddhist church in Los Angeles. It was very early, and misty, when we got there with our luggage. Mama had bought heavy coats for all of us. She grew up in eastern Washington and knew that anywhere inland in early April would be cold. I was proud of my new coat, and I remember sitting on a duffel bag trying to be

friendly with the Greyhound driver. I smiled at him. He didn't smile back. He was befriending no one. Someone tied a numbered tag to my collar and to the duffel bag (each family was given a number, and that became our official designation until the camps were closed), someone else passed out box lunches for the trip, and we climbed aboard.

I had never been outside Los Angeles County, never traveled more than ten miles from the coast, had never even ridden on a bus. I was full of excitement, the way any kid would be, and wanted to look out the window. But for the first few hours the shades were drawn. Around me other people played cards, read magazines, dozed, waiting. I settled back, waiting too, and finally fell asleep. The bus felt very secure to me. Almost half of its passengers were immediate relatives. Mama and my older brothers had succeeded in keeping most of us together, on the same bus, headed for the same camp. I didn't realize until much later what a job that was. The strategy had been, first, to have everyone living in the same district when the evacuation began, and then to get all of us included under the same family number, even though names had been changed by marriage. Many families weren't as lucky as ours and suffered months of anguish while trying to arrange transfers from one camp to another.

We rode all day. By the time we reached our destination, the shades were up. It was late afternoon. The first thing I saw was a yellow swirl across a blurred, reddish setting sun. The bus was being pelted by what sounded like splattering rain. It wasn't rain. This was my first look at something I would soon know very well, a billowing flurry of dust and sand churned up by the wind through Owens Valley.

We drove past a barbed-wire fence, through a gate, and into an open space where trunks and sacks and packages had been dumped from the baggage trucks that drove out ahead of us. I could see a few tents set up, the first rows of black barracks, and beyond them, blurred by sand, rows of barracks that seemed to spread for miles across this plain. People were sitting on cartons or milling around, with their backs to the wind, waiting to see which friends or relatives might be on this bus. As we approached, they turned or stood up, and some moved toward us expectantly. But inside the bus no one stirred. No one waved or spoke. They just stared out the windows, ominously silent. I didn't understand this. Hadn't we finally arrived, our whole family intact? I opened a window, leaned out, and yelled happily. "Hey! This whole bus is full of Wakatsukis!"

Outside, the greeters smiled. Inside there was an explosion of laughter, hysterical, tension-breaking laughter that left my brothers choking and whacking each other across the shoulders.

DISCUSSION

1. Japanese Americans at the beginning of World War II became innocent victims. How did the "hundred-year-old tradition of anti-Orientalism on the west coast" surface? What forms did this "distrust and irrational fear" take? How did it touch Jeanne Wakatsuki?

2. One of the most vivid scenes in the selection shows Mama hurling plates and "smashing cups and bowls and platters until the whole set lay in scattered blue and white fragments across the wooden floor" (page 637). What caused her to break her beautiful dishes?

3. Who asks the question in the title? Why is this question ironical?

4. Jeanne Wakatsuki Houston, one of the authors, is the speaker through whose eyes we see these events. What are her feelings about these wartime experiences? What is the tone of the selection?

For further activities, see page 652.

FROM TRAVELS WITH CHARLEY

JOHN STEINBECK

From the beginning of my journey, I had avoided the great high-speed slashes of concrete and tar called "thruways," or "superhighways." Various states have different names for them, but I had dawdled in New England, the winter grew apace, and I had visions of being snowbound in North Dakota. I sought out U.S. 90, a wide gash of a super-highway, multiple-lane carrier of the nation's goods. Rocinante[1] bucketed along. The minimum speed on this road was greater than any I had previously driven. I drove into a wind quartering in from my starboard bow and felt the buffeting, sometimes staggering blows of the gale I helped to make. I could hear the sough of it on the square surfaces of my camper top. Instructions screamed at me from the road once: "Do not stop! No stopping. Maintain speed." Trucks as long as freighters went roaring by, delivering a wind like the blow of a fist. These great roads are wonderful for moving goods but not for inspection of a countryside. You are bound to the wheel and your eyes to the car ahead and to the rearview mirror for the car behind and the side mirror for the car or truck about to pass, and at the same time you must read all the signs for fear you may miss some instructions or orders. No roadside stands selling squash juice, no antique stores, no farm products or factory outlets. When we get these thruways across the whole country, as we will and must, it will be possible to drive from New York to California without seeing a single thing.

At intervals there are places of rest and recreation, food, fuel and oil, postcards, steam-table food, picnic tables, garbage cans all fresh and newly painted, rest rooms and lavatories so spotless, so incensed with deodorants and with detergents that it takes a time to get your sense of smell back. For deodorants are not quite correctly named; they substitute one smell for another, and the substitute must be much stronger and more penetrating than the odor it conquers. I had neglected my own country too long. Civilization had made great

Charley: the author's French poodle.
[1] _Rocinante:_ Steinbeck's camper, named for Don Quixote's horse.

strides in my absence. I remember when a coin in a slot would get you a stick of gum or a candy bar, but in these dining palaces were vending machines where various coins could deliver handkerchiefs, comb-and-nail-file sets, hair conditioners and cosmetics, first-aid kits, minor drugs such as aspirin, mild physics, pills to keep you awake. I found myself entranced with these gadgets. Suppose you want a soft drink; you pick your kind—Sungrape or Cooly Cola—press a button, insert the coin, and stand back. A paper cup drops into place, the drink pours out and stops a quarter of an inch from the brim—a cold, refreshing drink guaranteed synthetic. Coffee is even more interesting, for when the hot black fluid has ceased, a squirt of milk comes down and an envelope of sugar drops beside the cup. But of all, the hot-soup machine is the triumph. Choose among ten—pea, chicken noodle, beef and veg., insert the coin. A rumbling hum comes from the giant and a sign lights up that reads "Heating." After a minute a red light flashes on and off until you open a little door and remove the paper cup of boiling-hot soup.

It is life at a peak of some kind of civilization. The restaurant accommodations, great scallops of counters with simulated leather stools, are as spotless as and not unlike the lavatories. Everything that can be captured and held down is sealed in clear plastic. The food is oven-fresh, spotless and tasteless; untouched by human hands. I remember with an ache certain dishes in France and Italy touched by innumerable human hands.

If one has driven a car over many years, as I have, nearly all reactions have become automatic. One does not think about what to do. Nearly all the driving technique is deeply buried in a machine-like unconscious. This being so, a large area of the conscious mind is left free for thinking. And what do people think of when they drive? On short trips perhaps of arrival at a destination or memory of events at the place of departure. But there is left, particularly on very long trips, a large area for daydreaming or even, God help us, for thought. No one can know what another does in that area. I myself have planned houses I will never build, have made gardens I will never plant, have designed a method for pumping the soft silt and decayed shells from the bottom of my bay up to my point of land at Sag Harbor, of leeching out the salt, thus making a rich and productive soil. I don't know whether or not I will do this, but driving along I have planned it in detail even to the kind of pump, the leeching bins, the tests to determine disappearance of salinity. Driving, I have created turtle traps in my mind, have written long, detailed letters never to be put to paper,

much less sent. When the radio was on, music has stimulated memory of times and places, complete with characters and stage sets, memories so exact that every word of dialogue is recreated. And I have projected future scenes, just as complete and convincing—scenes that will never take place. I've written short stories in my mind, chuckling at my own humor, saddened or stimulated by structure or content.

On my journey, which was designed for observation, I stayed as much as possible on secondary roads where there was much to see and hear and smell, and avoided the great wide traffic slashes which promote the self by fostering daydreams. I drove this wide, eventless way called U.S. 90 which bypassed Buffalo and Erie to Madison, Ohio, and then found the equally wide and fast U.S. 20 past Cleveland and Toledo, and so into Michigan.

On these roads out of the manufacturing centers there moved many mobile homes, pulled by specially designed trucks, and since these mobile homes comprise one of my generalities, I may as well get to them now. Early in my travels I had become aware of these new things under the sun, of their great numbers, and since they occur in increasing numbers all over the nation, observation of them and perhaps some speculation is in order. They are not trailers to be pulled by one's own car but shining cars long as pullmans. From the beginning of my travels I had noticed the sale lots where they were sold and traded, but then I began to be aware of the parks where they sit down in uneasy permanence. In Maine I took to stopping the night in these parks, talking to the managers and to the dwellers in this new kind of housing, for they gather in groups of like to like.

They are wonderfully built homes, aluminum skins, double-walled, with insulation, and often paneled with veneer of hardwood. Sometimes as much as forty feet long, they have two to five rooms, and are complete with air conditioners, toilets, baths, and invariably television. The parks where they sit are sometimes landscaped and equipped with every facility. I talked with the park men, who were enthusiastic. A mobile home is drawn to the trailer park and installed on a ramp, a heavy rubber sewer pipe is bolted underneath, water and electric power connected, the television antenna raised, and the family is in residence. Several park managers agreed that last year one in four new housing units in the whole community was a mobile home. The park men charge a small ground rent plus fees for water and electricity. Telephones are connected in nearly all of them simply by plugging in a jack. Sometimes the park has a general store for supplies, but if not the supermarkets which dot the countryside are available. Parking difficulties in the towns have caused these markets to move to the open country where they are immune from town taxes. This is also true of the trailer parks. The fact that these homes can be moved does not mean that they do move. Sometimes their owners stay for years in one place, plant gardens, build little walls of cinder blocks, put out awnings and garden furniture. It is a whole way of life that was new to me. These homes are never cheap and often are quite expensive and lavish. I have seen some that cost $20,000 and contained all the thousand appliances we live by—dishwashers, automatic clothes washers and driers, refrigerators and deep freezes.

The owners were not only willing but glad and proud to show their homes to me. The rooms, while small, were well proportioned. Every conceivable unit was built in. Wide windows, some even called picture windows, destroyed any sense of being closed in; the bedrooms and beds were spacious and the storage space unbelievable. It seemed to me a revolution in living and on a rapid increase. Why did a family choose to live in such a home? Well, it was comfortable, compact, easy to keep clean, easy to heat.

In Maine: "I'm tired of living in a cold barn with the wind whistling through, tired of the torment of little taxes and payments for this and that. It's warm and cozy and in the summer the air-conditioner keeps us cool."

"What is the usual income bracket of the mobiles?"

"That is variable but a goodly number are in the ten-thousand- to twenty-thousand-dollar class."

"Has job uncertainty anything to do with the rapid increase of these units?"

"Well perhaps there may be some of that. Who knows what is in store tomorrow? Mechanics, plant engineers, architects, accountants, and even here and there a doctor or a dentist live in the mobile. If a plant or a factory closes down, you're not trapped with property you can't sell. Suppose the husband has a job and is buying a house and there's a layoff. The value goes out of his house. But if he has a mobile home he rents a trucking service and moves on and he hasn't lost anything. He may never have to do it, but the fact that he can is a comfort to him."

"How are they purchased?"

"On time, just like an automobile. It's like paying rent."

And then I discovered the greatest selling appeal of all—one that crawls through nearly all American life. Improvements are made on these mobile homes every year. If you are doing well you turn yours in on a new model just as you do with an automobile if you can possibly afford to. There's status to that. And the turn-in value is higher

than that of automobiles because there's a ready market for used
homes. And after a few years the once expensive home may have a
poorer family. They are easy to maintain, need no paint since they are
usually of aluminum, and are not tied to fluctuating land values.

"How about schools?"

The school buses pick the children up right at the park and bring
them back. The family car takes the head of the house to work and
the family to a drive-in movie at night. It's a healthy life out in the
country air. The payments, even if high and festooned with interest,
are no worse than renting an apartment and fighting the owner for
heat. And where could you rent such a comfortable ground-floor
apartment with a place for your car outside the door? Where else
could the kids have a dog? Nearly every mobile home has a dog, as
Charley discovered to his delight. Twice I was invited to dinner in a
mobile home and several times watched a football game on television.
A manager told me that one of the first considerations in his business
was to find and buy a place where television reception is good. Since
I did not require any facilities, sewer, water, or electricity, the price to
me for stopping the night was one dollar.

The first impression forced on me was that permanence is neither
achieved nor desired by mobile people. They do not buy for the generations, but only until a new model they can afford comes out. The
mobile units are by no means limited to the park communities. Hundreds of them will be found sitting beside a farm house, and this was
explained to me. There was a time when, on the occasion of a son's
marriage and the addition of a wife and later of children to the farm,
it was customary to add a wing or at least a lean-to on the home
place. Now in many cases a mobile unit takes the place of additional
building. A farmer from whom I bought eggs and home-smoked bacon told me of the advantages. Each family has a privacy it never had
before. The old folks are not irritated by crying babies. The mother-in-
law problem is abated because the new daughter has a privacy she
never had and a place of her own in which to build the structure of a
family. When they move away, and nearly all Americans move away,
or want to, they do not leave unused and therefore useless rooms. Relations between the generations are greatly improved. The son is a
guest when he visits the parents' house, and the parents are guests in
the son's house.

Then there are the loners, and I have talked with them also. Driving along, you see high on a hill a single mobile home placed to command a great view. Others nestle under trees fringing a river or a lake.
These loners have rented a tiny piece of land from the owner. They

need only enough for the unit and the right of passage to get to it. Sometimes the loner digs a well and a cesspool, and plants a small garden, but others transport their water in fifty-gallon oil drums. Enormous ingenuity is apparent with some of the loners in placing the water supply higher than the unit and connecting it with plastic pipe so that a gravity flow is insured.

One of the dinners that I shared in a mobile home was cooked in an immaculate kitchen, walled in plastic tile, with stainless-steel sinks and ovens and stoves flush with the wall. The fuel is butane or some other bottled gas which can be picked up anywhere. We ate in a dining alcove paneled in mahogany veneer. I've never had a better or a more comfortable dinner. I had brought a bottle of whisky as my contribution, and afterward we sat in deep comfortable chairs cushioned in foam rubber. This family liked the way they lived and wouldn't think of going back to the old way. The husband worked as a garage mechanic about four miles away and made good pay. Two children walked to the highway every morning and were picked up by a yellow school bus.

Sipping a highball after dinner, hearing the rushing of water in the electric dishwasher in the kitchen, I brought up a question that had puzzled me. These were good, thoughtful, intelligent people. I said, "One of our most treasured feelings concerns roots, growing up rooted in some soil or some community." How did they feel about raising their children without roots? Was it good or bad? Would they miss it or not?

The father, a good-looking, fair-skinned man with dark eyes, answered me. "How many people today have what you are talking about? What roots are there in an apartment twelve floors up? What roots are in a housing development of hundreds and thousands of small dwellings almost exactly alike? My father came from Italy," he said. "He grew up in Tuscany in a house where his family had lived maybe a thousand years. That's roots for you, no running water, no toilet, and they cooked with charcoal or vine clippings. They had just two rooms, a kitchen and a bedroom where everybody slept, grandpa, father and all the kids, no place to read, no place to be alone, and never had had. Was that better? I bet if you gave my old man the choice he'd cut his roots and live like this." He waved his hands at the comfortable room. "Fact is, he cut his roots away and came to America. Then he lived in a tenement in New York—just one room, walk-up, cold water and no heat. That's where I was born and I lived in the streets as a kid until my old man got a job upstate in New York in the grape country. You see, he knew about vines, that's about all he knew. Now you take my wife. She's Irish descent. Her people had roots too."

"In a peat bog," the wife said. "And lived on potatoes." She gazed fondly through the door at her fine kitchen.

"Don't you miss some kind of permanence?"

"Who's got permanence? Factory closes down, you move on. Good times and things opening up, you move on where it's better. You got roots you sit and starve. You take the pioneers in the history books. They were movers. Take up land, sell it, move on. I read in a book how Lincoln's family came to Illinois on a raft. They had some barrels of whisky for a bank account. How many kids in America stay in the place where they were born, if they can get out?"

"You've thought about it a lot."

"Don't have to think about it. There it is. I've got a good trade. Long as there's automobiles I can get work, but suppose the place I work goes broke. I got to move where there's a job. I get to my job in three minutes. You want I should drive twenty miles because I got roots?"

Later they showed me magazines designed exclusively for mobile dwellers, stories and poems and hints for successful mobile living. How to stop a leak. How to choose a place for sun or coolness. And there were advertisements for gadgets, fascinating things, for cooking, cleaning, washing clothes, furniture and beds and cribs. Also there were full-page pictures of new models, each one grander and more shiny than the next.

"There's thousands of them," said the father, "and there's going to be millions."

"Joe's quite a dreamer," the wife said. "He's always figuring something out. Tell him your ideas, Joe."

"Maybe he wouldn't be interested."

"Sure I would."

"Well, it's not a dream like she said, it's for real, and I'm going to do it pretty soon now. Take a little capital, but it would pay off. I been looking around the used lots for the unit I want at the price I want to pay. Going to rip out the guts and set it up for a repair shop. I got enough tools nearly already, and I'll stock little things like windshield wipers and fan belts and cylinder rings and inner tubes, stuff like that. You take these courts are getting bigger and bigger. Some of the mobile people got two cars. I'll rent me a hundred feet of ground right near and I'll be in business. There's one thing you can say about cars, there's nearly always something wrong with them that's got to be fixed. And I'll have my house, this here one right beside my shop.

That way I would have a bell and give twenty-four-hour service."

"Sounds like a good deal," I said. And it does.

"Best thing about it," Joe went on, "if business fell off, why, I'd just move on where it was good."

His wife said, "Joe's got it all worked out on paper where everything's going to go, every wrench and drill, even an electric welder. Joe's a wonderful welder."

I said, "I take back what I said, Joe. I guess you've got your roots in a grease pit."

"You could do worse. I even worked that out. And you know, when the kids grow up, we could even work our way south in the winter and north in the summer."

"Joe does good work," said his wife. "He's got his own steady customers where he works. Some men come fifty miles to get Joe to work on their cars because he does good work."

"I'm a real good mechanic," said Joe.

Driving the big highway near Toledo I had a conversation with Charley on the subject of roots. He listened but he didn't reply. In the pattern-thinking about roots, I and most other people have left two things out of consideration. Could it be that Americans are a restless people, a mobile people, never satisfied with where they are as a matter of selection? The pioneers, the immigrants who peopled the continent, were the restless ones in Europe. The steady rooted ones stayed home and are still there. But every one of us, except the Negroes forced here as slaves, are descended from the restless ones, the wayward ones who were not content to stay at home. Wouldn't it be unusual if we had not inherited this tendency? And the fact is that we have. But that's the short view. What are roots and how long have we had them? If our species has existed for a couple of million years, what is its history? Our remote ancestors followed the game, moved with the food supply, and fled from evil weather, from ice and the changing seasons. Then after millennia beyond thinking they domesticated some animals so that they lived with their food supply. Then of necessity they followed the grass that fed their flocks in endlesss wanderings. Only when agriculture came into practice—and that's not very long ago in terms of the whole history—did a place achieve meaning and value and permanence. But land is a tangible, and tangibles have a way of getting into few hands. Thus it was that one man wanted ownership of land and at the same time wanted servitude because someone had to work it. Roots were in ownership of land, in tangible and immovable possessions. In this view we are a restless species with a very short history of roots, and those not widely distributed. Perhaps we have overrated roots as a psychic need. Maybe the greater the urge, the deeper and more ancient is the need, the will, the hunger to be somewhere else.

Since I hadn't seen the Middle West for a long time many impressions crowded in on me as I drove through Ohio and Michigan and Illinois. The first was the enormous increase in population. Villages had become towns and towns had grown to cities. The roads squirmed with traffic; the cities were so dense with people that all attention had to be devoted to not hitting anyone or not being hit. The next impression was of an electric energy, a force, almost a fluid of energy so powerful as to be stunning in its impact. No matter what the direction, whether for good or for bad, the vitality was everywhere. I don't think for a second that the people I had seen and talked to in New England were either unfriendly or discourteous, but they spoke tersely and usually waited for the newcomer to open communication. Almost on crossing the Ohio line it seemed to me that people were more open and more outgoing. The waitress in a roadside stand said good morning before I had a chance to, discussed breakfast as though she liked the idea, spoke with enthusiasm about the weather, sometimes even offered some information about herself without my delving. Strangers talked freely to one another without caution. I had forgotten how rich and beautiful is the countryside— the deep topsoil, the wealth of great trees, the lake country of Michigan handsome as a well-made woman, and dressed and jeweled. It seemed to me that the earth was generous and outgoing here in the heartland, and perhaps the people took a cue from it.

One of my purposes was to listen, to hear speech, accent, speech rhythms, overtones and emphasis. For speech is so much more than words and sentences. I did listen everywhere. It seemed to me that regional speech is in the process of disappearing, not gone but going. Forty years of radio and twenty years of television must have this impact. Communications must destroy localness, by a slow, inevitable process. I can remember a time when I could almost pinpoint a man's place of origin by his speech. That is growing more difficult now and will in some foreseeable future become impossible. It is a rare house or building that is not rigged with spiky combers of the air. Radio and television speech becomes standardized, perhaps better English than we have ever used. Just as our bread, mixed and baked, packaged and sold without benefit of accident or human frailty, is uniformly good and uniformly tasteless, so will our speech become one speech.

I who love words and the endless possibility of words am saddened by this inevitability. For with local accent will disappear local tempo. The idioms, the figures of speech that make language rich and full of the poetry of place and time must go. And in their place will be a national speech, wrapped and packaged, standard and tasteless. Localness is not gone but it is going. In the many years since I have listened to the land the change is very great. Traveling west along the northern routes I did not hear a truly local speech until I reached Montana. That is one of the reasons I fell in love again with Montana. The West Coast went back to packaged English. The Southwest kept a grasp but a slipping grasp on localness. Of course, the deep south holds on by main strength to its regional expressions, just as it holds and treasures some other anachronisms, but no region can hold out for long against the highway, the high-tension line, and the national television. What I am mourning is perhaps not worth saving, but I regret its loss nevertheless.

Even while I protest the assembly-line production of our food, our songs, our language, and eventually our souls, I know that it was a rare home that baked good bread in the old days. Mother's cooking was with rare exceptions poor, that good unpasteurized milk touched only by flies and bits of manure crawled with bacteria, the healthy old-time life was riddled with aches, sudden death from unknown causes, and that sweet local speech I mourn was the child of illiteracy and ignorance. It is the nature of a man as he grows older, a small bridge in time, to protest against change, particularly change for the better. But it is true that we have exchanged corpulence for starvation, and either one will kill us. The lines of change are down. We, or at least I, can have no conception of human life and human thought in a hundred years or fifty years. Perhaps my greatest wisdom is the knowledge that I do not know. The sad ones are those who waste their energy in trying to hold it back, for they can only feel bitterness in loss and no joy in gain.

DISCUSSION

1. In this selection several observations are made about roots. What point does the mechanic living in a trailer make? What thoughts about roots does Steinbeck have later? Do you agree with his suggestion that "perhaps we have overrated roots as a psychic need" (page 650)? Give reasons for your opinion.

2. What is the author's attitude toward "the assembly-line production of our food, our songs, our language" (page 651)? Do you agree?

For further activities, see page 652.

VOCABULARY

What Is an American? (page 628)

Crèvecoeur uses the Latin phrase "alma mater," which, like many other expressions from different languages, has become a part of English. Ten such words or phrases are listed below in the column at the left. On separate paper, match each with its meaning in the column at the right; then use each in an appropriate sentence. Check in a dictionary if you need to.

allegro	a mixture
coiffure	an expert
gauche	by or for each individual
connoisseur	briskly
per capita	relevant, pertinent
potpourri	hairdo
tête-à-tête	a kind of sculpture
bas-relief	a nickname
sobriquet	awkward
apropos	a private conversation

What Is Pearl Harbor? (page 632)

The FBI men who took Papa away were wearing *fedora* hats, soft felts with brims that may be turned up or down and low crowns that are creased lengthwise. Following are specific kinds of headgear. Identify those that you can, and check in a dictionary for a picture of those that are unfamiliar. Which belong to a specific period of time? Which are worn only by certain groups?

bowler	helmet	cloche	Panama
boater	skullcap	bonnet	sombrero
Homburg	beret	tam-o'-shanter	busby
fez	sailor	Stetson	top hat
turban	derby	porkpie	glengarry

Travels with Charley (page 641)

Steinbeck regrets the passing of dialects. He says, "The idioms, the figures of speech that make language rich and full of the poetry of place and time" are being replaced with the standardized language of radio and television. Is he right? How many of these idioms from the frontier

speech of a century ago do you know? Use a dictionary of idioms to find the meanings of any that you don't know.

to go like a house afire   bottom dollar
old stamping ground   to lock horns
lock, stock, and barrel   pig in a poke
to make the fur fly   to cut no ice
grubstake   pretty kettle of fish

COMPOSITION

The Sentimentality of William Tavener (page 608)

Think of two characters, real or imagined, to describe. You like one very much, and you dislike the other intensely. Write the descriptions, making your feeling for each clear from the tone of your writing rather than from any explicit statement. Your tone will be expressed by choice of words, by selection of details, by emphasis, and by the comments you make.

Early January (page 616)

Often the beginning of a new school year or a new romance or a new job gives us the hope that our lives will change—we will be different; we will be happier. The poet W. S. Merwin suggests that the new year is not a stranger, that the new school year, romance, or job will not change us and "it will be hard for us now to be sure it is here." Have you found this to be true in your experience? If so, write a composition telling about such an experience; if not, tell of one that *was* different, "a stranger."

What Is an American? (page 628)

Take part in a dialogue with Crèvecoeur. Choose four statements from this selection and, as if you were having a conversation with him, write your responses that will tell him how you see America. For example, how would you respond to "Behold fair cities, substantial villages, extensive fields, an immense country filled with decent houses, good roads. . . ."? Or "Here individuals of all nations are melted into a new race" of persons?

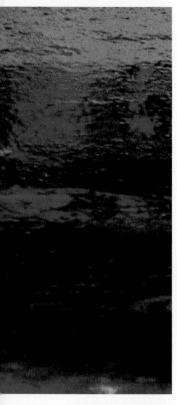

COMPOSITION

Ending a paper is often as difficult as beginning it. Yet the ending matters. After all, it contains the final impression that the writer leaves with the reader.

Seldom is it enough simply to stop. An ending must *conclude.* However, you should summarize and restate only if the material developed within the paper has been very complex indeed. Don't end the paper this way: "In conclusion, I have shown that. . . ." Either you *have* shown it (in which case the repetition is unnecessary), or you have not (in which case saying you have is inaccurate).

If you should not simply lift your pen and stop at the bottom of the last page, and if you should not simply restate what you have written earlier, how *should* you conclude your remarks? Again, as with openings, no one formula can be relied on *every* time. But keep these hints in mind as you approach your conclusion.

Can you echo something that was said at the beginning—a word, or a phrase, or a thought? This device (a very useful one) brings the reader back to the starting point, so that the paper seems well-formed rather than shapeless. Moreover, the repetition of an opening idea reminds the reader of how completely the paper has developed an idea.

CONCLUSIONS

Alternatively, can you end with a question? That device leaves the reader actively involved with what you have written, answering the question that your concluding remark has posed.

Finally, can you end with a paragraph that suggests the significance of what you have established? "All right," the reader may be thinking after absorbing your remarks. "I agree with what you've said. But what of it? So what? What am I to make of the information?" In a sentence or a final paragraph suggest the answer. By doing so, you will have written an effective conclusion, one that extends the reader's understanding.

ABOUT THE SELECTIONS

1. Of the various prose selections in this unit, which offered the most accurate insights into what life is *really* like, insofar as you have experienced and gained understanding of life? What knowledge have you gained, and what events have you experienced, that confirm the truth of what the selection records? In a paper, explain the view of reality that the selection reveals, and relate it to your own view.

2. Which of the poems in the unit did you most enjoy? Was it the subject matter, the diction, the imagery, the rhythm, the theme of the poem, a combination of some of those characteristics, or still others that appealed to you? Write a paper that shares your appreciation of the poem with a skeptical reader. To be persuasive, you will need to refer frequently and specifically to the poem itself.

3. Look again at how each prose selection in this unit ends. Do you notice any characteristics that all the endings share? In a paper examine what makes an effective ending, using selections in this unit to illustrate your remarks. Make sure that your own paper ends effectively!

ON YOUR OWN

1. All of us have experienced periods when our view of life was distorted. At such times, how things appeared to be was not how they really were. It may have been when we were sick, or in a strange place, or frightened, or angry. Pick one such occasion in your own life and describe it as vividly as you can. Try, through sensory language and sharp detail, to make the apparent world as real as it was in your imagination.

2. Suppose you had the opportunity of doing as John Steinbeck did (page 641). Suppose you could set out across the country with no schedule to keep and no people or places you had to visit. Your sole purpose in traveling would be to get to know America better. Where would you most like to head for? In a paper describe your arrival at that spot. How did you travel there? Why did you want to go there? What did you hear, smell, see when you arrived? What were your feelings?

3. Crèvecoeur (page 628) offers a definition of an American of the eighteenth century, including what makes such a person different from citizens of other nations. Write a definition of an American of the late twentieth century. You might imagine yourself corresponding with a foreign student interested in knowing more about your fellow Americans. Use examples, statistics, anecdotes, and facts to help make your definition clear.

4. Crane's ''The Open Boat'' and Porter's ''The Jilting of Granny Weatherall'' raise questions about the final meaning of life. For what purposes do we live? What is real, and what is only phony? The questions are profound. Think seriously about them. Then, without being intolerant toward views different from your own, express your views on these matters in writing. Support your remarks as specifically as you can.

ABOUT THE authors

Abigail Adams (1744–1818) The daughter of a Congregational minister in Weymouth, Massachusetts, Abigail Smith managed to educate herself without the benefit of any formal schooling. After her marriage to John Adams, Abigail helped him in his career as a lawyer and politician. For a period of ten years she managed the Adams farm on her own, increasing their property, educating their five children, and coping with the disruptions caused by the Revolutionary War. During this period also she began to write the letters to her husband which have made the period come alive for many later readers.

James Agee (1909–1958) Born in Knoxville, Tennessee, Agee went to Phillips Exeter Academy and Harvard University, where he won the poetry prize. His first collection of poems was called *Permit Me Voyage*. As a magazine writer, he was assigned to do a story on the Alabama sharecroppers; deeply affected by what he saw, he wrote a book about the lives of these people. It was illustrated with photographs by Walker Evans and was called *Let Us Now Praise Famous Men*. Agee adapted several stories and novels for the screen. *The African Queen* was made from his script.

Jack Agüeros (born 1934) Born in East Harlem, Jack Agüeros has worked in anti-poverty programs in Cleveland and New York and in a youth program on the Lower East Side of New York. His writing has been published in an anthology called *The Immigrant Experience*.

Liz Sohappy Bahe (born 1947) When Liz Sohappy Bahe was twenty-two she was given the Palouse name of her great-grandmother, Omnana Cheshirts, which means "Stopping on a Hill and Looking Down." She says, "My Indian name has made a great difference in my life. I really felt like a floating body until I received my name." Bahe grew up in Washington and then attended the Institute of American Indian Arts in Santa Fe. Until recently she lived in Chinle, Arizona, with her husband and two sons.

James Baldwin (born 1924) After graduating from high school in 1942, James Baldwin spent five years in the Greenwich Village area of New York City, working as handyman, office helper, factory worker, dishwasher, and waiter. His evenings he spent writing, and in 1948 he moved to Paris where he lived and wrote for the next ten years. Some of his best-known books are *Go Tell It on the Mountain, Tell Me How Long the Train's Been Gone, Notes of a Native Son,* and *The Fire Next Time*.

Toni Cade Bambara *The Liberator, Negro Digest,* and *Massachusetts Review* have all published stories by Toni Bambara, and her work has been included in many anthologies of black writing. She has also written stories for children and taught at Livingston College, Rutgers University, and at Harlem University.

Imamu Amiri Baraka (LeRoi Jones) (born 1934) Baraka grew up in Newark and attended Rutgers and Howard University. After a tour of duty in the Air Force, he studied philosophy at Columbia University and German at the New School for Social Research. His plays include, *A Black Mass, The Slave,* and *The Toilet.* He has written a novel, *The System of Dante's Hell,* and several collections of poems, including *The Dead Lecturer* and *Black Magic.*

Stephen Vincent Benét (1898–1943) Always fascinated by America's unique heritage, Benét recreated in his stories and poems that heritage and the people who shaped it. Two of his long poems, *Western Star* and *John Brown's Body,* were awarded Pulitzer Prizes.

Gina Berriault (born 1926)   Three of Gina Berriault's short stories have been selected as O. Henry Prize stories, one has won the Paris Review Fiction Prize, and one has been included in *Best American Short Stories of 1957.* She has worked as a journalist, bookstore clerk, librarian, and lecturer on creative writing. Besides her stories, collected in the volume *The Mistress,* she has written three novels: *Conference of Victims, The Descent,* and *The Son.*

Arna Bontemps (1902–1973)   After graduating from the University of Chicago, Arna Bontemps taught in several cities and worked as a college librarian. Most of his poetry was written during the 1920s. After that he concentrated on prose, and his writings cover a wide range of subjects. Among his best-known books are *The Story of the Negro, Famous Negro Athletes,* and anthologies like *American Negro Poetry* and *Golden Slippers.*

Richard Brautigan (born 1935)   A cult sprang up around Richard Brautigan with the publication of his novels *Trout Fishing in America* and *In Watermelon Sugar.* Brautigan was born in Tacoma, Washington but migrated to San Francisco where he haunted the North Beach section and began writing.

Gwendolyn Brooks (born 1917)   Awarded the Pulitzer Prize in 1950 for *Annie Allen,* her second book of poetry, Gwendolyn Brooks is also a fine prose writer. As one critic noted, she draws on the world she understands, but records insights about that world in such a way that they become "not merely personal or racial but universal in their implications."

William Cullen Bryant (1794–1878)   Bryant wrote "Thanatopsis," his most celebrated poem, before he was eighteen. During the next decade, while practicing law in a small Massachusetts village, he wrote poems that expressed his love of the American wilderness. Later in his life Bryant abandoned poetry almost entirely to devote himself to his work as editor of a large New York newspaper.

Truman Capote (born 1924)   Truman Capote won an O. Henry Memorial Award when he was only nineteen for his story "Miriam." From his first novel, *Other Voices, Other Rooms,* in 1948, to his enormously successful "nonfiction novel," *In Cold Blood,* he has produced many short stories, novels, and essays.

Willa Cather (1873–1947)   After college at the University of Nebraska, Willa Cather moved to Pittsburgh, where she taught English in high school for five years. Never marrying, she traveled widely. *O Pioneers!* and *My Ántonia* are her two most famous novels.

Diana Chang (born 1934)   The daughter of a Chinese father and a Eurasian mother, Diana Chang was born in New York but lived as a child in China. In addition to poetry, Chang has written novels—among them *The Frontiers of Love, The Only Game in Town,* and *Eye to Eye.* She edits *The American Pen.*

Fray Angélico Chávez (born 1910)   Born in Wagon Mound, New Mexico, Fray Angélico Chávez served with the Franciscan Order for thirty-four years, in missionary churches and as a combat Army chaplain. He loved poetry as a child, especially Robert Louis Stevenson's "Requiem." Chávez published his first book of poetry, *Clothed with the Sun,* at the age of twenty-nine and has published many collections since then, including *Selected Poems* and *Song of Francis.* Recently he published *My Penitente Land,* a spiritual biography of the Hispano people of New Mexico.

Frank Chin (born 1940)   Before becoming a television writer, Frank Chin worked as a clerk and brakeman for the Western Pacific and Southern Pacific railroads. He won the East-West Players Playwriting Award for *The Chickencoop Chinaman's Pregnant Pause.*

Kate Chopin (1851–1904)   Best known for her novel *The Awakening,* Kate Chopin did not write professionally until her husband's death. Then she wrote two novels and numerous short stories, usually focusing on the intricacies of love and marriage. Most of her stories are set in Louisiana, where she lived after her marriage.

Samuel Clemens (1835–1910)   Born in Missouri, Samuel Clemens made his famous trip West after the Civil War cut short his career as a steamboat pilot on the Mississippi River. Taking the pen name Mark Twain from a river expression meaning "safe water," he wrote newspaper sketches in Nevada and California. Books such as *The Adventures of Tom Sawyer, The Adventures of Huckleberry Finn,* and *A Connecticut Yankee in King Arthur's Court* soon made him a national celebrity.

Lucille Clifton (born 1936)   The author of numerous books for children and volumes of poetry that include *Good Times, An Ordinary Woman, Good News about the Earth,* and *Generations,* Lucille Clifton lives in Baltimore with her husband and six children. Her poems have appeared in *Black World* and *The Massachusetts Review.*

Stephen Crane (1871–1900)   The son of a Methodist minister, Crane became a newspaper reporter in New York after two years at college. At twenty-four he published his masterpiece, *The Red Badge of Courage.* Although he had never witnessed a battle himself, he recreated in his imagination the physical and psychological experiences of a common soldier during the Civil War. Crane then served as a war correspondent in Turkey and in Cuba. But his roving adventures ruined his health; after two years in England he died of tuberculosis before his thirtieth birthday.

St. Jean de Crèvecoeur (1735–1813)   Born and educated in France, St. Jean de Crèvecoeur sailed to the New World when he was twenty. As a surveyor, he traveled through wild country between the Great Lakes and the Ohio River. Then, in his thirties, he married an American girl and settled down for seven happy years on a farm in New York. There he wrote his famous *Letters from an American Farmer* "for the information of a friend in England." "What Is an American?" is a portion of one of those twelve letters.

Victor Hernández Cruz (born 1949)   Born in Aguas Buenas, Puerto Rico, Victor Hernández Cruz moved with his parents to New York when he was five. His volumes of poetry include *Snaps* and *Mainland.* He has also worked with various theater groups.

E. E. Cummings (1894–1962)   The son of a minister, E. E. Cummings grew up in Cambridge, Massachusetts. Following his graduation from Harvard University, he served as an ambulance driver in France during World War I. Like many other artists and writers of his generation, the young poet lived in Paris for some years after the war. His bold experiments with language and form have made him an important modern American poet.

James Dickey (born 1923)   A high school and college football star and a fighter pilot in both World War II and the Korean War, James Dickey might seem to some an unlikely poet. In fact, he wrote his first poem at the age of twenty-four—a description of football players dressing in a locker room. His novel *Deliverance* was made into a popular movie.

Emily Dickinson (1830–1886)   Except for a few brief trips to nearby cities, Emily Dickinson spent her life in the New England town of Amherst, Massachusetts. She lived much to herself, and wrote hundreds of poems, often jotting them down on any available piece of paper: a paper bag, a used envelope, the back of a recipe. All of them she tucked away in boxes and drawers. The poems were discovered and published after her death, but forty years went by before their excellence was recognized.

Isadora Duncan (1878–1927)   Isadora Duncan created a form of dance which she called "movement of the human body in harmony with the movements of the earth." Disappointed with lack of recognition in the U.S., the Duncan family went to Europe, where Isadora's barefoot, Greek-inspired dancing was acclaimed. She founded a dance school in Berlin and later taught dance in Moscow and married a Russian poet. Her two children drowned and she herself was killed in a sports car when her long scarf caught in a wheel.

Jonathan Edwards (1703–1758)   For nearly a quarter of a century Edwards served as minister at Northampton, Massachusetts, and from there he began the Great Awakening, a religious revival that eventually swept over the whole east coast of America.

James A. Emanuel (born 1921)   A poet from Nebraska who has held such diverse jobs as canteen steward, weighmaster, teacher of English, and Fulbright professor, Emanuel has taught for some years at City College, New York. His poems, collected in *The Treehouse and Other Poems* and *Panther Man,* have been widely printed in anthologies of black literature; but he feels his greatest satisfaction came from writing *Langston Hughes,* which he describes as "a book evolving from my racial pride."

Ralph Waldo Emerson (1803–1882)   His New England family was full of learned men and ministers, and for a while Ralph Waldo Emerson followed in the tradition. He worked his way through Harvard College and became pastor of a Boston church. But the creeds and formal sacraments of his church soon troubled him, and he gave up his pastorate. Following a brief trip to Europe, Emerson settled in the village of Concord, Massachusetts, where he began lecturing and writing his essays and poems. His bold, unconventional ideas were attacked by some, but they made Emerson one of the most popular lecturers of his time.

Mari Evans   A native of Toledo, Ohio, Mari Evans has been a Consultant for the National Endowment of the Arts and the producer/director of a weekly half-hour television series, "The Black Experience." She is writer-in-residence and assistant professor in black literature at Indiana University. She is the author of several juvenile books, and her poetry collections include *Where Is All the Music* and *I Am a Black Woman.*

William Faulkner (1897–1962)   "I didn't need to write about interesting foreign places," William Faulkner said. "There was more than enough in my own little postage stamp of earth to last me a lifetime." He proceeded to develop a whole world of people gathered in his mythical Yoknapatawpha County in northern Mississippi. His first important work, *The Sound and the Fury,* was published in 1929, and other novels followed: *As I Lay Dying, The Hamlet, Light in August, Absalom, Absalom,* among others. In 1949 he won the Nobel Prize for Literature.

Dorothy Canfield Fisher (1879–1958)   Born in Kansas, the daughter of an educator and an artist, young Dorothy was sent to Paris at age ten for a year of school. Later she attended Ohio State University, the Sorbonne in France, and then Columbia University in New York. Some of her works include *The Deepening Stream, Understood Betsy,* and *Seasoned Timber.*

Mary E. Wilkins Freeman (1852–1930)   For some of her life a New England spinster, like many of her characters, Mary Wilkins Freeman grew up in Randolph, Massachusetts, and Brattleboro, Vermont. For a time she acted as Oliver Wendell Holmes's secretary and met the New England writers of the day, but with the publication of *A New England Nun* she achieved recognition in her own right. In some two hundred short stories, twelve novels, and a play, Freeman wrote of the lives of New England villagers simply and objectively.

Robert Frost (1874–1963)   The only American poet to be awarded the Pulitzer Prize four times was Robert Frost. His poems, often set against a rural New England landscape, are notable for their conversational style and realistic portraits. Beneath their seeming simplicity, however, lie an irony and subtlety which exemplify Frost's belief that poetry is a question of "saying one thing and meaning another."

Nikki Giovanni (born 1943)   A popular poet who has read her poetry on television and put out a best-selling album, Nikki Giovanni was born in Knoxville, Tennessee. Her books of poetry include *Black Feeling, Black Talk, Black Judgement, Spin a Soft Black Song,* and *My House.*

Nathaniel Hawthorne (1804–1864)   For twelve years after his graduation from Bowdoin College, Nathaniel Hawthorne shut himself up in an old house in Salem, Massachusetts, to write, rarely leaving his room. *Twice-Told Tales* gained him some recognition. *The Scarlet Letter* was an immediate success, and largely because of this novel, he has come to be regarded as one of the best American writers of the nineteenth century.

Robert Hayden (1913–1980)   Both a student and teacher in Michigan, where he was born, Robert Hayden had several volumes of poetry published and won many honors. In 1966 he earned first prize at the First World Festival of Negro Arts at Dakar, Senegal, for a book entitled *A Ballad of Remembrance.*

Ernest Hemingway (1899–1961)   Experiences with his father, a doctor, on fishing trips in northern Michigan provided the young Ernest Hemingway with subjects for his early stories. Above all else he was an active man: a boxer, an expert fisherman, a skier, a big game hunter, and a war correspondent. Hemingway has written some of the best short stories in the language, as well as one or two outstanding novels. Some of his best-known novels are *The Sun Also Rises, A Farewell to Arms, For Whom the Bell Tolls,* and *The Old Man and the Sea.* He was awarded the Nobel Prize in 1954.

Patrick Henry (1736–1799)   More than any other individual, Patrick Henry was responsible for persuading Virginians that revolution was the only answer to British oppression. He was in his thirties when he made his famous "Give me liberty or give me death" speech, and he went on to become governor of Virginia and a delegate to the Constitutional Convention.

Oliver Wendell Holmes (1809–1894)   Upon graduating from Harvard in 1829, Oliver Wendell Holmes settled in Boston as a practicing physician. In 1847, he was appointed Professor of Anatomy and Physiology at Harvard, where he taught with great distinction for thirty-five years. Through the pages of the *Atlantic Monthly,* he became nationally famous as an essayist, author of the celebrated series *The Autocrat of the Breakfast Table.* Today, however, he is best remembered for his poetry.

Jeanne Wakatsuki Houston (born 1934)   The youngest of ten children born to an Inglewood, California, Japanese American family, Jeanne Wakatsuki Houston was interned along with her family at Manzanar Camp in California during World War II. Her husband, **James Houston** (born 1933), is a novelist. They now live with their three children in Santa Cruz.

Langston Hughes (1902–1967)   Born in Joplin, Missouri, Langston Hughes traveled so widely that he titled his autobiography *I Wonder As I Wander.* On one transatlantic voyage he ceremoniously broke free from his past ideas; he stood on the deck of the ship and, one by one, threw his books into the ocean. He published poems, short stories, novels, plays, movie scripts, songs, and several nonfiction studies of the black American.

Zora Neale Hurston (1903–1960)   Born in "the first incorporated Negro town in America," Eatonville, Florida, Zora Neale Hurston was the daughter of a Baptist minister. She studied first at Howard University, then at Barnard where she developed an interest in anthropology and folklore. She returned to the South to study folklore for four years. She began writing fiction in order to present what she felt to be an accurate picture of black life.

Washington Irving (1783–1859)   Son of a New York hardware merchant, Washington Irving rose to become the most popular American writer of his time. Once he was captured by Mediterranean pirates; For four years he served as U.S. minister to Spain. But Irving's best writing sprang from more ordinary experiences— his boyhood rambles over the countryside north of Manhattan and his seventeen years of wandering in Europe. Some of his best-known books are *Knickerbocker's History of New York, The Sketch Book* (containing "Rip Van Winkle" and "The Legend of Sleepy Hollow"), and *The Alhambra.*

Shirley Jackson (1919–1965)   Born in San Francisco, Jackson spent most of her life in Vermont, raising a family and writing two very different kinds of prose—comic descriptions of domestic life, like *Life among the Savages,* and tales of the morbid and the supernatural, like *We Have Always Lived in the Castle, The Haunting of Hill House,* and *The Sundial.*

Robinson Jeffers (1887–1962)   For fifty years Robinson Jeffers lived a fiercely private life in a house he built with his own hands on the rocky coast at Carmel, California. His seventeen volumes of poetry reveal his scorn for whatever in American life seemed to him easygoing, indulgent, or sentimental.

Thomas Jefferson (1743–1826)   His self-written epitaph reads: "Here was buried Thomas Jefferson, author of the Declaration of Independence, the Statute of Virginia for reli-

gious freedom, and father of the University of Virginia." Freedom—political, religious, intellectual—was his lifelong preoccupation. He was president of the United States, and vice president, secretary of state and ambassador to France. But Jefferson's epitaph makes clear the achievements by which he wanted to be remembered.

James Weldon Johnson (1871–1938)   This writer followed not one but several careers. Born in Jacksonville, Florida, he served as the principal of a high school there, studying law at the same time. In New York City a few years later, he became a successful composer, collaborating with his brother on popular songs and light opera. Next, a government appointment took him to Latin America as a diplomat. Then, when he was in his late forties, Johnson began to write, and devoted the rest of his life to writing and teaching.

Chief Joseph (1841–1904)   Hinmaton-Yalaktit (Thunder Traveling over the Mountains) was the Indian name of a man known in history as Chief Joseph, chief of the Wallamwatkin band of Nez Percé Indians of Oregon. (See the note on page 148.) After the Nez Percé surrender, Chief Joseph delivered a moving speech and later wrote an article entitled "An Indian's View of Indian Affairs" for the *North American Review.* Chief Joseph lived out his days on the Colville Reservation in Washington.

Martin Luther King, Jr. (1929–1968)   Civil rights leader and Nobel Prize winner Martin Luther King, Jr. grew up in Atlanta and earned his Ph.D. in theology from Boston University. King's rise to national prominence came when he organized the Montgomery bus boycott. Then King helped to organize the Southern Christian Leadership Conference to continue the fight for civil rights. Perhaps the culmination of King's work came with the August 1963 march on Washington when 250,000 people gathered to hear his famous "I have a dream" address. In 1964 King was awarded the Nobel Prize for Peace. He was shot by an assassin in Memphis on April 3, 1968.

Ring Lardner (1885–1933)   Short-story writer and journalist Ring Lardner got his start in newspaper work when he "stole" a position his brother had refused with the *South Bend* (Indiana) *Times*. In a later job, he covered the Chicago White Sox and became known as a sports writer. In 1914 Lardner wrote a series of humorous sketches based on the adventures of a White Sox pitcher. They were an immediate success. From then on Lardner wrote stories. In 1927 he published his autobiography, *The Story of a Wonder Man*.

Denise Levertov (born 1923)   British-born, Denise Levertov settled in the United States in 1948. Her vivid, impressionistic poems capture the essential details of sensuous experience and generate insight and emotional response. In addition to being the author of more than ten volumes of poetry—including *O Taste and See, Footprints,* and *The Freeing of the Dust*—Levertov is a teacher and lecturer.

Abraham Lincoln (1809–1865)   The son of a restless farmer, Abraham Lincoln was as nearly self-educated and self-made as a man can be. He was a village postmaster, a lawyer, a member of the Illinois legislature, a member of the House of Representatives in Washington for a single term. Lincoln as president became the inspiration to statesmen and common people not only in America in the nineteenth century, but all over the world into our own time.

Henry Wadsworth Longfellow (1807–1882)   The best-loved poet of his time, Longfellow saw beauty in everything from a ruined castle on the Rhine to a blacksmith shop in Cambridge. He created poetry out of everyday experiences. But Longfellow also loved the romantic memories of America's past which he recaptured and immor-

talized in poems such as *The Courtship of Miles Standish, Evangeline,* and *Hiawatha.* He remains the most quoted of American poets.

Amy Lowell (1874–1925)   Revolting against the conventional style of poetry and seeking to create new rhythms and single, tight images like those of the Japanese haiku poems, Amy Lowell was a leader of the Imagist movement in America. Some of her poetry met with disapproval from her fellow poets. After her death, she was awarded the Pulitzer Prize for her volume *What's O'Clock?*

Robert Lowell (1917–1978)   Born in Boston, Robert Lowell was a descendant of early New England colonists as well as a member of the family that produced the poets James Russell Lowell and Amy Lowell. After two years at Harvard, Lowell went to Kenyon College to study poetry with John Crowe Ransom. This, he once said, was "a happy decision." Regarded by many critics as the finest poet of his generation, he won several prizes—including the Pulitzer—for his intense and powerful poetry.

Carson McCullers (1917–1967)   Carson McCullers began writing when she was sixteen. She had wanted to be a concert pianist, but then, greatly admiring the playwright Eugene O'Neill, she decided that she wanted to write. McCullers went to New York to attend school but on the subway one day she lost her tuition money. Working during the day, she went to school at night. Soon one of her short stories was published in *Story* magazine. It was the beginning of her long career as an author. Her best-known works include *The Member of the Wedding* and *The Heart Is a Lonely Hunter*.

Claude McKay (1891–1948)   Born in Jamaica, British West Indies, Claude McKay came to the United States in his early twenties. His collection of poems *Harlem Shadows* (1922) established him as one of the significant black voices of the 1920s.

Archibald MacLeish (born 1892) "If poetry can call our numbed emotions into life," Archibald MacLeish has written, "its plain human usefulness needs no further demonstration." MacLeish has combined poetry with an active public and professional life.

Norman Mailer (born 1923) Mailer's *The Naked and the Dead* was one of the most successful and highly acclaimed novels to come out of World War II. It was followed by *Barbary Shore* and *The Deer Park,* which was made into a play. In 1969 Mailer won both the Pulitzer Prize and a National Book Award for *Armies of the Night: History as a Novel, the Novel as History.* Always something of a public personality, Mailer ran unsuccessfully for mayor of New York City in 1969 and has produced three films.

Edgar Lee Masters (1869–1950) Renouncing a successful law practice when he was past forty, Edgar Lee Masters turned all his energies to poetry. He began to write poems about people who had lived in Lewiston, Illinois, his boyhood home. *Spoon River Anthology* is that rare thing, a collection of poems that became a best seller.

Jesús Papoleto Meléndez From writing poems on bubble gum wrappers Jesús Papoleto Meléndez quickly progressed to publishing his first book of poems, *Street Poetry and other Poems,* at the age of twenty-one. He wrote about the New York barrio where he grew up and where he now lives with his wife and son. He has written two plays, *The Silent of Love* and *The Junkies Stole the Clock.*

Herman Melville (1819–1891) Hardship combined with "an everlasting itch for things remote" to drive Melville, then 17 years old, to sea. His first voyage was most difficult, yet at 21 he again took to the high seas—this time on a whaling voyage in the Pacific. The captain treated the crew so badly that after a year and a half Melville jumped ship in the Marquesas Islands. He was captured by the Taipis, a Polynesian tribe. Rescued by the crew of an Australian whaler, he returned to the United States. *Typee* and *Omoo,* novels of his sailing adventures, made Melville instantly famous. However, beginning with *Moby Dick* (1851), Melville turned to more serious and complicated themes.

W. S. Merwin (born 1927) The son of a Presbyterian minister in New York City, W. S. Merwin wrote hymns for his father's church as soon as he had learned to print. Merwin describes himself as an "unsatisfactory student" who spent most of his time in the library or out on the fields riding the ROTC horses. Merwin says, "Poetry is a matter of correspondences; one glimpses them, pieces of an order, or thinks one does, and tries to convey the sense of what one has seen to those to whom it may matter, including, if possible, one's self."

Edna St. Vincent Millay (1892–1950) By the time she was twenty, Edna St. Vincent Millay had achieved fame with "Renascence." Her poems expressed the disillusionment of the postwar generation and a romantic protest against traditions and conventions. Her early concern with her own identity—her relationship to others and to the universe—gradually shifted to a concern with broader social issues.

N. Scott Momaday (born 1934) Of both Kiowa and Cherokee descent, Scott Momaday grew up on Navaho, Apache, and Pueblo reservations throughout the Southwest. His father was an artist, his mother a teacher and writer. He is currently Professor of English at Stanford University. In 1969 his novel *House Made of Dawn* won the Pulitzer Prize. His other works include *The Way to Rainy Mountain, Angle of Geese and Other Poems,* and the autobiographical *The Names.*

Marianne Moore (1887–1972) Born in St. Louis, Marianne Moore had hoped to be a painter, but as she has explained, she had "a passion for rhythm and accent, so blundered into versifying." Her first volume entitled simply *Poems* appeared in 1921. Her *Collected Poems* was awarded the 1952 Pulitzer Prize. Her vivid and original images frequently derived from her astonishing range of interests: baseball, popular magazines, zoology, motion pictures, boxing, and Oriental art—to name only a handful of her many enthusiasms.

Ogden Nash (1902–1971)   America's best-known writer of humorous verse, Nash didn't start out to be a poet. After a year at Harvard he went to New York City and worked for two years as a bond salesman. "I sold one bond—to my godmother," he recalled. Nash then tried his hand at advertising, at book publishing, and at magazine work. On those jobs he discovered that misspellings often made a story or article unintentionally funny. Accordingly, he began writing verse with deliberate misspellings and unexpected rhymes. His poetry now fills more than twenty books.

Ted Palmanteer (born 1943)   Ted Palmanteer was born near Omak, Washington. He says he daydreamed and played hookey during his elementary school years, but later, he attended the Institute of American Indian Arts in Santa Fe where he studied painting, sculpture, and writing. Drafted during his freshman year in college, Palmanteer took part in the 1968 Tet Offensive in Vietnam, was wounded, and sent to Japan. After spending nearly a year in the hospital Palmanteer resumed his college studies.

Dorothy Parker (1893–1967)   As famous for her witty conversation as for her writing, Parker began writing light verse while working on the staff of a magazine. In 1926, *Enough Rope,* her first collection, was a best seller. After that she published additional volumes of poems, as well as several popular collections of biting short stories.

Marge Piercy (born 1936)   *Breaking Camp,* Marge Piercy's first book of poems, won for her a University of Michigan award for poetry and

drew admiration from critics who saw her poems as a courageous rejection of easy cynicism and modish cool to "believe again in language as thought and feeling and in metaphor as possibility." Among her recent works are *Woman on the Edge of Time* and *Living in the Open.*

Edgar Allan Poe (1809–1849)   In his short life, Poe achieved fame, but his story is tragic, full of frustration and sadness, poverty and loneliness. He lost both of his parents before he was three, one by death and the other by desertion. After a short stay at the University of Virginia, he began a career as a soldier, then as a writer and editor. His young wife died of tuberculosis in 1847. Two years later Poe was found unconscious on a Baltimore street and was taken to the charity hospital where he died.

Katherine Anne Porter (1894–1980)   Miss Porter wrote of her life: "I was born at Indian Creek, Texas, brought up in Texas and Louisiana, and educated in small Southern convent schools. I was precocious, nervous, rebellious, unteachable, and made life very uncomfortable for myself and I suppose for those around me. As soon as I learned to form letters on paper, at about three years, I began to write stories, and this has been the basic and absorbing occupation, the intact line of my life. . . ." She is famous for her short stories, collected in *Flowering Judas* and *Pale Horse, Pale Rider.* Her novel *Ship of Fools* gave her an even wider audience.

Ezra Pound (1885–1972)   One of the twentieth century's most significant and controversial literary figures, Ezra Pound roamed far from his Idaho birthplace. In over half a century of living in Europe, he served as friend and adviser to the poetic giants of the age, men such as Yeats, Frost, and Eliot. In addition, his own poetry has earned him a place among the most influential of all modern writers.

John Crowe Ransom (1888–1974)   For many years John Crowe Ransom taught at Kenyon

College, Ohio, where he founded the *Kenyon Review,* perhaps the most respected literary magazine in America. Ransom wrote only a relatively small amount of poetry, but each of his lyrics is virtually flawless.

Edwin Arlington Robinson (1869–1935) Edwin Arlington Robinson viewed the world as a harsh place. He wrote most forcefully about failures. "The failures are so much more interesting," he said. Although he was awarded the Pulitzer Prize three times, he remained a painfully shy, retiring man all his life. In his poetry he chose to depart from the conventions of the day.

Theodore Roethke (1908–1963) A teacher throughout much of his adult life, Theodore Roethke was also a fine athlete and excellent coach. "It took me ten years to complete one little book," he confessed about his first volume of verse. That book and the six that followed earned him many literary honors, including the 1954 Pulitzer Prize.

Luís Omar Salinas (born 1937) Luís Omar Salinas has lived on both sides of the Mexican–U.S. border. Born in Robstown, Texas, he lived in Mexico for several years, then went to live with an uncle and aunt in Bakersfield, California, where he attended high school. He worked his way through several California colleges as dishwasher, construction worker, and newspaper reporter. Salinas is the editor of *From the Barrio: A Chicano Anthology.*

Sonia Sanchez (born 1934) A poet and playwright who describes her politics as "Blackness," Sonia Sanchez has taught black literature at several different universities. She was born in Birmingham, Alabama, went to Hunter College, and now lives in New York with her three children. Her poems have been published in numerous anthologies of black poets and in her own works, among them *A Blues Book for Blue Black Magical Women.* She has edited an anthology of black poets called *Three*

Hundred and Sixty Degrees of Blackness Comin' at You. Among her plays are *The Bronx Is Next* and *Sister Son/ji.*

Carl Sandburg (1878–1967) Milkman, dishwasher, harvest hand, sign painter, brickmaker, and barbershop porter—all these jobs Carl Sandburg had tried before enrolling in Lombard College, not far from his Illinois home. With the publication of "Chicago" in 1914, Sandburg at last found the role for which he had unconsciously been preparing all his life. In the many poems that followed, Sandburg demonstrated his remarkable command of American speech rhythms, and colloquial idiom.

Alan Seeger (1888–1916) Alan Seeger was always a determined bohemian and individualist. He grew up in Staten Island and later lived in Mexico with his family. Seeger joined the French Foreign Legion in World War I and distinguished himself with risk-taking bravery. On July 5, 1916, in the Champagne region of France, Seeger was found dead of a shell wound.

Anne Sexton (1928–1974) Anne Sexton began to write seriously while she was recovering from a mental breakdown and later called the experience "a rebirth." Born in Newton, Massachusetts, Sexton grew up in Wellesley and lived as a wife and mother in Weston. She is often called a poet of the "confessional" school—one who writes of personal experiences and feelings in a very frank manner. Her collection *Live or Die* won the Pulitzer Prize; other collections include *To Bedlam and Part Way Back, Love Poems,* and *Transformations.* In September of 1974 she committed suicide.

Karl Shapiro (born 1913) In 1945 a Pulitzer Prize was awarded to Karl Shapiro for his collection *V–Letter and Other Poems,* which deals with the experience of being a Jewish soldier in the American army in World War II. He has been the editor of *Poetry* magazine and *Prairie Schooner.*

Leslie Silko (born 1948) "I'm a mixed breed Laguna Pueblo woman. If you know anything about Indian people, you'll know what this means." So Leslie Silko describes herself. Born in Albuquerque, New Mexico, and brought up on the Laguna Reservation, Silko now lives with her husband and two sons in Ketchikan, Alaska and devotes her time to writing fiction and poetry.

Virginia Sorensen (born 1912) Born in Provo, Utah and now living principally in Tangier, Morocco, Virginia Sorensen has traveled a great deal. Since she married English novelist Alec Waugh she "spends more time in Africa and London than in America," but plans to return to Utah for her later years, "having found no place in the world more beautiful or satisfying." Her work includes both adult novels and books for children.

William Stafford (born 1914) Stafford is both an author and an educator. He was born in Kansas, holds his doctorate of philosophy from the State University of Iowa, and has taught both in the Midwest and on the West Coast. In 1963, he was given the National Book Award for *Traveling Through the Dark*. His books of poetry include *West of Your City* and *The Rescued Year*.

John Steinbeck (1902–1968) Born in Salinas, California, Steinbeck first worked as a hod carrier, painter, chemist, surveyor, and fruit picker before finally achieving success as a novelist. His rich background of experience on different social levels gave him compassionate insight into the lives of all kinds of people, a compassion that is especially evident in such books as *Of Mice and Men* and *The Grapes of Wrath*. He was awarded the Nobel Prize for literature in 1962.

Wallace Stevens (1879–1955) Rising to the position of vice-president of a Connecticut insurance company, Wallace Stevens combined a successful business career with the writing of poetry. For Stevens poetry was an integral part of life; the role of the poet he said, "is to help people live their lives." His *Collected Poems* received the 1955 Pulitzer Prize.

May Swenson (born 1919) Although May Swenson lives now in New York, she was born in Logan, Utah, and has served as poet in residence at Purdue University. During a distinguished career she has been honored by many awards and grants. Her first collection of verse appeared in 1954, *Another Animal;* since then she has published numerous other volumes, including *A Cage of Spines* and *Half Sun Half Sleep.*

Sara Teasdale (1884–1933) Although she wrote gentle and polished lyrics, Sara Teasdale led a life that was turbulent and often unhappy. The last years of her life, ill and despondent, she spent in virtual seclusion. In 1933, Sara Teasdale took sleeping pills and died.

Henry David Thoreau (1817–1862) Henry David Thoreau "traveled a good deal in Concord," the New England village where he was born and where he died. He taught briefly in the Concord school but resigned when it was insisted that he flog the boys. Although *Walden* is considered Thoreau's masterpiece, his *Civil Disobedience* has influenced many people and political movements throughout the world.

James Thurber (1894–1961) In countless stories and essays, James Thurber described a chaotic world of bewildered men, seals in bedrooms, plump boneless dogs with flapping ears. Although nearly blinded by a childhood accident, Thurber rose above his handicap. "My one-eighth vision," he explained, "happily obscures sad and ungainly sights, leaving only the vivid and the radiant."

Tino Villanueva (born 1941) Currently a member of the Spanish faculty at Wellesley College and formerly director of a Boston radio program for the Spanish-speaking community, Tino Villanueva has contributed poems to many anthologies of Chicano writing, including *El Espejo/The Mirror* and periodicals such as *El Grito* and *Entre Nosotros*. He was born in San Marcos, Texas.

Kurt Vonnegut, Jr. (born 1922)   "All writers are going to have to learn more about science," claims Vonnegut, "simply because the scientific method is such an important part of their environment." Often mislabeled as a science-fiction writer, Vonnegut seeks deeper levels in his stories and novels. Among his published works are *Cat's Cradle, Welcome to the Monkey House,* and *Slaughterhouse-Five.*

Diane Wakoski (born 1937)   Born in Whittier, California, Diane Wakoski now lives in New York and teaches English to junior high school students. She has won the Robert Frost fellowship in poetry from Bread Loaf Writers Conference and published several volumes of poetry, including *Discrepancies and Apparitions, The George Washington Poems,* and *Motorcycle Betrayal Poems.*

Margaret Walker (born 1915)   In 1942 Margaret Walker's first book of poems, *For My People,* won the Yale Younger Poets award. She was born in Birmingham, Alabama, where her father was a minister. She worked as a newspaper reporter, social worker, and English teacher in North Carolina and West Virginia. For about twenty years after her poetry collection was published, Walker occupied herself with college teaching and bringing up her four children. Then, in 1966 she published a novel about the Civil War entitled *Jubilee.*

Marnie Walsh   Marnie Walsh grew up in North Dakota near Sioux land and has written many poems about Native Americans. Some of her poems have been published in *Dacotah Territory,* a periodical of Moorhead State College in Minnesota, and others were chosen for inclusion in the anthology *Wah'Kon-Tah: Contemporary Poetry of Native Americans.*

Eudora Welty (born 1909)   Eudora Welty was born in Jackson, Mississippi, where she has spent all her life. From Jackson she has written work that has won her a national reputation as one of the leading interpreters of her region of the country. Her first volume of stories was called *A Curtain of Green.* Her novels include *Delta Wedding* and *Losing Battles.*

Walt Whitman (1819–1892)   In 1855 Walt Whitman published a slender volume of poetry entitled *Leaves of Grass.* The poet may well have expected his book to cause wide critical comment, for he had abandoned regular rhymes, meters, and stanza patterns, aiming instead for a free verse form that grew out of content, "as loosely as lilacs or roses on a bush." From then until his death he continued to revise and add to it. Today, Whitman's poems are considered a major achievement in American poetry.

Richard Wilbur (born 1921)   "The business of poetry," according to Richard Wilbur, "is to make some kind of sense out of everyday experience." Born in New Jersey, Wilbur spent a childhood, he says, "among woods, orchards, cornfields, horses, cows, and haywagons." Wilbur's interest in nature is reflected in his poetry. His poems are tightly compressed. "The strength of the genie," Wilbur has written, "comes of his being confined in a bottle."

Thornton Wilder (1897–1975)   Born in Madison, Wisconsin, Thornton Wilder spent much of his boyhood in China, where his father was a consul general. Even as a boy he wrote plays for his sisters to act. His literary bent disturbed his father, who used to say, "Poor Thornton, poor Thornton, he'll be a burden all his life." With such plays as *Our Town* and *The Skin of Our Teeth,* Wilder began a new age in American drama. He was also a novelist—*The Bridge of San Luis Rey* is probably his best known

AUTHORS AND TITLES

Titles of selections are in italics. Biographical information for the authors can be found in *About the Authors,* beginning on page 656.

LITERARY SKILLS

The page number given indicates where the term is first introduced and defined.

credits continued

from *Songs and Satire* by Edgar Lee Masters. Printed with permission of Mrs. Edgar Lee Masters.
Meléndez, Jesús Papoleto. "OYE MUNDO/sometimes," from *Street Poetry & Other Poems* by Jesús Papoleto Meléndez, copyright © 1972 by Barlenmir House, Publishers, New York.
Merwin, W. S. "Early January," from *The Lice* by W. S. Merwin, copyright © 1967 by W. S. Merwin. Reprinted by permission of Atheneum Publishers.
Millay, Edna St. Vincent. "Dirge Without Music" and "Childhood Is the Kingdom Where Nobody Dies," from *Collected Poems,* Harper & Row. Copyright 1923, 1928, 1934, 1951,

1955, 1962, by Edna St. Vincent Millay and Norma Millay Ellis.

Momaday, N. Scott, "The Way to Rainy Mountain," pp. 128–136 in *House Made of Dawn* by N. Scott Momaday, Copyright © 1968 by N. Scott Momaday. Reprinted by permission of Harper & Row, Publishers, Inc. Slightly adapted. "Carriers of the Dream Wheel," from *Carriers of the Dream Wheel*, edited by Duane Niatum. Copyright © Harper & Row, 1975. Reprinted by permission.

Moore, Marianne. "The Fox and the Grapes," from *The Fables of La Fontaine*, translated by Marianne Moore. Copyright 1952 by Marianne Moore. Reprinted by permission of The Viking Press. "Silence," reprinted with permission of Macmillan Publishing Co., Inc. from *Collected Poems*, by Marianne Moore. Copyright 1935 by Marianne Moore. Renewed 1963 by Marianne Moore and T. S. Eliot.

Nash, Ogden. "Don't Cry, Darling, It's Blood All Right," from *Verses from 1929 On*, by Ogden Nash, by permission of Little, Brown and Co. Copyright 1934 by The Curtis Publishing Company.

Nee, Victor G. and Brett de Bary Nee. "Interview with Frank Chin," from *Longtime Californ'*, by Victor G. and Brett de Bary Nee. Copyright © 1972, 1973 by Victor G. and Brett de Bary Nee. Reprinted by permission of Pantheon Books, a Division of Random House.

Palmanteer, Ted. "Chinook Dance," from *The American Indian Reader*, published by The Indian Historical Press. All efforts to locate the copyright holder of this selection have proved unsuccessful. An appropriate fee for this use will be reserved by the publisher.

Parker, Dorothy. "One Perfect Rose," from *The Portable Dorothy Parker*. Copyright 1926, 1954 by Dorothy Parker. Reprinted by permission of The Viking Press.

Piercy, Marge. "A Work of Artifice," from *To Be of Use*, copyright © 1969, 1971, by Marge Piercy. Reprinted by permission of Doubleday & Co., Inc.

Porter, Katherine Anne. "The Jilting of Granny Weatherall," by Katherine Anne Porter. Copyright 1930, 1958 by Katherine Anne Porter. Reprinted from her volume *Flowering Judas and Other Stories* by permission of Harcourt Brace Jovanovich, Inc.

Pound, Ezra. "An Immorality," from *Lustra*. Copyright 1917 by Ezra Pound. All rights reserved. Reprinted by permission of New Directions Publishing Corporation for the Trustees of the Ezra Pound Literary Property Trust.

Ransom, John Crowe. "Bells for John Whiteside's Daughter," copyright 1924 by Alfred A. Knopf, Inc. and renewed 1952 by John Crowe Ransom. Reprinted from *Selected Poems*, Third Edition, revised and enlarged, by John Crowe Ransom, by permission of the publisher.

Robinson, Edwin Arlington. "Richard Cory" is reprinted by permission of Charles Scribner's Sons from *The Children of the Night* by Edwin Arlington Robinson. "Miniver Cheevy" (copyright 1907 Charles Scribner's Sons) is reprinted by permission of Charles Scribner's Sons from *The Town Down the River* by Edwin Arlington Robinson.

Roethke, Theodore. "Night Journey," copyright 1940 by Theodore Roethke. "The Waking," copyright 1948 by Theodore Roethke. From the book *The Collected Poems of Theodore Roethke*. Reprinted by permission of Doubleday & Co., Inc.

Salinas, Luís. "Pedro Infante," from *Crazy Gipsy*, 1969, Origines Press, Fresno University, California.

Sanchez, Sonia. "poem at thirty," from *Home Coming*, copyright © 1969, by Sonia Sanchez. Reprinted by permission of Broadside Press.

Sandburg, Carl. "Chicago" and "Limited," from *Chicago Poems* by Carl Sandburg, copyright 1916 by Holt, Rinehart and Winston, Inc.; copyright 1944 by Carl Sandburg. Reprinted by permission of Harcourt Brace Jovanovich, Inc. "Four Preludes on Playthings of the Wind," from *Smoke and Steel* by Carl Sandburg, copyright 1920 by Harcourt Brace Jovanovich, Inc.; renewed, 1948, by Carl Sandburg. Reprinted by permission of the publishers.

Seeger, Alan. "I Have a Rendezvous with Death" is reprinted by permission of Charles Scribner's Sons from *Poems* by Alan Seeger. Copyright 1916 Charles Scribner's Sons.

Sexton, Anne. "Young," from the book *All My Pretty Ones*, by Anne Sexton. Reprinted by permission of Houghton Mifflin Company. Copyright © 1962 by Anne Sexton.

ART CREDITS

ILLUSTRATIONS

PHOTOGRAPHS

GLOSSARY

Many unfamiliar words in this text have been footnoted. Other words that may be unfamiliar to you are defined in this glossary. If you look for a word and find it not listed in the glossary, reread the sentence or paragraph in which the word appeared. The word may not have been included here because the context gives clues to its meaning.

Guide words at the top of each page will help you locate the word you want. Use the pronunciation key found at the bottom of each page to learn how to pronounce a word correctly.

The pronunciations and definitions in this glossary are from *The American Heritage Dictionary of the English Language* and are used with permission.

A

a·bash (ə-băsh′) *tr.v.* **abashed, abashing, abashes.** To make ashamed or uneasy; disconcert.

a·bate (ə-bāt′) *v.* **abated, abating, abates.** —*tr.* **1.** To reduce in amount, degree, or intensity; lessen. **2.** To deduct from an amount; subtract.

ab·er·ra·tion (ăb′ə-rā′shən) *n.* **1.** A deviation from the proper or expected course. **2.** A departure from the normal or typical. **3.** An abnormal alteration in one's mental state; lapse in mental capacities.

a·bey·ance (ə-bā′əns) *n.* The condition of being temporarily set aside; suspension.

ab·hor (ăb-hôr′) *tr.v.* **-horred, -horring, -hors.** To regard with horror or loathing; abominate.

a·bode (ə-bōd′) *n.* A dwelling place or home.

a·bom·i·na·ble (ə-bŏm′ə-nə-bəl) *adj.* **1.** Detestable; loathsome. **2.** Thoroughly unpleasant.

ac·qui·esce (ăk′wē-ĕs′) *intr.v.* **-esced, -escing, -esces.** To consent or comply passively or without protest.

ac·quis·i·tive (ə-kwĭz′ə-tĭv) *adj.* Tending to acquire and retain ideas or information: *an acquisitive mind.*

ad·duce (ə-dōos′, ə-dyōos′, ă-) *tr.v.* **-duced, -ducing, -duces.** To cite as an example or means of proof in an argument; bring forward for consideration.

ad·her·ent (ăd-hîr′ənt) *n.* A supporter, as of a cause or individual: *"Rip's sole domestic adherent was his dog Wolf"* (Washington Irving).

ad·junct (ăj′ŭngkt′) *n.* Something attached to another thing but in a dependent or subordinate position.

ad·mo·ni·tion (ăd′mə-nĭsh′ən) *n.* **1.** Mild censure. **2.** Cautionary advice.

ad·ver·sar·y (ăd′vər-sĕr′ē) *n., pl.* **-ies.** An opponent; enemy.

af·flic·tion (ə-flĭk′shən) *n.* **1.** A condition of pain, suffering, or distress. **2.** A cause of pain, suffering, or distress.

a·ghast (ə-găst′, ə-gäst′) *adj.* Shocked by something horrible; terrified.

ag·i·tate (ăj′ə-tāt′) *v.* **-tated, -tating, -tates.** —*tr.* **1.** To move with violence or sudden forcefulness; excite physically: *a storm agitating the ocean.* **2.** To upset, disturb: *Grief agitated the widow.*

a·gue (ā′gyōo) *n.* A recurrent chill or fit of shivering.

a·kim·bo (ə-kĭm′bō) *adj.* With the hands on the hips and the elbows bowed outward.

a·lac·ri·ty (ə-lăk′rə-tē) *n.* Cheerful willingness; eagerness.

al·be·it (ôl-bē′ĭt, ăl-) *conj.* Although; even though; though; notwithstanding.

al·ien·ate (āl′yən-āt′, ā′lē-ən-) *tr.v.* **-ated, -ating, -ates.** **1.** To remove or dissociate (oneself, for example): *"man cannot alienate himself from his own consciousness"* (Wylie Sypher). **2.** To cause to be transferred; turn away: *"he succeeded . . . in alienating the affections of my only ward"* (Oscar Wilde).

al·lay (ə-lā′) *tr.v.* **-layed, -laying, -lays. 1.** To lessen or relieve (pain or grief, for example); reduce the intensity of. **2.** To calm or pacify; set to rest.

al·lu·sion (ə-lōo′zhən) *n.* **1.** The act of alluding; indirect mention. **2.** An indirect, but pointed or meaningful, reference.

am·bi·gu·i·ty (ăm'bĭ-gyōō'ə-tē) *n., pl.* **-ties. 1.** The state of being ambiguous. **2.** Something ambiguous.

am·big·u·ous (ăm-bĭg'yōō-əs) *adj.* **1.** Susceptible of multiple interpretation. **2.** Doubtful or uncertain.

a·mi·a·ble (ā'mē-ə-bəl) *adj.* **1.** Pleasantly disposed; goodnatured; agreeable. **2.** Cordial; friendly; sociable; congenial: *an amiable gathering.*

am·pli·tude (ăm'plə-tōōd', -tyōōd') *n.* **1.** Greatness of size; magnitude. **2.** Fullness; copiousness.

an·a·con·da (ăn'ə-kŏn'də) *n.* A large, nonvenomous, arboreal snake, *Eunectes murinus,* of tropical South America, that constricts its prey in its coils.

a·ne·mi·a (ə-nē'mē-ə) *n.* A pathological deficiency in the oxygen-carrying material of the blood, measured in unit volume concentrations of hemoglobin, red blood cell volume, and red blood cell number.

an·guish (ăng'gwĭsh) *n.* An agonizing physical or mental pain; torment; torture.

an·guished (ăng'gwĭsht) *adj.* **1.** Filled with anguish. **2.** Caused by or expressing anguish: *"On thy cold forehead starts the anguished dew."* (Coleridge).

an·nul (ə-nŭl') *tr.v.* **-nulled, -nulling, -nuls. 1.** To make or declare void or invalid; nullify or cancel, as a marriage or a law. **2.** To obliterate the existence or effect of; annihilate.

a·nom·a·lous (ə-nŏm'ə-ləs) *adj.* Deviating from the normal or common order, form, or rule; abnormal; deviant.

an·thra·cite (ăn'thrə-sīt') *n.* A hard coal having a high carbon content and little volatile matter that burns with a clean flame.

an·tip·a·thy (ăn-tĭp'ə-thē) *n., pl.* **-thies.** A strong feeling of aversion or opposition.

an·tiq·ui·ty (ăn-tĭk'wə-tē) *n., pl.* **-ties. 1.** *Sometimes capital* **A.** Ancient times, especially the times preceding the Middle Ages. **2.** The people, especially the writers, of ancient times.

a·pace (ə-pās') *adv.* At a rapid pace; rapidly; swiftly.

a·pex (ā'pĕks') *n., pl.* **apexes** or **apices** (ā'pə-sēz', ăp'ə-.) The pointed end of something; tip.

ap·pall (ə-pôl') *tr.v.* **-palled, -palling, -palls.** To fill with consternation or dismay.

ap·pa·ri·tion (ăp'ə-rĭsh'ən) *n.* **1.** A ghostly figure; specter. **2.** A sudden or unusual sight.

ap·pro·ba·tion (ăp'rə-bā'shən) *n.* Praise; commendation.

ar·che·type (är'kə-tīp') *n.* An original model or type after which other similar things are patterned; a prototype. **—ar'che·typ'al** (-tī'pəl) *adj.*

ar·dent (är'dənt) *adj.* **a.** Expressing or characterized by warmth of passion or desire. **b.** Displaying or characterized by strong enthusiasm or devotion; fervent; zealous.

ar·du·ous (är'jōō-əs) *adj.* **1.** Demanding great care, effort, or labor; strenuous: *"the arduous work of preparing a Dictionary of the English Language"* (Macaulay). **2.** Testing severely the powers of endurance; full of hardships: *"the effects of a long, arduous, and exhausting war"* (Alexander Hamilton).

ar·ray (ə-rā') *tr.v.* **-rayed, -raying, -rays. 1.** To arrange or draw up (troops, for example) in battle order. **2.** To deck in finery; adorn.

ar·roy·o (ə-roi'ō) *n., pl.* **-os. 1.** A deep gully cut by an intermittent stream; a dry gulch. **2.** A brook or creek.

as·cet·ic (ə-sĕt'ĭk) *n.* A person who renounces the comforts of society and leads a life of austere self-discipline, especially as an act of religious devotion.

a·skance (ə-skăns') *adv.* **1.** With a side or oblique glance; sidewise. **2.** With disapproval, suspicion, or distrust.

as·sail (ə-sāl') *tr.v.* **-sailed, -sailing, -sails. 1.** To attack with or as if with violent blows; assault. **2.** To attack verbally, as with ridicule or censure.

as·sent (ə-sĕnt') *intr.v.* **-sented, -senting, -sents.** To express agreement; concur.

as·si·du·i·ty (ăs'ə-dōō'ə-tē, -dyōō'ə-tē) *n., pl.* **-ties.** Close and constant application; unflagging effort; diligence.

as·sim·i·la·tion (ə-sĭm'ə-lā'shən) *n. Sociology.* The process whereby a group, as a minority or immigrant group, gradually adopts the characteristics of another culture.

a·stern (ə-stûrn') *adv. Nautical.* Behind a vessel.

a·troc·i·ty (ə-trŏs'ə-tē) *n., pl.* **-ties. 1.** Atrocious condition, quality, or behavior; monstrousness; vileness. **2.** An atrocious action, situation, or object; outrage.

at·trib·ute (ăt'rə-byōōt') *n.* A quality or characteristic belonging to a person or thing; a distinctive feature: *"Travel has lost the attributes of privilege and fashion."* (John Cheever).

au·gust (ô-gŭst') *adj.* **1.** Inspiring awe or admiration; majestic. **2.** Venerable for reasons of age or high rank.

au·re·ole (ôr'ē-ōl') *n.* **1.** A circle of light or radiance surrounding the head or body of a representation of a deity or holy person; a halo. **2.** A bright circumferential region around a luminous celestial body, as around the sun or moon, especially when observed through a haze or fog.

aus·tere (ô-stîr') *adj.* Severe or stern in disposition or appearance; somber; grave.

a·ver·sion (ə-vûr'zhən, -shən) *n.* **1.** Intense dislike. Used with *to.* **2.** A feeling of extreme repugnance.

awe (ô) *n.* An emotion of mingled reverence, dread, and wonder inspired by something majestic or sublime. *—tr.v.* **awed, awing** or **aweing, awes.** To inspire with awe.

a·wry (ə-rī') *adv.* Turned or twisted toward one side; askew.

B

bale·ful (bāl'fəl) *adj.* **1.** Harmful or malignant in intent or effect. **2.** Portending evil; dire. **—bale'ful·ly** *adv.*

ă pat/ā pay/âr care/ä father/b **bib**/ch **church**/d **deed**/ĕ pet/ē be/f **fife**/g **gag**/h hat/hw **which**/ĭ pit/ī pie/îr pier/j **judge**/k **kick**/l lid,
needle/m **mum**/n no, sudden/ng **thing**/ŏ pot/ō toe/ô paw, for/oi noise/ou out/ōō took/ōō boot/p pop/r roar/s sauce/sh ship, dish/

bar·bar·i·ty (bär-băr'ə-tē) *n., pl.* **-ties. 1.** Harsh or cruel conduct. **2.** An inhuman, brutal act. **3.** Crudity; coarseness.

bar·ren (băr'ən) *adj.* **1.** Unproductive of results or gains; unprofitable. **2.** Lacking in liveliness or interest; meager.

ba·salt (bə-sôlt', bā'sôlt') *n.* A hard, dense, dark volcanic rock composed chiefly of plagioclase, augite, and magnetite, and often having a glassy appearance.

bel·lig·er·ent (bə-lĭj'ər-ənt) *adj.* Given to or marked by hostile or aggressive behavior: *"Raymie bared his teeth like a belligerent mouse."* (Sinclair Lewis).

be·reave (bĭ-rēv') *tr.v.* **-reaved** or **-reft** (-rĕft'), **-reaving, -reaves. 1.** To deprive of (life or hope, for example): *"To a man bereft of the sense of purpose"* (G. Wilson Knight). **2.** To leave desolate, especially by death: *"cry aloud for the man who is dead, for the woman and children bereaved"* (Alan Paton).

bil·low (bĭl'ō) *n.* A large wave or ocean swell.

blight (blīt) *n.* **1.** An environmental condition that injures or kills plants or animals, as air pollution. **2.** One that withers hopes or ambitions, impairs growth, or halts prosperity.

bois·ter·ous (boi'stər-əs, -strəs) *adj.* **1.** Rough and stormy; violent and turbulent. **2.** Loud, noisy, and unrestrained.

bom·bast (bŏm'băst') *n.* Grandiloquent and pompous speech or writing.

bound (bound) *intr.v.* **bounded, bounding, bounds. 1.** To leap forward or upward; to spring. **2.** To progress by bounds.

brack·en (brăk'ən) *n.* **1.** A fern, *Pteridium aquilinum,* having tough stems and branching, finely divided fronds. Also called "brake." **2.** An area overgrown with this fern.

bra·va·do (brə-vä'dō) *n., pl.* **-does** or **-dos. 1.** Defiant or swaggering show of courage; false bravery. **2.** An instance of such behavior.

bridge·head (brĭj'hĕd') *n.* A military position established by advance troops on the enemy's side of a river or pass to afford protection for the main attacking force.

bro·cade (brō-kād') *n.* A heavy fabric interwoven with a rich, raised design.

bul·wark (bŏŏl'wərk, bŭl'-, -wôrk') *n. Usually plural.* The part of a ship's side that is above the upper deck.

burgh·er (bûr'gər) *n.* **1.** A member of the mercantile class of a medieval city. **2.** A solid citizen; bourgeois.

C

cab·a·ret (kăb'ə-rā') *n.* A restaurant providing short programs of live entertainment.

cam·bric (kām'brĭk) *n.* A finely woven white linen or cotton fabric.

can·did (kăn'dĭd) *adj.* Without prejudice; impartial; fair.

car·a·van (kăr'ə-văn') *n.* A company of travelers journeying together, especially across a desert.

ca·reen (kə-rēn') *v.* **-reened, -reening, -reens.** —*intr.* To move rapidly and in an uncontrolled manner; to lurch or swerve in motion.

cat·a·mount (kăt'ə-mount') *n.* Also **cat·a·moun·tain** (kăt'ə-moun'tən). Any of various wild felines, such as a mountain lion or a lynx.

ca·vort (kə-vôrt') *intr.v.* **-vorted, -vorting, -vorts. 1.** To bound or prance about in a sprightly manner; to caper. **2.** To make merry; to sport; to frolic.

ce·ram·ic (sə-răm'ĭk) *n.* Any of various hard, brittle, heat-resistant and corrosion-resistant materials made by firing clay or other minerals and consisting of one or more metals in combination with a nonmetal, usually oxygen. —**ce·ram'ic** *adj.*

chas·tise (chăs-tīz') *tr.v.* **-tised, -tising, -tises.** To punish, usually by beating.

chi·me·ra (kī-mîr'ə, kə-) *n.* A creation of the imagination; an impossible and foolish fancy.

chiv·al·rous (shĭv'əl-rəs) *adj.* **1.** Having the qualities of gallantry and honor attributed to an ideal knight. **2.** Of or pertaining to chivalry. —**chiv·al·rous·ly** *adv.* —**chiv·al·rous·ness** *n.*

chiv·al·ry (shĭv'əl-rē) *n., pl.* The qualities idealized by knighthood, such as bravery, courtesy, and honesty.

chron·ic (krŏn'ĭk) *adj.* **1.** Of long duration; continuing; constant. **2.** Prolonged; lingering, as certain diseases.

cleave (klēv) *intr.v.,* **cleaved, cleaving, cleaves. 1.** To adhere, cling, or stick fast. Used with *to.* **2.** To be faithful. Used with *to.*

cli·che (klē-shā') *n.* A trite or overused expression or idea.

co·erce (kō-ûrs') *tr.v.* **-erced, -ercing, -erces.** To force to act or think in a given manner; to compel by pressure or threat.

co·er·cion (kō-ûr'shən) *n.* **1.** The act or practice of coercing. **2.** A coercive power.

co·her·ence (kō-hîr'əns, kō-hĕr'-) *n.* The quality or state of logical or orderly relationship of parts; consistency; congruity.

come·ly (kŭm'lē) *adj.* **-lier, -liest.** Having a pleasing appearance; attractive; handsome; graceful.

com·mo·di·ous (kə-mō'dē-əs) *adj.* Spacious; roomy.

com·mun·ion (kə-myōōn'yən) *n.* **1.** A possessing or sharing in common; participation. **2.** A sharing of thoughts or feelings; intimate talk.

com·pen·sa·tion (kŏm'pən-sā'shən) *n.* **1. a.** The act of compensating or making amends. **b.** The state of being compensated. **2.** Something given or recieved as an equivalent or as reparation for a loss, service, or debt; a recompense; an indemnity.

com·plai·sant (kəm-plā'sənt, -zənt, kŏm'plā-zănt') *adj.* Showing a desire or willingness to please; cheerfully obliging.

com·pli·ance (kəm-plī'əns) *n.* Also **com·pli·an·cy** (-ən-sē). **1.** A yielding to a wish, request, or demand; acquiescence. **2.** A disposition or tendency to yield to others.

---

t tight/th thin, path/*th* this, bathe/ŭ cut/ûr urge/v valve/w with/y yes/z zebra, size/zh vision/ə about, item, edible, gallop, circus/ á *Fr.* ami/œ *Fr.* feu, *Ger.* schön/ü *Fr.* tu, *Ger.* über/КН *Ger.* ich, *Scot.* loch/N *Fr.* bon.

com·posed (kəm-pōzd′) *adj.* Calm; serene; self-possessed.

com·pre·hend (kŏm′prĭ-hĕnd′) *tr.v.* **-hended, -hending, -hends. 1.** To grasp mentally; understand or know. **2.** To take in, include, or embrace; comprise.

com·punc·tion (kəm-pŭngk′shən) *n.* **1.** A strong uneasiness caused by a sense of guilt; remorse. **2.** A slight uneasiness or regret.

con·cil·i·ate (kən-sĭl′ē-āt′) *tr.v.* **-ated, -ating, -ates. 1.** To overcome the distrust or animosity of; win over; placate; soothe. **2.** To gain, win, or secure (favor, friendship, or good will, for example) by friendly overtures.

con·fla·gra·tion (kŏn′flə-grā′shən) *n.* A large and destructive fire.

con·jec·ture (kən-jĕk′chər) *v.* **-tured, -turing, -tures.** —*tr.* To infer from inconclusive evidence; to guess. —*n.* Inference based on inconclusive or incomplete evidence; guesswork.

con·se·crate (kŏn′sə-krāt′) *tr.v.* **-crated, -crating, -crates.** To make, declare, or set apart as sacred.

con·sis·ten·cy (kən-sĭs′tən-sē) *n., pl.* **-cies.** Compatibility or agreement among successive acts, ideas, or events.

con·ster·na·tion (kŏn′stər-nā′shən) *n.* Sudden confusion, amazement, or frustration.

con·strain (kən-strān′) *tr.v.* **-strained, -straining, -strains.** To compel by physical, moral, or circumstantial force; oblige.

con·sum·mate (kŏn′sə-māt′) *tr.v.* **-mated, -mating, -mates.** To bring to completion, perfection, or fulfillment; achieve.

con·temp·tu·ous (kən-tĕmp′chōō-əs) *adj.* Manifesting or feeling contempt; scornful; disdainful. Often used with *of.* —**con·temp′tu·ous·ly** *adv.*

con·trite (kən-trīt′, kŏn′trīt′) *adj.* Humbled by guilt and repentant for one's sins; penitent.

con·trive (kən-trīv′) *v.* **-trived, -triving, -trives.** —*tr.* **1.** To plan or devise with cleverness or ingenuity. **2.** To invent or fabricate, especially by improvisation.

cop·ing (kō′pĭng) *n.* The top part of a wall or roof, usually slanted.

cor·dial (kôr′jəl) *adj.* **1.** Hearty; warm; sincere. **2.** Invigorating; stimulating; reviving. —**cor′dial′i·ty** (kôr′jăl′ə-tē, -jē-ăl′ə-tē, -dē-ăl′ə-tē) *n.*

cor·rob·o·rate (kə-rŏb′ə-rāt′) *tr.v.* **-rated, -rating, -rates.** To strengthen or support (other evidence); attest the truth or accuracy of.

cos·mo·pol·i·tan (kŏz′mə-pŏl′ə-tən) *adj.* **1.** Common to the whole world. **2.** At home in all parts of the earth or in many spheres of interest. —*n.* A cosmopolite.

coun·ter·pane (koun′tər-pān′) *n.* A coverlet for a bed; bedspread.

coy (koi) *adj.* **coyer, coyest. 1.** Shy and demure; retiring. **2.** Pretending shyness or modesty; affectedly shy. **3.** Annoyingly unwilling to commit oneself; affectedly devious.

cran·ny (krăn′ē) *n., pl.* **-nies.** A small opening, as in a wall or rock face; crevice; fissure. —**cran′nied** *adj.*

crest·fall·en (krĕst′fô′lən) *adj.* Dejected; dispirited; depressed.

crys·tal·line (krĭs′tə-lĭn) *adj.* Resembling crystal; transparent.

cum·ber (kŭm′bər) *tr.v.* **-bered, -bering, -bers. 1.** To weigh down; burden. **2.** To hamper; obstruct.

cyn·i·cal (sĭn′ĭ-kəl) *adj.* Scornful of the motives or virtue of others; bitterly mocking; sneering.

cyn·i·cism (sĭn′ə-sĭz′əm) *n.* A cynical attitude or character.

D

dap·per (dăp′ər) *adj.* **1.** Neatly dressed; trim. **2.** Small and active.

deb·o·nair (dĕb′ə-nâr′) *adj.* **1.** Suave; nonchalant; urbane. **2.** Affable; gracious; genial. **3.** Carefree; gay; jaunty.

de·cease (dĭ-sēs′) *intr.v.* **-ceased, -ceasing, -ceases.** To die. —*n.* Death.

de·claim (dĭ-klām′) *v.* **-claimed, -claiming, -claims.** —*tr.* To utter or recite with rhetorical effect.

de·cry (dĭ-krī′) *tr.v.* **-cried, -crying, -cries.** To belittle or disparage openly; to censure.

de·gen·er·ate (dĭ-jĕn′ə-rāt′) *intr.v.* **-ated, -ating, -ates.** To deteriorate. —*adj.* (dĭ-jĕn′ər-ĭt). **1.** Characterized by deterioration. **2.** Marked by or exhibiting degeneracy. —*n.* (dĭ-jĕn′ər-ĭt). A morally degraded person.

de·jec·tion (dĭ-jĕk′shən) *n.* A state of depression; melancholy.

de·mean·or (dĭ-mē′nər) *n.* The way in which a person behaves or conducts himself; deportment; manner.

de·ment·ed (dĭ-mĕnt′tĭd) *adj.* Insane.

de·mo·ni·ac (dĭ-mō′nē-ăk′) *adj.* Also **de·mo·ni·a·cal** (dē′mə-nī′ə-kəl). **1.** Arising or seeming to arise from possession by a demon. **2.** Befitting or suggestive of a devil; fiendish; frenzied.

de·nun·ci·a·tion (dĭ-nŭn′sē-ā′shən, -shē-ā′shən) *n.* **1.** The act of denouncing; open condemnation or censure. **2.** The act of accusing another of a crime before a public prosecutor.

de·ploy (dĭ-ploi′) *v.* **-ployed, -ploying, -ploys.** —*tr.* To station (persons or forces) systematically over an area. —**de·ploy′ment** *n.*

dep·u·ta·tion (dĕp′yə-tā′shən) *n.* A person or group appointed to represent another or others; delegation.

de·ri·sive (dĭ-rī′sĭv) *adj.* Mocking; scoffing.

de·scry (dĭ-skrī′) *tr.v.* **-scried, -scrying, -scries. 1.** To discern (something difficult to catch sight of): *"through the mists they could descry the long arm of the mountains"* (J.R.R. Tolkien). **2.** To discover by careful observation or investigation.

des·o·late (dĕs′ə-lĭt) *adj.* **1.** Devoid of inhabitants; deserted: *"streets which were usually so thronged now grown desolate"* (Defoe). **2.** Rendered unfit for habitation; laid waste; devastated. **3.** Dreary; dismal; gloomy.

de·volve (dĭ-vŏlv′) *v.* **-volved, -volving, -volves.**

ă pat/ā pay/âr care/ä father/b bib/ch church/d deed/ĕ pet/ē be/f fife/g gag/h hat/hw which/ĭ pit/ī pie/îr pier/j judge/k kick/l lid, needle/m mum/n no, sudden/ng thing/ŏ pot/ō toe/ô paw, for/oi noise/ou out/ŏŏ took/ōō boot/p pop/r roar/s sauce/sh ship, dish/

—*intr.* To be passed on to a substitute or successor; be conferred. Used with *on*, *to*, or *upon*.

de·vour (dĭ-vour′) *tr.v.* **-voured, -vouring, -vours.** To take in greedily with the senses or mind: *devour a novel.*

di·a·bol·ic (dī′ə-bŏl′ĭk) *adj.* Also **di·a·bol·i·cal** (-ĭ-kəl). **1.** Of, concerning, proceeding from, or having the characteristics of the devil; satanic; hellish. **2.** Appropriate to a devil; extremely wicked; fiendishly cruel.

di·lap·i·dat·ed (dĭ-lăp′ə-dā′tĭd) *adj.* Fallen into a state of disrepair; broken-down.

di·late (dī-lāt′, dī′lāt′, dĭ-lāt′) *v.* **-lated, -lating, -lates.** —*tr.* To make wider or larger; cause to expand.

dil·i·gent (dĭl′ə-jənt) *adj.* Industrious; assiduous.

dire·ful (dīr′fəl) *adj.* Dreadful; frightful; dire.

dirge (dûrj) *n.* A funeral hymn or lament.

dis·cern (dĭ-sûrn′, -zûrn′) *v.* **-cerned, -cerning, -cerns.** —*tr.* To perceive (something obscure or concealed); detect.

dis·con·cert·ed (dĭs′kən-sûr′tĭd) *adj.* Bereft of composure; perturbed.

dis·con·so·late (dĭs-kŏn′sə-lĭt) *adj.* **1.** Beyond consolation; hopelessly sad. **2.** Cheerless; gloomy; dismal.

dis·course (dĭs′kôrs′, -kōrs′) *n.* **1.** Verbal expression in speech or writing. **2.** Verbal exchange; conversation.

dis·cre·tion (dĭs-krĕsh′ən) *n.* The quality of being discreet, prudent or cautious reserve.

dis·dain (dĭs-dān′) *tr.v.* **-dained, -daining, -dains. 1.** To regard or treat with haughty contempt; despise. **2.** To consider unworthy of oneself; reject with scorn.

dis·joint·ed (dĭs-join′tĭd) *adj.* **1.** Separated at the joints. **2.** Out of joint; dislocated. **3.** Lacking order or coherence; disconnected.

dis·man·tle (dĭs-măn′tl) *tr.v.* **-tled, -tling, -ties.** To take apart; tear down.

dis·par·age (dĭs-păr′ĭj) *tr.v.* **-aged, -aging, -ages. 1.** To belittle; slight. **2.** To reduce in esteem or rank.

dis·pel (dĭs-pĕl′) *tr.v.* **-pelled, -pelling, -pels.** To rid of by or as if by driving away or scattering; dispense with: *"the effect of his tone was to dispel her shyness"* (Henry James).

dis·si·pate (dĭs′ə-pāt′) *v.* **-pated, -pating, -pates.** —*tr.* To exhaust or expend intemperately; to waste; squander.

dis·so·lu·tion (dĭs′ə-lōō′shən) *n.* **1.** Decomposition into fragments or parts; disintegration. **2.** Extinction of life; death.

dis·tort (dĭs-tôrt′) *tr.v.* **-torted, -torting, -torts. 1.** To twist out of a proper or natural relation of parts; misshape; contort. **2.** To cast false light on; alter misleadingly; misrepresent.

dis·tor·tion (dĭs-tôr′shən) *n. Optics.* A distorted image resulting from imperfections in an optical system, such as a lens.

dis·traught (dĭs-trôt′) *adj.* Anxious or agitated; harried; worried.

di·ver·si·ty (dĭ-vûr′sə-tē, dī-) *n., pl.* **-ties. 1. a.** The fact or quality of being diverse; difference. **b.** A point or respect in which things differ. **2.** Variety; multiformity: *a healthy diversity in one's diet.*

di·vine (dĭ-vīn′) *v.* **-vined, -vining, -vines.** —*tr.* **1.** To foretell or reveal through the art of divination. **2. a.** To know by inspiration, intuition, or reflection: *"if we can divine the future, out of what we can collect from the past"* (Burke). **b.** To guess.

di·vin·i·ty (dĭ-vĭn′ə-tē) *n., pl.* **-ties.** The state or quality of being divine.

doc·ile (dŏs′əl; *British* dō′sīl′) *adj.* **1.** Capable of being taught; ready and willing to receive training; teachable. **2.** Submissive to training or management; tractable. **3.** Yielding to handling or treatment; easily shaped or formed.

dog·ged (dô′gĭd, dŏg′ĭd) *adj.* Not yielding readily; willful; stubborn: *"his manner displayed a kind of dogged self-assertion which had nothing aggressive in it"* (Conrad).

dole·ful (dōl′fəl) *adj.* Filled with grief; mournful; melancholy.

do·main (dō-mān′) *n.* A territory or range of rule or control; realm.

do·min·ion (də-mĭn′yən) *n.* Control or the exercise of control; rule; sovereignty.

dor·mant (dôr′mənt) *adj.* **1.** Asleep or lying as if asleep; not awake or active. **2.** Latent but capable of being activated: *"a harrowing experience which . . . lay dormant but still menacing"* (Charles Jackson).

dray (drā) *n.* A low, heavy cart without sides, used for haulage.

dray·man (drā′mən) *n., pl.* **-men** (-mĭn). A driver of a dray.

du·bi·ous (dōō′bē-əs, dyōō′-) *adj.* Reluctant to concur; skeptical; doubtful.

dun (dŭn) *tr.v.* **dunned, dunning, duns.** To importune (a debtor) persistently for payment.

E

ed·i·fice (ĕd′ə-fĭs) *n.* A building, especially one of imposing appearance or size.

ef·fuse (ĭ-fyōōz′) *tr.v.* **effused, -fusing, -fuses.** To pour or spread out; disseminate.

ef·fu·sive (ĭ-fyōō′sĭv) *adj.* **1.** Irrepressibly demonstrative. **2.** Unrestrained in emotional expression; gushy.

e·jac·u·late (ĭ-jăk′yə-lāt′) *v.* **-lated, -lating, -lates.** —*tr.* To utter suddenly and passionately; exclaim.

e·lix·ir (ĭ-lĭk′sər) *n.* **1.** A sweetened aromatic solution of alcohol and water, containing or serving as a vehicle for medicine. **2.** Any medicinal potion thought to have generalized curative or restorative powers.

e·lu·sive (ĭ-lōō′sĭv) *adj.* Tending to elude grasp, perception, or mental retention: *"the edge of the sea remains an elusive and indefinable boundary"* (Rachel Carson).

em·bit·ter (ĕm-bĭt′ər, ĭm-) *tr.v.* **-tered, -tering, -ters. 1.** To make bitter. **2.** To arouse bitter feelings in; make resentful or hostile.

---

t tight/th **thin,** path/*th* **this,** bathe/ŭ **cut**/ûr **urge**/v **valve**/w **with**/y **yes**/z **zebra,** size/zh **vision**/ə **about, item, edible, gallop, circus**/ā *Fr.* ami/œ *Fr.* feu, *Ger.* schön/ü *Fr.* tu, *Ger.* über/ᴋʜ *Ger.* ich, *Scot.* loch/ɴ *Fr.* bon.

em·i·nent (ĕm′ə-nənt) *adj.* **a.** Outstanding in performance or character; distinguished: *an eminent historian.* **b.** Of high rank or station.

en·cap·su·late (ĕn-kăp′sə-lāt′, ĭn-) *v.* -**lated, -lating, -lates.** —*tr.* To encase in or as if in a capsule. —**en·cap′su·la′tion** *n.*

en·cum·ber (ĕn-kŭm′bər, ĭn-) *tr.v.* -**bered, -bering, -bers.** **1.** To weigh down unduly; lay too much upon. **2.** To hinder, impede, or clutter, as with useless articles or unwanted additions.

en·hance (ĕn-hăns′, -häns′, ĭn-) *tr.v.* -**hanced, -hancing, -hances.** To increase or make greater, as in value, cost, beauty, or reputation; augment.

en·ig·mat·ic (ĕn′ĭg-măt′ĭk) *adj.* Also **en·ig·mat·i·cal** (-ĭ-kəl). Of or resembling an enigma; puzzling: *"a smile that was at once worldly, wan, and enigmatic"* (J.D. Salinger).

en·mi·ty (ĕn′mə-tē) *n., pl.* -**ties.** Deep-seated hatred, as between rivals or opponents; antagonism.

en·nui (än′wē′) *n.* Listlessness and dissatisfaction resulting from lack of interest; boredom.

en·sconce (ĕn-skŏns′, ĭn-) *tr.v.* -**sconced, -sconcing, -sconces.** **1.** To settle (oneself) securely or comfortably: *"She was ensconced in a ponderous fauteuil of figured velvet."* (Ronald Firbank). **2.** To place, fix, or conceal in a secure place.

en·thrall (ĕn-thrôl′, ĭn-) *tr.v.* -**thralled, -thralling, -thralls.** **1.** To hold spellbound; captivate; charm. **2.** To reduce to thralldom; enslave.

en·tice (ĕn-tīs′) *tr.v.* -**ticed, -ticing, -tices.** To attract by arousing hope or desire; lure.

en·treat (ĕn-trēt′, ĭn-) *v.* -**treated, -treating, -treats.** —*tr.* **1.** To ask (someone) earnestly; beseech; implore; beg. **2.** To ask for (something) earnestly; petition for.

en·treat·y (ĕn-trē′tē, ĭn-) *n., pl.* -**ies.** An earnest request; plea.

e·nun·ci·a·tion (ĭ-nŭn′sē-ā′shən, ĭ-nŭn′shē-) *n.* The manner in which a speaker articulates words or speech sounds.

ep·i·thet (ĕp′ə-thĕt′) *n.* An abusive or contemptuous word or phrase used to describe a person.

e·pit·o·me (ĭ-pĭt′ə-mē) *n.* **1.** A summary of a book, article, event, or the like; an abridgment; abstract. **2.** One that is consummately representative or expressive of an entire class or type; embodiment.

e·qui·nox (ē′kwə-nŏks′, ĕk′wə-) *n.* Either of the two times during a year when the sun crosses the celestial equator and when the length of day and night are approximately equal.

e·quiv·o·cal (ĭ-kwĭv′ə-kəl) *adj.* Of doubtful nature, as categorically or ethically; questionable; not genuine: *"He struck me as a smooth, smiling, equivocal sort of person"* (G.K. Chesterton).

er·rat·ic (ĭ-răt′ĭk) *adj.* **1.** Without a fixed or regular course; straying; wandering: *"The tears coursed their erratic way down her checks"* (Elizabeth Bowen). **2.** Lacking consistency, regularity, or uniformity.

es·ca·pade (ĕs′kə-pād′) *n.* A carefree or reckless adventure; a fling; caper.

ev·a·nesce (ĕv′ə-nĕs′) *intr.v.* -**nesced, -nescing,** -**nesces.** To dissipate like vapor; disappear gradually; fade away; vanish. **ev′a·nes′cence** *n.*

e·vince (ĭ-vĭns′) *tr.v.* **evinced, evincing, evinces.** To show or demonstrate clearly or convincingly; manifest; exhibit.

ex·hil·a·rate (ĕg-zĭl′ə-rāt′, ĭg-) *tr.v.* -**rated, -rating, rates.** To invigorate; stimulate.

ex·pe·di·ent (ĕk-spē′dē-ənt) *n.* **1.** That which answers the immediate purpose; a means to an end: *"Advertisers regard acting merely as a sales expedient."* (Charles Marowitz). **2.** A contrivance adopted to meet an urgent need; a device; recourse.

ex·pe·dite (ĕk′spə-dīt′) *tr.v.* -**dited, -diting, -dites.** To speed up the progress of; help along; assist; facilitate: *"a broad way now is pav'd/To expedite your glorious march"* (Milton).

ex·pire (ĕk-spīr′, ĭk-) *v.* -**pired, -piring, -pires.** —*intr.* **1.** To come to an end; terminate; cease to be effective: *His membership expired.* **2.** To breathe one's last breath; die.

ex·ploit (ĕks′ploit′) *n.* An act or deed, especially a brilliant or heroic feat.

ex·qui·site (ĕks′kwĭ-zĭt) *adj.* Intense; keen: *an exquisite pain.* —**ex′qui·site·ly** *adv.*

ex·tem·po·ra·ne·ous (ĕk-stĕm′pə-rā′nē-əs, ĭk-) *adj.* Provided, made, or adapted as an expedient; improvised; makeshift.

ex·tinc·tion (ĕk-stĭngk′shən, ĭk-) *n.* **1.** The act of extinguishing or making extinct: *"They aim at the extinction of the belief in individuality"* (Edward Conze). **2.** The fact or condition of being extinguished or extinct.

ex·ult (ĕg-zŭlt′, ĭg-) *intr.v.* -**ulted, -ulting, -ults.** To rejoice greatly; be jubilant or triumphant.

F

fac·ile (făs′əl, -īl) *adj.* Arrived at without due care, effort, or examination; superficial.

fa·cil·i·tate (fə-sĭl′ĭ-tāt′) *tr.v.* -**tated, -tating, -tates.** To free from difficulties or obstacles; make easier; aid; assist.

farce (färs) *n.* Something ludicrous; an empty show; mockery: *"childish family portraits, with their farce of sentiment and smiling lies"* (Thackeray).

fath·om (făth′əm) *n., pl.* **fathoms** or **fathom.** A unit of length equal to six feet, and used principally in the measurement and specification of marine depths.

fe·do·ra (fĭ-dôr′ə, -dōr′ə) *n.* A soft felt hat with a brim that can be turned up or down and a rather low crown creased lengthwise.

feign (fān) *v.* **feigned, feigning, feigns.** —*tr.* **1. a.** To give a false appearance of; pretend; to sham: *jump into bed and feign sleep.* **b.** To represent falsely; pretend to: *feign authorship of a novel.* **2.** To invent; make up; fabricate: *feign an experience.* —*intr.* To pretend; dissemble.

fe·lic·i·ty (fĭ-lĭs′ə-tē) *n., pl.* -**ties. a.** Great happiness; bliss. **b.** An instance of this.

fer·vent (fûr′vənt) *adj.* Having or showing great emotion or warmth; passionate; ardent.

fes·toon (fĕs-tōon′) *n.* A string or garland of leaves, flowers, ribbon, or the like, suspended in a loop or curve between two points. —*tr.v.* **festooned, -tooning, -toons.** To decorate with or as with a festoon or festoons.

fet·ter (fĕt′ər) *tr.v.* **fettered, -tering, -ters. 1.** To put fetters on; to shackle. **2.** To restrict the freedom of movement or thought of; confine; impede.

fir·ma·ment (fûr′mə-mənt) *n.* The vault or expanse of the heavens; sky.

fis·sure (fĭsh′ər) *n.* **1.** A narrow crack or cleft, as in a rock face. **2.** The process of separation or division. **3.** A schism; a split.

flac·cid (flăk′sĭd) *adj.* Lacking firmness; soft and limp; flabby.

fla·grant (flā′grənt) *adj.* Extremely or deliberately conspicuous; notorious; shocking: *a flagrant miscarriage of justice.*

flay (flā) *tr.v.* **flayed, flaying, flays.** To assail with stinging criticism; excoriate.

foal (fōl) *v.* **foaled, foaling, foals.** —*tr.* To give birth to (a foal).

fo·ment (fō-mĕnt′) *tr.v.* **-mented, -menting, -ments.** To promote the growth or arousal of; stir up; instigate.

fore·cas·tle (fōk′səl, fōr′kăs′əl, -käs′əl, fōr′-) *n.* Also **fo′c's′le** (fōk′səl). **1.** The section of the upper deck of a ship located at the bow, forward of the foremast. **2.** A superstructure at the bow of a merchant ship, where the crew is housed.

fore·shad·ow (fōr-shăd′ō, fōr-) *tr.v.* **-owed, -owing, -ows.** To present an indication or suggestion of beforehand; to presage.

for·mi·da·ble (fōr′mə-də-bəl) *adj.* **1.** Arousing fear, dread, or alarm. **2.** Admirable or awe-inspiring. **3.** Difficult to surmount, defeat, or undertake; awesome.

forth·right (fōrth′rīt, fōrth′-) *adj.* Proceeding straight ahead; straightforward; frank; candid: *a forthright appraisal.*

for·ti·tude (fōr′tə-tōod′, -tyōod′) *n.* Strength of mind that allows one to endure pain or adversity with courage.

fos·sil (fŏs′əl) *n.* **1.** A remnant or trace of an organism of a past geological age, such as a skeleton, footprint, or leaf imprint, embedded in the earth's crust. **2.** One that is outdated or antiquated; especially, a person with outmoded ideas; a fogy.

frag·ile (frăj′əl, -īl′) *adj.* Easily broken or damaged; brittle.

frip·per·y (frĭp′ə-rē) *n., pl.* **-ies. 1.** Pretentious finery; excessively ornamented dress. **2.** Pretentious elegance; ostentation.

fu·gi·tive (fyōo′jə-tĭv) *adj.* Running or having run away; fleeing, as from justice, the law, or the like.

furl (fûrl) *v.* **furled, furling, furls.** —*tr.* To roll up and secure (a flag or sail) to a pole, yard, or mast.

fur·tive (fûr′tĭv) *adj.* **1.** Characterized by stealth; surreptitious. **2.** Expressive of hidden motives or purposes; shifty.

G

gait (gāt) *n.* A way of moving on foot; a particular fashion of walking, running, or the like.

gal·lant·ry (găl′ən-trē) *n., pl.* **-ries. 1.** Nobility of spirit or action; courage. **2.** Chivalrous attention toward women; courtliness; courteousness.

gam·bol (găm′bəl) *intr.v.* **-boled,** or **-bolled, -boling,** or **-bolling, -bols.** To leap about playfully; to frolic; skip.

garb (gärb) *n.* Clothing; especially, the distinctive attire of one's occupation or station: *sailors' garb.*

gaud·y (gô′dē) *adj.* **-ier, -iest.** Characterized by tasteless or showy colors; garish.

ga·zette (gə-zĕt′) *tr.v.* **gazetted, -zetting, -zettes.** *British.* To announce or publish in a gazette.

ge·ni·al·i·ty (jē′nē-ăl′ə-tē) *n.* The quality of being genial; friendliness; cordiality.

gi·gan·tic (jī-găn′tĭk) *adj.* **1.** Pertaining to or suitable for a giant. **2. a.** Exceedingly large of its kind: *a gigantic toadstool.* **b.** Very large or extensive: *a gigantic radio network.*

gin·ger·ly (jĭn′jər-lē) *adv.* **1.** With great care or delicacy. **2.** Cautiously; carefully; timidly.

glad·i·a·tor (glăd′ē-ā′tər) *n.* **1.** A professional combatant, slave, captive, or condemned prisoner trained to entertain the public by engaging in mortal combat in the ancient Roman arena. **2.** A controversialist or disputant, especially one chosen to represent his faction or party in a public debate.

goad (gōd) *n.* That which prods or urges; a stimulus or irritating incentive. —*tr.v.* **goaded, goading, goads.** To prod with or as if with a goad; give impetus to; incite.

gos·sa·mer (gŏs′ə-mər) *n.* **1.** A fine film of cobwebs often seen floating in the air or caught on bushes or grass. **2.** Anything delicate, light, or insubstantial.

grav·i·ty (grăv′ə-tē) *n.* Solemnity or dignity of manner.

grim (grĭm) *adj.* **grimmer, grimmest.** Unrelenting; rigid; stern.

guile (gīl) *n.* Insidious, treacherous cunning; craftiness; dissimulation.

H

hal·low (hăl′ō) *tr.v.* **-lowed, -lowing, -lows.** To make or set apart as holy; sanctify; consecrate.

ham·mock (hăm′ək) *n.* A hanging, easily swung cot or lounge of canvas or netting suspended between two trees or other supports.

ha·rangue (hə-răng′) *n.* **1.** A long, pompous speech; especially, one delivered before a gathering. **2.** A speech characterized by strong feeling or vehement expression; tirade. —*v.* **harangued, -ranguing, -rangued.** —*tr.* To deliver a harangue to.

har·ass (hăr′əs, hə-răs′) *tr.v.* **-assed, -assing, -asses.** To disturb or irritate persistently.

has·ten (hā′sən) v. **-tened, -tening, -tens.** —intr. To move swifty. —tr. To hurry.

head·wa·ters (hĕd′wô′tərz, -wŏt′ərz) pl.n. The waters from which a river rises.

he·li·o·trope (hē′lē-ə-trōp′) n. Any of several plants of the genus *Heliotropium;* especially, *H. arborescens,* native to South America, having small, fragrant, purplish flowers.

hie (hī) intr.v. **hied, hieing,** or **hying, hies.** To go quickly; hasten; hurry.

hoar·y (hôr′ē, hōr′ē) adj. **-ier, -iest. 1.** Gray or white with or as if with age. **2.** Very old; ancient.

home·ly (hōm′lē) adj. **-lier, -liest. 1.** Of a nature associated or suited to the home; domestic; familiar; homey: *homely virtues.* **2.** Of a simple or unpretentious nature; uncomplicated; plain. **3.** Lacking elegance or refinement; crude.

hos·tile (hŏs′təl) adj. Feeling or showing enmity; antagonistic.

hov·el (hŭv′əl, hŏv′-) n. A small, miserable dwelling.

hov·er (hŭv′ər, hŏv′-) intr.v. **-ered, -ering, -ers. 1.** To fly, soar, or float as if suspended: *gulls hovering over the waves.* **2.** To remain or linger in close proximity; move back and forth in or near a place.

hue (hyōō) n. **1.** A particular gradation of color; tint; shade. **2.** Color.

hus·band (hŭz′bənd) tr.v. **husbanded, -banding, -bands.** To spend or use economically; to budget; to conserve: *husband one's energy.*

hy·per·bo·le (hī-pûr′bə-lē) n. An exaggeration or extravagant statement used as a figure of speech; for example, *I could sleep for a year. This book weighs a ton.*

hy·poc·ri·sy (hĭ-pŏk′rə-sē) n., pl. **-sies. 1.** The feigning of beliefs, feelings, or virtues that one does not hold or possess; insincerity. **2.** An instance of such falseness.

I

im·mac·u·late (ĭ-măk′yə-lĭt) adj. **1.** Free from stain or blemish; spotless; pure. **2.** Free from fault or error.

im·pale (ĭm-pāl′) tr.v. **-paled, -paling, -pales.** To pierce with a sharp stake or point.

im·pas·sive (ĭm-păs′ĭv) adj. **1.** Devoid of or not subject to emotion; apathetic. **2.** Revealing no emotion; expressionless.

im·pend·ing (ĭm-pĕn′dĭng) adj. Likely or due to happen soon; imminent.

im·per·cep·ti·ble (ĭm′pər-sĕp′tə-bəl) adj. **1.** Not perceptible. **2.** Barely perceptible.

im·pe·ri·al (ĭm-pîr′ē-əl) adj. Of or pertaining to an empire or emperor.

im·pe·ri·ous (ĭm-pîr′ē-əs) adj. **1.** Domineering; overbearing. **2.** Regal; imperial.

im·per·turb·a·ble (ĭm′pər-tûr′bə-bəl) adj. Not capable of being perturbed.

im·pet·u·ous (ĭm-pĕch′ōō-əs) adj. Having great

impetus; rushing with violence: *impetuous, heaving waves.*

im·pla·ca·ble (ĭm-plā′kə-bəl, -plăk′ə-bəl) adj. **1.** Not placable; incapable of appeasement; inexorable. **2.** Unalterable; inflexible.

im·por·tune (ĭm′pôr-tōōn′, -tyōōn′, ĭm-pôr′chən) tr.v. **-tuned, -tuning, -tunes.** To beset with repeated and insistent requests.

im·por·tu·ni·ty (ĭm′pôr-tōō′nə-tē, -tyōō′nə-tē) n., pl. **-ties. 1. a.** The act of importuning. **b.** The state or quality of being importunate. **2.** *Plural.* Insistent demands or requests.

im·pro·vise (ĭm′prə-vīz′) v. **-vised, -vising, -vises.** —intr. To invent, compose, recite, or execute something offhand.

im·pu·ni·ty (ĭm-pyōō′nə-tē) n., pl. **-ties. 1.** Exemption from punishment or penalty. **2.** Immunity or preservation from recrimination, regret, or the like; escape from what is probable, certain, or just.

in·ar·tic·u·late (ĭn′är-tĭk′yə-lĭt) adj. Uttered without the use of normal words or syllables; incomprehensible as speech or language.

in·au·gu·rate (ĭn-ô′gyə-rāt′) tr.v. **-rated, -rating, -rates.** To begin or start officially.

in·can·ta·tion (ĭn′kăn-tā′shən) n. Ritual recitation of verbal charms or spells to produce a magical effect.

in·car·nate (ĭn-kär′nĭt) adj. **a.** Invested with bodily nature and form. **b.** Personified.

in·cen·tive (ĭn-sĕn′tĭv) n. Something inciting to action or effort, as the fear of punishment or the expectation of reward.

in·ces·sant (ĭn-sĕs′ənt) adj. Continuing without respite or interruption; unceasing. **—in·ces′sant·ly** adv.

in·cite (ĭn-sīt′) tr.v. **-cited, -citing, -cites.** To provoke to action, stir up, or urge on.

in·co·her·ent (ĭn′kō-hîr′ənt) adj. **1.** Not coherent; disordered; unconnected; inharmonious. **2.** Unable to think or express one's thoughts in a clear or orderly manner: *incoherent with grief.* **—in′co·her′ent·ly** adv.

in·cred·u·lous (ĭn-krĕj′ə-ləs) adj. **1.** Disbelieving; skeptical. **2.** Expressing disbelief: *an incredulous stare.* **—in·cred′u·lous·ly** adv.

in·cum·bent (ĭn-kŭm′bənt) adj. Lying, leaning, or resting upon something else.

in·di·gence (ĭn′də-jəns) n. Want or neediness.

in·dis·crim·i·nate (ĭn′dĭs-krĭm′ə-nĭt) adj. **1.** Random; haphazard. **2.** Not properly restricted or restrained; promiscuous.

in·dis·posed (ĭn′dĭs-pōzd′) adj. **1.** Mildly ill. **2.** Disinclined; unwilling.

in·di·vis·i·ble (ĭn′də-vĭz′ə-bəl) adj. Incapable of being divided.

in·ef·fa·ble (ĭn-ĕf′ə-bəl) adj. Beyond expression; indescribable or unspeakable: *ineffable delight.* **—in·ef′fa·bly** adv.

in·fi·nite (ĭn′fə-nĭt) adj. **1.** Having no boundaries or limits. **2.** Immeasurably or uncountably large.

in·fin·i·tes·i·mal (ĭn′fĭn-ə-tĕs′ə-məl) adj. Immeasurably or incalculably minute.

in·firm (ĭn-fûrm′) *adj.* Weak in body, especially from old age; feeble.

in·flex·i·ble (ĭn-flĕk′sə-bəl) *adj.* Incapable of being changed; unalterable: *inflexible standards.* —**in·flex′i·bil′i·ty** *n.*

in·her·ent (ĭn-hîr′ənt, -hĕr′ənt) *adj.* Existing as an essential constituent or characteristic; intrinsic. —**in·her′ent·ly** *adv.*

in·iq·ui·ty (ĭ-nĭk′wə-tē) *n., pl.* **-ties.** Moral turpitude or sin; wickedness.

in·or·di·nate (ĭn-ôrd′n-ĭt) *adj.* **1.** Exceeding reasonable limits; immoderate; unrestrained. **2.** Not regulated; disorderly.

in·scru·ta·ble (ĭn-skrōō′tə-bəl) *adj.* Not able to be fathomed or understood; impenetrable; enigmatic. —**in·scru′ta·bil′i·ty** *n.*

in·so·lent (ĭn′sə-lənt) *adj.* **1.** Presumptuous and insulting in manner or speech; arrogant. **2.** Audaciously impudent; impertinent.

in·stru·men·tal·i·ty (ĭn′strə-mĕn-tăl′ə-tē) *n., pl.* **-ties. 1.** The quality or circumstance of being instrumental. **2.** Agency; means.

in·suf·fer·a·ble (ĭn-sŭf′ər-ə-bəl) *adj.* Not endurable; intolerable.

in·su·per·a·ble (ĭn-sōō′pər-ə-bəl) *adj.* Incapable of being overcome; insurmountable: *an insuperable barrier.*

in·sur·gent (ĭn-sûr′jənt) *n.* One who revolts against authority; especially, a member of a political party who rebels against its leadership.

in·tem·per·ate (ĭn-tĕm′pər-ĭt) *adj.* Not temperate or moderate.

in·ter·mi·na·ble (ĭn-tûr′mə-nə-bəl) *adj.* Tiresomely protracted; endless.

in·ter·mit (ĭn′tər-mĭt′) *v.* **-mitted, -mitting, -mits.** —*intr.* To suspend activity temporarily or repeatedly.

in·tern (ĭn′tûrn′) *n.* One who is interned; an internee. —*v.* **interned, -terning, -terns.** —*intr.* (ĭn′tûrn′). To train or serve as an intern. —*tr.* (ĭn-tûrn′). To detain or confine, especially in wartime.

in·tern·ment (ĭn-tûrn′mənt) *n.* The act of interning or the state of being interned.

in·ti·ma·cy (ĭn′tə-mə-sē) *n., pl.* **-cies. 1.** The condition of being intimate. **2.** An instance of being intimate.

in·ti·mate[1] (ĭn′tə-māt′) *tr.v.* **-mated, -mating, -mates.** To communicate with a hint or other indirect sign; imply subtly.

in·ti·mate[2] (ĭn′tə-mĭt) *adj.* **1.** Marked by close acquaintance, association, or familiarity. **2.** Pertaining to or indicative of one's deepest nature.

in·tim·i·date (ĭn-tĭm′ə-dāt′) *tr.v.* **-dated, -dating, -dates. 1.** To make timid; frighten. **2.** To discourage or inhibit by or as if by threats.

in·trep·id (ĭn-trĕp′ĭd) *adj.* Resolutely courageous; fearless; bold.

in·trude (ĭn-trōōd′) *v.* **-truded, -truding, -trudes.** —*tr.* To interpose (oneself or something) without invitation, fitness, or leave. —**in·trud′er** *n.*

in·var·i·a·ble (ĭn-vâr′ē-ə-bəl) *adj.* Not changing or subject to change; constant. —**in·var′i·a·bly** *adv.*

in·vest (ĭn-vĕst′) *v.* **-vested, -vesting, -vests.** —*tr.* To endow with rank, authority, or power.

in·vet·er·ate (ĭn-vĕt′ər-ĭt) *adj.* **1.** Firmly established by long standing; deep-rooted. **2.** Persisting in an ingrained habit; habitual: *an inveterate liar.*

in·vi·o·late (ĭn-vī′ə-lĭt) *adj.* Not violated; intact.

ir·ra·tion·al (ĭ-răsh′ən-əl) *adj.* Not endowed with reason.

ir·res·o·lute (ĭ-rĕz′ə-lōōt′) *adj.* **1.** Unresolved as to action or procedure: *"greatly oppressed in my mind, irresolute, and not knowing what to do"* (Defoe). **2.** Lacking in resolution; vacillating; wavering; indecisive. —**ir·res′o·lu′tion** *n.*

ir·rev·o·ca·ble (ĭ-rĕv′ə-kə-bəl) *adj.* Incapable of being retracted or revoked; irreversible.

J

ja·pan (jə-păn′) *n.* **1.** A black enamel or lacquer of a type originating in the Orient, used to produce a durable glossy finish. **2.** Any object decorated and varnished in the Japanese manner. —*adj.* Relating to or varnished with japan.

jeop·ard·ize (jĕp′ər-dīz′) *tr.v.* **-dized, -dizing, -dizes.** To invite loss of or injury to; make vulnerable or precarious; imperil.

jo·cose (jō-kōs′) *adj.* **1.** Given to good-humored joking; merry. **2.** Characterized by joking; humorous. —**jo·cose′ly** *adv.*

jo·vi·al (jō′vē-əl) *adj.* Marked by hearty conviviality.

ju·ris·dic·tion (jŏŏr-əs-dĭk′shən) *n.* **1.** The right and power to interpret and apply the law. **2.** Authority or control.

K

keel (kēl) *n. Poetic.* A ship.

ker·o·sene (kĕr′ə-sēn′, kĕr′ə-sēn′) *n.* A thin oil distilled from petroleum or shale oil, used as a fuel and alcohol denaturant.

key (kē) *n., pl.* **keys.** A low offshore island or reef, often of coral or sand; a cay.

knead (nēd) *tr.v.* **kneaded, kneading, kneads. 1.** To mix and work (a substance) into a uniform mass, especially to fold, press, and stretch dough with the hands. **2.** To make (bread) by kneading.

L

lach·ry·mose (lăk′rə-mōs′) *adj.* **1.** Weeping or inclined to weep; tearful. **2.** Causing tears; sorrowful.

lack·lus·ter (lăk′lŭs′tər) *adj.* Also *chiefly British* **lack·lus·tre.** Lacking luster, brightness, or vitality; dull.

la·tent (lā′tənt) *adj.* Present or potential, but not manifest: *latent talent.*

lee (lē) *n.* **1.** The side or quarter away from the

direction from which the wind blows; the side sheltered from the wind. **2.** Any place sheltered from the wind.

leech (lēch) *n.* One who preys on or clings to another; a parasite.

lee·ward (lē'wərd, lōō'ərd) *adj.* Located on or moving toward the side toward which the wind is blowing. —*n.* The lee side or quarter. —*adv.* Toward the lee side.

leg·a·cy (lĕg'ə-sē) *n., pl.* **-cies. 1.** Money or property bequeathed to someone by will. **2.** Something handed down from an ancestor or predecessor, or from the past.

le·thal (lē'thəl) *adj.* **1.** Sufficient to cause or capable of causing death. **2.** Of, pertaining to, or causing death.

lev·ee (lĕv'ē) *n.* **1.** An embankment raised to prevent a river from overflowing. **2.** A landing place on a river; pier.

lib·er·al (lĭb'ər-əl, lĭb'rəl) *adj.* **a.** Tending to give freely; generous: *a liberal benefactor.* **b.** Generously given; bountiful: *a liberal serving.*

lib·er·al·i·ty (lĭb'ə-răl'ə-tē) *n., pl.* **-ties. 1.** The quality or state of being liberal. **2.** A generous gift.

lithe (līth) *adj.* **1.** Readily bent; supple; limber. **2.** Marked by effortless grace.

liv·id (lĭv'ĭd) *adj.* **1.** Ashen or pallid, as with anger, rage, or illness. **2.** Extremely angry; furious.

loathe (lōth) *tr.v.* **loathed, loathing, loathes.** To detest greatly; abhor.

loi·ter (loi'tər) *intr. v.* **-tered, -tering, -ters.** To stand idly about; linger aimlessly; loaf.

lope (lōp) *intr.v.* **loped, loping, lopes.** To run or ride with a steady, easy gait. —*n.* A steady, easy gait.

lot·ter·y (lŏt'ə-rē) *n., pl.* **-ies.** A contest in which tokens are distributed or sold, the winning token or tokens being secretly predetermined or ultimately selected in a chance drawing.

loy·al·ist (loi'ə-lĭst) *n.* **1.** One who maintains loyalty to a lawful government, political party, or sovereign, especially during war or revolutionary change. **2.** A Tory.

lu·di·crous (lōō'dĭ-krəs) *adj.* Laughable or hilarious through obvious absurdity or incongruity.

lu·gu·bri·ous (lōō-gōō'brē-əs, lōō-gyōō'-) *adj.* Mournful or doleful, especially to a ludicrous degree. —**lu·gu'bri·ous·ness** *n.*

lu·mi·nous (lōō'mə-nəs) *adj.* Intelligible; clear.

lurch (lûrch) *intr.v.* **lurched, lurching, lurches.** To roll or pitch suddenly or erratically, as a ship during a storm.

lu·rid (lōōr'ĭd) *adj.* **1.** Causing shock or horror. **2.** Glowing or glaring through a haze. **3.** Sallow in color; pallid.

lux·u·ri·ant (lŭg-zhōōr'ē-ənt, lŭk-shōōr'-) *adj.* Growing abundantly, vigorously, or lushly.

M

mag·na·nim·i·ty (măg'nə-nĭm'ĭ-tē) *n.* The quality of being magnanimous.

mag·nan·i·mous (măg-năn'ə-məs) *adj.* Noble of mind and heart; generous in forgiving; above revenge or resentment; unselfish; gracious.

mag·ni·tude (măg'nĭ-tōōd', -tyōōd') *n.* Greatness in significance or influence.

ma·lev·o·lence (mə-lĕv'ə-ləns) *n.* **1.** Ill will toward others; rancor; malice. **2.** Evil influence, especially supernatural.

mal·ice (măl'ĭs) *n.* The desire to harm others, or to see others suffer; ill will; spite.

ma·li·cious (mə-lĭsh'əs) *adj.* Resulting from or having the nature of malice.

ma·lig·nant (mə-lĭg'nənt) *adj.* **1.** Showing great malevolence; actively evil in nature. **2.** Highly injurious; pernicious.

mal·le·a·ble (măl'ē-ə-bəl) *adj.* **1.** Capable of being shaped or formed, as by hammering or pressure: *a malleable metal.* **2.** Capable of being altered or influenced; tractable, pliable.

ma·ni·a (mā'nē-ə, mān'yə) *n.* An inordinately intense desire or enthusiasm for something; craze.

man·i·fold (măn'ə-fōld) *adj.* Of many kinds; varied; multiple.

mar·row (măr'ō) *n.* The inmost, choicest, or essential part; pith.

mar·tial (mär'shəl) *adj.* Characteristic of or befitting a warrior.

mas·tiff (măs'tĭf) *n.* A large dog of an ancient breed, probably originating in Asia, having a short fawn-colored coat.

maud·lin (môd'lĭn) *adj.* Effusively sentimental.

max·im (măk'sĭm) *n.* A succinct formulation of some fundamental principle or rule of conduct.

me·di·o·cre (mē'dē-ō'kər) *adj.* Neither good nor bad; average; ordinary; commonplace. Usually used disparagingly.

me·di·oc·ri·ty (mē'dē-ŏk'rə-tē) *n., pl.* **-ties.** The state or quality of being mediocre.

mel·io·ra·tion (mēl'yə-rā'shən, mē'lē-ə-) *n.* The act or process of improving something or the state of being improved.

men·ace (mĕn'ĭs) *n.* A threat.

mer·ci·less (mûr'sĭ-lĭs) *adj.* Having no mercy; pitiless; cruel.

mi·gra·to·ry (mī'grə-tôr'ē, -tōr'ē) *adj.* **1.** Characterized by migration; migrating periodically: *migratory birds.* **2.** Of or relating to a migration. **3.** Roving; nomadic.

mirth (mûrth) *n.* **1.** Rejoicing or enjoyment, especially when expressed in merrymaking. **2.** Gladness and gaiety, especially when expressed by laughter.

mis·con·strue (mĭs'kən-strōō') *tr.v.* **-strued, -struing, -strues.** To mistake the meaning of; misinterpret; misunderstand.

mite (mīt) *n.* Any very small object, creature, or particle.

mit·i·gate (mĭt'ə-gāt') *v.* **-gated, -gating, -gates.** —*tr.* To moderate (a quality or condition) in force or intensity; alleviate.

mot·ley (mŏt'lē) *adj.* Having components of great variety; heterogeneous: "*I did not realize how motley are the qualities that go to make up a human being.*" (Maugham).

---

murk·y (mûr′kē) *adj.* **-ier, -iest.** Also **mirk·y.** **1.** Dark or gloomy. **2.** Cloudy in color; having no brightness.

mus·ing (myoo′zĭng) *adj.* Absorbed in thought; contemplative. —*n.* Contemplation; meditation.

myr·i·ad (mĭr′ē-əd) *n.* A vast number; a great multitude.

N

na·bob (nā′bŏb′) *n.* A man of wealth and prominence.

naught (nôt) *n.* Also **nought.** **1.** Nothing. **2.** A cipher; zero; the figure 0. —*adj.* Also **nought.**

net·tle (nĕt′l) *tr.v.* **nettled, -tling, -tles.** To irritate; vex.

neu·tral·ize (noo′trə-līz′, nyoo′-) *tr.v.* **-ized, -izing, -izes.** **1.** To make neutral. **2.** To make ineffective; counterbalance and bring to nothing.

nim·ble (nĭm′bəl) *adj.* **-bler, -blest.** **1.** Quick and agile in movement or action; deft. **2.** Quick and deft at devising; cleverly alert; acute.

noc·tur·nal (nŏk-tûr′nəl) *adj.* Of, suitable to, or occurring at night.

no·mad·ic (nō-măd′ĭk) *adj.* Also **no·mad·i·cal** (-ĭ-kəl). Leading the life of a nomad; wandering; roving.

non·cha·lance (nŏn′shə-läns′) *n.* Debonair lack of concern.

non·com·mit·tal (nŏn′kə-mĭt′l) *adj.* Refusing commitment to any particular course of action or opinion; revealing no preference or purpose.

non·con·form·ist (nŏn′kən-fôr′mĭst) *n.* One who refuses to be bound by the accepted rules, beliefs, or practices of a group. —**non′con·form′i·ty** *n.*

no·to·ri·ous (nō-tôr′ē-əs, -tōr′ē-əs) *adj.* Known widely and regarded unfavorably; infamous. —**no·to′ri·ous·ly** *adv.*

nov·ice (nŏv′ĭs) *n.* A person new to any field or activity; beginner.

O

ob·du·rate (ŏb′dyoo-rĭt, ŏb′doo-) *adj.* Hardened against feeling; unyielding; hardhearted.

o·blig·a·to·ry (ə-blĭg′ə-tôr′ē, -tōr′ē, ŏb′lĭ-gə-) *adj.* **1.** Legally or morally constraining; binding. **2.** Imposing or recording an obligation: *a bill obligatory.* **3.** Of the nature of an obligation; compulsory: *Attendance is obligatory.*

o·blit·er·ate (ə-blĭt′ə-rāt′) *tr.v.* **-ated, -ating, -ates.** To do away with completely; destroy so as to leave no trace.

o·bliv·i·ous (ə-blĭv′ē-əs) *adj.* Unaware or unmindful.

ob·nox·ious (ŏb-nŏk′shəs, əb-) *adj.* Highly disagreeable or offensive; odious.

ob·scu·ri·ty (ŏb-skyoor′ə-tē, əb-) *n., pl.* **-ties.** The condition of being unknown.

ob·se·qui·ous (ŏb-sē′kwē-əs, əb-) *adj.* Full of servile compliance; fawning.

ob·sid·i·an (ŏb-sĭd′ē-ən) *n.* An acid-resistant, lustrous volcanic glass, usually black or banded and displaying curved, shiny surfaces when fractured.

ob·sti·nate (ŏb′stə-nĭt) *adj.* Stubbornly adhering to an attitude, opinion, or course of action; resistant to argument or entreaty; inflexible; obdurate.

ob·strep·er·ous (ŏb-strĕp′ər-əs, əb-) *adj.* Noisily defiant; unruly; boisterous; unmanageable.

o·paque (ō-pāk′) *adj.* Impenetrable by light; neither transparent nor translucent.

op·press (ə-prĕs′) *tr.v.* **-pressed, -pressing, -presses.** **1.** To subjugate or persecute by unjust or tyrannical use of force or authority. **2.** To weigh heavily upon, especially so as to depress the mind or spirits.

op·pres·sion (ə-prĕsh′ən) *n.* The act of oppressing, or the state of being oppressed.

op·pro·bri·ous (ə-prō′brē-əs) *adj.* Expressing or carrying a sense of disgrace or contemptuous scorn: *opprobrious epithets.*

op·u·lent (ŏp′yə-lənt) *adj.* Having or characterized by great wealth; rich; affluent. —**op′u·lence** *n.*

os·cil·late (ŏs′ə-lāt′) *intr.v.* **-lated, -lating, -lates.** To swing back and forth with a steady uninterrupted rhythm.

os·ten·ta·tious (ŏs′tĕn-tā′shəs, ŏs′tən-) *adj.* Characterized by or given to ostentation; showy; pretentious.

out·crop (out′krŏp′) *n. Geology.* A portion of bedrock or other stratum protruding through the soil level.

P

pal·pa·ble (păl′pə-bəl) *adj.* **1.** Capable of being handled, touched, or felt; tangible. **2.** Easily perceived; obvious.

pal·try (pôl′trē) *adj.* **-trier, -triest.** **1.** Petty; trifling; insignificant. **2.** Worthless; contemptible.

pan·de·mo·ni·um (păn′də-mō′nē-əm) *n.* **1.** Any place characterized by uproar and noise. **2.** Wild uproar or noise.

pan·o·ram·a (păn′ə-răm′ə, -rä′mə) *n.* An unlimited view of all visible objects over a wide area.

pa·rab·o·la (pə-răb′ə-lə) *n. Geometry.* A plane curve formed by: **a.** A conic section taken parallel to an element of the intersected cone. **b.** The locus of points equidistant from a fixed line and a fixed point not on the line.

par·a·bol·ic (păr′ə-bŏl′ĭk) *adj.* **1.** Of or like a parable. **2.** Of or having the form of a parabola.

par·a·pher·na·lia (păr′ə-fər-nāl′yə, -fə-nāl′yə) *n.* The articles used in some activity; equipment; gear.

par·ti·al·i·ty (pär′shē-ăl′ə-tē, pär-shăl′-) *n., pl.* **-ties.** **1.** The state or condition of being partial. **2.** Favorable prejudice or bias. **3.** A special fondness; predilection.

pas·sive (păs′ĭv) *adj.* **1.** Receiving or subjected to an action without responding or initiating an action in return. **2.** Accepting without objection or resistance; submissive; compliant.

---

t tight/th thin, path/*th* this, bathe/ŭ cut/ûr urge/v valve/w with/y yes/z zebra, size/zh vision/ə about, item, edible, gallop, circus/ à *Fr.* ami/œ *Fr.* feu, *Ger.* schön/ü *Fr.* tu, *Ger.* über/ᴋʜ *Ger.* ich, *Scot.* loch/ɴ *Fr.* bon.

pa·thet·ic (pə-thĕt′ĭk) *adj.* **1.** Of, pertaining to, expressing, or arousing pity, sympathy, or tenderness; full of pathos. **2.** Distressing and inadequate. —**pa·thet′i·cal·ly** *adv.*

path·o·log·i·cal (păth′ə-lŏj′ĭ-kəl) *adj.* Disordered in behavior: *a pathological liar.* —**path′o·log′i·cal·ly** *adv.*

pa·thos (pā′thŏs′, -thôs′) *n.* A quality in something or someone that arouses feelings of pity, sympathy, tenderness, or sorrow in another.

pa·tri·arch (pā′trē-ärk′) *n.* **1.** Someone regarded as the founder or original head of an enterprise, organization, or tradition. **2.** A very old and venerable man; an elder.

pa·tron·ize (pā′trə-nīz′, păt′rə-) *tr.v.* **-ized, -izing, -izes.** To treat in an offensively condescending manner.

pe·cu·ni·ar·y (pĭ-kyoo′nē-ĕr′ē) *adj.* Consisting of or pertaining to money: *a pecuniary loss; pecuniary motives.*

pen·sive (pĕn′sĭv) *adj.* **1.** Engaged in deep thoughtfulness. **2.** Suggesting or expressing deep, often melancholy thoughtfulness.

pen·u·ry (pĕn′yə-rē) *n.* Extreme want or poverty; destitution.

per·emp·to·ry (pə-rĕmp′tə-rē) *adj.* Having the nature of or expressing a command; urgent.

per·func·to·ry (pər-fŭngk′tə-rē) *adj.* Done or acting routinely and with little interest or care.

per·me·ate (pûr′mē-āt′) *v.* **-ated, -ating, -ates.** —*tr.* To spread or flow throughout; pervade.

per·pet·u·al (pər-pĕch′oo-əl) *adj.* Ceaselessly repeated or continuing without interruption.

per·son·age (pûr′sən-ĭj) *n.* **1.** A character in a literary work. **2. a.** A person. **b.** A person of distinction.

per·tain (pər-tān′) *intr.v.* **-tained, -taining, -tains.** To have reference; relate: *evidence pertaining to the accident.*

per·ti·na·cious (pûr′tə-nā′shəs) *adj.* Stubbornly or perversely persistent.

per·ti·nac·i·ty (pûr′tə-năs′ə-tē) *n.* The quality or state of being pertinacious.

per·tur·ba·tion (pûr′tər-bā′shən) *n.* **a.** The act of perturbing. **b.** The state or condition of being perturbed; agitation.

pe·ruse (pə-rooz′) *tr.v.* **-rused, -rusing, -ruses.** To read or examine, especially with great care.

per·va·sive (pər-vā′sĭv, -zĭv) *adj.* Having the quality or tendency to pervade or permeate.

per·verse (pər-vûrs′) *adj.* **1.** Marked by a disposition to oppose and contradict. **2.** Cranky; peevish.

pes·ti·lent (pĕs′tə-lənt) *adj.* Likely to cause an epidemic disease.

pet·tish (pĕt′ĭsh) *adj.* Ill-tempered; peevish; petulant. —**pet′tish·ness** *n.*

pet·u·lant (pĕch′oo-lənt) *adj.* Unreasonably irritable or ill-tempered; peevish.

pi·e·ty (pī′ə-tē) *n., pl.* **-ties. 1.** Religious devotion and reverence to God. **2.** Devotion and reverence to parents and family. **3.** A pious act or thought. **4.** The state or quality of being pious.

pi·quant (pē′kənt, -känt′, pē-känt′) *adj.* Pleasantly disturbing; appealingly provocative: *touched by the piquant faces of children.* —**pi′quan·cy** *n.*

pique (pēk) *tr.v.* **piqued, piquing, piques.** To cause to feel resentment or vexation; injure the feelings of.

plac·id (plăs′ĭd) *adj.* Having an undisturbed surface or aspect; outwardly calm or composed.

plau·si·ble (plô′zə-bəl) *adj.* Seemingly or apparently valid, likely, or acceptable.

plight (plīt) *tr.v.* **plighted, plighting, plights.** To promise or bind by a solemn pledge; especially, to betroth. —**plight one's troth.** To become engaged to marry.

plow·share (plou′shâr′) *n.* The cutting blade of a plow; a share.

ply (plī) *v.* **plied, plying, plies.** —*tr.* **1.** To use diligently as a tool or weapon; wield: *He plies an ax with the assurance of a lumberjack.* **2.** To engage in (a trade, for example); practice diligently. **3.** To traverse or sail over regularly.

pom·mel (pŭm′əl, pŏm′-) *tr.v.* **pommeled, -meling, -mels.** To beat; pummel.

pontoon bridge. A temporary floating bridge using pontoons for support. Also called "bateau bridge."

por·tend (pôr-tĕnd′, pōr-) *tr.v.* **-tended, -tending, -tends.** To serve as an omen or warning of; presage.

pos·ter·i·ty (pŏ-stĕr′ə-tē) *n.* All of a person's descendants.

po·tent (pōt′nt) *adj.* Capable of commanding attention; able to convince: *potent arguments.*

pre·car·i·ous (prĭ-kâr′ē-əs) *adj.* **1.** Dangerously lacking in security or stability. **2.** Subject to chance or unknown conditions.

prec·i·pice (prĕs′ə-pĭs) *n.* An extremely steep or overhanging mass of rock, such as a crag or the face of a cliff.

pre·cip·i·tate (prĭ-sĭp′ə-tāt′) *v.* **-tated, -tating, -tates.** —*tr.* To cause to happen before anticipated or required.

pre·cip·i·ta·tion (prĭ-sĭp′ə-tā′shən) *n.* **1.** A headlong fall or rush. **2.** Abrupt or impulsive haste.

pre·cur·sor (prĭ-kûr′sər, prē′kûr′sər) *n.* One that precedes and indicates or announces someone or something to come; forerunner; harbinger.

pre·dom·i·nate (prĭ-dŏm′ə-nāt′) *v.* **-nated, -nating, -nates.** —*intr.* To be of greater power, importance, or quantity; be most important or outstanding.

pre·em·i·nent (prē-ĕm′ə-nənt) *adj.* Superior to or notable above all others; outstanding. —**pre·em′i·nent·ly** *adv.*

pre·ten·sion (prĭ-tĕn′shən) *n.* A claim to something, such as a privilege, right, or other position of distinction or importance.

pro·di·gious (prə-dĭj′əs) *adj.* **1.** Impressively great in size, force, or extent; enormous. **2.** Extraordinary; marvelous.

pro·fuse (prə-fyoos′, prō-) *adj.* **1.** Plentiful; overflowing; copious. **2.** Giving or given freely and abundantly; extravagant. —**pro·fuse′ly** *adv.*

ă pat/ā pay/âr care/ä father/b **bib**/ch **church**/d **deed**/ĕ pet/ē be/f **fife**/g **gag**/h **hat**/hw **which**/ĭ pit/ī pie/îr **pier**/j **judge**/k **kick**/l **lid**,
needle/m **mum**/n no, sudden/ng **thing**/ŏ pot/ō **toe**/ô paw, for/oi noise/ou out/oo took/oo boot/p **pop**/r roar/s sauce/sh **ship, dish**/

pro·fu·sion (prə-fyōō′zhen, prō-) *n.* **1.** The state of being profuse; abundance. **2.** Lavish or unrestrained expense.

proph·e·sy (prŏf′ə-sī′) *v.* **-sied, -sying, -sies.** —*tr.* **1.** To reveal by divine inspiration. **2.** To predict. **3.** To prefigure; foreshow.

prop·o·si·tion (prŏp′ə-zĭsh′ən) *n.* **1.** A plan or scheme suggested for acceptance. **2.** *Informal.* A matter requiring special handling: *a difficult proposition.*

pro·pri·e·tor (prə-prī′ə-tər) *n. Abbr.* **prop., propr.** A person who has legal title to something; an owner. —**pro·pri′e·tor·ship′** *n.*

pro·sa·ic (prō-zā′ĭk) *adj.* Lacking in imagination and spirit; dull; ordinary.

pros·trate (prŏs′trāt′) *tr.v.* **-trated, -trating, -trates.** To make (oneself) bow or kneel down in humility or adoration.

prov·ince (prŏv′ĭns) *n. Plural.* Areas of a country situated away from the capital or population center. Preceded by *the.*

pro·voc·a·tive (prə-vŏk′ə-tĭv) *adj.* Tending to provoke; exciting; stimulating.

pru·dent (prōōd′ənt) *adj.* **1.** Wise in handling practical matters; exercisng good judgment or common sense. **2.** Careful in regard to one's own interests; provident.

Q

quaff (kwŏf, kwăf, kwôf) *v.* **quaffed, quaffing, quaffs.** —*tr.* To drink heartily.

quar·ry (kwôr′ē, kwŏr′ē) *n., pl.* **-ries.** An open excavation or pit from which stone is obtained by digging, cutting, or blasting.

qui·es·cent (kwī-ĕs′ənt, kwē-) *adj.* Inactive or still; dormant.

quilt (kwĭlt) *n.* A bed coverlet or blanket made of two layers of fabric with a layer of cotton, wool, feathers, or down in between, all stitched firmly together, usually in a crisscross design.

quirk (kwûrk) *n.* **1.** A peculiarity of behavior that eludes prediction or suppression. **2.** An unpredictable or unaccountable act or event; vagary.

R

ran·sack (răn′săk′) *tr.v.* **-sacked, -sacking, -sacks.** To search or examine thoroughly.

rash (răsh) *adj.* **rasher, rashest. 1.** Acting without forethought or due caution; impetuous. **2.** Characterized by ill-considered haste or boldness.

ra·tion·al (răsh′ən-əl) *adj.* **1.** Having or exercising the ability to reason. **2.** Of sound mind; sane. **3.** Manifesting or based upon reason; logical.

rec·ti·tude (rĕk′tə-tōōd′, -tyōōd′) *n.* **1.** Moral uprightness. **2.** Rightness, as of intellectual judgment.

re·dress (rĭ-drĕs′, rē′drĕs) *n.* Satisfaction or amends for wrong done.

re·dun·dan·cy (rĭ-dŭn′dən-sē) *n., pl.* **-cies.** *Technol-*ogy. Duplication or repetition of elements in electronic or mechanical equipment to provide alternative functional channels in case of failure.

re·frain (rĭ-frān′) *v.* **-frained, -fraining, -frains.** —*intr.* To hold oneself back; forbear. Used with *from: Kindly refrain from singing.*

re·miss (rĭ-mĭs′) *adj.* Lax in attending to duty; negligent. —**re·miss′ness** *n.*

re·mon·strate (rĭ-mŏn′strāt′) *v.* **-strated, -strating, -strates.** —*tr.* To say or plead in protest, objection, or reproof.

re·morse (rĭ-môrs′) *n.* Moral anguish arising from repentance for past misdeeds; bitter regret.

re·mu·ner·ate (rĭ-myōō′nə-rāt′) *tr.v.* **-ated, -ating, -ates.** To compensate for; make up for: *remunerate his efforts.*

rend (rĕnd) *v.* **rent** (rĕnt) or **rended, rending, rends.** —*tr.* To penetrate and disturb as if by tearing: *screams that rend the silence.*

ren·e·gade (rĕn′ə-gād′) *n.* One who rejects his religion, cause, allegiance, or group for another; a traitor; deserter. —*adj.* Of or like a renegade; traitorous.

re·nown (rĭ-noun′) *n.* The quality of being widely honored and acclaimed; celebrity.

re·pel·lent (rĭ-pĕl′ənt) *adj.* **1.** Serving or tending to repel; capable of repelling something. **2.** Inspiring aversion and distaste; repulsive.

re·pose (rĭ-pōz′) *n.* **1. a.** The act of resting; a rest. **b.** The state of being at rest; relaxation. **2.** Peace of mind; freedom from anxiety; composure.

re·pres·sion (rĭ-prĕsh′ən) *n.* **a.** The action of repressing. **b.** The state of being repressed. —**re·pres′sive** (-prĕs′ĭv) *adj.*

rep·ri·mand (rĕp′rə-mănd′, -mänd′) *tr.v.* **-manded, -manding, -mands.** To rebuke or censure severely. —*n.* A severe or formal rebuke or censure.

re·pug·nance (rĭ-pŭg′nəns) *n.* The state of feeling extreme dislike or aversion.

re·spire (rĭ-spīr′) *v.* **-spired, -spiring, -spires.** —*intr.* To breathe in and out; inhale and exhale.

res·pite (rĕs′pĭt) *n.* A temporary cessation or postponement, usually of something disagreeable; an interval of rest or relief.

res·tive (rĕs′tĭv) *adj.* Impatient or nervous under restriction, delay, or pressure; uneasy; restless.

ret·i·cent (rĕt′ə-sənt) *adj.* Restrained or reserved in style.

rev·eil·le (rĕv′ə-lē) *n.* The sounding of a bugle early in the morning to awaken and summon persons in a camp or garrison.

rev·e·la·tion (rĕv′ə-lā′shən) *n.* **1.** Something revealed. **2.** An act of revealing, especially a dramatic disclosure of something not previously known or realized.

re·ver·ber·ate (rĭ-vûr′bə-rāt′) *v.* **-ated, -ating, -ates.** —*intr.* To re-echo; resound. —**re·ver′ber·a′tion** *n.*

re·vile (rĭ-vīl′) *v.* **-viled, -viling, -viles.** —*tr.* To denounce with abusive language; rail against. —*intr.* To use abusive language.

re·volve (rĭ-vŏlv′) *v.* **-volved, -volving, -volves.** —*intr.* **1.** To orbit a central point. **2.** To turn on an axis; rotate.

---

t tight/th thin, path/*th* this, bathe/ŭ cut/ûr urge/v valve/w with/y yes/z zebra, size/zh vision/ə about, item, edible, gallop, circus/ä *Fr.* ami/œ *Fr.* feu, *Ger.* schön/ü *Fr.* tu, *Ger.* über/ᴋʜ *Ger.* ich, *Scot.* loch/ɴ *Fr.* bon.

ric·o·chet (rĭk′ə-shā′, -shĕt′) *intr.v.* **-cheted** (-shād′) or **-chetted** (-shĕt′ĭd), **-cheting** (-shā′ĭng) or **-chetting** (-shĕt′ĭng), **-chets.** To rebound at least once from a surface or surfaces.

ri·fle (rī′fəl) *tr.v.* **-fled, -fling, -fles. 1.** To search with intent to steal. **2.** To ransack or plunder; pillage. **3.** To rob; strip bare.

rit·u·al (rĭch′ōō-əl) *n.* The prescribed form or order of conducting a religious or solemn ceremony.

roist·er (rois′tər) *intr.v.* **-ered, -ering, -ers.** To engage in boisterous merrymaking; revel noisily.

ros·trum (rŏs′trəm) *n., pl.* **-trums** or **-tra** (-trə). A dais, platform, or similar raised place for public speaking.

rus·tic (rŭs′tĭk) *adj.* **1.** Typical of country life. **2.** Simple; unsophisticated; bucolic.

ruth·less (rōōth′lĭs) *adj.* Having no compassion or pity; merciless.

S

sa·ga·cious (sə-gā′shəs) *adj.* Possessing or showing sound judgment and keen perception; wise.

sa·vant (sə-vänt′, săv′ənt; *French* sȧ-väN′) *n.* A learned scholar; a wise man.

scathe (skā*th*) *tr.v.* **scathed, scathing, scathes. 1.** To harm or injure severely, especially by fire or heat; wither; sear. **2.** To criticize severely. —*n.* Harm; injury.

scav·en·ger (skăv′ĭn-jər) *n.* **1.** An animal that feeds on dead animal flesh or other decaying organic matter. **2.** One who scavenges.

schiz·o·phre·ni·a (skĭt′sə-frē′nē-ə, -frĕn′ē-ə) *n.* Any of a group of psychotic reactions characterized by withdrawal from reality with highly variable accompanying affective, behavioral, and intellectual disturbances.

scourge (skûrj) *tr.v.* **scourged, scourging, scourges. 1.** To flog. **2.** To chastise severely; excoriate.

scru·ple (skrōō′pəl) *n.* Ethical objection to certain actions; principle; dictate of conscience.

scull (skŭl) *n.* A long oar twisted from side to side over the stern of a boat to propel it. —*v.* **sculled, sculling, sculls.** —*tr.* To propel (a boat) with a scull or sculls.

sed·u·lous (sĕj′ōō-ləs) *adj.* Diligent; painstaking; industrious.

seis·mic (sīz′mĭk) *adj.* Of, subject to, or caused by an earthquake or earth vibration.

seis·mom·e·ter (sīz-mŏm′ə-tər) *n.* A detecting device that receives seismic impulses.

sen·si·bil·i·ty (sĕn′sə-bĭl′ə-tē) *n., pl.* **-ties. a.** Keen intellectual perception: *the sensibility of a painter to color.* **b.** Mental or emotional responsiveness toward something, as the feelings of another.

sen·ti·nel (sĕnt′n-əl) *n.* One that keeps guard; a sentry.

ser·vile (sûr′vəl, -vīl′) *adj.* Slavish in character or attitude; obsequious; submissive.

ser·vi·tude (sûr′və-tōōd′, -tyōōd′) *n.* Submission to a master; slavery.

sev·er (sĕv′ər) *v.* **-ered, -ering, -ers.** —*tr.* To cut or break forcibly into two or more parts.

se·ver·i·ty (sə-vĕr′ə-tē) *n., pl.* **-ties. 1.** Harshness; rigor. **2.** Extreme strictness; rigid conformity. **3.** Austerity; gravity.

sex·til·lion (sĕks-tĭl′yən) *n.* The cardinal number represented by 1 followed by 21 zeros, usually written 10^{21}.

sex·ton (sĕks′tən) *n.* A maintenance man in a church, responsible for the care and upkeep of the church property and sometimes for bell-ringing or supervising burials in the churchyard.

shale (shāl) *n.* A fissile rock composed of laminated layers of claylike, fine-grained sediments.

shift·less (shĭft′lĭs) *adj.* **1.** Showing a lack of ambition or purpose; lazy. **2.** Showing a lack of resourcefulness or efficiency; not capable. —**shift′-less·ness** *n.*

sin·is·ter (sĭn′ĭ-stər) *adj.* **1.** Suggesting an evil force or motive: *a sinister smile.* **2.** Presaging trouble; ominous.

sol·ace (sŏl′ĭs) *tr.v.* **solaced, -acing, -aces. 1.** To comfort, cheer, or console, as in trouble or sorrow. **2.** To allay or assuage.

so·lic·it (sə-lĭs′ĭt) *v.* **-ited, -iting, -its.** —*tr.* To seek to obtain by persuasion, entreaty, or formal application: *solicit votes.*

so·lic·i·tous (sə-lĭs′ə-təs) *adj.* Anxious and concerned; attentive.

so·lil·o·quy (sə-lĭl′ə-kwē) *n., pl.* **-quies.** The act of speaking to oneself in or as in solitude.

spav·in (spăv′ən) *n.* Either of two diseases affecting the hock joint of horses: *bog spavin,* an infusion of lymph that enlarges the joint, and *bone spavin,* a bony deposit that stiffens the joint.

spec·u·la·tive (spĕk′yə-lə-tĭv, -lā′tĭv) *adj.* Of, characterized by, or based upon contemplative speculation; conjectural in nature rather than pragmatic or positive. —**spec′u·la·tive·ly** *adv.*

spit·toon (spĭ-tōōn′) *n.* A bowl-shaped, usually metal vessel for spitting into. Also called "cuspidor."

spon·ta·ne·i·ty (spŏn′tə-nē′ə-tē) *n., pl.* **-ties. 1.** The condition or quality of being spontaneous. **2.** Spontaneous behavior, impulse, or movement.

spon·ta·ne·ous (spŏn-tā′nē-əs) *adj.* **1.** Voluntary and impulsive; unpremeditated: *spontaneous applause.* **2.** Unconstrained and unstudied in manner or behavior.

spright·ly (sprīt′lē) *adj.* **-lier, -liest.** Buoyant or animated; full of life.

squan·der (skwŏn′dər) *tr.v.* **-dered, -dering, -ders.** To spend wastefully or extravagantly; dissipate.

staid (stād) *adj.* Prudently reserved and colorless in style, manner, or behavior; grave; sober.

stan·chion (stăn′chən, -shən) *n.* One of the vertical posts used to secure cattle in a stall.

stat·ure (stăch′ər) *n.* A level achieved; status; caliber.

stealth (stĕlth) *n.* **1.** The act of moving, proceeding, or acting in a covert way. **2.** Furtiveness; covertness.

stol·id (stŏl′ĭd) *adj.* Having or showing little emotion; impassive.

ă pat/ā pay/âr care/ä father/b **bib**/ch **church**/d **deed**/ĕ pet/ē be/f **fife**/g **gag**/h **hat**/hw **which**/ĭ pit/ī **pie**/îr **pier**/j **judge**/k **kick**/l lid, needle/m **mum**/n no, sudden/ng **thing**/ŏ pot/ō toe/ô paw, for/oi noise/ou out/ŏŏ took/ōō **boot**/p pop/r roar/s sauce/sh **ship, dish**/

stul·ti·fy (stŭl′tə-fī′) *tr.v.* **-fied, -fying, -fies.** To render useless or ineffectual; cripple.

stu·pe·fy (stoō′pə-fī′, styoō′-) *tr.v.* **-fied, -fying, -fies.** **1.** To dull the senses of; put into a stupor. **2.** To amaze; astonish.

sub·due (səb-doō′, -dyoō′) *tr.v.* **-dued, -duing, -dues.** **1.** To conquer and subjugate; put down; vanquish. **2.** To make less intense or prominent; tone down: *A vote of approval subdued his anger.*

sub·or·di·nate (sə-bôr′də-nĭt) *adj.* **1.** Belonging to a lower or inferior class or rank; minor; secondary. **2.** Subject to the authority or control of another.

sub·ter·fuge (sŭb′tər-fyoōj′) *n.* An evasive tactic used to avoid censure or other awkward confrontation.

sub·tle (sŭt′l) *adj.* **-tler, -tlest. 1. a.** So slight as to be difficult to detect or analyze; elusive. **b.** Not immediately obvious; abstruse. **2.** Able to make fine distinctions; keen.

suc·cinct (sək-sĭngkt′) *adj.* Clearly expressed in few words; concise; terse. **—suc·cinct′ly** *adv.*

suc·cumb (sə-kŭm′) *intr.v.* **-cumbed, -cumbing, -cumbs.** To yield or submit to an overpowering force or overwhelming desire; give in or give up.

suf·fer·ance (sŭf′ər-əns, sŭf′-rəns) *n.* The capacity to tolerate pain or distress.

suf·fice (sə-fīs′) *v.* **-ficed, -ficing, -fices.** *—intr.* To meet present needs or requirements; be sufficient or adequate: *These rations will suffice until next week.*

suf·fuse (sə-fyoōz′) *tr.v.* **-fused, -fusing, -fuses.** To spread through or over, as with liquid, color, or light.

su·per·an·nu·at·ed (soō′pər-ăn′yoō-ā′tĭd) *adj.* **1.** Retired or discharged because of age or infirmity. **2.** Obsolete; antiquated.

sup·pli·cate (sŭp′lĭ-kāt′) *v.* **-cated, -cating, -cates.** *—tr.* **1.** To ask for humbly or earnestly, as by praying. **2.** To make a humble entreaty to; beseech. **—sup′pli·ca′tion** *n.*

sur·mise (sər-mīz′) *v.* **-mised, -mising, -mises.** *—tr.* To infer (something) without sufficiently conclusive evidence.

sur·ro·gate (sûr′ə-gĭt, -gāt′) *n.* **1.** A person or thing that is substituted for another; a substitute. **2.** In New York and some other states, a judge having jurisdiction over the probate of wills and the settlement of estates.

sus·cep·ti·ble (sə-sĕp′tə-bəl) *adj.* Readily subject to an influence, agency, or force; unresistant; yielding.

sus·tain (sə-stān′) *tr.v.* **-tained, -taining, -tains.** To support the spirits, vitality, or resolution of.

swain (swān) *n.* A country youth; especially, a young shepherd.

swath (swäth, swôth) *n.* Also **swathe** (swäth, swôth). **1.** The width of a scythe stroke or a mowing-machine blade. **2.** Something likened to a swath. **—cut a (wide) swath.**

syn·chro·nize (sĭn′krə-nīz′, sĭng′-) *v.* **-nized, -nizing, -nizes.** *—tr.* To cause to operate with exact coincidence in time or rate.

T

tab·leau (tăb′lō, tă-blō′) *n., pl.* **tableaux** (tăb′lōz′, tă-blōz′) or **-leaus.** A striking incidental scene, as of a picturesque group of people.

te·na·cious (tə-nā′shəs) *adj.* Holding or tending to hold firmly; persistent; stubborn.

ten·u·ous (tĕn′yoō-əs) *adj.* Of little significance; weak; unsubstantial; flimsy: *a tenuous argument.*

tep·id (tĕp′ĭd) *adj.* Moderately warm; lukewarm.

ter·ma·gant (tûr′mə-gənt) *n.* A quarrelsome or scolding woman; a shrew. *—adj.* Abusive; shrewish.

terse (tûrs) *adj.* **terser, tersest.** Effectively concise; free of superfluity. **—terse′ly** *adv.*

tinc·ture (tĭngk′chər) *tr.v.* **tinctured, -turing, -tures.** **1.** To stain or tint with a color. **2.** To infuse, as with a quality; impregnate.

tor·pid (tôr′pĭd) *adj.* Lethargic; apathetic.

tra·jec·to·ry (trə-jĕk′tə-rē) *n., pl.* **-ries.** The path of a moving particle or body, especially such a path in three dimensions.

tran·quil (trăn′kwəl) *adj.* **-quiler** or **-quiller, -quilest** or **-quillest.** Free from agitation or other disturbance; calm; unruffled; serene.

trans·fig·ure (trăns-fĭg′yər) *tr.v.* **-ured, -uring, -ures.** To transform the figure or appearance of; alter radically.

trans·fix (trăns-fĭks′) *tr.v.* **-fixed, -fixing, -fixes.** To render motionless, as with terror, amazement, or awe.

tran·sient (trăn′shənt, -zhənt, -zē-ənt) *n.* One that is transient; especially, a person staying a single night at a hotel.

trans·mit·ter (trăns-mĭt′ər, trănz-) *n.* Electronic equipment that generates and amplifies a carrier wave, modulates it with a meaningful signal, as derived from speech or other sources, and radiates the resulting signal from an antenna.

trav·es·ty (trăv′ĭ-stē) *n., pl.* **-ties.** An exaggerated or grotesque imitation with intent to ridicule; a burlesque.

trite (trīt) *adj.* **triter, tritest.** Overused and commonplace; lacking interest or originality.

truf·fle (trŭf′əl) *n.* Any of various fleshy subterranean fungi, chiefly of the genus *Tuber*, often esteemed as food.

tu·mul·tu·ous (tə-mŭl′choō-əs) *adj.* Confusedly or violently agitated: *a tumultuous heart.*

tur·bu·lent (tûr′byə-lənt) *adj.* Violently agitated or disturbed; tumultuous: *turbulent rapids.*

tur·ret (tûr′ĭt) *n.* A small ornamented tower or tower-shaped projection on a building.

U

un·can·ny (ŭn′kăn′ē) *adj.* **-nier, -niest.** Exciting wonder and fear; inexplicable; strange: *an uncanny laugh.*

unc·tion (ŭngk′shən) *n.* Affected or exaggerated earnestness, especially in language; unctuousness.

un·flinch·ing (ŭn′flĭn′chĭng) *adj.* Not betraying fear or indecision; unshrinking; resolute.

un·guent (ŭng′gwənt) *n.* A salve for soothing or healing; an ointment.

u·nique (yōō-nēk′) *adj.* **1.** Being the only one of its kind; solitary; sole. **2.** Being without an equal or equivalent; unparalleled.

u·ni·ver·sal (yōō′nə-vûr′səl) *adj. Abbr.* **univ. 1.** Of, pertaining to, extending to, or affecting the entire world or all within the world; worldwide. **2.** Including, pertaining to, or affecting all members of the class or group under consideration: *the universal skepticism of philosophers.*

un·mit·i·gat·ed (ŭn′mĭt′ə-gā′tĭd) *adj.* **1.** Not diminished or moderated in intensity or severity; unrelieved. **2.** Absolute.

un·ob·tru·sive (ŭn′əb-trōō′sĭv) *adj.* Not readily noticeable. **—un′ob·tru′sive·ly** *adv.*

un·re·lent·ing (ŭn′rĭ-lĕn′tĭng) *adj.* **1.** Inexorable. **2.** Not diminishing in intensity, speed, or effort.

un·sheathe (ŭn′shēth′) *tr.v.* **-sheathed, -sheathing, -sheathes.** To draw from or as if from a sheath or scabbard.

un·ut·ter·a·ble (ŭn′ŭt′ər-ə-bəl) *adj.* Not capable of being uttered or expressed; too profound for oral expression. **—un′ut′ter·a·bly** *adv.*

u·su·rer (yōō′zhər-ər) *n.* A person who lends money at an exorbitant or unlawful rate of interest.

u·sur·pa·tion (yōō′sər-pā′shən, yōō′zər-) *n.* **1.** The act of usurping; especially, the illegal seizure of royal sovereignty. **2.** *Law.* The illegal encroachment upon or exercise of authority or privilege belonging to another.

V

va·grant (vā′grənt) *n.* **1.** A person who wanders from place to place without a fixed home or livelihood and ekes out a living by begging or stealing; a tramp; vagabond. **2.** A wanderer; rover.

ven·er·a·ble (vĕn′ər-ə-bəl) *adj.* Worthy of reverence or respect by virtue of dignity, character, position, or age.

ven·er·ate (vĕn′ə-rāt′) *tr.v.* **-ated, -ating, -ates.** To regard with respect, reverence, or heartfelt deference.

ver·ba·tim (vûr-bā′tĭm) *adj.* Using exactly the same words; word for word. *—adv.* In exactly the same words.

ves·tige (vĕs′tĭj) *n.* A visible trace, evidence, or sign of something that has once existed but exists or appears no more.

vin·di·cate (vĭn′dĭ-kāt′) *tr.v.* **-cated, -cating, -cates.** To justify or prove the worth of, especially in light of later developments.

vir·tu·o·so (vûr′chōō-ō′sō) *n., pl.* **-sos** or **-si** (-sē). **1.** A musician with masterly ability, technique, or personal style; a brilliant performer. **2.** One with masterly skill or technique in any field, especially in the arts.

vis·age (vĭz′ĭj) *n.* The face or facial expression of a person; countenance.

vi·tu·per·a·tive (vī-tōō′pər-ə-tĭv, vī-tyōō′-, vĭ-) *adj.* Harshly abusive; acrimonious: *"Five minutes won't be ample time for a vituperative phone call"* (Kingsley Amis).

vo·cif·er·ous (vō-sĭf′ər-əs) *adj.* **1.** Making an outcry; clamorous. **2.** Characterized by loudness and vehemence. **—vo·cif′er·ous·ly** *adv.*

void (void) *n.* **1.** Something that is void; an empty space; a vacuum. **2.** An open space or break in continuity; a gap.

vouch·safe (vouch·sāf′) *tr.v.* **-safed, -safing, -safes.** To condescend to grant or bestow (a reply, favor, or privilege, for example); to deign.

W

wan (wŏn) *adj.* **wanner, wannest. 1.** Unnaturally pale, as from physical or emotional distress. **2.** Suggestive of or indicating weariness, illness, or unhappiness; languid; melancholy: *a wan expression.* **—wan′ly** *adv.*

wan·ton (wŏn′tən) *adj.* Maliciously cruel; merciless.

wean (wēn) *tr.v.* **weaned, weaning, weans.** To detach (a person) from that to which he is accustomed or devoted.

whee·dle (hwēd′l) *v.* **-dled, -dling, -dles.** *—tr.* **1.** To persuade or attempt to persuade by flattery or guile; cajole. **2.** To obtain through the use of flattery or guile. *—intr.* To use flattery or cajolery to achieve one's ends.

wile (wīl) *n.* **1.** A deceitful stratagem or trick. **2.** Trickery; cunning; deceit.

wist·ful (wĭst′fəl) *adj.* Full of a melancholy yearning; longing pensively; wishful. **—wist′ful·ly** *adv.*

with·al (wĭth-ôl′) *adv.* Besides; in addition.

with·ers (wĭth′ərz) *pl.n.* The high point of the back of a horse, or of a similar or related animal, located at the base of the neck and between the shoulder blades.

wrack (răk) *n.* Damage or destruction by violent means: *bring to wrack and ruin.*

wrath·ful (răth′fəl, räth′-) *adj.* **1.** Full of wrath; fiercely angry. **2.** Proceeding from or expressing wrath: *wrathful vengeance.*

wreathe (rēth) *v.* **wreathed, wreathing, wreathes.** *—tr.* **1.** To twist or entwine into a wreath. **2.** To twist or curl into a wreathlike shape or contour. **3.** To crown or decorate with or as with a wreath. **4.** To coil or curl.

wrest (rĕst) *tr.v.* **wrested, wresting, wrests. 1.** To obtain by or as by pulling with violent twisting movements: *wrest a book out of another's hands.* **2.** To usurp forcefully: *wrest power.*

writ (rĭt) *n. Law.* A written order issued by a court, commanding the person to whom it is addressed to perform or cease performing some specified act.

ă pat/ā pay/âr care/ä father/b bib/ch church/d deed/ĕ pet/ē be/f fife/g gag/h hat/hw which/ĭ pit/ī pie/îr pier/j judge/k kick/l lid, needle/m mum/n no, sudden/ng thing/ŏ pot/ō toe/ô paw, for/oi noise/ou out/ōō took/ōō boot/p pop/r roar/s sauce/sh ship, dish/ t tight/th thin, path/th this, bathe/ŭ cut/ûr urge/v valve/w with/y yes/z zebra, size/zh vision/ə about, item, edible, gallop, circus/ à *Fr.* ami/œ *Fr.* feu, *Ger.* schön/ü *Fr.* tu, *Ger.* über/KH *Ger.* ich, *Scot.* loch/N *Fr.* bon.

EFGHIJ-D-8987